Critical acclaim for *PC Magazine Visual Basic Programmer's Guide to the Windows API*

"An excellent book. Dan's book shows you how to do things with VB that you can't otherwise do. A very complete reference guide. The only book our reviewer wanted to keep."

—Robert Scoble, Associate Editor, *BasicPro Magazine*

"…indispensable and highly recommended. It's not the sort of book you'll sit down and read cover to cover, but it won't be long before it's the most dog-eared volume on your shelf."

—Robert Fulton, *Microsoft Mindshare Forum* and *Tuscon Computer Society Journal*

"…the definitive reference for Visual Basic programmers on using the Windows API…also contains a wealth of background information on how Windows works…"

—Allan Colby, Chairman of Visual Basic Special Interest Group, Palo Alto

PC Magazine Visual Basic Programmer's Guide to the Windows API

PC Magazine
Visual Basic
Programmer's
Guide to the
Windows API

Daniel Appleman

Ziff-Davis Press
Emeryville, California

Editor	Terry Somerson
Technical Reviewer	Don Malin
Project Coordinator	Sheila McGill
Proofreader	Pat Mannion
Cover Design	Ken Roberts
Cover Illustration	Ken Roberts
Book Design	Laura Lamar/MAX, San Francisco
Technical Illustration	Cherie Plumlee Computer Graphics & Illustration
Screen Graphics Editor	Dan Brodnitz
Word Processing	Howard Blechman and Cat Haglund
Page Layout	Steph Bradshaw, Anna. L. Marks, M. D. Barrera, and Tony Jonick
Indexer	Mark Kmetzko

This book was produced on a Macintosh IIfx, with the following applications: FrameMaker®, Microsoft® Word, MacLink®*Plus*, Aldus® FreeHand™, Adobe Photoshop™, and Collage Plus™.

Ziff-Davis Press
5903 Christie Avenue
Emeryville, CA 94608
1-800-688-0448

ISBN 1-56276-073-4

Manufactured in the United States of America

10 9 8 7 6 5 4

CONTENTS AT A GLANCE

TABLE OF CONTENTS

Part 3   Windows Messages

ACKNOWLEDGMENTS

I WOULD LIKE TO THANK A NUMBER OF PEOPLE WHO HAVE BEEN CRITICAL IN bringing this project to life. Words cannot describe the amazing folks at Ziff-Davis Press. Cindy Hudson, Cheryl Holzaepfel, Sheila McGill, and their staff not only did a phenomenal job, but made my first project with Ziff-Davis an absolute pleasure.

I could not have asked for a better editor than Terry Somerson, who brought to the development process not only an amazing eye for the details of formatting and grammar, but a broad viewpoint that was indispensable in tightening up the overall structure.

And many thanks to Don Malin of Crescent Software who somehow managed to catch so many of those little, but oh so important omissions and errors during his technical reviews.

Thanks also to the many people I've met since founding Desaware who provided encouragement during this project. I'd especially like to thank the gang at Microsoft: Michael Risse, Solveig Whittle, Kris Reynolds, and Rick Raddatz. In addition to help with this book, they provided the opportunity to contribute to the professional edition of Visual Basic. I'd also like to thank Jim Fawcette at BasicPro, who helped in many ways, and Corrine Restivo and the crew at Cinnamon Software for their manufacturing wizardry.

None of this would have been possible without those at MicroLabs who helped provide the motivation (albeit unintentionally) to undertake this project and others in the first place.

I can't begin to name all of the friends who provided encouragement and support during this project: Andy, Marian, Bob, Greg, Mona, Clint, Franky, The Doppelts and Papos, the Pyrzqxgl/XBBS crowd, and Dr. Seuss AZA #195—a million thanks.

Ronit—what can I say? You've always been there.

First, last, and foremost, I wish to thank my parents. My mother—also an author—whose book is far more important to the world than this one could possibly be. And to my father, who reviewed every chapter before it was sent in—I thank God every day that you could be here to see this in print.

ABOUT TWO YEARS AGO I SAW MICROSOFT'S VISUAL BASIC FOR THE FIRST time and decided that I was looking at the future of computer programming—period. I started writing programs for Windows in 1985 for the original version 1.0, and knew full well the amount of effort that was required for even the simplest Windows program—not to mention the months it took to learn Windows in the first place. Suddenly, here was a tool that allowed me to write applications in hours that literally used to take weeks. What's more, it was powerful and extensible enough for use in serious professional applications.

I was so certain that Visual Basic would be a success that I founded a company, Desaware, with the sole intent to provide enhancements and tools that would extend the language's capabilities. Through developing these tools and following and participating in the Visual Basic forums on CompuServe, it became clear to me that Visual Basic was potentially far more flexible and powerful than most people realized, and that there was an enormous need for add-on products of various types.

But it also became clear that there was one add-on that was both vastly underutilized and misunderstood, yet was part of every single Windows system—one that contains over 700 powerful and thoroughly tested functions: that is, the Windows Application Program Interface (API) itself. The problem was this: all of the available documentation for the Windows API is written primarily for C or C++ programmers. As such, it provides no insight on how to use the Windows API functions with Visual Basic. Not only that, the documentation contains a great deal of information that is useless to the Visual Basic programmer because it is either incompatible with VB or already duplicates functionality that Visual Basic supports.

After mulling over this for a while, I approached Cindy Hudson at Ziff-Davis Press with the idea for a book on the Windows API that would be targeted directly to Visual Basic programmers. This book is the result.

What Is in This Book

When I first began working on this book, I set out three main goals.

First, I was well aware of the fact that a large number of Visual Basic programmers have absolutely no experience programming in Windows. I wanted this book to be accessible to them as well. But I did not want it to be simply a set of techniques and boilerplate code to copy blindly. The true power of the Windows API demands some understanding of how Windows works and how Visual Basic fits into it.

As a result, this book contains a fairly thorough Windows primer. Key concepts such as windows and device contexts are introduced and demonstrated through code examples. The reader's knowledge of Visual Basic is used as a basis for introducing the corresponding concepts in Windows. In addition, no knowledge of C is assumed—all of the code in the book is written in Visual Basic.

Second, I wanted the book to be immediately useful for both beginning and experienced programmers. In order to accomplish this, the book is divided into general subject areas, each of which is self-contained with an introduction, one or two sample programs, and a function reference listing the Windows functions that are related to that subject. The introduction not only describes the underlying theory of how and why the Windows API functions work, but how Visual Basic fits into the picture.

Finally, I wanted this book to be comprehensive. As such it describes every Windows API function and message that is likely to be even remotely useful to the Visual Basic programmer. Even experienced Windows programmers will find this book useful for its reference sections that describe the use of each function under Visual Basic along with one or more declarations for its use.

 As a bonus, this book contains a dynamic link library APIGUIDE.DLL that offers a number of valuable support functions. For example, it includes functions that support printer device setup for any printer. It also contains a unique control CBK.VBX that is a subset of Desaware's SpyWorks-VB package. This control allows you to use Windows API functions known as *callback functions*, which require that a function address be provided to Windows.

A Quick Tour of the Contents

Part 1 introduces Windows and its relationship to Visual Basic. Chapters 1 and 2 provide the theoretical framework to understand the Windows API. Chapter 3 focuses on the Visual Basic to Windows interface, describing it in enough depth so that the reader will be able to take the C language specification of any dynamic link library and create a Visual Basic interface for it. Techniques for reducing the possibilities of errors are stressed—including the use of aliasing to enforce type-checking on DLL function calls.

Each chapter in Part 2 discusses an aspect of Windows, beginning with the basics such as Windows information and drawing functions, and proceeding to specialized techniques such as bitmap manipulation, printing, memory management, and so on.

Part 3 focuses on Windows messages with an emphasis on how they can be used to extend the functionality of the standard Visual Basic controls.

This book ends with a set of appendixes that define the common data structures and file formats used by Windows, and other reference information.

The sample programs provided on the disk that accompanies this book are intended to demonstrate use of API functions and to teach certain concepts.

While many are useful in actual applications development (I frequently use WinView and APICons during development), they are not intended to be examples of complete or commercial-quality code. They are, however, designed to be easy to extend and I encourage you to do so. Modifying the code and adding your own features is the best way to gain experience in using the Windows API.

How to Use This Book

This book assumes that you already know Visual Basic at least moderately well. It makes no effort to explain how to program in Visual Basic or to define Visual Basic keywords, properties, or events.

If you have little or no experience with Windows, you may find it best to use this book as a textbook. Read all of Part 1 carefully, then read the beginning of each chapter, skipping the function reference.

If you are already well acquainted with Windows, you will probably find the function reference and code samples most useful. You may wish to skim through the chapters as well—especially the sections that deal with Visual Basic compatibility.

Visual Basic Version Compatibility

Over 700 functions are described in this book, along with dozens of data structures and Windows messages. Every effort has been made to characterize these functions as they relate to Visual Basic. Each function and message has a heading in its function reference called "Use with VB." This is where any known incompatibilities or quirks are listed. If "No problem" is indicated, it means that I know of no problems in using that function and have done some testing with that function or one that is closely related. At the same time, it does not guarantee that the function will work under every circumstance. You should be sure to test your application thoroughly. If you do find any problems, please notify me so that any necessary changes may be incorporated into future editions.

The original printing of this book was released for version 2.0 of Visual Basic. This printing has been revised as needed to be compatible with both Visual Basic 2.0 and 3.0. The changes were quite minor because while Visual Basic has changed, the underlying Windows API has not. All of the sample files and listings have been tested with Visual Basic 3.0; however, they are still presented in version 2.0 format to ensure compatibility with both versions.

Some discussion of Visual Basic 1.0 has been left in this revision where appropriate. The listing for the RectPlay example in Chapter 4 discusses how to interpret listings for version 1.0 if necessary.

Conventions

Throughout this book, variables will be defined and used with their Visual Basic type identifier appended. This is done both for clarity and in order to promote a type-safe programming style. Thus the variable declaration form:

```
Dim a%
```

will be preferred over:

```
Dim a as integer
```

Throughout this book, keywords are printed in boldface.

This book is written for use with Windows 3.1. Appendixes E and F list those functions and messages that are not available under Windows 3.1 and should thus be left out of any application that needs to be Windows 3.0 compatible. All of the sample programs except for the CommDemo project are compatible with both versions of Windows.

Closing Notes

I don't think I realized when I started quite how big a project this would turn out to be, and I never imagined how well-received this book would be by the Visual Basic community. As large as this book is, it can't possibly contain all of the information available on Windows. The Windows Software Development Kit documentation itself contains six major volumes plus additional smaller books.

I've been as careful as possible to leave out only that information that is not likely to be useful to the Visual Basic programmer. Examples of this are the owner draw and nonclient messages that are incompatible with Visual Basic, or OLE, DDE, and Common Dialogs that are implemented adequately in Visual Basic and involve significant effort to access directly.

I've also made every effort to ensure the technical accuracy of this book—especially with regard to Visual Basic compatibility issues where much of the information is based on experimentation and deduction.

Nevertheless, you may find some shortcomings in the form of errors, omissions, or areas where difficult concepts are not explained clearly enough. I hope you will feel free to contact me with any suggestions so that they can be incorporated into future editions of this book. I can be reached via CompuServe mail at 70303,2252 (or Internet via 70303.2252@compuserve-.com), and by fax at Desaware: (408) 371-3530. If you don't have access to either of these, write me at the following address:

Daniel Appleman
c/o Ziff-Davis Press
5903 Christie Avenue
Emeryville, CA 94608

DLLs and APIs

Getting a Handle on Windows

The Visual Basic–Windows Interface

1

The Windows API

DLLs and APIs

Moving from DOS to Windows

Dynamic Link Libraries (DLLs)

Application Programmer's Interface (API)

FOR USERS OF MICROSOFT WINDOWS, FEW PRODUCTS IN RECENT HISTORY have generated as much excitement as Visual Basic. One reason for this is that Visual Basic is the first programming tool that truly allows people to write Windows applications without being a Windows expert.

Moving from DOS to Windows

Visual Basic is a comprehensive programming language. It is certainly adequate for a great many applications. There is a good chance, however, that sooner or later you will run into a requirement that Visual Basic does not support directly. For example, sound support, I/O port access, and many bitmap operations are not part of the Visual Basic language.

But this is not really a flaw in Visual Basic. No language can contain every command and function that might be needed by every programmer. In the DOS world, this problem is solved by creating and using libraries of functions that extend the capabilities of the language. These functions can be linked into your programs as needed.

In the Windows world, things are a bit more complex. For one thing, the operating environment is considerably more complicated than DOS—the simple act of displaying a line on the screen involves the use of objects known as Windows handles, display contexts, and pens. The process of linking in external functions is different—Windows applications often use a technique known as dynamic linking instead of the static linking common in DOS (linking will be described in detail later in this chapter).

As long as you are using only Visual Basic functions and commands, this complexity remains mostly in the background. As soon as you are ready to go beyond the built-in features of the language, you are sure to face some of these issues.

Don't panic.

Like any serious programming language, Visual Basic is highly extensible. While a great deal of press has been devoted to the third party add-ons and libraries available for VB, the fact is that the greatest add-on library of them all is included automatically with every copy of the language. That is Windows itself.

There has been a great deal of talk about how complex Windows programming is—and it is, for people writing entire programs in C or Pascal. As a Visual Basic programmer, you already have a good general understanding of how Windows works (though you may not realize it). That is because Visual Basic is very closely tied to Windows. VB events correspond closely to Windows messages. VB properties often correspond closely to Windows styles and properties. In a sense, Visual Basic is a programmable shell for Windows.

The first part of this book covers the relationship between Windows and Visual Basic. This chapter focuses on the transition from DOS to Windows and the issue of extensibility in general. Chapter 2 looks inside Windows and shows how it corresponds to Visual Basic. Chapter 3 is a thorough review of everything you need to know to access Windows functions and DLL functions in general from Visual Basic.

To appreciate the differences between DOS and Windows programming, it is a good idea to take a moment and review the three big differences between DOS and Windows itself.

First, Windows is multitasking—it's able to run more than one program at the same time. Multitasking poses an interesting set of problems. Which program gets access to the screen? How is memory shared? If more than one program are using the screen, which program gets keyboard input? Which one gets mouse input? What if two programs want to use the same serial port? Almost every difference between DOS and Windows programming relates in some way to multitasking.

Second, Windows is event driven. Many DOS programs are written as loops that perform I/O operations as needed. The programmer decides when it is time to check for keyboard or mouse input. Windows programs can receive external events at almost any time, and are not allowed to use continuous loops, which tie up the system and prevent other applications from running.

Third, Windows is device independent. DOS programs frequently need to take into account every possible printer or graphics device type (it is not unusual for a DOS program to ship with dozens of printer drivers, and separate graphics drivers for EGA, VGA, monochrome, and Super VGA graphics mode—and sometimes even for different brands of VGA cards!). Windows provides a graphics device interface (called GDI) that makes it possible to support any graphics device directly—Windows takes care of providing the individual drivers. GDI translates graphics commands so that they appear identical (or at least as similar as possible) on all devices.

Many of the programming issues that will be discussed here derive from these differences. The development of dynamic linking is one such issue.

Dynamic Link Libraries (DLLs)

Linking refers to the process in which external functions are incorporated into an application. The terms *static* and *dynamic* describe this process. Static linking takes place during creation of the program. Dynamic linking takes place when the program is running.

Static Linking

Programming languages are typically extended in two ways. First, most languages provide some capability to access the underlying operating system. In DOS, this is accomplished with interrupt 21 calls to DOS. Second, most languages allow you to create libraries of functions that can be merged into your program. These functions then appear to the programmer as if they were built into the language.

Program modules containing functions are precompiled into object (.OBJ) files. These object files are often grouped into library (.LIB) files using a program called a librarian (such as LIB.EXE).

When it is time to create a final executable version of an application, a program known as a linker scans your application's object files for references to functions that are not defined. It then searches through any specified library files for the missing functions. The linker extracts any program modules containing the required functions and copies them into the new executable file, "linking" them to your program. This process, shown in Figure 1.1, is known as *static linking* because all of the addressing information needed by your program to access the library functions is fixed when the executable file is created, and remains unchanged (static) when the program is running.

Figure 1.1
Static linking

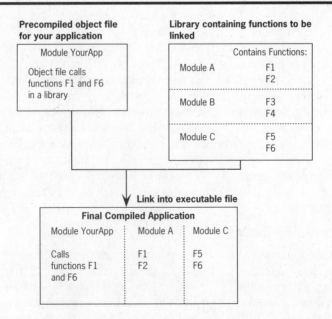

Precompiled object file for your application

| Module YourApp |
| Object file calls functions F1 and F6 in a library |

Library containing functions to be linked

	Contains Functions:
Module A	F1 F2
Module B	F3 F4
Module C	F5 F6

Link into executable file

Final Compiled Application		
Module YourApp	Module A	Module C
Calls functions F1 and F6	F1 F2	F5 F6

Linkers traditionally include entire modules when linking in an executable file, thus functions F2 and F5 in Figure 1.1 are included in the application even though they are not called by module YourApp. Newer compilers and linkers, especially those used by the C++ language, allow inclusion of functions on an individual basis.

Static linking has one minor drawback. Consider the example in Figure 1.2. Imagine you have a function called ShowMessage that displays a message on the screen and requests a user prompt. Say this function is 20k in size and you use it in five different programs.

Figure 1.2
Disk space used
under static linking

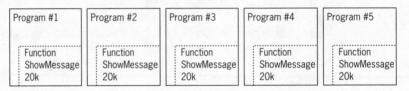

Total space used by function ShowMessage = 100k

As Figure 1.2 shows, 80k of disk space is essentially wasted in copies of the same function. If a typical application uses library functions totaling 100k, it is clear that this can quickly add up.

Still, it's only disk space. It's almost impossible today to find a disk with a capacity under 40 megabytes, so this really isn't much of a problem.

That is, until you start writing Windows applications. Windows is multitasking, meaning that it is quite possible for all five programs to be running at the same time. Now that 80k of wasted space is tying up scarce memory as well.

Another problem that arises with Windows is the issue of accessing the underlying system. With DOS applications, a few dozen operating system commands can be accessed through a simple interrupt scheme. Windows has hundreds of commands. Microsoft addressed these problems by implementing a technique called *dynamic linking* which is described in the next section.

Dynamic Linking

Under dynamic linking, program modules containing functions are also precompiled into object (.OBJ) files. Instead of grouping them into library files, they are linked into a special form of Windows executable file known as a *dynamic link library* (DLL). When a DLL is created, the programmer specifies which of the functions included should be accessible from other running applications. This is known as *exporting* the function.

When you create a Windows executable file, the linker scans your program's object files and makes a list of those functions that are not present and the DLL in which they can be found. The process of specifying where each function can be found is known as *importing* the function.

The dynamic linking process is shown in Figure 1.3.

Figure 1.3

Dynamic linking

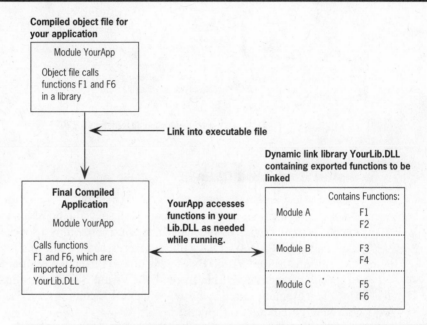

When your application runs, any time it needs a function that is not in the executable file, Windows loads the dynamic link library so that all of its functions become accessible to your application. At that time, the address of each function is resolved and dynamically linked into your application—hence the term *dynamic* linking. Figure 1.4 updates the example shown in Figure 1.2, illustrating how memory is saved by having all applications share the same dynamic link library.

Dynamic link libraries typically have the extension .DLL, but this is not a requirement. Visual Basic custom controls are also DLLs (though they have some special features) and use the extension .VBX. Windows system DLLs use the standard executable extension .EXE.

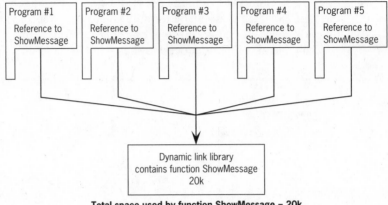

Figure 1.4
Disk space used
under dynamic
linking

Visual Basic and DLLs

Visual Basic does create executable (.EXE) files, but they are not normal Windows executable files. Instead, they contain a special kind of intermediate code known as pseudo code or P-code, which is interpreted by a special Visual Basic DLL called VBRUNxxx.DLL (the xxx corresponds to the version number).

This means that Visual Basic does not go through a regular link sequence to specify external functions. Instead, the Visual Basic programmer uses the Declare statement to tell Windows which DLL contains the desired function and what parameters it expects.

Another side effect of Visual Basic's P-code approach is that Visual Basic cannot itself be used to create dynamic link libraries. Fortunately, Windows offers hundreds of functions and there are many low-cost add-on DLLs available for Visual Basic, so chances are you won't need to create custom DLLs very often.

For those situations where you just have to create your own dynamic link libraries, you will need a more traditional development system and language. The most common tools for DLL development at this time are provided by Microsoft (Visual C++) and Borland International (Borland C++ for Windows and Turbo C++ for Windows). This is a rapidly changing field, however, and new tools appear frequently, so you may want to do additional research if you choose to take this approach.

But, once again, you will find that between Visual Basic, the Windows API, and various third party tools, your inability to directly create DLLs with Visual Basic is no great loss.

Application Programmer's Interface (API)

API is one of those acronyms that seems to be used primarily to intimidate people. An API is simply a set of functions available to an application programmer. The DOS interrupt functions can technically be considered the DOS API. If you write database programs in dBase, the dBase functions you use can be considered the dBase API.

The term is most often used to describe a set of functions that are part of one application but are being accessed by another application. When a Visual Basic program uses Dynamic Data Exchange to execute an Excel spreadsheet function, you can say that it is accessing the Excel API.

So, the Windows API refers to the set of functions that are part of Windows and are accessible to any Windows application. It is difficult to overstate the significance of this concept. Consider the following example.

Bring up the Windows Program Manager and invoke the About command under the Help menu. A dialog box will come up showing information about the system including the amount of memory free in Windows.

Obviously there is a method within Windows for determining how much free memory is present. As it turns out, that function is called **GetFreeSpace** and is exported by Windows (thus it is part of the API and is available to any Windows application).

Try the following trivial Visual Basic program:

```
' Create a new project

' In a module place the following statement:
Declare Function GetFreeSpace& Lib "KERNEL" (byval wFlags%)

' In the form_Click event for form1 place the following line:
Print Int(GetFreeSpace&(0)/1024); "KB Free"
```

Now run the program. When you click anywhere on the form, it will display the amount of available system memory. Almost every aspect of the Windows environment and the API functions associated with it are accessible from Visual Basic.

The Windows API and Visual Basic

When you consider that the Windows API has literally hundreds of functions, it becomes apparent that there is a great deal of capability available.

This may seem overwhelming—after all, learning hundreds of functions can be somewhat time consuming, almost as time consuming as trying to figure out which ones to use in any given case. Fortunately there are a number of factors that help bring this down to size. From the point of view of the Visual Basic programmer, the Windows API functions can be divided into four categories.

1. *API functions that correspond to Visual Basic features.* Many API functions are already built into Visual Basic, so there is no need to access them via the Declare statement. These functions will be covered briefly, as they are of little use to the VB programmer.

2. *API functions that cannot be used from Visual Basic.* There are a number of API functions that for reasons that will become clear later, simply cannot be accessed from Visual Basic. In most cases this is because they require parameters that are incompatible with VB. In other cases they implement operations that are necessary for an independent Windows program that VB handles behind the scenes. Most of these will also be mentioned briefly in Appendix E, but will not be covered in any detail.

3. *API functions that are useful for Visual Basic programmers.* These functions will be covered in detail with examples.

4. *API functions that cannot be called directly from Visual Basic, but can be accessed through a simple interface that performs certain parameter conversions or allows access to information that cannot be obtained directly.* The disk provided with this book includes the dynamic link library APIGUIDE.DLL, which provides support for these functions; thus they will also be covered in detail with examples. As an added bonus, the APIGUIDE.DLL library also contains a number of extra functions (such as port I/O support) that help fill in some of the few remaining gaps. (APIGUIDE.DLL is described in Appendix A.)

The Major Windows DLLs

The Windows API is divided into three major dynamic link libraries and a number of smaller DLLs as shown in Table 1.1.

Before we look more closely at Windows DLLs, let's learn a little bit about Windows itself.

Table 1.1   Windows DLLs

DLL Name	Description
KERNEL.EXE	Low-level operating functions. Memory management, task management, resource handling, and related operations are found here.
USER.EXE	Functions relating to Windows management. Messages, menus, cursors, carets, timers, communications, and most other nondisplay functions can be found here.
GDI.EXE	The Graphics Device Interface library. This DLL contains functions relating to device output. Most drawing, display context, metafile, coordinate, and font functions are in this DLL.
Printer DLLs (generally have the extension .DRV)	Each printer driver has its own dynamic link library that includes printer setup and control functions. These are accessible through an interface provided in APIGUIDE.DLL.
TOOLHELP.DLL LZEXPAND.DLL VER.DLL	These DLLs are part of Windows 3.1 and provide additional capabilities for examining memory, file compression, and version control. In some cases the capabilities are accessible directly; in others you will need to use APIGUIDE.DLL.
APIGUIDE.DLL	Provided on disk with this book. This DLL provides VB interfaces for some incompatible Windows API functions, plus a few additional utility functions.

CHAPTER

2

Getting a Handle on Windows

AS A VISUAL BASIC PROGRAMMER, YOU ALREADY HAVE A GOOD UNDER-
standing of how Windows works. As you read this chapter you will
start to acquire the background that will enable you to use the Windows API effectively.

Relating Visual Basic to Windows

Visual Basic is more than just a language that runs in the Windows environment. It is closely tied to Windows. Visual Basic features and characteristics
almost always have a close correspondence to a feature or characteristic of
Windows. This chapter takes advantage of these similarities to allow you to
use your knowledge of Visual Basic to understand Windows.

An Overview of Visual Basic

Before discussing Windows itself, it's worth taking a moment to review the architecture of Visual Basic. The point here is not to teach Visual Basic (which
you know already), but to identify some of its key concepts with an eye toward later showing the corresponding Windows concepts.

Multitasking

A Visual Basic program can run at the same time as other Visual Basic programs and other Windows applications, a process known as multitasking.
Moreover, unless you specify otherwise, it is possible to run more than one
copy of the same program at one time. For example, if you create a clock program in VB and run it more than once (without closing the previous copy),
you can have more than one clock on the screen running simultaneously.
Each "clock" is considered an *instance* of the clock program.

Each Visual Basic program or instance owns its own forms, and each
form may contain controls.

Forms and Controls

In Visual Basic, forms and controls are objects that represent a rectangular
area of the screen. A form can contain controls that can be considered
"child" controls. Some controls (like the frame and picture controls) can contain other controls as children in a similar manner. Each form and control has
the following capabilities:

- *Properties.* Properties reflect attributes of the form or control. Some attri-
  butes are simple, like the position of the object or whether it is visible.
  Others are more sophisticated and trigger a complex set of operations.
  For example, setting the **path** property for a directory control causes the
  control to be updated based on the path you specified and generates a
  Change event.

- *Events*. Each form or control object can be notified when certain events occur. You have the option of attaching program code to these events. The code will be executed each time the event occurs.

- *Methods*. Each form or control object can be acted on by special functions known as methods. For example, the **Refresh** method causes a form or control to be erased and then redrawn.

System Objects

Visual Basic contains a number of other system objects. These include the Menu, Clipboard, Screen, and Printer objects. Each of these objects allows you to access some underlying capability in Windows. These objects can also have properties and methods associated with them.

An Overview of Windows

Visual Basic really has a very simple and straightforward architecture. You create forms and controls, define their attributes using properties, and write code to handle the various events that occur. Additional code can be written to add functionality (using the command language along with form and control methods), and to work with additional systems objects. Finally, Visual Basic can create an executable file that can run in a multitasking environment.

Now consider the other Windows applications you are acquainted with. They incorporate the following features of the Windows environment.

Multitasking

The earlier definition of multitasking used the clock application as an example. It is clear that it is possible to not only run different applications at the same time, but multiple instances of those applications that allow it. Every application can have virtually any number of windows.

Windows and Controls

Like Visual Basic's form, a window is an object that represents a rectangular area of the screen. A window can contain other windows known as child windows. Windows have functionality associated with them, which can be completely defined by the application programmer. Alternatively, the programmer can assign the attributes and functionality of a standard built-in window such as the list box or edit box. Child windows used in dialog boxes typically use one of the standard window definitions or one defined in a DLL, and are usually called *controls*.

A window has the following features:

- *Attributes*. The concept of a window is extremely flexible; thus it is not surprising that a window has many attributes. These vary from attributes related to appearance such as size, position, and visibility, to functional attributes that define the performance of the window, how it handles keystrokes and mouse events, and so on.

- *Messages*. Every window has associated with it a special function called a Windows function. This function receives messages from a variety of sources, the most important in most cases being event messages from the Windows environment itself.

- *Functionality*. Each window has some underlying functionality. This can be quite sophisticated, as is the case with an edit control, or quite simple as in the case of a window that simply displays text (such as an About box). The functionality of a window can be triggered by external messages through the Windows function, or directly through API function calls.

System and Environment Calls

Windows supports a vast array of underlying system resources and tools. Some are obvious: printer support, menus, and the clipboard come to mind. Some are less well known: information functions, drawing tools, memory management, communications, and sound support only begin the list. As important as these features are, most are incidental to understanding the architecture of the Windows operating environment. Once you understand the basic concepts of the system, these features will fall quickly into place.

Translating Visual Basic Concepts to Windows

Visual Basic and Windows are very similar. A Visual Basic form corresponds very closely to a window in Windows. Visual Basic controls correspond closely to Windows controls. Visual Basic properties and events reflect Windows attributes and messages. Visual Basic system objects provide an interface to Windows system capabilities.

In truth, the similarity is far closer than you might expect. Yes, Visual Basic forms correspond to windows, but that's because they *are* windows. Visual Basic controls contain standard Windows controls. Many VB properties and events correspond on a one-to-one basis with standard Windows attributes and messages.

This correspondence between Visual Basic features and Windows is critical, and one of the things that make Visual Basic the powerful tool that it is. Because a VB form is a window, virtually every Windows API function or message can be used with a VB form. Because a VB control encapsulates a standard Windows control, virtually every API function or message that accesses Windows controls will also work on a Visual Basic control.

As a result, a very large percentage of the hundreds of functions provided by Windows are not only accessible but are also useful to the Visual Basic programmer.

Inside Windows

It is one thing to say that Visual Basic and Windows are similar. Taking advantage of it is something else. Visual Basic provides a very-easy-to-use interface. The attributes of a form or control are accessed easily through a limited number of properties. A window actually has a great many attributes beyond those accessible through the standard Visual Basic properties. The API interface to that information is correspondingly more complex.

In the next section we'll look in greater detail at the internal workings of Windows. This will help you better understand both the API and Visual Basic itself.

What Is a Window?

The most important thing to recognize about Windows is this: If it is on the screen, it is in a window. If it is not on the screen, it is probably still in a window. Forms are windows. Controls such as scroll bars, edit controls, list boxes, and buttons are windows. The icons in the Program Manager are windows, as are the ones on the bottom of your desktop (which are actually two windows—one for the icon, one for the text label!).

This leads to an interesting question. How can two objects as different as a scroll bar and an edit control be windows? How does the system differentiate between the two?

To understand this, it is necessary to look at the different types of attributes that a window can have.

Windows Have Class

All Windows belong to a class. When a window is assigned to a class, it is given a set of attributes that define fundamental aspects of its functionality and appearance, as shown in Table 2.1.

Class information is helpful in determining the type of window you are looking at; however, since changing a class attribute changes the characteristics of every window in the class, it has little utility to the Visual Basic programmer.

For example, let's say you change the class cursor. You can use API functions to load any cursor or create your own, and set it as the default cursor for a class. Unfortunately, doing so changes the cursor for every window of the

class. Since Visual Basic classes are shared by all VB applications, changing the cursor in this manner may affect every application written in Visual Basic that is currently running.

Table 2.1	Class Attributes	
Class Attribute	**Description**	
Class Style	Defines various basic attributes of each window in the class. Examples include whether the window can receive double clicks, if it should be automatically redrawn when the window size changes, and others (see Chapter 4).	
Class Function	The default Windows Function for the class.	
Class and Window Extra Bytes	Class extra bytes are used to hold data that is shared by all windows in a class. Window extra bytes specify extra data area allocated with each window in a class.	
Instance	Specifies which instance owns the class. Most classes that you will deal with in Visual Basic belong either to the system or to the Visual Basic runtime library.	
Icon	Specifies the default icon that appears on the Windows desktop when a window of this class is minimized.	
Cursor	Specifies the default cursor that is used when the mouse is positioned over a window in this class.	
Background	Specifies the default background color for windows in this class.	
Menu	Specifies the default menu for windows in this class.	

Changes made to a class in this manner affect the current runtime environment only (since the information for a class is kept in memory once loaded). It does not modify any application files. The original class definition will be restored when the class is reloaded after being unloaded from the system (or *registered*, as it is called in Windows). When this occurs depends on whether the class is defined by an application, within a DLL, or by the system. Application-defined classes are unregistered when the application terminates. DLL-defined classes are typically unregistered when all applications using the DLL terminate. System classes are registered when Windows loads, so you may need to exit Windows to reload a system class that has been modified. It's enough to say that it is a good idea for any application that modifies a class to restore the original state when it terminates.

Table 2.2 describes commonly used system classes that are built into Windows.

Table 2.2   **Standard Windows Classes**

Class Name	Description
BUTTON	Used for buttons, option buttons, and check boxes.
COMBOBOX	Used for windows that combine an edit control and list box.
EDIT	Used for single and multiline edit controls.
LISTBOX	Used for single- and multiple-select list boxes.
SCROLLBAR	Used for scroll bars.
STATIC	Used for windows that display text.
MDICLIENT	Used for Multiple Document Interface (MDI) windows.

Windows Have Style

Every window has a class defined when the window is created; however, class alone is not enough to define a window. For example, the LISTBOX class includes both single-select and multiple-select list boxes. The EDIT class includes single and multiline edit controls, with and without scroll bars.

Windows uses an attribute called the window Style to define the characteristics of a window within a class. The window Style is a 32-bit flag that is passed to the Windows operating system during the creation process. Figure 2.1 shows some of the common variations determined by the window Style. A window's Style also helps determine its appearance attributes such as border style, presence of a caption and system menu, modality, presence of scroll bars, text alignment, and more.

Chapter 4 goes into detail on how you can examine and in some cases modify the style of Visual Basic forms and controls.

Other Windows Attributes

Windows have a large number of other attributes that can be determined and set by a variety of Windows API calls. Many of these, like position and size, are self-explanatory. A few deserve a closer look.

Parent and Child Relationship

Every window may have a parent window and child windows. This relationship is crucial for managing windows in an application.

Figure 2.1

Sample of control variations based on window Style

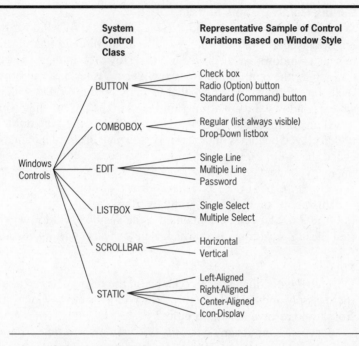

A window without a parent is a top level window. An application typically has a single top level window, which is the main window for the application. When it is minimized, an icon for that window appears on the desktop. It is possible for an application to have several top level windows, though that requires additional effort on the part of the programmer. Visual Basic forms are all top level windows, but Visual Basic takes care of any overhead that this requires.

There are two types of windows that have parents. Owned windows may appear anywhere on the screen. The most common type of owned window, the Pop-up window, is frequently used for dialog boxes. Child windows are confined to the display area of the window to which they belong.

When a window has a parent, it is affected by the parent window in a number of ways:

- When a parent window is shown (made visible), all visible child and owned windows are displayed after the parent window.

- When a parent window is hidden, all child and owned windows are hidden.

- When a parent window is destroyed, all child and owned windows are automatically destroyed first.

- When a parent window is moved, child windows are moved with the parent.

Sibling Relationships and the Z-Order

When a parent window is made visible, all of its child windows that are visible are displayed. As long as windows have a parent-child relationship, the order in which windows are displayed is clear. However, in many cases child windows share the same parent; for example, in Visual Basic all controls drawn directly on a form window have that form as a parent. These windows are called *sibling* windows and are at the same level in the parent-child window hierarchy.

If any of these child windows overlap each other, the order in which they are displayed becomes important. The display order of sibling windows is called the *Z-Order*. This term is derived from the concept of windows appearing in layers stacked up on an imaginary Z axis rising up from the screen. A window at the top of the Z-Order is drawn after its sibling windows and thus appears above them if there is any overlap.

The Z-Order can be controlled using Windows API functions and the Visual Basic **Z-Order** method. which is new to Visual Basic version 2.0.

Focus

Dozens of individual windows can be on the display screen at a time, but there is only one keyboard. How does Windows know which window or control should receive keyboard input?

Keyboard input can go to only one window at a time. The window receiving keyboard input is considered to have the input focus. The way a window indicates focus varies with the type of the window. A button displays a dashed rectangle around the button text. An edit control shows a blinking vertical line called a caret (which indicates the text insertion point) when it has the focus. Focus is usually shifted with the Tab key, but you can control the focus directly using Windows API calls and Visual Basic methods.

The Windows Function

Every window has a Windows function that processes messages very much like a Visual Basic program contains code to process events. Each Windows message has a message number assigned to it. For example, the message that a window receives when it receives the input focus is the WM_SETFOCUS message, which is assigned number 7. This event corresponds to the Visual Basic **GotFocus** event.

The Windows function receives four parameters. The first parameter is the window handle, which will be described later in this chapter. The second parameter is the message number. The third and fourth parameters are 16-bit and 32-bit parameters, respectively, that vary depending on the message. For example, when a window receives the WM_SETFOCUS message, the 16-bit parameter contains a handle identifying the window that has just lost the input focus.

Windows functions are usually written in C; however, if it were possible to write a Windows function in Visual Basic, it would look something like this:

```
' Typical Windows Function
Function WindowsProc&(Byval hwnd%, Byval message%, Byval⇔
wparam%, Byval lparam&)
    Select Case message%
        Case WM_PAINT
            ' The window receives this message when it is
            ' time to update the screen.
        Case WM_SETFOCUS
            ' Place code here describing what to do when
            ' the window receives the focus.
        ' Add cases for additional messages as needed
    End Select
    ' Function DefWindowProc& provides a default response
    ' for each Windows message that needs one.
    WindowProc& = DefWindowProc&(hwnd%, message%,⇔
wparam%, lparam&)
End Function
```

There is one outstanding benefit of this simple message-passing protocol. A Windows Function can be called directly by the application programmer, even if the caller belongs to a different application. This can be done in Visual Basic via the **SendMessage** and **PostMessage** Windows API functions. Part 3 of this book describes this technique in detail.

Superclassing and Visual Basic Controls

Each class provides a default Windows function that is used by every window in the class. However, a window need not use that default function. It is possible for a window to call a user-defined Windows function. This user-defined function can process any messages necessary, and can then call the original default Windows function. This technique is called *subclassing* of a window, because the subclassed window exhibits some of the characteristics of the original class along with those that are newly defined.

When a new class is created it can define a default Windows function from scratch or it can make use of the default function of an existing class. This new class function can handle some messages directly, and pass the rest to the existing class function. This in effect allows creation of a *superclass* of the original class. All windows created in this new class will have a default Windows function that has some of the characteristics of the base class along with whatever functionality was created by the new class function.

There is no limit to this capability. A class can be a superclass of another superclass. Windows of a superclass can in turn be subclassed.

Visual Basic uses superclassing to create the classes for its controls, as shown in Figure 2.2.

Figure 2.2

Visual Basic encapsulation of standard Windows controls

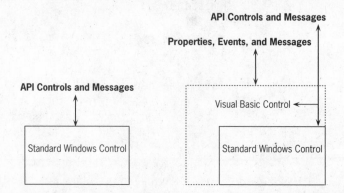

Table 2.3 shows the class names for the standard VB controls for Visual Basic 2.0 and 1.0 and known base classes.

Table 2.3   **Visual Basic Class Names**

Control	Class Name[1]	Windows Base Class
Check	ThunderCheckBox	BUTTON
Combo	ThunderComboBox	COMBOBOX
Command	ThunderCommandButton	BUTTON
Dir	ThunderDirListBox	LISTBOX
Drive	ThunderDriveListBox	COMBOBOX
File	ThunderFileListBox	LISTBOX
Form	ThunderForm	—
Frame	ThunderFrame	BUTTON
Label	ThunderLabel[2]	STATIC
List	ThunderListBox	LISTBOX

Table 2.3   **Visual Basic Class Names (Continued)**

Control	Class Name[1]	Windows Base Class
MDIForm	ThunderMDIForm[3]	—
Option	ThunderOptionButton	BUTTON
Picture	ThunderPictureBox	—
Scroll (Horiz)	ThunderHScrollBar	SCROLLBAR
Scroll (Vert)	ThunderVScrollBar	SCROLLBAR
Text	ThunderTextBox	EDIT
Timer	ThunderTimer	—

1 Thunder was the original code name for Visual Basic within Microsoft.

2 Visual Basic 1.0 only. VB 2.0 and later implements this control as a graphical control.

3 Contains child window of class MDIClass at runtime.

When a message is received by a Visual Basic control that has a base class, the message is processed by the Visual Basic class Windows Function if necessary, then it's frequently sent to the default Windows Function for the base class. This means that many of the messages that work with standard Windows classes will work equally well on the Visual Basic superclass.

Consider this simple example that allows you to quickly find a string inside a list control.

```
VERSION 2.00
Begin Form Form1
    Caption         =    "Form1"
    Height          =    4425
    Left            =    1035
    LinkTopic       =    "Form1"
    ScaleHeight     =    4020
    ScaleWidth      =    7365
    Top             =    1140
    Width           =    7485
    Begin ListBox List1
        Height          =    2370
        Left            =    600
        TabIndex        =    2
        Top             =    720
        Width           =    2475
```

```
        End
        Begin CommandButton Command2
           Caption         =    "Command2"
           Height          =    615
           Left            =    4080
           TabIndex        =    1
           Top             =    1500
           Width           =    1875
        End
        Begin CommandButton Command1
           Caption         =    "Command1"
           Height          =    675
           Left            =    4080
           TabIndex        =    0
           Top             =    660
           Width           =    1875
        End
    End
End

' Declarations
Option Explicit
Const LB_FINDSTRINGEXACT = &H423
Declare Function GetFocus% Lib "USER" ()
Declare Function SendMessage& Lib "USER" (ByVal hWnd%, ⇔
ByVal message%, ByVal wparam%, ByVal lparam$)

'
' Fill the listbox with some sample text
'
Sub Command1_Click ()
    Dim x%
    For x% = 1 To 1000
        List1.AddItem "Listbox entry #" + Str$(x%)
    Next x%
End Sub

'
' This code demonstrates a fast search for a string in
' the list box
'
Sub Command2_Click ()
    Dim hw%, t&
        ' The following two lines can be used to obtain the
```

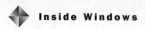

```
    ' window handle for a VB 1.0 list box. The VB 2.0
    ' list box has a hWnd property.
    ' list1.SetFocus
    ' hw% = GetFocus%()
    hw% = List1.hWnd
    t& = SendMessage&(hw%, LB_FINDSTRINGEXACT, -1, ⇔
    "Listbox entry # 15")
    MsgBox "Listbox entry found at " + Str$(t&)
End Sub
```

The form for this small sample program contains a list box and two command buttons. Clicking on the Command1 button causes the list box to be loaded with sample data strings. Clicking on the Command2 button causes an API function to be called that searches for a specific string and displays the number of the entry that contains that string.

This example also illustrates one advantage of using Windows messages to work with Visual Basic controls. Searching for a string in a list control using Visual Basic requires a loop similar to the one shown in the listing for the **Command1_Click** event to fill the list control. This process can be quite slow on list controls with many entries. The message-based technique is extremely fast. This technique is frequently used with the **LB_RESETCONTENT** message on VB 1.0 list controls to quickly clear the control—as VB 1.0 list controls do not support the **Clear** method.

The Visual Basic-Windows Connection Revisited

From the above description, it may seem that defining classes and Windows Functions is a fairly complex proposition. As a matter of fact, it is. This is why the smallest "Hello World" program written in C can take over a hundred lines of code.

Fortunately, Visual Basic handles all of this overhead for you. Some of these tasks (like creating classes, subclassing, and directly creating windows) cannot be accomplished from within Visual Basic without extensive DLL support. Nevertheless, while the concepts introduced in this chapter will be indispensable when it comes to using the API functions and messages effectively, by and large you will be able to let Visual Basic do its work, adding API functions only as needed.

When Is a Window Not a Window?

Version 2.0 of Visual Basic introduced a new type of control called a **graphical control**. Graphical controls are unique in that they are not actually windows, even though they often act like them. A graphical control is an object defined within Visual Basic itself that defines the characteristics of a part of a form or control. For example, the line graphical control describes how a line should be drawn; the label graphical control describes a block of text.

Graphical controls do not support many of the capabilities of a window; for example, they cannot receive the input focus and so cannot accept keyboard input. However, these limitations are offset by the fact that they require much less overhead than a standard control.

The real catch with this type of control is that since it is not a window, it does not have a window handle—an identifier used by Windows to identify a particular window. This means that, generally, it is not possible to use API functions with graphical controls even though they do have a Windows function. The APIGUIDE.DLL library included in this book contains function **agSendControlMessage** that can be used to send messages to graphical controls. It also contains additional functions to work with this type of control.

Further information on graphical controls and how they work with Windows can be found in Chapter 6.

System Objects

The system objects in Visual Basic (such as the Clipboard, Screen, and Printer objects) have no direct corresponding entity in Windows. These system resources are accessed by API functions and are covered in detail in later chapters.

There is, however, one other area of Windows that deserves some attention as it affects almost everything related to display and drawing operations. That is the subject of graphic output and device contexts.

Graphic Output in Windows

One of the great advantages of Windows over other operating environments is that Windows provides a graphical user interface (GUI) to the user. With features such as "point and click" with a mouse, dragging of objects, toolbars, and menus, applications written for GUIs tend to be easier to use and understand than traditional character-based applications.

The Graphical Device Interface (GDI)

It is possible to write a GUI program that runs directly under DOS without Windows, just as it is possible to incorporate graphics into any DOS program, but this involves considerably more work than doing so under Windows.

Consider the task of drawing a colored line across a screen. Conceptually, the task can be divided into several steps.

1. Figure out the screen resolution (pixel height and width).

2. Determine which pixels are in the line and thus need to be set to the specified color.

3. Set the pixels by accessing the graphics hardware.

Not too difficult—until you consider one problem with the typical DOS system; that is, there is no such thing as a typical DOS system. Unless you are willing to limit yourself to one hardware configuration, your line-drawing program must include hardware support for CGA, EGA, MGA, VGA, SVGA, and untold numbers of ultra-VGAs with color support ranging from monochrome to full 24-bit color.

Of course, there are drawing function libraries that help by providing a general interface to the graphics hardware, but what happens when you want to send your output to a printer? Many printers have their own proprietary command languages. Some printer languages like PCL5 and Postscript can take quite a lot of work to support.

Clearly, writing code that supports every probable output device is unacceptable.

Windows therefore provides a device independent graphics library called the *Graphical Device Interface* (GDI). GDI provides an intermediate layer between your code and the hardware. It supports a large set of drawing functions and graphical objects along with the ability to determine the characteristics of the device you are drawing to. It also provides mapping capabilities that allow you to draw to any coordinate system, with GDI performing any scaling or conversion necessary to map your coordinate system to the target device. Above all, Windows provides drivers for literally hundreds of display and print devices, and GDI is able to convert your drawing commands into the language or command stream necessary for each one of them.

Device Contexts

At any given time when you are drawing under Windows, the area being drawn to has a number of specific characteristics. The size of the area available (window size or page size when printing), the color you are using, the background color, and the type of device (display or printer) are just some of these characteristics. They represent the current drawing context. In Windows, this drawing context is described by an object known as a *device context* (DC). A device context that represents a window on the display screen is sometimes referred to as a *display context*.

Figure 2.3 provides a graphical view of the process of drawing under Windows.

A device context describes the characteristics of the current drawing environment for a particular device or window. Table 2.4 describes the more important attributes of a device context.

All the attributes shown in Table 2.4 are described in detail elsewhere in the book (especially Chapter 6). Windows provides a large set of API functions to get and set DC attributes.

Figure 2.3
The Graphical
Device Interface

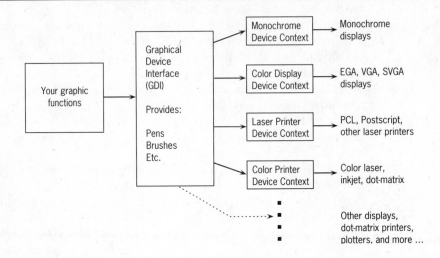

Table 2.4   Device Context Attributes

DC Attribute	Description
Background Color	Used for the background of styled lines and hatched brushes, and when converting bitmaps from color to monochrome and vice versa.
Bitmap	A DC may have a bitmap selected into it. This bitmap can then be transferred to another DC or to the device.
Brush	Brushes are used for filling graphic objects.
Clipping	A clipping region specifies the area within the context that can be drawn on.
Coordinate System	The mapping mode (similar to VB scale mode) and coordinate system to use (see Chapter 6).
Font	The font to be used for text output.
Pen	Pens are used for all line drawing. Pens have several attributes including width, color, style (solid or dashed).
Pen Position	The current location (start point) for drawing operations.
Text Color	Color of text.

Consider once again the task of drawing a color line—this time under Windows. The steps are as follows:

1. Get a device context to use for drawing to a window.

2. Determine the start position and use a GDI API function to set the start position for the line (function **MoveTo**).

3. Set the drawing color by selecting a pen of the desired color into the DC.

4. Call the appropriate GDI API function to draw a line (function **LineTo**).

Windows takes care of accessing the display hardware regardless of the type of display being used. If the display is monochrome, Windows automatically converts the line to monochrome. If the display cannot handle the exact pen color you requested, Windows chooses the closest color available.

The real power of this technique comes into play when it is time to print. If you have a function that draws a line to the display, the same function can be used to draw a line to a printer. All that is necessary is to use a printer device context in place of the window device context. This works on more complex tasks as well. You can create a subroutine that draws a pie chart that accepts a DC as a parameter. If you pass it a device context for a window, it will draw the pie chart on the window. If you pass it a device context for a printer, it will draw the pie chart on the printer. You can even arrange things so that the function will automatically scale the pie chart based on the area available for drawing.

Visual Basic provides access to device contexts for forms, picture controls, and the Printer object, making it easy to call advanced GDI drawing functions for those objects.

Memory Device Contexts

A special type of device context available under Windows is a memory device context. A memory device context essentially simulates a device in memory. A common use of memory DCs is to prepare images in memory before sending them to a device. A complex image can be prepared and saved in a memory bitmap (a block of memory set aside to hold pixels of image data). Once the image is complete, it can be transferred to a compatible physical device context using an extremely fast BitBlt transfer (BitBlt is short for bit block transfer—a very fast function for copying bitmaps).

A Handle for Every Object

Windows, device contexts, program instances, pens, brushes, bitmaps, cursors—these represent some of the most important objects in the Windows environment. They can all be accessed or used in one way or another via Windows API functions. This means that there must be some way to identify these objects and to pass them as parameters to a function.

Windows identifies each of these objects with a 16-bit integer known as a *handle*. Each handle has a type identifier starting with a lowercase h, which is typically used when passing the parameter as a function; for example, a window handle is referred to as hWnd, so the definition of a function like **SetFocus** that accepts a window handle will typically be **SetFocus(hWnd)**. Function definitions and type identifiers will be discussed further in Chapter 3. Table 2.5 provides a brief summary of the most important handles, their common type identifiers, and what they are used for.

Table 2.5   **Windows Handles**

Object	Identifier	Description
Bitmap	hBitmap	An area in memory that holds image information.
Brush	hBrush	Used during drawing to fill areas.
Cursor	hCursor	A mouse cursor. Up to a 32x32 monochrome image that can be assigned to represent the mouse position.
Device Context	hDC	Device context.
Font	hFont	Represents a text font.
Icon	hIcon	An icon. Typically a 32x32 color or monochrome image.
Instance	hInstance	Represents an instance of a running Windows application.
Memory	hMem	Refers to a block of memory.
Menu	hMenu	Menu bar or pop-up menu.
Metafile	hMF hMetaFile	An object in which you can record drawing operations for later playback.
Module	hModule hLibModule	Refers to a code module such as a DLL or application module. Often used to access resources within a module such as fonts, icons, cursors, and so on.
Palette	hPalette	Color palette.
Pen	hPen	Determines the type of line during drawing.

Table 2.5 **Windows Handles (Continued)**

Object	Identifier	Description
Region	hRgn	An area on the window—usually used to specify clipping (the part of the window that can be drawn on).
Task	hTask	Describes an independently running application.
Window	hWnd hDlg hCtl	Represents a window on the display. **hDlg** is sometimes used if the window is a dialog box and **hCtl** if the window is a control—but they are still window handles and can be used interchangeably.

There are a number of other handles that are used less frequently. These will be described along with the functions that use them elsewhere in this book.

Objects can be created under program control or, in some cases, loaded from existing program modules (application modules or dynamic link libraries). When an object (such as a font, bitmap, or icon) is available to be loaded from a module, it is called a *resource*.

Using Handles

Handles refer to objects that are managed by the Windows environment. As such, you must be cautious when using them. When you create an object, it is frequently necessary to destroy that object when you are through with it. Failing to do so prevents the memory used by the object from being freed by the system. Ultimately the amount of available resources and memory will be reduced to the point that other applications will not run and it will be necessary to exit and reenter Windows to continue.

By the same token, deleting or destroying an object that is still in use elsewhere in the system can lead to serious problems including the dreaded "unrecoverable application error" (UAE) or general protection fault (GPF).

Some objects can be "locked." This fixes the location of the object in memory and allows some GDI functions to access it. Locked objects must be unlocked when you are finished using them.

All of the details relating to creating, destroying, locking, and unlocking various objects will be covered when each object is introduced in Part 2.

The Next Step

There is a lot more to be said about Windows, but this brief overview should be helpful. In Part 2 you will find in-depth explanations of many of the concepts introduced here along with the API functions and messages that are necessary to put this information to use. With a good understanding of the material covered in this chapter, you should have no trouble deciphering many of the otherwise cryptic API calls.

One more step is needed before diving into the reference material—that is, a thorough review of the interface between Visual Basic and Windows (or other dynamic link libraries).

3

The Visual Basic–
Windows Interface

The Declare Statement

DLL Parameters

Programming
Techniques

THERE ARE TWO APPROACHES TO TAKE IN LEARNING TO CALL DLL FUNCtions from Visual Basic. One is simply to look at a set of "boilerplate" definitions for the Windows API and use them as given. This approach is certainly fast and easy, but can lead to difficulty when things don't work right, and provides little help in dealing with other dynamic link libraries.

This chapter will present the second approach by helping you understand the procedures involved in accessing dynamic link libraries from Visual Basic. It will begin with an in-depth review of the Visual Basic **Declare** statement, followed by an analysis of the parameter-passing conventions, with emphasis on understanding how Visual Basic data types correspond to those frequently used in DLLs and how to convert from one to another. Finally, this chapter will explore some of the problems related to debugging when using DLLs.

The Declare Statement

The Visual Basic **Declare** statement is used to import a DLL function into Visual Basic. It informs VB where a DLL function may be found, and serves to let Visual Basic know what types of parameters a DLL function expects and what values it returns. Once a DLL function is properly declared, it appears to the VB programmer like any other Basic function or subroutine.

The key words here are "properly declared." The function declaration in VB must correspond exactly to the DLL function in terms of numbers and types of parameters and the type of value returned. Any errors in this declaration are likely to lead to general protection faults (GPFs) or unrecoverable application errors (UAEs), which will, at the very least, cause you to lose all work done in your Visual Basic project since it was last saved.

The syntax for the Visual Basic **Declare** statement is as follows for subroutines that do not return a value:

```
Declare Sub globalname Lib libname$ [Alias aliasname$]⇔
[(argument list)]
```

For functions that return a value it is:

```
Declare Function globalname Lib libname$ [Alias aliasname$]⇔
[(argument list)]
```

In the **Declare** statement, *globalname* is the name of the function in the dynamic link library. If you are defining a function, you should append a type specifier to the name (for example, *globalname%*, *globalname&*, *etc.*) to indicate the type of value returned by the function. Alternatively, you can add the **AS** *typename* specifier to the end of the function declaration where *typename* is one of **Integer**, **Long**, **Single**, **Double**, **Currency**, **String**, or **Variant**. In all cases, this book uses the type specifier character appended to the variable name to specify type. This tends to encourage stronger typing throughout the program, improves clarity, and keeps lines shorter (which can be an issue for some of the longer DLL declarations).

libname$ is the name of the dynamic link library that contains the function and specifies to Visual Basic where to look for that function. This is a string type and thus must be enclosed in quotes. The name must include the file extension of the DLL unless it is one of the three Windows DLLs USER, KERNEL, or GDI, in which case no extension is needed.

These two examples illustrate use of the *globalname* and *libname* parameters:

```
Declare Function agGetInstance% Lib "apiguide.dll"()
```

```
Declare Function GetVersion% Lib "Kernel" ()
```

The **Alias** *aliasname$* option is used when you wish the function to be called in Visual Basic by a name other than the one defined in the dynamic link library. One case where this is useful is where the function name in the DLL contains a character that cannot be used in a Visual Basic function name. For example, the **_lopen** function in Windows has a leading underscore. It can still be used in Visual Basic by defining it as follows:

```
Declare Function lopen% Lib "Kernel" Alias "_lopen" (ByVal⇔
lpPathName$, ByVal iReadWrite%)
```

Aliasing can also be used to provide improved type checking for DLL functions that can accept parameters that reflect multiple types. This will be described later in this chapter.

Argument Lists

An argument list is a list of dummy parameter names indicating the parameters that are passed to the function. The terms *argument* and *parameter* both have the same meaning in this context. Visual Basic tends to use the term argument in its documentation, while Windows uses parameter. This book follows the Windows convention.

The "dummy" variable names in an argument list are merely placeholders—they have no significance outside of the declaration. This means that if you define an argument list like this:

```
ByVal dummy1%, ByVal dummy2%
```

dummy1% and *dummy2%* are not significant outside of this line, nor will they conflict with other variables of the same name elsewhere in the program.

Call by Reference versus Call by Value

The default calling convention for Visual Basic is *call by reference*. This means that Visual Basic passes to the DLL a pointer to the argument variable itself. The DLL can modify the actual parameter because it has a pointer indicating where in memory the parameter is located.

Call by value is a calling convention in which a copy of the parameter value is passed to the DLL. This is specified for numeric data types by preceding the parameter with the word **ByVal**. Figure 3.1 illustrates the differences between these calling conventions.

Figure 3.1

Numeric calling conventions

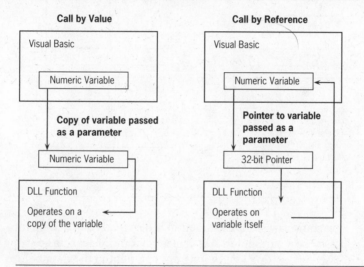

Calling Conventions for String Parameters

Visual Basic is somewhat inconsistent in the use of **ByVal** with string variables.

There are two types of strings supported in the interface between Visual Basic and the DLL interface. If the **ByVal** keyword is absent, Visual Basic will pass to the DLL function a VB string handle (known as the **HLSTR** data type). This string handle can only be recognized by DLLs that are designed specifically for Visual Basic.

Windows API functions expect string parameters to be passed as a pointer to a null terminated string, that is, a string of characters, where the end of the string is identified by a character with the ASCII value of 0. This is the string format used by the C programming language. When the **ByVal** keyword is used with a string parameter, Visual Basic converts the string into C language format by adding a null termination character. Because the parameter is a pointer, the DLL is capable of modifying the string even though the

ByVal keyword is specified. Figure 3.2 shows the differences between the two string calling conventions.

Figure 3.2
String calling
conventions

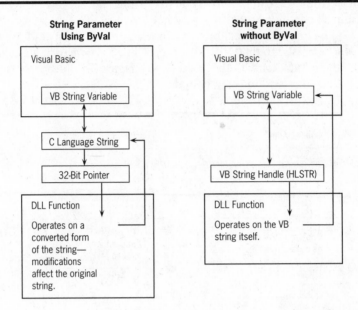

In some cases, a DLL function is designed to load data into a string that is passed as a parameter. It is critical that the Visual Basic string variable be preassigned a string length long enough to hold the data before it is passed as a parameter to the DLL function. This can be done by using a fixed length string, or by setting the string length using the **String$** function. Additional issues relating to string parameters will be covered later in this chapter.

The calling convention specified in the **Declare** statement must match that expected by the DLL function (this applies to both numeric and string data types). The most common cause of UAEs or "bad DLL calling convention" errors is the failure to include the **ByVal** keyword when it is needed, or failure to omit it when omission is necessary. How to determine if a DLL expects a parameter to be called by value or by reference will be discussed later in this chapter.

DLL Parameters

In order to understand how to create argument lists for dynamic link libraries, it is necessary to first examine the types of parameters that DLLs may use. Since dynamic link libraries are typically written in C, they can use a

wide variety of parameters that are not supported directly by Visual Basic. The choice of appropriate Visual Basic variable types is not always obvious. In fact, it is not always possible to find a type or create a Visual Basic type definition to match a given DLL parameter.

DLL Parameter Types and Notation

Table 3.1 lists parameter types that are available to DLLs created using the C or C++ programming language. The type listed indicates the C language data type—information that is frequently provided as part of the documentation for DLL functions. This table is based on current 16-bit compiler technology; 32-bit compilers often define **int** as a 32-bit number.

Table 3.1   **C/C++ Data Types Commonly Used in DLLs**

Type	Description
BOOL	16-bit Boolean value.
BYTE	Eight-bit unsigned integer. A full 16 bits are used when passing BYTE parameters.
char	Eight-bit signed integer. A full 16 bits are used when passing char parameters.
FARPROC	32-bit (far) pointer to a function or procedure.
HANDLE	Handle to a Windows object. A 16-bit unsigned integer.
int, short	16-bit signed integer.
long	32-bit signed integer (VB Long integer).
LP....	32-bit (Long) pointer to a structure or other data item.
LPINT	32-bit (Long) pointer to a 16-bit signed integer.
LPSTR	32-bit (Long) pointer to a C type null terminated string.
NP....	16-bit (Near) pointer to a structure or other data item.
NPSTR	16-bit (Near) pointer to a C type null terminated string.
unsigned int, unsigned short, WORD	16-bit unsigned integer.
unsigned long, DWORD	32-bit unsigned integer. Also referred to as a "double word."

Table 3.2 covers the basic and most common types of DLL parameters. There are some notational conventions that can help determine the type of DLL parameters. These notations take the form of a one- or two-character prefix to the variable type and are commonly used with DLL documentation.

Table 3.2 **Notation Conventions**

Notation	Description	Example
b	Indicates Boolean.	bVisible
c	Indicates character.	cVar
dw	Indicates 32-bit unsigned integer (double word).	dwVar
f	Flag bits within a 16- or 32-bit variable.	fReset
h	Indicates a handle.	hWnd
l	Indicates a 32-bit integer.	lParam
lp	Indicates a 32-bit (Long) pointer.	lpString
n	Indicates a 16-bit integer.	nChars
p	Indicates a 16-bit pointer.	pInt
w	Indicates a 16-bit unsigned integer (word).	wParam

These notation conventions can be helpful in keeping track of the types of parameters that a DLL function takes. The correct Visual Basic data type to use depends first on the width of the parameter (16 or 32 bits). If the parameter is a pointer, the data or structure referred to by the pointer is the next most important factor.

The remainder of this section reviews interface techniques for each of the various parameter types.

Eight- and 16-Bit Numeric Parameters

The eight- and 16-bit numeric parameters include the following DLL parameter types: int, short, unsigned int, unsigned short, BOOL, and WORD. These are all 16-bit data types that are called by value. Thus the Visual Basic parameter for this type will always be (**ByVal** *param* **As Integer**) or (**ByVal** *paramname* %).

Booleans

Both Visual Basic and C define a Boolean FALSE as zero, and all nonzero values as TRUE. It is important to note, however, that in C programming the value for TRUE is typically 1, whereas in Visual Basic the value of TRUE is typically –1. This difference can lead to confusion in cases where a programmer makes assumptions about the value of the TRUE condition. For example, to determine if a window is visible using the **IsWindowVisible**() API, use:

```
If IsWindowVisible(hWnd%) then .... '
```

The following probably won't work:

```
If IsWindowVisible(hWnd%)= -1 then ....
```

The latter example may not work because Windows does not specify that IsWindowVisible will return –1 when a window is visible, only that the result will be nonzero.

16-Bit Signed Integers

Signed integers (**int**, **short**) are some of the easiest data types to handle from Visual Basic. The Visual Basic integer data type works perfectly.

16-Bit Unsigned Integers

The Visual Basic signed integer has a range of –32768 to 32767. An unsigned integer has a range of 0 to 65535. Converting to and from signed variables can be accomplished as follows: To pass an unsigned 16-bit integer value from 32768 to 65535 to a DLL, use a signed long value from 32768 to 65535 inclusive. (The value is likely to be in a long anyway, as Visual Basic cannot handle this range of values in the **Integer** data type). Subtract 65536 from the value (hex value &h10000). The result is a negative number that corresponds to the required unsigned value.

```
SignedEquivalent%= cint(UnsignedNumber&-&h10000&)
```

The trick here is this: The DLL expects an unsigned 16-bit value. Even though Visual Basic interprets **SignedEquivalent%** as a negative number, the DLL will interpret the same 16 bits as a positive number in the 32768 to 65535 range.

The same situation exists in reverse when a DLL function returns an unsigned value. The 16 bits returned will be interpreted by Visual Basic as a negative number. When using a DLL that can return 16-bit unsigned values greater than 32767, the integer returned should be loaded into a long integer using the following equation:

```
LongResult& = (Clng(IntegerResult%) and &h0ffff&)
```

In this case the negative number is first converted into a long via the **Clng** function. This results in a long negative number. The value is then masked to remove the high 16 bits. The result is a positive 16-bit number in a long variable.

Eight-Bit Signed and Unsigned Integers
Eight-bit parameters are passed to DLL functions as 16-bit values. Thus they also use the Visual Basic integer definition:

```
ByVal cParam As Integer
```

Eight-bit signed integers can range from –128 to 127. Eight-bit unsigned integers can range from 0 to 255. As long as the Visual Basic variable is within the correct range, it will be passed correctly to the DLL function. No conversions are necessary. The same applies for DLL functions that return eight-bit values.

32-Bit Numeric Parameters

The 32-bit numeric parameters include the following DLL parameter types: **long**, **unsigned long**, **DWORD**. These are all 32-bit data types that are called by value. Thus the Visual Basic parameter for this type will always be

```
ByVal param As Long
```

(or **ByVal** *paramname* **&**).

32-Bit Signed Integers
The Visual Basic **Long** data type is fully compatible with this data type and can be used directly without conversion both as a parameter and as a function return value.

32-Bit Unsigned Integers
A 32-bit signed integer has a range of –2,147,483,648 to 2,147,483,647 whereas a 32-bit unsigned integer has a range of 0 to 4,294,967,295. In the unlikely event that you need to perform an unsigned to signed conversion in the range 2,147,483,647 to 4,294,967,295, use the same technique as that shown for 16-bit values, but use the **Currency** or **Double** data type to hold the intermediate values. The single precision type does not provide enough precision.

Currency Parameters

The Windows API does not use the Visual Basic **Currency** data type. Any dynamic link libraries that use this data type should pose no conversion problems (assuming they work correctly). Treat **Currency** as any other numeric type.

Floating-Point Parameters

The Windows API does not use floating-point variables (this fact is surprising to many). Any dynamic link libraries that use the **Single** or **Double** data type can be converted easily, assuming the DLLs work correctly. In general, you may treat singles and doubles as any other numeric type.

There are, however, two areas where caution may be needed. First, be careful that your **Declare** statement matches the DLL function parameters and return type correctly—**Single** and **Double** are *not* interchangeable.

Second, be sure that the DLL you are using is compatible with Visual Basic in terms of floating-point calling conventions. There are two issues to be concerned with relating to the floating-point calling convention. First, the compiler must use the IEEE floating-point standard. Second, the compiler must use the Microsoft calling convention for floating-point numbers. Microsoft languages pass floating-point values using CPU registers for singles, and by passing a pointer to a temporary area on the stack for doubles. Some other compilers pass floating-point numbers using coprocessor registers. These are not compatible with Visual Basic.

Variants

The Windows API does not use the Visual Basic **Variant** data type. Any dynamic link library that uses this data type will have been designed for use with Visual Basic and should pose no conversion problem. Variants were not available in Visual Basic version 1.0.

Object Handles

All handles under Windows can be represented as 16-bit (two-byte) integers and are passed by value. As such, the integer calling convention:

```
(ByVal param As Integer)
```

or

```
(ByVal paramname%)
```

is used. Keep in mind that object handles are identifiers to internal Windows objects and that no mathematical operations should be performed on them.

Flags and Bitfields

Many DLL functions interpret individual bits in an integer parameter or result as flags, each with its own meaning. It is therefore important to know how to set and retrieve the values of individual bits and groups of bits in a 16-bit or 32-bit integer.

Bit Numbering

Bits are numbered in an integer from the least significant bit (rightmost) to the most significant bit. Bits are numbered starting at 0, as shown in Figure 3.3.

Figure 3.3
Bit numbering for 16- and 32-bit integers

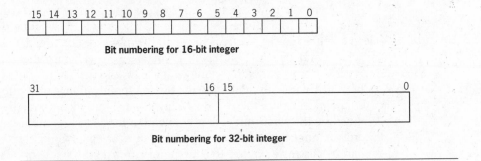

Using Hexadecimal

This book makes extensive use of hexadecimal numbers when discussing flags and bitfields. This is because it is much easier to determine which bits are being manipulated in hex than in decimal. Table 3.3 shows the bit patterns and values for hex numbers one through &H0F.

Table 3.3   **Hexadecimal Bit Patterns and Decimal Values**

Hex Value	Bit Pattern	Decimal Equivalent
0	0000	0
1	0001	1
2	0010	2
3	0011	3
4	0100	4
5	0101	5

Table 3.3   **Hexadecimal Bit Patterns and Decimal Values (Continued)**

Hex Value	Bit Pattern	Decimal Equivalent
6	0110	6
7	0111	7
8	1000	8
9	1001	9
A	1010	10
B	1011	11
C	1100	12
D	1101	13
E	1110	14
F	1111	15

Table 3.3 shows that if you wanted a number in which only bit 2 was set, number 4 satisfies that condition. At first glance, hexadecimal seems to be no easier than decimal.

Now consider the case where you want a 16-bit integer in which only bit 6 is set.

In decimal, this requires a fair amount of math. Each binary position represents a power of two (bit 0 is 2^0, bit 1 is 2^1, etc.) so bit 6 is 2^6, which is 64.

In hexadecimal, the solution is much easier. A 16-bit hexadecimal number is made up of four hexadecimal digits. The first digit represents bits 0 through 3, the second digit represents bits 4-7, and so on. Bit 6 is the third bit (bit 2) in the second digit. Bit 2 is represented by the number 4—thus the solution is &H40.

Assume that you wanted to set bit 3 as well. In decimal a number with bits 6 and 3 set is calculated via $2^6+2^3 = 72$. In hexadecimal, the second hex digit remains the same, and bit 3 is set in the first hex digit leading to the result &H48.

If you are still not convinced of the advantages of hexadecimal, consider the problem of determining which bits are set in the following 32-bit number 6029316 (decimal). Not a pleasant prospect. Now consider the same number portrayed in hex: &H05C0004. Each hex digit represents four bits, so the bits set can be determined easily by using Table 3.3 to find the bits set for each hex digit, and taking into account which bits in the 32-bit number are represented by that digit. This is shown in Table 3.4.

Table 3.4   **Determining Bit Values in a Number (Example &H05C0004)**

Hex Digit	Hex Value	Bits Included	Bits Set
0	4	0-3	2
1	0	4-7	none
2	0	8-11	none
3	0	12-15	none
4	C	16-19	19 and 18
5	5	20-23	22 and 20

Three Boolean operators are used frequently in manipulating bits in numbers. These are the **Or**, **And**, and **Not** operators and are described in the Visual Basic manuals.

Setting, Retrieving, and Testing a Flag Bit

Bits are set using the Visual Basic **Or** operator. This is a case where hexadecimal notation comes in very handy—as it makes it easy to see the location of the bits being set. Consider the following examples where f% represents any integer variable:

```
f% = f% or &h0001%          ' Set bit 0
f% = f% or &h0200%          ' Set bit 9
f% = f% or &h0001 or &h0200% ' Set bit 0 and 9
f% = f% or &h0405&          ' Set bits 0,2 and 10
```

Testing of bit values is made easy by the definition that a FALSE condition is described by the value zero. A mask can be created that has set only those bits that need to be tested, as shown here:

```
if f% and &h0001% then ...  ' True if bit 0 is set
if f% and &h0200% then ...  ' True if bit 9 is set
if f% and (&h0001% or &h0200%) then ... ' True if bit 0 ⇔
and 9 are both set.
if (f% and &h0001%) or (f% and &h0200%) then ... ' True if ⇔
bit 0 is set or bit 9 is set.
```

Clearing flag bits is accomplished by using the Visual Basic **And** operator and the complement of the bit you wish to reset. For example:

```
f% = f% and (not &h0001%)  ' Clear bit 0
f% = f% and (not &h0200%)  ' Clear bit 9
f% = f% and (not (&h0200% or &h001%)) ' Clear bits 0 and 9
f% = f% and (not &h0201%)  ' Same as above
```

Working with Bitfields

Many DLL functions use pointers to structures that contain bitfields. A bitfield is simply a group of bits within a 16-bit or 32-bit integer. When one of these bitfields consists of a single bit, it is a flag bit and can be dealt with as shown in the previous section.

When a bitfield has more than one bit, it becomes necessary to perform a shift operator to access it. Consider an example in which bits 2 through 4 are a bitfield in an integer. With three bits, this bitfield can have a value from 0 to 7.

To set the value of this bitfield it is necessary to first clear the previous value, then combine the two values using the **Or** operator. The value can be cleared using:

```
f% = f% and (not &h001c%) ' Bits 2,3,4 are cleared
```

The new value must be shifted left two spaces, then merged with the existing value. Visual Basic does not have built-in shift operators, but this task is easily accomplished through multiplication:

```
f% = f% or (newval% * 4)
```

The multiplier needed to shift n spaces to the left is 2^n.

To determine the existing value, it is necessary to extract the bitfield and shift it to the right. This is done using division:

```
groupval% = (f% and &h001c)/4  ' Get value of group
```

Problems occur when you attempt to access the high order bit (bit 15) of a 16-bit integer. If you begin to get overflow errors, you should convert the variable into a long integer and perform long integer arithmetic.

The Visual Basic function **Hex$()** is quite useful in determining hexadecimal values when working with individual bits—especially when it comes to reviewing intermediate results during debugging.

Bitfield Definitions

When you refer to the DLL documentation for a bitfield, you will see it defined in a C structure as follows:

```
struct tagStructName {
    unsigned short field1:1  ' Single bitfield
    unsigned short field2:1  ' Another single bitfield
    unsigned short field3:3  ' 3 bit bitfield
```

```
unsigned short fieldx:n  ' n = # of bits in field
}
```

Bitfields in Microsoft C are assigned from the low order bits; thus in this example **field1** will be in bit 0, **field2** in bit 1, **field3** a three-bit bitfield including bits 2 through 4, and so on.

Strings

Strings include the **LPSTR** and **LPBYTE** data types (pointer to characters, or pointer to unsigned characters). As mentioned earlier, most dynamic link libraries expect null-terminated C language strings. Visual Basic can pass these parameters by using the

```
(ByVal paramname As String)
```

or

```
(ByVal paramname$)
```

convention.

These DLL functions cannot return Visual Basic strings. They do on occasion return **LPSTR** pointers, which can then be copied into Visual Basic strings or user-defined types using API functions. This process is covered in "Inside Strings and Structures" in Chapter 16 and "Global Memory" in Chapter 12.

API Functions That Modify Strings

DLL functions may not return VB strings directly, but they can modify strings that are passed to them. It is therefore absolutely essential that you predefine the length of any VB string parameter that may be changed by a DLL call.

This can be accomplished by either defining a fixed-length string, or using the **String$** function to set the initial length of the string. DLL functions that can change string parameters will allow you to specify the maximum length of the buffer as one of the parameters, or the DLL will provide another function that allows you to determine the length of the string buffer required.

When allocating string length, be sure to allocate enough space for the null termination character used in C language strings. If a string is to hold N characters, you must allocate a string buffer of length N+1.

Note that Visual Basic strings may contain null characters, but C language strings may not (since they use the null character to indicate the end of the string). If you find that strings are being truncated, you may have null characters hidden in them.

Visual Basic Strings

The Windows API uses C language null-terminated strings exclusively. Some dynamic link libraries that are designed for use with Visual Basic (such as APIGUIDE.DLL, for example) can accept Visual Basic strings as parameters. To pass a VB string directly use the (*param* **As String**) or (*param*$) convention; do not use the **ByVal** keyword.

Be sure that the DLL specifically states that the parameter expects a Visual Basic string (or **HLSTR**) format—VB string and C language string parameters are not compatible.

It is also possible for a function to return a Visual Basic string, in which case the function name will have the string type specifier ($), or the declaration will be followed by the **As String** specifier.

NULL Strings versus NULL Values

Some DLL functions that accept string parameters can also accept a NULL value in place of the string. It is important to recognize the difference between a NULL string and a NULL (or zero) value. A NULL string is an empty string. An empty string can be assigned in VB using

```
stringname$ = ""
```

When you pass a NULL string pointer to a DLL function using **ByVal**, you are passing a pointer to a string that contains only the null terminating character. When passing it without the **ByVal** specifier, you are passing a valid **HLSTR** handle to an empty string. In both cases you are passing a valid pointer or handle to the DLL function.

When a DLL function accepts a NULL value in place of a string, it expects the actual value zero rather than a pointer or handle to an empty string. This can only be passed in VB using the **Long** data type. Thus the DLL function has a parameter that effectively permits both the **String** and **Long** data types. Methods for handling functions that accept more than one data type are covered later in this chapter.

Pointers to Numeric Values

Pointers to numeric values include the **LPINT** data type, and other pointers to numeric types as defined by the individual DLL functions. It is extremely common for pointers to be used in this way as parameters.

Visual Basic can pass a pointer to a numeric data type simply by not using the **ByVal** keyword (call by reference). The DLL function can then use this pointer to access the actual variable, and may also modify this variable in some cases. This technique can be used with any numeric data type.

Pointers to Structures

A DLL structure is the same as a Visual Basic user-defined type as created with the **Type** keyword. In many cases it is possible to create a VB user-defined type that exactly matches the structure expected by the DLL. In other cases, that becomes somewhat tricky.

Once you have a compatible VB type definition, it can be passed by reference as a parameter (you cannot pass a user-defined type by value to a DLL).

Converting a DLL Structure to a VB Structure

A DLL structure can contain any number of variables, each with any data type. The standard Windows API structures are defined in the file API-TYPES.TXT, which is provided with this book; however, if you use other commercial or shareware DLLs, you may need to adapt a DLL structure to VB yourself. Table 3.5 shows how various DLL structure data types can be handled in a VB user-defined type.

Table 3.5   **DLL Data Types in a VB User-Defined Type**

Data Type	Entry in VB User-Defined Type
BYTE	Fixed string of length 1 (String * 1).
16-bit number	Integer.
32-bit number	Long.
Bitfields	Combine every 16 bits of bitfields into an Integer. Use techniques described in this chapter to access the bitfields.
Character Array (fixed length)	Fixed length string.
FARPROC (pointer to a function)	Long. Not supported directly by VB. For details refer to the discussion on FARPROCs later in this chapter.
Handle	Integer.
HLSTR (VB string handle)	Variable length string.
LPSTR (pointer to C string)	Long. Use techniques described in Chapter 16 and Appendix A to obtain a long value to use as an address for a VB string.
Number Array (fixed length)	Number array of the appropriate type for VB 2.0 or later. A fixed length string or individual integers for VB 1.0.
Pointer to structure	Long. See LPSTR.
Single or Double	Single or Double (type must match).

Pointers to Arrays

Some DLL functions accept pointers to arrays of numbers or structures. These can be handled by specifying the parameter data type as that of the array data type and using the call by reference convention. You can then use the first element of the array as the parameter. This passes a pointer to the start of the array.

In cases where the DLL function can modify the contents of the array, it is critical that the array be predefined to be large enough to hold any changes. Refer to the documentation on the specific API function to determine its array size requirements.

The following example shows how to pass the first element of an array to a DLL function:

```
' Declarations is:
Declare Sub SendToDLL Lib "alib.dll" (x%)

' In the subroutine use:
ReDim x(10) As Integer
SendToDLL x(0)
```

Under version 2.0 of Visual Basic it is possible to pass an array to a DLL function using the standard array passing syntax as follows:

```
' Declaration
Declare Sub SendToDLL Lib "alib.dll" (x() As Integer)

' In subroutine use:
SendToDLL x()
```

This technique passes a special Visual Basic array descriptor called an **HAD** to the DLL function and should not be used with Windows API functions. Only dynamic link libraries that are specifically designed to work with Visual Basic arrays can use this method.

Pointers to Functions

Pointers to functions include FARPROC, DLGPROC, and other data types that define 32-bit pointers to functions. Many Windows API functions use pointers to functions as parameters in order to allow Windows to call a function in a user application. The user function that is called by Windows is referred to as a *callback* function.

Visual Basic provides no support for callback functions; thus DLL functions and structures that have pointers to functions as parameters cannot normally be used with Visual Basic.

The disk accompanying this book includes a custom control called CBK.VBX, which will enable you to use pointers to functions in some situations by providing a 32-bit pointer to an internal function that in turn triggers a control event when called by Windows. Refer to Appendix A for information on using this control.

Parameters Accepting More Than One Type

In some cases DLL functions are defined to accept more than one type. An example of this is the **LoadCursor** function, which is defined as follows:

```
HCURSOR LoadCursor(hInstance, lpCursorName)
```

where **HCURSOR** is a 16-bit handle to a cursor object, **hInstance** is a 16-bit instance handle, and **lpCursorName** is either the name of the cursor or a 32-bit integer ID for the cursor resource. To support both types of **lpCursorName** parameters it would take the following two declarations:

```
Declare Function LoadCursor% Lib "USER" (ByVal hInstance%, ⇔
ByVal lpCursorName As string)
```

and

```
Declare Function LoadCursor% Lib "USER" (ByVal hInstance%, ⇔
ByVal lpCursorName As long)
```

Of course, both of these definitions cannot coexist in the same program, as Visual Basic would flag a duplicate declaration error if they did.

In order to allow use of functions that accept more than one data type for a parameter, Visual Basic defines the special data type **Any** to declare a parameter that has no type checking. The type of parameter passed is always that of the parameter passed when the function is called. The declaration for LoadCursor would therefore be:

```
Declare Function LoadCursor% Lib "USER" (ByVal hInstance%,⇔
lpCursorName As Any)
```

In this case to call **LoadCursor** with a string parameter you would use the command:

```
res% = LoadCursor%(hmodule%, ByVal cursorname$)
```

where *hmodule* is the handle of the module that contains the cursor and *cursorname$* is the name of the cursor resource. Note the necessity of using the **ByVal** keyword to force the string to be passed correctly as a null terminated C language string.

To use the cursor resource ID you would use the command:

```
res% = LoadCursor%(hmodule%, ByVal cursorid&)
```

where *cursorid* is the long value identifying a cursor resource. Note that both the **ByVal** and **&** specifiers must be included. **ByVal** forces the call by value convention to be used. The **&** type specifier informs Visual Basic that the value is a 32-bit **Long**.

Neglecting to use the **ByVal** in either case, or the **&** type specifier in the later case, will lead to an error, and can cause a general protection fault or other system crash.

The **As Any** type forces the parameter passing convention and data type to be defined entirely by the calling procedure. Any data type can be passed to the DLL either by reference or by value. It is the programmer's responsibility to be certain that the DLL function can accept the parameter as it is passed—Visual Basic does not perform any conversions.

It is possible to move the **ByVal** specifier into the declaration for cases where a parameter is always called by value. The following declaration of **LoadCursor** accomplishes this:

```
Declare Function LoadCursor% Lib "USER" (ByVal hInstance%, ⇔
    ByVal lpCursorName As Any)
```

It is still necessary to include a type specifier with the *lpCursorName* parameter. See "Aliasing" below for a better solution to this problem.

Programming Techniques

There are a number of techniques available to VB programmers that are helpful when accessing the Windows API and other DLLs.

Aliasing

As shown earlier, the **As Any** declaration in an argument list allows any parameter type to be passed as a DLL parameter. This makes it possible to support DLL functions that can accept more than one data type for a particular parameter.

This does have one disadvantage, however. Using **As Any** turns off all type checking for the specified parameter. Consider once again the definition for **LoadCursor**:

```
Declare Function LoadCursor% Lib "USER" (ByVal hInstance%, ⇔
    ByVal lpCursorName As Any)
```

It is true that **lpCursorName** can now be passed a string or long parameter. It is also true that **lpCursorName** can be passed a 16-bit integer, a double, a control handle, or any other data type. This opens the door to all sorts of disastrous possibilities including general protection faults. All it takes is to call the function accidentally with a variable that has an incorrect data type.

One way to enforce strict type checking and help prevent these problems is to use the **Alias** technique in the function declaration. Consider the following two declarations:

```
Declare Function LoadCursorByName% Lib "USER" Alias ⇔
"LoadCursor" (ByVal hInstance%, ByVal lpCursorName As string)
```

and

```
Declare Function LoadCursorByID% Lib "USER" Alias ⇔
"LoadCursor" (ByVal hInstance%, ByVal lpCursorName As long)
```

LoadCursorByName accesses the DLL function LoadCursor using a string as the **lpCursorName** parameter. **LoadCursorByID** accesses the same **LoadCursor** DLL function, but uses a long integer as the **lpCursorName** parameter. Each of these functions enforces strict type checking on the **lpCursorName** parameter allowing Visual Basic to detect incorrect variable types before calling the DLL function and minimizing the chance of a GPF or other system crash.

The Advantages of Type-Safe Declarations

The availability of aliasing poses the Visual Basic programmer with an interesting philosophical dilemma. A look at the WIN31API.TXT file that is provided with the professional version of Visual Basic shows that Microsoft has chosen the first approach for the declaration library that they provide. In cases where a Windows API function parameter accepts multiple data types, the declaration either specifies the more common data type or uses the **As Any** type specifier.

This book advocates using the second approach. The APIDECS.TXT file provided on the included disk includes type-safe declarations for most Windows API functions. Use of the **As Any** specifier places all of the responsibility for accurately defining API parameters in the program code itself. Each time an API function is used, there is the possibility of an error. Not only that, but even an error as minor as a missing type specifier or incorrect use of a **ByVal** command can lead to a system crash.

Using strict type checking does increase the number of function declarations, but it moves the responsibility for defining API parameters to the declaration itself. This minimizes the chances of programming errors and reduces their severity when they do occur. The benefits of this technique, especially on large projects or those that involve more than one programmer, more than justify the extra overhead in function declarations.

Aliasing and Function Ordinal Numbers

Most functions in Windows dynamic link libraries have associated with them a number called an *ordinal number*. It is possible to access functions by ordinal number instead of the function name by specifying the number in the alias string preceded with a # sign. This technique can provide a slight improvement in performance. For example, the **GetVersion** API function is normally declared as:

```
Declare Function GetVersion& Lib "KERNEL"()
```

The **GetVersion** function has the ordinal value of 3, and can thus be accessed using this declaration:

```
Declare Function GetVersion& Lib "KERNEL" Alias "#3" ()
```

Ordinal values for functions can be determined using a utility program that analyzes the header of an executable file or DLL, for example, the EXE-HDR.EXE program that is part of the Windows software development kit and some language products. It is not included with Visual Basic.

Sending Messages

Chapter 2 discussed the fact that Visual Basic has the ability to send messages to controls. There are actually two Windows API functions that are commonly used to send messages: SendMessage and PostMessage. They are declared as follows:

```
Declare Function SendMessage& Lib "User" (ByVal hWnd%, ⇔
ByVal wMsg%, ByVal wParam%, ByVal lParam As Any)
```

```
Declare Function PostMessage Lib "User" (ByVal hWnd%, ⇔
ByVal wMsg%, ByVal wParam%, lParam As Any)
```

SendMessage sends a message by immediately calling the Windows function for the window specified. **PostMessage** sends a message by posting a message into the message queue for the window (that is, the list of messages that are in line to be processed by the window). Messages sent via **PostMessage** will be processed by the window in due course, after the current event has been processed or when a **DoEvents** function is executed.

Part 3 of this book covers the use of these two functions in detail.

Software Support

The disk that comes with this book contains a number of files that provide programming support.

Visual Basic Declaration Files

These files contain the function declarations and the structure and constant definitions that are necessary to access the Windows API from Visual Basic. They are based on the file WIN31API.TXT that is provided with the professional version of Visual Basic; however, several changes have been incorporated into these files to make them easier to use and to help reduce overhead.

WIN31API.TXT suffers two major problems—first, it is impossible to include the entire file in an application module without running out of memory. Programmers need to extract only those declarations and definitions needed for the application using an editor. Second, the file contains declarations for many API functions that are not usable under Visual Basic.

To help solve this problem, instead of providing a single file containing constant, type, and function declarations, three separate files are included on the disk that comes with this book.

- APIDECS.TXT contains all of the Visual Basic declarations for the Windows API functions that are useful under Visual Basic. This file is based on the Windows 3.1 API. Appendix E lists those functions that are new to Windows 3.1 and thus should not be used by programs that need to be compatible with Windows 3.0.

- APITYPES.TXT contains the Visual Basic user type definitions for structures used by Windows.

- APICONST.TXT contains the constant definitions used by Windows. This file is still too large to include in a Visual Basic module, but the supplied program APICONS.EXE makes it easy to extract constants or groups of constants from this file. The complete source of this program is included and described in Chapter 19.

This book also includes file APIDECS.BAS, which contains the full contents of APIDECS.TXT and APITYPES.TXT in the form of a Visual Basic module. This provides a very easy way to add Windows API functions to your programs. All you need to do is add the APIDECS.BAS file to your project and all of the Windows structures and API declarations are immediately available.

For Visual Basic version 1.0, it is necessary to load the contents of file APITYPES.TXT into your global module. Then create a new module and copy into it the contents of file APIDECS.TXT.

APIGUIDE.DLL

Many of the Windows API functions require parameters that are difficult to obtain directly from Visual Basic. APIGUIDE.DLL contains functions that allow you to obtain the instance handle of an application, the window handle of controls that do not provide an **hWnd** property, and much more. It also includes functions to convert among data types and to obtain address information for Visual Basic variables.

A number of other useful functions are included in this DLL and will be introduced as needed. They are also covered in Appendix A.

CBK.VBX

CBK.VBX is a custom control that allows you to use pointers to functions in many Windows API functions from Visual Basic. This capability will also be introduced as needed and covered in Appendix A.

Avoiding General Protection Faults

A general protection fault (GPF) is an error that occurs when an application attempts to access an invalid block of memory. This type of error is also known as an unrecoverable application error (UAE) under Windows 3.0.

When a GPF occurs, you should allow Windows to close your application. In some cases you may need to exit Windows or reboot your system, depending on where memory has been corrupted.

When you are programming exclusively in Visual Basic, the language protects you from many common errors, such as trying to assign a string to a number, or passing illegal parameters between functions.

This protection is limited when dealing with dynamic link libraries, as Visual Basic has no built-in way of knowing what parameters a DLL expects other than in the grossest sense. VB can detect a bad calling convention in cases where the total size of the argument list does not match what is expected, but that is about all. Errors in DLL function parameters are frequently fatal, leading to GPFs or completely crashing Windows (requiring a system reboot).

Visual Basic must rely on your function declarations to determine the interface to each DLL function. It is therefore critical that the declarations be accurate. The rest of this chapter reviews some of the techniques that you can use to minimize the chances of GPFs occurring, and to speed the debugging process when using Windows API functions.

Save Your Work Frequently

When an API function is passed an illegal parameter, it can lead to a GPF. It is strongly suggested that you save your project before testing code that accesses Windows API functions.

Review Your DLL Function Declarations

These must be accurate. Pay special attention to the use of the **ByVal** keyword. A common error that many people make is failure to specify **ByVal** on integer and string parameters.

Watch String and Buffer Sizes

Many Windows API functions return data by modifying the contents of a string, structure, or array that they receive as a parameter. Be sure that the string or array is long enough to hold the data that will be set by Windows, and that any structures are defined correctly.

When Windows modifies a buffer that has not been allocated to the correct length, it will write over the end of the buffer and can easily corrupt critical system data. This can lead to an immediate GPF or, worse, plant the seeds for a GPF to occur later on when the system attempts to access the corrupted data. This type of bug can be notoriously difficult to find because the GPF may not occur until long after the erroneous code is executed.

Use Aliasing to Provide Strong Type Checking

Any DLL function that defines a parameter with the **As Any** data type opens the door to GPFs any time the function is called accidentally with an incorrect parameter. By using aliasing to provide type-safe DLL function declarations, you can eliminate this type of error.

Check for Valid Parameters

Many Windows API functions require that parameters be valid before they are called. For example: passing an invalid window handle to a function can lead to a GPF. Windows 3.1 provides improved parameter checking for Windows API functions (as compared to Windows 3.0), but it is no substitute for verifying the values of variables before they are used as DLL function parameters. Most Windows API functions provide a mechanism for determining if the returned result is valid or if an error occurred.

Windows Control and Information Functions

Hardware and System Functions

Device Contexts

Drawing Functions

Bitmaps, Icons, and Raster Operations

Working with Menus

Text and Fonts

Printing

Menu, Task, and Resource Management

File Operations

Serial Communications

The Clipboard, Sound Drivers, and Other Topics

Advanced Topics

PART

2

Windows API
Functions

4

Windows Control and Information Functions

T HIS CHAPTER COVERS THE WINDOWS API FUNCTIONS THAT DEAL DI-
rectly with the Windows objects that were introduced in Chapter 2.
In Visual Basic, these include both forms and controls. In addition,
two sample programs are presented. The RectPlay program demonstrates use of rectangle functions with Windows. The WinView program allows you to determine the hierarchy of windows in a system and obtain
various types of information about them.

Rectangle and Point Functions

Before we discuss Windows objects themselves, it is important for you to understand two data structures that are used extensively in Windows: the rectangle (**RECT**) and the point (**POINTAPI**). These structures are used as
parameters to many API functions.

A window by its very nature represents a rectangular area on the screen,
so many functions that involve specification of all or part of a window's area
use the **RECT** structure. The **POINTAPI** structure is frequently used in cases
where an X,Y coordinate needs to be specified.

RECT Type Definition

The RECT structure is defined in Visual Basic as follows:

```
Type RECT    '8 Bytes
     left As Integer
     top As Integer
     right As Integer
     bottom As Integer
End Type
```

The **RECT** structure is used to represent a rectangular area. The **left** and
top fields describe the location of the first corner of the rectangle (normally
the upper left corner). The **right** and **bottom** fields determine the size of the
rectangle. The units and coordinate system for these fields can vary depending on the scaling in effect, the object being described, and the API function
being called.

In most cases, the field names are merely conventions and have no functional connotations. For example, there is no absolute requirement that the
contents of the **bottom** field be greater than the contents of the **top** field. The
two locations described may be located anywhere, and may in fact be negative. Figure 4.1 shows some possible rectangles.

Figure 4.1
RECT structure
examples

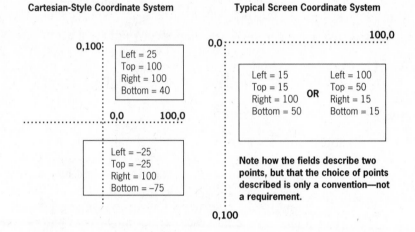

Determining Rectangle Size

One of the slightly confusing subtleties in dealing with **RECT** structures is that the point specified by the **right** and **bottom** fields is generally not part of the rectangle. Consider the rectangle **left**=0, **top**=0, **right**=1, **bottom**=1, where the units are screen pixels. Intuitively, one might expect this to be a rectangle that is two units on each side (thus the rectangle would contain four pixels).

In fact, this rectangle describes a single pixel located at 0,0. The second point (1,1) is not part of the rectangle. This has two very important consequences for the programmer.

First, calculating the height and width of a rectangle is simple:

```
' rc is defined as type RECT
' Note that this example assumes a typical screen
' coordinate system in which the right, bottom fields
' do in fact describe the lower right corner.
' For other coordinate systems, you would need to take
' the absolute value of width% and height%
width% = rc.right - rc.left
height% = rc.bottom - rc.top
```

Note that rectangles with widths or heights greater than 32,767 units are not considered valid rectangles.

Second, the rectangle **left**=0, **top**=0, **right**=0, **bottom**=0 describes an empty rectangle (one that contains no pixels).

Using RECT Parameters

RECT structures are passed to Windows functions by reference. The parameter list for a **RECT** parameter will contain the entry **(rcname As RECT)**.

POINTAPI Type Definition

The **POINTAPI** structure is defined in Visual Basic as follows:

```
Type POINTAPI  '4 Bytes - Synonymous with LONG
     x As Integer
     y As Integer
End Type
```

The **POINTAPI** structure corresponds to the Windows POINT structure, but is defined as **POINTAPI** in Visual Basic to avoid conflict with the VB **Point** keyword.

POINTAPI is used to describe a location. As with the **RECT** structure, the units of the **x** and **y** fields depend on the object and API function being used.

Unlike the **RECT** parameter, which is passed as a function parameter by reference, Windows functions that accept **POINTAPI** structures as parameters sometimes expect them as a 32-bit Long value with the **x** field in the low order 16 bits and the **y** field in the high order 16 bits. You can convert the **POINTAPI** structure to a Long mathematically as follows:

```
' EndPoint is defined as a POINTAPI structure
tlong& = EndPoint.x + CLng(EndPoint.y) * &H10000
```

Alternatively, you can use the **agPOINTAPItoLong()** function in the **APIGUIDE** DLL provided with this book to convert a **POINTAPI** structure directly to a Long.

Rectangle Functions

Table 4.1 describes the Windows API functions that directly manipulate rectangles. Note that rectangles are used extensively by many other functions as well. These functions are described in full detail in the reference section of this chapter.

Example: RectPlay

RectPlay is a program designed to illustrate use of some of the Windows API rectangle functions. Figure 4.2 shows the RectPlay program in action.

Table 4.1   **Rectangle Functions**

Function	Description
CopyRect	Copies the contents of one rectangle to another.
EqualRect	Returns TRUE (nonzero) if two rectangles are equal.
InflateRect	Increases or decreases the size of a rectangle.
IntersectRect	Obtains a rectangle that represents the intersection of two rectangles. This means that all points in the new rectangle are present in both source rectangles.
IsRectEmpty	Returns TRUE (nonzero) if a rectangle is empty.
OffsetRect	Moves the location of a rectangle by the offset specified.
PtInRect	Determines if a specified point is in a rectangle.
SetRect	Sets the fields of a rectangle via function (instead of assigning the fields directly).
SetRectEmpty	Sets a rectangle to empty by setting all fields to 0.
SubtractRect	Subtracts one rectangle from another. It effectively uses one rectangle to "cut off" part of another.
UnionRect	Obtains a rectangle that represents the union of two rectangles. This is the smallest rectangle that fully contains both source rectangles.

Figure 4.2

RectPlay program screen

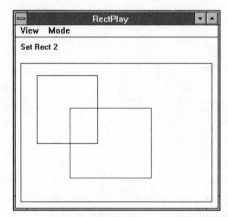

The RectPlay program defines two global **RECT** variables: **Rect1** and
Rect2. It lets you specify the rectangles using the mouse. It can display both
rectangles, as well as the corresponding intersection and union rectangles.
A point mode brings up a message box describing whether the point is in any
of these rectangles.

Project Description

The RectPlay project includes four files. RECTPLAY.FRM is the only form used
by the program. RECTPLAY.BAS is the only module in the program and contains the constant type and global definitions and some program code.
APIDECS.BAS is the type-safe API declaration file provided with this book.
APIGUIDE.BAS contains the declarations for the APIGUIDE.DLL dynamic link library.

Listing 4.1 shows the project file for the RectPlay program.

Listing 4.1   **Project Listing File RECTPLAY.MAK**

```
RECTPLAY.FRM
RECTPLAY.BAS
APIDECS.BAS
APIGUIDE.BAS
ProjWinSize=152,402,248,215
ProjWinShow=2
```

Form Description

Listing 4.2 contains the header from file RECTPLAY.FRM that describes the
control setup for the form.

Listing 4.2   **RECTPLAY.FRM Header**

```
VERSION 2.00
Begin Form RectPlay
    Caption         =   "RectPlay"
    Height          =   4680
    Left            =   1035
    LinkMode        =   1   'Source
    LinkTopic       =   "Form1"
    ScaleHeight     =   3990
    ScaleWidth      =   4950
    Top             =   1140
    Width           =   5070
    Begin PictureBox Picture1
        ForeColor       =   &H00000000&
        Height          =   3255
        Left            =   120
```

Listing 4.2   RECTPLAY.FRM Header (Continued)

```
      ScaleHeight    =    215
      ScaleMode      =    3  'Pixel
      ScaleWidth     =    311
      TabIndex       =    0
      Top            =    600
      Width          =    4695
   End
   Begin Label Label1
      Caption        =    "Label1"
      Height         =    255
      Left           =    120
      TabIndex       =    1
      Top            =    120
      Width          =    3735
   End
```

Checking the menu entry in the MenuViewBar popup menu causes the corresponding rectangle to be displayed.

```
   Begin Menu MenuViewBar
      Caption        =    "View"
      Begin Menu MenuView
         Caption     =    "Rect&1"
         Checked     =    -1  'True
         Index       =    0
      End
      Begin Menu MenuView
         Caption     =    "Rect&2"
         Checked     =    -1  'True
         Index       =    1
      End
      Begin Menu MenuView
         Caption     =    "&Union"
         Index       =    2
      End
      Begin Menu MenuView
         Caption     =    "&Intersect"
         Index       =    3
      End
   End
```

Each menu command in the ModeViewBar menu sets the global variable **SettingState%** to specify the action of the mouse on the picture control.

```
   Begin Menu ModeViewBar
      Caption        =    "Mode"
      Begin Menu MenuMode
         Caption     =    "Point"
         Index       =    0
```

```
        End
        Begin Menu MenuMode
            Caption         =    "SetRect1"
            Index           =    1
        End
        Begin Menu MenuMode
            Caption         =    "SetRect2"
            Index           =    2
        End
    End
End
```

Using RectPlay

The Mode menu defines the three operating modes for the RectPlay program. The three entries in this menu set the **SettingState%** global variable to one of its three allowed values. When **SettingState%** is 1 (the initial value), it is possible to draw a rectangle on the picture control by clicking the left mouse button at the first point, dragging the mouse while holding the button down, then releasing the mouse button at the second point. This defines a rectangle that is stored in variable **Rect1**. **SettingState%** of 2 is similar, except that the rectangle defined is stored in variable **Rect2**.

When **SettingState%** is 0, it is possible to click anywhere in the picture control. If the click position is anywhere within either of the two rectangles, their intersection, or their union, that information is displayed in a message box.

The View menu has four entries: Rect1, Rect2, Union, and Intersection, which indicate which rectangles will be displayed. Each rectangle is displayed in a different color.

RectPlay Program Listings

Before we look at our first program example, let's briefly review the conventions followed in presenting the listings. (See "How to Use This Book" for a full discussion of conventions.) Program listings appear as saved in Visual Basic version 2.0 ASCII file format, but they are also compatible with version 3.0. The listings divide into two parts. The header section describes the properties of both the form and the controls on the form. This header is fairly intuitive as can be seen from Listing 4.2 above, which shows the header for the RectPlay program. A detailed description of this format can be found in the appendix of the *Visual Basic Programmer's Guide.*

The balance of the listing describes the variables and procedures of the form or module. Use the declaration of each **Sub** or **function** to determine the object to which a subroutine is attached if you are using the Visual Basic editor to type in the code. For example,

```
Sub MenuView_Click(Index As Integer)
```

is code attached to the MenuView menu array.

In many cases, a Visual Basic line is too long to place on one line in the program listing. The ⇔ character at the end of a line indicates that the following line is actually part of the same line.

All of the listings and executable programs provided with this book are compatible with versions 2.0 and 3.0 of Visual Basic. Unless otherwise noted, the programs in this book are also compatible with Visual Basic 1.0. In order to load the program into VB 1.0 you will need to perform several steps. The following sequence applies to the RectPlay project, but is applicable to any of the examples in this book.

1. Create a new APIDECS.BAS by loading file APIDECS.TXT into a new module and saving that module as APIDECS.BAS.

2. Copy RECTPLAY.BAS into an empty global module. Merge file API-TYPES.TXT into the beginning of this global module.

3. Create a form and controls based on the header section of RECTPLAY-.FRM. Use an editor to remove the header section, then use the Visual Basic Load-Text command to load the file into the form.

Listing 4.3   **Module RECTPLAY.BAS**

```
' Rectplay
'
' Demonstration of rectangle operations
'
'
'-----------------------------------------------------------
'
'                     Application Globals
'
'-----------------------------------------------------------

' Global rectangles

Global Rect1 As RECT
Global Rect2 As RECT
Global RectUnion As RECT
Global RectIntersect As RECT

Global SettingState%      ' 0 = Point detect mode
                          ' 1 = Setting Rect1
                          ' 2 = Setting Rect2

Global StartPoint As POINTAPI
Global EndPoint As POINTAPI
Global HasCapture% ' Indicates that mouse tracking is in effect
```

Rect1 and Rect2 hold two rectangles set by the user. **RectUnion** and **RectIntersect** are set to the union and intersection of the rectangle. **StartPoint** and **EndPoint** are used during mouse tracking when the user is drawing the rectangles.

Listing 4.4   **RECTPLAY.FRM**

```
'    Displays information about the point in the EndPoint
'    global variable (which is set during the Picturel
'    MouseUp event.
'
Sub DoPointDisplay ()
    Dim outstring$, crlf$
    Dim tlong&

    ' Define a newline string
    crlf$ = Chr$(13) + Chr$(10)

    ' We use PtInRectBynum% as a type checked alias of the
    ' PtInRect API command.
    If PtInRectBynum%(Rect1, agPOINTAPItoLong(EndPoint)) Then
        outstring$ = "is in Rect1" + crlf$
    End If
    If PtInRectBynum%(Rect2, agPOINTAPItoLong(EndPoint)) Then
        outstring$ = outstring$ + "is in Rect2" + crlf$
    End If
    If PtInRectBynum%(RectUnion, agPOINTAPItoLong(EndPoint)) Then
        outstring$ = outstring$ + "is in RectUnion" + crlf$
    End If

    ' Here's a way to pass a POINTAPI structure without using
    ' agPOINTAPItoLong
    tlong& = EndPoint.x + CLng(EndPoint.y) * &H10000
    If PtInRectBynum%(RectIntersect, tlong&) Then
        outstring$ = outstring$ + "is in RectIntersect" + crlf$
    End If
    If outstring$ = "" Then outstring$ = "is not in any rectangle"
    MsgBox outstring$, 0, "Selected Point"
End Sub

Sub Form_Load ()
    SettingState% = 1    ' Set the initial value
End Sub

'    Set the Label1 control based on the SettingState%
'    global variable to indicate to the user what the
'    operating mode is.
'
Sub Form_Paint ()
    Select Case SettingState%
        Case 0
            Label1.Caption = "Point Detect"
```

Listing 4.4   RECTPLAY.FRM (Continued)

```
        Case 1
                Label1.Caption = "Set Rect 1"
        Case 2
                Label1.Caption = "Set Rect 2"
    End Select

End Sub

'   Set the SettingState% variable according to the
'   mode command selected.
'
Sub MenuMode_Click (Index As Integer)
    SettingState% = Index
    RectPlay.Refresh
End Sub

'   Check or uncheck the item to view
'   Then redraw the picture box
'
Sub MenuView_Click (Index As Integer)
    If MenuView(Index).Checked Then
        MenuView(Index).Checked = 0
    Else MenuView(Index).Checked = -1
    End If
    Picture1.Refresh
End Sub
```

The **MouseDown**, **MouseMove**, and **MouseUp** events demonstrate a well-known technique for drawing a rectangle by dragging the mouse. The **Mouse-Down** event records the start location, or anchor of the rectangle. The drawing mode is set to exclusive or, meaning that drawing inverts the pixels on the screen. For example, on a white screen, the inversion process will draw a black line. However, if the same line is drawn a second time, the inversion process will restore the previous state—erasing the line.

The **MouseMove** event erases any existing rectangle using this technique, then draws a new rectangle from the anchor point to the current mouse position. Finally, the **MouseUp** procedure erases the final rectangle, records it in the appropriate global variable, and forces the entire display to be updated.

```
'   Record the current mouse location in StartPoint, and
'   set the drawing mode to exclusive or
'
Sub Picture1_MouseDown (Button As Integer, Shift As Integer, x As Single, y ⇔
As Single)
    ' This conversion is safe, as we are in pixels
    StartPoint.x = CInt(x)
    StartPoint.y = CInt(y)
    EndPoint.x = CInt(x)
```

```
      EndPoint.y = CInt(y)
      ' Drawing will be exclusive Or
      Picture1.DrawMode = 10
      HasCapture% = -1
End Sub


'    If mouse tracking is in effect, and a rectangle
'    is being drawn, erase the prior rectangle and draw
'    one based on the new location.
'
Sub Picture1_MouseMove (Button As Integer, Shift As Integer, x As Single, y ⇔
As Single)
      If SettingState% <> 0 And HasCapture% Then
            Picture1.Line (StartPoint.x, StartPoint.y)-(EndPoint.x, EndPoint.y), , B
            Picture1.Line (StartPoint.x, StartPoint.y)-(x, y), , B
      End If
      EndPoint.x = x
      EndPoint.y = y
End Sub


'    Erase the prior rectangle and save the information
'    in the appropriate global rectangle.
'
'
Sub Picture1_MouseUp (Button As Integer, Shift As Integer, x As Single, y ⇔
As Single)

      ' If we're not mouse tracking, exit the subroutine
      If Not HasCapture% Then Exit Sub

      If SettingState% <> 0 Then
            Picture1.Line (StartPoint.x, StartPoint.y)-(EndPoint.x, EndPoint.y), , B
      End If
      EndPoint.x = x
      EndPoint.y = y
      Select Case SettingState%
            Case 0
                  DoPointDisplay  ' Show point information
            Case 1
                  SetRect Rect1, StartPoint.x, StartPoint.y, EndPoint.x, EndPoint.y
            Case 2
                  SetRect Rect2, StartPoint.x, StartPoint.y, EndPoint.x, EndPoint.y
      End Select
      HasCapture% = 0
      ' Restore the original drawing mode
      Picture1.DrawMode = 13
      Picture1.Refresh
End Sub


'    Draw each of the rectangles that are requested,
'    each in a different color.
'
```

```
Sub Picture1_Paint ()


    ' Find the union and intersection rectangles
    ' Using API calls
    dummy% = IntersectRect(RectIntersect, Rect1, Rect2)
    dummy% = UnionRect(RectUnion, Rect1, Rect2)

    If MenuView(0).Checked Then ' Rect1
        Picture1.Line (Rect1.Left, Rect1.Top)-(Rect1.Right, Rect1.Bottom), ⇔
        QBColor(1), B
    End If
    If MenuView(1).Checked Then ' Rect2
        Picture1.Line (Rect2.Left, Rect2.Top)-(Rect2.Right, Rect2.Bottom), ⇔
        QBColor(2), B
    End If
    If MenuView(2).Checked Then ' Union
        Picture1.Line (RectUnion.Left, RectUnion.Top)-(RectUnion.Right, ⇔
        RectUnion.Bottom), QBColor(8), B
    End If
    If MenuView(3).Checked Then
        Picture1.Line (RectIntersect.Left, RectIntersect.Top)-⇔
        (RectIntersect.Right, RectIntersect.Bottom), QBColor(4), B
    End If

End Sub
```

Suggestions for Practice

You should consider the following suggestions for improving RectPlay to gain
additional experience working with the rectangle API functions.

- Add a command (menu or button) to clear **Rect1** or **Rect2** (use **SetRect-Empty**).

- Add a **RectSubtract** rectangle similar to the **RectUnion** and **RectIntersect** so that you can experiment with the **SubtractRect** API function.

- Add a text field that allows you to enter offset information (x and y) that can then be used to offset or change the size of **Rect1** and **Rect2** (use **InflateRect** and **OffsetRect**).

- Implement a warning box that notifies you if **Rect1** and **Rect2** are equal.

Window Control and Information Functions

This section describes the Windows API functions that relate to the control
and identification of Windows objects.

The functions described here can work on any window in the system. This fact has far-reaching ramifications. It means that it is possible for a VB program to directly manipulate the windows of any running application. It is possible to find out if a particular application is running, and launch it if it is not. It is possible to rearrange all of the windows on the screen, or to minimize or maximize other applications.

This means that the VB programmer must use these API functions very cautiously. One of the nice features of the Visual Basic environment is that it protects you from yourself—in theory it is impossible for VB to crash the system or crash other applications (but in practice, there are a number of bugs that can cause general protection faults). When used incorrectly, the API functions can cause many kinds of GPFs in both VB and other applications. Read the function reference carefully before using these functions.

All of the functions described in this section are usable, if not always useful, to the Visual Basic programmer. There are a number of functions that relate primarily to creation of windows that are either not compatible with Visual Basic, or can be used only with great difficulty or risk. These are described in Appendix E.

Window Hierarchy and Identification Functions

The Windows API provides a number of functions that allow you to obtain information about windows. This includes both information relating to the attributes of a window and information relating to the relationship of windows to each other.

Obtaining the Handle of a Window

All the functions in this section require a window handle as one of their parameters. Visual Basic forms and most VB controls provide the window handle via the **hWnd** property of the form or control. Some custom controls and most VB 1.0 controls do not have a **hWnd** property. For these controls, two common methods are used to obtain the control's window handle.

One technique is to invoke the **SetFocus** method for the control. You can then use the **GetFocus** API function to obtain the handle of the window that has the focus. The disadvantage of this technique is that it demands careful programming to avoid confusion on the part of the user due to unexpected changes in focus and window activation.

The preferred method is to use the **agGetControlHwnd** function that is included in the APIGUIDE.DLL dynamic link library provided by this book or its equivalent. Virtually every available third party DLL for Visual Basic has a function that performs this task, and they can be used interchangeably.

Identifying a Form or Control from Its Window Handle

Many of the functions in this section enable you to find or search for windows in various way. There are two techniques for identifying which form or control is associated with a window handle.

The first technique is to obtain the window handle for known controls and compare them to the handle under question. The second technique is to obtain the form or control name using the **agGetControlName** function in the APIGUIDE.DLL dynamic link library. This function returns an empty string if the window in question is not a VB form or control, making it easy to determine if a window is part of a Visual Basic program.

Graphical Controls

Graphical controls are not actually windows. They do not have an associated window handle or **hWnd** property. As such, they cannot be used with the API functions described in this chapter. As far as Windows is concerned, graphical controls are part of their parent container or form, thus a label or image control on a form is simply part of the form itself.

Window Hierarchy

Chapter 2 discussed how windows exist in a hierarchy of top level windows, owned windows, and child windows. Windows maintains an internal list of every window in the system. The Windows API provides a number of functions that make it possible to search for particular windows and list windows, and otherwise determine the hierarchy of every window in the system.

These functions, listed in Table 4.2, are covered in detail in the reference section of this chapter.

Table 4.2   **Window Hierarchy Functions**

Function	Description
EnumChildWindows	Requires the CBK.VBX custom control provided with this book. Enumerates child windows of a specified window by triggering an event in CBK.VBX for each child window.
EnumTaskWindows	Requires the CBK.VBX custom control. Enumerates all windows that belong to a specified task by triggering an event in CBK.VBX for each window.
EnumWindows	Requires the CBK.VBX custom control. Enumerates all top level and owned windows in the system by triggering an event in CBK.VBX for each window.
FindWindow	Finds a window by class name and/or window name (the window caption).

Table 4.2	Window Hierarchy Functions (Continued)	
	GetActiveWindow	Returns the handle of the active window. The active window is the top level window that is associated with the input focus.
	GetFocus	Returns the handle of the window that has the input focus.
	GetLastActivePopup	Obtains the handle of the last active popup window for a specified window.
	GetNextWindow	Given a window handle, this function obtains the handle of the next (or previous) window in the internal list of windows. If the specified window is a child window, this function will obtain the handle of the next (or previous) child window.
	GetParent	Obtains the handle of the parent window of the specified window.
	GetSysModalWindow	Obtains the handle of the current system modal window if any exists. When a system modal window exists, no other window can be activated.
	GetTopWindow	Obtains the handle of the first (highest-level) child window for the specified window.
	SetActiveWindow	Sets the active window.
	SetFocus	Selects a window to receive the input focus.
	SetParent	Allows you to change the parent window of any window.
	SetSysModalWindow	Makes the specified window system modal, meaning that no other window in the system can be activated.

Examples of many of these functions can be found in the sample program WinView that is presented later in this chapter.

Window Location and Size Functions

Each window has location and size characteristics regardless of whether it is visible or not. The Windows API functions described here always use screen pixel units. If the window is a VB form or control, the **ScaleMode** property has no effect on the parameters, or the values returned by these functions.

This section refers to both screen and client coordinates. *Screen coordinates* are measured in pixels, with the upper left corner of the screen being 0,0. The *client area* of a window is the usable space of the window (not counting the borders, caption, and menu bars). The term *client coordinates* refers to pixel coordinates within the client area, with the upper left corner of the window being 0,0.

The functions listed in Table 4.3 relate to window location and size and are covered in detail in the reference section of this chapter.

Table 4.3   **Window Location and Size Functions**

Function	Description
ArrangeIconicWindows	Can be used to rearrange iconic (minimized) windows that are contained in another window.
AdjustWindowRect AdjustWindowRectEx	Calculate the required size of a window to obtain a specified client area size.
BeginDeferWindowPos DeferWindowPos EndDeferWindowPos	Make it possible to reposition a group of windows at once by building a window position list. **BeginDeferWindowPos** creates a window list handle. Each call to **DeferWindowPos** specifies the new location or visibility of a specified window. When **EndDeferWindowPos** is called, all of the changes will be made at once.
BringWindowToTop	Brings the specified window to the top of the list of visible windows, making it visible if it is wholly or partially obscured. The window is also activated.
ChildWindowFromPoint	Obtains the handle of the child window at the specified coordinates if one exists. The coordinates are client coordinates relative to the parent window.
ClientToScreen	Determines the screen coordinates for the specified point in a window's client area.
GetClientRect	Obtains a rectangle that describes the client area of a window. This is a convenient way to determine the size of the client area in pixels.
GetWindowPlacement	Retrieves a **WINDOWPLACEMENT** structure for the specified window showing the state of the window, and its location when minimized, maximized, and normal.
GetWindowRect	Used to obtain a rectangle describing the location and size of the window rectangle in screen coordinates. The window rectangle includes the border, caption, menu bars, and so on.
InvalidateRect	Specifies that all or part of the client area of a window needs to be redrawn.
MapWindowPoints	Converts one or more points in the client coordinates of one window into the client coordinates of a second window.
MoveWindow	Allows you to move and change the size of the specified window.

Table 4.3   **Window Location and Size Functions (Continued)**

ScreenToClient | Determines the client coordinates in a particular window for the specified point on the screen.

SetWindowPos | Allows you to change the position and size of a window, and to modify its position in the internal windows list that controls display order.

SetWindowPlacement | Sets characteristics for the specified window according to a **WINDOWPLACEMENT** structure. This structure provides the state of the window, and its location when minimized, maximized, and normal.

Window Information Functions and Styles

The Windows API contains a number of functions that provide information on the current state of the window. These are listed in Table 4.4 and are described in further detail in the reference section of this chapter.

Table 4.4   **Window Information Functions**

Function	Description
GetClassInfo	Retrieves the class information structure for the specified window's class.
GetClassLong GetClassWord SetClassLong SetClassWord	Use to retrieve or set information from a window's class.
GetDesktopWindow	Obtains the window handle of the entire desktop (or screen).
GetWindowLong GetWindowWord SetWindowLong SetWindowWord	Use to retrieve or set information about a window.
IsChild	Use to determine if one window is a child window or descendent of a second window.
IsIconic	Use to determine if a window is minimized.
IsWindow	Use to determine if a specified handle is a window handle.
IsWindowEnabled	Use to determine if a window is enabled.

Table 4.4   Window Information Functions (Continued)

IsWindowVisible	Use to determine if a window is visible.
IsZoomed	Use to determine if a window is maximized.

Every class has a class style word associated with it that can be accessed with the **GetClassWord** and **SetClassWord** functions. This style word is defined with the **WNDCLASS** structure listed in Appendix B.

Every window has a 32-bit style and a 32-bit extended style that can be accessed with the **GetWindowLong** and **SetWindowLong** API commands. These are described later in this chapter.

Other Window Functions

The Windows API functions listed in Table 4.5 relate to window objects but don't fall cleanly into any of the categories presented so far. They are described in detail in the reference section of this chapter.

Table 4.5   Miscellaneous Window Object Functions

Function	Description
AnyPopup	Use to determine if any popup window is visible.
CloseWindow	Use to minimize the specified window if it is a top level window. It has no effect on popup and child windows.
DestroyWindow	Destroys the specified window and all child and owned windows for which that window is the parent.
EnableWindow	Enables or disables the specified window.
GetUpdateRect	Determines the portion of a window that needs to be updated.
InvalidateRect	Specifies that all or part of the client area of a window needs to be updated.
LockWindowUpdate	Enables or disables drawing for the specified window.
PostMessage	Use to post a message into the window's application queue. The message will be received by the window during the normal course of event processing by Windows.
RedrawWindow	A powerful function to control the redrawing of all or part of a window.

Table 4.5	**Miscellaneous Window Object Functions (Continued)**	
	ScrollWindow ScrollWindowEx	Use to scroll all or part of the client area of a window.
	SendMessage	Use to send a message by calling the window function for the window. The message is thus processed immediately.
	ShowOwnedPopups	Hides or shows all owned popup windows belonging to the window specified.
	ShowScrollBar	Hides or shows the scroll bars belonging to a window.
	ShowWindow	Use to set the state of a window, including hiding, showing, minimizing, maximizing, and activating the window.
	UpdateWindow	Causes an immediate update of any portions of a window that require updating.
	ValidateRect	Specifies that all or part of a rectangle has been updated or no longer requires updating.

Let's look closer at the **InvalidateRect**, **ValidateRect**, and **UpdateWindow** commands. Each window maintains information internally on whether any part of it needs to be drawn. For example, when a window is created the entire window needs updating. When part of a window is revealed due to the closing of a higher-level window or dialog box, only part of the window may need to be updated. The process of notifying a window that an update is needed is called *invalidating*, and is done with the **InvalidateRect** function.

When all or part of a window is invalidated, it is not drawn immediately. Instead, the window keeps track of the area and combines the area specified by multiple **InvalidateRect** calls into a single invalid area.

When the Windows system has idle time available, it generates a **WM_-PAINT** message to the window, which tells the window to update the specified area. A program can force an immediate update by using the **UpdateWindow** function. If a program draws all or part of a window, it may use the **ValidateRect** function to inform Windows that part of the window no longer needs updating.

Windows 3.1 also added the **RedrawWindow** API function that provides a great deal of flexibility in invalidating and redrawing all or part of a window.

Example: WinView

WinView is a program that illustrates some of the Windows API functions described in this chapter. It includes several functions from each category discussed, with an emphasis on the hierarchy functions. Figure 4.3 shows the WinView program in action.

Figure 4.3

WinView program screen

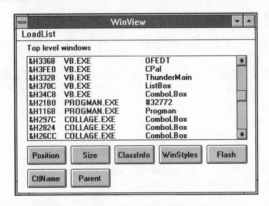

The list box shown in Figure 4.3 contains a list of the windows in the system. Menu commands can be used to display lists of all top level windows, or of the owned or child windows for a selected window. Alternatively, it is possible to point to any window on the screen and add it to the list.

Once a window in the list is selected, command buttons are used to bring up message boxes containing various types of information on the windows selected.

Project Description

The WinView system includes five files. WINVIEW.FRM is the only form used in the program. WINVIEW.BAS is the only module in the program and contains the constant type and global definitions and some program code. APIDECS.BAS is the type-safe API declaration file provided with this book. APIGUIDE.BAS contains the declarations for the APIGUIDE.DLL dynamic link library. CBK.VBX is the generic callback custom control, included on the program disk of this book, that enables use of callback functions with Visual Basic. This custom control is described in detail in Appendix A.

Listing 4.5 shows the project file for the WinView program.

Listing 4.5   **Project Listing File WINVIEW.MAK**

```
WINVIEW.FRM
CBK.VBX
WINVIEW.BAS
APIDECS.BAS
APIGUIDE.BAS
ProjWinSize=175,439,248,215
ProjWinShow=2
```

Form Description

Listing 4.6 contains the header from file WINVIEW.FRM that describes the control setup for the form.

Listing 4.6   **WINVIEW.FRM Header**

```
VERSION 2.00
Begin Form Winview
      Caption        =    "WinView"
      Height         =    4245
      Left           =    1035
      LinkMode       =    1   'Source
      LinkTopic      =    "Form1"
      ScaleHeight    =    237
      ScaleMode      =    3   'Pixel
      ScaleWidth     =    386
      Top            =    1140
      Width          =    5910
      Begin ccCallback Callback1
         Left        =    2580
         Top         =    3000
         Type        =    6   'EnumWindows
      End
```

The List1 list box is loaded with lists of windows. Each entry includes a window handle, followed by the name of the application that owns the window, and then by the name of the class to which the window belongs. The selected window in the list (if any) can be operated on by the command buttons.

```
   Begin ListBox List1
      Height         =    1980
      Left           =    240
      TabIndex       =    8
      Top            =    360
      Width          =    5355
   End
```

The command buttons are used to obtain information about the window selected in the List1 box. The CmdPosition and CmdSize buttons display the location and size of the selected window. The CmdClassInfo button displays the class style of the selected window. The CmdWinStyles button displays the window styles of the selected window that are common to all classes. The CmdFlash button demonstrates the **FlashWindow** API function. The CmdName button is used to display the Visual Basic form name or control name if the window is a Visual Basic form or control.

```
Begin CommandButton CmdPosition
    Caption          =    "Position"
    Height           =    435
    Left             =    240
    TabIndex         =    2
    Top              =    2460
    Width            =    975
End
Begin CommandButton CmdSize
    Caption          =    "Size"
    Height           =    435
    Left             =    1320
    TabIndex         =    3
    Top              =    2460
    Width            =    975
End
Begin CommandButton CmdClassInfo
    Caption          =    "ClassInfo"
    Height           =    435
    Left             =    2400
    TabIndex         =    4
    Top              =    2460
    Width            =    975
End
Begin CommandButton CmdWinStyles
    Caption          =    "WinStyles"
    Height           =    435
    Left             =    3480
    TabIndex         =    5
    Top              =    2460
    Width            =    1035
End
Begin CommandButton CmdFlash
    Caption          =    "Flash"
    Height           =    435
    Left             =    4620
    TabIndex         =    6
    Top              =    2460
    Width            =    975
End
Begin CommandButton CmdCtlName
    Caption          =    "CtlName"
    Height           =    435
    Left             =    240
    TabIndex         =    7
    Top              =    3000
    Width            =    975
End
Begin CommandButton CmdParent
    Caption          =    "Parent"
    Height           =    435
    Left             =    1320
```

```
            TabIndex        =   1
            Top             =   3000
            Width           =   975
         End
```

The **Label1** control displays the type of windows being displayed in the
List1 control. In Point mode, this label indicates the window that is being
pointed to.

```
    Begin Label Label1
        Height          =   195
        Left            =   240
        TabIndex        =   0
        Top             =   60
        Width           =   5415
    End
```

The MenuLoadList popup menu contains menu commands to fill the
List1 control with lists of all top level windows, all owned windows of a selected window, and all child windows of a selected window. The MenuPointed
menu entry causes the program to enter point mode in which you can move
the cursor over the screen and add any window into the window list. The Me-
nuClear menu entry can be used to clear the window list.

```
    Begin Menu MenuLoadList
        Caption         =   "LoadList"
        Begin Menu MenuTopLevel
            Caption         =   "&TopLevel"
            Shortcut        =   ^T
        End
        Begin Menu MenuChildren
            Caption         =   "&Children"
            Shortcut        =   ^C
        End
        Begin Menu MenuOwned
            Caption         =   "&Owned"
            Shortcut        =   ^O
        End
        Begin Menu MenuPointed
            Caption         =   "&Pointed"
            Shortcut        =   ^P
        End
        Begin Menu MenuClear
            Caption         =   "C&lear"
        End
    End
End
```

Using WinView

WinView is a windows information viewer designed to demonstrate some of
the API functions that deal with windows objects. WinView operations fall

into two categories: finding or selecting a window, and viewing information about the window.

Finding and selecting windows is accomplished with the LoadList menu, which has five commands in a popup menu. The TopLevel command loads the list box with a list of every top level window in the system (see Figure 4.3). The window information includes the window handle, application name, and class name. The Children command loads the list box with a list of child windows for the currently selected window. The Owned command loads the list box with a list of owned windows for the currently selected window. Note that since owned windows may also be top level windows, these windows also appear in the top level window list.

The Pointed command allows you to point to any window on the screen and add it to the list box. The Clear command clears the list box.

Once a window is in the list box, it may be selected. Information about the selected window can be obtained by clicking on any of the command buttons.

WinView Program Listings

Module WINVIEW.BAS contains the constant declarations and global variables used by the program.

Listing 4.7   **Module WINVIEW.BAS**

```
'' Winview sample program
'
' The following constants are included from APICONST.TXT
Global Const GWL_WNDPROC = (-4)
Global Const GWW_HINSTANCE = (-6)
Global Const GWW_HWNDPARENT = (-8)
Global Const GWW_ID = (-12)
Global Const GWL_STYLE = (-16)
Global Const GWL_EXSTYLE = (-20)
Global Const GCL_MENUNAME = (-8)
Global Const GCW_HBRBACKGROUND = (-10)
Global Const GCW_HCURSOR = (-12)
Global Const GCW_HICON = (-14)
Global Const GCW_HMODULE = (-16)
Global Const GCW_CBWNDEXTRA = (-18)
Global Const GCW_CBCLSEXTRA = (-20)
Global Const GCL_WNDPROC = (-24)
Global Const GCW_STYLE = (-26)
Global Const WM_USER = &H400
Global Const WS_OVERLAPPED = &H0&
Global Const WS_POPUP = &H80000000
Global Const WS_CHILD = &H40000000
Global Const WS_MINIMIZE = &H20000000
Global Const WS_VISIBLE = &H10000000
Global Const WS_DISABLED = &H8000000
Global Const WS_CLIPSIBLINGS = &H4000000
```

Listing 4.7   Module WINVIEW.BAS (Continued)

```
Global Const WS_CLIPCHILDREN = &H2000000
Global Const WS_MAXIMIZE = &H1000000
Global Const WS_CAPTION = &HC00000
Global Const WS_BORDER = &H800000
Global Const WS_DLGFRAME = &H400000
Global Const WS_VSCROLL = &H200000
Global Const WS_HSCROLL = &H100000
Global Const WS_SYSMENU = &H80000
Global Const WS_THICKFRAME = &H40000
Global Const WS_GROUP = &H20000
Global Const WS_TABSTOP = &H10000
Global Const WS_MINIMIZEBOX = &H20000
Global Const WS_MAXIMIZEBOX = &H10000
Global Const WS_TILED = WS_OVERLAPPED
Global Const WS_ICONIC = WS_MINIMIZE
Global Const WS_SIZEBOX = WS_THICKFRAME
Global Const WS_OVERLAPPEDWINDOW = (WS_OVERLAPPED Or WS_CAPTION Or ⇔
WS_SYSMENU Or WS_THICKFRAME Or WS_MINIMIZEBOX Or WS_MAXIMIZEBOX)
Global Const WS_POPUPWINDOW = (WS_POPUP Or WS_BORDER Or WS_SYSMENU)
Global Const WS_CHILDWINDOW = (WS_CHILD)
Global Const WS_TILEDWINDOW = (WS_OVERLAPPEDWINDOW)
Global Const WS_EX_DLGMODALFRAME = &H1&
Global Const WS_EX_NOPARENTNOTIFY = &H4&
Global Const CS_VREDRAW = &H1
Global Const CS_HREDRAW = &H2
Global Const CS_KEYCVTWINDOW = &H4
Global Const CS_DBLCLKS = &H8
Global Const CS_OWNDC = &H20
Global Const CS_CLASSDC = &H40
Global Const CS_PARENTDC = &H80
Global Const CS_NOKEYCVT = &H100
Global Const CS_NOCLOSE = &H200
Global Const CS_SAVEBITS = &H800
Global Const CS_BYTEALIGNCLIENT = &H1000
Global Const CS_BYTEALIGNWINDOW = &H2000
Global Const CS_GLOBALCLASS = &H4000
Global Const GW_HWNDFIRST = 0
Global Const GW_HWNDLAST = 1
Global Const GW_HWNDNEXT = 2
Global Const GW_HWNDPREV = 3
Global Const GW_OWNER = 4
Global Const GW_CHILD = 5
Global Const ES_LEFT = &H0&
Global Const ES_CENTER = &H1&
Global Const ES_RIGHT = &H2&
Global Const ES_MULTILINE = &H4&
Global Const ES_UPPERCASE = &H8&
Global Const ES_LOWERCASE = &H10&
Global Const ES_PASSWORD = &H20&
Global Const ES_AUTOVSCROLL = &H40&
Global Const ES_AUTOHSCROLL = &H80&
Global Const ES_NOHIDESEL = &H100&
Global Const ES_OEMCONVERT = &H400&
Global Const BS_PUSHBUTTON = &H0&
```

Listing 4.7   Module WINVIEW.BAS (Continued)

```
Global Const BS_DEFPUSHBUTTON = &H1&
Global Const BS_CHECKBOX = &H2&
Global Const BS_AUTOCHECKBOX = &H3&
Global Const BS_RADIOBUTTON = &H4&
Global Const BS_3STATE = &H5&
Global Const BS_AUTO3STATE = &H6&
Global Const BS_GROUPBOX = &H7&
Global Const BS_USERBUTTON = &H8&
Global Const BS_AUTORADIOBUTTON = &H9&
Global Const BS_PUSHBOX = &HA&
Global Const BS_OWNERDRAW = &HB&
Global Const BS_LEFTTEXT = &H20&
Global Const SS_LEFT = &H0&
Global Const SS_CENTER = &H1&
Global Const SS_RIGHT = &H2&
Global Const SS_ICON = &H3&
Global Const SS_BLACKRECT = &H4&
Global Const SS_GRAYRECT = &H5&
Global Const SS_WHITERECT = &H6&
Global Const SS_BLACKFRAME = &H7&
Global Const SS_GRAYFRAME = &H8&
Global Const SS_WHITEFRAME = &H9&
Global Const SS_USERITEM = &HA&
Global Const SS_SIMPLE = &HB&
Global Const SS_LEFTNOWORDWRAP = &HC&
Global Const SS_NOPREFIX = &H80&
Global Const DS_ABSALIGN = &H1&
Global Const DS_SYSMODAL = &H2&
Global Const DS_LOCALEDIT = &H20&
Global Const DS_SETFONT = &H40&
Global Const DS_MODALFRAME = &H80&
Global Const DS_NOIDLEMSG = &H100&
Global Const LB_RESETCONTENT = (WM_USER + 5)
Global Const LB_SETTABSTOPS = (WM_USER + 19)
Global Const LBS_NOTIFY = &H1&
Global Const LBS_SORT = &H2&
Global Const LBS_NOREDRAW = &H4&
Global Const LBS_MULTIPLESEL = &H8&
Global Const LBS_OWNERDRAWFIXED = &H10&
Global Const LBS_OWNERDRAWVARIABLE = &H20&
Global Const LBS_HASSTRINGS = &H40&
Global Const LBS_USETABSTOPS = &H80&
Global Const LBS_NOINTEGRALHEIGHT = &H100&
Global Const LBS_MULTICOLUMN = &H200&
Global Const LBS_WANTKEYBOARDINPUT = &H400&
Global Const LBS_EXTENDEDSEL = &H800&
Global Const LBS_STANDARD = (LBS_NOTIFY Or LBS_SORT Or WS_VSCROLL Or ⇔
WS_BORDER)
Global Const CBS_SIMPLE = &H1&
Global Const CBS_DROPDOWN = &H2&
Global Const CBS_DROPDOWNLIST = &H3&
Global Const CBS_OWNERDRAWFIXED = &H10&
Global Const CBS_OWNERDRAWVARIABLE = &H20&
Global Const CBS_AUTOHSCROLL = &H40&
```

Listing 4.7 Module WINVIEW.BAS (Continued)

```
Global Const CBS_OEMCONVERT = &H80&
Global Const CBS_SORT = &H100&
Global Const CBS_HASSTRINGS = &H200&
Global Const CBS_NOINTEGRALHEIGHT = &H400&
Global Const SBS_HORZ = &H0&
Global Const SBS_VERT = &H1&
Global Const SBS_TOPALIGN = &H2&
Global Const SBS_LEFTALIGN = &H2&
Global Const SBS_BOTTOMALIGN = &H4&
Global Const SBS_RIGHTALIGN = &H4&
Global Const SBS_SIZEBOXTOPLEFTALIGN = &H2&
Global Const SBS_SIZEBOXBOTTOMRIGHTALIGN = &H4&
Global Const SBS_SIZEBOX = &H8&
'-----------------------------------------------------------
'          Application global constants
'-----------------------------------------------------------
Global PointMode% ' True when pointing
```

PointMode% is used to determine if the system is in point mode. When in point mode, the WinView form has the mouse capture (explained in the next listing) and is using the form's **MouseMove** event to update the **Label1** control with information about the window that the cursor is over.

Listing 4.8 WINVIEW.FRM

```
'   Builds a string describing the window in format
'   handle, source application, class
'   separated by tabs
'
Function GetWindowDesc$ (Hwnd%)
    Dim desc$
    Dim tbuf$
    Dim inst%

    ' Include the windows handle first
    desc$ = "&H" + Hex$(Hwnd%) + Chr$(9)

    ' Get name of source app
    tbuf$ = String$(256, 0) ' Predefine string length
    ' Get instance for window
    inst% = GetWindowWord(Hwnd%, GWW_HINSTANCE)

    ' Get the module filename
    dummy% = GetModuleFileName(inst%, tbuf$, 255)
    tbuf$ = GetBaseName(tbuf$)


    ' The following two lines are equivalent
```

Listing 4.8   WINVIEW.FRM (Continued)

```
        tbuf$ = agGetStringFromLPSTR$(tbuf$)
        ' If InStr(tbuf$, Chr$(0)) Then tbuf$ = Left$(tbuf$, InStr(tbuf$, ⇔
        Chr$(0)) - 1)

        ' And add it to the description
        desc$ = desc$ + tbuf$ + Chr$(9)

        ' Finally, add the class name
        tbuf$ = String$(256, 0)' Initialize space again
        dummy% = GetClassName(Hwnd%, tbuf$, 255)
        tbuf$ = agGetStringFromLPSTR$(tbuf$)

        desc$ = desc$ + tbuf$

        ' And return the description
        GetWindowDesc$ = desc$

End Function
```

The **GetModuleFileName** function shown above obtains the executable module name for an application given the instance handle. It is described further in Chapter 12.

When an API function loads a string into a buffer as is done with functions **GetClassName** and **GetModuleFileName**, it simply copies the data into the string buffer with a null character to indicate the end of the string. It does not actually change the length of the string as known to Visual Basic. In order to set the VB string to the correct length, you may use the **InStr** function to determine the position of the terminating null character. The APIGUIDE-.DLL dynamic link library also provides function **agGetStringFromLPSTR$**, which performs the same task.

```
' If source$ is a path, this function retrieves the
' basename, or filename sans path
' source$ MUST be a valid filename
'
Function GetBaseName$ (ByVal source$)
    Do While InStr(source$, "\") <> 0
        source$ = Mid$(source$, InStr(source$, "\") + 1)
    Loop
    If InStr(source$, ":") <> 0 Then
        source$ = Mid$(source$, InStr(source$, ":") + 1)
    End If
    GetBaseName$ = source$
End Function


'   Loads the listbox with a list of all top level
'   windows.
```

```
'
Sub MenuTopLevel_Click ()
    Dim Hwnd%

    ' Clear the listbox
    dummy% = SendMessageBynum&(agGetControlHwnd(List1), LB_RESETCONTENT, ⇔
    0, 0&)

    ' The desktop is the highest window
    Hwnd% = GetDeskTopWindow()

    ' Its first child is the 1st top level window
    Hwnd% = GetWindow(Hwnd%, GW_CHILD)

    ' Now load all top level windows
    Do
        List1.AddItem GetWindowDesc$(Hwnd%)
        Hwnd% = GetWindow(Hwnd%, GW_HWNDNEXT)
    Loop While Hwnd% <> 0
    Label1.Caption = "Top level windows"

End Sub

Sub Form_Load ()
    ReDim tabsets%(2)
    tabsets%(0) = 35
    tabsets%(1) = 110
    dummy% = SendMessage&(agGetControlHwnd%(List1), LB_SETTABSTOPS, 2, ⇔
    tabsets%(0))
End Sub
```

Refer to Chapter 18 for more information on setting tab stops in a list box.

```
Sub MenuChildren_Click ()
    Dim Hwnd%
    Dim windowdesc$

    ' Is there a window selected?
    If List1.ListIndex < 0 Then
        MsgBox "No Window Selected", 0, "Error"
        Exit Sub
    End If
    windowdesc$ = List1.Text

    Hwnd% = Val(windowdesc$)      ' Extract window handle

    ' Its first child is the specified window
    Hwnd% = GetWindow(Hwnd%, GW_CHILD)

    If Hwnd% = 0 Then
        MsgBox "No children found for this window", 0, "Error"
        Exit Sub
```

```
    End If

    ' Clear the listbox
    dummy% = SendMessageBynum&(agGetControlHwnd(List1), LB_RESETCONTENT, ⇔
    Ø, Ø&)

    ' You can use the VB command List1.Clear to clear
    ' the list box under VB version 2.Ø. The message
    ' version is included here to demonstrate use of the
    ' SendMessage function and to preserve VB 1.Ø compatibility.


    ' Now load all the child windows
    Do
        List1.AddItem GetWindowDesc$(Hwnd%)
        Hwnd% = GetWindow(Hwnd%, GW_HWNDNEXT)
    Loop While Hwnd% <> Ø
    Label1.Caption = "Children of: " + "&" + windowdesc$

End Sub

Sub CmdParent_Click ()
    Dim Hwnd%, newhwnd%
    Dim windowdesc$

    If List1.ListIndex < Ø Then
        MsgBox "No Window Selected", Ø, "Error"
        Exit Sub
    End If
    Hwnd% = Val(List1.Text)
    newhwnd% = GetParent%(Hwnd%)
    If newhwnd% = Ø Then
        MsgBox "Window has no parent", Ø, "Window &H" + Hex$(Hwnd%)
        Exit Sub
    End If
    windowdesc$ = GetWindowDesc$(newhwnd%)
    MsgBox windowdesc$, Ø, "Parent of &H" + Hex$(Hwnd%) + " is"
End Sub

'    lpData was passed by the EnumWindows call and contains
'    the parent window handle that we are looking for.
'
Sub Callback1_EnumWindows (Hwnd As Integer, lpData As Long, retval As Integer)
    ' If hWnd is owned by window in lpData,
    ' Add it to the listbox
    If GetParent(Hwnd) = CInt(lpData) Then
        List1.AddItem GetWindowDesc$(Hwnd)
    End If
    retval = 1  ' Continue enumeration
End Sub


'   Show owned windows of the currently selected window
```

```
'
'
Sub MenuOwned_Click ()
    Dim Hwnd%
    Dim windowdesc$

    ' Is there a window selected?
    If List1.ListIndex < Ø Then
        MsgBox "No Window Selected", Ø, "Error"
        Exit Sub
    End If
    windowdesc$ = List1.Text

    Hwnd% = Val(windowdesc$)     ' Extract window handle

    ' Clear the listbox
    dummy% = SendMessageBynum&(agGetControlHwnd(List1), LB_RESETCONTENT, ⇔
    Ø, Ø&)

    ' This uses the cbk.vbx control to obtain a callback
    ' address for EnumWindows.
    ' This will trigger the Callback1_EnumWindows event
    ' for each top level window.  This technique could
    ' also have been used in place of the GetWindow loop
    ' in the MenuTopLevel_Click event.
    dummy% = EnumWindows(Callback1.ProcAddress, CLng(Hwnd%))

    If List1.Listcount = Ø Then
        MsgBox "No owned windows found for this window", Ø, "Error"
        Label1.Caption = ""
        Exit Sub
    End If

    Label1.Caption = "Owned windows of: " + "&" + windowdesc$

End Sub

Sub Form_MouseMove (Button As Integer, Shift As Integer, X As Single, Y As ⇔
Single)
    Dim pt As POINTAPI
    Dim foundhWnd%

    ' Only record window if we're in point mode
    If Not PointMode% Then Exit Sub
    pt.X = X
    pt.Y = Y
    ClientToScreen WinView.Hwnd, pt
    foundhWnd% = WindowFromPointBynum%(agPOINTAPItoLong&(pt))
    Label1.Caption = GetWindowDesc$(foundhWnd%)


End Sub
```

The **MouseMove** event receives coordinates X,Y in client coordinates based on the **ScaleMode** property, which for this form is set as pixels. Because the form has the capture (see the description for the **MenuPointed_Click** event), it will receive **MouseMove** events regardless of where the cursor is on the screen. The coordinates are converted from client to screen coordinates by function **ClientToScreen**; then function **WindowFromPointBynum** is used to determine the window for that position. One technique for understanding this better is to create a label control on the form and set the caption to display the client and screen coordinate values as the mouse moves.

```
Sub MenuPointed_Click ()

    ' Let system know that we're in point mode
    PointMode% = -1
    dummy% = SetCapture(WinView.Hwnd)
End Sub
```

Normally, each window receives mouse events only when the mouse cursor is over that particular window. When a window has the capture, all mouse events are sent to that window regardless of where the mouse is on the screen. Chapter 5 discusses this in further detail.

```
'   If we're in point mode, record the current window
'   in the listbox
'
Sub Form_MouseDown (Button As Integer, Shift As Integer, X As Single, Y ⇔
As Single)
    If Not PointMode% Then Exit Sub
    List1.AddItem Label1.Caption
    PointMode% = 0
    Label1.Caption = ""
    ' If capture is still held, release it - this is
    ' actually not necessary in VB 1.0 as it seems to
    ' release the capture anyway!
    If GetCapture() = WinView.Hwnd Then ReleaseCapture
End Sub

'   Just clear the listbox
'
Sub MenuClear_Click ()
    ' Clear the listbox
    dummy% = SendMessageBynum&(agGetControlHwnd(List1), LB_RESETCONTENT, ⇔
    0, 0&)

End Sub

' Show the position of the selected window
'
Sub CmdPosition_Click ()
    Dim WindowRect As RECT
```

```
    Dim useHwnd%
    Dim crlf$

    Dim outstring$, titlestring$

    crlf$ = Chr$(13) + Chr$(10)

    If List1.ListIndex < 0 Then
        MsgBox "No windows selected", 0, "Error"
        Exit Sub
    End If

    titlestring$ = List1.Text
    useHwnd% = Val(titlestring$)

    ' Get the rectangle describing the window
    GetWindowRect useHwnd%, WindowRect

    If IsIconic%(useHwnd%) Then
        outstring$ = "Is Iconic" + crlf$
    End If

    If IsZoomed%(useHwnd%) Then
        outstring$ = outstring$ + "Is Zoomed" + crlf$
    End If

    If IsWindowEnabled%(useHwnd%) Then
        outstring$ = outstring$ + "Is Enabled" + crlf$
    Else
        outstring$ = outstring$ + "Is Disabled" + crlf$
    End If

    If IsWindowVisible%(useHwnd%) Then
        outstring$ = outstring$ + "Is Visible" + crlf$
    Else
        outstring$ = outstring$ + "Is NOT Visible" + crlf$
    End If

    outstring$ = outstring$ + "Rect: " + Str$(WindowRect.left) + ","
    outstring$ = outstring$ + Str$(WindowRect.top) + ","
    outstring$ = outstring$ + Str$(WindowRect.right) + ","
    outstring$ = outstring$ + Str$(WindowRect.bottom)

    MsgBox outstring$, 0, titlestring$
End Sub

' Show the size of the selected window
'
Sub CmdSize_Click ()
    Dim WindowClientRect As RECT
    Dim useHwnd%
    Dim crlf$
```

```
    Dim outstring$, titlestring$

    crlf$ = Chr$(13) + Chr$(10)

    If List1.ListIndex < 0 Then
        MsgBox "No windows selected", 0, "Error"
        Exit Sub
    End If

    titlestring$ = List1.Text
    useHwnd% = Val(titlestring$)

    ' Get the rectangle describing the window
    GetClientRect useHwnd%, WindowClientRect

    outstring$ = "Horiz Pixels: " + Str$(WindowClientRect.right) + crlf$
    outstring$ = outstring$ + "Vert Pixels: " + Str$(WindowClientRect.bottom)

    MsgBox outstring$, 0, titlestring$


End Sub

' Show class styles for the selected window
'
Sub CmdClassInfo_Click ()
    Dim clsextra%, wndextra%
    Dim style%
    Dim useHwnd%
    Dim crlf$

    Dim outstring$, titlestring$

    crlf$ = Chr$(13) + Chr$(10)

    If List1.ListIndex < 0 Then
        MsgBox "No windows selected", 0, "Error"
        Exit Sub
    End If

    titlestring$ = List1.Text
    useHwnd% = Val(titlestring$)

    ' Get the class info
    clsextra% = GetClassWord%(useHwnd%, GCW_CBCLSEXTRA)
    wndextra% = GetClassWord%(useHwnd%, GCW_CBWNDEXTRA)
    style% = GetClassWord%(useHwnd%, GCW_STYLE)

    outstring$ = "Class & Word Extra = " + Str$(clsextra%) + "," + ⇔
    Str$(wndextra%) + crlf$
    If style% And CS_BYTEALIGNCLIENT Then
```

```
        outstring$ = outstring$ + "CS_BYTEALIGNCLIENT" + crlf$
End If
If style% And CS_BYTEALIGNWINDOW Then
        outstring$ = outstring$ + "CS_BYTEALIGNWINDOW" + crlf$
End If
If style% And CS_CLASSDC Then
        outstring$ = outstring$ + "CS_CLASSDC" + crlf$
End If
If style% And CS_DBLCLKS Then
        outstring$ = outstring$ + "CS_DBLCLKS" + crlf$
End If
If style% And CS_GLOBALCLASS Then
        outstring$ = outstring$ + "CS_GLOBALCLASS" + crlf$
End If
If style% And CS_HREDRAW Then
        outstring$ = outstring$ + "CS_HREDRAW" + crlf$
End If
If style% And CS_NOCLOSE Then
        outstring$ = outstring$ + "CS_NOCLOSE" + crlf$
End If
If style% And CS_OWNDC Then
        outstring$ = outstring$ + "CS_OWNDC" + crlf$
End If
If style% And CS_PARENTDC Then
        outstring$ = outstring$ + "CS_PARENTDC" + crlf$
End If
If style% And CS_SAVEBITS Then
        outstring$ = outstring$ + "CS_SAVEBITS" + crlf$
End If
If style% And CS_VREDRAW Then
        outstring$ = outstring$ + "CS_VREDRAW" + crlf$
End If

' Note: We could tap the style& variable for class
' styles as well (especially since it is easy to
' determine the class for a window), but that is
' beyond the scope of this sample program.


MsgBox outstring$, 0, titlestring$



End Sub

' Show window styles for the selected window

Sub CmdWinStyles_Click ()
    Dim style&
    Dim useHwnd%
    Dim crlf$
```

```
Dim outstring$, titlestring$

crlf$ = Chr$(13) + Chr$(10)

If List1.ListIndex < 0 Then
    MsgBox "No windows selected", 0, "Error"
    Exit Sub
End If

titlestring$ = List1.Text
useHwnd% = Val(titlestring$)

' Get the class info
style& = GetWindowLong&(useHwnd%, GWL_STYLE)

If style& And WS_BORDER Then
    outstring$ = outstring$ + "WS_BORDER" + crlf$
End If
If style& And WS_CAPTION Then
    outstring$ = outstring$ + "WS_CAPTION" + crlf$
End If
If style& And WS_CHILD Then
    outstring$ = outstring$ + "WS_CHILD" + crlf$
End If
If style& And WS_CLIPCHILDREN Then
    outstring$ = outstring$ + "WS_CLIPCHILDREN" + crlf$
End If
If style& And WS_CLIPSIBLINGS Then
    outstring$ = outstring$ + "WS_CLIPSIBLINGS" + crlf$
End If
If style& And WS_DISABLED Then
    outstring$ = outstring$ + "WS_DISABLED" + crlf$
End If
If style& And WS_DLGFRAME Then
    outstring$ = outstring$ + "WS_DLGFRAME" + crlf$
End If
If style& And WS_GROUP Then
    outstring$ = outstring$ + "WS_GROUP" + crlf$
End If
If style& And WS_HSCROLL Then
    outstring$ = outstring$ + "WS_HSCROLL" + crlf$
End If
If style& And WS_MAXIMIZE Then
    outstring$ = outstring$ + "WS_MAXIMIZE" + crlf$
End If
If style& And WS_MAXIMIZEBOX Then
    outstring$ = outstring$ + "WS_MAXIMIZEBOX" + crlf$
End If
If style& And WS_MINIMIZE Then
    outstring$ = outstring$ + "WS_MINIMIZE" + crlf$
End If
If style& And WS_MINIMIZEBOX Then
```

```
            outstring$ = outstring$ + "WS_MINIMIZEBOX" + crlf$
        End If
        If style& And WS_POPUP Then
            outstring$ = outstring$ + "WS_POPUP" + crlf$
        End If
        If style& And WS_SYSMENU Then
            outstring$ = outstring$ + "WS_SYSMENU" + crlf$
        End If
        If style& And WS_TABSTOP Then
            outstring$ = outstring$ + "WS_TABSTOP" + crlf$
        End If
        If style& And WS_THICKFRAME Then
            outstring$ = outstring$ + "WS_THICKFRAME" + crlf$
        End If
        If style& And WS_VISIBLE Then
            outstring$ = outstring$ + "WS_VISIBLE" + crlf$
        End If
        If style& And WS_VSCROLL Then
            outstring$ = outstring$ + "WS_VSCROLL" + crlf$
        End If

        ' Note: We could tap the style& variable for class
        ' styles as well (especially since it is easy to
        ' determine the class for a window), but that is
        ' beyond the scope of this sample program.

        MsgBox outstring$, 0, titlestring$


    End Sub


    ' Flashes the caption of the selected window. This feature
    ' is typically attached to a timer when the code needs to
    ' "flash" a window caption to attract the user's attention.
    ' Try clicking this button several times quickly for a
    ' visible window that has a caption to see the effect.
    '
    Sub CmdFlash_Click ()
        Dim titlestring$
        Dim useHwnd%

        If List1.ListIndex < 0 Then
            MsgBox "No windows selected", 0, "Error"
            Exit Sub
        End If

        titlestring$ = List1.Text
        useHwnd% = Val(titlestring$)
        dummy% = FlashWindow(useHwnd%, -1)

    End Sub
```

```
' Obtains the control name or form name of a Visual
' Basic form or control given the window handle.
' Non-VB windows will have no form or control name.
'
Sub CmdCtlName_Click ()
    Dim titlestring$
    Dim outputstring$
    Dim useHwnd%

    If List1.ListIndex < Ø Then
        MsgBox "No windows selected", Ø, "Error"
        Exit Sub
    End If

    titlestring$ = List1.Text
    useHwnd% = Val(titlestring$)
    outputstring$ = agGetControlName(useHwnd%)

    If outputstring$ = "" Then
        MsgBox "Not a VB Form or Control", Ø, titlestring$
    Else
        MsgBox "CtlName or FormName = " + outputstring$, Ø, titlestring$
    End If

End Sub
```

Suggestions for Practice

You may wish to consider the following list of exercises for improving Win-View and gaining additional experience working with Windows API functions:

■ Add a menu command to move up one level in the hierarchy. Given a selected window, this command would add the parent window and all its siblings to the list box. The **GetWindow** and **GetNextWindow** functions will help here.

■ Extend the window style viewer to take into account the window style bits unique to each of the standard classes.

■ Add a Find Window command that looks for the handle of a window given its caption.

■ Create a tiling program that will divide the screen among all running applications. Use the **DeferWindowPos** functions. Hint for determining the screen size: What happens when you use the **GetWindowRect** on the desktop window?

■ Create a project where you print text to the form, then randomly scroll rectangular areas on the form from one part of the form to another. The result will be a jumble, but a good demonstration of the use of the **Scroll-Window** and **ScrollWindowEx** API calls.

Window Style Reference

The 32-bit window style data is divided into two parts. The high 16 bits are used to define general window styles common to all classes. The interpretation of the low 16 bits depends on the class. Chapter 2 discusses how Visual Basic controls correspond to the standard windows classes listed below.

Style bits do generally reflect the current state of a window; however, changing a style bit via **SetWindowLong** does not cause a corresponding change in the window—at least not immediately. Some style bits may be changed at runtime successfully (frequently taking effect when the window is redrawn), but most take effect correctly only when the window is created (meaning that they cannot be set from VB). Microsoft does not document which style bits may be changed safely at runtime; thus you should do so at your own risk and only after thorough experimentation.

By the same token, experimentation is the best way to learn about style bits. Simply retrieve the current style for a form or control, use the bit setting techniques described in Chapter 1 to modify the style, and set the new style. It is beyond the scope of this book to completely characterize the style combinations for every Visual Basic control. Instead, this chapter documents all of the standard window styles, and points out particular cases that are useful. If you see a feature that interests you, try it out and see if it works. If you find something particularly interesting, please send it to the publisher for incorporation into future editions of this book. Also, keep in mind that the WinView project provides a powerful tool for examining window styles.

Windows does provide API functions to perform most tasks that affect a window style (such as controlling visibility, window state, and so on.), so it should rarely be necessary to directly modify the window style.

Each style bit is represented by a constant name and a value in hexadecimal that indicates the bit that is set. Normal style bits are retrieved via:

```
GetWindowLong(hWnd%, GWL_STYLE)
```

and set via:

```
SetWindowLong(hWnd%, GWL_STYLE, value&)
```

To access the extended Windows style bits, substitute

```
GWL_EXSTYLE
```

for

```
GWL_STYLE
```

Keep in mind that each time a program is run, the style bits are reset from the VB project files; thus any changes to style bits must take place at runtime. This is often done in the form **Load** event.

General Windows Style Bits Table

Constant Name	Hex Value	Description
WS_BORDER	800000	Window has a border.
WS_CAPTION	C00000	Window has a title bar.
WS_CHILD	40000000	Window is a child window.
WS_CLIPCHILDREN	2000000	Prevents drawing to a parent window from drawing over a child window. This bit is controlled by the Visual Basic **ClipControls** property for forms and controls that can contain other controls.
WS_CLIPSIBLINGS	4000000	Prevents drawing into one child window from drawing over the client area of another child window that shares the same parent window. Under VB 1.0, this bit is not set for forms and controls. Setting it makes it possible to use overlapping controls.
WS_DISABLED	8000000	Window is disabled.
WS_DLGFRAME	400000	Window has a double border but no title bar.
WS_GROUP	20000	Window is the beginning of a group of controls in a dialog box.

Constant Name	Hex Value	Description
WS_HSCROLL	100000	Window has a horizontal scroll bar.
WS_MAXIMIZE	1000000	Window is maximized.
WS_MAXIMIZEBOX	10000	Window has a maximize box to the right of its title bar.
WS_MINIMIZE	20000000	Window is minimized.
WS_MINIMIZEBOX	20000	Window has a minimize box to the right of its title bar.
WS_OVERLAPPED	0	Default (no bits set) is an overlapped top level window with a caption and border.
WS_POPUP	80000000	Window is a popup window.
WS_SYSMENU	80000	Window has a system menu box at the left of its title bar.
WS_TABSTOP	10000	Window has a tab stop. This means that you may use the tab key to set the focus to this control in a dialog box.
WS_THICKFRAME	40000	Window has a thick frame (or border) that can be used to size the window.
WS_VISIBLE	10000000	Window is visible.
WS_VSCROLL	200000	Window has a vertical scroll bar.

Extended Windows Style Bits Table

Constant Name	Hex Value	Description
WS_EX_ACCEPTFILES	10	Window accepts drag-drop files from file manager.

Constant Name	Hex Value	Description
WS_EX_DLGMODALFRAME	1	Window has a double border. If **WS_CAPTION** is also specified, it will have a title bar.
WS_EX_NOPARENTNOTIFY	4	Windows will not send a **WM_PARENTNOTIFY** message to the parent when destroyed.
WS_EX_TOPMOST	8	This window should be placed over all windows (except others with this bit set). The **SetWindowPos** API function can be used to change this attribute.
WS_EX_TRANSPARENT	20	Creates a transparent window that does not obscure windows below it.

Of these, the most intriguing are the **WS_EX_ACCEPTFILES** and **WS_EX_TRANSPARENT** styles. Unfortunately, both cannot be used under VB without resorting to a custom control or DLL (both require subclassing to implement). Still, you might want to try setting the **WS_EX_TRANSPARENT** bit on a form (such as the form for the RectPlay project)—the results are interesting, especially if you minimize and then restore the program.

Dialog Box Style Bits Table

These styles are included for completeness, but have little use to the VB programmer.

Constant Name	Hex Value	Description
DS_LOCALEDIT	20	Edit controls use application's local heap. **EM_GETHANDLE** and **EM_SETHANDLE** messages work.

Constant Name	Hex Value	Description
DS_MODALFRAME	80	Dialog has a frame that can be combined with a title bar and system menu.
DS_NOIDLEMSG	100	**WM_ENTERIDLE** messages are not sent to the dialog's owner.
DS_SETFONT	40	Sets the font for a dialog box.
DS_SYSMODAL	2	Dialog box is system modal.

MDIClient Class Style Bits Table

This style is set for the Visual Basic MDIClient window. This is the window that covers the client area of an MDI form. It is not applicable to Visual Basic 1.0. Feel free to experiment.

Constant Name	Hex Value	Description
MDIS_ALLCHILD -STYLES	1	Enables MDI window to use all child style bits.

Button Class Style Bits Table

Constant Name	Hex Value	Description
BS_3STATE	5	A check box that has a third "gray" state. Has no effect on VB controls.
BS_AUTO3STATE	6	A 3 State check box that cycles through the three states, changing each time it is selected. Has no effect on VB controls.
BS_AUTOCHECKBOX	3	Specifies a check box that toggles the selection state each time the user selects the control.

Constant Name	Hex Value	Description
BS_AUTORADIOBUTTON	9	A radio button that automatically checks itself and unchecks all other radio buttons in its group when it is selected.
BS_CHECKBOX	2	Button is a check box.
BS_DEFPUSHBUTTON	1	Creates a default button. Similar to setting the Default property on the VB command button.
BS_GROUPBOX	7	Similar to the VB Frame control.
BS_LEFTTEXT	20	Places text to the left of a check box or radio button. This bit may be changed on a VB check box or option button.
BS_OWNERDRAW	B	A button that must be drawn by the application. This feature is not available from VB.
BS_RADIOBUTTON	4	Similar to a VB Option Button control.

ComboBox Class Style Bits Table

Constant Name	Hex Value	Description
CBS_AUTOHSCROLL	40	See **ES_HSCROLL** for edit control.
CBS_DISABLENOSCROLL	800	Vertical scroll is always shown (instead of being shown only when there are more entries than fit).
CBS_DROPDOWN	2	List box is displayed only when user selects the dropdown icon.

Constant Name	Hex Value	Description
CBS_DROPDOWNLIST	3	Like **CBS_DROP-DOWN** except that instead of an edit control, there is a static control that reflects the selected list box entry.
CBS_NOINTEGRALHEIGHT	400	Combo box can be any size. Normally the box is sized so that partial lines are not shown.
CBS_OEMCONVERT	80	See **ES_OEMCON-VERT**.
CBS_OWNERDRAWFIXED	10	Styles for combo boxes
CBS_OWNERDRAWVARIABLE	20	drawn under application
CBS_HASSTRINGS	200	control. Not used in VB.
CBS_SIMPLE	1	List box is displayed at all times.
CBS_SORT	100	List box entries are sorted.

Edit Class Style Bits Table

Constant Name	Hex Value	Description
ES_AUTOHSCROLL	80	Control automatically scrolls horizontally when typing at the end of a line. Without this bit, the text length is limited to what will fit in the box.
ES_AUTOVSCROLL	40	Control automatically scrolls up a page when the Enter key is pressed on the last line.
ES_CENTER	1	Text is centered.
ES_LEFT	0	Default: Text is left-justified.

Constant Name	Hex Value	Description
ES_LOWERCASE	10	Characters are converted to lower-case as they are typed in.
ES_MULTILINE	4	Multiline edit control.
ES_NOHIDESEL	100	Normally, when a control loses the focus the selected text no longer appears selected. This bit disables that behavior.
ES_OEMCONVERT	400	Text in the control is converted to the OEM character set. See Chapter 5.
ES_PASSWORD	20	The asterisk character (*) is displayed in the box as characters are typed in.
ES_READONLY	800	Text in this control cannot be edited by the user.
ES_RIGHT	2	Text is right-justified.
ES_UPPERCASE	8	Characters are converted to upper-case as they are typed in.
ES_WANTRETURN	1000	Pressing the Enter key inserts a carriage return into the text on multiline edit controls. This overrides the default push button if present.

The bad news is that these styles need to be set when the control is created and thus modifying them for an existing VB text control has no effect. The good news is that many of them can be simulated by intercepting the VB **KeyDown** and **KeyPressed** events. Also, many third-party edit controls take advantage of these features.

ListBox Class Style Bits Table

Constant Name	Hex Value	Description
LBS_DISABLENOSCROLL	1000	Vertical scroll is always shown (instead of being shown only when there are more entries than fit in the control window).
LBS_EXTENDEDSEL	800	Shift and control combinations can be used to select multiple entries. See **LBS_MULTIPLESEL**.
LBS_MULTICOLUMN	200	List box supports multiple columns. See **LBS_MULTIPLESEL**.
LBS_MULTIPLESEL	8	List box allows multiple selections.
LBS_NOINTEGRALHEIGHT	100	List box can be any size. Normally the box is sized so that partial lines are not shown.
LBS_NOREDRAW	4	Prevents update of the list box while changes are made. See Chapters 17 and 19.
LBS_NOTIFY	1	Parent window receives event notification for this control.
LBS_OWNERDRAWFIXED	10	Used for list boxes drawn under program control. Not usable under VB.
LBS_OWNERDRAWVARIABLE	20	
LBS_HASSTRINGS	40	
LBS_SORT	2	List box is sorted.

Constant Name	Hex Value	Description
LBS_USETABSTOPS	80	Allows alignment by tab stops. This is set by default in VB list box controls.
LBS_WANTKEYBOARDINPUT	400	List box receives all keyboard input allowing special processing for keyboard input.

ScrollBar Class Style Bits Table

Constant Name	Hex Value	Description
SBS_HORZ	0	Default: Horizontal scroll bar.
SBS_SIZEBOX	8	Creates a size box (maximize or minimize button).
SBS_TOPALIGN SBS_LEFTALIGN SBS_BOTTOMALIGN SBS_RIGHTALIGN	2 2 4 4	Used during creation of the scroll bar to align the scroll bar to the specified side of a rectangle. **Top** and **Bottom** apply to horizontal scroll bars, **Left** and **right** to vertical.
SBS_VERT	1	Vertical scroll bar.
SBS_SIZEBOXTOPLEFT-ALIGN SBS_SIZEBOXBOTTOM-RIGHTALIGN	2 4	Used to align size boxes to the top left or bottom right of a rectangle.

Static Class Style Bits Table

Constant Name	Hex Value	Description
SS_BLACKFRAME	7	Box whose frame is in the color used to draw window frames (default=black).

Constant Name	Hex Value	Description
SS_BLACKRECT	4	Solid rectangle in the color used to draw window frames (default=black).
SS_CENTER	1	Text is centered.
SS_GRAYFRAME	8	Box whose frame is in the color used to draw the screen background (default=gray).
SS_GRAYRECT	5	Solid rectangle in the color used to draw the screen background (default=gray).
SS_ICON	3	When used in a dialog box, this displays an icon. The text contains a resource ID to the icon in the file.
SS_LEFT	0	Default: left-aligned.
SS_LEFTNOWORD-WRAP	C	Same as **SS_SIMPLE** except that tabs are expanded.
SS_NOPREFIX	80	The & character does not cause the next character to be underlined. Normally, &Hello would display as <u>H</u>ello.
SS_RIGHT	2	Text is right-aligned.
SS_SIMPLE	B	Simple box containing fixed text to display.
SS_WHITEFRAME	9	Box whose frame is in the color used to fill windows backgrounds (default=white).
SS_WHITERECT	6	Solid rectangle in the color used to fill window backgrounds (default=white).

Function Reference

This section contains an alphabetical reference for the functions described in this chapter.

■ AdjustWindowRect, AdjustWindowRectEx

VB Declaration `Declare Sub AdjustWindowRect Lib "User" (lpRect As RECT, ByVal dwStyle&, ByVal ⇔ bMenu%)`

`Declare Sub AdjustWindowRectEx Lib "User" (lpRect As RECT, ByVal dwStyle&, ByVal ⇔ bMenu%, ByVal dwExStyle&)`

Description Calculates the size of a window rectangle needed to obtain a specified client rectangle given a window style.

Use with VB Works, but is not particularly useful.

Parameter	Type/Description
lpRect	**RECT**—Initially contains the desired client area, is set by the function to the target window rectangle size.
dwStyle	**Long**—Window style.
bMenu	**Integer**—Set TRUE (nonzero) if window has a menu.
dwExStyle	**Long**—(**AdjustWindowRectEx** only). The extended window style.

Comments These functions do not take into account the size of title bars, borders, and extra menu rows. They are commonly used when creating windows, so they are not of much use to the VB programmer.

■ AnyPopup

VB Declaration `Declare Function AnyPopup% Lib "User" ()`

Description Determines if a popup window exists anywhere on the screen.

Use with VB No problem.

Return Value **Integer**—TRUE (nonzero) if a popup exists.

Comments A popup for this function includes any visible, unowned top level windows, both popup and overlapped.

■ ArrangeIconicWindows

VB Declaration `Declare Function ArrangeIconicWindows% Lib "User" (ByVal hWnd%)`

Description Arranges the minimized child windows of a parent window.

Use with VB	Useful for arranging icons on the desktop.

Parameter	Type/Description
hWnd	**Integer**—Handle of the parent window.

Return Value   **Integer**—The height of a row of icons. Zero on failure.

Comments   Use **GetDesktopWindow** to obtain the window handle of the desktop to arrange the desktop icons. You may also be able to use this on a custom control that can contain iconized child windows.

▪ BeginDeferWindowPos

VB Declaration   `Declare Function BeginDeferWindowPos% Lib "User" (ByVal nNumWindows%)`

Description   Begins the process of building a list of new window positions for simultaneous updating. This function returns a handle to an internal structure that will hold the window positions. This structure is then filled by calls to **DeferWindowPos**. When you are ready to update all the window positions, a call to **EndDeferWindowPos** changes all of the window positions in the structure simultaneously.

Use with VB   No problem.

Parameter	Type/Description
nNumWindows	**Integer**—Initial number of windows to allocate space for in the structure. The structure will automatically be resized if necessary during each **DeferWindowPos** call.

Return Value   **Integer**—Handle to the internal structure. Zero on error.

▪ BringWindowToTop

VB Declaration   `Declare Sub BringWindowToTop Lib "User" (ByVal hWnd%)`

Description   Brings the specified window to the top of the window list, uncovering it if it is partially or entirely obscured by other windows. Popup, top level, and MDI child windows are also activated by this function.

Use with VB   No problem.

Parameter	Type/Description
hWnd	**Integer**—The handle of the window to bring to the top.

Comments   This function may be used with child windows as well.

■ ChildWindowFromPoint, ChildWindowFromPointBynum

VB Declaration   Declare Function ChildWindowFromPoint% Lib "User" (ByVal hWnd%, ByVal Pnt As ANY)

Declare Function ChildWindowFromPointBynum% Lib "User" Alias ⇔ "ChildWindowFromPoint" (ByVal hWnd%, ByVal Pnt&)

Description   Returns the handle of the first child window in a parent window that contains the specified point.

Use with VB   No problem. Can be used to identify controls given a coordinate point on a form. **ChildWindow-FromPontBynum** is the type-safe version of this function. The use of aliasing to provide parameter type checking is described in Chapter 3.

Parameter	Type/Description
hWnd	**Integer**—Handle of parent window.
Pnt	**Long**—Point value. Use **agPOINTAPItoLong** to obtain this value from a point structure.

Return Value   **Integer**—Window handle of the first child window found containing the specified point. If no window is found, returns **hWnd** (the handle of the parent window). If the point is outside of the parent window, returns 0.

■ ClientToScreen

VB Declaration   Declare Sub ClientToScreen Lib "User" (ByVal hWnd%, lpPoint As POINTAPI)

Description   Determines the screen coordinates for a point given in the client coordinates of a window.

Use with VB   No problem.

Parameter	Type/Description
hWnd	**Integer**—Handle of the window that determines the client coordinates to use.
lpPoint	**POINTAPI**—Point in client coordinates of **hWnd**. On return, this parameter will contain the same point in screen coordinates.

■ CloseWindow

VB Declaration   Declare Sub CloseWindow Lib "User" (ByVal hWnd%)

Description   Minimizes the specified window.

Use with VB   Use the **WindowState** property to minimize VB forms.

Parameter	Type/Description
hWnd	**Integer**—Handle of the window to minimize.

Comments   This function has no effect on popup and child windows.

■ CopyRect

VB Declaration   Declare Function CopyRect% Lib "User" (lpDestRect As RECT, lpSourceRect As RECT)

Description   The contents of rectangle **lpSourceRect** are copied into rectangle **lpDestRect**.

Use with VB   No problem.

Parameter	Type/Description
lpDestRect	**RECT**—Destination rectangle structure.
lpSourceRect	**RECT**—Source rectangle.

Return Value   Has no significance.

■ DeferWindowPos

VB Declaration   Declare Function DeferWindowPos% Lib "User" (ByVal hWinPosInfo%, ByVal hWnd%, ⇔
ByVal hWndInsertAfter%, ByVal x%, ByVal y%, ByVal cx%, ByVal cy%, ByVal wFlags%)

Description   This function specifies a new window position for the specified window and enters it into the structure created by **BeginDeferWindowPos** for later update. Refer to the **BeginDeferWindowPos** function for more information.

Use with VB   No problem.

Parameter	Type/Description
hWinPosInfo	**Integer**—Handle of structure returned by **BeginDeferWindowPos** for subsequent calls to **DeferWindowPos**.
hWnd	**Integer**—Window to position.
hWndInsertAfter	**Integer**—Window handle. Window **hWnd** will be placed after this window handle in the window list. May also be one of the following values: **HWND_BOTTOM**: Place window at bottom of the window list. **HWND_TOP**: Place window at the top of the Z-order, the order in which windows are displayed for the given level of the window in the hierarchy. **HWND_TOPMOST**: Place window at the top of the list, ahead of any topmost windows (see **WS_EX_TOPMOST** style bit). **HWND_NOTOPMOST**: Place window at the top of the list, behind any topmost windows.
x	**Integer**—The new x coordinate of the window. If **hWnd** is a child window, x is given in the client coordinates of the parent window.
y	**Integer**—The new y coordinate of the window. If **hWnd** is a child window, x is given in the client coordinates of the parent window.
cx	**Integer**—Specifies the new window width.

Parameter	Type/Description
cy	**Integer**—Specifies the new window height.
flags	**Integer**—An integer containing flags from the following: **SWP_DRAWFRAME**: Draws a frame around the window. **SWP_HIDEWINDOW**: Hides the window. **SWP_NOACTIVATE**: Do not activate the window. **SWP_NOMOVE**: Retains current position (x and y are ignored). **SWP_NOREDRAW**: Window is not automatically redrawn. **SWP_NOSIZE**: Retains current size (cx and cy are ignored). **SWP_NOZORDER**: Retains current position in the window list (**hWndInsertAfter** is ignored). **SWP_SHOWWINDOW**: Display the window.

Return Value   **Integer**—Returns a new handle to the structure containing the position update information. This handle should be used on further calls to **DeferWindowPos** and the ending call to **EndDeferWindowPos**. Returns zero on error.

Comments   When a window is made into a topmost window, all its owned windows are also made topmost. When it is made non-topmost, all of its owned and owner windows are also made non-topmost. Z-order refers to the order of windows from the top to the bottom of an imaginary Z-axis extending outward from the screen.

■ DestroyWindow

VB Declaration   `Declare Function DestroyWindow% Lib "User" (ByVal hWnd%)`

Description   Destroys the specified window and all its child windows.

Use with VB   Do not use on VB forms or controls.

Parameter	Type/Description
hWnd	**Integer**—Handle of window to destroy.

Return Value   **Integer**—TRUE (nonzero) on success. Zero on error.

■ EnableWindow

VB Declaration   `Declare Function EnableWindow% Lib "User" (ByVal hWnd%, ByVal aBOOL%)`

Description   Enables or disables all mouse and keyboard input to the specified window.

Use with VB   Use the **Enabled** property on VB forms and controls.

Parameter	Type/Description
hWnd	**TYPE**—Window handle.
aBool	**Integer**—TRUE (nonzero) to enable the window. False to disable.

Return Value   Integer—TRUE (nonzero) if the window was previously enabled, zero if disabled.

■ EndDeferWindowPos

VB Declaration   `Declare Sub EndDeferWindowPos% Lib "User" (ByVal WinPosInfo%)`

Description   Simultaneously updates the positions and states of all windows specified by calls to **DeferWindowPos**.

Use with VB   No problem.

Parameter	Type/Description
WinPosInfo	**Integer**—Structure handle as returned by the most recent call to **DeferWindowPos**.

■ EnumChildWindows

VB Declaration   `Declare Function EnumChildWindows% Lib "User" (ByVal hWndParent%, ByVal ⇔`
`lpEnumFunc&, ByVal lParam&)`

Description   Enumerates the child windows for the specified parent window.

Use with VB   Requires the CBK.VBX custom control.

Parameter	Type/Description
hWndParent	**Integer**—Handle of parent window for which to enumerate child windows.
lpEnumFunc	**Long**—Pointer to function to call for each child window. Use the **ProcAddress** property of the CBK.VBX custom control to obtain a function pointer for callbacks.
lParam	**Long**—Value that is passed to the **EnumWindows** event of the CBK.VBX custom control during enumeration. The meaning of this value is defined by the programmer.

Return Value   Integer—TRUE (nonzero) if the function is successful.

Comments   Refer to Appendix A for details on using the CBK.VBX custom control with enumeration functions. Child windows of child windows are also enumerated by this function.

■ EnumTaskWindows

VB Declaration   `Declare Function EnumTaskWindows% Lib "User" (ByVal hTask%, ByVal lpEnumFunc&, ⇔`
`ByVal lParam&)`

Description   Enumerates the windows associated with the specified task.

Use with VB   Requires the CBK.VBX custom control.

Parameter	Type/Description
hTask	**Integer**—Handle of the specified task.
lpEnumFunc	**Long**—Pointer to function to call for each child window. Use the **ProcAddress** property of the CBK.VBX custom control to obtain a function pointer for call-backs.
lParam	**Long**—Value that is passed to the **EnumWindows** event of the CBK.VBX custom control during enumeration. The meaning of this value is defined by the programmer.

Return Value   **Integer**—TRUE (nonzero) if the function is successful.

Comments   Refer to Appendix A for details on using the CBK.VBX custom control with enumeration functions.

■ EnumWindows

VB Declaration   `Declare Function EnumWindows% Lib "User" (ByVal lpEnumFunc&, ByVal lParam&)`

Description   Enumerates all parent windows (top level and owned) in the window list.

Use with VB   Requires the CBK.VBX custom control.

Parameter	Type/Description
lpEnumFunc	**Long**—Pointer to function to call for each child window. Use the **ProcAddress** property of the CBK.VBX custom control to obtain a function pointer for callbacks.
lParam	**Long**—Value that is passed to the **EnumWindows** event of the CBK.VBX custom control during enumeration. The meaning of this value is defined by the programmer.

Return Value   **Integer**—TRUE (nonzero) if the function is successful.

Comments   Refer to Appendix A for details on using the CBK.VBX custom control with enumeration functions.

■ EqualRect

VB Declaration   `Declare Function EqualRect% Lib "User" (lpRect1 As RECT, lpRect2 As RECT)`

Description   Determines if two rectangles structures are equal.

Use with VB   No problem.

Parameter	Type/Description
lpRect1	**RECT**—Rectangle to compare.
lpRect2	**RECT**—Rectangle to compare.

Return Value   **Integer**—TRUE (nonzero) if the upper left and lower right coordinates of the two rectangles are equal, zero otherwise.

■ FindWindow, FindWindowBynum, FindWindowBystring

VB Declaration
```
Declare Function FindWindow% Lib "User" (Byval lpClassName As Any, Byval ⇔
lpWindowName As Any)

Declare Function FindWindowBynum% Lib "User" Alias "FindWindow" (Byval ⇔
lpClassName&, Byval lpWindowName&)

Declare Function FindWindowBystring% Lib "User" Alias "FindWindow" (Byval ⇔
lpClassName$, Byval lpWindowName$)
```

Description   Finds the first window in the window list that meets the specified conditions.

Use with VB   No problem.

Parameter	Type/Description
lpClassName	**Long** or **String**—Pointer to null terminated (C language) string containing the name of the class for the window, or zero to accept any class.
lpWindowName	**Long** or **String**—Pointer to null terminated (C language) string containing the window text (or title), or zero to accept any window title.

Return Value   **Integer**—The handle of the first window found, or zero if no window is found that meets the requirements.

Comments   **FindWindowBynum** and **FindWindowBystring** provide type-safe declarations for the **FindWindow** function. When using **FindWindowBynum**, you may use the **agGetAddressForLPSTR$** function in APIGUIDE.DLL to obtain a pointer to a null terminated string in Long type format.

■ FlashWindow

VB Declaration   `Declare Function FlashWindow% Lib "User" (ByVal hWnd%, ByVal bInvert%)`

Description   Flashes the specified window. This means that the title or caption is changed as if switching from active to inactive or vice versa. This function is commonly used for inactive windows to attract the user's attention.

Use with VB   No problem.

Parameter	Type/Description
hWnd	**Integer**—Handle of the window to flash.
bInvert	**Integer**—TRUE (nonzero) to toggle the window caption. FALSE to return to the original state.

Return Value   **Integer**—TRUE (nonzero) if the window was active before the call.

Comments   This function is frequently used in combination with a timer to cause repeated flashing. **fInvert** is ignored on minimized windows.

■ GetActiveWindow

VB Declaration   Declare Function GetActiveWindow% Lib "User" ()

Description   Obtains the handle of the active window.

Use with VB   No problem.

Return Value   Integer—The handle of the active window, or zero if no window is active.

Comments   The active window is the top level window that has the input focus unless **SetActiveWindow** was used to explicitly set a different window.

■ GetClassInfo

VB Declaration   Declare Function GetClassInfo% Lib "User" (ByVal hInstance%, ByVal lpClassName$, ⇔ lpWndClass as WNDCLASS)

Description   Retrieves a copy of the **WNDCLASS** structure containing information about the specified class.

Use with VB   No problem.

Parameter	Type/Description
hInstance	Integer—A handle to the instance that owns the class. NULL to obtain information on standard Windows classes.
lpClassName$	String—The name of the class to search for. May also be a Long value resource ID in which case a new declaration accepting a Long variable in this parameter is required.
lpWndClass	WNDCLASS—structure to contain the results.

Return Value   Integer—TRUE (nonzero) on success, zero if a matching class is not found.

Comments   Refer to Appendix B for information on the **WNDCLASS** data structure.

■ GetClassLong

VB Declaration: Declare Function GetClassLong& Lib "User" (ByVal hWnd%, ByVal nIndex%)

Description   Obtains one of the Long variable entries for the window class.

Use with VB   No problem.

Parameter	Type/Description
hWnd	Integer—Window handle for which to obtain class information.

Parameter	Type/Description
nIndex	**Integer**—Information to retrieve, may be one of the following constants: **GCL_MENUNAME**: Retrieves the name or resource ID for the class menu. **GCL_WNDPROC**: Retrieves the address of the class window function (the default window function for windows in this class). Positive values represent a byte offset used to obtain class information allocated in the extra bytes for this class.

Return Value   **Long**—As specified by **nIndex**.

■ GetClassName

VB Declaration   `Declare Function GetClassName% Lib "User" (ByVal hWnd%, ByVal lpClassName$, ⟺ ByVal nMaxCount%)`

Description   Retrieves the class name for the specified window.

Use with VB   No problem.

Parameter	Type/Description
hWnd	**Integer**—Window handle for which to obtain the class name.
lpClassName	**String**—Buffer to load with the class name. Must be preallocated to at least **nMaxCount+1** characters.
nMaxCount	**Integer**—Length of the buffer provided by lpClassName.

Return Value   **Integer**—The length in bytes of the class name excluding the final null terminating character.

■ GetClassWord

VB Declaration   `Declare Function GetClassWord% Lib "User" (ByVal hWnd%, ByVal nIndex%)`

Description   Obtains one of the **Integer** variable entries for the window class.

Use with VB   No problem.

Parameter	Type/Description
hWnd	**Integer**—Window handle for which to obtain class information.
nIndex	**Integer**—Information to retrieve, may be one of the following constants: **GCW_CBCLSEXTRA**: Number of extra bytes allocated in this class structure. **GCW_CBWNDEXTRA**: Number of extra bytes allocated in the window structure for each window in this class. **GCW_HBRBACKGROUND**: Handle to the default brush to use when painting the background of each window of this class (see Chapter 7). **GCW_HCURSOR**: Handle to the default cursor for windows in this class. **GCW_HICON**: Handle to the default icon for windows in this class. **GCW_HMODULE**: Handle to the module for this class. **GCW_STYLE**: Style of this class. Positive values obtain class information allocated in the extra bytes for this class.

Return Value   Integer—As specified by **nIndex**.

Comments   Refer to the definition of the **WNDCLASS** structure in Appendix B for further information including the definition of the GCW_ style attribute.

■ GetClientRect

VB Declaration   `Declare Sub GetClientRect Lib "User" (ByVal hWnd%, lpRect As RECT)`

Description   Returns the size of the client rectangle for the specified window.

Use with VB   No problem.

Parameter	Type/Description
hWnd	**TYPE**—Window for which to obtain the size.
lpRect	**RECT**—Rectangle to load with the size of the client area in pixels.

Comments   The left and top fields of **lpRect** are always set to zero by this function.

■ GetDesktopWindow

VB Declaration   `Declare Function GetDesktopWindow% Lib "User" ()`

Description   Obtain a window handle representing the entire screen.

Use with VB   No problem.

Return Value   Integer—Handle of the desktop window.

Comments   All desktop icons are drawn on this window. It is also used for screen savers.

■ GetFocus

VB Declaration   `Declare Function GetFocus% Lib "User" ()`

Description   Obtain the handle of the window that has the input focus.

Use with VB   No problem.

Return Value   Integer—Handle of the window with the focus. Zero if no window has the focus.

■ GetNextWindow

VB Declaration   `Declare Function GetNextWindow% Lib "User" (ByVal hWnd%, ByVal wFlag%)`

Description   Retrieves the handle for the next or previous window in the internal Windows list. If **hWnd** is a top level window, this function finds the next (or previous) top level window. If **hWnd** is a child window, this function returns the next (or previous) child window.

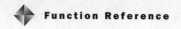

Use with VB	No problem.

Parameter	Type/Description
hWnd	**Integer**—Window handle to search from.
wFlag	**Integer**—One of the following constants: **GW_HWNDNEXT**: to find the next window. **GW_HWNDPREV**: to find the previous window.

Return Value   **Integer**—Handle of the window found. Zero if no window is found.

■ GetParent

VB Declaration   `Declare Function GetParent% Lib "User" (ByVal hWnd%)`

Description   Determine the parent window of the specified window.

Use with VB   No problem.

Return Value   **Integer**—Handle of the parent window. Zero if the window has no parent.

■ GetSysModalWindow

VB Declaration   `Declare Function GetSysModalWindow% Lib "User" ()`

Description   Obtains the handle of the system modal window if one is present. When a system modal window exists, no other window can receive mouse or keyboard input.

Use with VB   No problem.

Return Value   **Integer**—Handle of the system modal window. Zero if no windows are system modal.

■ GetTopWindow

VB Declaration   `Declare Function GetTopWindow% Lib "User" (ByVal hWnd%)`

Description   Searches the internal window list for the handle of the first child window belonging to the specified window.

Use with VB   No problem.

Parameter	Type/Description
hWnd	**Integer**—Window for which to find the top level child.

Return Value   **Integer**—The handle of the top level child window for the window specified.

■ GetUpdateRect

VB Declaration `Declare Function GetUpdateRect% Lib "User" (ByVal hWnd%, lpRect As RECT, ByVal ⇔ bErase%)`

Description Obtains a rectangle describing the portion of the specified window that needs to be updated.

Use with VB No problem.

Parameter	Type/Description
hWnd	**Integer**—Window for which to determine the update area.
lpRect	**RECT**—Rectangle to load with the update coordinates.
bErase	**Integer**—Set TRUE (nonzero) to erase the update area.

Return Value **Integer**—TRUE (nonzero) if the update area is not empty.

Comments If the window class style has **CS_OWNDC** set and the window mapping mode is not **MM_TEXT**, the update rectangle will be in logical coordinates. Refer to Chapter 6 for a description of these terms.

■ GetWindow

VB Declaration `Declare Function GetWindow% Lib "User" (ByVal hWnd%, ByVal wCmd%)`

Description Obtains the handle of a window with a specified relationship to a source window.

Use with VB No problem.

Parameter	Type/Description
hWnd	**Integer**—Source window.
wCmd	**Integer**—Specifies the relationship of the result window to the source window based on the following constants: **GW_CHILD**: Find the first child window of the source window. **GW_HWNDFIRST**: Find the first sibling window for a source child window, or the first top level window. **GW_HWNDLAST**: Find the last sibling for a source child window, or the last top level window. **GW_HWNDNEXT**: Find the next sibling window for the source window. **GW_HWNDPREV**: Find the previous sibling window for the source window. **GW_OWNER**: Find the owner of the window.

Return Value **Integer**—Window handle as specified by wCmd.

Comments Sibling windows refer to windows on the same level of the hierarchy. If a window has five child windows, those five windows are siblings.

GetWindowLong

VB Declaration   Declare Function GetWindowLong& Lib "User" (ByVal hWnd%, ByVal nIndex%)

Description   Obtains information from the window structure for the specified window.

Use with VB   No problem.

Parameter	Type/Description
hWnd	**Integer**—Handle of window for which to obtain information.
nIndex	**Integer**—Information to retrieve; may be one of the following constants: **GWL_EXSTYLE**: The extended window style. **GWL_STYLE**: The window style. **GWL_WNDPROC**: The address of the window function for this window. Dialog boxes also specify the following constants: **DWL_DLGPROC**: Address of the dialog function for this window. **DWL_MSGRESULT**: Value returned by a message processed within the dialog function. **DWL_USER**: Defined by the application. Positive values obtain window information allocated in the extra bytes for this window.

Return Value   **Long**—As specified by **nIndex**.

GetWindowPlacement

VB Declaration   Declare Function GetWindowPlacement% Lib "User" (ByVal hWnd%, lpwndpl As ⇔ WINDOWPLACEMENT)

Description   Obtains window state and location information for a window.

Use with VB   No problem.

Parameter	Type/Description
hWnd	**Integer**—Handle of window for which to obtain the information.
lpwndpl	**WINDOWPLACEMENT**—Structure containing location and state information for the window. See Appendix B for details.

Return Value   **Integer**—TRUE (nonzero) on success, zero otherwise.

GetWindowRect

VB Declaration   Declare Sub GetWindowRect Lib "User" (ByVal hWnd%, lpRect As RECT)

Description   Obtains the bounding rectangle for the entire window including borders, title bars, scroll bars, menus, and so on.

Use with VB   No problem.

Parameter	Type/Description
hWnd	**Integer**—Handle of window for which to obtain the bounding rectangle.
lpRect	**RECT**—Rectangle to load with the window dimensions in screen coordinates.

Comments   Use this with the handle obtained from **GetDesktopWindow** to obtain a rectangle describing the entire visible display.

■ GetWindowText

VB Declaration   `Declare Function GetWindowText% Lib "User" (ByVal hWnd%, ByVal lpString$, ByVal ⇔ aint%)`

Description   Retrieve the title (caption) text of a window or contents of a control.

Use with VB   Use the **Caption** or **Text** property (as appropriate) for VB forms or controls.

Parameter	Type/Description
hWnd	**Integer**—Handle of window for which to obtain the text.
lpString	**String**—Predefined string buffer of at least **aint**+1 characters to load with the window text.
aint	**Integer**—Length of **lpString** buffer.

Return Value   **Integer**—The length of the string copied into lpString not including the null terminating character.

■ GetWindowTextLength

VB Declaration   `Declare Function GetWindowTextLength% Lib "User" (ByVal hWnd%)`

Description   Obtains the length of the title (caption) text or the contents of the control.

Use with VB   You may use the VB **Len** function on the **Text** or **Caption** property (as appropriate) for VB forms or controls, however, this function may be faster.

Parameter	Type/Description
hWnd	**Integer**—Handle of window for which to obtain the text.

Return Value   **Integer**—The length of the window text.

■ GetWindowWord

VB Declaration   `Declare Function GetWindowWord% Lib "User" (ByVal hWnd%, ByVal nIndex%)`

Description   Obtains information from the window structure for the specified window.

Use with VB	No problem.	
	Parameter	**Type/Description**
	hWnd	**Integer**—Handle of window for which to obtain information.
	nIndex	**Integer**—Information to retrieve; may be one of the following constants: **GWW_HINSTANCE**: The handle of the instance that owns the window. **GWW_HWNDPARENT**: The handle of the parent of this window. Do not use **SetWindowWord** to change this value. **GWW_ID**: The identifier of a child window within a dialog box. Positive values obtain window information allocated in the extra bytes for this window.

Return Value   **Word**—As specified by **nIndex**.

■ InflateRect

VB Declaration   `Declare Sub InflateRect Lib "User" (lpRect As RECT, ByVal X%, ByVal Y%)`

Description   This function increases or decreases the size of a rectangle. X% is added to the **right** field and subtracted from the **left** field. This serves to increase the width of the rectangle if X% is positive, and reduce it if X% is negative. Y% does the same for the **top** and **bottom** fields.

Use with VB	No problem.	
	Parameter	**Type/Description**
	lpRect	**RECT**—Rectangle structure to modify.
	X%	**Integer**—Inflate width by this number.
	Y%	**Integer**—Inflate height by this number.

Comments   Note that the actual change in width and height will be twice the value of the X% and Y% parameters. A rectangle may not have a width or height greater than 32,767 units. This function does not check X% and Y% to prevent this type of error.

■ IntersectRect

VB Declaration   `Declare Function IntersectRect% Lib "User" (lpDestRect As RECT, lpSrc1Rect ⇔`
`As RECT, lpSrc2Rect As RECT)`

Description   This function loads into rectangle **lpDestRect** a rectangle that describes the intersection of **lpSrc1Rect** and **lpSrc2Rect**. This is the rectangle that includes all points that are common to both rectangles. If the two source rectangles do not overlap at all, **lpDestRect** will be set to be an empty rectangle.

Use with VB	No problem.	
	Parameter	**Type/Description**
	lpDestRect	**RECT**—Destination rectangle that will contain the intersection of **lpSrc1Rect** and **lpSrc2Rect**.

Parameter	Type/Description
lpSrc1Rect	**RECT**—First source rectangle.
lpSrc2Rect	**RECT**—Second source rectangle.

Return Value   **Integer**—Nonzero if the destination rectangle is not empty, zero otherwise.

Comments   The RectPlay example program provides a graphical illustration of this function in action.

■ InvalidateRect

VB Declaration   Declare Sub InvalidateRect Lib "User" (ByVal hWnd%, lpRect As RECT, ByVal ⇔
bErase%)

Declare Sub InvalidateRectBynum Lib "User" Alias "InvalidateRect" (ByVal ⇔
hWnd%, Byval lpRect&, ByVal bErase%)

Description   This function invalidates all or part of the client area of a window. This will cause that part of the window to be redrawn in due course.

Use with VB   No problem. Unlike the VB **Refresh** method, this does not cause an immediate redraw.

Parameter	Type/Description
hWnd	**Integer**—Handle of window to invalidate.
lpRect	**RECT**—Rectangle structure describing the part of the rectangle to invalidate. Use **InvalidateRectBynum** with **lpRect** set to zero (**Long** data type) to invalidate the entire window.
bErase	**Integer**—TRUE (nonzero) to cause the specified area to be erased before it is redrawn.

Comments   Windows causes the window to be redrawn when the system has some idle time available with which to update the screen.

■ IsChild

VB Declaration   Declare Function IsChild% Lib "User" (ByVal hWndParent%, ByVal hWnd%)

Description   Determines if one window is the child or descendent of another.

Use with VB   No problem.

Parameter	Type/Description
hWndParent	**Integer**—Window handle of parent.
hWnd	**Integer**—Window handle to test.

Return Value   **Integer**—TRUE (nonzero) if **hWnd** is a child or descendent of **hWndParent**.

■ IsIconic

VB Declaration   `Declare Function IsIconic% Lib "User" (ByVal hWnd%)`

Description   Determines if the window is minimized.

Use with VB   No problem.

Parameter	Type/Description
hWnd	**Integer**—Handle of window to test.

Return Value   **Integer**—TRUE (nonzero) if window is minimized.

■ IsRectEmpty

VB Declaration   `Declare Function IsRectEmpty% Lib "User" (lpRect As RECT)`

Description   Determines if a rectangle is empty.

Use with VB   No problem.

Parameter	Type/Description
lpRect	**RECT**—Rectangle to check.

Return Value   **Integer**—TRUE (nonzero) if the rectangle is empty, zero otherwise.

■ IsWindow

VB Declaration   `Declare Function IsWindow% Lib "User" (ByVal hWnd%)`

Description   Determines if a window handle is valid.

Use with VB   No problem.

Parameter	Type/Description
hWnd	**Integer**—Handle to test.

Return Value   **Integer**—TRUE (nonzero) if the handle is a valid window handle.

■ IsWindowEnabled

VB Declaration   `Declare Function IsWindowEnabled% Lib "User" (ByVal hWnd%)`

Description   Determines if the window is enabled.

Use with VB   No problem.

Parameter	Type/Description
hWnd	Integer—Handle of window to test.

Return Value   Integer—TRUE (nonzero) if window is enabled.

■ IsWindowVisible

VB Declaration   `Declare Function IsWindowVisible% Lib "User" (ByVal hWnd%)`

Description   Determines if the window is visible.

Use with VB   No problem.

Parameter	Type/Description
hWnd	Integer—Handle of window to test.

Return Value   Integer—TRUE (nonzero) if the window is visible.

Comments   A window can be visible and still obscured by other visible windows that are on top of it (precede it in the internal window list).

■ IsZoomed

VB Declaration   `Declare Function IsZoomed% Lib "User" (ByVal hWnd%)`

Description   Determines if the window is maximized.

Use with VB   No problem.

Parameter	Type/Description
hWnd	Integer—Handle of window to test.

Return Value   Integer—TRUE (nonzero) if the window is maximized, zero otherwise.

■ LockWindowUpdate

VB Declaration   `Declare Function LockWindowUpdate% Lib "User" (ByVal hWnd%)`

Description   Locks the specified window from being updated. Only one window may be locked at a time.

Use with VB   No problem.

Parameter	Type/Description
hWnd	Integer—Handle of window to lock. Specify zero to unlock the window.

Return Value   Integer—TRUE (nonzero) on success. FALSE (zero) if another window is currently locked.

Comments Windows keeps track of areas in the locked window that are invalid and causes them to be re-drawn after the window is unlocked.

■ MapWindowPoints

VB Declaration `Declare Sub MapWindowPoints Lib "User" (ByVal hWndFrom%, ByVal hWndTo%, lppt As` ⇔
`POINTAPI, ByVal cPoints%)`

Description Converts points in the client coordinates of one window into the client coordinates of a second window.

Use with VB Be careful to pass to the function either a single point, or the first **POINTAPI** structure in an array, and that the number of entries in the array is at least **cPoints**.

Parameter	Type/Description
hWndFrom	**Integer**—Handle of window that defines the source coordinates. Use zero, or the desktop window handle to specify screen coordinates.
hWndTo	**Integer**—Handle of window that defines the destination coordinates. Use zero, or the desktop window handle to specify screen coordinates.
lppt	**POINTAPI**—First entry in an array of point structures to convert.
cPoints	**Integer**—The number of points to convert.

■ MoveWindow

VB Declaration `Declare Sub MoveWindow Lib "User" (ByVal hWnd%, ByVal X%, ByVal Y%, ByVal` ⇔
`nWidth%, ByVal nHeight%, ByVal bRepaint%)`

Description Used to change the position and size of the specified window. Top level windows may be bound by minimum or maximum sizes that will override the parameters provided.

Use with VB No problem. Identical to the Visual Basic **Move** statement. Changing the VB **Top**, **Left**, **Height**, and **Width** properties achieves the same effect for VB forms and controls.

Parameter	Type/Description
hWnd	**Integer**—Handle of the window to move.
X	**Integer**—New left position for the window.
Y	**Integer**—New top position for the window.
nWidth	**Integer**—New width for the window.
nHeight	**Integer**—New height for the window.
bRepaint	**Integer**—TRUE (nonzero) if window should be redrawn. FALSE (zero) indicates that the application will explicitly redraw the window.

■ OffsetRect

VB Declaration   `Declare Sub OffsetRect Lib "User" (lpRect As RECT, ByVal X%, ByVal Y%)`

Description   This function moves a rectangle by applying a specified offset. X% is added to the **right** and **left** fields, Y% to the **top** and **bottom** fields. The direction of offset depends on whether the parameters are positive or negative, and the coordinate system in use.

Use with VB   No problem.

Parameter	Type/Description
lpRect	**RECT**—Rectangle to be offset.
X%	**Integer**—Horizontal offset.
Y%	**Integer**—Vertical offset.

Comments   A rectangle may not have a width or height greater than 32,767 units. This function does not check X% and Y% to prevent this type of error.

■ PostAppMessage, PostAppMessageBynum, PostAppMessageBystring

VB Declaration   `Declare Function PostAppMessage% Lib "User" (ByVal hTask%, ByVal wMsg%, ⇔`
`ByVal wParam%, lParam As Any)`

`Declare Function PostAppMessageBynum% Lib "User" Alias "PostAppMessage" ⇔`
`(ByVal hTask%, ByVal wMsg%, ByVal wParam%, Byval lParam&)`

`Declare Function PostAppMessageBystring% Lib "User" Alias "PostAppMessage" ⇔`
`(ByVal hTask%, ByVal wMsg%, ByVal wParam%, Byval lParam$)`

Description   Posts a message to the message queue of an application without directing it to a specific window. Posted messages are processed in due course during Windows event processing. **PostAppMessageBystring** and **PostAppMessageBynum** are type-safe declarations of **PostAppMessage**.

Use with VB   Only useful if you are aware of a particular application that can receive application messages of this type.

Parameter	Type/Description
hTask	**Integer**—Handle to the task to receive the message.
wMsg	**Integer**—Message ID.
wParam	**Integer**—16-bit parameter depending on message.
lParam	**Varies**—32-bit **Long** or **String** parameter depending on the message.

Return Value   **Integer**—TRUE (nonzero) if the message is posted successfully.

Comments   Most applications only process messages that are destined to particular windows, thus this function is of limited use under VB.

■ PostMessage, PostMessageBynum, PostMessageBystring

VB Declaration   Declare Function PostMessage% Lib "User" (ByVal hWnd%, ByVal wMsg%, ByVal ⇔ wParam%, lParam As Any)

Declare Function PostMessageBynum% Lib "User" Alias "PostMessage" (ByVal ⇔ hWnd%, ByVal wMsg%, ByVal wParam%, Byval lParam&)

Declare Function PostMessageByString% Lib "User" Alias "PostMessage" (ByVal ⇔ hWnd%, ByVal wMsg%, ByVal wParam%, Byval lParam$)

Description   Posts a message to the message queue of the specified window. Posted messages are processed in due course during Windows event processing, at which time the Windows function for the specified window is called with the posted message. **PostMessageBystring** and **PostMessageBynum** are type-safe declarations of **PostMessage**.

Use with VB   Good for sending window messages that do not need to be processed immediately.

Parameter	Type/Description
hWnd	**Integer**—Handle of the window to receive the message.
wMsg	**Integer**—Message ID.
wParam	**Integer**—16-bit parameter depending on message.
lParam	**Varies**—32-bit **Long** or **String** parameter depending on the message.

Return Value   **Integer**—TRUE (nonzero) if the message is posted successfully.

Comments   If **lParam** is a handle or pointer to a global memory block, that block must be allocated with the **GMEM_SHARE** flag. See Chapter 12 for details.

■ PtInRect

VB Declaration   Declare Function PtInRect% Lib "User" (lpRect As RECT, ByVal Pnt As Any)

Declare Function PtInRectBynum% Lib "User" Alias "PtInRect" (lpRect As ⇔ RECT, ByVal Pnt&)

Description   This function determines if the specified point is located in rectangle **lpRect**. **PtInRectBynum%** is a type-safe version of **PtInRect**.

Use with VB   No problem.

Parameter	Type/Description
lpRect	**RECT**—Rectangle to use for test.
Pnt	**Long**—Long representation of **POINTAPI** structure containing the point to check. The X value is in the low-order word, the Y value in the high-order word.

Return Value   **Integer**—TRUE (nonzero) if the point is in the specified rectangle, zero otherwise.

Comments   A point is considered to be inside a rectangle if it is within the four boundaries of the rectangle, or on the top or left side of the rectangle. A point located on the right or bottom side is not considered to be in the rectangle. You can use the **agPOINTAPItoLong()** function in the **APIGUIDE.DLL** library to convert a **POINTAPI** structure into a **Long**.

■ RedrawWindow

VB Declaration
```
Declare Function RedrawWindow% Lib "User" (ByVal hWnd%, lprcUpdate As RECT, ⇔
ByVal hrgnUpdate%, ByVal fuRedraw%)
```

Description   Redraws all or part of a window according to the **fuRedraw** flag.

Use with VB   No problem.

Parameter	Type/Description
hWnd	**Integer**—Handle of the window to redraw.
lprcUpdate	**RECT**—Rectangle describing the area in the window to redraw.
hrgnUpdate	**Integer**—Handle to a region describing the area to redraw. (Regions are described in Chapter 6.)
fuRedraw	**Integer**—Flags specifying the redraw operation to perform. The constants in the following table may be combined to specify the redraw operation.

fuRedraw Constant	Description
RDW_ERASE	The background of the redraw area is erased before drawing. **RDW_INVALIDATE** must also be specified.
RDW_FRAME	Updates the nonclient area if included in the redraw area. **RDW_INVALIDATE** must also be specified.
RDW_INTERNALPAINT	A WM_PAINT message is posted to the window even if it is not invalid.
RDW_INVALIDATE	Invalidates the redraw area.
RDW_NOERASE	Prevents the background of the redraw area from being erased.
RDW_NOFRAME	Prevents the nonclient area from being redrawn if it is part of the redraw area. **RDW_VALIDATE** must also be specified.
RDW_NOINTERNALPAINT	Prevents any pending **WM_PAINT** messages that were generated internally or by this function. **WM_PAINT** messages will still be generated for invalid areas.
RDW_VALIDATE	Validates the redraw area.
RDW_ERASENOW	Erases the specified redraw area immediately.
RDW_UPDATENOW	Updates the specified redraw area immediately.

fuRedraw Constant	Description
RDW_ALLCHILDREN	Redraw operation includes child windows if present in the redraw area.
RDW_NOCHILDREN	Redraw operation excludes child windows if present in the redraw area.

Return Value **Integer**—TRUE (nonzero) on success, zero otherwise.

Comments If this function is used on the desktop window, the application must use the **RDW_ERASE** flag to redraw the desktop.

■ ScreenToClient

VB Declaration `Declare Sub ScreenToClient Lib "User" (ByVal hWnd%, lpPoint As POINTAPI)`

Description Determines the client coordinates for a given point on the screen.

Use with VB No problem.

Parameter	Type/Description
hWnd	**Integer**—Handle of window defining the client coordinate system to use.
lpPoint	**POINTAPI**—Structure containing the point on the screen in screen coordinates. This function loads the structure with the corresponding client coordinates based on **hWnd**.

■ ScrollWindow

VB Declaration `Declare Sub ScrollWindow Lib "User" (ByVal hWnd%, ByVal XAmount%, ByVal ⇔ YAmount%, lpRect As RECT, lpClipRect As RECT)`

`Declare Sub ScrollWindowBynum Lib "User" Alias "ScrollWindow" (ByVal ⇔ hWnd%,ByVal XAmount%, ByVal YAmount%, ByVal lpRect&, ByVal lpClipRect&)`

Description Scrolls all or part of a window's client area. **ScrollWindowBynum** specifies the rectangle pointers as **Long** to facilitate passing zero as a parameter.

Use with VB When scrolling a form with the **AutoRedraw** property set to TRUE, this function does not affect the persistent bitmap; thus the contents of the client area (except for control positions) will be restored when the window is redrawn.

Parameter	Type/Description
hWnd	**Integer**—Handle of the window to scroll.
XAmount	**Integer**—Distance to scroll horizontally. Positive values scroll right, negative values scroll left.
YAmount	**Integer**—Distance to scroll vertically. Positive values scroll down, negative values scroll up.

Parameter	Type/Description
lpRect	**RECT**—Rectangle in client coordinates defining the portion of the client area to scroll. When NULL, the entire client area is scrolled. When NULL, child windows and controls are offset as well, along with any invalid areas. Otherwise child windows and invalid areas are not offset; thus it is advisable to call the **UpdateWindow** function before scrolling when **lpRect** is specified.
lpClipRect	**RECT**—Clipping rectangle. Only the area within this rectangle may be scrolled. This rectangle takes priority over **lpRect**. May be NULL.

Comments **ScrollWindowBynum** provides a declaration that calls for **Long** variables containing pointers to the specified rectangles. This allows you to specify zero (NULL) as the rectangle parameters. You may use **agGetAddressForObject** to obtain a **Long** pointer to a rectangle object. For example, to scroll the part of a window specified by rectangle **rcname** up ten pixels without specifying a clipping rectangle use

```
ScrollWindowBynum(formname.hWnd, 0, -10, agGetAddressForObject(rcname), 0&)
```

Areas uncovered by scrolling are invalidated and will be redrawn by Windows in due course during normal event processing.

■ ScrollWindowEx

VB Declaration
```
Declare Sub ScrollWindowEx Lib "User" (ByVal hWnd%, ByVal dx%, ByVal dy%, ⇔
lprcScroll As RECT, lprcClip As RECT, ByVal hrgnUpdate%, lprcUpdate As RECT, ⇔
ByVal fuScroll%)

Declare Sub ScrollWindowEx Lib "User" Alias "ScrollWindowEx" (ByVal hWnd%, ⇔
ByVal dx%, ByVal dy%, lprcScroll As RECT, lprcClip As RECT, ByVal hrgnUpdate%, ⇔
lprcUpdate As RECT, ByVal fuScroll%)
```

Description Scrolls all or part of a window's client area with additional options. **ScrollWindowExBynum** specifies the rectangle pointers as **Long** to facilitate passing zero as a parameter.

Use with VB See comments for **ScrollWindow**.

Parameter	Type/Description
hWnd	**Integer**—Handle of the window to scroll.
dx	**Integer**—Distance to scroll horizontally. Positive values scroll right, negative values scroll left.
dy	**Integer**—Distance to scroll vertically. Positive values scroll down, negative values scroll up.
lprcScroll	**RECT**—Rectangle in client coordinates defining the portion of the client area to scroll. When zero, the entire client area is scrolled.
lprcClip	**RECT**—Clipping rectangle. Only the area within this rectangle may be scrolled. This rectangle takes priority over **lpRect**. May be zero in which case no clipping takes place.
hrgnUpdate	**Integer**—Region to load with the area invalidated during scrolling. May be zero. Refer to Chapter 6 for information on regions.

Parameter	Type/Description
lprecUpdate	**RECT**—Rectangle structure that will be loaded with a rectangle defining the area invalidated during scrolling. May be zero.
fuScroll	**Integer**—Flags that control scrolling. May be a combination of the following constants: **SW_ERASE**: Erases the background of the newly invalidated area. **SW_INVALDATE**: Invalidates the area uncovered by scrolling. **SW_SCROLLCHILDREN**: Child windows within the scroll area are moved by the amount scrolled. Be sure that child windows or controls are either entirely in the scroll area or entirely outside the scroll area when using this function to prevent invalid results.

Comments See comments for **ScrollWindow**.

■ SendMessage, SendMessageBynum, SendMessageBystring

VB Declaration
```
Declare Function SendMessage& Lib "User" (ByVal hWnd%, ByVal wMsg%, ByVal ⇔
wParam%, lParam As Any)

Declare Function SendMessageBynum& Lib "User" Alias "SendMessage" (ByVal ⇔
hWnd%, ByVal wMsg%, ByVal wParam%, Byval lParam&)

Declare Function SendMessageBystring& Lib "User" Alias "SendMessage" (ByVal ⇔
hWnd%, ByVal wMsg%, ByVal wParam%, Byval lParam$)
```

Description Sends a message to a window by calling the window function for that window. This function does not return until the message is processed. **SendMessageBystring** and **SendMessageBynum** are type-safe declarations of **SendMessage**.

Use with VB No problem.

Parameter	Type/Description
hWnd	**Integer**—Handle of the window to receive the message.
wMsg	**Integer**—Message ID.
wParam	**Integer**—16-bit parameter depending on message.
lParam	Varies—32-bit **Long** or **String** parameter depending on the message.

Return Value **Long**—Depends on the message.

Comments If **lParam** is a handle or pointer to a global memory block, that block must be allocated with the **GMEM_SHARE** flag. See Chapter 12 for details.

■ SetActiveWindow

VB Declaration `Declare Function SetActiveWindow% Lib "User" (ByVal hWnd%)`

Description Activates the specified window.

Use with VB   Use with caution. This function does not change the input focus, thus it is possible for the focus to be set to an inactive window—generally an undesirable situation. It is preferable to use the **SetFocusAPI** function to activate a window.

Parameter	Type/Description
hWnd	**Integer**—Handle of window to activate.

Return Value   **Integer**—Handle of the previously active window.

■ SetClassLong

VB Declaration   ```Declare Function SetClassLong& Lib "User" (ByVal hWnd%, ByVal nIndex%, ByVal ⇔ dwNewLong&)```

Description   Sets one of the **Long** variable entries for the window class.

Use with VB   See comments.

Parameter	Type/Description
hWnd	**Integer**—Window handle for which to set class information.
nIndex	**Integer**—See description for the **nIndex** parameter to the **Get-ClassLong** function. Do not use the **GCL_MENUNAME** index.
dwNewLong	**Long**—New value for the class information specified by **nIndex**.

Return Value   **Long**—The previous value for the class information specified by **nIndex**.

Comments   Changing the **GCL_WNDPROC** data is dangerous and should not be done by a VB application.

■ SetClassWord

VB Declaration   ```Declare Function SetClassWord% Lib "User" (ByVal hWnd%, ByVal nIndex%, ByVal ⇔ wNewWord%)```

Description   Sets one of the **Integer** variable entries for the window class.

Use with VB   See comments.

Parameter	Type/Description
hWnd	**Integer**—Window handle for which to obtain class information.
nIndex	**Integer**—See description for the **nIndex** parameter to the **GetClassWord** function. Do not use the **GCW_CBCLSEXTRA**, **GCW_CBWNDEX-TRA** and **GCW_HMODULE** indexes.
dwNewWord	**Word**—New value for the class information specified by **nIndex**.

Return Value   **Integer**—The previous value for the class information specified by **nIndex**.

Comments   Use with care. Remember that changes affect all windows of the specified class, but that changes may not take effect until the window is redrawn.

◼ SetFocusAPI

VB Declaration   `Declare Function SetFocusAPI% Lib "User" Alias "SetFocus" (ByVal hWnd%)`

Description   Sets the input focus to the specified window. Activates the window if necessary.

Use with VB   The **SetFocus** method is preferred for VB forms and controls.

Parameter	Type/Description
hWnd	**Integer**—Handle of the window that will receive the focus.

Return Value   **Integer**—Handle of the window that previously had the focus.

Comments   This function uses the alias **SetFocusAPI** to avoid conflicts with the Visual Basic **SetFocus** method.

◼ SetParent

VB Declaration   `Declare Function SetParent% Lib "User" (ByVal hWndChild%, ByVal hWndNewParent%)`

Description   Specifies the new parent for a window.

Use with VB   Makes it possible for VB to support child windows in many cases.

Parameter	Type/Description
hWndChild	**Integer**—Handle of child window.
hWndNewParent	**Integer**—New parent for **hWndChild**.

Return Value   The handle of the previous parent window.

Comments   This function can be used to place VB controls inside of container controls at runtime (such as making a button a child window of a **picture** or **frame** control), or moving controls from one container control to another. When a control is moved to another parent, its position is based on the coordinate system of the new parent, thus it may be necessary to reposition the control in order for it to appear in the desired location.

◼ SetRect

VB Declaration   `Declare Sub SetRect Lib "User" (lpRect As RECT, ByVal X1%, ByVal Y1%, ByVal ⇔`
`X2%, ByVal Y2%)`

Description   Sets the contents of the specified rectangle.

Use with VB   No problem.

Parameter	Type/Description
lpRect	**RECT**—Rectangle to set.
X1	**Integer**—Value for **left** field.

Parameter	Type/Description
Y1	**Integer**—Value for **top** field.
X2	**Integer**—Value for **right** field.
Y2	**Integer**—Value for **bottom** field.

Comments This function provides a convenient way to set the contents of a rectangle with a single function instead of requiring four assignments. Keep in mind that the width and height of a rectangle must be less than 32,767.

■ SetRectEmpty

VB Declaration `Declare Sub SetRectEmpty Lib "User" (lpRect As RECT)`

Description Sets **lpRect** to be an empty rectangle (all fields=0).

Use with VB No problem.

Parameter	Type/Description
lpRect	**RECT**—Rectangle to set to empty.

■ SetSysModalWindow

VB Declaration `Declare Function SetSysModalWindow% Lib "User" (ByVal hWnd%)`

Description Makes the specified window into the system modal window. When a window is system modal, no other window can be activated or receive input.

Use with VB Use with caution. Among the windows that cannot be activated once a window is system modal are the VB immediate mode window and VB control window (which contains the Run, Break, and End menus); thus it is possible to enter a state where the system is hung and needs to be reset in order to continue.

Parameter	Type/Description
hWnd	**Integer**—Specifies handle of window to make system modal.

Return Value **Integer**—Handle of the previous system modal window.

Comments The window must be destroyed to end the system modal state.

■ SetWindowLong

VB Declaration `Declare Function SetWindowLong& Lib "User" (ByVal hWnd%, ByVal nIndex%, ByVal ⇔ dwNewLong&)`

Description Sets information in the window structure for the specified window.

Use with VB	See comments.

Parameter	Type/Description
hWnd	**Integer**—Handle of window for which to obtain information.
nIndex	**Integer**—See description for the **nIndex** parameter to the **GetWindowLong** function.
dwNewLong	**Long**—New value for the window information specified by **nIndex**.

Return Value   The previous value of the specified data.

Comments   Changing the **GWL_WNDPROC** data is dangerous and should not be done by a VB application. Refer to the style reference in this chapter for information on windows style bits that may be changed.

■ SetWindowPlacement

VB Declaration   `Declare Function SetWindowPlacement% Lib "User" (ByVal hWnd%, lpwndpl As ⇔ WINDOWPLACEMENT)`

Description   Sets window state and location information for a window.

Use with VB   No problem.

Parameter	Type/Description
hWnd	**Integer**—Handle of window for which to set placement information.
lpwndpl	**WINDOWPLACEMENT**—Structure containing location and state information for the window. See Appendix B for details.

Return Value   **Integer**—TRUE (nonzero) on success, zero otherwise.

■ SetWindowPos

VB Declaration   `Declare Sub SetWindowPos Lib "User" (ByVal hWnd%, ByVal hWndInsertAfter%, ByVal ⇔ X%, ByVal Y%, ByVal cx%, ByVal cy%, ByVal wFlags%)`

Description   This function specifies a new position and state for a window. It can also change the position of the window in the internal window list. This function is similar to the **DeferWindowPos** function, except that it takes effect immediately.

Use with VB   No problem.

Parameter	Type/Description
hWnd	**Integer**—Window to position.
hWndInsertAfter	**Integer**—See description of the **hWndInsertAfter** parameter to the **DeferWindowPos** function.
x	**Integer**—See description of the **x** parameter to the **DeferWindowPos** function.

Parameter	Type/Description
y	Integer—See description of the **y** parameter to the **DeferWindowPos** function.
cx	Integer—See description of the **cx** parameter to the **DeferWindowPos** function.
cy	Integer—See description of the **cy** parameter to the **DeferWindowPos** function.
flags	Integer—See description of the **hWndInsertAfter** parameter to the **DeferWindowPos** function.

Comments   See comments for the **DeferWindowPos** function.

■ SetWindowText

VB Declaration   `Declare Function SetWindowText% Lib "User" (ByVal hWnd%, ByVal lpString$)`

Description   Sets the title (caption) text of a window or contents of a control.

Use with VB   Use the **Caption** or **Text** property (as appropriate) for VB forms or controls.

Parameter	Type/Description
hWnd	Integer—Handle of a window for which to set the text.
lpString	String—Text to set into **hWnd**.

■ SetWindowWord

VB Declaration   `Declare Function SetWindowLong& Lib "User" (ByVal hWnd%, ByVal nIndex%, ByVal ⇔ dwNewWord%)`

Description   Sets information in the window structure for the specified window.

Use with VB   Use with caution.

Parameter	Type/Description
hWnd	Integer—Handle of window for which to obtain information.
nIndex	Integer—See description for the **nIndex** parameter to the **GetWindowWord** function. Do not use this function with the **GWW_HWNDPARENT** index (use the **SetParent** API function instead).
dwNewWord	Integer—New value for the window information specified by **nIndex**.

Return Value   The previous value of the specified data.

ShowOwnedPopups

VB Declaration   Declare Sub ShowOwnedPopups Lib "User" (ByVal hWnd%, ByVal fShow%)

Description   Shows or hides all popup windows owned by the specified window.

Use with VB   No problem.

Parameter	Type/Description
hWnd	**Integer**—Handle to parent window.
fShow	**Integer**—TRUE (nonzero) to show all popup windows owned by **hWnd**; FALSE (zero) to hide them.

ShowScrollBar

VB Declaration   Declare Sub ShowScrollBar Lib "User" (ByVal hWnd%, ByVal wBar%, ByVal bShow%)

Description   This function can be used to hide or show scroll bars.

Use with VB   Use the **Visible** property to hide or show VB scroll bar controls. This function may be used on VB controls that have scroll bars (such as the edit control and list box), but be sure to carefully verify the operation of the control before using it in an application.

Parameter	Type/Description
hWnd	**Integer**—Window handle; depends on the value of **wBar**.
wBar	**Integer**—One of the following constants: **SB_CTL:** **hWnd** specifies the window handle of a scroll bar control. **SB_HORZ:** **hWnd** specifies a window that has a horizontal scroll bar. **SB_VERT:** **hWnd** specifies a window that has a vertical scroll bar. **SB_BOTH:** **hWnd** specifies a window that has both horizontal and vertical scroll bars.
fShow	**Integer**—TRUE (nonzero) to show the scroll bar designated by **wBar**; FALSE (zero) to hide it.

Comments   When using a custom control that provides instantaneous scroll events, do not use this function during the scroll event.

ShowWindow

VB Declaration   Declare Function ShowWindow% Lib "User" (ByVal hWnd%, ByVal nCmdShow%)

Description   Use to control the visibility of a window.

Use with VB   Use the VB property that corresponds to a **ShowWindow** command for VB forms and controls.

Parameter	Type/Description
hWnd	**Integer**—Handle of the window on which to apply the command specified by **nCmdShow**.

Parameter	Type/Description
nCmdShow	**Integer**—Specifies a visibility command for the window. Use one of the following constants:

SW_HIDE: Hides the window. Activation passes to another window.

SW_MINIMIZE: Minimizes the window. Activation passes to another window.

SW_RESTORE: Displays a window at its original size and location and activates it.

SW_SHOW: Displays a window at its current size and location, and activates it.

SW_SHOWMAXIMIZED: Maximizes a window and activates it.

SW_SHOWMINIMIZED: Minimizes a window and activates it.

SW_SHOWMINNOACTIVE: Minimizes a window without changing the active window.

SW_SHOWNA: Displays a window at its current size and location. Does not change the active window.

SW_SHOWNOACTIVATE: Displays a window at its most recent size and location. Does not change the active window.

SW_SHOWNORMAL: Same as **SW_RESTORE**.

Return Value   **Integer**—TRUE (nonzero) if window was previously visible. FALSE (zero) otherwise.

■ SubtractRect

VB Declaration   `Declare Function SubtractRect% Lib "User" (lpDestRect As RECT, lpSrc1Rect ⇔`
`As RECT, lpSrc2Rect As RECT)`

Description   This function loads into rectangle **lpDestRect** a rectangle that describes the result when rectangle **lpSrc2Rect** is subtracted from **lpSrc1Rect**.

Use with VB   No problem.

Parameter	Type/Description
lpDestRect	**RECT**—Destination rectangle that will contain the result of **lpSrc2Rect** subtracted from **lpSrc1Rect**.
lpSrc1Rect	**RECT**—First source rectangle.
lpSrc2Rect	**RECT**—Second source rectangle.

Return Value   **Integer**—TRUE (nonzero) if the function was successful, zero otherwise.

Comments   **lpSrc2Rect** must completely intersect **lpSrc1Rect** either horizontally or vertically. In other words, when the part of **lpSrc1Rect** that intersects **lpSrc2Rect** is removed from **lpSrc1Rect**, the result must be a rectangle. If it is not, **lpDestRect** is simply set to **lpSrc1Rect**.

■ UnionRect

VB Declaration   `Declare Function UnionRect% Lib "User" (lpDestRect As RECT, lpSrc1Rect As RECT, ⇔`
`lpSrc2Rect As RECT)`

Description This function loads into rectangle **lpDestRect** a rectangle that describes the union of **lpSrc1Rect** and **lpSrc2Rect**. This is the rectangle that includes all points in both rectangles.

Use with VB No problem.

Parameter	Type/Description
lpDestRect	**RECT**—Destination rectangle that will contain the union of **lpSrc1Rect** and **lpSrc2Rect**.
lpSrc1Rect	**RECT**—First source rectangle.
lpSrc2Rect	**RECT**—Second source rectangle.

Return Value **Integer**—TRUE (nonzero) if the resulting rectangle is not empty, zero otherwise.

Comments The RectPlay example program provides a graphical illustration of this function in action.

■ UpdateWindow

VB Declaration `Declare Sub UpdateWindow Lib "User" (ByVal hWnd%)`

Description Forces an immediate update of a window. All areas in the window that were previously invalidated are redrawn.

Use with VB If any part of a VB form or control needs updating, this is similar to the **Refresh** method.

Parameter	Type/Description
hWnd	**Integer**—Handle of the window to update.

■ ValidateRect, ValidateRectBynum

VB Declaration `Declare Sub ValidateRect Lib "User" (ByVal hWnd%, lpRect As RECT)`

`Declare Sub ValidateRectBynum Lib "User" Alias "ValidateRect" (ByVal hWnd%, ⇔ ByVal lpRect&)`

Description Validates all or part of the client area of a window. This informs Windows that the specified area does not need to be redrawn.

Use with VB No problem.

Parameter	Type/Description
hWnd	**Integer**—Handle of window to invalidate.
lpRect	**RECT**—Rectangle structure describing the part of the rectangle to be validated. Use **ValidateRectBynum** with **lpRect** set to zero (**Long** data type) to validate the entire window.

■ WindowFromPoint, WindowFromPointBynum

VB Declaration   Declare Function WindowFromPoint% Lib "User" (ByVal Pnt As Any)

Declare Function WindowFromPointBynum% Lib "User" Alias "WindowFromPoint" ⇔ (ByVal Pnt&)

Description   Returns the handle of the window that contains the specified point. Ignores disabled, hidden, and transparent windows.

Use with VB   No problem. Can be used to identify forms and controls given their position in screen coordinates.

Parameter	Type/Description
Pnt	**Long**—Point value in screen coordinates. Use **agPOINTAPItoLong** to obtain this value from a point structure.

Return Value   **Integer**—Handle of the window that contains the specified point. Zero if no window exists at the point specified.

5

Hardware and System Functions

HE WINDOWS API PROVIDES ACCESS TO A VARIETY OF SYSTEM INFORMA-
tion and hardware functions that can be useful to the Visual Basic programmer. This chapter reviews those functions relating to the mouse and
cursor, the caret, keyboard input, time, and other system information.

Mouse, Cursor, and Caret Functions

Visual Basic provides support for the mouse and the cursor it controls (or
MousePointer, as it is called in Visual Basic). The cursor is a system-wide resource. This means that only one cursor may be selected at a time. It is possible for any application to change the cursor regardless of where the mouse is
on the screen, so caution should be used when dealing with these functions.

The caret is used to indicate a position within a control. Like the cursor,
the caret is a system resource—only one may exist in the system at a time.

Unless otherwise noted, all mouse and cursor positions are specified in
pixel screen coordinates.

Cursor Clipping

Windows provides the ability to restrict the mouse to a specified area on the
screen, a process called *clipping*. The cursor clipping functions are shown in
Table 5.1.

Table 5.1 **Cursor Clipping Functions**

Function	Description
ClipCursor	Specifies the clipping rectangle.
GetClipCursor	Retrieves the current cursor clipping area if one is present.

Cursor Position

Table 5.2 describes the Windows API functions that may be used to set and retrieve the cursor position.

Table 5.2 **Cursor Position Functions**

Function	Description
SetCursorPos	Moves the cursor to the location specified.
GetCursorPos	Retrieves the current cursor position.

Other Mouse and Cursor Functions

Windows provides a number of other mouse related functions that—with limitations—may be used with Visual Basic.

Custom Cursors

A cursor is made up of a pair of monochrome bitmaps whose dimensions may be up to 32x32 pixels. It is very similar internally to a monochrome icon. Like other Windows objects, a cursor object is represented by a 16-bit handle.

Windows provides functions to create cursors and select them for use. Unfortunately, Visual Basic is not truly compatible with these API functions. When a custom cursor is selected using the **SetCursor** API function, VB tends to reset the cursor to the original value without notice.

You can use the **SetCursor** API function to change the cursor only during uninterrupted operations in a procedure. As soon as normal event processing takes place through use of the **DoEvents** function or exiting an event procedure, the cursor is changed to the value appropriate for the form or control over which it appears. It is possible to use the **SetClassWord** API function to set the class cursor for a particular class to a user-defined cursor; however, this affects all windows that belong to that class. Alternatively, there are third-party products, such as Desaware's CCF-Cursors, that allow full use of custom cursors with VB.

Cursor resources may be loaded from program files or DLL files or may be created directly using the **CreateCursor** API function, which is described in Chapter 8.

Mouse Capture

Mouse events (such as **MouseUp**, **MouseMove**, **MouseDown**, and **DblClick**) normally go to the window in which they take place. It is possible for a window to "capture" the mouse. This means that all mouse events go to the window that has the capture, regardless of where the mouse is on the screen. The mouse capture functions are not fully compatible with Visual Basic, as VB tends to automatically release the capture in many cases when the mouse is clicked outside of the window that has the capture. However, the capture can on occasion be used to good effect as shown in the WinView project example presented in Chapter 4.

When you set the capture to a Visual Basic window it will receive **MouseMove** events regardless of where the cursor is on the screen. It will also receive the first **MouseDown** event when the mouse is clicked. After that, the mouse capture is automatically released. Table 5.3 summarizes the remaining API functions relating to the mouse and cursor.

Table 5.3 **Additional Mouse and Cursor Functions**

Function	Description
CopyCursor	Makes a copy of a cursor.
CreateCursor	Creates a cursor from two bitmaps (see Chapter 8).
DestroyCursor	Destroys a cursor and frees all system resources that it uses.
GetCapture	Determines which window if any has the mouse capture.
GetCursor	Retrieves the handle of the current cursor.
GetDoubleClickTime	Determines the time during which two consecutive mouse clicks will be considered a double click.
LoadCursor	Loads a cursor resource from a file.
ReleaseCapture	Cancels the mouse capture.
SetCapture	Sets the mouse capture to the specified window.
SetCursor	Selects the cursor to use.
SetDoubleClickTime	Sets the time during which two consecutive mouse clicks will be considered a double click.
ShowCursor	Controls the visibility of the cursor.
SwapMouseButton	Swaps the meanings of the right and left mouse buttons.

Caret Functions

The *caret* is a shared system resource that is commonly used to indicate a position with text. It is generally a flashing line or block, though any bitmap can be used as the caret. There can be only one caret in the system at a time.

The caret API functions are of limited use under Visual Basic. Normally, a window should set the caret when it receives the input focus, and destroy it when it loses the focus. Unfortunately, in Visual Basic the **GotFocus** and **LostFocus** events occur only when a control loses focus to another control in the current application. They do not occur when the focus is switched to other applications. This makes it difficult to know when to set the caret for a particular control. It is of course possible to use a timer to detect when a control has the focus and to set the caret based on the results, but this is a cumbersome technique.

The SysInfo project described later in this chapter demonstrates use of a custom caret in an edit box. The caret functions are listed in Table 5.4.

Table 5.4   **Caret Functions**

Function	Description
CreateCaret	Creates and selects a caret.
DestroyCaret	Destroys a caret.
GetCaretPos	Determines the position of the caret in logical coordinates.
GetCaretBlinkTime	Gets the flash rate for the caret.
HideCaret	Hides the caret.
SetCaretBlinkTime	Sets the flash rate for the caret.
SetCaretPos	Sets the position of the caret in logical coordinates.
ShowCaret	Makes the caret visible.

Keyboard and Other Input Functions

The Windows API provides a number of functions that can be used to control and process keyboard input. In order to understand how to use them, it is necessary to know a little bit about the way that Windows processes characters.

The OEM and Windows Character Sets

A character is generally represented in Windows as an eight-bit unsigned character type. String data is made up of a sequence of these eight-bit characters. These eight bits are sufficient to define 256 characters. Many of these characters are defined by a standard known as ASCII (American Standard Code for Information Interchange); for example, ASCII character #10 is defined as a line feed character that indicates a break between lines.

Windows does provide support for extended two-byte character sets such as those used to represent Kanji (a Japanese alphabet), but a complete review of those character sets is beyond the scope of this book.

A character set describes the appearance of each of the 256 possible characters. Different languages frequently have different character sets in order to provide support for the characters unique to that language. The MS-DOS operating system describes a character set as a *code page*, and provides standard code pages for a number of different languages. Computer manufacturers will generally provide a keyboard that matches the default code page for a particular system, thus a DOS-based computer sold in Germany will have a

German keyboard and default to the German MS-DOS code page. Windows refers to this character set as the OEM (original equipment manufacturer) character set. All DOS-related activities, such as command lines and file names, use the OEM character set.

Windows internally uses its own character set based on ANSI (American National Standards Institute) called the ANSI or Windows character set. Windows does communicate with DOS in many cases, so a number of translation functions exist to convert OEM to ANSI and vice versa. The mapping from one character set to another is not one-to-one, thus if you convert a string from OEM to ANSI and back, it may not match the original string.

One example of this is the Ê character (ASCII #202 decimal). This character does not exist in the MS-DOS code page #437 (U.S. standard). An attempt to save a file using this character would lead to an error, or a file that could not be accessed from the keyboard. The **AnsiToOem** API function will convert this character to the letter E. The **OemToAnsi** function will obviously not convert the letter E back to Ê. The API conversion functions for OEM and ANSI character sets are shown in Table 5.5.

Table 5.5   **OEM and ANSI Conversion Functions**

Function	Description
AnsiToOem AnsiToOemBuff	Converts a string from the ANSI character set to the OEM character set.
OemToAnsi OemToAnsiBuff	Converts a string from the OEM character set to the ANSI character set.

Scan Codes and Virtual Keys

Keys on the keyboard produce different scan codes based on their position. A scan code is a hardware-dependent code that the keyboard sends to the computer to indicate that a keyboard operation took place. Scan codes can vary by the type of keyboard and type of computer being used, so software that uses scan codes directly may not be compatible with every computer that runs Windows. In order to provide low-level access to the keyboard that does not depend on the scan code, Windows defines *virtual keys*. Virtual keys are defined by constants with a VK_ prefix and are listed in Table 5.7 later in this chapter. They are also defined in the APICONST.TXT file provided with this book.

An overview of character processing can be seen in Figure 5.1.

Table 5.6 lists the keyboard processing API functions.

Figure 5.1

Keyboard
processing in
Windows

**How Windows
Processes Characters**

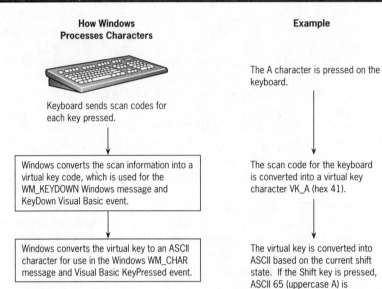

Keyboard sends scan codes for
each key pressed.

↓

Windows converts the scan information into a
virtual key code, which is used for the
WM_KEYDOWN Windows message and
KeyDown Visual Basic event.

↓

Windows converts the virtual key to an ASCII
character for use in the Windows WM_CHAR
message and Visual Basic KeyPressed event.

Example

The A character is pressed on the
keyboard.

↓

The scan code for the keyboard
is converted into a virtual key
character VK_A (hex 41).

↓

The virtual key is converted into
ASCII based on the current shift
state. If the Shift key is pressed,
ASCII 65 (uppercase A) is
generated; otherwise ASCII 97
(lowercase a) is generated. Other
values may be generated
depending on the states of the
Control and Alt keys.

Table 5.6　　**Keyboard Processing API Functions**

Function	Description
GetAsyncKeyState	Retrieves the state of the specified virtual key at the time the function is called.
GetKBCodePage	Retrieves the number of the code page currently in effect for Windows and used to translate to and from the OEM character set.
GetKeyboardState	Retrieves the current state of all 256 virtual keys.
GetKeyboardType	Determines the type of keyboard in use.
GetKeyNameText	Determines the name of a particular virtual key. For example, the spacebar on U.S. keyboards is called "Space."
GetKeyState	Retrieves the state of the specified virtual key.
MapVirtualKey	Converts characters to and from virtual keys, scan codes, and ASCII values.

Table 5.6	**Keyboard Processing API Functions (Continued)**
OemKeyScan	Converts ASCII codes to OEM scan codes and shift states.
SetKeyboardState	Sets the state of the 256 virtual keys as perceived by Windows.
ToAscii	Converts a scan code and shift state to an ASCII code.
VkKeyScan	Converts ASCII codes to virtual key codes and shift states.

Virtual Key Codes

Table 5.7 shows the virtual key codes used in Windows.

Table 5.7	**Virtual Key Codes**

Virtual Key Code	Value
VK_LBUTTON	&H01
VK_RBUTTON	&H02
VK_CANCEL	&H03
VK_MBUTTON	&H04
VK_BACK	&H08
VK_TAB	&H09
VK_CLEAR	&H0C
VK_RETURN	&H0D
VK_SHIFT	&H10
VK_CONTROL	&H11
VK_MENU	&H12
VK_PAUSE	&H13
VK_CAPITAL	&H14
VK_ESCAPE	&H1B
VK_SPACE	&H20
VK_PRIOR	&H21

Table 5.7　　　**Virtual Key Codes (Continued)**

VK_NEXT	&H22
VK_END	&H23
VK_HOME	&H24
VK_LEFT	&H25
VK_UP	&H26
VK_RIGHT	&H27
VK_DOWN	&H28
VK_SELECT	&H29
VK_PRINT	&H2A
VK_EXECUTE	&H2B
VK_SNAPSHOT	&H2C
VK_INSERT	&H2D
VK_DELETE	&H2E
VK_HELP	&H2F
VK_NUMPAD0	&H60
VK_NUMPAD1	&H61
VK_NUMPAD2	&H62
VK_NUMPAD3	&H63
VK_NUMPAD4	&H64
VK_NUMPAD5	&H65
VK_NUMPAD6	&H66
VK_NUMPAD7	&H67
VK_NUMPAD8	&H68
VK_NUMPAD9	&H69
VK_MULTIPLY	&H6A
VK_ADD	&H6B
VK_SEPARATOR	&H6C

Table 5.7	Virtual Key Codes (Continued)	
	VK_SUBTRACT	&H6D
	VK_DECIMAL	&H6E
	VK_DIVIDE	&H6F
	VK_F1	&H70
	VK_F2	&H71
	VK_F3	&H72
	VK_F4	&H73
	VK_F5	&H74
	VK_F6	&H75
	VK_F7	&H76
	VK_F8	&H77
	VK_F9	&H78
	VK_F10	&H79
	VK_F11	&H7A
	VK_F12	&H7B
	VK_F13	&H7C
	VK_F14	&H7D
	VK_F15	&H7E
	VK_F16	&H7F
	VK_F17	&H80
	VK_F18	&H81
	VK_F19	&H82
	VK_F20	&H83
	VK_F21	&H84
	VK_F22	&H85
	VK_F23	&H86
	VK_F24	&H87

Table 5.7	**Virtual Key Codes (Continued)**
VK_NUMLOCK	&H90
VK_SCROLL	&H91
VK_A—VK_Z	same as ASCII values for A–Z
VK_0—VK_9	same as ASCII values for 0–9

Input Control Functions

Windows provides a number of additional input control functions, which are listed in Table 5.8.

Table 5.8	**Input Control Functions**	
	Function	**Description**
	EnableHardwareInput	Enables or disables all mouse and keyboard input to the system.
	GetInputState	Determines if any keyboard or mouse events are in the system queue ready to be processed.
	GetQueueStatus	Determines what types of messages are in the application queue ready to be processed.
	IsDBCSLeadByte	Determines if a character is the first byte in a double-byte character set such as Kanji.
	LockInput	Used to lock or unlock input to all tasks other than the current task.

Time and System Functions

The Windows API includes a number of functions that make it possible to obtain information about the Windows system and to control various features in Windows. Some of these functions duplicate the functionality of the Windows Control Panel application (CONTROL.EXE).

Time Functions

The functions listed in Table 5.9 are used to retrieve information on Windows timing. Note that PC-based systems measure time internally by timer ticks, each of which is typically 50 milliseconds long (though it can vary by system). The timer tick duration determines the resolution of the time results returned by these functions.

Table 5.9 **Windows Time Functions**

Function	Description
GetCurrentTime	Retrieves the number of milliseconds that the current Windows session has been running.
GetMessageTime	Returns the time (measured in milliseconds) that the most recent message was posted to the application message queue measured from when the current Windows session was started.
GetTickCount	Identical to **GetCurrentTime**.
GetTimerResolution	Determines the duration of a timer tick in microseconds. This is also the resolution of the Windows time functions.

The Windows API also includes functions to control the internal Windows timers; however, these should not be used by Visual Basic applications. The VB timer control duplicates their functionality.

System Information and Control Functions

The functions listed in Table 5.10 may be used to determine information about the Windows system and perform various system operations.

Table 5.10 **System Information Functions**

Function	Description
ExitWindows	Exits Windows.
ExitWindowsExec	Exits Windows and causes a DOS application to run.
GetFreeSpace	Determines the amount of free memory.
GetFreeSystemResources	May be used to determine the percentage of available resources in the kernel, user, and GDI private heaps.
GetSysColor	Determines the current color setting for a Windows object (for example, the color of a button or the color of the title bar of an active window).

Table 5.10   **System Information Functions (Continued)**

GetSystemMetrics	Determines a variety of system metrics such as the height of a menu bar or window caption, the width of a vertical scroll bar, the minimum size of a window, etc.
GetVersion	Determines the versions of Windows and DOS that are running.
GetWinFlags	Determines the operating mode of Windows and the type of CPU and coprocessor present.
SetSwapAreaSize	Sets the amount of memory that an application may use for its code segments.
SetSysColors	Sets the current color setting for a Windows object (for example, the color of a scroll bar or the color of the title bar of an inactive window).
SystemParametersInfo	This powerful function can be used to retrieve and set a large number of system parameters such as the Windows screensaver, the desktop wallpaper, the keyboard delay and repeat rate, and more. Refer to the function reference for details.

Example: SysInfo—A System Information Viewer

SysInfo is a program designed to illustrate some of the Windows API functions described in this chapter. It includes several functions from each category presented above. The program allows you to calculate the amount of free space and system resources, the Windows mode and CPU, current system colors, system metrics, and other Windows system parameters. It can be easily extended to provide other kinds of information.

SysInfo also demonstrates some of the keyboard and caret functions. Refer to the WinView program in Chapter 4 for examples of some of the mouse functions.

Figure 5.2 shows the SysInfo program when retrieving system color information. Figure 5.3 shows the SysInfo form during design time (to help identify control locations).

Using SysInfo

A list box and associated label control are visible on the screen only when checking system colors after invoking the System-Colors menu command. Selecting an entry causes the background color of the label control to be set to the system color for the specified object.

Figure 5.2

SysInfo program
screen (running)

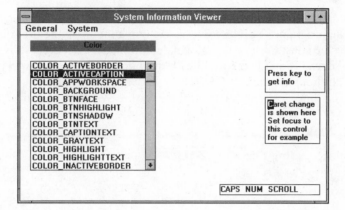

Figure 5.3

SysInfo main form
(design time)

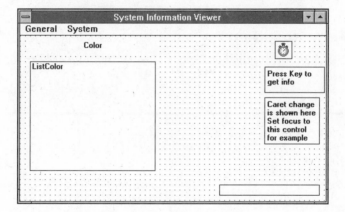

Two text controls are present on the form. When the upper text control has the focus, pressing any key will cause the key name to appear in the control. When the lower text control receives the input focus, a square caret will be created and shown.

A label control at the lower right of the form is used in conjunction with a timer control to show the current state of the CapsLock, NumLock, and ScrollLock keys.

Project Description

The SysInfo project includes four files. SYSINFO.FRM is the only form used in the program. SYSINFO.BAS is the only module in the program and contains the constant type and global definitions. APIDECS.BAS is the type-safe API declaration file provided with this book. APIGUIDE.BAS contains the declarations for the APIGUIDE.DLL dynamic link library.

Listing 5.1 shows the project file for the SysInfo program.

Listing 5.1   Project Listing File SYSINFO.MAK

```
SYSINFO.FRM
SYSINFO.BAS
APIDECS.BAS
APIGUIDE.BAS
ProjWinSize=174,387,248,215
ProjWinShow=2
Title="SYSINFO"
```

Form Description

Listing 5.2 contains the header from file SYSINFO.FRM that describes the control setup for the form.

Listing 5.2   SYSINFO.FRM Header

```
VERSION 2.00
Begin Form SysInfo
   Caption         =   "System Information Viewer"
   Height          =   4560
   Left            =   1035
   LinkMode        =   1  'Source
   LinkTopic       =   "Form1"
   ScaleHeight     =   3870
   ScaleWidth      =   7365
   Top             =   1140
   Width           =   7485
   Begin Timer Timer1
      Interval     =     250
      Left         =    6120
      Top          =     120
   End
```

When the MenuColor menu command is selected, the ListColor list box will be made visible and will show a list of Windows objects that have associated colors.

```
Begin ListBox ListColor
   Height         =    2565
   Left           =    240
   TabIndex       =    2
   Top            =    600
   Visible        =    0    'False
   Width          =    3015
End
```

When the **KeyCheck** control has the focus, any keystroke causes the name of the key found to be displayed in the control. For letters, the key name is the same as the character. For control keys and function keys, the key name describes the key.

```
Begin TextBox KeyCheck
   Height         =    615
   Left           =    5880
   MultiLine      =    -1   'True
   TabIndex       =    0
   Text           =    "Press Key to get info"
   Top            =    720
   Width          =    1455
End
Begin TextBox Text1
   Height         =    1095
   Left           =    5880
   MultiLine      =    -1   'True
   TabIndex       =    1
   Text           =    "Caret change is shown here Set focus to this ⇔
   control for example"
   Top            =    1440
   Width          =    1335
End
```

The background color of the **LabelColor** control is set to the system color for the object selected in the ListColor list box.

```
Begin Label LabelColor
   Alignment      =    2    'Center
   Caption        =    "Color"
   Height         =    255
   Left           =    240
   TabIndex       =    3
   Top            =    120
   Visible        =    0    'False
   Width          =    3015
End
```

The **LabelKeyState** control will be updated with the state of the CapsLock, NumLock, and ScrollLock keys during each timer event.

```
Begin Label LabelKeyState
    BorderStyle     =   1   'Fixed Single
    Height          =   255
    Left            =   4800
    TabIndex        =   4
    Top             =   3480
    Width           =   2415
End
```

The MenuGeneral menus commands are used to obtain statistics on the system. These include the system free memory and resource space, time information and the type of hardware in use.

```
Begin Menu MenuGeneral
    Caption         =   "General"
    Begin Menu MenuFreeSpace
        Caption         =   "Free&Space"
    End
    Begin Menu MenuTimes
        Caption         =   "&Times"
    End
    Begin Menu MenuFlags
        Caption         =   "&Flags"
    End
End
```

The MenuSystem menu commands can be used to determine the colors of various system objects, and to view other system metrics including standard object size information and additional system parameters.

```
Begin Menu MenuSystem
    Caption         =   "System"
    Begin Menu MenuColors
        Caption         =   "Colors"
    End
    Begin Menu MenuMetrics
        Caption         =   "&Metrics"
    End
    Begin Menu MenuParameters
        Caption         =   "&Parameters"
    End
End
End
```

SysInfo Listing

Module SYSINFO.BAS contains the constant declarations and global variables used by the program.

Listing 5.3   Module SYSINFO.BAS

```
' Sysinfo.txt

' Chapter 5 demonstration program


' General Purpose Defines

Global Const NULL = 0

' System information constants

Global Const GFSR_SYSTEMRESOURCES = 0
Global Const GFSR_GDIRESOURCES = 1
Global Const GFSR_USERRESOURCES = 2
Global Const WF_PMODE = &H1
Global Const WF_CPU286 = &H2
Global Const WF_CPU386 = &H4
Global Const WF_CPU486 = &H8
Global Const WF_STANDARD = &H10
Global Const WF_WIN286 = &H10
Global Const WF_ENHANCED = &H20
Global Const WF_WIN386 = &H20
Global Const WF_CPU086 = &H40
Global Const WF_CPU186 = &H80
Global Const WF_LARGEFRAME = &H100
Global Const WF_SMALLFRAME = &H200
Global Const WF_80x87 = &H400
Global Const VK_LBUTTON = &H1
Global Const VK_RBUTTON = &H2
Global Const VK_CANCEL = &H3
Global Const VK_MBUTTON = &H4
Global Const VK_BACK = &H8
Global Const VK_TAB = &H9
Global Const VK_CLEAR = &HC
Global Const VK_RETURN = &HD
Global Const VK_SHIFT = &H10
Global Const VK_CONTROL = &H11
Global Const VK_MENU = &H12
Global Const VK_PAUSE = &H13
Global Const VK_CAPITAL = &H14
Global Const VK_ESCAPE = &H1B
Global Const VK_SPACE = &H20
Global Const VK_PRIOR = &H21
Global Const VK_NEXT = &H22
Global Const VK_END = &H23
Global Const VK_HOME = &H24
Global Const VK_LEFT = &H25
```

Listing 5.3   Module SYSINFO.BAS (Continued)

```
Global Const VK_UP = &H26
Global Const VK_RIGHT = &H27
Global Const VK_DOWN = &H28
Global Const VK_SELECT = &H29
Global Const VK_PRINT = &H2A
Global Const VK_EXECUTE = &H2B
Global Const VK_SNAPSHOT = &H2C
Global Const VK_INSERT = &H2D
Global Const VK_DELETE = &H2E
Global Const VK_HELP = &H2F
Global Const VK_NUMPAD0 = &H60
Global Const VK_NUMPAD1 = &H61
Global Const VK_NUMPAD2 = &H62
Global Const VK_NUMPAD3 = &H63
Global Const VK_NUMPAD4 = &H64
Global Const VK_NUMPAD5 = &H65
Global Const VK_NUMPAD6 = &H66
Global Const VK_NUMPAD7 = &H67
Global Const VK_NUMPAD8 = &H68
Global Const VK_NUMPAD9 = &H69
Global Const VK_MULTIPLY = &H6A
Global Const VK_ADD = &H6B
Global Const VK_SEPARATOR = &H6C
Global Const VK_SUBTRACT = &H6D
Global Const VK_DECIMAL = &H6E
Global Const VK_DIVIDE = &H6F
Global Const VK_F1 = &H70
Global Const VK_F2 = &H71
Global Const VK_F3 = &H72
Global Const VK_F4 = &H73
Global Const VK_F5 = &H74
Global Const VK_F6 = &H75
Global Const VK_F7 = &H76
Global Const VK_F8 = &H77
Global Const VK_F9 = &H78
Global Const VK_F10 = &H79
Global Const VK_F11 = &H7A
Global Const VK_F12 = &H7B
Global Const VK_F13 = &H7C
Global Const VK_F14 = &H7D
Global Const VK_F15 = &H7E
Global Const VK_F16 = &H7F
Global Const VK_NUMLOCK = &H90
Global Const VK_SCROLL = &H91
Global Const WM_USER = &H400
Global Const SM_CXSCREEN = 0
Global Const SM_CYSCREEN = 1
Global Const SM_CXVSCROLL = 2
Global Const SM_CYHSCROLL = 3
Global Const SM_CYCAPTION = 4
Global Const SM_CXBORDER = 5
Global Const SM_CYBORDER = 6
Global Const SM_CXDLGFRAME = 7
Global Const SM_CYDLGFRAME = 8
```

Listing 5.3   Module SYSINFO.BAS (Continued)

```
Global Const SM_CYVTHUMB = 9
Global Const SM_CXHTHUMB = 10
Global Const SM_CXICON = 11
Global Const SM_CYICON = 12
Global Const SM_CXCURSOR = 13
Global Const SM_CYCURSOR = 14
Global Const SM_CYMENU = 15
Global Const SM_CXFULLSCREEN = 16
Global Const SM_CYFULLSCREEN = 17
Global Const SM_CYKANJIWINDOW = 18
Global Const SM_MOUSEPRESENT = 19
Global Const SM_CYVSCROLL = 20
Global Const SM_CXHSCROLL = 21
Global Const SM_DEBUG = 22
Global Const SM_SWAPBUTTON = 23
Global Const SM_RESERVED1 = 24
Global Const SM_RESERVED2 = 25
Global Const SM_RESERVED3 = 26
Global Const SM_RESERVED4 = 27
Global Const SM_CXMIN = 28
Global Const SM_CYMIN = 29
Global Const SM_CXSIZE = 30
Global Const SM_CYSIZE = 31
Global Const SM_CXFRAME = 32
Global Const SM_CYFRAME = 33
Global Const SM_CXMINTRACK = 34
Global Const SM_CYMINTRACK = 35
Global Const SM_CMETRICS = 36
Global Const SPI_GETBEEP = 1
Global Const SPI_SETBEEP = 2
Global Const SPI_GETMOUSE = 3
Global Const SPI_SETMOUSE = 4
Global Const SPI_GETBORDER = 5
Global Const SPI_SETBORDER = 6
Global Const SPI_GETKEYBOARDSPEED = 10
Global Const SPI_SETKEYBOARDSPEED = 11
Global Const SPI_LANGDRIVER = 12
Global Const SPI_ICONHORIZONTALSPACING = 13
Global Const SPI_GETSCREENSAVETIMEOUT = 14
Global Const SPI_SETSCREENSAVETIMEOUT = 15
Global Const SPI_GETSCREENSAVEACTIVE = 16
Global Const SPI_SETSCREENSAVEACTIVE = 17
Global Const SPI_GETGRIDGRANULARITY = 18
Global Const SPI_SETGRIDGRANULARITY = 19
Global Const SPI_SETDESKWALLPAPER = 20
Global Const SPI_SETDESKPATTERN = 21
Global Const SPI_GETKEYBOARDDELAY = 22
Global Const SPI_SETKEYBOARDDELAY = 23
Global Const SPI_ICONVERTICALSPACING = 24
Global Const SPI_GETICONTITLEWRAP = 25
Global Const SPI_SETICONTITLEWRAP = 26
Global Const SPI_GETMENUDROPALIGNMENT = 27
Global Const SPI_SETMENUDROPALIGNMENT = 28
Global Const SPI_SETDOUBLECLKWIDTH = 29
```

Listing 5.3 **Module SYSINFO.BAS (Continued)**

```
Global Const SPI_SETDOUBLECLKHEIGHT = 30
Global Const SPI_GETICONTITLELOGFONT = 31
Global Const SPI_SETDOUBLECLICKTIME = 32
Global Const SPI_SETMOUSEBUTTONSWAP = 33
Global Const SPI_SETICONTITLELOGFONT = 34
Global Const SPI_GETFASTTASKSWITCH = 35
Global Const SPI_SETFASTTASKSWITCH = 36
Global Const SPIF_UPDATEINIFILE = 1
Global Const SPIF_SENDWININICHANGE = 2
Global Const COLOR_SCROLLBAR = 0
Global Const COLOR_BACKGROUND = 1
Global Const COLOR_ACTIVECAPTION = 2
Global Const COLOR_INACTIVECAPTION = 3
Global Const COLOR_MENU = 4
Global Const COLOR_WINDOW = 5
Global Const COLOR_WINDOWFRAME = 6
Global Const COLOR_MENUTEXT = 7
Global Const COLOR_WINDOWTEXT = 8
Global Const COLOR_CAPTIONTEXT = 9
Global Const COLOR_ACTIVEBORDER = 10
Global Const COLOR_INACTIVEBORDER = 11
Global Const COLOR_APPWORKSPACE = 12
Global Const COLOR_HIGHLIGHT = 13
Global Const COLOR_HIGHLIGHTTEXT = 14
Global Const COLOR_BTNFACE = 15
Global Const COLOR_BTNSHADOW = 16
Global Const COLOR_GRAYTEXT = 17
Global Const COLOR_BTNTEXT = 18
Global Const COLOR_INACTIVECAPTIONTEXT = 19
Global Const COLOR_BTNHIGHLIGHT = 20

'---------------------------------------------------

'                Application Global Variables

'---------------------------------------------------

' Holder for the original caret blink time
Global OriginalCaretBlinkTime%
```

Listing 5.4 **SYSINFO.FRM**

```
'   This shows how a custom caret can be used in a text
'   box. Note that an arbitrary bitmap could be used as
'   well (refer to the function reference for the
'   CreateCaret function - also Chapter 8 for information
'   on bitmaps).
'   Also note that VB may change the caret back to the
'   default without notice (like when a menu or other
'   application is selected)
```

Listing 5.4   SYSINFO.FRM (Continued)

```
'
Sub Text1_GotFocus ()

    ' Save the original blink time - it will be used to
    ' restore the original value during the LostFocus event
    OriginalCaretBlinkTime% = GetCaretBlinkTime%()

    ' Create a different shaped caret
    CreateCaret agGetControlHwnd%(Text1), 0, 10, 15

    ' Creating the new caret caused the prior one (the
    ' default for the edit control) to be destroyed and
    ' thus hidden. So we must show the new caret.
    ShowCaret agGetControlHwnd%(Text1)

    ' And change to an obnoxiously fast blink time - just
    ' to show how it's done.
    SetCaretBlinkTime 150
End Sub

'   Be sure to set the caret blink time back to its
'   original value when the control loses the focus
'
Sub Text1_LostFocus ()
    SetCaretBlinkTime OriginalCaretBlinkTime%
End Sub

Sub MenuFreeSpace_Click ()
    ShowColors 0
    SysInfo.Cls
    Print
    Print GetFreeSpace&(0); "Bytes free in Global Heap"
    Print GetFreeSystemResources%(GFSR_SYSTEMRESOURCES); "% free system ⇔
    resources."
    Print GetFreeSystemResources%(GFSR_GDIRESOURCES); "% free GDI resources."
    Print GetFreeSystemResources%(GFSR_USERRESOURCES); "% free USER ⇔
    resources."
End Sub

Sub MenuTimes_Click ()
    ShowColors 0
    SysInfo.Cls
    Print
    Print "Caret blinks every "; GetCaretBlinkTime%(); " ms"
    Print "It's been "; GetCurrentTime&(); " ms since Windows was started"
    Print "The last Windows message was processed at "; GetMessageTime&(); ⇔
    " ms"
    Print "Two clicks within "; GetDoubleClickTime%(); " ms of each other ⇔
    are a double click"
    Print "Timer resolution is "; GetTimerResolution&(); "microseconds per ⇔
    tick"

End Sub
```

Listing 5.4   SYSINFO.FRM (Continued)

```
Sub MenuFlags_Click ()
    Dim flagnum&
    Dim vernum&, verword%

    ShowColors 0
    SysInfo.Cls
    Print
    ' Get the windows flags and version numbers
    flagnum& = GetWinFlags&()
    vernum& = GetVersion&()
    verword% = CInt(vernum& / &H10000)
    Print "Running MS-DOS version "; verword% / 256; "."; verword% And &HFF
    verword% = CInt(vernum& And &HFFFF&)
    Print "Running Windows version "; verword% And &HFF; "."; CInt(verword% ⇔
/ 256)
    If flagnum& And WF_80x87 Then Print "80x87 coprocessor present"
    If flagnum& And WF_CPU086 Then Print "8086 present"
    If flagnum& And WF_CPU186 Then Print "80186 present"
    If flagnum& And WF_CPU286 Then Print "80286 present"
    If flagnum& And WF_CPU386 Then Print "80386 present"
    If flagnum& And WF_CPU486 Then Print "80486 present"
    If flagnum& And WF_ENHANCED Then Print "Windows 386-enhanced mode"
    If flagnum& And WF_PAGING Then Print "Memory paging active"
    If flagnum& And WF_PMODE Then Print "Protected mode operation"
    If flagnum& And WF_WLO Then Print "Windows emulation in non-Windows ⇔
system"

End Sub

Sub Form_Load ()
    ListColor.AddItem "COLOR_ACTIVEBORDER"
    ListColor.AddItem "COLOR_ACTIVECAPTION"
    ListColor.AddItem "COLOR_APPWORKSPACE"
    ListColor.AddItem "COLOR_BACKGROUND"
    ListColor.AddItem "COLOR_BTNFACE"
    ListColor.AddItem "COLOR_BTNHIGHLIGHT"
    ListColor.AddItem "COLOR_BTNSHADOW"
    ListColor.AddItem "COLOR_BTNTEXT"
    ListColor.AddItem "COLOR_CAPTIONTEXT"
    ListColor.AddItem "COLOR_GRAYTEXT"
    ListColor.AddItem "COLOR_HIGHLIGHT"
    ListColor.AddItem "COLOR_HIGHLIGHTTEXT"
    ListColor.AddItem "COLOR_INACTIVEBORDER"
    ListColor.AddItem "COLOR_INACTIVECAPTION"
    ListColor.AddItem "COLOR_INACTIVECAPTIONTEXT"
    ListColor.AddItem "COLOR_MENU"
    ListColor.AddItem "COLOR_MENUTEXT"
    ListColor.AddItem "COLOR_SCROLLBAR"
    ListColor.AddItem "COLOR_WINDOW"
    ListColor.AddItem "COLOR_WINDOWFRAME"
    ListColor.AddItem "COLOR_WINDOWTEXT"
End Sub
```

Listing 5.4　　SYSINFO.FRM (Continued)

```
' (The colors of these system objects can be set using the control panel
' (CONTROL.EXE) and are specified in the WIN.INI initialization file. They
' can also be retrieved and set using the GetSysColor and SetSysColor
' API functions.)

Sub ListColor_Click ()
    Dim colindex%
    Select Case ListColor.ListIndex
        Case Ø
            colindex% = COLOR_ACTIVEBORDER
        Case 1
            colindex% = COLOR_ACTIVECAPTION
        Case 2
            colindex% = COLOR_APPWORKSPACE
        Case 3
            colindex% = COLOR_BACKGROUND
        Case 4
            colindex% = COLOR_BTNFACE
        Case 5
            colindex% = COLOR_BTNHIGHLIGHT
        Case 6
            colindex% = COLOR_BTNSHADOW
        Case 7
            colindex% = COLOR_BTNTEXT
        Case 8
            colindex% = COLOR_CAPTIONTEXT
        Case 9
            colindex% = COLOR_GRAYTEXT
        Case 10
            colindex% = COLOR_HIGHLIGHT
        Case 11
            colindex% = COLOR_HIGHLIGHTTEXT
        Case 12
            colindex% = COLOR_INACTIVEBORDER
        Case 13
            colindex% = COLOR_INACTIVECAPTION
        Case 14
            colindex% = COLOR_INACTIVECAPTIONTEXT
        Case 15
            colindex% = COLOR_MENU
        Case 16
            colindex% = COLOR_MENUTEXT
        Case 17
            colindex% = COLOR_SCROLLBAR
        Case 18
            colindex% = COLOR_WINDOW
        Case 19
            colindex% = COLOR_WINDOWFRAME
        Case 20
            colindex% = COLOR_WINDOWTEXT
    End Select
    LabelColor.BackColor = GetSysColor&(colindex%) And &HFFFFFF

End Sub
```

Listing 5.4   **SYSINFO.FRM (Continued)**

```
'    The following is a selection of the system metrics
'    that can be determined - see the reference section
'    under the GetSystemMetrics function for more.
'
Sub MenuMetrics_Click ()
    ShowColors Ø
    SysInfo.Cls
    Print
    Print "Non sizeable border width,height = "; ⇔
    GetSystemMetrics%(SM_CXBORDER); ","; GetSystemMetrics%(SM_CYBORDER)
    Print "Caption height = "; GetSystemMetrics%(SM_CYCAPTION)
    Print "Cursor width,height = "; GetSystemMetrics%(SM_CXCURSOR); ",";⇔
    GetSystemMetrics%(SM_CYCURSOR)
    Print "Icon width,height = "; GetSystemMetrics%(SM_CXICON); ","; ⇔
    GetSystemMetrics%(SM_CYICON)
    Print "Width,Height of client area of full screen window = "; ⇔
    GetSystemMetrics%(SM_CXFULLSCREEN); ","; GetSystemMetrics(SM_CYFULLSCREEN)
    Print "Menu bar height = "; GetSystemMetrics%(SM_CYMENU)
    Print "Minimum width,height of window = "; GetSystemMetrics(SM_CXMIN); ⇔
    ","; GetSystemMetrics(SM_CYMIN)

End Sub

'    Use to show or hide the colors listbox and label
'
Sub ShowColors (bflag%)
    If bflag% Then  ' Show them
        ListColor.Visible = -1
        LabelColor.Visible = -1
    Else     ' Hide them
        ListColor.Visible = Ø
        LabelColor.Visible = Ø
    End If

End Sub

Sub MenuColors_Click ()
    SysInfo.Cls
    ShowColors -1
End Sub

'    A few examples of the many system parameters that can
'    be set and retreived using the SystemParametersInfo
'    function
'
Sub MenuParameters_Click ()
    Dim intval%
    ShowColors Ø
    SysInfo.Cls
    Print
    dummy% = SystemParametersInfo(SPI_GETKEYBOARDDELAY, Ø, intval%, Ø)
    Print "Keyboard Delay is "; intval%
    dummy% = SystemParametersInfo(SPI_GETKEYBOARDSPEED, Ø, intval%, Ø)
```

Listing 5.4   **SYSINFO.FRM (Continued)**

```
        Print "Keyboard Speed is "; intval%
        dummy% = SystemParametersInfo(SPI_GETSCREENSAVEACTIVE, 0, intval%, 0)
        Print "Screen Save Active = "; intval%
        dummy% = SystemParametersInfo(SPI_GETSCREENSAVETIMEOUT, 0, intval%, 0)
        Print "Screen Save Dealy is "; intval%; " seconds"


End Sub

'   Update a label field to show the current state
'   of the capslock, numlock and scroll lock keys
'
Sub Timer1_Timer ()
        Dim numlock%, scrolllock%, capslock%
        Dim res$

        capslock% = GetKeyState%(VK_CAPITAL)
        numlock% = GetKeyState%(VK_NUMLOCK)
        scrolllock% = GetKeyState%(VK_SCROLL)

        ' The low bit indicates the state of the toggle
        If capslock% And 1 Then res$ = res$ + "CAPS  "
        If numlock% And 1 Then res$ = res$ + "NUM  "
        If scrolllock% And 1 Then res$ = res$ + "SCROLL"

        LabelKeyState.Caption = res$
End Sub

Sub KeyCheck_KeyPress (KeyAscii As Integer)
        KeyAscii = 0    ' Ignore keys in this control
End Sub

'   Display in the edit control the name of the key
'
Sub KeyCheck_KeyDown (KeyCode As Integer, Shift As Integer)
        Dim scancode&
        Dim keyname As String * 256

        ' Get the scancode
        scancode& = MapVirtualKey%(KeyCode, 0)
        ' Shift the scancode to the high word and get the
        ' key name
        dummy% = GetKeyNameText(scancode& * &H10000, keyname, 255)
        KeyCheck.Text = keyname
End Sub

Sub KeyCheck_LostFocus ()
        KeyCheck.Text = "Press key to get info"
End Sub
```

Function Reference

■ AnsiToOem

VB Declaration   `Declare Function AnsiToOem% Lib "Keyboard" (ByVal lpAnsiStr$, ByVal lpOemStr$)`

Description   Converts a string in the ANSI character set to the OEM character set.

Use with VB   No problem.

Parameter	Type/Description
lpAnsiStr	**String**—String in the ANSI character set.
lpOemStr	**String**—Preallocated string to load with the converted string. Must be the same length as **lpAnsiStr** or longer.

Return Value   Not used.

■ AnsiToOemBuff

VB Declaration   `Declare Sub AnsiToOemBuff Lib "Keyboard" (ByVal lpAnsiStr$, ByVal lpOemStr$, ⇔`
`ByVal nLength%)`

Description   Converts a buffer in the ANSI character set to the OEM character set.

Use with VB   No problem.

Parameter	Type/Description
lpAnsiStr	**String**—String in the ANSI character set.
lpOemStr	**String**—Preallocated string to load with the converted string. Must be the same length as **lpAnsiStr** or longer.
nLength	**Integer**—Length of the string to convert.

■ ClipCursor, ClipCursorClear, ClipCursorRect

VB Declaration   `Declare Sub ClipCursor Lib "User" (lpRect As Any)`

`Declare Sub ClipCursorClear Lib "User" Alias "ClipCursor" (ByVal lpRect&)`

`Declare Sub ClipCursorRect Lib "User" Alias "ClipCursor" (lpRect As RECT)`

Description   Restricts the cursor to the area specified. **ClipCursorRect** and **ClipCursorClear** are type-safe versions of the **ClipCursor** function.

Use with VB	No problem.

Parameter	Type/Description
lpRect	**RECT** or **LONG**—RECT: specifies the rectangle describing in pixel screen coordinates the area in which the cursor may be positioned. **LONG** uses the value 0 to the **ClipCursorClear** form of the function to disable cursor clipping and restore normal operation.

■ CopyCursor

VB Declaration `Declare Function CopyCursor% Lib "User" (ByVal hinst%, ByVal hcur%)`

Description Makes a copy of the specified cursor. The copy will belong to the specified application instance.

Use with VB No problem. Use the **agGetInstance** in APIGUIDE.DLL to obtain the instance of your VB application.

Parameter	Type/Description
hInst	**Integer**—Handle of the instance that will own the new cursor.
hcur	**Integer**—Handle of the cursor to copy.

Return Value **Integer**—Handle of the new cursor.

Comments When you load a cursor from a DLL or instance, that cursor can be used only as long as the DLL or instance remains loaded. This function allows you to make a copy of a cursor that belongs to your application. This cursor must be destroyed when it's no longer needed using the **DestroyCursor** API function to free up the system resources used.

■ CreateCaret

VB Declaration `Declare Sub CreateCaret Lib "User" (ByVal hWnd%, ByVal hBitmap%, ByVal nWidth%,⇔`
`ByVal nHeight%)`

Description Creates a caret as specified and selects it as the caret for the specified window. The caret is a line, block, or bitmap that is generally used to indicate text position within a text box.

Use with VB Works, but the standard VB text controls do not process **GotFocus** and **LostFocus** events when switching between applications, thus it is difficult to know when to set the caret for a control. Also, VB controls the position of the caret based on the assumption that it is a vertical line, so other carets may not be positioned correctly.

Parameter	Type/Description
hWnd	**Integer**—Handle of the window that will own the caret.
hBitmap	**Integer**—Handle to a bitmap to use as the caret. May be zero or one, in which case a caret is created using the **nWidth** and **nHeight** parameters. If one, the new caret will be gray instead of black.

Parameter	Type/Description
nWidth	**Integer**—The width of the caret in logical units (see Chapter 6 for more on logical units).
nHeight	**Integer**—The height of the caret in logical units.

Comments   The caret is a shared system resource. Creating a new caret destroys the previous caret, as does the **DestroyCaret** function. Do not attempt to destroy a caret using **DestroyCaret** during the Visual Basic **LostFocus** event. This is because the **LostFocus** event in VB is not received until another window already has the focus, so calling **DestroyCaret** at that time will destroy the other window's caret.

■ DestroyCaret

VB Declaration   `Declare Sub DestroyCaret Lib "User" ()`

Description   Destroys a caret.

Use with VB   Can be used to eliminate a caret from a control. Otherwise does not seem to have any practical use.

Comments   See comments for the **CreateCaret** function.

■ DestroyCursor

VB Declaration   `Declare Function Lib "User" (ByVal hCursor%)`

Description   Destroys the specified cursor and frees up all system resources that it uses. Do not use this function on system cursor resources loaded with the **LoadCursor** function.

Use with VB   No problem.

Parameter	Type/Description
hcursor	**Integer**—Handle to a cursor object to destroy.

Return Value   **Integer**—TRUE on success, FALSE otherwise.

■ EnableHardwareInput

VB Declaration   `Declare Function EnableHardwareInput% Lib "User" (ByVal bEnableInput%)`

Description   Enables or disables all mouse and keyboard input for the system.

Use with VB   Not recommended.

Parameter	Type/Description
bEnableInput	**Integer**—TRUE (nonzero) to enable hardware input. FALSE to disable.

Return Value   Integer—TRUE if input was enabled prior to calling this function. FALSE otherwise.

■ ExitWindows

VB Declaration   `Declare Function ExitWindows% Lib "User" (ByVal dwReturnCode&, ByVal reserved%)`

Description   Exits Windows to DOS

Use with VB   No problem.

Parameter	Type/Description
dwReturnCode	**Long**—The return value to pass to MS-DOS or one of the following constants: **EW_REBOOTSYSTEM**: Causes the system to reboot. **EW_RESTARTWINDOWS**: Causes Windows to restart after exiting to DOS.
reserved	**Integer**—Set to zero.

Return Value   Integer—Zero if any applications refuse to terminate.

■ ExitWindowsExec

VB Declaration   `Declare Function ExitWindowsExec% Lib "User" (ByVal lpszExe$, ByVal lpszParams$)`

Description   Exits Windows, runs the specified DOS program, then restarts Windows.

Use with VB   No problem.

Parameter	Type/Description
lpszExe	**String**—The complete path name of the DOS program to run.
lpszParams	**String**—A string containing command line parameters to pass to the DOS program.

Return Value   Integer—Zero if any applications refuse to terminate.

■ GetAsyncKeyState

VB Declaration   `Declare Function GetAsyncKeyState Lib "User" (ByVal vKey%)`

Description   Determines the state of the specified virtual key at the time the function is called.

Use with VB   No problem.

Parameter	Type/Description
vKey	**Integer**—The key code of the virtual key to test.

Return Value	**Integer**—Bit 0 is 1 if the key has been pressed since the last call to **GetAsyncKeyState**, 0 otherwise. Bit 15 is 1 if the key is currently down, 0 if up.
Comments	If **VK_LBUTTON** or **VK_RBUTTON** is specified, the button state is reported based on the actual button regardless of whether the mouse buttons were swapped with **SwapMouseButton**.

■ GetCapture

VB Declaration	`Declare Function GetCapture% Lib "User" ()`
Description	Determines the window that has captured mouse events. Refer to the **SetCapture** API function for details.
Use with VB	No problem.
Return Value	**Integer**—The handle of the window that has the mouse capture. Zero if no window has the mouse capture.

■ GetCaretBlinkTime

VB Declaration	`Declare Function GetCaretBlinkTime% Lib "User" ()`
Description	Determines the flash or blink rate of the caret.
Use with VB	No problem.
Return Value	**Integer**—The time between flashes of the caret in milliseconds.

■ GetCaretPos

VB Declaration	`Declare Sub GetCaretPos Lib "User" (lpPoint As POINTAPI)`
Description	Determines the current position of the caret.
Use with VB	No problem.

Parameter	Type/Description
lpPoint	**POINTAPI**—This structure is loaded with the position of the caret in client coordinates of the window containing the caret.

■ GetClipCursor

VB Declaration	`Declare Sub GetClipCursor Lib "User" (lprc As Rect)`
Description	Retrieves a rectangle describing the current clipping area for the cursor as defined by the **SetClipCursor** function.

Use with VB	No problem.

Parameter	Type/Description
lprc	**RECT**—Rectangle to load with the current clipping rectangle in screen coordinates. The rectangle will reflect the size of the display screen if no clipping is in effect.

■ GetCurrentTime

VB Declaration	`Declare Function GetCurrentTime& Lib "User" ()`
Description	Determines the number of milliseconds that the current Windows session has been running.
Use with VB	No problem.
Return Value	**Long**—Time since Windows started in milliseconds. Wraps around after about 49 days.

■ GetCursor

VB Declaration	`Declare Function GetCursor% Lib "User" ()`
Description	Retrieves the handle of the currently selected cursor.
Use with VB	No problem.
Return Value	**Integer**—The handle of the cursor currently in use. Zero if no cursor exists.

■ GetCursorPos

VB Declaration	`Declare Sub GetCursorPos Lib "User" (lpPoint As POINTAPI)`
Description	Retrieves the current position of the cursor.
Use with VB	No problem.

Parameter	Type/Description
lpPoint	**POINTAPI**—Structure to load with the position of the cursor in screen pixel coordinates.

■ GetDoubleClickTime

VB Declaration	`Declare Function GetDoubleClickTime% Lib "User" ()`
Description	Determines the time between two consecutive mouse clicks that will cause them to be considered a single double click event.
Use with VB	No problem.

Return Value　Integer—The double click time in milliseconds.

■ GetFreeSpace

VB Declaration　Declare Function GetFreeSpace& Lib "Kernel" (ByVal wFlags%)

Description　Determines the amount of free memory.

Use with VB　No problem.

Parameter	Type/Description
wFlags	Integer—Set to zero.

Return Value　Long—Number of bytes of memory free in the global heap.

■ GetFreeSystemResources

VB Declaration　Declare Function GetFreeSystemResources% Lib "User" (ByVal fuSysResource%)

Description　Determines the percentage of free resources available.

Use with VB　No problem.

Parameter	Type/Description
fuSysResource	Integer—One of the following constants: **GFSR_SYSTEMRESOURCES**: Function returns the percentage of free system resources. **GFSR_GDIRESOURCES**: Function returns the percentage of free space for GDI objects. These include display contexts, drawing objects, regions, and fonts. **GFSR_USERRESOURCES**: Function returns percentage of free space for USER objects. These include windows and menus.

Return Value　Integer—A percentage defined by the **fuSysResource** parameter.

■ GetInputState

VB Declaration　Declare Function GetInputState% Lib "User" ()

Description　Determines if there are any mouse or keyboard events pending.

Use with VB　No problem.

Return Value　Integer—TRUE if there are any mouse or keyboard events in the system queue that need to be processed.

■ GetKBCodePage

VB Declaration   `Declare Function GetKBCodePage% Lib "Keyboard" ()`

Description   Determines the Windows code page used to translate between the OEM and ANSI character sets.

Use with VB   No problem.

Return Value   **Integer**: One of the following values:

437	Default: United States
850	International
860	Portugal
861	Iceland
863	French Canadian
865	Norway/Denmark

■ GetKeyboardState, GetKeyboardStateBystring

VB Declaration   `Declare Sub GetKeyboardState Lib "User" (LpKeyState As Any)`

`Declare Sub GetKeyboardStateBystring Lib "User" Alias "GetKeyboardState" ⇔ (ByVal LpKeyState$)`

Description   Retrieves the current state of each virtual key on the keyboard.

Use with VB   No problem.

Parameter	Type/Description
lpKeyState	**String**—A 256-character fixed-length string. Each character will be loaded with the state of its corresponding virtual key. Bit 0 is 1 for toggle keys (CapsLock, NumLock, and ScrollLock) if the key is toggled (on). Bit 7 is 1 if the key is currently down, 0 if up.

■ GetKeyboardType

VB Declaration   `Declare Function GetKeyboardType% Lib "Keyboard" (ByVal nTypeFlag%)`

Description   Determines information about the keyboard in use.

Use with VB   No problem.

Parameter	Type/Description
nTypeFlag	**Integer**— One of the following: 0—Return the type of keyboard. 1—Return the subtype of the keyboard. 2—Return the number of function keys on the keyboard.

Return Value Integer—Zero on error. Otherwise as shown here:

nTypeFlag=0

1	PC or compatible 83-key keyboard
2	Olivetti 102-key keyboard
3	AT or compatible 84-key keyboard
4	Enhanced (IBM) 101- or 102-key keyboard
5	Nokia 1050 keyboard
6	Nokia 9140 keyboard
7	Japanese keyboard

nTypeFlag=1

Any value	Depends on the manufacturer

nTypeFlag=2

1	10 function keys
2	12 or 18 function keys
3	10 function keys
4	12 function keys
5	10 function keys
6	24 function keys
7	Depends on the manufacturer

■ GetKeyNameText

VB Declaration Declare Function GetKeyNameText% Lib "Keyboard" (ByVal lParam&, ByVal ⇔
lpBuffer$, ByVal nSize%)

Description Determines the name of a key given the scan code.

Use with VB No problem.

Parameter	Type/Description
lParam	**Long**: Bits 0–5 = 0 Bits 16-23 = the scan code of the key. Bit 24 = extended bit on enhanced keyboards. Bit 25 = set to 1 to ignore differentiation between the left and right shift and control keys.
lpBuffer	**String**—String preinitialized to at least **nSize+1** bytes that will be loaded with the key name.
nSize	**Integer**—Maximum length of the string.

Return Value   **Integer**—Actual length of the key name loaded into lpBuffer.

■ GetKeyState

VB Declaration   `Declare Function GetKeyState% Lib "User" (ByVal nVirtKey%)`

Description   Determines the state of the specified virtual key at the time the most recent input message for that key was processed.

Use with VB   No problem.

Parameter	Type/Description
nVirtKey	**Integer**—The key code of the virtual key to test. Use the actual ASCII value for alphanumeric characters (A–Z, a–z, 0–9).

Return Value   **Integer**—Bit 0 is 1 for toggle keys (CapsLock, NumLock, ScrollLock) if the key is toggled (on). Bit 15 is 1 if the key is currently down, 0 if up.

■ GetMessageTime

VB Declaration   `Declare Function GetMessageTime& Lib "User" ()`

Description   Determines the time at which the most recent message was processed in milliseconds since the start of the current Windows session.

Use with VB   Works, but is not particularly useful.

Return Value   **Long**—See description.

■ GetQueueStatus

VB Declaration   `Declare Function GetQueueStatus& Lib "User" (ByVal fuFlags%)`

Description   Determines the type of messages that are pending in an application's message queue.

Use with VB   Not particularly useful.

Parameter	Type/Description
fuFlags	**Integer**—A flag word indicating which messages to check for. The flag bits are defined by the following constants: **QS_KEY**: **WM_CHAR** messages (will cause VB KeyPressed events). **QS_MOUSE**: Any mouse message. **QS_MOUSEMOVE**: MouseMove message or event. **QS_MOUSEBUTTON**: Mouse button message or related event. **QS_PAINT**: Paint message pending. **QS_POSTMESSAGE**: Other posted message. **QS_SENDMESSAGE**: Message sent from another application. **QS_TIMER**: Timer message.

Return Value   **Long**—The high word is a 16-bit flag word containing the messages pending. Bits are determined by the same constants defined for the **fuFlags** parameter. The low word is a matching flag word, where each bit indicates messages added since the last call to this function, or since messages were last processed.

■ GetSysColor

VB Declaration   `Declare Function GetSysColor& Lib "User" (ByVal nIndex%)`

Description   Determines the color of the specified Windows display object.

Use with VB   No problem.

Parameter	Type/Description
nIndex	**Integer**—Constant specifying a Windows display object as shown in the table that follows.

Constant Definition	Windows Object
COLOR_ACTIVEBORDER	Border of active window
COLOR_ACTIVECAPTION	Caption of active window
COLOR_APPWORKSPACE	Background of MDI desktop
COLOR_BACKGROUND	Windows desktop
COLOR_BTNFACE	Button
COLOR_BTNHIGHLIGHT	3D highlight of button
COLOR_BTNSHADOW	3D shading of button
COLOR_BTNTEXT	Button text
COLOR_CAPTIONTEXT	Text in window caption
COLOR_GRAYTEXT	Gray text, or zero if dithering is used
COLOR_HIGHLIGHT	Selected item background
COLOR_HIGHLIGHTTEXT	Selected item text
COLOR_INACTIVEBORDER	Border of inactive window
COLOR_INACTIVECAPTION	Caption of inactive window
COLOR_INACTIVECAPTIONTEXT	Text of inactive window
COLOR_MENU	Menu
COLOR_MENUTEXT	Menu text
COLOR_SCROLLBAR	Scroll Bar
COLOR_WINDOW	Window background

Constant Definition	Windows Object
COLOR_WINDOWFRAME	Window frame
COLOR_WINDOWTEXT	Window text

Return Value   **Long**—RGB color of the specified object.

GetSystemMetrics

VB Declaration   `Declare Function GetSystemMetrics% Lib "User" ByVal nIndex%)`

Description   Returns information about the Windows environment.

Use with VB   No problem.

Parameter	Type/Description
nIndex	**Integer**—Constant specifying information to retrieve as shown in the table that follows.

Constant Definition	Information Retrieved
SM_CXBORDER	Width of non-sizeable border
SM_CXCURSOR	Cursor width
SM_CXDLGFRAME	Width of dialog box border
SM_CXDOUBLECLK	Width of double click area (see comments)
SM_CXFRAME	Width of sizeable border
SM_CXFULLSCREEN	Width of client area of maximized window
SM_CXHSCROLL	Width of arrow on horizontal scroll bar
SM_CXHTHUMB	Width of scroll box on horizontal scroll bar
SM_CXICON	Width of icon
SM_CXICONSPACING	Horizontal space between desktop icons
SM_CXMIN	Minimum width of a window
SM_CXMINTRACK	Minimum tracking width of window
SM_CXSCREEN	Width of screen
SM_CXSIZE	Width of title bar bitmaps
SM_CXVSCROLL	Width of arrow in vertical scroll bar
SM_CYBORDER	Height of non-sizeable border
SM_CYCAPTION	Height of window caption
SM_CYCURSOR	Cursor height
SM_CYDLGFRAME	Height of dialog box border

Constant Definition	Information Retrieved
SM_CYDOUBLECLK	Height of double click area (see comments)
SM_CYFRAME	Height of sizeable border
SM_CYFULLSCREEN	Height of client area of maximized window
SM_CYHSCROLL	Height of arrow on horizontal scroll bar
SM_CYICON	Height of icon
SM_CYICONSPACING	Vertical space between desktop icons
SM_CYKANJIWINDOW	Height of Kanji window
SM_CYMENU	Height of menu
SM_CYMIN	Minimum height of window
SM_CYMINTRACK	Maximum tracking height of window
SM_CYSCREEN	Height of screen
SM_CYSIZE	Height of title bar bitmaps
SM_CYVSCROLL	Height of arrow on vertical scroll bar
SM_CYVTHUMB	Height of scroll box on vertical scroll bar
SM_DBCSENABLED	TRUE if double byte characters are supported
SM_DEBUG	TRUE if debugging version of windows is running
SM_MENUDROPALIGNMENT	Zero if popup menus are aligned to the left of the menu bar item, TRUE if the popup menu is aligned to the right of the menu bar item
SM_MOUSEPRESENT	TRUE if a mouse is present
SM_PENWINDOWS	The handle of the pen windows support DLL if loaded
SM_SWAPBUTTON	TRUE if left and right mouse buttons are swapped

Return Value   Integer—As specified for each index.

Comments   The double click area specifies the proximity in which two mouse clicks must take place on the display to be considered a double click.

■ GetTickCount

VB Declaration   `Declare Function GetTickCount& Lib "User" ()`

Description   See **GetCurrentTime**.

■ GetTimerResolution

VB Declaration   `Declare Function GetTimerResolution& Lib "User" ()`

Description	Determines the resolution of time functions.
Use with VB	No problem.
Return Value	**Long**—The number of microseconds in each timer tick.

■ GetVersion

VB Declaration	`Declare Function GetVersion& Lib "Kernel" ()`
Description	Determines the version of Windows and DOS currently running.
Use with VB	No problem.
Return Value	**Long**—The low 16 bits contain the Windows version—the low byte contains the major version number (3 for Windows 3.10), the high byte contains the minor version as a two-digit decimal number (10 for Windows 3.10). The high 16 bits contain the DOS version—the high byte contains the major version number and the low byte contains the minor version number.

■ GetWinFlags

VB Declaration	`Declare Function GetWinFlags& Lib "Kernel" ()`
Description	Retrieves information on the Windows configuration and system CPU and coprocessors.
Use with VB	No problem.
Return Value	**Long**—A 32-bit flag variable containing bits set according to the constants in the following table.

WF_80x87	Intel compatible coprocessor present
WF_CPU286	80286 present
WF_CPU386	80386 present
WF_CPU486	80486 present
WF_ENHANCED	Windows is in enhanced mode
WF_PAGING	Paged memory is active
WF_PMODE	Windows is in protected mode
WF_STANDARD	Windows is in standard mode
WF_WIN286	Same as WF_STANDARD
WF_WIN386	Same as WF_ENHANCED
WF_WLO	Non-Windows OS running windows emulation libraries

■ HideCaret

VB Declaration   Declare Sub HideCaret Lib "User" (ByVal hWnd%)

Description   Hides the caret in the specified window.

Use with VB   Works, but be aware that Visual Basic will reset and redisplay the caret when a control obtains the focus.

Parameter	Type/Description
hWnd	**Integer**—Handle of the window that contains the caret. May be zero, in which case the caret will be hidden only if it is contained in a window that is owned by the active task (See Chapter 12 for information on tasks).

Comments   Windows maintains an internal counter for caret display similar to that used for the **ShowCursor** function. Thus calls to **HideCaret** and **ShowCaret** must be balanced.

■ IsDBCSLeadByte

VB Declaration   Declare Function IsDBCSLeadByte% Lib "Kernel" (ByVal bTestChar%)

Description   Determines if this is the first character in a two-byte character when using a double-byte character set.

Use with VB   Should work in any version of Visual Basic that supports double-byte character sets.

Parameter	Type/Description
bTestChar	**Integer**—Character to test.

Return Value   **Integer**—TRUE if this is the first byte of a two-byte character.

Comments   Double-byte character sets are used for character sets such as Kanji that require over 256 characters.

■ LoadCursor, LoadCursorBynum, LoadCursorBystring

VB Declaration   Declare Function LoadCursor% Lib "User" (ByVal hInstance%, ByVal ⇔
lpCursorName As Any)

Declare Function LoadCursorBynum% Lib "User" Alias "LoadCursor" (ByVal ⇔
hInstance%, ByVal lpCursorName&)

Declare Function LoadCursorBystring% Lib "User" Alias "LoadCursor" (ByVal ⇔
hInstance%, ByVal lpCursorName$)

Description   Loads a cursor from the specified module or application instance. **LoadCursorBynum** and **Load-CursorBystring** are type-safe versions of the **LoadCursor** function.

Use with VB   No problem.

Parameter	Type/Description
hInstance	**Instance**—Module handle for a dynamic link library, or instance handle that specifies the executable file that contains the cursor.
lpCursorName	**String** or **Long**—As a **String**, specifies the name of the cursor resource to load. As a **Long**, specifies the resource ID to load or a constant representing one of the stock system cursors. When loading a stock system cursor, the **hInstance** parameter should be set to 0. The constants are as follows: **IDC_ARROW**: Arrow cursor. **IDC_CROSS**: Crosshair cursor. **IDC_IBEAM**: Text-style I cursor. **IDC_ICON**: An empty icon. **IDC_SIZE**: Rectangle with small rectangle at its lower right corner. **IDC_SIZENEWSW**: Northeast and southwest pointing arrows. **IDC_SIZENS**: North and south arrows. **IDC_SIZENWSE**: Northwest and southeast pointing arrows. **IDC_SIZEWE**: East and west arrows. **IDC_UPARROW**: Arrow pointing up. **IDC_WAIT**: The hourglass cursor.

Return Value   **Integer**—A handle to the loaded cursor.

Comments   Do not destroy stock system cursors or cursors belonging to other applications. Be careful that **lpCursorName** refers to a cursor resource.

■ LockInput

VB Declaration   `Declare Function LockInput% Lib "User" (ByVal hReserved%, ByVal hwndInput%, ⇔ ByVal fLock%)`

Description   Locks or unlocks input to all tasks other than the current one.

Use with VB   Not recommended as it may interfere with the performance of other applications..

Parameter	Type/Description
hReserved	**Integer**—Set to zero.
hwndInput	**Integer**—Handle of window in the current task that will receive all input.
fLock	**Integer**—TRUE (nonzero) to lock input, FALSE to unlock.

Return Value   **Integer**—TRUE on success, FALSE otherwise.

■ MapVirtualKey

VB Declaration   `Declare Function MapVirtualKey% Lib "Keyboard" (ByVal wCode%, ByVal wMapType%)`

Description   Performs various scan code and character conversions depending on the mapping type specified.

Use with VB   No problem.

Parameter	Type/Description
wCode	**Integer**—The source character or scan code to convert.
wMapType	**Integer**—Controls the type of mapping as follows: 0—**wCode** is a virtual key code. The function returns the corresponding scan code. 1—**wCode** is a scan code. The function returns the corresponding virtual key code. 2—**wCode** is a virtual key code. The function returns the corresponding ASCII value (unshifted).

Return Value   **Integer**—As specified by the **wMapType** parameter.

■ OemKeyScan

VB Declaration   `Declare Function OemKeyScan& Lib "Keyboard" (ByVal wOemChar%)`

Description   Determines the scan code and shift states for an ASCII character in the OEM character set.

Use with VB   No problem.

Parameter	Type/Description
wOemChar	**Integer**—ASCII value of the character to convert.

Return Value   **Long**—The low word contains the scan code. The high word contains the following flags: Bit 0 indicates that the shift key is down. Bit 1 indicates that the control key is down. If both words are –1, the character is not defined in the OEM character set.

■ OemToAnsi

VB Declaration   `Declare Function OemToAnsi% Lib "Keyboard" (ByVal lpOemStr$, ByVal lpAnsiStr$)`

Description   Converts a string in the OEM character set to the ANSI character set.

Use with VB   No problem.

Parameter	Type/Description
lpOemStr	**String**—String in the OEM character set.
lpAnsiStr	**String**—Preallocated string to load with the converted string. Must be the same length as **lpOemStr** or longer.

Return Value   Not used.

OemToAnsiBuff

VB Declaration   Declare Sub OemToAnsiBuff Lib "Keyboard" (ByVal lpOemStr$, ByVal ⇔
lpAnsiStr$, ByVal nLength%)

Description   Converts a buffer in the OEM character set to the ANSI character set.

Use with VB   No problem.

Parameter	Type/Description
lpOemStr	**String**—String in the OEM character set.
lpAnsiStr	**String**—Preallocated string to load with the converted string. Must be the same length as **lpOemStr** or longer.
nLength	**Integer**—Length of the string to convert.

ReleaseCapture

VB Declaration   Declare Sub ReleaseCapture Lib "User" ()

Description   Cancels mouse capture. Refer to the **SetCapture** function for information on the mouse capture.

Use with VB   VB releases the capture when the mouse is clicked on other applications and other screen objects, so in practice this function is rarely necessary for VB.

SetCapture

VB Declaration   Declare Function SetCapture% Lib "User" (ByVal hWnd%)

Description   Sets the capture to the specified window. This means that all mouse events will go to this window regardless of where the mouse is on the screen.

Use with VB   VB releases the capture when the mouse is clicked outside of the VB application that sets the capture and possibly under other circumstances as well. This limits the usefulness of this feature. Refer to the WinView project in Chapter 4 for an example.

Parameter	Type/Description
hWnd	**Integer**—The handle of the window that will receive all mouse events.

Return Value   **Integer**—The handle of the window that previously had the mouse capture. Zero if no window had the capture.

SetCaretBlinkTime

VB Declaration   Declare Sub SetCaretBlinkTime Lib "User" (ByVal wMSeconds%)

Description   Determines the flash or blink rate of the caret.

Use with VB	No problem.	
	Parameter	**Type/Description**
	wMSeconds	**Integer**—The new time between flashes of the caret in milliseconds.

Comments The caret is a system resource, so the blink time affects the caret for all applications. You can use the **GetCaretBlinkTime** function to obtain the initial blink time setting, which can be used then to restore the initial value when appropriate.

■ SetCaretPos

VB Declaration `Declare Sub SetCaretPos Lib "User" (ByVal X%, ByVal Y%)`

Description Specifies the position of the caret.

Use with VB	No problem.	
	Parameter	**Type/Description**
	X	**Integer**—X position for the caret in client coordinates.
	Y	**Integer**—Y position for the caret in client coordinates.

Comments The caret is a shared system resource. Applications should be sure that the caret is in a window owned by the current task before changing its position.

■ SetCursor

VB Declaration `Declare Function SetCursor% Lib "User" (ByVal hCursor%)`

Description Selects the specified cursor to be the current cursor.

Use with VB	Does not work well with Visual Basic due to VB's habit of changing the cursor back at various times.	
	Parameter	**Type/Description**
	hCursor	**Integer**—Handle of the cursor to set as the current cursor. Zero to specify that no cursor will be displayed.

Return Value **Integer**—The value of the previous cursor.

■ SetCursorPos

VB Declaration `Declare Sub SetCursorPos Lib "User" (ByVal X%, ByVal Y%)`

Description Sets the cursor position.

Use with VB   No problem.

Parameter	Type/Description
X	**Integer**—X position for the cursor in screen pixel coordinates.
Y	**Integer**—Y position for the cursor in screen pixel coordinates.

■ SetDoubleClickTime

VB Declaration   `Declare Sub SetDoubleClickTime Lib "User" (ByVal wCount%)`

Description   Sets the time between two consecutive mouse clicks that will cause them to be considered a single double click event.

Use with VB   No problem.

Parameter	Type/Description
wCount	**Integer**—The new **DoubleClick** time delay in milliseconds.

■ SetKeyboardState, SetKeyboardStateBystring

VB Declaration   `Declare Sub SetKeyboardState Lib "User" (lpKeyState As Any)`

`Declare Sub SetKeyboardStateBystring Lib "User" Alias "SetKeyboardState"` ⇔
`(ByVal lpKeyState$)`

Description   Sets the current state of each virtual key on the keyboard.

Use with VB   No problem.

Parameter	Type/Description
lpKeyState	**String**—A 256-character fixed-length string. Each character in the internal Windows keyboard state table will be set according to the state of its corresponding virtual key in this table. The state of each key is the same as the result of the **GetKeyState** function.

Comments   This function can be used to set the states of the CapsLock, NumLock, and ScrollLock keys.

■ SetSwapAreaSize

VB Declaration   `Declare Function SetSwapAreaSize& Lib "Kernel" (ByVal rsSize%)`

Description   Specifies the amount of memory that the current application may use for its code segments.

Use with VB   Not recommended.

Parameter	Type/Description
rsSize	**Integer**—Number of code paragraphs to allocate to the current task.

Return Value   **Long**—The low-order word contains the number of paragraphs actually allocated to the application. The high word contains the maximum number of paragraphs that could be allocated.

Comments   Increasing the number of code paragraphs may improve the performance of an application by reducing swapping of code segments. It may, however, impair the performance of other applications and reduce the amount of memory available for data.

■ SetSysColors

VB Declaration   `Declare Sub SetSysColors Lib "User" (ByVal nChanges%, lpSysColor%, ⇔`
`lpColorValues&)`

Description   Sets the color of the specified Windows display object.

Use with VB   No problem.

Parameter	Type/Description
nChanges	**Integer**—Number of objects to change.
lpSysColor	**Integer**—Passed by reference. This is the first element in an integer array with **nChanges** elements. Each entry contains a constant specifying a Windows display object. Refer to the **GetSysColors** function for a complete list of objects whose colors may be set.
lpColorValues	**Long**—Passed by reference. This is the first element in a long array of RGB values that will be used to set the colors of the objects in the **lpSysColor** array.

■ ShowCaret

VB Declaration   `Declare Sub ShowCaret Lib "User" (ByVal hWnd%)`

Description   Shows the caret in the specified window.

Use with VB   See the description of the **HideCaret** function.

Parameter	Type/Description
hWnd	**Integer**—Handle of the window that contains the caret. May be zero, in which case the caret will be shown only if it is contained in a window that is owned by the active task (see Chapter 12 for information on tasks).

Comments   See the description of the **HideCaret** function.

ShowCursor

VB Declaration   `Declare Function ShowCursor% Lib "User" (ByVal bShow%)`

Description   Controls the visibility of the cursor.

Use with VB   No problem.

Parameter	Type/Description
bShow	**Integer**—TRUE (nonzero) to display the cursor, FALSE to hide it.

Return Value   The display count (see comments).

Comments   Windows maintains an internal display count that is incremented for each call of this function if **bShow** is TRUE and decremented if **bShow** is FALSE. The cursor will be displayed when this count is greater than or equal to zero. Keep in mind that the cursor is a shared resource and that changes will affect all applications.

SwapMouseButton

VB Declaration   `Declare Function SwapMouseButton% Lib "User" (ByVal bSwap%)`

Description   Determines if the functions of the left and right mouse buttons are reversed.

Use with VB   No problem.

Parameter	Type/Description
bSwap%	**Integer**—When TRUE (nonzero) the functions of the mouse buttons are swapped (meaning that the left button triggers right button events and vice versa). FALSE restores normal operation.

Return Value   **Integer**—TRUE if the mouse buttons were reversed prior to this call, FALSE otherwise.

Comments   The mouse is a shared resource so this function affects all applications in the system.

SystemParametersInfo, SystemParametersInfoByval

VB Declaration   `Declare Function SystemParametersInfo% Lib "User" (ByVal uAction%, ByVal ⇔`
`uParam%, lpvParam As Any, ByVal fuWinIni%)`

`Declare Function SystemParametersInfoByval% Lib "User" Alias ⇔`
`"SystemParametersInfo" (ByVal uAction%, ByVal uParam%, ByVal lpvParam As Any, ⇔`
`ByVal fuWinIni%)`

Description   Allows the retrieval and setting of a number of Windows system parameters. **SystemParametersInfoByval** is used when **lpvParam** is a string or is used to pass a long parameter.

Use with VB	No known problems.

Parameter	Type/Description
uAction	**Integer**—Specifies the parameter to set. Refer to the constants in the table that follows.
uParam	**Integer**—Refer to **uAction** table below.
lpvParam	**Integer, Long, String,** or **data** structure—**Integer, Long,** and **data** structures are called by reference. Use **SystemParametersInfoByval** with **String** data. Refer to **uAction** table below for use.
fuWinIni	**Integer**—Specifies whether the WIN.INI file should be updated when setting system parameters. May be zero (to prevent WIN.INI update) or one of the following constants: **SPIF_UPDATEINIFILE**: Updates WIN.INI. **SPIF_SENDWININICHANGE**: Causes a WM_WININICHANGE message to be sent to all applications when **SPIF_UPDATEINIFILE** is also set. Otherwise has no effect. This message informs applications that WIN.INI has been changed.

uAction Table   Refer to your Windows manual for information on these parameters and the WIN.INI file. Parameters that are not specified for an action are not used.

SPI_GETBEEP	**lpvParam** is an integer that will be set TRUE if the beep sound is on.
SPI_GETBORDER	**lpvParam** is an integer that receives a multiplier that controls the sizeable window border size.
SPI_GETFASTTASKSWITCH	**lpvParam** is an integer that will be set TRUE if fast task switching is enabled.
SPI_GETGRIDGRANULARITY	**lpvParam** is an integer that will be set to the grid granularity value.
SPI_GETICONTITLELOGFONT	**lpvParam** points to a **LOGFONT** structure that will be set according to the font used for icon titles.
SPI_GETICONTITLEWRAP	**lpvParam** is an integer that will be set TRUE if icon title wrapping is enabled.
SPI_GETKEYBOARDDELAY	**lpvParam** is an integer that will be set to the keyboard repeat delay.
SPI_GETKEYBOARDSPEED	**lpvParam** is an integer that will be set to the keyboard repeat speed.
SPI_GETMENUDROPALIGNMENT	**lpvParam** is an integer that will be set FALSE if popup menus are left aligned (default), TRUE for right aligned.
SPI_GETMOUSE	**lpvParam** is the first entry in a three-element integer array. Entry 0 is set to the WIN.INI **MouseThreshold1** field, entry 1 to **MouseThreshold2**, and entry 2 to **MouseSpeed**.

SPI_GETSCREENSAVEACTIVE	**lpvParam** points to an integer that will be set TRUE if the screen saver is active, FALSE otherwise.
SPI_GETSCREENSAVETIMEOUT	**lpvParam** points to an integer that will be set to the screen save time-out in seconds.
SPI_ICONHORIZONTALSPACING	If **lpvParam** is NULL, **uParam** is the new width for icon spacing on the desktop in pixels. Otherwise **lpvParam** is an integer to receive the current icon spacing.
SPI_ICONVERTICALSPACING	Same as **SPI_ICONHORIZONTALSPACING** for the vertical icon spacing.
SPI_LANGDRIVER	**lpvParam** is a string with the new language driver file name.
SPI_SETBEEP	**uParam** is TRUE to turn the beep sound on, FALSE to turn it off.
SPI_SETBORDER	**uParam** is the multiplier that controls the sizeable window border size.
SPI_SETDESKPATTERN	If **lpvParam** is NULL and **uParam** is –1, the value is read from the WIN.INI file. Otherwise, **lpvParam** is a string defining the desktop pattern in a series of eight numbers.
SPI_SETDESKWALLPAPER	**lpvParam** is a string containing the name of a bitmap file to use as the desktop wallpaper.
SPI_SETDOUBLECLKHEIGHT	**uParam** is the new double click height. See the comments for the **GetSystemMetrics** function for details.
SPI_SETDOUBLECLKWIDTH	**uParam** is the new double click width. See the comments for the **GetSystemMetrics** function for details.
SPI_SETFASTTASKSWITCH	**uParam** is TRUE to turn on fast task switching, FALSE to turn it off.
SPI_SETGRIDGRANULARITY	**uParam** is the new grid granularity.
SPI_SETICONTITLELOGFONT	**lpvParam** is a **LOGFONT** structure that will define the font to use for icon titles. **uParam** is the size of the **LOGFONT** structure. If both are NULL, the font defined during system startup will be used.
SPI_SETICONTITLEWRAP	**uParam** is TRUE to turn on icon title wrapping.
SPI_SETKEYBOARDDELAY	**uParam** is the new keyboard repeat delay.
SPI_SETKEYBOARDSPEED	**uParam** is the new keyboard repeat speed.
SPI_SETMENUDROPALIGNMENT	**uParam** is FALSE to set left aligned popup menus, TRUE for right aligned.

SPI_SETMOUSE	**lpvParam** is the first entry in a three-element integer array containing mouse settings. See **SPI_GETMOUSE** for details.
SPI_SETMOUSEBUTTONSWAP	**uParam** is TRUE to swap the meaning of the left and right mouse buttons, FALSE to use original values.
SPI_SETSCREENSAVEACTIVE	**uParam** is TRUE to activate the screen saver, FALSE to deactivate.
SPI_SETSCREENSAVETIMEOUT	**uParam** is the new screen save time-out in seconds.

Return Value   Integer—TRUE on success, FALSE otherwise.

■ ToAscii, ToAsciiByString

VB Declaration
```
Declare Function ToAscii% Lib "Keyboard" (ByVal wVirtKey%, ByVal ⇔
wScanCode%, lpKeyState As Any, lpChar As Any, ByVal wFlags%)

Declare Function ToAsciiBystring% Lib "Keyboard" Alias "ToAscii" (ByVal ⇔
wVirtKey%, ByVal wScanCode%, ByVal lpKeyState$, lpChar&, ByVal wFlags%)
```

Description   Determines the ASCII value of a virtual key based on the states of the various shift and control keys on the keyboard. **ToAsciiBystring** is a type-safe version of **ToAscii**.

Use with VB   No problem.

Parameter	Type/Description
wVirtKey	**Integer**—The virtual key to translate.
wScanCode	**Integer**—Optional: the scan code of the key. The high bit is 0 if the key is pressed, 1 otherwise.
lpKeyState	**String**—256-byte string indicating the state of the keyboard as obtained by function **GetKeyboardState**. The high bit of each byte is 1 if the key is pressed.
lpChar	**Long**—Passed by reference. Is set to the ASCII result. May be two characters (function keys and some control Alt combinations produce a two-character sequence on DOS systems).
wFlags	**Integer**—Set to 1 if a menu is active, 0 otherwise.

Return Value   Integer—One of the following values:
0—The character cannot be translated based on **lpKeyState**.
1—One character was loaded into **lpChar**.
2—Two characters were loaded into **lpChar**.

■ VkKeyScan

VB Declaration   `Declare Function VkKeyScan% Lib "Keyboard" (ByVal cChar%)`

Description   Determines the virtual key code and shift states for an ASCII character in the Windows character set.

Use with VB   No problem.

Parameter	Type/Description
cChar	**Integer**—ASCII value of the character to convert.

Return Value   **Long**—The low word contains the virtual key code. The high word contains the following flags:
Bit 0 indicates that the shift key is down.
Bit 1 indicates that the control key is down.
Bit 6 indicates a Ctrl-Alt combination.
Bit 7 indicates a Shift-Ctrl-Alt combination.
If both words are -1, the character is not defined.

Comments   Translations for the numeric keypad are ignored. This function can be used to obtain the correct parameters to use when sending **WM_KEYDOWN** and **WM_KEYUP** messages.

6

Device Contexts

WINDOWS SUPPORTS A NUMBER OF DIFFERENT TYPES OF DEVICES FOR both input and output. The two most common devices are the display screen and the printer, although Windows also supports other devices such as the plotter and image acquisition devices. This chapter describes the programmer's interface to these physical devices. It includes two sample programs: Devview, which allows you to obtain information about a device, and Clipview, which shows how to control the area on the device to which drawing is permitted. The chapter also includes an extensive discussion of coordinate systems—a powerful feature for promoting device independence.

Before reading this chapter, it is strongly recommended that you review the last part of Chapter 2, which introduced device contexts.

Introduction to Device Contexts

A *device context* (DC) is a Windows object that allows drawing to a window or device. All graphic and text output to a device takes place through a device context. To use the Windows API effectively, it is important that you understand the concept of the device context. See Chapters 2 and 7 for more information about device contexts.

The Philosophy behind the Device Context

The two most frequently used devices under Windows are the display screen and the printer. There obviously needs to be some mechanism for sending data to these devices. Under Windows, this data will most frequently be graphics information such as lines and fills, and text information.

Under MS-DOS, when you write data to a device you are accessing all parts of the device at all times. In other words, a program drawing graphics on a VGA screen has access to the entire screen, and a program sending output to a printer has access to the entire page. If you wish a program to draw only on a portion of the display or page, it is the responsibility of the program itself to calculate where it may or may not draw. Consider the following example.

You have written a word processing program that needs to display and print a page that contains text, a graphic logo, and an image. The page contains a graphic logo area, a text area, and an image (or picture) area.

MS-DOS provides no protection when drawing in one area to prevent the program from drawing over the other areas. Thus the application program must be very careful to draw the image only in the picture area. If the image is too large to fit, the program must either scale it or check each pixel to make sure that it falls within the picture area before drawing it. This applies to the text and graphic logo areas as well. Also, the program must calculate the position on the screen for each element in each area. If the picture image is offset by 100 pixels from the top of the screen, the position of each pixel in the image must be offset by 100 pixels before it is drawn. All of the coordinate calculations must be performed manually by the program.

Consider then what happens when you take the code that draws a page to the screen and try to adapt it to a printer. The printer resolution is different from that of the display screen. The aspect ratio is probably different as well. This adds considerable complexity to a program, and does not even take into account the fact that you will probably want the program to support a number of different display devices and printers.

Windows provides two features that eliminate much of this complexity: built-in *clipping* and *coordinate transformation*.

Clipping

With clipping, every time a program calls a graphics or text output function, Windows checks to see if the output falls within a clipping area. It does this on a pixel-by-pixel basis. With regard to our word processing example, this means that each area may be protected from the other. When you are drawing the graphic logo, you can specify that the graphic logo area be the clipping region. If the graphic image extends beyond that area it will automatically be clipped and there is no risk of it affecting other areas. This makes it easy to handle the problem described earlier of images that exceed the picture area—if the image is too large it will automatically be clipped to the desired space.

The most common use of clipping is within Windows to prevent drawing in one window from affecting others. You can see this by creating a Visual Basic form and placing a command button in the center. Use the **Line** command to draw a line that starts at one end of the form and passes through the command button to the other side. Note how the line appears on both sides of the command button but does not appear on the command button itself. This is because the command button is a window that is not part of the clipping region for the form.

The default clipping region for any window is the window itself. It is important to note, however, that the clipping region may be set to any portion of a window. In the same way, clipping may be used to allow drawing onto only part of a printer page. The Clipview example program shows how this is done.

Coordinate Transformation

Windows also provides the ability to translate a coordinate system from one used by the physical device to any coordinate system you choose. This is an extremely powerful technique as can be seen once again with our word processing example.

Consider the graphic logo. Assume that you want this logo to always fill the entire width of the window or page, and that you always want the height to be a fixed percentage of the width, say 10 percent.

Without coordinate transformations, you must first determine the pixel location on the screen of the start of the logo area. Then it is necessary to calculate the height and width of the logo area. All of these figures will vary from device to device. The actual drawing routine must be designed to use these calculated values to draw the graphic.

With coordinate transformation, all of these calculations become unnecessary. Your program need only define the coordinate system for the graphic logo area. It can specify, for example, that the lower left corner of the area will be the coordinates 0,0, and that the width of the area will always be 1000 units and the height will always be 100 units. These units are called *logical units*. The Windows drawing functions always use logical units, and it is the responsibility of Windows to convert these logical units into the actual device physical units.

Now the graphic logo drawing routine can be simplified—it can be set up to always draw into a 1000x100 unit area. Windows will perform the coordinate transformations required to draw the logo correctly on any device once the coordinate system has been set up.

Device Contexts Revisited

So far this section has shown how specifying a clipping area and a coordinate system can both simplify output to a device and provide device independence. The question then is how do you specify the clipping area and coordinate system for a device?

You are already acquainted with Windows objects from Chapter 4. Windows objects do provide automatic clipping to other windows as shown in the example where a line was drawn "through" a command button, but a window provides no ability to specify a clipping region within the window. Nor does a window help with regard to printed output. A window is only useful for specifying an area on the display screen (which is a very important "only"—but still does not address the current problem).

Windows therefore provides an object known as a device context. A device context may be associated with a window, with a device, or with a block of memory that simulates a device (called a memory device context). A device context may also have associated with it a clipping region and a coordinate system.

All drawing under Windows takes place through a device context rather than directly to a window or device. This provides the mechanism by which clipping and coordinate transformations may take place. You can think of a device context as a black box—graphics and text output commands go in one side, are processed and translated according to the attributes that are selected for the device context, and then are sent to the actual window or device.

Introduction to Using Device Contexts

Windows provides a pool of five built-in device contexts that are available for use to draw into windows or devices. When you wish to draw to a window or device, you request a device context from this pool, specify the attributes for the context, and then use it for drawing. Once you no longer need it, you release it. The device context is returned to the pool and becomes available for use by this or other applications.

Windows also provides the capability of creating device contexts in cases where you do not wish to use one from the general context pool. You can also specify that each window in a specific class have its own device context or that all windows in a class share a device context. These possibilities are described later in this chapter.

So far only two device context attributes have been discussed: clipping regions and coordinate systems. In fact, a device context has a number of other important attributes. These are listed in Table 6.1 along with the default values assigned to a device context when it is newly created or retrieved from the device context pool. Don't worry if some of these attributes are unclear—they will all be explained later in this chapter and in Chapter 7.

Table 6.1   **Default Device Context Attributes**

Attribute	Default Value	See Chapter
Background color	White	7
Background mode	Opaque	7
Bitmap	None	8
Brush	White brush	7
Brush origin	0,0	7
Clipping region	Entire window or device surface	6
Color palette	Default palette	7,16
Pen position	0,0	7
Drawing mode	R2_COPYPEN	7
Font	System font	10
Intercharacter spacing	0	10
Mapping mode	MM_TEXT	6

Table 6.1   **Default Device Context Attributes (Continued)**

Attribute	Default Value	See Chapter
Pen	Black	7
Polygon-filling mode	ALTERNATE	7
Stretching mode	BLACKONWHITE	8
Text color	Black	10
Viewport origin	0,0	6
Viewport extents	1,1	6
Window origin	0,0	6
Window extents	1,1	6

Obtaining a Device Context

A device context handle is used as a parameter to most Windows drawing functions. The device context itself is an internal Windows data structure that occupies about 800 bytes. Windows provides several ways to create or obtain device contexts:

- *Private device contexts*   When a window belongs to a class with the CS_OWNDC, CS_PARENTDC, or CS_CLASSDC class style bits set, it is given a private device context. In the case of CS_CLASSDC, a single device context is shared by all windows in a class. The CS_PARENTDC style gives a window the device context of its parent window. In the case of CS_OWNDC, each window has its own device context. The advantage of this is that the device context is always available for drawing into the window. The Windows system does not modify the device context in any way. The disadvantage lies in the extra 800 bytes taken up by each window. Visual Basic forms and picture controls have the CS_OWNDC style. The handle for a private device context is obtained using the **GetDC** or **GetDCEx** function.

- *Cached device contexts*   In order to conserve resources, Windows provides a cache of five internal device contexts that are shared by all applications and that may be used with any window. These contexts are also obtained using the **GetDC** or **GetDCEx** function. When a cached DC is obtained, it is initialized to the default attributes shown in Table 6.1. It is essential, when using cached DCs, to release them when they are no longer needed using the **ReleaseDC** function. This is necessary in order to prevent the system from locking up due to lack of available device contexts.

■ *Created device contexts*   It is possible to create a device context using the **CreateDC** and **CreateCompatibleDC** function. You may create as many of these as needed.

Table 6.2 describes the API functions used in obtaining and freeing device contexts.

Table 6.2   **Device Context API Functions**

Function	Description
CreateCompatibleDC	Creates a memory device context that is compatible to a source DC. A memory device context can be considered a simulation of a device in memory. Selecting a bitmap into the device allows creation of a memory image that is compatible with the device.
CreateDC	Creates a device context for the specified device. It is most often used to create a DC for a printer.
CreateIC	Creates an information context (IC) for the specified device. An IC is similar to a device context, except that it takes less overhead. It can be used to obtain information about a device but may not be used for drawing operations.
DeleteDC	Deletes a created device context. This should be used to free device contexts created using the **CreateDC**, **CreateIC**, and **CreateCompatibleDC** functions.
GetDC GetDCEx	Obtains a device context for the specified window. If the window's class uses a private DC, that device context is retrieved by this function. Otherwise the function obtains a DC from the Windows cache. The **GetDCEx** function makes it possible to obtain a cached context even for windows that normally use private DCs.
GetWindowDC	This function is similar to **GetDC** except that it retrieves a device context for the entire window rectangle (not just the client area of the window).
ReleaseDC	Releases a window obtained using **GetDC**, **GetDCEx**, or **GetWindowDC**. If the DC is a private device context, this function has no effect. Otherwise, the DC is returned to the cache.

It's important to differentiate between the device contexts retrieved by the **GetDC** and **GetDCEx** functions and the **CreateDC** and **CreateCompatibleDC** functions. The former retrieve a device context from the Windows device context pool. This is a pool of five device contexts that are available to any

Windows application. Device contexts obtained using these functions must never be destroyed—they must be released using the **ReleaseDC** function, which causes the DC to be returned to the Windows device context pool when it is no longer needed. They must be returned as soon as possible, as these five DCs are shared by all Windows applications.

When the **CreateDC** and **CreateCompatibleDC** functions are used to obtain a device context, a new device context is actually created. This involves a fair amount of overhead in both time and memory, but contexts created in this manner may be held as long as you wish. When they are no longer needed they should be destroyed using the **DestroyDC** function, which frees up the memory allocated during the creation process.

Device Context Attributes

Table 6.1 lists the attributes of a device context. All of these attributes may be set using API function calls. Generally speaking, it is necessary to set the DC attributes before drawing into a device context. If a window uses cached device contexts, the attributes need to be set each time a DC is obtained for drawing.

Drawing Objects

Drawing objects are selected into a DC using the **SelectObject** API function described in Chapter 7. For example, it is possible to select a red pen into a DC in order to draw a red line in a window. The **SelectObject** function returns as its result a handle to the original drawing object for that DC. It is very important to select that original object back into the device context before releasing or destroying the DC.

Drawing Attributes and Mapping Modes

A device context describes drawing attributes such as the drawing mode and intercharacter spacing. It also defines the mapping mode and coordinate system to use for drawing. Unlike drawing objects there is no need to clear these settings before releasing or destroying the DC.

Color Palettes

With version 2.0 and greater, Visual Basic supports the use of color palettes to provide a selection of up to 256 colors to use from the millions available on many super-VGA devices. The use of color palette API functions with Visual Basic is described in detail in "Color Palettes" in Chapter 16.

Using Device Contexts with Visual Basic

Visual Basic forms and picture controls use private device contexts. You can retrieve a DC for a form or picture control using the **hDC** property or the

GetDC function (both techniques return the same handle when **AutoRedraw** is FALSE).

Saving the Device Context State

It is absolutely essential that a Visual Basic DC be restored to its original state before returning control to Visual Basic. Windows provides two handy API functions (shown in Table 6.3) that allow you to save and restore the state of a device context.

Table 6.3	**Device Context Stack Functions**	
	Function	Description
	SaveDC	Saves the state and attributes of the specified device context on a device context stack.
	RestoreDC	Restores the state and attributes of a device context from the Windows device context stack.

The following sequence of operations is commonly used when using Windows API functions to draw to a VB form or control:

1. Retrieve a device context handle using the **hDC** property.

2. Save the state of the device context using the **SaveDC** function.

3. Select the desired drawing objects and coordinate system.

4. Perform the drawing operations.

5. Restore the state of the device context using the **RestoreDC** function.

This process is described in further detail in the example programs in Chapter 7.

Device Contexts and the AutoRedraw Property

To effectively use the Windows API drawing functions, it is important to understand how Visual Basic uses device contexts and bitmaps internally. Figure 6.1 shows the architecture of the VB drawing environment.

Each form or picture control may have two bitmap images associated with it. The background bitmap image contains a bitmap that is to be used as the background for the window. The handle to this bitmap may be set and retrieved by the **Picture** property. The persistent image bitmap is used only when the **AutoRedraw** property is set to TRUE (-1). In this case, all drawing goes to a memory bitmap that is compatible with the window. This technique allows the VB programmer to draw an image once, and let VB automatically copy the persistent image bitmap to the window whenever the window needs updating. This also means that when **AutoRedraw** is 0, the persistent image bitmap does not exist and is not modified during drawing. You can still retrieve an image bitmap by reading the **Image** property, in which case Visual Basic will create a bitmap containing the background picture and return a handle to that bitmap.

Figure 6.1
Visual Basic drawing
architecture

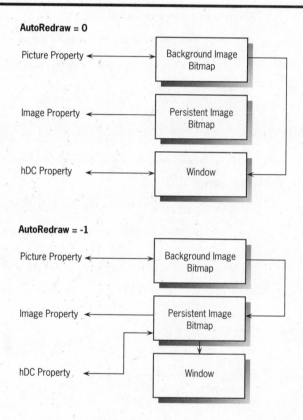

When the **AutoRedraw** property is FALSE, all drawing goes directly to the window. This is much faster and requires less overhead, since the extra memory for the persistent bitmap is not required and drawing to a window is frequently faster than copying a bitmap—especially if the bitmap is large. However, since VB does not maintain a persistent image for the window, it is necessary for the VB program to detect paint events and draw the window upon receipt of a **Paint** event.

Tables 6.4 and 6.5 describe the values of the VB properties associated with drawing and the process of updating a window.

Table 6.4	**Drawing with AutoRedraw = 0**
hDC property	Handle to a device context for the window.
Image property	Handle to a bitmap for the persistent image for the window. This image is not changed during drawing.
Picture property	Handle to the background image bitmap for the window.
Effect of **Cls** method	Clears the window to the background color or bitmap.
Window update process	Windows copies the Picture bitmap (if one exists) to the window, then sends a **Paint** event. All drawing goes directly to the window by way of the **hDC** device context.

Table 6.5	**Drawing with AutoRedraw = -1**
hDC property	Handle to a device context for a memory device context that is compatible with the window and contains a bitmap the size of the window. This bitmap is called the persistent image bitmap or screen for the window.
Image property	Handle to a bitmap for the persistent image for the window. This is the bitmap selected into the device context described by the **hDC** property.
Picture property	Handle to the background image bitmap for the window. Changing this property causes the persistent image bitmap to be immediately updated to reflect this bitmap.
Effect of **Cls** method	Clears the persistent bitmap to the background color and copies the background image bitmap (if one exists) to the persistent bitmap.
Window update process	Windows copies the persistent image bitmap to the window. All drawing goes directly to the persistent image bitmap by way of the **hDC** device context. No **Paint** events are sent.

The Windows API drawing functions can be used in either drawing mode. When drawing to the device context retrieved by the **hDC** property, drawing will go to the persistent bitmap or the window depending on the state of the **AutoRedraw** property.

There are some subtleties to be aware of when drawing to the persistent image bitmap when **AutoRedraw** is TRUE. First, unlike the VB drawing functions, the API functions do not inform VB that the window needs to be updated. Therefore it is necessary to invoke the **Refresh** method on the window or to invalidate the window to cause the persistent image to be transferred to the window. This also means that creating a complex drawing using API functions when **AutoRedraw** is TRUE is much faster than using the VB functions that update the display after each drawing operation.

Second, when **AutoRedraw** is set to TRUE, it is still possible to obtain a device context to the window itself using the **GetDC** API function and draw directly to the window. This is a subtle difference that is important to understand. When you use the **hDC** property to retrieve a device context when **AutoRedraw** is TRUE and draw into it, you are drawing into a memory device context that contains the persistent image bitmap. When you use the **GetDC** function to obtain a device context for a window, you are accessing the window itself.

Images drawn in this manner will not be placed in the persistent image bitmap. Due to the lack of **Paint** events, your program will have no way of knowing when that information is overwritten due to an update from the persistent image bitmap.

You should make no assumptions regarding the state of the device context retrieved using the **GetDC** function when **AutoRedraw** is TRUE. You should save the device context state and select any needed drawing objects before drawing into this DC.

The ClipControls Property and Graphical Controls

The Windows API drawing functions work identically to the Visual Basic drawing methods with regard to the **ClipControls** property and Graphical controls.

Forms, picture controls, and frame controls can be containers of other controls. This means that they can have child windows or controls contained within their client area. The **ClipControls** and **AutoRedraw** properties combine to determine whether the control is excluded from the clipping region. When the control is excluded from the clipping region, any drawing on the area of that control will be prevented. Tables 6.6 and 6.7 indicate whether drawing over a control will take place or not.

Table 6.6 **Drawing over a Window-Based Child Control**

	AutoRedraw = TRUE	AutoRedraw = FALSE
ClipControls = TRUE	No	No
ClipControls = FALSE	No	Yes

Table 6.7   **Drawing over a Graphical Child Control**

	AutoRedraw = TRUE	AutoRedraw = FALSE
ClipControls = TRUE	No	Yes
ClipControls = FALSE	No	Yes

Visual Basic graphical controls do not have a window associated with them. This means that you cannot obtain a device context for a graphical control. You can draw into the area occupied by a graphical control by obtaining a device context for the container control and drawing into it as long as **AutoRedraw** is set to FALSE for the container.

If you expect to be drawing on container objects, you will probably want to experiment with the various drawing methods and properties.

Device Context Information Functions

The Windows General Device Interface (GDI) provides a mechanism for obtaining information about devices in the form of the **GetDeviceCaps** function. The most important information from the programmer's point of view are the various device dimensions including resolution, aspect ratio, and colors supported. The RASTERCAPS capabilities field allows the programmer to determine if a device supports certain raster capabilities such as the BitBlt operation, device-independent bitmap functions, and bitmaps that are greater than 64k in size. A plotter, for example, is usually unable to handle raster operations.

GetDeviceCaps also allows you to determine which GDI functions are supported internally by the device. For example, some devices are able to draw lines and circles using built-in hardware accelerators. In such cases, GDI will usually allow the driver to perform the operation. Otherwise, GDI will perform the graphic function itself. This information is usually not important to the programmer.

Example: DevView—A Device Information Viewer

DevView is a program that can display information about a given device. It does not include all of the information provided by the **GetDeviceCaps** function, but is easily extensible.

Figure 6.2 shows the DevView program in action and shows the location of the project's controls on the form.

Figure 6.2

DevView program screen

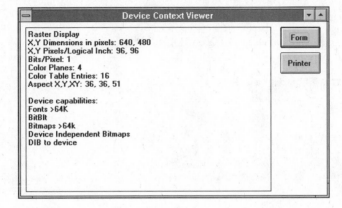

Using DevView

This simple program has only two controls. The Form button obtains a device context for the form and displays information for that context. The Printer button does the same for the default printer.

Project Description

The DevView project includes three files. DEVVIEW.FRM is the only form used in the program. DEVVIEW.BAS is the only module in the program and contains the constant type and global definitions. APIDECS.BAS is the type-safe API declaration file provided with this book.

Listing 6.1 shows the project file for the DevView program.

Listing 6.1   **Project Listing File DEVVIEW.MAK**

```
DEVVIEW.FRM
DEVVIEW.BAS
APIDECS.BAS
ProjWinSize=175,439,248,215
ProjWinShow=2
Title="DEVVIEW"
```

Listing 6.2 contains the header from file DEVVIEW.FRM that describes the control setup for the form.

Listing 6.2   DEVVIEW.FRM Header

```
VERSION 2.00
Begin Form DevView
    Caption         =   "Device Context Viewer"
    Height          =   4470
    Left            =   1035
    LinkMode        =   1  'Source
    LinkTopic       =   "Form1"
    ScaleHeight     =   4065
    ScaleWidth      =   7365
    Top             =   1140
    Width           =   7485
    Begin TextBox Text1
        Height          =   3855
        Left            =   120
        MultiLine       =   -1 'True
        TabIndex        =   0
        Top             =   120
        Width           =   5895
    End
    Begin CommandButton Command1
        Caption         =   "Form"
        Height          =   495
        Left            =   6240
        TabIndex        =   1
        Top             =   120
        Width           =   975
    End
    Begin CommandButton Command2
        Caption         =   "Printer"
        Height          =   495
        Left            =   6240
        TabIndex        =   2
        Top             =   720
        Width           =   975
    End
End
```

DevView Listing

Module DEVVIEW.BAS contains the constant declarations and global variables used by the program.

Listing 6.3   Module DEVVIEW.BAS

```
' DevView.bas


' Global Constants used in devview
Global Const DRIVERVERSION = 0
Global Const TECHNOLOGY = 2
Global Const HORZSIZE = 4
Global Const VERTSIZE = 6
Global Const HORZRES = 8
Global Const VERTRES = 10
Global Const BITSPIXEL = 12
Global Const PLANES = 14
Global Const NUMBRUSHES = 16
Global Const NUMPENS = 18
Global Const NUMMARKERS = 20
Global Const NUMFONTS = 22
Global Const NUMCOLORS = 24
Global Const PDEVICESIZE = 26
Global Const CURVECAPS = 28
Global Const LINECAPS = 30
Global Const POLYGONALCAPS = 32
Global Const TEXTCAPS = 34
Global Const CLIPCAPS = 36
Global Const RASTERCAPS = 38
Global Const ASPECTX = 40
Global Const ASPECTY = 42
Global Const ASPECTXY = 44
Global Const LOGPIXELSX = 88
Global Const LOGPIXELSY = 90
Global Const SIZEPALETTE = 104
Global Const NUMRESERVED = 106
Global Const COLORRES = 108
Global Const DT_PLOTTER = 0
Global Const DT_RASDISPLAY = 1
Global Const DT_RASPRINTER = 2
Global Const DT_RASCAMERA = 3
Global Const DT_CHARSTREAM = 4
Global Const DT_METAFILE = 5
Global Const DT_DISPFILE = 6
Global Const CC_NONE = 0
Global Const CC_CIRCLES = 1
Global Const CC_PIE = 2
Global Const CC_CHORD = 4
Global Const CC_ELLIPSES = 8
Global Const CC_WIDE = 16
Global Const CC_STYLED = 32
Global Const CC_WIDESTYLED = 64
Global Const CC_INTERIORS = 128
```

Listing 6.3　Module DEVVIEW.BAS (Continued)

```
Global Const LC_NONE = 0
Global Const LC_POLYLINE = 2
Global Const LC_MARKER = 4
Global Const LC_POLYMARKER = 8
Global Const LC_WIDE = 16
Global Const LC_STYLED = 32
Global Const LC_WIDESTYLED = 64
Global Const LC_INTERIORS = 128
Global Const PC_NONE = 0
Global Const PC_POLYGON = 1
Global Const PC_RECTANGLE = 2
Global Const PC_WINDPOLYGON = 4
Global Const PC_TRAPEZOID = 4
Global Const PC_SCANLINE = 8
Global Const PC_WIDE = 16
Global Const PC_STYLED = 32
Global Const PC_WIDESTYLED = 64
Global Const PC_INTERIORS = 128
Global Const CP_NONE = 0
Global Const CP_RECTANGLE = 1
Global Const TC_OP_CHARACTER = &H1
Global Const TC_OP_STROKE = &H2
Global Const TC_CP_STROKE = &H4
Global Const TC_CR_90 = &H8
Global Const TC_CR_ANY = &H10
Global Const TC_SF_X_YINDEP = &H20
Global Const TC_SA_DOUBLE = &H40
Global Const TC_SA_INTEGER = &H80
Global Const TC_SA_CONTIN = &H100
Global Const TC_EA_DOUBLE = &H200
Global Const TC_IA_ABLE = &H400
Global Const TC_UA_ABLE = &H800
Global Const TC_SO_ABLE = &H1000
Global Const TC_RA_ABLE = &H2000
Global Const TC_VA_ABLE = &H4000
Global Const TC_RESERVED = &H8000
Global Const RC_BITBLT = 1
Global Const RC_BANDING = 2
Global Const RC_SCALING = 4
Global Const RC_BITMAP64 = 8
Global Const RC_GDI20_OUTPUT = &H10
Global Const RC_DI_BITMAP = &H80
Global Const RC_PALETTE = &H100
Global Const RC_DIBTODEV = &H200
Global Const RC_BIGFONT = &H400
Global Const RC_STRETCHBLT = &H800
Global Const RC_FLOODFILL = &H1000
Global Const RC_STRETCHDIB = &H2000
```

Listing 6.3   Module DEVVIEW.BAS (Continued)

```
Global Const PC_RESERVED = &H1
Global Const PC_EXPLICIT = &H2
Global Const PC_NOCOLLAPSE = &H4
```

The DevView project displays the device information in a text control. This technique was chosen in order to make it easy to scroll information should you choose to expand the program to display additional information. In the DEVVIEW.FRM listing that follows, note the use of the **crlf$** to insert line breaks into the text string.

Listing 6.4   DEVVIEW.FRM

```
'   Loads the edit box with information about the DC
'
Sub LoadInfo (nhDC%)
    Dim a$
    Dim r%
    Dim crlf$

    crlf$ = Chr$(13) + Chr$(10)

    r% = GetDeviceCaps(nhDC%, TECHNOLOGY)
    If r% And DT_RASPRINTER Then a$ = "Raster Printer"
    If r% And DT_RASDISPLAY Then a$ = "Raster Display"
    ' You can detect other technology types here - see the
    ' GetDeviceCaps function description for technology
    ' types
    If a$ = "" Then a$ = "Other technology"
    a$ = a$ + crlf$
    a$ = a$ + "X,Y Dimensions in pixels:" + Str$(GetDeviceCaps(nhDC%, ⇔
HORZRES)) + "," + Str$(GetDeviceCaps(nhDC%, VERTRES)) + crlf$
    a$ = a$ + "X,Y Pixels/Logical Inch:" + Str$(GetDeviceCaps(nhDC%, ⇔
LOGPIXELSX))+ "," + Str$(GetDeviceCaps(nhDC%, LOGPIXELSY)) + crlf$
    a$ = a$ + "Bits/Pixel:" + Str$(GetDeviceCaps(nhDC%,BITSPIXEL)) + crlf$
    a$ = a$ + "Color Planes:" + Str$(GetDeviceCaps(nhDC%,PLANES)) + crlf$
    a$ = a$ + "Color Table Entries:" + Str$(GetDeviceCaps(nhDC%, ⇔
NUMCOLORS)) + crlf$
    a$ = a$ + "Aspect X,Y,XY:" + Str$(GetDeviceCaps(nhDC%, ASPECTX)) + "," ⇔
+Str$(GetDeviceCaps(nhDC%, ASPECTY)) + "," +Str$(GetDeviceCaps(nhDC%, ⇔
ASPECTXY)) + crlf$
    r% = GetDeviceCaps(nhDC%, RASTERCAPS)
    a$ = a$ + crlf$ + "Device capabilities:" + crlf$
    If r% And RC_BANDING Then a$ = a$ + "Banding" + crlf$
    If r% And RC_BIGFONT Then a$ = a$ + "Fonts >64K" +crlf$
    If r% And RC_BITBLT Then a$ = a$ + "BitBlt" + crlf$
```

Listing 6.4   **DEVVIEW.FRM (Continued)**

```
        If r% And RC_BITMAP64 Then a$ = a$ + "Bitmaps >64k" +crlf$
        If r% And RC_DI_BITMAP Then a$ = a$ +"Device Independent Bitmaps" + crlf$
        If r% And RC_DIBTODEV Then a$ = a$ + "DIB to device"+ crlf$
        If r% And RC_FLOODFILL Then a$ = a$ + "Flood fill" +crlf$
        If r% And RC_SCALING Then a$ = a$ + "Scaling" + crlf$
        If r% And RC_STRETCHBLT Then a$ = a$ + "StretchBlt" +crlf$
        If r% And RC_STRETCHDIB Then a$ = a$ + "StretchDIB" +crlf$
        Text1.Text = a$
End Sub

Sub Command1_Click ()
        LoadInfo CInt(Devview.hDC)
End Sub

Sub Command2_Click ()
        LoadInfo CInt(Printer.hDC)
End Sub
```

Scaling and Coordinate Systems

GDI provides extensive coordinate transformation and scaling capabilities. This is critical to providing device independence. Without such capabilities, it would be necessary for a program to take into account the resolution of each device.

Consider the task of drawing a bar chart. Without scaling and coordinate transformations, it would be necessary to determine the coordinate value of the origin, the direction of the scales, and the number of pixels or bits on each scale. A screen would typically have the origin at the upper left corner of the screen with coordinate values increasing to the right and down. A printer might have the origin at the lower left corner of the page with coordinate values increasing toward the top and right. The screen resolution might be anything from 640x350 to 1280x1024 or more. The printer resolution may range from a few hundred dots per inch on each axis to thousands of dots per inch on a high resolution laser printer. The complexity of the bar chart drawing program is increased by the need to determine the information about the device and then adjust every drawing operation accordingly.

Logical versus Device Coordinates

GDI solves this problem by having drawing take place into a device context that provides its own coordinate system that is independent of the actual physical device. This coordinate system is referred to as the *logical coordinate system* and it defines a *logical window* as compared to *device coordinates* that define a physical or device window.

Consider again the task of drawing a bar chart. Instead of creating a bar chart routine that handles every possible device, it is possible to create a bar chart routine that draws to a logical window. For example, the routine can be designed to draw into a 4000x3000 pixel logical coordinate system with the origin at the lower left. It is then possible to use the API scaling functions to map this logical window to any device.

The advantage of using a very-high-resolution logical window is that it allows the graphic routines to automatically take advantage of a high-resolution device such as a printer, while still producing the best possible image on lower-resolution devices such as monitors.

The bar chart routine could also be designed to use full 24-bit color. Windows will then attempt to find the nearest color match that the device supports.

This coordinate mapping system provides an additional feature that can be extremely useful to a programmer. It is possible to choose a coordinate system that is based on real physical dimensions, such as inches, centimeters, or twips (1/1440 inch). This makes it easy for a programmer to create graphics that are accurately scaled.

The accuracy of the output will vary by device. A device such as a printer, which has an exact physical resolution expressed as the number of dots per inch, can produce extremely accurate output. If the program draws a line that is one inch long in the logical coordinate system, it will appear exactly one inch long on paper.

Display monitors do not have the same precision. A 640x480 pixel display will appear different on a 13-inch monitor than it does on a 21-inch monitor. Windows does not know the size of the monitor you are using, so it defines a logical inch for displays that are usually close to a physical inch. The determination of how many display pixels are in a logical inch is made by the device driver, and can be determined using the **GetDeviceCaps** DC information function.

It is important to differentiate between logical and device coordinates when using Windows API functions. Logical coordinates are used for most GDI drawing operations and describe the logical window that you are drawing to. Physical or device coordinates are used for most Windows management functions and describe actual physical pixels or bits on a device. Device coordinates on a display screen are usually given as client coordinates—these coordinates are based on the client area of a window and have an origin at the upper left corner of the client area. This contrasts with window rectangle coordinates that describe the entire window rectangle including scroll bars, captions, and menus. The necessary parameters for each Windows function are described in the function reference.

It is possible to convert logical coordinates to and from device coordinates using the functions in Table 6.8.

Table 6.8   **Logical to Physical Coordinate Conversion Functions**

Function	Description
DPtoLP	Converts a point in the device coordinate system to the logical coordinate system for a device context.
LPtoDP	Converts a point in the logical coordinate system for a device context to the physical or device coordinate system.

Mapping Modes

Windows provides a number of mapping modes that define or partially define the logical coordinate system for a device context. These are shown in Table 6.9.

Table 6.9   **Windows Mapping Modes**

Mapping Mode	Description
MM_ANISOTROPIC	This is similar to the VB **ScaleMode** property being set to 0. The mapping between the logical coordinate system and the device coordinate system is completely arbitrary. Images in the logical window may be stretched or shifted in any direction when drawn.
MM_HIENGLISH	Each unit in the logical coordinate system is 0.001 inch long. The origin is at the lower left corner of the device, with values incrementing toward the top and right.
MM_HIMETRIC	Each unit in the logical coordinate system is 0.01 millimeter long. The origin is at the lower left corner of the device, with values incrementing toward the top and right.
MM_ISOTROPIC	The mapping between the logical coordinate system and the device coordinate system is completely arbitrary with one exception: Windows guarantees that the horizontal and vertical units represent the same physical length. For example, a line 100 units long will appear the same length regardless of whether it is horizontal or vertical. Thus a square in the logical window will appear square when drawn. Images in the logical window may be scaled and shifted in any manner.
MM_LOENGLISH	Each unit in the logical coordinate system is 0.01 inch long. The origin is at the lower left corner of the device, with values incrementing toward the top and right.

Table 6.9 **Windows Mapping Modes (Continued)**

Mapping Mode	Description
MM_LOMETRIC	Each unit in the logical coordinate system is 0.1 millimeter long. The origin is at the lower left corner of the device, with values incrementing toward the top and right.
MM_TEXT	This is the default mapping for a device context and is the mapping used in Visual Basic forms or picture controls regardless of the value of the VB **ScaleMode** property. This is similar to the **ScaleMode** property being set to 3. Each unit in the logical coordinate system represents one pixel in the device coordinate system. The origin is at the upper left corner of the device increasing toward the bottom and right. The logical and device coordinate systems are thus effectively the same.
MM_TWIPS	This is similar to the VB **ScaleMode** property being set to 1. Each unit represents one twip (or 1/1440 inch). The origin is at the lower left corner of the device increasing toward the top and right.

Keep in mind that setting the mapping mode and coordinate system for a device context only affects future drawing operations onto that context. Any existing image on the device remains unchanged.

Some of the Windows mapping modes correspond to the mapping modes provided by Visual Basic using the **ScaleMode** property. There are some critical differences between them and some subtleties when using Windows mapping modes on Visual Basic controls. One of the key differences is that Visual Basic uses floating point values to describe coordinates (thus in the VB inches scale, each unit represents one inch and fractional units are possible). Windows uses integer arithmetic only. For this reason, Windows API functions will tend to have better performance than VB drawing functions when extensive scaling is used.

Windows and Viewports—Extents and Origins

The idea of a logical window has already been introduced. The height and width of the logical window are known as the *extents* of the window. It is also possible to define where in the logical window the origin lies. The origin of a logical window is the point that has X,Y coordinates of 0,0. This point may be located anywhere in the logical window.

The area on the device that corresponds exactly to the logical window is known as the *viewport*. The height and width of the viewport are called the viewport extents. The offset of the viewport from the device origin is known as the viewport origin.

It is essential to note that the extents and origin of the logical window do not restrict drawing to that window. In other words, it is possible to draw outside of the logical window using the same logical coordinate system. In this case, the drawing will also appear outside of the viewport. The window and viewport extents are used only to define the scaling on each axis. The window and viewport origins are used only to define the offset. The equations describing the logical-to-physical mapping are as follows:

Variable Definitions

DevX = device X coordinate

DevY = device Y coordinate

LogX = logical X coordinate

LogY = logical Y coordinate

xWO = logical window origin on the X axis

yWO = logical window origin on the Y axis

xWE = Logical window extents on the X axis

yWE = Logical window extents on the Y axis

xVO = viewport origin on the X axis (device coordinates)

yVO = viewport origin on the Y axis (device coordinates)

xVE = viewport extents on the X axis (device coordinates)

yVE = viewport extents on the Y axis (device coordinates)

Mapping Equations

DevX = (LogX - xWO) * xVE/xWE+xVO

DevY = (LogY - yWO) * yVE/yWE+yVO

LogX = (DevX - xVO) * xWE/xVE+xWO

LogY = (DevY - yVO) * yWE/yVE+yWO

Windows and viewport extents are used only with the MM_ANISOTROPIC and MM_ISOTROPIC modes. The scaling in the other mapping modes is fixed by Windows. Figures 6.3 and 6.4 illustrate possible use of the MM_ANISOTROPIC and MM_ISOTROPIC mapping modes.

Figure 6.3
MM_ISOTROPIC
mapping

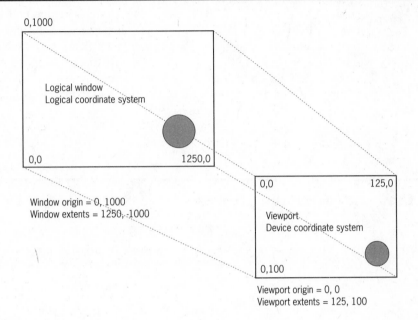

Window origin = 0, 1000
Window extents = 1250, -1000

Viewport origin = 0, 0
Viewport extents = 125, 100

Figure 6.4
MM_ANISOTROPIC
mapping

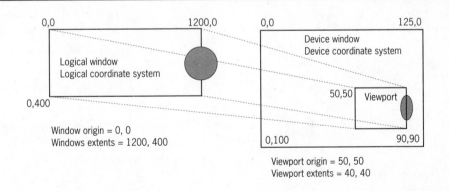

Window origin = 0, 0
Windows extents = 1200, 400

Viewport origin = 50, 50
Viewport extents = 40, 40

As shown in Figure 6.3, MM_ISOTROPIC mode allows arbitrary positioning of the origin of the logical coordinate system and arbitrary scaling. It assures that the aspect ratio remains constant. In other words, a square in the logical coordinate system will appear square on the device. Note the use of a negative window extent to reverse the direction of the vertical scale.

MM_ANISOTROPIC mode, shown in Figure 6.4, is completely uncon-strained. The area defined by the window extents is mapped into the area de-fined by the viewport. In Figure 6.4, the viewport is also shifted within the client window by setting the viewport origin to the center of the client win-dow. Note that setting the extents does not restrict drawing unless clipping is explicitly set. In this case the gray circle on the right of the logical window is mapped into an oval at the right of the viewport. Unlike MM_ISOTROPIC mode, the aspect ratio is not preserved.

Table 6.10 shows the Windows API functions that are used to control the mapping of logical to device coordinates.

Table 6.10   **Windows Mapping Functions**

Function	Description
GetDCOrg	Determines the position of the origin of the client area of a window in screen coordinates.
GetMapMode	Determines the current mapping mode of a DC.
GetViewportExt GetViewportExtEx	Obtains the extents of the specified viewport.
GetViewportOrg GetViewportOrgEx	Obtains the origins of the specified viewport.
GetWindowExt GetWindowExtEx	Obtains the extents of the specified logical window.
GetWindowOrg GetWindowOrgEx	Obtains the origins of the specified logical window.
OffsetViewportOrg OffsetViewportOrgEx	Offsets the origin of the specified viewport.
OffsetWindowOrg OffsetWindowOrgEx	Offsets the origin of the specified window.
ScaleViewportExt ScaleViewportExtEx	Scales the extents of the specified viewport.
ScaleWindowExt ScaleWindowExtEx	Scales the extents of the specified logical window.
SetMapMode	Sets the mapping mode for the specified device context.
SetViewportExt SetViewportExtEx	Sets the extents of the specified viewport.

Table 6.10 **Windows Mapping Functions (Continued)**

Function	Description
SetViewportOrg	Sets the origin of the specified viewport.
SetViewportOrgEx	
SetWindowExt	Sets the extents of the specified logical window.
SetWindowExtEx	
SetWindowOrg	Sets the origin of the specified window.
SetWindowOrgEx	

Windows Coordinate Systems and Visual Basic

All of the coordinate transformations described in this section work with Visual Basic windows. However, it is important to understand how Visual Basic handles scaling.

Visual Basic does not use the Windows mapping modes to control scaling. It leaves device contexts in the MM_TEXT mapping mode and does all scaling internally. This allows VB to handle floating point coordinates (unlike Windows, which uses integer coordinate values only).

As a result, when using device context mapping it is absolutely critical to restore the device context mapping mode to its original value once you are finished using API drawing functions. The easiest way to do this is by using the **SaveDC** and **RestoreDC** functions to save the original device context information.

Examples of this technique, along with examples of the use of Windows mapping modes during drawing can be found in Chapter 7, which discusses drawing with API functions.

Clipping, Regions, and Other Device Context Control Functions

Windows provides a number of functions for controlling the process of drawing into device contexts. These require a mechanism for specifying an area in a device context.

Regions

Just as rectangles are important for controlling Windows, regions are important for controlling device contexts. A region is a GDI object that describes an area in a device context. Each region has an object handle and like any GDI object, should be deleted using the **DeleteObject** API function when it is no longer needed (see Chapter 7). This area can be as simple as a rectangle, or arbitrarily complex. It can include several areas that are detached from each other. It can include polygons and circles. The functions used to create and manipulate regions are shown in Table 6.11.

Table 6.11   **Region Functions**

Function	Description
CombineRgn	Combines two regions in the manner specified.
CreateEllipticRgn CreateEllipticRgnIndirect	Creates circular and elliptical regions.
CreatePolygonRgn CreatePolyPolygonRgn	Creates a region out of one or more polygons.
CreateRectRgn CreateRectRgnIndirect	Creates rectangular regions.
CreateRoundRectRgn	Creates a region from a rectangle with rounded corners.
EqualRgn	Determines if two regions are equal.
GetRgnBox	Obtains a rectangle that bounds the specified region.
OffsetRgn	Offsets the specified region.
PtInRegion	Determines if a point is inside the specified region.
RectInRegion	Determines if any part of a rectangle is in the specified region.
SetRectRgn	Changes the specified region to describe a rectangular area.

Clipping

It is possible to restrict the drawing to a device context to specific parts of the logical window. This can be intuitively seen by the fact that when you draw graphics onto a Visual Basic form, it will not draw over the form's controls unless clipping is explicitly disabled by setting the **ClipControls** property to FALSE. Windows excludes the area covered by controls from the drawing area of the form's device context. This process is known as *clipping* and the drawing area is referred to as the *clipping region*. (Clipping was discussed earlier in this chapter.) Table 6.12 lists the device context clipping functions.

Table 6.12   **Region Clipping Functions**

Function	Description
ExcludeClipRect	Excludes the specified rectangle from the clipping region.
GetClipBox	Retrieves a rectangle that bounds the clipping region.
IntersectClipRect	Sets the clipping region to the intersection of the current region and the specified rectangle.
OffsetClipRgn	Offsets the clipping region by a specified amount.
PtVisible	Determines if the specified point is visible (lies within the current clipping region).
RectVisible	Determines if any part of the specified rectangle is visible (lies within the current clipping region).
SelectClipRgn	Selects a region to be the clipping region for the specified device context.

Validation

Chapter 1 discussed the process of updating windows and described how part of a window may be invalidated for update at some future time. Just as rectangle functions are used to invalidate all or part of a window, region functions can be used to invalidate or validate all or part of a display context. Table 6.13 lists these functions.

Table 6.13   **Device Context Validation Functions**

Function	Description
ExcludeUpdateRgn	Excludes the invalidated parts of the window (the update region) from the clipping region. This can be used to prevent drawing to those parts of the window that will be updated later by Windows.
GetBoundsRect	Retrieves the bounding rectangle. Refer to the function reference in this chapter for information on this function.
GetUpdateRgn	Obtains a region describing the invalid area in the window.
InvalidateRgn	Invalidates the specified region in the device context.
ScrollDC	Scrolls a region within a device context.
ValidateRgn	Validates the specified region in the device context.

Performance Considerations

When Windows is drawing into a device context, it is necessary to check every pixel to see if it is within the clipping region. This means that clipping may have a significant impact on performance. This is, in fact, the reason that Visual Basic provides a **ClipControls** property. Setting this property to FALSE can dramatically improve drawing speed on a form or picture control that contains child controls. When clipping is used, it is always advisable to use rectangular clipping regions if possible.

Example: ClipView—A Brief Clipping Demonstration

ClipView is a program that can display the effect of clipping regions on drawing. It provides a template that you can extend to experiment with more complex region functions. Figure 6.5 shows the ClipView program in action.

Figure 6.5
ClipView program
screen

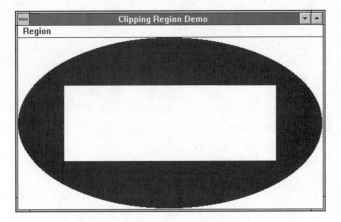

Using ClipView

This simple program has only two menu commands: Elliptic and Elliptic-Rect. The Elliptic command creates an elliptic region that fills the form and selects it as the clipping region. The clipping is demonstrated when the program attempts to fill the form to black. The Elliptic-Rect command demonstrates a more complex region in which a rectangle is excluded from the region before it is selected as the clipping region.

Project Description

The ClipView project includes four files. CLIPVIEW.FRM is the only form used in the program. CLIPVIEW.BAS is the only module in the program and contains the constant type and global definitions. APIDECS.BAS is the type-safe API declaration file provided with this book. APIGUIDE.BAS contains the declarations for the APIGUIDE.DLL dynamic link library.

Listing 6.5 shows the project file for the ClipView program.

Listing 6.5   **Project Listing File CLIPVIEW.MAK**

```
CLIPVIEW.FRM
CLIPVIEW.BAS
APIDECS.BAS
APIGUIDE.BAS
ProjWinSize=80,392,248,215
ProjWinShow=2
```

Form Description

Listing 6.6 contains the header from file CLIPVIEW.FRM that describes the control setup for the form.

Listing 6.6   **CLIPVIEW.FRM Header**

```
VERSION 2.00
Begin Form ClipView
    Caption         =   "Clipping Region Demo"
    Height          =   4710
    Left            =   1035
    LinkMode        =   1  'Source
    LinkTopic       =   "Form1"
    ScaleHeight     =   4020
    ScaleWidth      =   7365
    Top             =   1140
    Width           =   7485
    Begin Menu MenuRegion
        Caption         =   "Region"
        Begin Menu MenuElliptic
            Caption         =   "Elliptic"
        End
        Begin Menu MenuEllipticNorect
            Caption         =   "Elliptic-Rect"
        End
    End
End
```

ClipView Listing

Module CLIPVIEW.BAS contains the constant declarations and global variables used by the program.

Listing 6.7 Module CLIPVIEW.BAS

```
' Clipper - Region clipping demonstration program
'
'
'-------------------------------------------------------
'            Global Variable and constants
'
Global Const RGN_AND = 1
Global Const RGN_OR = 2
Global Const RGN_XOR = 3
Global Const RGN_DIFF = 4
Global Const RGN_COPY = 5


Global ClippingRegion%
```

Listing 6.8 Form Listing CLIPVIEW.FRM

```
'    Create an elliptical region that fits in the window
'
Sub MenuElliptic_Click ()
    Dim rc As RECT
    GetClientRect hWnd, rc
    ClippingRegion% = CreateEllipticRgnIndirect(rc)
    ' ShowClip selects the ellipse as the clipping region,
    ' then fills the window to show the clipping effect.
    ShowClip ClippingRegion%
    ' Be sure to delete the region when done.
    dummy% = DeleteObject(ClippingRegion%)
End Sub

' Selects the specified region as the clipping region,
' then fills the form.  Only the area in the region will be
' filled - the rest is "clipped" out.
'
Sub ShowClip (rgn%)
    Clipper.Cls
    dummy% = SelectClipRgn%(Clipper.hDC, rgn%)
    Line (0, 0)-(Clipper.ScaleWidth,Clipper.ScaleHeight), , BF
    dummy% = SelectClipRgn%(Clipper.hDC, 0)
End Sub
```

Listing 6.8   Form Listing CLIPVIEW.FRM (Continued)

```
' This shows the creation of a more complex region.
'
Sub MenuEllipticNorect_Click ()
    Dim rc As RECT, rc2 As RECT
    Dim rgn2%

    GetClientRect hWnd, rc
    ' Start with the same clipping region used in
    ' MenuElliptic
    ClippingRegion% = CreateEllipticRgnIndirect(rc)

    ' Make a copy of a rectangle describing the form size
    dummy% = CopyRect(rc2, rc)
    ' Shrink it by 75 pixels on a side
    InflateRect rc2, -75, -75
    ' Then convert the rectangle into a region
    rgn2% = CreateRectRgnIndirect(rc2)

    ' Combine the regions using the difference operation
    dummy% = CombineRgn(ClippingRegion%, ClippingRegion%,rgn2%, RGN_DIFF)

    ' And now select this as the clipping region.
    ShowClip ClippingRegion%

    ' Delete both regions when done
    dummy% = DeleteObject(ClippingRegion%)
    dummy% = DeleteObject(rgn2%)

End Sub
```

Function Reference

■ CombineRgn

VB Declaration   `Declare Function CombineRgn% Lib "GDI" (ByVal hDestRgn%, ByVal hSrcRgn1%, By⇔`
`Val hSrcRgn2%, ByVal nCombineMode%)`

Description   Combines two regions to form a new region.

Use with VB   No problem.

Parameter	Type/Description
hDestRgn	**Integer**—Handle to a region that will contain the combined result.
hSrcRgn1	**Integer**—First source region.
hSrcRgn2	**Integer**—Second source region.
nCombineMode	**Integer**—Method in which to combine the two regions. May be one of the following constants defined in APICONST.TXT: **RGN_AND**: **hDestRgn** is set to the intersection of the two source regions (the area common to both). **RGN_COPY**: **hDestRgn** is set to a copy of **hSrcRgn1**. **RGN_DIFF**: **hDestRgn** is set to the area in **hSrcRgn1** that is not present in **hSrcRgn2**. **RGN_OR**: **hDestRgn** is set to the union of the two source regions (the area that appears in either source region). **RGN_XOR**: **hDestRgn** is the exclusive OR (XOR) of the two source regions (the area that appears in either source region, but not both).

Return Value   **Integer**—Returns one of the following constants:
COMPLEXREGION: if the region has borders that overlap each other.
SIMPLEREGION: if the borders of the region do not overlap each other.
NULLREGION: if the region is empty.
ERROR: if the combined region could not be created.

■ CreateCompatibleDC

VB Declaration   `Declare Function CreateCompatibleDC% Lib "GDI" (ByVal hDC%)`

Description   Creates a memory device context that is compatible with the specified device context.

Use with VB   Refer to "Using Device Contexts with Visual Basic," earlier in this chapter.

Parameter	Type/Description
hDC	**Integer**—Handle to a device context. The new device context will be compatible with this one. May be zero to create a device context compatible with the screen.

Return Value   **Integer**—A handle to the new device context or zero on error.

Comments   A bitmap needs to be selected for this device context before it can be drawn on. The device context should be deleted with the **DeleteDC** function when it's no longer needed. All objects selected into the DC should be unselected and replaced with the original selected objects before the device context is deleted.

■ CreateDC

VB Declaration   `Declare Function CreateDC% Lib "GDI" (ByVal lpDriverName$, ByVal lpDevice⇔`
`Name$, ByVal lpOutput$,ByVal lpInitData&)`

Description   Creates a device context for the specified device.

Use with VB   Refer to "Using Device Contexts with Visual Basic," earlier in this chapter.

Parameter	Type/Description
lpDriverName	**String**—The DOS file name of the device driver to use (without extension).
lpDeviceName	**String**—The name of the particular device to use. This parameter is used when a driver supports more than one device.
lpOutput	**String**—The name of the DOS file name or device to use for output.
lpInitData	**Long**—Zero to use the default initialization values for the device, or the address of a DEVMODE structure containing initialization values to use. This address may be obtained using the **agGetAddressForObject** function.

Return Value   **Integer**—A handle to the new device context or zero on error.

Comments   The device context should be deleted with the **DeleteDC** function when it's no longer needed. All objects selected into the DC should be unselected and replaced with the original selected objects before the device context is deleted. The driver, device, and output strings can typically be obtained for installed printers from the WIN.INI file. Refer to Chapter 13 for information on accessing WIN.INI information.

The line

`CreateDC("Display","","",0)`

may be used to obtain a device context for the entire display screen.

■ CreateEllipticRgn

VB Declaration   `Declare Function CreateEllipticRgn% Lib "GDI" (ByVal X1%,ByVal Y1%, ByVal ⇔`
`X2%, ByVal Y2%)`

Description   Creates a region in the shape of an ellipse that fits in the rectangle described by the points X1,Y1 and X2,Y2.

Use with VB   No problem.

Parameter	Type/Description
X1, Y1	**Integers**—X,Y coordinates describing the upper left corner of the bounding rectangle.
X2, Y2	**Integers**—X,Y coordinates describing the lower right corner of the bounding rectangle.

Return Value   Integer—A region handle on success, zero on error.

Comments   Be sure to delete the region with the **DeleteObject** function when it is no longer needed.

■ CreateEllipticRgnIndirect

VB Declaration   `Declare Function CreateEllipticRgnIndirect% Lib "GDI" (lpRect As RECT)`

Description   Creates a region in the shape of an ellipse that fits in the specified rectangle.

Use with VB   No problem.

Parameter	Type/Description
lpRect	**RECT**—Rectangle that specifies the size of the elliptic region to create.

Return Value   Integer—A region handle on success, zero on error.

Comments   Be sure to delete the region with the **DeleteObject** function when it is no longer needed.

■ CreateIC

VB Declaration   `Declare Function CreateIC% Lib "GDI" (ByVal lpDriverName$, ByVal lpDevice⇔`
`Name$, ByVal lpOutput$,ByVal lpInitData&)`

Description   Creates an information context for the specified device. An information context can be used to quickly retrieve information about a device without the overhead of creating a device context. It can be passed as a parameter to information functions such as **GetDeviceCaps** in place of the device context parameter.

Use with VB   Refer to "Using Device Contexts with Visual Basic," earlier in this chapter.

Parameter	Type/Description
lpDriverName	**String**—The DOS file name of the device driver to use (without extension).
lpDeviceName	**String**—The name of the particular device to use. This parameter is used when a driver supports more than one device.

Parameter	Type/Description
lpOutput	**String**—The name of the DOS file or device to use for output.
lpInitData	**Long**—Zero to use the default initialization values for the device, or the address of a DEVMODE structure containing initialization values to use. This address may be obtained using the **agGetAddress-ForObject** function.

Return Value   **Integer**—A handle to the information context or zero on error.

Comments   The device context should be deleted with the **DeleteDC** function when it's no longer needed. The driver, device, and output strings can typically be obtained for installed printers from the WIN.INI file. Refer to Chapter 13 for information on accessing WIN.INI information.
     The line

```
CreateIC("Display","","",0)
```

may be used to obtain an information context for the entire display screen.

■ CreatePolygonRgn

VB Declaration   Declare Function CreatePolygonRgn% Lib "GDI" (lpPoints AsPOINTAPI, ByVal ⇔
nCount%, ByVal nPolyFillMode%)

Description   Creates a region out of an arbitrary series of points. Windows automatically closes the polygon by connecting the last and first points.

Use with VB   No problem.

Parameter	Type/Description
lpPoints	**POINTAPI**—The first **POINTAPI** structure in an array of **nCount POINTAPI** structures.
nCount	**Integer**—Number of points in the polygon.
nPolyFillMode	**Integer**—Describes the polygon filling mode. May be either the **ALTERNATE** or the WINDING constant. Refer to the **SetPolyFillMode** function in Chapter 7 for an explanation of polygon fill modes.

Return Value   **Integer**—The handle of the region created, or zero on error.

Comments   Be sure to delete the region with the **DeleteObject** function when it's no longer needed.

■ CreatePolyPolygonRgn

VB Declaration   Declare Function CreatePolyPolygonRgn% Lib "GDI" (lpPoints As POINTAPI, ⇔
lpPolyCounts%, ByVal nCount%,ByVal nPolyFillMode%)

Description   Creates a region made up of any number of polygons. Each polygon must be closed.

Use with VB	No problem.

Parameter	Type/Description
lpPoints	**POINTAPI**—The first **POINTAPI** structure in an array of **nCount** **POINTAPI** structures.
lpPolyCounts	**Integer**—The first integer in an array of integers. Each entry contains the number of points that make up a closed polygon. The **lpPoints** array consists of a series of closed polygons, each of which has an entry in the **lpPolyCounts** array.
nCount	**Integer**—Total number of points in the **lpPoints** array.
nPolyFillMode	**Integer**—Describes the polygon filling mode. May be either the **ALTERNATE** or the **WINDING** constant. Refer to the **SetPolyFillMode** function in Chapter 7 for an explanation of polygon fill modes.

Return Value Integer—The handle of the region created, or zero on error.

Comments Be sure to delete the region with the **DeleteObject** function when it's no longer needed.

■ CreateRectRgn

VB Declaration `Declare Function CreateRectRgn% Lib "GDI" (ByVal X1%, ByVal Y1%, ByVal X2%, ⇔`
`ByVal Y2%)`

Description Creates a region in the shape of a rectangle described by the points X1,Y1 and X2,Y2.

Use with VB No problem.

Parameter	Type/Description
X1, Y1	**Integers**—X,Y coordinates describing the upper left corner of the rectangle.
X2, Y2	**Integers**—X,Y coordinates describing the lower right corner of the rectangle.

Return Value Integer—A region handle on success, zero on error.

Comments Be sure to delete the region with the **DeleteObject** function when it's no longer needed.

■ CreateRectRgnIndirect

VB Declaration `Declare Function CreateRectRgnIndirect% Lib "GDI" (lpRect As RECT)`

Description Creates a region in the shape of a rectangle described by **lpRect**.

Use with VB No problem.

Parameter	Type/Description
lpRect	**RECT**—Rectangle that defines the region to create.

Return Value Integer—A region handle on success, zero on error.

Comments Be sure to delete the region with the **DeleteObject** function when it's no longer needed.

■ CreateRoundRectRgn

VB Declaration Declare Function CreateRoundRectRgn% Lib "GDI" (ByVal X1%, ByVal Y1%, ByVal ⇔
X2%, ByVal Y2%, ByVal X3%,ByVal Y3%)

Description Creates a region in the shape of a rectangle with rounded corners described by the points X1,Y1 and X2,Y2. X3 and X4 define the ellipse used to round the corners.

Use with VB No problem.

Parameter	Type/Description
X1, Y1	**Integers**—X,Y coordinates describing the upper left corner of the rectangle.
X2, Y2	**Integers**—X,Y coordinates describing the lower right corner of the rectangle.
X3	**Integer**—The width of the ellipse used to round the corners.
Y3	**Integer**—The height of the ellipse used to round the corners.

Return Value Integer—A region handle on success, zero on error.

Comments Be sure to delete the region with the **DeleteObject** function when it's no longer needed.

■ DeleteDC

VB Declaration Declare Function DeleteDC% Lib "GDI" (ByVal hDC%)

Description Deletes the specified device context or information context and frees all associated windows resources. Do not use with device contexts obtained using the **GetDC** function.

Use with VB Do not use on device context handles obtained using the VB **hDC** property.

Parameter	Type/Description
hDC	**Integer**—Device context to delete.

Return Value Integer—TRUE (nonzero) on success, zero otherwise.

Comments If objects have been selected into the device context, they should be selected out before calling this function. This is done by selecting the original objects back into the DC.

■ DPtoLP

VB Declaration Declare Function DPtoLP% Lib "GDI" (ByVal hDC%, lpPointsAs POINTAPI, ByVal ⇔
nCount%)

Description   Converts an array of points from device coordinates into logical coordinates in the specified display context.

Use with VB   Refer to "Scaling and Coordinate Systems," earlier in this chapter.

Parameter	Type/Description
hDC	**Integer**—Handle to a device context that defines a logical coordinate system.
lpPoints	**POINTAPI**—The first entry in an array of one or more **POINTAPI** structures containing points in device coordinates. Each entry will be converted to logical coordinates.
nCount	**Integer**—The number of entries in the **lpPoints** array.

Return Value   **Integer**—TRUE (nonzero) on success, zero otherwise.

■ EqualRgn

VB Declaration   `Declare Function EqualRgn% Lib "GDI" (ByVal hSrcRgn1%, ByVal hSrcRgn2%)`

Description   Determines if two regions are equivalent.

Use with VB   No problem.

Parameter	Type/Description
hSrcRgn1	**Integer**—Handle to a region.
hSrcRgn2	**Integer**—Handle to a region.

Return Value   **Integer**—TRUE (nonzero) if the two regions are equal. Zero otherwise.

■ ExcludeClipRect

VB Declaration   `Declare Function ExcludeClipRect% Lib "GDI" (ByVal hDC%,ByVal X1%, ByVal ⇔`
`Y1%, ByVal X2%, ByVal Y2%)`

Description   Excludes the rectangle defined by points X1,Y1 and X2,Y2 from the clipping area in the specified device context. Drawing will not take place inside this rectangle.

Use with VB   Refer to "Clipping, Regions, and Other Device Context Control Functions," earlier in this chapter.

Parameter	Type/Description
hDC	**Integer**—Device context to modify.
X1, Y1	**Integers**—X,Y coordinates describing the upper left corner of the rectangle in logical coordinates.
X2, Y2	**Integers**—X,Y coordinates describing the lower right corner of the rectangle in logical coordinates.

Return Value   **Integer**—Returns one of the following constants:
COMPLEXREGION: if the region has borders that overlap each other.
SIMPLEREGION: if the borders of the region do not overlap each other.
NULLREGION: if the region is empty.
ERROR: new clipping region could not be created.

ExcludeUpdateRgn

VB Declaration   `Declare Function ExcludeUpdateRgn% Lib "User" (ByVal hDC%, ByVal hWnd%)`

Description   Excludes the update region of the specified window from the clipping region of the specified device context. This prevents drawing into areas that are invalid (and thus due to be updated at a later time).

Use with VB   Refer to "Clipping, Regions, and Other Device Context Control Functions," earlier in this chapter.

Parameter	Type/Description
hDC	**Integer**—Device context. The clipping region of this device context will be modified by excluding the update region of window **hWnd**.
hWnd	**Integer**—Handle to a window.

Return Value   See function **ExcludeClipRect** for return values.

GetBoundsRect

VB Declaration   `Declare Function GetBoundsRect% Lib "GDI" (ByVal hDC%, lprcBounds As RECT,` ⇔
`ByVal flags%)`

Description   Retrieves the bounding rectangle for the specified device context. Each device context has a bounding rectangle that may be used by the programmer to accumulate information representing the bounds of the current image.

Use with VB   No known problems.

Parameter	Type/Description
hDC	**Integer**—Device context for the bounding rectangle.
lprcBounds	**RECT**—Rectangle to load with the current bounding rectangle for device context **hDC**.
flags%	**Integer**—May be set to constant **DCB_RESET** to clear the bounding rectangle. Otherwise set to zero.

Return Value   **Integer**—One of the following constants:
DCB_SET or **DCB_ACCUMULATE:** if the bounding rectangle is not empty.
DCB_RESET: if the bounding rectangle is empty.

■ GetClipBox

VB Declaration `Declare Function GetClipBox% Lib "GDI" (ByVal hDC%,lpRect As RECT)`

Description Retrieves the smallest rectangle that completely contains the clipping region for the specified device context.

Use with VB Refer to "Clipping, Regions, and Other Device Context Control Functions," earlier in this chapter.

Parameter	Type/Description
hDC	**Integer**—Handle to a display context.
lpRect	**RECT**—Rectangle structure to load with a rectangle that contains the clipping region for display context **hDC**.

Return Value See function **ExcludeClipRect** for return values.

■ GetDC

VB Declaration `Declare Function GetDC% Lib "User" (ByVal hWnd%)`

Description Retrieves a device context for the specified window.

Use with VB Refer to "Clipping, Regions, and Other Device Context Control Functions," earlier in this chapter.

Parameter	Type/Description
hWnd	**Integer**—Handle of window for which a device context is obtained. Zero to retrieve a DC for the entire screen.

Return Value **Integer**—The handle of a device context to the specified window. Zero on error.

Comments If the window belongs to a class with the **CS_OWNDC, CS_CLASSDC** or **CS_PARENTDC** style bits set, the context retrieved will be that of the Window or class. This is the case with VB forms and picture controls. You should make no assumptions regarding the default attributes of the retrieved device context for a form or picture control especially with regard to drawing objects. In addition, the default attributes will differ depending on setting of the **AutoRedraw** property for the control or form. You must restore the attributes of the device context to their original values before the device context is released. Device contexts for windows that do not have the **CS_OWNDC, CS_CLASSDC,** or **CS_PARENTDC** style bits set will be retrieved from the general Windows cache and will have all attributes set to their default values.

■ GetDCEx

VB Declaration `Declare Function GetDCEx% Lib "User" (ByVal hWnd%, ByVal hrgnClip%, ByVal ⇔ fdwOptions&)`

Description Retrieves a device context for the specified window. This function provides additional options as compared to **GetDC**.

Use with VB   Refer to "Using Device Contexts with Visual Basic," earlier in this chapter.

Parameter	Type/Description
hWnd	**Integer**—Handle of window for which a device context is obtained.
hrgnClip	**Integer**—A clipping region to use with the window.
fdwOptions	**Long**—A flag word with bits set according to the following constants: **DCX_CACHE**: The device context is retrieved from the Windows cache regardless of the class style setting for the window. **DCX_CLIPCHILREN**: The area of all visible child windows is excluded from the DC's clipping region. **DCX_CLIPSIBLINGS**: The area of all visible sibling windows above window **hWnd** is excluded from the DC's clipping region. **DCX_EXCLUDERGN**: Excludes the region specified by **hrgnClip** from the DC's clipping region. **DCX_INTERSECTRGN**: Intersects the region specified by **hrgn-Clip** with the clipping region for the device context. **DCX_LOCKWINDOWUPDATE**: This flag allows drawing to the window even if it is locked due to a call to **LockWindowUpdate**. **DCX_PARENTCLIP**: Overrides the **CS_PARENTDC** class style setting. The DC's origin is set to the upper left corner of window **hWnd**. **DCX_WINDOW**: A device context is returned for the entire window rectangle rather than just the client area of the window.

Return Value   **Integer**—The handle of a device context to the specified window. Zero on error.

Comments   If the window belongs to a class with the **CS_OWNDC**, **CS_CLASSDC**, or **CS_PARENTDC** style bits set, the context retrieved will be that of the window or class. In this case, the attributes of the device context will be unchanged from their previous values. This is usually the case with VB forms and controls. Otherwise, the **DCX_CACHE** bit must be set to retrieve a device context from the general Windows cache. If it is not set, this function will return zero. The DC will have all attributes set to their default values. Device contexts from the cache must be released after use with the **ReleaseDC** function to prevent the system from locking up, as Windows only has five cached DCs available.

■ GetDCOrg

VB Declaration   `Declare Function GetDCOrg& Lib "GDI" (ByVal hDC%)`

Description   Retrieves the location of the origin of the specified device context in screen coordinates. For example, if the DC origin is the upper left corner of a window client area, this function retrieves the position of that corner on the screen in screen pixel coordinates.

Use with VB   No problem.

Parameter	Type/Description
hDC	**Integer**—Display context.

Return Value   **Long**—The low word contains the X screen coordinate, the high word contains the Y screen coordinate.

■ GetDeviceCaps

VB Declaration   `Declare Function GetDeviceCaps% Lib "GDI" (ByVal hDC%,ByVal nIndex%)`

Description   Retrieves information regarding the capabilities of the device for the specified device context.

Use with VB   No problem.

Parameter	Type/Description
hDC	**Integer**—Device context for the device for which information is requested.
nIndex	**Integer**—Specifies the type of information to retrieve based on constants shown in Table 6.14.

Return Value   Refer to Table 6.14.

Table 6.14   **GetDeviceCaps Index Table**

Constant	Information Returned
DRIVERVERSION	Device driver version.
TECHNOLOGY	One of the following constants:
	DT_PLOTTER: Plotter. **DT_RASDISPLAY**: Raster display. **DT_RASPRINTER**: Raster printer. **DT_RASCAMERA**: Raster camera. **DT_CHARSTREAM**: Character stream. **DT_METAFILE**: Metafile. **DT_DISPFILE**: Display file.
HORZSIZE	Display width in millimeters.
VERTSIZE	Display height in millimeters.
HORZRES	Display width in pixels.
VERTRES	Display height in pixels.
LOGPIXELSX	Pixels/logical inch (horizontal).
LOGPIXELSY	Pixels/logical inch (vertical).
BITSPIXEL	Bits/pixel (on each color plane).
PLANES	Number of color planes.
NUMBRUSHES	Number of built-in device brushes.
NUMPENS	Number of built-in device pens.

Table 6.14   **GetDeviceCaps Index Table (Continued)**

Constant	Information Returned
NUMMARKERS	Number of built-in device markers.
NUMFONTS	Number of built-in device fonts.
NUMCOLORS	Entries in the device color table.
ASPECTX	Width of device pixel (see ASPECTXY).
ASPECTY	Height of device pixel (see ASPECTXY).
ASPECTXY	Diagonal size of device pixel. These values are relative to each other such that the $((ASPECTX^2)+(ASPECTY^2))^{.5} = ASPECTXY$.
PDEVICESIZE	Size of PDEVICE internal structure.
CLIPCAPS	One of the following constants: **CP_NONE**: Device has no built in clipping. **CP_RECTANGLE**: Device can clip to rectangles. **CP_REGION**: Device can clip to regions.
SIZEPALETTE	Entries in the system palette (see **RASTERCAPS RC_PALETTE** flag).
NUMRESERVED	Reserved entries in the system palette.
COLORRES	Color resolution in bits/pixel (see **RASTERCAPS RC_PALETTE** flag).
RASTERCAPS	A flag made up of the following values: **RC_BANDING:** Device supports banding. **RC_BIGFONT:** Fonts larger than 64k okay. **RC_BITBLT:** BitBlt is supported. **RC_BITMAP64K:** Bitmaps larger than 64k okay. **RC_DI_BITMAP: SetDIBits** and **GetDIBits** functions are supported. **RC_DIBTODEV: SetDIBitsToDevice** supported. **RC_FLOODFILL: Floodfill** API function is supported. **RC_NONE:** No raster operations supported. **RC_PALETTE:** Palette-based device. **RC_SAVEBITMAP:** Can save bitmaps. **RC_SCALING:** Scaling is built-in. **RC_STRETCHBLT: StretchBlt** supported. **RC_STRETCHDIB: StretchDIBits** supported.
CURVECAPS	A flag describing built-in curve generation capabilities. Refer to the **CC_xxx** constants in file APICONST.TXT for a complete list.
LINECAPS	A flag describing built-in line generation capabilities. Refer to the **LC_xxx** constants in file APICONST.TXT for a complete list.
POLYGONCAPS	A flag describing built-in polygon generation capabilities. Refer to the **PC_xxx** constants in file APICONST.TXT for a complete list.

Table 6.14   **GetDeviceCaps Index Table (Continued)**

Constant	Information Returned
TEXTCAPS	A flag made up of the following values: **TC_OP_CHARACTER**: Fonts can be placed in any location. **TC_OP_STROKE**: Device can omit any stroke on a built-in font. **TC_CP_STROKE**: Built-in fonts can be clipped at any pixel. **TC_CR_90**: Characters can be rotated 90 degrees. **TC_CR_ANY**: Character rotation supported. **TC_SF_X_YINDEP**: Separate X and Y scaling of characters is supported. **TC_SA_DOUBLE**: Built-in fonts may be doubled in size. **TC_SA_INTEGER**: Built-in fonts may be scaled by integer multipliers. **TC_SA_CONTIN**: Built-in fonts may be scaled continuously. **TC_EA_DOUBLE**: Device can create bold fonts. **TC_IA_ABLE**: Device can create italic fonts. **TC_UA_ABLE**: Device can underline fonts. **TC_SO_ABLE**: Device can strikeout fonts. **TC_RA_ABLE**: Supports raster fonts. **TC_VA_ABLE**: Supports vector fonts.

■ GetMapMode

VB Declaration   `Declare Function GetMapMode% Lib "GDI" (ByVal hDC%)`

Description   Retrieves the mapping mode for the specified device context.

Use with VB   Refer to "Scaling and Coordinate Systems," earlier in this chapter.

Parameter	Type/Description
hDC	Integer—Handle to the device context to check.

Return Value   **Integer**—The current mapping mode for the device context. Refer to the **SetMapMode** function for a description of mapping modes.

■ GetRgnBox

VB Declaration   `Declare Function GetRgnBox% Lib "GDI" (ByVal hRgn%, lpRect As RECT)`

Description   Retrieves the smallest rectangle that completely contains the specified region.

Use with VB   No problem.

Parameter	Type/Description
hRgn	Integer—Handle to a region.
lpRect	RECT—Rectangle structure to load with a rectangle that completely contains the specified region.

Return Value   See function **ExcludeClipRect** for return values.

■ GetUpdateRgn

VB Declaration   `Declare Function GetUpdateRgn% Lib "User" (ByVal hWnd%,ByVal hRgn%, ByVal ⇔`
`fErase%)`

Description   Determines the update region of the specified window. This is the region that is currently invalid
and needs to be updated.

Use with VB   No problem.

Parameter	Type/Description
hWnd	**Integer**—Handle of window for which to determine the update region.
hRgn	**Integer**—Handle to a region to load with the update region for window **hWnd**.
fErase	**Integer**—TRUE (nonzero) to specify that the window background should be erased and parts of the window outside of the client area should be redrawn.

Return Value   See function **ExcludeClipRect** for return values.

■ GetViewportExt

VB Declaration   `Declare Function GetViewportExt& Lib "GDI" (ByVal hDC%)`

Description   Retrieves the extents of the device context's viewport.

Use with VB   Refer to "Scaling and Coordinate Systems," earlier in this chapter.

Parameter	Type/Description
hDC	**Integer**—Handle to a device context.

Return Value   **Long**—Low word contains the horizontal extent, high word contains the vertical extent of the
DC viewport. Extents are specified in device units.

Comments   Refer to "Windows and Viewpoints—Extents and Origins," earlier in this chapter.

■ GetViewportExtEx

VB Declaration   `Declare Function GetViewportExtEx% Lib "GDI" (ByVal hDC%,lpSize As SIZEAPI)`

Description   Retrieves the extents of the device context's viewport.

Use with VB   Refer to "Scaling and Coordinate Systems," earlier in this chapter.

Parameter	Type/Description
hDC	**Integer**—Handle to a device context.
lpSize	**SIZEAPI**—SIZEAPI structure to load with the horizontal and vertical extents of the DC viewport in device units.

Return Value   **Integer**—TRUE (nonzero) on success, zero otherwise.

Comments   Refer to "Windows and Viewpoints—Extents and Origins," earlier in this chapter.

■ GetViewportOrg

VB Declaration   `Declare Function GetViewportOrg& Lib "GDI" (ByVal hDC%)`

Description   Retrieves the origin of the device context's viewport.

Use with VB   Refer to "Scaling and Coordinate Systems," earlier in this chapter.

Parameter	Type/Description
hDC	**Integer**—Handle to a device context.

Return Value   **Long**—Low word contains the horizontal origin, high word contains the vertical origin of the DC viewport. Results are in device coordinates.

Comments   Refer to "Windows and Viewpoints—Extents and Origins," earlier in this chapter.

■ GetViewportOrgEx

VB Declaration   `Declare Function GetViewportOrgEx% Lib "GDI" (ByVal hDC%,lpSize As SIZEAPI)`

Description   Retrieves the origins of the device context's viewport.

Use with VB   Refer to "Scaling and Coordinate Systems," earlier in this chapter.

Parameter	Type/Description
hDC	**Integer**—Handle to a device context.
lpSize	**SIZEAPI**—SIZEAPI structure to load with the horizontal and vertical origin of the DC viewport in device coordinates.

Return Value   **Integer**—TRUE (nonzero) on success, zero otherwise.

Comments   Refer to "Windows and Viewpoints—Extents and Origins," earlier in this chapter.

■ GetWindowDC

VB Declaration   Declare Function GetWindowDC% Lib "User" (ByVal hWnd%)

Description   Retrieves a display context for the entire window specified (including borders, scroll bars, captions, menus, and so on).

Use with VB   Works, but is not recommended.

Parameter	Type/Description
hWnd	**Integer**—Handle of a window for which to retrieve a device context.

Return Value   **Integer**—Device context for the window, zero on error.

■ GetWindowExt

VB Declaration   Declare Function GetWindowExt& Lib "GDI" (ByVal hDC%)

Description   Retrieves the window extents of the specified device context.

Use with VB   Refer to "Scaling and Coordinate Systems," earlier in this chapter.

Parameter	Type/Description
hDC	**Integer**—Handle to a device context.

Return Value   **Long**—Low word contains the horizontal extent, high word contains the vertical extent of the DC window. Extents are specified in logical units.

Comments   Refer to "Windows and Viewpoints—Extents and Origins," earlier in this chapter.

■ GetWindowExtEx

VB Declaration   Declare Function GetWindowExtEx% Lib "GDI" (ByVal hDC%,lpSize As SIZEAPI)

Description   Retrieves the window extents of the specified device context.

Use with VB   Refer to "Scaling and Coordinate Systems," earlier in this chapter.

Parameter	Type/Description
hDC	**Integer**—Handle to a device context.
lpSize	**SIZEAPI**—SIZEAPI structure to load with the horizontal and vertical extents of the DC window in logical units.

Return Value   **Integer**—TRUE (nonzero) on success, zero otherwise.

Comments   Refer to "Windows and Viewpoints—Extents and Origins," earlier in this chapter.

■ GetWindowOrg

VB Declaration   `Declare Function GetWindowOrg& Lib "GDI" (ByVal hDC%)`

Description   Retrieves the window origin for the specified device context.

Use with VB   Refer to "Scaling and Coordinate Systems," earlier in this chapter.

Parameter	Type/Description
hDC	**Integer**—Handle to a device context.

Return Value   **Long**—Low word contains the horizontal origin, high word contains the vertical origin of the DC window. Results are in logical coordinates.

Comments   Refer to "Windows and Viewpoints—Extents and Origins," earlier in this chapter.

■ GetWindowOrgEx

VB Declaration   `Declare Function GetWindowOrgEx% Lib "GDI" (ByVal hDC%,lpSize As SIZEAPI)`

Description   Retrieves the window origin for the specified device context.

Use with VB   Refer to "Scaling and Coordinate Systems," earlier in this chapter.

Parameter	Type/Description
hDC	**Integer**—Handle to a device context.
lpSize	**SIZEAPI**—**SIZEAPI** structure to load with the horizontal and vertical origin of the DC window in logical coordinates.

Return Value   **Integer**—TRUE (nonzero) on success, zero otherwise.

Comments   Refer to "Windows and Viewpoints—Extents and Origins," earlier in this chapter.

■ IntersectClipRect

VB Declaration   `Declare Function IntersectClipRect% Lib "GDI" (ByVal hDC%, ByVal X1%, ByVal ⇔ Y1%, ByVal X2%, ByVal Y2%)`

Description   Specifies a new clipping region for the specified display context from the intersection of the current clipping region and the rectangle defined by points X1,Y1 and X2,Y2.

Use with VB   Refer to "Clipping, Regions, and Other Device Context Control Functions," earlier in this chapter.

Parameter	Type/Description
hDC	**Integer**—Device context to modify.
X1, Y1	**Integers**—X,Y coordinates describing the upper left corner of the rectangle in logical coordinates.

Parameter	Type/Description
X2, Y2	**Integers**—X,Y coordinates describing the lower right corner of the rectangle in logical coordinates.

Return Value   See function **ExcludeClipRect** for return values.

■ InvalidateRgn

VB Declaration   `Declare Sub InvalidateRgn Lib "User" (ByVal hWnd%, ByVal hRgn%, ByVal bErase%)`

Description   Invalidates the specified region in a window, adding it to the update region of the window so that it may be redrawn in due course.

Use with VB   No problem.

Parameter	Type/Description
hWnd	**Integer**—Handle of window to invalidate.
hRgn	**Integer**—Handle to region defining the area to invalidate. The region is specified in window client coordinates.
fErase	**Integer**—TRUE (nonzero) if the region is to be erased before being updated.

Comments   If **fErase** is TRUE, the entire update area will be erased before update, not just the specified region.

■ LPtoDP

VB Declaration   `Declare Function LPtoDP% Lib "GDI" (ByVal hDC%, lpPointsAs POINTAPI, ByVal ⇔ nCount%)`

Description   Converts an array of points from logical coordinates in the specified display context to device coordinates.

Use with VB   Refer to "Scaling and Coordinate Systems," earlier in this chapter.

Parameter	Type/Description
hDC	**Integer**—Handle to a device context that defines a logical coordinate system.
lpPoints	**POINTAPI**—The first entry in an array of one or more **POINTAPI** structures containing points in logical coordinates. Each entry will be converted to device coordinates.
nCount	**Integer**—The number of entries in the **lpPoints** array.

Return Value   **Integer**— TRUE (nonzero) on success, zero otherwise.

■ OffsetClipRgn

VB Declaration   Declare Function OffsetClipRgn% Lib "GDI" (ByVal hDC%,ByVal X%, ByVal Y%)

Description   Moves the clipping region of the specified device context by the amount specified.

Use with VB   No problem.

Parameter	Type/Description
hDC	**Integer**—Device context.
X	**Integer**—Horizontal offset in logical coordinates.
Y	**Integer**—Vertical offset in logical coordinates.

Return Value   See function **ExcludeClipRect** for return values.

■ OffsetRgn

VB Declaration   Declare Function OffsetRgn% Lib "GDI" (ByVal hRgn%, ByVal X%, ByVal Y%)

Description   Moves the specified region by the offset specified.

Use with VB   No problem.

Parameter	Type/Description
hRgn	**Integer**—Handle to a region.
X	**Integer**—Horizontal offset in logical coordinates.
Y	**Integer**—Vertical offset in logical coordinates.

Return Value   See function **ExcludeClipRect** for return values.

■ OffsetViewportOrg

VB Declaration   Declare Function OffsetViewportOrg& Lib "GDI" (ByVal hDC%, ByVal X%, ByVal Y%)

Description   Offsets the origin of the device context's viewport.

Use with VB   Refer to "Scaling and Coordinate Systems," earlier in this chapter.

Parameter	Type/Description
hDC	**Integer**—Handle to a device context.
X,Y	**Integer**—Horizontal and vertical offset to add to the viewport origins.

Return Value   **Long**—The previous viewport origins in device coordinates. The low word contains the horizontal origin and the high word contains the vertical origin of the DC viewport.

Comments   Refer to the "Windows and Viewpoints—Extents and Origins," earlier in this chapter.

■ OffsetViewportOrgEx

VB Declaration   `Declare Function SetViewportOrgEx% Lib "GDI" (ByVal hDC%,ByVal X%, ByVal ⇔`
                       `Y%, lpPoint As POINTAPI)`

Description   Offsets the origin of the device context's viewport.

Use with VB   Refer to "Scaling and Coordinate Systems," earlier in this chapter.

Parameter	Type/Description
hDC	**Integer**—Handle to a device context.
X,Y	**Integer**—Horizontal and vertical offset to add to the viewport origins in device coordinates.
lpPoint	**POINTAPI—POINTAPI** structure to load with the previous horizontal and vertical origins of the DC viewport in device coordinates.

Return Value   **Integer**—TRUE (nonzero) on success, zero otherwise.

Comments   Refer to "Windows and Viewpoints—Extents and Origins," earlier in this chapter.

■ OffsetWindowOrg

VB Declaration   `Declare Function OffsetWindowOrg& Lib "GDI" (ByValh DC%, ByVal X%, ByVal Y%)`

Description   Offsets the window origin for the specified device context.

Use with VB   Refer to "Scaling and Coordinate Systems," earlier in this chapter.

Parameter	Type/Description
hDC	**Integer**—Handle to a device context.
X,Y	**Integer**—Horizontal and vertical offset to add to the window origins.

Return Value   **Long**—The previous window origins in logical coordinates. The low word contains the horizontal origin and the high word contains the vertical origin.

Comments   Refer to "Windows and Viewpoints—Extents and Origins," earlier in this chapter.

■ OffsetWindowOrgEx

VB Declaration   `Declare Function SetWindowOrgEx% Lib "GDI" (ByVal hDC%,ByVal X%, ByVal Y%, ⇔`
                       `lpPoint As POINTAPI)`

Description   Offsets the window origin for the specified device context.

Use with VB   Refer to "Scaling and Coordinate Systems," earlier in this chapter.

Parameter	Type/Description
hDC	**Integer**—Handle to a device context.
X,Y	**Integer**—Horizontal and vertical window origins in logical coordinates.
lpPoint	**POINTAPI**—**POINTAPI** structure to load with the previous horizontal and vertical origins of the DC window in logical coordinates.

Return Value   **Integer**—TRUE (nonzero) on success, zero otherwise.

Comments   Refer to "Windows and Viewpoints—Extents and Origins," earlier in this chapter.

■ PtInRegion

VB Declaration   `Declare Function PtInRegion% Lib "GDI" (ByVal hRgn%,ByVal X%, ByVal Y%)`

Description   Determines if a point is in a specified region.

Use with VB   No problem.

Parameter	Type/Description
hRgn	**Integer**—Handle to a region.
X	**Integer**—X coordinate of a point in logical coordinates.
Y	**Integer**—Y coordinates of a point in logical coordinates.

Return Value   **Integer**—TRUE (nonzero) if the point is in the region. FALSE (zero) otherwise.

■ PtVisible

VB Declaration   `Declare Function PtVisible% Lib "GDI" (ByVal hDC%, ByVal X%, ByVal Y%)`

Description   Determines if the specified point is visible (that is, inside the clipping region of the specified display context).

Use with VB   No problem.

Parameter	Type/Description
hDC	**Integer**—Handle to a display context.
X,Y	**Integers**—The X,Y coordinates of the point to check.

Return Value   **Integer**—TRUE (non-zero) if the point is visible, FALSE otherwise.

◼ RectInRegion

VB Declaration   Declare Function RectInRegion% Lib "GDI" (ByVal hRgn%,lpRect As RECT)

Description   Determines if any part of a rectangle is in a specified region.

Use with VB   No problem.

Parameter	Type/Description
hRgn	**Integer**—Handle to a region.
lpRect	**RECT**—Rectangle structure to test against region **hRgn**.

Return Value   **Integer**—TRUE (nonzero) if all or part of the rectangle is in the region. FALSE (zero) otherwise.

◼ RectVisible

VB Declaration   Declare Function RectVisible% Lib "GDI" (ByVal hDC%,lpRect As RECT)

Description   Determines if any part of the specified rectangle is visible (that is, inside the clipping region of the specified display context).

Use with VB   No problem.

Parameter	Type/Description
hDC	**Integer**—Handle to a display context.
lpRect	**RECT**—The rectangle to test for visibility. The rectangle is specified in logical coordinates.

Return Value   **Integer**—TRUE (nonzero) if any part of the rectangle is visible, FALSE otherwise.

◼ ReleaseDC

VB Declaration   Declare Function ReleaseDC% Lib "User" (ByVal hWnd%,ByVal hDC%)

Description   Releases the specified device context that was obtained through calls to **GetDC** or **GetWindowDC**. It has no effect on class or private device contexts.

Use with VB   Refer to "Using Device Contexts with Visual Basic," earlier in this chapter.

Parameter	Type/Description
hDC	**Integer**—Handle to the display context to release.

Return Value   **Integer**—1 on success, 0 otherwise.

■ RestoreDC

VB Declaration   `Declare Function RestoreDC% Lib "GDI" (ByVal hDC%,ByVal nSavedDC%)`

Description   Restores a previously saved device context from the device context stack.

Use with VB   Refer to "Using Device Contexts with Visual Basic," earlier in this chapter.

Parameter	Type/Description
hDC	**Integer**—Handle of the device context to restore.
nSavedDC	**Integer**—ID number of the device context to restore as returned by the **SaveDC** function. Use -1 to restore the most recently saved device context.

Return Value   **Integer**—TRUE (nonzero) on success, zero on error.

Comments   If **nSavedDC** refers to a DC that is not on the top of the stack, all device contexts above **nSavedDC** on the stack are removed from the stack as well.

■ SaveDC

VB Declaration   `Declare Function SaveDC% Lib "GDI" (ByVal hDC%)`

Description   Saves the state of the specified device context on the Windows device context stack. The DC mapping mode, window and viewport scaling, clipping region, and list of selected objects are saved. This function is often used before making a temporary change to the device context. The DC attributes are restored by the **RestoreDC** function.

Use with VB   Refer to "Using Device Contexts with Visual Basic," earlier in this chapter.

Parameter	Type/Description
hDC	**Integer**—Handle of the device context to save.

Return Value   An integer identifying the device context so that it may be restored using the **RestoreDC** function. Zero on error.

Comments   The number of device contexts that may be saved is limited only by memory.

■ ScaleViewportExt

VB Declaration   `Declare Function ScaleViewportExt& Lib "GDI" (ByVal hDC%, ByVal Xnum%, ByVal ⇔ Xdenom%, ByVal Ynum%,ByVal Ydenom%)`

Description   Sets the extents of the device context's viewport.

Use with VB   Refer to "Scaling and Coordinate Systems," earlier in this chapter.

Parameter	Type/Description
hDC	**Integer**—Handle to a device context.

Parameter	Type/Description
Xnum, Ynum	**Integers**—The current X and Y extents are multiplied by these numbers.
Xdenom, Ydenom	**Integers**—The product of the current X and Y extents multiplied by **Xnum** and **Ynum** are divided by these numbers.

Return Value   **Long**—The previous viewport extents in device units. The low word contains the horizontal extent, the high word contains the vertical extent of the DC viewport.

Comments   Refer to "Using Device Contexts with Visual Basic," earlier in this chapter. Only valid in the MM_ISOTROPIC and MM_ANISOTROPIC mapping modes. In MM_ISOTROPIC mode you must set the window extents before the viewport extents.

■ ScaleViewportExtEx

VB Declaration   ```
Declare Function ScaleViewportExtEx% Lib "GDI" (ByVal hDc%, ByVal Xnum%, ByVal ⇔
Xdenom%, ByVal Ynum%, ByVal Ydenom%, lpSize As SIZEAPI
```

**Description**    Sets the extents of the device context's viewport.

**Use with VB**    Refer to "Scaling and Coordinate Systems," earlier in this chapter.

| Parameter | Type/Description |
|---|---|
| hDC | **Integer**—Handle to a device context. |
| Xnum, Ynum | **Integers**—The current X and Y extents are multiplied by these numbers. |
| Xdenom, Ydenom | **Integers**—The product of the current X and Y extents multiplied by **Xnum** and **Ynum** are divided by these numbers. |
| lpSize | **SIZEAPI**—**SIZEAPI** structure to load with the previous horizontal and vertical viewport extents. |

**Return Value**    **Integer**—True (non-zero) on sucess, zero otherwise.

**Comments**    Refer to the chapter text for an explanation of viewport and window extents and origins. Only valid in the MM_ISOTROPIC and MM_ANISOTROPIC mapping modes. In MM_ISOTROPIC mode you must set the window extents before the viewport extents.

## ■ ScaleWindowExt

**VB Declaration**    ```
Declare Function ScaleWindowExt& Lib "GDI" (ByVal hDC%,ByVal Xnum%, ByVal ⇔
Xdenom%, ByVal Ynum%, ByVal Ydenom%)
```

Description   Scales the window extents for the specified device context.

Use with VB   Refer to "Scaling and Coordinate Systems," earlier in this chapter.

Parameter	Type/Description
hDC	**Integer**—Handle to a device context.
Xnum, Ynum	**Integers**—The current X and Y extents are multiplied by these numbers.
Xdenom, Ydenom	**Integers**—The product of the current X and Y extents multiplied by **Xnum** and **Ynum** are divided by these numbers.

Return Value   **Long**—The previous window extents in logical units. The low word contains the horizontal extent, and the high word contains the vertical extent.

Comments   Refer to "Windows and Viewpoints—Extents and Origins," earlier in this chapter. Only valid in the MM_ISOTROPIC and MM_ANISOTROPIC mapping modes. In MM_ISOTROPIC mode you must set the window extents before the viewport extents.

■ ScaleWindowExtEx

VB Declaration
```
Declare Function ScaleWindowExtEx& Lib "GDI" (ByVal hDC%,ByVal nXnum%, ⇔
ByVal nXdenom%, ByVal nYnum%, ByVal nYdenom%, lpSize As SIZEAPI)
```

Description   Scales the window extents for the specified device context.

Use with VB   Refer to "Scaling and Coordinate Systems," earlier in this chapter.

Parameter	Type/Description
hDC	**Integer**—Handle to a device context.
nXnum, nYnum	**Integers**—The current X and Y extents are multiplied by these numbers.
nXdenom, nYdenom	**Integers**—The product of the current X and Y extents multiplied by **nXnum** and **nYnum** are divided by these numbers.
lpSize	**SIZEAPI**—SIZEAPI structure to load with the previous horizontal and vertical window extents of the DC viewport in logical units.

Return Value   **Integer**—TRUE (nonzero) on success, zero otherwise.

Comments   Refer to "Windows and Viewpoints—Extents and Origins," earlier in this chapter. Only valid in the MM_ISOTROPIC and MM_ANISOTROPIC mapping modes. In MM_ISOTROPIC mode you must set the window extents before the viewport extents.

■ ScrollDC

VB Declaration
```
Declare Function ScrollDC% Lib "User" (ByVal hDC%, ByVal dx%, ByVal dy%, ⇔
lprcScroll As RECT, lprcClip As RECT, ByVal hRgnUpdate%, lprcUpdate As RECT)
```

Description   Scrolls a rectangle in a window represented by a device context horizontally and/or vertically.

Use with VB	Refer to "Scaling and Coordinate Systems," earlier in this chapter.

Parameter	Type/Description
hDC	**Integer**—Handle to a device context.
dx	**Integer**—Horizontal units to scroll.
dy	**Integer**—Vertical units to scroll.
lprcScroll	**RECT**—The rectangle to scroll.
lprcClip	**RECT**—A rectangle that specifies the clipping rectangle. Scrolling only occurs within this rectangle.
hRgnUpdate	**Integer**—This region will be set to the area uncovered by the scrolling operation in the client coordinate system. May be zero, in which case the update region will not be set.
lprcUpdate	**RECT**—This rectangle will be set to the area uncovered by the scrolling operation in the client coordinate system. May be zero (this requires that the VB declaration be modified to accept a long parameter as **lprcUpdate**).

Return Value **Integer**—TRUE (nonzero) on success, zero on error.

Comments If both **hrgnUpdate** and **lprcUpdate** are NULL, Windows will not compute the update region for this DC.

■ SelectClipRgn

VB Declaration `Declare Function SelectClipRgn% Lib "GDI" (ByVal hDC%,ByVal hRgn%)`

Description Selects a new clipping region for the specified device context.

Use with VB Refer to "Clipping, Regions, and Other Device Context Control Functions," earlier in this chapter.

Parameter	Type/Description
hDC	**Integer**—Display context for which to set a new clipping region.
hRgn	**Integer**—Handle to a clipping region to set for the display context. This region uses device coordinates.

Return Value See function **ExcludeClipRect** for return values.

Comments This function makes a copy of the specified region, thus the same region may be used on multiple device contexts or deleted without affecting the clipping region on each display context. Some printers have different coordinate systems for text and graphics. In these cases, use the coordinate system that provides the higher resolution, for example, a dot matrix printer that uses dithering. The text resolution will be higher than the graphics resolution. In this case the text coordinate system should be used.

■ SetBoundsRect

VB Declaration   `Declare Function SetBoundsRect% Lib "GDI" (ByVal hDC%,lprcBounds As RECT, ⇔`
                    `ByVal flags%)`

Description   Sets the bounding rectangle for the specified device context. Each device context has a bounding
                    rectangle that may be used by the programmer to accumulate information representing the
                    bounds of the current image.

Use with VB   No known problems.

Parameter	Type/Description
hDC	**Integer**—Device context for the bounding rectangle.
lprcBounds	**RECT**—Rectangle from which to set the bounding rectangle.
flags%	**Integer**—Flag integer that may be a combination of the following constants: **DCB_ACCUMULATE**: The new bounding rectangle is the union of the current bounding rectangle and **lprcBounds**. **DCB_DISABLE**: Turns off bounds accumulation. This is the default. **DCB_ENABLE**: Turns on bounds accumulation.

Return Value   **Integer**—A flag with bits set based on the following constants:
                    DCB_ACCUMULATE: The bounding rectangle is not empty. This bit is always set after calling
                    this function.
                    DCB_DISABLE: Bounds accumulation is disabled.
                    DCB_ENABLE: Bounds accumulation is enabled.

■ SetMapMode

VB Declaration   `Declare Function SetMapMode% Lib "GDI" (ByVal hDC%, ByVal nMapMode%)`

Description   Sets the mapping mode for the specified device context.

Use with VB   Refer to "Scaling and Coordinate Systems," earlier in this chapter. Changing the mapping mode
                    without the proper precautions will lead to incorrect drawing on the part of VB drawing functions.

Parameter	Type/Description
hDC	**Integer**—Handle to the device context to change.
nMapMode	**Integer**—One of the following constants: **MM_ANISOTROPIC**: Viewport and window extents may be completely arbitrary. **MM_HIENGLISH**: Logical units are 0.001 inch. Origin is the lower left corner. **MM_HIMETRIC**: Logical units are 0.01 millimeter. Origin is the lower left corner. **MM_ISOTROPIC**: Viewport and window extents are arbitrary except that the X and Y logical units are the same size. **MM_LOENGLISH**: Logical units are 0.01 inch. Origin is the lower left corner. **MM_HIMETRIC**: Logical units are 0.1 millimeter. Origin is the lower left corner. **MM_TEXT**: Logical units are one pixel. **MM_TWIPS**: Logical units are one twip (1/1440 inch). Origin is the lower left corner.

Return Value   **Integer**—The previous mapping mode for the device context.

Comments   Refer to "Scaling and Coordinate Systems," earlier in this chapter.

■ SetRectRgn

VB Declaration   `Declare Sub SetRectRgn Lib "GDI" (ByVal hRgn%, ByVal X1%,ByVal Y1%, ByVal ⇔`
`X2%, ByVal Y2%)`

Description   Sets the specified region to a rectangle described by the points X1,Y1 and X2,Y2.

Use with VB   No problem.

Parameter	Type/Description
hRgn	**Integer**—This region is set to the specified rectangle.
X1, Y1	**Integers**—X,Y coordinates describing the upper left corner of the rectangle.
X2, Y2	**Integers**—X,Y coordinates describing the lower right corner of the rectangle.

Comments   This function is similar to **CreateRectRgn** except that it sets an existing region rather than creating a new region.

■ SetViewportExt

VB Declaration   `Declare Function SetViewportExt& Lib "GDI" (ByVal hDC%, ByVal X%, ByVal Y%)`

Description   Sets the extents of the device context's viewport.

Use with VB   Refer to "Scaling and Coordinate Systems," earlier in this chapter.

Parameter	Type/Description
hDC	**Integer**—Handle to a device context.
X,Y	**Integer**—Horizontal and vertical viewport extents.

Return Value   **Long**—The previous viewport extents in device units. The low word contains the horizontal extent, the high word contains the vertical extent of the DC viewport.

Comments   Refer to "Windows and Viewpoints—Extents and Origins," earlier in this chapter. Only valid in the MM_ISOTROPIC and MM_ANISOTROPIC mapping modes. In MM_ISOTROPIC mode you must set the window extents before the viewport extents.

■ SetViewportExtEx

VB Declaration   `Declare Function SetViewportExtEx% Lib "GDI" (ByVal hDC%,ByVal X%, ByVal ⇔`
`Y%, lpSize As SIZEAPI)`

Description	Sets the extents of the device context's viewport.
Use with VB	Refer to "Scaling and Coordinate Systems," earlier in this chapter.

Parameter	Type/Description
hDC	**Integer**—Handle to a device context.
X,Y	**Integer**—Horizontal and vertical viewport extents.
lpSize	**SIZEAPI**—**SIZEAPI** structure to load with the previous horizontal and vertical extents of the DC viewport in device units.

Return Value	**Integer**—TRUE (nonzero) on success, zero otherwise.
Comments	Refer to "Windows and Viewpoints—Extents and Origins," earlier in this chapter. Only valid in the MM_ISOTROPIC and MM_ANISOTROPIC mapping modes. In MM_ISOTROPIC mode you must set the window extents before the viewport extents.

■ SetViewportOrg

VB Declaration	`Declare Function SetViewportOrg& Lib "GDI" (ByVal hDC%, ByVal X%, ByVal Y%)`
Description	Sets the origin of the device context's viewport.
Use with VB	Refer to "Scaling and Coordinate Systems," earlier in this chapter.

Parameter	Type/Description
hDC	**Integer**—Handle to a device context.
X,Y	**Integer**—Horizontal and vertical viewport origins in device units.

Return Value	**Long**—The previous viewport origins in device units. The low word contains the horizontal origin and the high word contains the vertical origin of the DC viewport.
Comments	Refer to "Windows and Viewpoints—Extents and Origins," earlier in this chapter.

■ SetViewportOrgEx

VB Declaration	`Declare Function SetViewportOrgEx% Lib "GDI" (ByVal hDC%,ByVal X%, ByVal ⇔` `Y%, lpSize As SIZEAPI)`
Description	Sets the origin of the device context's viewport.
Use with VB	Refer to "Scaling and Coordinate Systems," earlier in this chapter.

Parameter	Type/Description
hDC	**Integer**—Handle to a device context.
X,Y	**Integer**—Horizontal and vertical viewport origins in device coordinates.

Parameter	Type/Description
lpSize	**SIZEAPI**—**SIZEAPI** structure to load with the previous horizontal and vertical origins of the DC viewport in device coordinates.

Return Value   **Integer**—TRUE (nonzero) on success, zero otherwise.

Comments   Refer to "Windows and Viewpoints—Extents and Origins," earlier in this chapter.

■ SetWindowExt

VB Declaration   `Declare Function SetWindowExt& Lib "GDI" (ByVal hDC%, ByVal X%, ByVal Y%)`

Description   Sets the window extents for the specified device context.

Use with VB   Refer to "Scaling and Coordinate Systems," earlier in this chapter.

Parameter	Type/Description
hDC	**Integer**—Handle to a device context.
X,Y	**Integer**—Horizontal and vertical window extents.

Return Value   **Long**—The previous window extents in logical units. The low word contains the horizontal extent, and the high word contains the vertical extent.

Comments   Refer to "Windows and Viewpoints—Extents and Origins," earlier in this chapter. Only valid in the MM_ISOTROPIC and MM_ANISOTROPIC mapping modes. In MM_ISOTROPIC mode you must set the window extents before the viewport extents.

■ SetWindowExtEx

VB Declaration   `Declare Function SetWindowExtEx% Lib "GDI" (ByVal hDC%,ByVal X%, ByVal Y%, ⇔`
`lpSize As SIZEAPI)`

Description   Sets the window extents for the specified device context.

Use with VB   Refer to "Scaling and Coordinate Systems," earlier in this chapter.

Parameter	Type/Description
hDC	**Integer**—Handle to a device context.
X,Y	**Integer**—Horizontal and vertical window extents.
lpSize	**SIZEAPI**—**SIZEAPI** structure to load with the previous horizontal and vertical window extents of the DC viewport in logical units.

Return Value   **Integer**—TRUE (nonzero) on success, zero otherwise.

Comments   Refer to "Windows and Viewpoints—Extents and Origins," earlier in this chapter. Only valid in the MM_ISOTROPIC and MM_ANISOTROPIC mapping modes. In MM_ISOTROPIC mode you must set the window extents before the viewport extents.

■ SetWindowOrg

VB Declaration `Declare Function SetWindowOrg& Lib "GDI" (ByVal hDC%,ByVal X%, ByVal Y%)`

Description Sets the window origin for the specified device context.

Use with VB Refer to "Scaling and Coordinate Systems," earlier in this chapter.

Parameter	Type/Description
hDC	**Integer**—Handle to a device context.
X,Y	**Integer**—Horizontal and vertical window origins in logical coordinates.

Return Value **Long**—The previous window origins in logical coordinates. The low word contains the horizontal origin and the high word contains the vertical origin.

Comments Refer to "Windows and Viewpoints—Extents and Origins," earlier in this chapter.

■ SetWindowOrgEx

VB Declaration `Declare Function SetWindowOrgEx% Lib "GDI" (ByVal hDC%,ByVal X%, ByVal Y%,` ⇔
`lpSize As SIZEAPI)`

Description Sets the window origin for the specified device context.

Use with VB Refer to "Scaling and Coordinate Systems," earlier in this chapter.

Parameter	Type/Description
hDC	**Integer**—Handle to a device context.
X,Y	**Integer**—Horizontal and vertical window origins in logical coordinates.
lpSize	**SIZEAPI**—**SIZEAPI** structure to load with the previous horizontal and vertical origins of the DC window in logical coordinates.

Return Value **Integer**—TRUE (nonzero) on success, zero otherwise.

Comments Refer to "Windows and Viewpoints—Extents and Origins," earlier in this chapter.

■ ValidateRgn

VB Declaration `Declare Sub ValidateRgn Lib "User" (ByVal hWnd%, ByVal hRgn%)`

Description Validates the specified region in a window, removing it from the update region.

Use with VB   No problem.

Parameter	Type/Description
hWnd	**Integer**—Handle of window to invalidate.
hRgn	**Integer**—Handle to region defining the area to validate. The region is specified in window client coordinates.

CHAPTER

7

Drawing Functions

THIS CHAPTER COVERS THE WINDOWS API FUNCTIONS THAT CONTROL graphic output. The creation and use of drawing objects such as pens and brushes are discussed, along with their use with Visual Basic. An example program, QuikDraw, illustrates the use of many of these functions and demonstrates the ability of Windows to record sequences of graphics operations in metafiles.

Overview of Graphic Output

The process of drawing in Windows involves a number of different objects:

- *Device:* This can be a display window, a printer page, or any other output device for which a device context can be obtained.

- *Device context:* This determines all aspects of drawing onto a device. The drawing objects listed below are selected into a device context before drawing. The DC also specifies the coordinate system to use when drawing.

- *Pen:* A pen is an object that defines the way that lines are drawn. Pens have several attributes including width, color, and dashing.

- *Brush:* A brush is an object that defines the way that areas are filled. Brushes may be solid, hatched, or defined using a bitmap pattern.

- *Drawing attributes:* These define how the line or area being drawn on by the pen or brush is combined with the existing image on a device.

- *Clipping area:* This defines the area in the device context that can actually be drawn on. Clipping is discussed in Chapter 6.

- *Color palette:* This GDI object defines the colors that are visible on a window. The subject is discussed further in Chapter 16.

Figure 7.1 illustrates the process of drawing onto a device.

GDI Drawing Objects

A GDI drawing object is an internal Windows object that defines an aspect of the drawing operation. In this chapter, the focus is on pens and brushes, though much of the discussion also applies to GDI objects such as regions and metafiles. These objects are "owned" by GDI, the Graphical Device Interface portion of the Windows system. The issue of ownership is important here, as it dictates a number of rules for using these objects.

Figure 7.1

Overview of drawing under Windows

Drawing Objects and Attributes   **Description**

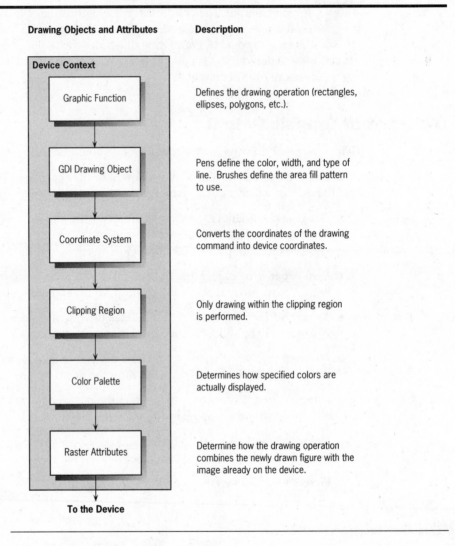

Defines the drawing operation (rectangles, ellipses, polygons, etc.).

Pens define the color, width, and type of line. Brushes define the area fill pattern to use.

Converts the coordinates of the drawing command into device coordinates.

Only drawing within the clipping region is performed.

Determines how specified colors are actually displayed.

Determine how the drawing operation combines the newly drawn figure with the image already on the device.

Creation of GDI Drawing Objects

Pens and brushes are obtained using one of the functions listed in Table 7.1.

Selection and Deletion Rules for GDI Objects

In order to use a pen or a brush it is necessary to select it into a device context using the **SelectObject** function. A device context may have only one object of each type selected at a time. When an object is selected into a DC, the **SelectObject** function returns as a result the object of that type that was previously selected into the device context. For example, when a pen is selected into a DC, a handle to the previously selected pen is returned.

Table 7.1   **Pen and Brush Creation Functions**

Function	Description
CreateBrushIndirect	Creates a brush using a **LOGBRUSH** data structure.
CreateDIBPatternBrush	Creates a brush based on a device-independent bitmap pattern.
CreateHatchBrush	Creates a hatched brush.
CreatePatternBrush	Creates a brush based on a bitmap pattern.
CreatePen	Creates a pen.
CreatePenIndirect	Creates a pen based on a **LOGPEN** data structure.
CreateSolidBrush	Creates a solid color brush.
GetStockObject	Retrieves a system pen or brush.

This handle should be saved so that it may be restored into the device context before the DC is deleted. *Always restore the original GDI objects into a device context before that context is deleted.*

Pens and brushes are owned by GDI. This means that the data for the object is kept in the internal Windows resource heaps. Since they are owned by Windows and not the application, these objects are not automatically freed by Windows when an application closes. It is therefore important that your application delete any GDI objects that it creates before it exits in order to free the resources for use by other applications. *Never delete a GDI object that is selected into a device context!*

The **GetStockObject** function retrieves a stock system object. Objects returned by this function must not be deleted with the **DeleteObject** function.

Table 7.2 shows the API functions used when working with GDI objects.

Table 7.2   **GDI Object Control**

Function	Description
DeleteObject	Deletes a GDI object.
EnumObjects	Enumerates the objects available to a device context.

Table 7.2   **GDI Object Control (Continued)**

Function	Description
GetObjectAPI	Retrieves information about a GDI object.
IsGDIObject	Determines if a handle is not a GDI object.
SelectObject	Selects a GDI object into a device context.

Pens

A pen is a GDI object that defines how lines are drawn. Pens are selected into device context using the **SelectObject** function. A line has three attributes: color, width, and style.

A pen's color specifies the desired RGB color for lines. The actual color used will depend on the device. GDI will always choose the closest color that the device can actually render.

The width attribute specifies the width of a line in logical coordinates.

Pens can be created with a number of styles including solid, invisible, and several varieties of dashed and dotted lines. Only the solid and invisible styles may be used with line widths greater than one. Table 7.1 describes the API functions used to create pens.

Brushes

A brush is a GDI object that defines how areas are filled. A brush is an 8×8 pixel area that is painted on the area that is to be filled.

Attributes

Brush attributes define the contents of the 8×8 pixel area defined by the brush. In the case of pattern brushes, the area contains a user-defined bitmap. For solid brushes, the entire area is a single solid color. For hatched brushes, a bitmap is defined such that a cross-hatched pattern is created when the area is filled.

A brush's color specifies the desired RGB color for the brush. The actual color used will depend on the device. GDI will always choose the closest color that the device can actually render.

Table 7.1 describes the API functions used to create brushes.

Origins

A brush, as mentioned earlier, represents an 8×8 pixel area used in filling areas on a display device. Imagine a brush that consists of a horizontal line at the top of the brush area, and consider what happens when you fill a window using that brush. If the brush begins filling from the upper-left corner of a window, the window will be filled with horizontal lines eight pixels apart where the first line is at the top of the window. It doesn't matter where you start painting on the window—the horizontal lines will always match up. This is because the brush origin is aligned with the top of the window. But what if you wanted the horizontal lines to start at the second or third pixel from the top of the window? This might be necessary if a window has been scrolled by a number of pixels that is not divisible by 8 as shown in Figure 7.2. Figure 7.2 shows that the pattern painted with the brush in the area uncovered after a scroll will not match the scrolled area.

You could create a new brush where the vertical line starts at the second or third row in the 8×8 area, but an easier solution is to offset the origin of the brush to start at the desired row. This is a two-part process. First, the origin of the brush is changed using the **SetBrushOrg** or **SetBrushOrgEx** function. Next, the **UnrealizeObject** function is used on the brush. This function tells Windows to delete any existing physical representation of the brush. This is necessary because Windows actually uses the logical brush object to create a physical brush that is used internally to do the actual drawing.

The exact process for aligning brushes is as follows:

1. Be sure that the brush to be realigned is not selected into a device context. If necessary, select a different brush into the device context temporarily.

2. Use the **SetBrushOrg** function to set the new brush origin.

3. Use the **UnrealizeObject** function to realign the brush. This informs Windows that it should re-create the internal bitmap based on the new origin when the brush is selected into a device context.

4. Select the realigned brush into the device context.

Do not change the origin of the system stock brushes (those obtained by the **GetStockObject** function).

Table 7.3 shows the API functions used when working with brushes.

Table 7.3 **API Brush Origin Functions**

Function	Description
GetBrushOrg GetBrushOrgEx	Retrieves the origin of a brush.
SetBrushOrg	Realigns the origin of a brush.
UnrealizeObject	Forces Windows to re-create the internal brush bitmap when a brush is selected into a DC. Also used with palettes (see Chapter 16).

Figure 7.2
Aligning brush origins

Illustration of Brush Alignment

A window is filled with a horizontally hatched brush.

The window is scrolled up by a number of pixels that is not divisible by 8. The shaded area indicates the area of the window that was uncovered.

Painting into the uncovered area with the current hatched brush shows how the newly filled area is not aligned with the scrolled area. The brush must be realigned in order to obtain the correct pattern.

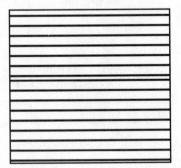

GDI Objects and Visual Basic

As mentioned in Chapter 6, Visual Basic forms and picture controls use private device contexts. The pen and brush selected into that device depend on the various properties of the VB control. These include the **FillColor**, **FillStyle**, **DrawStyle**, and **DrawWidth** properties.

It is important to restore these original objects into the device context if other pens or brushes are used during API drawing operations.

Drawing Attributes

A device context also specifies a number of drawing attributes. These define the way that brushes and pens interact with the current contents of the window or device surface. Table 7.4 lists the API functions that are used to control drawing attributes.

Table 7.4   **Drawing Attribute Control Functions**

Function	Description
GetBkColor	Retrieves the current background color.
GetBkMode	Retrieves the current background mode.
GetCurrentPosition GetCurrentPositionEx	Retrieves the current pen position.
GetNearestColor	Given a color, obtains the nearest color that can actually be rendered by a device.
GetPolyFillMode	Retrieves the current polygon filling mode. See **SetPolyFillMode** in the function reference section of this chapter for details.
GetROP2	Retrieves the current line raster operation mode.
MoveTo, MoveToEx	Sets the pen position.
SetBkColor	Sets the background color.
SetBkMode	Sets the background mode.
SetPolyFillMode	Sets the current polygon filling mode. Refer to the description of this function in the function reference section of this chapter for details.
SetROP2	Sets the line raster operation mode.

Line Raster Operations

Normally, when you think of drawing with a pen, you assume that the pen color is simply drawn on the display or device. Windows actually supports 16 different line drawing modes that define how a line is combined with information already present on the display. These modes are called *line raster operations* (also known as raster-ops, binary raster operations, or ROP2 mode) and are referred to in Visual Basic as the drawing mode. The ROP2 raster operations are identical to the VB **DrawMode** property.

One commonly used raster operation is the exclusive-or mode. Drawing a line once in this mode causes a line to appear in which the pixels are inverted wherever the line is drawn. Drawing the line again causes the original display to be restored. This technique is used in the RectPlay program in Chapter 4 to allow creation of a rectangle by dragging the mouse.

Background Mode

Hatched brushes, dashed pens, and text all have a background. For hatched brushes it is the area between the hatch lines. For dashed pens it is the area between the dots or dashes. For text it is the background of each character cell.

The background mode defines how Windows handles this background area. It can be opaque or transparent. When opaque, the background area is set to the background color. When transparent, the background area remains undisturbed.

Current Position

Each device context has a current pen position specified. The pen position is primarily used by the **LineTo** function, which draws from the current pen position to a specified point, then updates the current pen position.

Drawing Functions

Windows provides a robust set of drawing functions beyond those provided by Visual Basic. Each function is described in detail in the function reference section of this chapter. Table 7.5 lists the functions.

Table 7.5   **Windows API Drawing Functions**

Function	Description
Arc	Draws an arc.
Chord	Draws a chord (an ellipse bisected by a line).
DrawFocusRect	Draws a rectangle with a fine dotted line as commonly used to indicate the control that has the focus.
Ellipse	Draws an ellipse.

Table 7.5 **Windows API Drawing Functions (Continued)**

Function	Description
ExtFloodFill	Fills an area on the screen.
FillRect	Fills a rectangle.
FillRgn	Fills a region.
FloodFill	Fills an area on the screen.
FrameRect	Draws a frame around a rectangle.
FrameRgn	Draws a frame around a region.
GetPixel	Retrieves the color of a pixel.
LineDDA	Retrieves a list of all pixels that will be set by a specified line.
LineTo	Draws a line.
PaintRgn	Fills a region based on the current brush.
Pie	Draws a pie shape.
Polygon	Draws a polygon.
PolyLine	Draws a series of connected line segments.
PolyPolygon	Draws a series of polygons.
Rectangle	Draws a rectangle.
RoundRect	Draws a rectangle with rounded corners.
SetPixel	Sets the color of a single pixel.

Metafiles

A *metafile* is an object that can record GDI drawing operations for later play-back. Metafiles can be stored in memory or on disk and are useful for any situation where an image needs to be saved. Metafiles have an advantage over bitmaps in that they usually consume less space, are device-independent, and are scalable. Each record in a metafile contains a single GDI output command. A complete list of GDI commands that can be represented by metafile records can be found in Appendix B under the **METARECORD** data structure.

It is possible to obtain the data for a metafile and save it on disk or to open a metafile file for playback in an application. Metafiles can also be transferred to and from the clipboard.

A metafile is created by using the **CreateMetaFile** function to create a metafile device context. Note that a metafile device context is not the same thing as a metafile handle. Your application can draw on a metafile device context in the same way as it would draw on any other device context. When the drawing is complete, the **CloseMetaFile** function is called to close the metafile device context and create a metafile handle. This metafile handle can then be used to play back the drawing commands on another device context.

Table 7.6 lists the metafile functions.

Table 7.6 **Metafile Functions**

Function	Description
CloseMetaFile	Closes a metafile device context and retrieves a metafile handle.
CopyMetaFile	Copies a metafile.
CreateMetaFile	Creates a metafile device context that is ready to be drawn on.
DeleteMetaFile	Deletes a metafile.
EnumMetaFile	Enumerates records in a metafile.
GetMetaFile	Retrieves a metafile handle to a DOS file containing a metafile.
GetMetaFileBits	Extracts the data from a metafile into a block of memory.
PlayMetaFile	Plays back the commands in a metafile.
PlayMetaFileRecord	Plays back a single metafile record.
SetMetaFileBits, SetMetaFileBitsBetter	Creates a metafile handle for a block of memory that contains a metafile.

Example: QuikDraw—Drawing with API Functions

QuikDraw is a program that demonstrates several aspects of drawing with API functions. It illustrates the operation of a number of the API drawing functions and how they can be safely used with Visual Basic. It also shows how Windows scales images by changing coordinate systems, and the creation and use of drawing objects. Finally, the program demonstrates the use of metafiles to record drawing commands for later playback.

Figure 7.3 shows the design-time screen of the QuikDraw program.

Figure 7.3

QuikDraw program screen

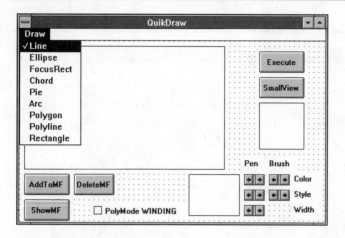

Using QuikDraw

The QuikDraw menu allows you to specify a Windows API drawing command to execute when the Execute button is pressed. Each drawing command needs two or more points as parameters. The points are specified by clicking the mouse in the large picture control. The maximum number of points that can be specified depends on the type of figure selected; for example, a line only has two points.

The Execute command button causes the current figure to be drawn. Clicking in the large picture control after the Execute button is pressed starts the definition of a new object.

The SmallView command button causes the current figure to be drawn into the small picture control. The figure is scaled so that the entire area of the large picture control is mapped into the smaller picture control.

The five scroll bars at the lower right of the screen allow you to specify the pen and brush style, pen and brush color, and pen width for drawing. The current figure will be drawn using these drawing objects. Click on the Execute or SmallView button after changing the drawing objects to show the current figure drawn with the new attributes. The small rectangle picture control (Picture3) shows a rectangle drawn with the currently selected pen and brush.

The AddToMF button adds the current figure to a global metafile. The ShowMF button plays the metafile on the large and small picture controls. These two commands allow you to build a more complex image. The DeleteMF button deletes the current metafile. The PolyMode WINDING check box sets the polygon fill mode. Refer to Figure 7.7 for a description of this value. Figure 7.4 shows the QuikDraw runtime program screen after drawing a complex metafile created with the program.

Figure 7.4
QuikDraw runtime screen

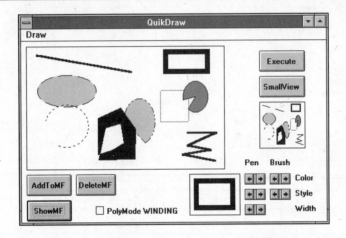

Project Description

The QuikDraw project includes four files. QUIKDRAW.FRM is the only form used in the program. QUIKDRAW.BAS is the only module in the program and contains the constant type and global definitions. APIDECS.BAS is the type-safe API declaration file provided with this book. APIGUIDE.BAS contains the declarations for the APIGUIDE.DLL dynamic link library.

Listing 7.1 shows the project file for the QuikDraw program.

Listing 7.1   **Project Listing File QUIKDRAW.MAK**

```
QUIKDRAW.FRM
QUIKDRAW.BAS
APIDECS.BAS
APIGUIDE.BAS
ProjWinSize=175,439,248,215
ProjWinShow=2
```

Form Description

Listing 7.2 contains the header from file QUIKDRAW.FRM that describes the control setup for the form.

Listing 7.2 **QUIKDRAW.FRM Header**

```
VERSION 2.00
Begin Form QuikDraw
   Caption        =   "QuikDraw"
   Height         =   4935
   Left           =   1035
   LinkMode       =   1  'Source
   LinkTopic      =   "Form1"
   ScaleHeight    =   4245
   ScaleWidth     =   7365
   Top            =   1140
   Width          =   7485
   Begin HScrollBar ScrollObject
      Height      =   255
      Index       =   4
      Left        =   5400
      Max         =   9
      TabIndex    =   16
      Top         =   3840
      Value       =   1
      Width       =   495
   End
   Begin CheckBox ChkPoly
      Caption     =   "PolyMode WINDING"
      Height      =   255
      Left        =   1800
      TabIndex    =   18
      Top         =   3840
      Width       =   2175
   End
   Begin CommandButton CmdShowMF
      Caption     =   "ShowMF"
      Height      =   495
      Left        =   120
      TabIndex    =   6
      Top         =   3720
      Width       =   1095
   End
   Begin HScrollBar ScrollObject
      Height      =   255
      Index       =   3
      Left        =   6000
      Max         =   7
      Min         =   -1
      TabIndex    =   11
      Top         =   3480
      Value       =   6
      Width       =   495
   End
```

Listing 7.2   QUIKDRAW.FRM Header (Continued)

```
Begin HScrollBar ScrollObject
   Height        =    255
   Index         =    2
   Left          =    5400
   Max           =    5
   Min           =    -1
   TabIndex      =    10
   Top           =    3480
   Width         =    495
End
Begin HScrollBar ScrollObject
   Height        =    255
   Index         =    1
   Left          =    6000
   Max           =    16
   Min           =    -1
   TabIndex      =    9
   Top           =    3120
   Value         =    15
   Width         =    495
End
Begin HScrollBar ScrollObject
   Height        =    255
   Index         =    0
   Left          =    5400
   Max           =    16
   Min           =    -1
   TabIndex      =    8
   Top           =    3120
   Width         =    495
End
Begin PictureBox Picture3
   Height        =    975
   Left          =    4080
   ScaleHeight   =    945
   ScaleWidth    =    1185
   TabIndex      =    7
   Top           =    3120
   Width         =    1215
End
Begin CommandButton CmdDeleteMF
   Caption       =    "DeleteMF"
   Height        =    495
   Left          =    1320
   TabIndex      =    5
   Top           =    3120
   Width         =    975
End
```

Listing 7.2   QUIKDRAW.FRM Header (Continued)

```
Begin CommandButton CmdExecute
    Caption         =   "AddToMF"
    Height          =   495
    Index           =   2
    Left            =   120
    TabIndex        =   4
    Top             =   3120
    Width           =   1095
End
Begin PictureBox Picture2
    Height          =   1095
    Left            =   5760
    ScaleHeight     =   71
    ScaleMode       =   3   'Pixel
    ScaleWidth      =   71
    TabIndex        =   3
    Top             =   1440
    Width           =   1095
End
Begin CommandButton CmdExecute
    Caption         =   "SmallView"
    Height          =   495
    Index           =   1
    Left            =   5760
    TabIndex        =   2
    Top             =   840
    Width           =   1095
End
Begin CommandButton CmdExecute
    Caption         =   "Execute"
    Height          =   495
    Index           =   0
    Left            =   5760
    TabIndex        =   1
    Top             =   240
    Width           =   1095
End
Begin PictureBox Picture1
    Height          =   2895
    Left            =   120
    ScaleHeight     =   191
    ScaleMode       =   3   'Pixel
    ScaleWidth      =   319
    TabIndex        =   0
    Top             =   120
    Width           =   4815
End
Begin Label Label5
```

Listing 7.2   QUIKDRAW.FRM Header (Continued)

```
        Caption        =    "Width"
        Height         =    255
        Left           =    6600
        TabIndex       =    17
        Top            =    3840
        Width          =    615
    End
    Begin Label Label4
        Caption        =    "Style"
        Height         =    255
        Left           =    6600
        TabIndex       =    15
        Top            =    3480
        Width          =    615
    End
    Begin Label Label3
        Caption        =    "Color"
        Height         =    255
        Left           =    6600
        TabIndex       =    14
        Top            =    3120
        Width          =    615
    End
    Begin Label Label2
        Caption        =    "Brush"
        Height         =    255
        Left           =    6000
        TabIndex       =    13
        Top            =    2760
        Width          =    615
    End
    Begin Label Label1
        Caption        =    "Pen"
        Height         =    255
        Left           =    5400
        TabIndex       =    12
        Top            =    2760
        Width          =    495
    End
```

The MenuDraw menu contains an entry for each API function that is available for drawing with this program.

```
    Begin Menu MenuDraw
        Caption        =    "Draw"
```

```
       Begin Menu MenuDrawType
          Caption         =   "Line"
          Checked         =   -1  'True
          Index           =   0
       End
       Begin Menu MenuDrawType
          Caption         =   "Ellipse"
          Index           =   1
       End
       Begin Menu MenuDrawType
          Caption         =   "FocusRect"
          Index           =   2
       End
       Begin Menu MenuDrawType
          Caption         =   "Chord"
          Index           =   3
       End
       Begin Menu MenuDrawType
          Caption         =   "Pie"
          Index           =   4
       End
       Begin Menu MenuDrawType
          Caption         =   "Arc"
          Index           =   5
       End
       Begin Menu MenuDrawType
          Caption         =   "Polygon"
          Index           =   6
       End
       Begin Menu MenuDrawType
          Caption         =   "Polyline"
          Index           =   7
       End
       Begin Menu MenuDrawType
          Caption         =   "Rectangle"
          Index           =   8
       End
    End
End
```

The five scroll bars in QuikDraw are in a control array with property
CtlName = ScrollObject. Their design-time property settings are shown in
Table 7.7. The color values are indexes into the **QBColor** function that returns an RGB color. These scroll bars have code attached to their **Change**
event that causes them to wrap around. In other words, when the value of
the scroll is set to **Max**, the code will immediately set the value to **Min+1**.

Table 7.7	**QuikDraw Scroll Bar Controls**				

Index	Min	Max	Value	Description
0	-1	16	0	Pen color
1	-1	16	15	Brush color
2	-1	5	0	Pen style
3	-1	7	6	Brush style. 0-4 are hatch styles, 5 for a solid brush.
4	0	9	1	Pen width

QuikDraw Program Listings

Module QUIKDRAW.BAS contains the constant declarations and global variables used by the program.

Listing 7.3	**Module QUIKDRAW.BAS**

```
' QuikDraw program example


' Global constants imported from APICONST.TXT
Global Const R2_BLACK = 1
Global Const R2_NOTMERGEPEN = 2
Global Const R2_MASKNOTPEN = 3
Global Const R2_NOTCOPYPEN = 4
Global Const R2_MASKPENNOT = 5
Global Const R2_NOT = 6
Global Const R2_XORPEN = 7
Global Const R2_NOTMASKPEN = 8
Global Const R2_MASKPEN = 9
Global Const R2_NOTXORPEN = 10
Global Const R2_NOP = 11
Global Const R2_MERGENOTPEN = 12
Global Const R2_COPYPEN = 13
Global Const R2_MERGEPENNOT = 14
Global Const R2_MERGEPEN = 15
Global Const R2_WHITE = 16
Global Const ALTERNATE = 1
Global Const WINDING = 2
Global Const TRANSPARENT = 1
Global Const OPAQUE = 2
```

Listing 7.3   Module QUIKDRAW.BAS (Continued)

```
Global Const MM_TEXT = 1
Global Const MM_LOMETRIC = 2
Global Const MM_HIMETRIC = 3
Global Const MM_LOENGLISH = 4
Global Const MM_HIENGLISH = 5
Global Const MM_TWIPS = 6
Global Const MM_ISOTROPIC = 7
Global Const MM_ANISOTROPIC = 8
Global Const ABSOLUTE = 1
Global Const RELATIVE = 2
Global Const WHITE_BRUSH = 0
Global Const LTGRAY_BRUSH = 1
Global Const GRAY_BRUSH = 2
Global Const DKGRAY_BRUSH = 3
Global Const BLACK_BRUSH = 4
Global Const NULL_BRUSH = 5
Global Const HOLLOW_BRUSH = NULL_BRUSH
Global Const WHITE_PEN = 6
Global Const BLACK_PEN = 7
Global Const NULL_PEN = 8
Global Const OEM_FIXED_FONT = 10
Global Const ANSI_FIXED_FONT = 11
Global Const ANSI_VAR_FONT = 12
Global Const SYSTEM_FONT = 13
Global Const DEVICE_DEFAULT_FONT = 14
Global Const DEFAULT_PALETTE = 15
Global Const SYSTEM_FIXED_FONT = 16
Global Const PS_SOLID = 0
Global Const PS_DASH = 1
Global Const PS_DOT = 2
Global Const PS_DASHDOT = 3
Global Const PS_DASHDOTDOT = 4
Global Const PS_NULL = 5
Global Const PS_INSIDEFRAME = 6
Global Const HS_HORIZONTAL = 0
Global Const HS_VERTICAL = 1
Global Const HS_FDIAGONAL = 2
Global Const HS_BDIAGONAL = 3
Global Const HS_CROSS = 4
Global Const HS_DIAGCROSS = 5


' Application global variables
Global MaxPoints%    ' Maximum points to use this drawing mode
Global PointsUsed%   ' Number of points used.
' Array of points
Global PointArray(32) As POINTAPI
```

Listing 7.3   Module QUIKDRAW.BAS (Continued)

```
' Current drawing mode - most recent Draw menu index
Global LastDrawIndex%

' This flag is set to -1 after the Execute button is pressed.
' This is an indication that the next click in Picture1 should
' start a new object.
Global LastWasExecute%

' Metafile to hold objects
Global hndMetaFile%

' Private Pen and Brush to use
Global hndPen%
Global hndBrush%
```

Listing 7.4   Form QUIKDRAW.FRM

```
DefStr A-Z


'
' We default to the line mode with no points defined.
'
Sub Form_Load ()
    MaxPoints% = 2
    PointsUsed% = Ø
End Sub


'
'    It is important to delete these GDI objects (if they
'    were created) before closing the application so that
'    the Windows resources may be properly freed.
'
Sub Form_Unload (Cancel As Integer)
    If hndMetaFile% <> Ø Then di% = DeleteMetaFile%(hndMetaFile%)
    If hndPen% <> Ø Then di% = DeleteObject(hndPen%)
    If hdnBrush% <> Ø Then di% = DeleteObject(hndBrush%)

End Sub


'
'    Mouse clicks in Picture1
'
```

Listing 7.4   Form QUIKDRAW.FRM (Continued)

```
Sub Picture1_MouseDown (Button As Integer, Shift As Integer, X As Single, Y ⇔
As Single)
    Dim pt%, px%, py%

    ' If last command was an execute, clear the points to
    ' start a new image
    If LastWasExecute% Then
        PointsUsed% = 0
        LastWasExecute% = 0
    End If


    ' If the maximum number of points has been exceeded
    ' Shift all of the points down
    If PointsUsed% >= MaxPoints% Then
        For pt% = 1 To MaxPoints%
            PointArray(pt% - 1) = PointArray(pt%)
        Next pt%
        PointsUsed% = PointsUsed% - 1
    End If
    ' Add the current point to the list
    PointArray(PointsUsed%).X = CInt(X)
    PointArray(PointsUsed%).Y = CInt(Y)
    PointsUsed% = PointsUsed% + 1
    Picture1.Cls

    ' Draw small + indicators to show where the points are.
    For pt% = 0 To PointsUsed% - 1
        px% = PointArray(pt%).X
        py% = PointArray(pt%).Y
        Picture1.Line (px% - 2, py%)-(px% + 3, py%)
        Picture1.Line (px%, py% - 2)-(px%, py% + 3)
    Next pt%
End Sub


'
'
' This function handles the menu commands. Each one
' defines a different object to draw when the Execute
' command button is selected.
'
Sub MenuDrawType_Click (Index As Integer)
    ' Clear out the current object.
    PointsUsed% = 0
    Picture1.Cls
    ' LastDrawIndex is a global that shows which GDI
    ' drawing function is being tested.
    LastDrawIndex% = Index
```

Listing 7.4   Form QUIKDRAW.FRM (Continued)

```
' Uncheck all of the menu entries
For X% = 0 To 8
    MenuDrawType(X%).Checked = 0
Next X%
' And check this one only.
MenuDrawType(Index).Checked = -1
' Each GDI drawing tool has a maximum number of points
' that it needs in order to perform the drawing.
Select Case Index
    Case 0, 1, 2, 8
        MaxPoints% = 2
    Case 3, 4, 5
        MaxPoints% = 4
    ' Polygons are limited to the size of the point
    ' data array
    Case 6, 7
        MaxPoints% = 32
End Select
End Sub


'   Draw the current object on the picture
'   Index = 0 is the Execute button which draws the current
'   object into the large Picture1 control
'
'   Index = 2 is the SmallView button which draws the
'   current object into the small Picture2 control
'
'   Index = 3 is the AddToMF button which adds the current
'   object into the current metafile.
'
Sub CmdExecute_Click (Index As Integer)
    Dim dc%, saved%
    Dim rc As RECT
    Dim oldpen%, oldbrush%, oldpolymode%

    Select Case Index
        Case 0  ' Execute button - draw into Picture1 after
                ' clearing the control.
            dc% = Picture1.hDC
            Picture1.Cls
        Case 1  ' SmallView button - draw into Picture2
            picture2.Cls
            dc% = picture2.hDC
            ' We're going to be changing the scaling,
            ' better save the current state of the DC or
            ' the VB drawing routines will no longer draw
            ' correctly.
            saved% = SaveDC%(dc%)
```

Listing 7.4   Form QUIKDRAW.FRM (Continued)

```
                    ' The entire area of Picture1 is scaled to fit
                    ' Picture2 exactly - this requires a change of
                    ' the mapping mode.
                    di% = SetMapMode%(dc%, MM_ANISOTROPIC)

                    ' The logical window is the size of Picture1.
                    ' Mapping this to the area of Picture2 is done
                    ' by making all of Picture2 the viewport.
                    dl& = SetWindowExt&(dc%, Picture1.scalewidth, ⇔
                    Picture1.scaleheight)
                    dl& = SetViewportExt&(dc%, picture2.scalewidth, ⇔
                    picture2.scaleheight)

            Case 2  ' AddToMeta button - Add the current object
                    ' to the global metafile.
                    ' First create a new metafile device context.
                    dc% = CreateMetaFileBynum%(0)
                    If hndMetaFile% <> 0 Then
                        ' If a global metafile already exists,
                        ' first play the existing metafile into the
                        ' new one.
                        di% = PlayMetaFile(dc%, hndMetaFile%)
                        ' Then delete the existing metafile.
                        di% = DeleteMetaFile(hndMetaFile%)
                        hndMetaFile% = 0
                        ' The drawing commands that follow will add
                        ' the current object to the new metafile
                        ' device context.
                    End If

            End Select

    ' Select in the private pen and brush if we're using
    ' them
    If hndPen% <> 0 And hndBrush% <> 0 Then
        oldpen% = SelectObject%(dc%, hndPen%)
        oldbrush% = SelectObject%(dc%, hndBrush%)
    End If
    ' Also change the polygon filling mode to winding if
    ' necessary
    If ChkPoly.Value = 1 Then oldpolymode% = SetPolyFillMode(dc%, WINDING)

    ' The object drawn depends on global LastDrawIndex
    ' which was set by the Draw menu commands.
    ' The PointsUsed% global indicates how many points have
    ' been drawn in Picture1.
    Select Case LastDrawIndex%
```

Listing 7.4   Form QUIKDRAW.FRM (Continued)

```
Case Ø  ' Draw a line
    If PointsUsed% = 2 Then
        ' Set the current position of the pen
        dl& = MoveTo&(dc%, PointArray(Ø).X, PointArray(Ø).Y)
        ' and draw to the specified point.
        di% = LineTo%(dc%, PointArray(1).X, PointArray(1).Y)
    End If
Case 1  ' Draw an ellipse
    If PointsUsed% = 2 Then
        di% = Ellipse(dc%, PointArray(Ø).X, PointArray(Ø).Y, ⇔
                PointArray(1).X, PointArray(1).Y)
    End If
Case 2 ' Draw a focus rectangle
    If PointsUsed% = 2 Then
        SetRect rc, PointArray(Ø).X, PointArray(Ø).Y, ⇔
        PointArray(1).X, PointArray(1).Y
        DrawFocusRect dc%, rc
    End If
Case 3  ' Draw a chord
    If PointsUsed% = 4 Then
        di% = Chord(dc%, PointArray(Ø).X, PointArray(Ø).Y, ⇔
                PointArray(1).X, PointArray(1).Y, PointArray(2).X, ⇔
                PointArray(2).Y, PointArray(3).X, PointArray(3).Y)
    End If
Case 4  ' Draw a pie
    If PointsUsed% = 4 Then
        di% = Pie(dc%, PointArray(Ø).X, PointArray(Ø).Y, ⇔
                PointArray(1).X, PointArray(1).Y, PointArray(2).X, ⇔
                PointArray(2).Y, PointArray(3).X, PointArray(3).Y)
    End If
Case 5  ' Draw an arc
    If PointsUsed% = 4 Then
        di% = arc(dc%, PointArray(Ø).X, PointArray(Ø).Y, ⇔
                PointArray(1).X, PointArray(1).Y, PointArray(2).X, ⇔
                PointArray(2).Y, PointArray(3).X, PointArray(3).Y)
    End If
Case 6 ' Draw a polygon
    If PointsUsed% > 1 Then
        di% = Polygon(dc%, PointArray(Ø), PointsUsed%)
    End If
Case 7 ' Draw a polyline
    If PointsUsed% > 1 Then
        di% = PolyLine(dc%, PointArray(Ø), PointsUsed%)
    End If
Case 8 ' Draw a rectangle
    If PointsUsed% = 2 Then
        di% = Rectangle(dc%, PointArray(Ø).X, PointArray(Ø).Y, ⇔
                PointArray(1).X, PointArray(1).Y)
```

Listing 7.4   Form QUIKDRAW.FRM (Continued)

```
            End If

        End Select

    ' Be sure to restore the original GDI objects!
    If oldpen% <> Ø Then di% = SelectObject%(dc%, oldpen%)
    If oldbrush% <> Ø Then di% = SelectObject%(dc%, oldbrush%)
    If ChkPoly.Value = 1 Then di% = SetPolyFillMode(dc%, oldpolymode%)

    Select Case Index
        Case Ø
            ' Notify the mouse down routine that the last
            ' command was an execute
            ' This informs the system that the next mouse
            ' click in Picture1 is the start of a new
            ' object.
            LastWasExecute% = -1
        Case 1   ' Restore the previous state of the Picture2 DC
            di% = RestoreDC%(dc%, saved%)
        Case 2   ' Close the metafile device context and
                 ' obtain a metafile handle.
            hndMetaFile% = CloseMetaFile%(dc%)
            dc% = Picture1.hDC
    End Select
End Sub


'
' Delete the current metafile
'
Sub CmdDeleteMF_Click ()
    If hndMetaFile% Then
        di% = DeleteMetaFile%(hndMetaFile%)
        hndMetaFile% = Ø
    End If

End Sub


'
'
' Show the current global metafile if one exists. It will
'   be shown in both Picture1 and Picture2
'
Sub CmdShowMF_Click ()
    Dim saved%, dc%, di%, dl&
    ' Because the original drawing was into Picture1,
    ' playing the metafile into Picture1 is trivial.
    Picture1.Cls
    di% = PlayMetaFile(Picture1.hDC, hndMetaFile%)
```

Listing 7.4   Form QUIKDRAW.FRM (Continued)

```
' Picture 2 is trickier. First we clear it and save the
' current DC state.
picture2.Cls
dc% = picture2.hDC
saved% = SaveDC%(dc%)
' Now set the new coordinate system. See the
' CmdExecute()_Click
' command for further explanation
di% = SetMapMode%(dc%, MM_ANISOTROPIC)
dl& = SetWindowExt&(dc%, Picture1.scalewidth, Picture1.scaleheight)
dl& = SetViewportExt&(dc%, picture2.scalewidth, picture2.scaleheight)
' All of the drawing objects that were used on the
' original objects were saved with the metafile, thus
' the metafile will automatically draw each object in
' the correct color and style.
di% = PlayMetaFile(dc%, hndMetaFile%)
' And restore the original DC state
di% = RestoreDC%(dc%, saved%)

End Sub


'
'   These scroll bars are used to select colors, styles and
'   pen widths.  The Min and Max properties are selected
'   such that the Scrollbar value parameter may be used
'   directly in the GDI object creation function.
'
Sub ScrollObject_Change (Index As Integer)

    ' Wrap around when increasing
    If ScrollObject(Index).Value = ScrollObject(Index).Max Then
        ScrollObject(Index).Value = ScrollObject(Index).Min + 1
        Exit Sub
    End If
    ' Wrap around when decrementing
    If ScrollObject(Index).Value = ScrollObject(Index).Min Then
        ScrollObject(Index).Value = ScrollObject(Index).Max - 1
        Exit Sub
    End If


    ' Delete the current objects
    If hndPen% Then di% = DeleteObject(hndPen%)
    If hndBrush% Then di% = DeleteObject(hndBrush%)

    ' Now create the new pen
    hndPen% = CreatePen(ScrollObject(2).Value, ScrollObject(4).Value, ⇔
```

Listing 7.4   **Form QUIKDRAW.FRM (Continued)**

```
                    QBColor(ScrollObject(0).Value))

    ' Now create the new brush
    ' Value 6 indicates that we should create a solid brush
    ' 0-5 indicate styles of hatched brushes.
    If ScrollObject(3).Value = 6 Then
        hndBrush% = CreateSolidBrush%(QBColor(ScrollObject(1).Value))
    Else
        hndBrush% = CreateHatchBrush%(ScrollObject(3).Value, ⇔
                    QBColor(ScrollObject(1).Value))
    End If

    ' Draw a sample rectangle using the current pen&Brush
    ' This forces the Paint event to be triggered.
    Picture3.Refresh

End Sub


'
'   This picture control shows a rectangle drawn in the
'   current pen and brush.
'
Sub Picture3_Paint ()
    Dim rc As RECT
    Dim hwnd%
    Dim oldpen%, oldbrush%

    ' Get the window handle for Picture3
    hwnd% = agGetControlHwnd%(Picture3)
    ' Get a rectangle with the client area size...
    GetClientRect hwnd%, rc
    '.. and shrink it by 10 pixels on a side.
    InflateRect rc, -10, -10

    ' Select in our private pen and brush
    If hndPen% <> 0 And hndBrush% <> 0 Then
        oldpen% = SelectObject%(Picture3.hDC, hndPen%)
        oldbrush% = SelectObject%(Picture3.hDC, hndBrush%)
    End If

    ' Draw the rectangle
    di% = Rectangle(Picture3.hDC, rc.left, rc.top, rc.right, rc.bottom)

    ' Be sure to restore the original GDI objects!
    If oldpen% <> 0 Then di% = SelectObject%(Picture3.hDC, oldpen%)
    If oldbrush% <> 0 Then di% = SelectObject%(Picture3.hDC, oldbrush%)

End Sub
```

Suggestions for Modifying QuikDraw

Like the other example programs in this book, QuikDraw was designed to illustrate the use of API functions. As such, it is far from a polished application. You may wish to add some of these features for practice:

- The ability to save and load metafiles from disk.

- Support for additional GDI drawing functions.

- The ability to preview the current object with the metafile before adding it to the metafile.

- Support for different ROP2 (line drawing) and background modes.

- A more sophisticated user interface.

- The ability to delete an object from a metafile (hint: this is done by creating a new metafile device context, enumerating the source metafile, and using the **PlayMetaFileRecord** command to play into the DC only those objects that you wish to copy).

Function Reference

This section contains an alphabetical reference for the functions described in this chapter.

■ Arc

VB Declaration   `Declare Function Arc% Lib "GDI" (ByVal hDC%, ByVal X1%, ByVal Y1%, ByVal ⇔`
`X2%, ByVal Y2%, ByVal X3%, ByVal Y3%, ByVal X4%, ByVal Y4%)`

Description   Draws an arc as shown in Figure 7.5. X1,Y1,X2,Y2 specify a bounding rectangle of an ellipse. The point at which a line drawn from the center of the rectangle to points X3,Y3 intersects the ellipse determines the start of the arc. A similar line through X4,Y4 determines the end of the arc.

Figure 7.5
Arc, chord, and pie graphics functions

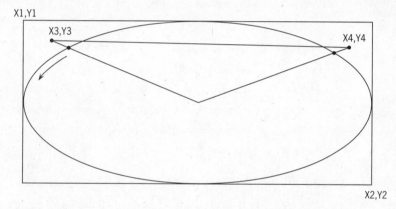

The **Arc**, **Chord,** and **Pie** functions use the same parameters. X1, Y1, X2, Y2 define a bounding rectangle that defines an ellipse. X3, Y3, X4, Y4 define two lines that intersect the ellipse. The three functions produce these drawings:

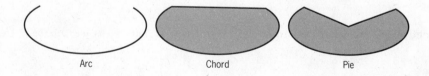

Use with VB   No problem.

Parameter	Type/Description
hDC	**Integer**—Handle to a display context.
X1,Y1	**Integers**—Specify the upper left corner of a rectangle that bounds an ellipse.
X2,Y2	**Integers**—Specify the lower right corner of a rectangle that bounds an ellipse.

Parameter	Type/Description
X3,Y3	**Integers**—Specify the arc starting point.
X4,Y4	**Integers**—Specify the arc ending point.

Return Value   Integer—TRUE on success, FALSE otherwise.

Comments   The width and height of the bounding rectangle must be between 3 and 32766 units in size.

■ Chord

VB Declaration   `Declare Function Chord% Lib "GDI" (ByVal hDC%, ByVal X1%, ByVal Y1%, ByVal ⇔`
`X2%, ByVal Y2%, ByVal X3%, ByVal Y3%, ByVal X4%, ByVal Y4%)`

Description   Draws a chord as shown in Figure 7.5. X1,Y1,X2,Y2 specify a bounding rectangle of an ellipse. The chord is the area between the ellipse and the line defined by X3,Y3 and X4,Y4.

Use with VB   No problem.

Parameter	Type/Description
hDC	**Integer**—Handle to a display context.
X1,Y1	**Integers**—Specify the upper left corner of a rectangle that bounds an ellipse.
X2,Y2	**Integers**—Specify the lower right corner of a rectangle that bounds an ellipse.
X3,Y3	**Integers**—Specify one point of a line that intersects the ellipse.
X4,Y4	**Integers**—Specify the second point of a line that intersects the ellipse.

Return Value   Integer—TRUE on success, FALSE otherwise.

Comments   The width and height of the bounding rectangle must be between 3 and 32766 units in size.

■ CloseMetaFile

VB Declaration   `Declare Function CloseMetaFile% Lib "GDI" (ByVal hMF%)`

Description   Closes the specified metafile device context and returns a handle to the newly created metafile.

Use with VB   No problem.

Parameter	Type/Description
hMF	**Integer**—A metafile device context as returned by the **CreateMetaFile** function.

Return Value   Integer—A handle to the metafile. The **PlayMetaFile** function may be used to play the metafile.

Comments   Be sure to use the **DeleteMetaFile** function to delete the metafile and free its resources when the metafile is no longer needed.

■ CopyMetaFile, CopyMetaFileBynum

VB Declaration `Declare Function CopyMetaFile% Lib "GDI" (ByVal hMF%, ByVal lpFilename$)`
`Declare Function CopyMetaFileBynum% Lib "GDI" (ByVal hMF%, ByVal hDest&)`

Description Makes a copy of the specified metafile. **CopyMetaFileBynum** is used to copy a metafile to a memory metafile.

Use with VB No problem.

Parameter	Type/Description
hMF	**Integer**—Handle to a metafile to copy.
lpFileName$	**String**—File name for the new metafile.
hDest&	**Long**—When set to zero in **CopyMetaFileBynum**, causes a memory metafile to be created.

Return Value **Integer**—A handle to the new metafile.

■ CreateBrushIndirect

VB Declaration `Declare Function CreateBrushIndirect% Lib "GDI" (lpLogBrush As LOGBRUSH)`

Description Creates a brush based on a **LOGBRUSH** data structure.

Use with VB No problem.

Parameter	Type/Description
lpLogBrush	**LOGBRUSH**—**LOGBRUSH** data structure as defined in Appendix B.

Return Value **Integer**—A handle to the new brush on success, zero otherwise.

Comments Use the **DeleteObject** function to delete the brush when it is no longer needed.

■ CreateDIBPatternBrush

VB Declaration `Declare Function CreateDIBPatternBrush% Lib "GDI" (ByVal hPackedDIB%, ByVal wUsage%)`

Description Creates a brush using a device-independent bitmap to specify the brush pattern.

Use with VB No problem.

Parameter	Type/Description
hPackedDIB	**Integer**—A global memory handle to a block of memory containing a **BITMAPINFO** structure followed by a device-independent bitmap. The bitmap dimensions should be 8x8 pixels. If a monochrome DIB is specified, the DIB colors are ignored and the text and background colors are used instead. Refer to Chapter 8 for information on device-independent bitmaps and Chapter 12 for information on using global memory blocks.

Parameter	Type/Description
wUsage	**Integer**—One of the following constants: **DIB_PAL_COLORS**: The DIB color table contains indexes to the current logical palette. **DIB_RGB_COLORS**: The DIB color table contains 32-bit RGB color values.

Return Value   **Integer**—A handle to the new brush on success, zero otherwise.

Comments   Use the **DeleteObject** function to delete the brush when it is no longer needed.

■ CreateHatchBrush

VB Declaration   `Declare Function CreateHatchBrush% Lib "GDI" (ByVal nIndex%, ByVal crColor&)`

Description   Creates a brush with a hatched pattern as shown in Figure 7.6.

Figure 7.6
Hatched patterns for
brushes

HS_HORIZONTAL HS_BDIAGONAL HS_FDIAGONAL HS_VERTICAL HS_CROSS HS_DIAGCROSS

Note: Refer to the APICONST.TXT file for constant definitions.

Use with VB   No problem.

Parameter	Type/Description
nIndex	**Integer**—Specifies the type of hatching as shown in Figure 7.6.
crColors	**Long**—Specifies the RGB foreground color of the brush.

Return Value   **Integer**—A handle to the new brush on success, zero otherwise.

Comments   Use the **DeleteObject** function to delete the brush when it is no longer needed.

■ CreateMetaFile, CreateMetaFileBynum, CreateMetaFileBystring

VB Declaration   `Declare Function CreateMetaFile% Lib "GDI" (ByVal lpString As Any)`

`Declare Function CreateMetaFileBynum% Lib "GDI" Alias "CreateMetaFile"` ⇔
`(ByVal lpString&)`

`Declare Function CreateMetaFileBystring% Lib "GDI" Alias "CreateMetaFile"` ⇔
`(ByVal lpString$)`

Description	Creates a metafile device context. Drawing operations may be performed on this device context. When the CloseMetaFile function is called to close this device context, a metafile handle is created that contains the recorded sequence of drawing commands, which can then be played back into any device context. CreateMetaFileBynum and CreateMetaFileBystring are type-safe declarations for this function.
Use with VB	No problem.

Parameter	Type/Description
lpString	**String** or **Long**—The name of the file to hold the metafile. When called with the value zero, the metafile is created in memory.

Return Value	**Integer**—A handle to the metafile device context.

■ CreatePatternBrush

VB Declaration   `Declare Function CreatePatternBrush% Lib "GDI" (ByVal hBitmap%)`

Description   Creates a brush using a bitmap to specify the brush pattern.

Use with VB   No problem.

Parameter	Type/Description
hPackedDIB	**Integer**—A handle to a bitmap. The bitmap dimensions should be 8x8 pixels. If a monochrome bitmap is specified, the text and background colors are used in the pattern. Refer to Chapter 8 for information on bitmaps.

Return Value	**Integer**—A handle to the new brush on success, zero otherwise.
Comments	Use the **DeleteObject** function to delete the brush when it is no longer needed.

■ CreatePen

VB Declaration   `Declare Function CreatePen% Lib "GDI" (ByVal nPenStyle%, ByVal nWidth%, ⇔`
`ByVal crColor&)`

Description   Creates a pen with the specified style, width, and color.

Use with VB　　No problem.

Parameter	Type/Description
nPenStyle	**Integer**—Specifies the pen style based on the following constants: **PS_SOLID**: Pen is a solid color. **PS_DASH**: Pen is dashed (**nWidth** must be 1). **PS_DOT**: Pen is dotted (**nWidth** must be 1). **PS_DASHDOT**: Pen alternates dashes and dots (**nWidth** must be 1). **PS_DASHDOTDOT**: Pen alternates dashes and double dots (**nWidth** must be 1). **PS_NULL**: Pen does not draw. **PS_INSIDEFRAME**: Pen draws inside the frame of closed objects produced by **Ellipse**, **Rectangle**, **RoundRect**, **Pie**, and **Chord**. If the exact RGB color specified does not exist, dithering is used.
nWidth	**Integer**—Width of the pen in logical units.
crColor	**Long**—RGB color of the pen

Return Value　　**Integer**—A handle to the new pen on success, zero otherwise.

Comments　　Use the **DeleteObject** function to delete the pen when it is no longer needed.

■ CreatePenIndirect

VB Declaration　　`Declare Function CreatePenIndirect% Lib "GDI" (lpLogPen As LOGPEN)`

Description　　Creates a pen based on the specified **LOGPEN** structure.

Use with VB　　No problem.

Parameter	Type/Description
lpLogPen	**LOGPEN**—Logical pen structure.

Return Value　　**Integer**—A handle to the new pen on success, zero otherwise.

Comments　　Use the **DeleteObject** function to delete the pen when it's no longer needed.

■ CreateSolidBrush

VB Declaration　　`Declare Function CreateSolidBrush% Lib "GDI" (ByVal crColor&)`

Description　　Creates a brush with a solid color.

Use with VB　　No problem.

Parameter	Type/Description
crColor	**Long**—RGB color of the brush.

Return Value　　**Integer**—A handle to the new brush on success, zero otherwise.

Comments　　Use the **DeleteObject** function to delete the brush when it is no longer needed.

■ DeleteMetaFile

VB Declaration   `Declare Function DeleteMetaFile% Lib "GDI" (ByVal hMF%)`

Description   Deletes the specified metafile.

Use with VB   No problem.

Parameter	Type/Description
hMF	**Integer**—A handle to a metafile.

Return Value   **Integer**—TRUE (nonzero) on success, zero otherwise.

Comments   If the metafile is based on a disk file, the file itself is not deleted by this function. It may thus be reopened with the **GetMetaFile** function.

■ DeleteObject

VB Declaration   `Declare Function DeleteObject% Lib "GDI" (ByVal hObject%)`

Description   This function is used to delete GDI objects such as pens, brushes, fonts, bitmaps, regions, and palettes. All system resources used by the object are released.

Use with VB   No problem.

Parameter	Type/Description
hObject	**Integer**—Handle to a GDI object (pen, brush, font, bitmap, region, or palette).

Return Value   **Integer**—TRUE (nonzero) on success, zero otherwise.

Comments   The GDI object must not have been selected into a device context when it is deleted. Do not delete system objects obtained using the **GetStockObject** function.

■ DrawFocusRect

VB Declaration   `Declare Sub DrawFocusRect Lib "User" (ByVal hDC%, lpRect As RECT)`

Description   Draws a focus rectangle. The rectangle is drawn using the exclusive-or operation in the style used to indicate the focus (typically a dotted line). Call this function a second time with the same parameters to erase the focus rectangle.

Use with VB   No problem.

Parameter	Type/Description
hDC	**Integer**—Handle to a device context.
lpRect	**RECT**—Rectangle to draw in logical coordinates.

■ Ellipse

VB Declaration   Declare Function Ellipse% Lib "GDI" (ByVal hDC%, ByVal X1%, ByVal Y1%, ⟺
ByVal X2%, ByVal Y2%)

Description   Draws an ellipse that is bounded by the specified rectangle. The ellipse is drawn using the currently selected pen and filled using the currently selected brush.

Use with VB   No problem.

Parameter	Type/Description
hDC	**Integer**—Handle to a device context.
X1,Y1	**Integers**—Upper left point in logical coordinates of the bounding rectangle.
X2,Y2	**Integers**—Lower right point in logical coordinates of the bounding rectangle.

Return Value   **Integer**—TRUE (nonzero) on success, zero otherwise.

■ EnumMetaFile

VB Declaration   Declare Function EnumMetaFile% Lib "GDI" (ByVal hDC%, ByVal hMF%, ByVal ⟺
lpCallbackFunc&, ByVal lpClientData&)

Description   Enumerates the individual metafile records for a metafile. Each metafile record contains a single GDI command. This can be used along with the **PlayMetaFileRecord** function to selectively play portions of a metafile.

Use with VB   Requires the CBK.VBX custom control provided with this book.

Parameter	Type/Description
hDC	**Integer**—Handle to a device context.
hMF	**Integer**—Handle to a metafile.
lpCallbackFunc	**Long**—Pointer to function to call for each GDI object. Use the **ProcAddress** property of the CBK.VBX custom control to obtain a function pointer for callbacks.
lpClientData	**Long**—Value that is passed to the **EnumMetaFile** event of the CBK.VBX custom control during enumeration.

Return Value   **Integer**—TRUE (nonzero) if all of the metafile records were enumerated, zero otherwise.

Comments   Refer to Appendix A for details on using the CBK.VBX custom control with enumeration functions.

■ EnumObjects

VB Declaration   Declare Function EnumObjects% Lib "GDI" (ByVal hDC%, ByVal nObjectType%, ⟺
ByVal lpObjectFunc&, ByVal lpData&)

Description   Enumerates the pens and brushes that may be used with the specified device context.

Use with VB   Requires the CBK.VBX custom control provided with this book.

Parameter	Type/Description
hDC	**Integer**—Handle to a device context.
nObjectType	**Integer**—The type of object to enumerate based on the following constants: **OBJ_BRUSH**: Enumerates brushes. **OBJ_PEN**: Enumerates pens.
lpObjectFunc	**Long**—Pointer to function to call for each GDI object. Use the **ProcAddress** property of the CBK.VBX custom control to obtain a function pointer for callbacks.
lParam	**Long**—Value that is passed to the **EnumObjects** event of the CBK.VBX custom control during enumeration.

Return Value   **Integer**—The last value returned by the callback function.

Comments   Refer to Appendix A for details on using the CBK.VBX custom control with enumeration functions.

■ ExtFloodFill

VB Declaration   `Declare Function ExtFloodFill% Lib "GDI" (ByVal hDC%, ByVal X%, ByVal Y%, ⇔`
`ByVal crColor&, ByVal wFillType%)`

Description   Fills an area in the specified device context using the currently selected brush.

Use with VB   No problem.

Parameter	Type/Description
hDC	**Integer**—Handle to a device context.
X,Y	**Integers**—Point at which to begin filling in logical coordinates.
crColor	**Long**—Boundary color to use.
wFillType	**Integer**—Type of filling to perform based on one of the following constants: **FLOODFILLBORDER**: Same as performed by the **FloodFill** function. **FLOODFILLSURFACE**: Fills outward from the specified point as long as color **crColor** is found.

Return Value   **Integer**—TRUE (nonzero) on success. Zero if the area could not be filled.

Comments   If **FLOODFILLBORDER** is specified, point X,Y must not have color **crColor**. If **FLOOD-FILLSURFACE** is specified, point X,Y must have color **crColor**. This function only works on raster devices.

■ FillRect

VB Declaration   Declare Function FillRect% Lib "User" (ByVal hDC%, lpRect As RECT, ByVal ⇔
hBrush%)

Description   Fills a rectangle using the specified brush.

Use with VB   No problem.

Parameter	Type/Description
hDC	**Integer**—Handle to a device context.
lpRect	**RECT**—Rectangle describing the area to fill in logical coordinates.
hBrush	**Integer**—Handle of the brush to use.

Return Value   Not used.

Comments   The value of the top field of **lpRect** must be smaller than that of the bottom field. The value of the left field of **lpRect** must be smaller than that of the right field.

■ FillRgn

VB Declaration   Declare Function FillRgn% Lib "GDI" (ByVal hDC%, ByVal hRgn%, ByVal hBrush%)

Description   Fills the specified region using the specified brush.

Use with VB   No problem.

Parameter	Type/Description
hDC	**Integer**—Handle to a device context.
hRgn	**Integer**—Handle to a region to fill in device coordinates.
hBrush	**Integer**—Handle of the brush to use.

Return Value   **Integer**—TRUE (nonzero) on success, zero otherwise.

■ FloodFill

VB Declaration   Declare Function FloodFill% Lib "GDI" (ByVal hDC%, ByVal X%, ByVal Y%, ⇔
ByVal crColor&)

Description   Fills an area in the specified device context using the currently selected brush. The area is defined by color **crColor**.

Use with VB   No problem.

Parameter	Type/Description
hDC	**Integer**—Handle to a device context.

Parameter	Type/Description
X,Y	**Integers**—Point at which to begin filling in logical coordinates.
crColor	**Long**—Boundary color to use. The surface bounded by this color is filled.

Return Value   **Integer**—TRUE (nonzero) on success. Zero if the area could not be filled.

Comments   Point X,Y must not have color **crColor**, and must be within the clipping region. This function only works on raster devices.

■ FrameRect

VB Declaration

```
Declare Function FrameRect% Lib "User" (ByVal hDC%, lpRect As RECT, ByVal ⇔
hBrush%)
```

Description   Draws a border one logical unit wide around a rectangle using the specified brush.

Use with VB   No problem.

Parameter	Type/Description
hDC	**Integer**—Handle to a device context.
lpRect	**RECT**—Rectangle specifying the border to draw. This is identical to the border drawn using the Rectangle function when the pen is one unit wide.
hBrush	**Integer**—Handle of the brush to use.

Return Value   Not used.

Comments   The value of the top field of **lpRect** must be smaller than that of the bottom field. The value of the left field of **lpRect** must be smaller than that of the right field.

■ FrameRgn

VB Declaration

```
Declare Function FrameRgn% Lib "GDI" (ByVal hDC%, ByVal hRgn%, ByVal ⇔
hBrush%, ByVal nWidth%, ByVal nHeight%)
```

Description   Draws a frame around the specified region using the specified brush.

Use with VB   No problem.

Parameter	Type/Description
hDC	**Integer**—Handle to a device context.
hRgn	**Integer**—Handle to a region to fill in device coordinates.
hBrush	**Integer**—Handle of the brush to use.
nWidth	**Integer**—Width in device units of the vertical borders.
nHeight	**Integer**—Height in device units of the horizontal borders.

Return Value   Integer—TRUE (nonzero) on success, zero otherwise.

■ GetBkColor

VB Declaration   `Declare Function GetBkColor& Lib "GDI" (ByVal hDC%)`

Description   Retrieves the current background color for the specified device context.

Use with VB   No problem.

Parameter	Type/Description
hDC	**Integer**—Handle to a device context.

Return Value   **Long**—RGB value of the current background color.

■ GetBkMode

VB Declaration   `Declare Function GetBkMode% Lib "GDI" (ByVal hDC%)`

Description   Retrieves the current background filling mode for the specified device context.

Use with VB   No problem.

Parameter	Type/Description
hDC	**Integer**—Handle to a device context.

Return Value   One of the following constants:
OPAQUE: The background of text, hatched brushes, and dashed pen lines is set to the current background color.
TRANSPARENT: The background of text, hatched brushes, and dashed pen lines is not modified.

■ GetBrushOrg

VB Declaration   `Declare Function GetBrushOrg& Lib "GDI" (ByVal hDC%)`

Description   Retrieves the origin of the currently selected brush in the specified device context. Refer to "Brushes," earlier in this chapter.

Use with VB   No problem.

Parameter	Type/Description
hDC	**Integer**—Handle to a device context.

Return Value   **Long**—The low word of the result contains the X coordinate in device coordinates. The high word contains the Y coordinate.

■ GetBrushOrgEx

VB Declaration   `Declare Function GetBrushOrgEx% Lib "GDI" (ByVal hDC%, lpPoint As POINTAPI)`

Description   Retrieves the origin of the currently selected brush in the specified device context. Refer to "Brushes," earlier in this chapter.

Use with VB   No problem.

Parameter	Type/Description
hDC	**Integer**—Handle to a device context.
lpPoint	**POINTAPI**—**POINTAPI** structure to load with the current brush origin.

Return Value   **Integer**—TRUE (nonzero) on success, zero on error.

■ GetCurrentPosition

VB Declaration   `Declare Function GetCurrentPosition& Lib "GDI" (ByVal hDC%)`

Description   Retrieves the current pen position in the device context.

Use with VB   No problem.

Parameter	Type/Description
hDC	**Integer**—Handle to a device context.

Return Value   **Long**—The low word of the result contains the X coordinate in device coordinates. The high word contains the Y coordinate.

■ GetCurrentPositionEx

VB Declaration   `Declare Function GetCurrentPositionEx% Lib "GDI" (ByVal hDC%, lpPoint As ⇔ POINTAPI)`

Description   Retrieves the current pen position in the specified device context.

Use with VB   No problem.

Parameter	Type/Description
hDC	**Integer**—Handle to a device context.
lpPoint	**POINTAPI**—**POINTAPI** structure to load with the current position.

Return Value   **Integer**—TRUE (nonzero) on success, zero on error.

■ GetMetaFile

VB Declaration Declare Function GetMetaFile% Lib "GDI" (ByVal lpFilename$)

Description Retrieves a metafile handle to a metafile contained in a disk file.

Use with VB No problem.

Parameter	Type/Description
lpFilename$	**String**—Name of the disk file containing a metafile.

Return Value Integer—TRUE (nonzero) on success, zero otherwise.

■ GetMetaFileBits

VB Declaration Declare Function GetMetaFileBits% Lib "GDI" (ByVal hMF%)

Description Copies the specified metafile into a global memory handle. The contents of this handle must not be modified. This function may be used to retrieve the raw data for a metafile in order to save it to a disk file.

Use with VB No problem.

Parameter	Type/Description
hMF	**Integer**—Handle to a metafile. This handle will no longer be valid after this function is called.

Return Value Integer—A global memory handle on success, zero otherwise.

Comments Refer to Chapter 12 for information on using global memory handles.

■ GetNearestColor

VB Declaration Declare Function GetNearestColor& Lib "GDI" (ByVal hDC%, ByVal crColor&)

Description Retrieves the closest solid color to the specified color that the device can actually display.

Use with VB No problem.

Parameter	Type/Description
hDC	**Integer**—Handle to a device context.
crColor	**Long**—RGB color to check.

Return Value Long—The RGB color closest to **crColor** that the device can actually draw.

■ GetObject

VB Declaration `Declare Function GetObjectAPI% Lib "GDI" Alias "Getobject" (ByVal hObject%, ByVal nCount%, ByVal ⇔`
`lpObject&)`

Description Retrieves a structure describing the specified object.

Use with VB No problem.

Parameter	Type/Description
hObject	**Integer**—Handle to a pen, brush, font, or bitmap.
nCount	**Integer**—Number of bytes of data to retrieve. Usually the size of the structure defined by **lpObject**.
lpObject	**Long**—Address of a buffer to load with object data. This will typically be a **LOGPEN** structure for pens, **LOGBRUSH** for fonts, **LOGFONT** for fonts, and **BITMAP** for bitmaps. For palettes, this should point to an integer variable that will be loaded with the number of entries in the palette. Use the **agGetAddressForObject** function in APIGUIDE.DLL to obtain the address for a data structure.

Return Value **Integer**—The number of bytes of data loaded.

Comments Refer to Appendix B for information on logical object data structures. The **bmBits** field of the **BITMAP** data structure is not valid when retrieving information for a bitmap.

You can remove the **ByVal** from the **lpObject** parameter, in which case you may pass the actual **LOGPEN**, **LOGBRUSH**, **LOGFONT**, and **BITMAP** structures as parameters without using the **agGetAddressForObject** function.

■ GetPixel

VB Declaration `Declare Function GetPixel& Lib "GDI" (ByVal hDC%, ByVal X%, ByVal Y%)`

Description Retrieves the RGB value of a pixel in the specified device context.

Use with VB No problem.

Parameter	Type/Description
hDC	**Integer**—Handle to a device context.
X,Y	**Integers**—Point to check in logical coordinates.

Return Value **Long**—RGB color of the specified point.

■ GetPolyFillMode

VB Declaration `Declare Function GetPolyFillMode% Lib "GDI" (ByVal hDC%)`

Description Retrieves the polygon filling mode for the specified device context. Refer to the **SetPolyFillMode** function description for details.

Use with VB   No problem.

Parameter	Type/Description
hDC	Integer—Handle to a device context.

Return Value   Integer—The constant **ALTERNATE** or **WINDING**. Refer to Figure 7.7 for a description of the two filling modes.

Figure 7.7
Polygon filling modes

Polygon fill mode = ALTERNATE

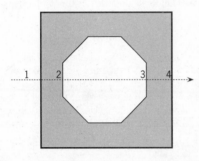

Windows traverses each scan line from left to right and counts each polygon vertex. It then alternates filling - filling between the first and second vertex, the third and fourth, and so on.

Polygon fill mode = WINDING

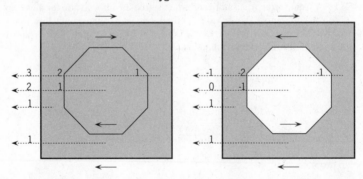

For each point on the scan line, Windows draws an imaginary line to the outside of the figure. Each time the imaginary line passes through a vertex that was drawn clockwise, a count is incremented. When it passes through a vertex that was drawn counter-clockwise, the count is decremented. The area at the point is filled if the resulting count is not zero.
The drawings above show the effect of the drawing direction (indicated by arrows) on the filling. The imaginary lines used to determine filling are shown as dashed lines. The numbers indicate the count.

■ GetROP2

VB Declaration	`Declare Function GetROP2% Lib "GDI" (ByVal hDC%)`
Description	Retrieves the current drawing mode for the specified device context. This defines how drawing operations combine with the image already on the display.
Use with VB	This is identical to reading the **DrawMode** property for VB forms or picture controls.

Parameter	Type/Description
hDC	**Integer**—Handle to a device context.

Return Value	**Integer**—Table 7.8 shows the name of the constant specifying a drawing mode from the API-CONST.TXT file, the equivalent VB **DrawMode** property value, and a brief description of the drawing mode.
Comments	This function only works on raster devices. For a more thorough description of how raster operations are used to combine a color with an existing image on a device, refer to the discussion in Chapter 8 on raster operations.

Table 7.8 **APICONST.TXT Drawing Mode Constants**

Constant	Draw Mode	Pixel Value
R2_BLACK	1	Black.
R2_WHITE	16	White.
R2_NOP	11	Unchanged.
R2_NOT	6	The inverse of the current display color.
R2_COPYPEN	13	The pen color.
R2_NOTCOPYPEN	4	The inverse of **R2_COPYPEN**.
R2_MERGEPENNOT	14	The inverse of the display color ORed with the pen color.
R2_MASKPENNOT	5	Inverse of the display color ANDed with the pen color.
R2_MERGENOTPEN	12	Inverse of the pen color ORed with the display color.
R2_MASKNOTPEN	3	Inverse of the pen color ANDed with the display color
R2_MERGEPEN	15	The pen color ORed with the display color.
R2_NOTMERGEPEN	2	Inverse of **R2_MERGEPEN**.
R2_MASKPEN	9	The display color ANDed with the pen color.

Table 7.8	**APICONST.TXT Drawing Mode Constants (Continued)**		

Constant	Draw Mode	Pixel Value
R2_NOTMASKPEN	8	Inverse of **R2_MASKPEN**.
R2_XORPEN	7	The exclusive-or of the display and pen colors.
R2_NOTXORPEN	10	The inverse of **R2_XORPEN**.

■ GetStockObject

VB Declaration   Declare Function GetStockObject% Lib "GDI" (ByVal nIndex%)

Description   Retrieves a stock object. This is one of the standard Windows objects that may be used by any application.

Use with VB   No problem.

Parameter	Type/Description
nIndex	Integer—One of the constants specified in the following table:

Value of nIndex	System Object Retrieved
BLACK_BRUSH	Black brush.
DKGRAY_BRUSH	Dark gray brush.
GRAY_BRUSH	Gray brush.
HOLLOW_BRUSH	Hollow brush.
LTGRAY_BRUSH	Light gray brush.
NULL_BRUSH	Empty brush.
WHITE_BRUSH	White brush.
BLACK_PEN	Black pen.
NULL_PEN	Empty pen.
WHITE_PEN	White pen.
ANSI_FIXED_FONT	Fixed pitched font using the Windows (ANSI) character set.
ANSI_VAR_FONT	Variable width font using the Windows (ANSI) character set.
DEVICE_DEFAULT_FONT	Default font used by the device.
OEM_FIXED_FONT	Fixed font in the OEM character set.

Value of nIndex	System Object Retrieved
SYSTEM_FONT	Screen system font. This is the default variable width font used for menus, dialog boxes, and so on.
SYSTEM_FIXED_FONT	Screen system font. This is the default fixed pitch font used for menus, dialog boxes, and so on, before Windows 3.0.
DEFAULT_PALETTE	Default color palette.

Return Value   **Integer**—A handle to the specified object.

Comments   Origins of stock brushes may not be changed. These objects should not be deleted using **Delete-Object**. Do not use the **DK_GRAY_BRUSH**, **GRAY_BRUSH**, and **LTGRAY_BRUSH** brushes on windows that do not have the **CS_HREDRAW** and **CS_VREDRAW** class styles.

■ InvertRect

VB Declaration   `Declare Sub InvertRect Lib "User" (ByVal hDC%, lpRect As RECT)`

Description   Inverts the specified rectangle on a device context by inverting the value of each pixel.

Use with VB   No problem.

Parameter	Type/Description
hDC	**Integer**—A handle to a device context.
lpRect	**RECT**— The rectangle to invert specified in logical coordinates.

■ InvertRgn

VB Declaration   `Declare Sub InvertRgn Lib "User" (ByVal hDC%, ByVal hRgn%)`

Description   Inverts the specified region on a device context by inverting the value of each pixel.

Use with VB   No problem.

Parameter	Type/Description
hDC	**Integer**—A handle to a device context.
lpRect	**RECT**—The region on the device to invert.

Return Value   **Integer**—TRUE (nonzero) on success, zero otherwise.

■ IsGDIObject

VB Declaration   `Declare Function IsGDIObject% Lib "GDI" (ByVal hobj%)`

Description   Determines if **hobj** is a valid GDI object.

Use with VB   No problem.

Parameter	Type/Description
hobj	Integer—A handle to check.

Return Value   Integer—FALSE (zero) if **hobj** is not a handle to a valid GDI object. If TRUE, it may or may not be a valid handle.

■ LineDDA

VB Declaration   `Declare Sub LineDDA Lib "GDI" (ByVal X1%, ByVal Y1%, ByVal X2%, ByVal Y2%, ⇔`
`ByVal lpLineFunc&, ByVal lpData&)`

Description   Enumerates all points in the specified line.

Use with VB   Requires the CBK.VBX custom control provided with this book.

Parameter	Type/Description
X1,Y1	**Integers**—Starting point of the line to check.
X2,Y2	**Integers**—Ending point of the line to check. This point is not considered part of the line.
lpLineFunc	**Long**—Pointer to function to call for each point that would be set when drawing the specified line. Use the **ProcAddress** property of the CBK.VBX custom control to obtain a function pointer for callbacks.
lParam	**Long**—Value that is passed to the **LineDDAProc** event of the CBK.VBX Custom control during enumeration.

Comments   Refer to Appendix A for details on using the CBK.VBX custom control with enumeration functions.

■ LineTo

VB Declaration   `Declare Function LineTo% Lib "GDI" (ByVal hDC%, ByVal X%, ByVal Y%)`

Description   Draws a line using the current pen from the current position to the point specified. The new current position will be point X,Y after this function is called.

Use with VB   No problem.

Parameter	Type/Description
hDC	Integer—Handle to a device context.
X,Y	Integers—End position for the point in logical coordinates. This point is not drawn; it's not part of the line.

Return Value   Integer—TRUE (nonzero) on success, zero otherwise.

■ MoveTo

VB Declaration   `Declare Function MoveTo& Lib "GDI" (ByVal hDC%, ByVal X%, ByVal Y%)`

Description   Specifies a new current pen position for the specified device context.

Use with VB   No problem.

Parameter	Type/Description
hDC	**Integer**—Handle to a device context.
X,Y	**Integers**—New pen position in logical coordinates.

Return Value   **Long**—The low word of the result contains the X coordinate in device coordinates. The high word contains the Y coordinate.

■ MoveToEx

VB Declaration   `Declare Function MoveToEx% Lib "GDI" (ByVal hDC%, ByVal nX%, ByVal nY%, ⇔`
`lpPoint As POINTAPI)`

Description   Specifies a new current pen position for the specified device context. The previous position is stored in **lpPoint**.

Use with VB   No problem.

Parameter	Type/Description
hDC	**Integer**—Handle to a device context.
X,Y	**Integers**—New pen position in logical coordinates.
lpPoint	**POINTAPI**—**POINTAPI** in which to store the previous pen position.

Return Value   **Integer**—TRUE (nonzero) on success, zero otherwise.

■ PaintRgn

VB Declaration   `Declare Function PaintRgn% Lib "GDI" (ByVal hDC%, ByVal hRgn%)`

Description   Fills the specified region using the currently selected brush.

Use with VB   No problem.

Parameter	Type/Description
hDC	**Integer**—Handle to a device context.
hRgn	**Integer**—Handle to a region to fill in device coordinates.

Return Value   **Integer**—TRUE (nonzero) on success, zero otherwise.

■ Pie

VB Declaration   Declare Function Pie% Lib "GDI" (ByVal hDC%, ByVal X1%, ByVal Y1%, ByVal ⇔
X2%, ByVal Y2%, ByVal X3%, ByVal Y3%, ByVal X4%, ByVal Y4%)

Description   Draws a pie as shown in Figure 7.5. X1,Y1,X2,Y2 specify a bounding rectangle of an ellipse. The point at which lines drawn from the center of the rectangle to points X3,Y3 and X4,Y4 define the wedge in the pie figure.

Use with VB   No problem.

Parameter	Type/Description
hDC	**Integer**—Handle to a display context.
X1,Y1	**Integers**—Specify the upper left corner of a rectangle that bounds an ellipse.
X2,Y2	**Integers**—Specify the lower right corner of a rectangle that bounds an ellipse.
X3,Y3	**Integers**—Specify one side of the pie wedge.
X4,Y4	**Integers**—Specify the side of the pie wedge not specified by X3,Y3.

Return Value   Integer—TRUE on success, FALSE otherwise.

Comments   The width and height of the bounding rectangle must be between 3 and 32766 units in size.

■ PlayMetaFile

VB Declaration   Declare Function PlayMetaFile% Lib "GDI" (ByVal hDC%, ByVal hMF%)

Description   Plays a metafile into the specified device context. The GDI operations that were recorded in the metafile are executed for the DC.

Use with VB   A metafile is capable of changing objects and mapping modes for a device context. Be sure to save the state of a VB form or picture control DC before calling this function.

Parameter	Type/Description
hDC	**Integer**—Handle to a device context on which to play the metafile.
hMF	**Integer**—Handle to a metafile to play.

Return Value   Integer—TRUE (nonzero) on success, zero otherwise.

■ PlayMetaFileRecord

VB Declaration   Declare Sub PlayMetaFileRecord Lib "GDI" (ByVal hDC%, lpHandletable%, ⇔
lpMetaRecord As METARECORD, ByVal nHandles%)

Description   Plays a single record from a metafile (each record contains a single GDI drawing command). This can be used in combination with the **EnumMetaFile** function to play only selected metafile records. The parameters to this function are similar to those returned by the **EnumMetaFile** event of the CBK.VBX custom control.

Use with VB   No problem.

Parameter	Type/Description
hDC	**Integer**—Handle to a device context on which to play the metafile record's GDI command.
lpHandleTable	**Integer**—The first entry in an integer array of handles to GDI objects used by the metafile.
lpMetaRecord	**METARECORD**—A single metafile record. Appendix B contains a description of this data structure.
nHandles	**Integer**—The number of handles in the metafile's handle table.

■ Polygon

VB Declaration   Declare Function Polygon% Lib "GDI" (ByVal hDC%, lpPoints As POINTAPI, ⇔
ByVal nCount%)

Description   Draws a polygon consisting of an arbitrary series of two or more points. Windows automatically closes the polygon by connecting the last and first points. The border of the polygon is drawn with the currently selected pen. The polygon is filled using the currently selected brush.

Use with VB   No problem.

Parameter	Type/Description
lpPoints	**POINTAPI**—The first **POINTAPI** structure in an array of **nCount** **POINTAPI** structures.
nCount	**Integer**—Number of points in the polygon.

Return Value   **Integer**—TRUE (nonzero) on success, zero otherwise.

Comments   The **GetPolyFillMode** and **SetPolyFillMode** functions determine how the polygon is filled.

■ PolyLine

VB Declaration   Declare Function Polyline% Lib "GDI" (ByVal hDC%, lpPoints As POINTAPI, ⇔
ByVal nCount%)

Description   Draws a series of lines using the current pen. The current position is not modified by this function.

Use with VB	No problem.

Parameter	Type/Description
lpPoints	**POINTAPI**—The first **POINTAPI** structure in an array of **nCount** **POINTAPI** structures.
nCount	**Integer**—Number of points in the **lpPoints** array. A line is drawn from the first point to the second, and so on.

Return Value   **Integer**—TRUE (nonzero) on success, zero otherwise.

■ PolyPolygon

VB Declaration   Declare Function PolyPolygon% Lib "GDI" (ByVal hDC%, lpPoints As POINTAPI, ⇔
lpPolyCounts%, ByVal nCount%)

Description   Draws two or more polygons using the currently selected pen. Fills them using the currently selected brush based on the polygon fill mode specified by the **SetPolyFillMode** function. Each
polygon must be closed.

Use with VB   No problem.

Parameter	Type/Description
lpPoints	**POINTAPI**—The first **POINTAPI** structure in an array of **nCount** **POINTAPI** structures.
lpPolyCounts	**Integer**—The first integer in an array of integers. Each entry contains the number of points that make up a closed polygon. The **lpPoints** array consists of a series of closed polygons, each one of which has an entry in the **lpPolyCounts** array.
nCount	**Integer**—Total number of polygons to be drawn. Must be at least 2.

Return Value   **Integer**—TRUE (nonzero) on success, zero otherwise.

■ Rectangle

VB Declaration   Declare Function Rectangle% Lib "GDI" (ByVal hDC%, ByVal X1%, ByVal Y1%, ⇔
ByVal X2%, ByVal Y2%)

Description   Draws the rectangle specified with the currently selected pen and fills it with the currently selected brush.

Use with VB   No problem.

Parameter	Type/Description
hDC	**Integer**—Handle to a device context.
X1,Y1	**Integers**—Point specifying the upper-left corner of the rectangle.
X2,Y2	**Integers**—Point specifying the lower-right corner of the rectangle.

Return Value   Integer—TRUE (nonzero) on success, zero otherwise.

■ RoundRect

VB Declaration   `Declare Function RoundRect% Lib "GDI" (ByVal hDC%, ByVal X1%, ByVal Y1%,` ⇔

`ByVal X2%, ByVal Y2%, ByVal X3%, ByVal Y3%)`

Description   Draws the rectangle with rounded corners with the currently selected pen and fills it with the currently selected brush. X3 and Y3 define the ellipse used to round the corners.

Use with VB   No problem.

Parameter	Type/Description
X1, Y1	**Integers**—X,Y coordinates describing the upper left corner of the rectangle.
X2, Y2	**Integers**—X,Y coordinates describing the lower right corner of the rectangle.
X3	**Integer**—The width of the ellipse used to round the corners.
Y3	**Integer**—The height of the ellipse used to round the corners.

Return Value   Integer—TRUE (nonzero) on success, zero otherwise.

■ SelectObject

VB Declaration   `Declare Function SelectObject% Lib "GDI" (ByVal hDC%, ByVal hObject%)`

Description   Each device context may have graphics objects selected into it. These include bitmaps, brushes, fonts, pens, and regions. Only one of each object may be selected into a device context at a time. The selected object is used during drawing to the DC; for example, the currently selected pen determines the color and style of lines drawn into the device context.

Use with VB   No problem.

Parameter	Type/Description
hDC	**Integer**—A handle to a device context.
hObject	**Integer**—A handle to a bitmap, pin, brush, font, or region.

Return Value   Integer—A handle to the object of the same type of **hObject** that was previously selected into the device context.

Comments   The return value is typically used to obtain the original value of the objects selected into the DC when new objects are selected. This original object is usually selected back into the device context after the graphic operations are complete. It is important to restore the original objects before destroying a device context.

■ SetBkColor

VB Declaration   Declare Function SetBkColor& Lib "GDI" (ByVal hDC%, ByVal crColor&)

Description   Sets the background color for the specified device context. The background color is used to fill the gaps in hatched brushes, dashed pens, and characters if the background mode is OPAQUE. It is also used during bitmap color conversions as described in Chapter 8.

Use with VB   No problem.

Parameter	Type/Description
hDC	**Integer**—Handle to a device context.
crColor	**Long**—RGB color value of new background color.

Return Value   **Long**—The previous background color. &H80000000& on error.

Comments   The background color will actually be the closest color to **crColor** that the device can display.

■ SetBkMode

VB Declaration   Declare Function SetBkMode% Lib "GDI" (ByVal hDC%, ByVal nBkMode%)

Description   Specifies the way that gaps in hatched brushes, dashed pens, and characters are filled.

Use with VB   No problem.

Parameter	Type/Description
hDC	**Integer**—Handle to a device context.
nBkMode	**Integer**—One of the following constant values: **OPAQUE**: Use the current background color to fill in gaps in dashed pens, hatched brushes, and characters. **TRANSPARENT**: Do not fill in gaps as described above.

Return Value   **Integer**—The value of the previous background mode.

■ SetBrushOrg

VB Declaration   Declare Function SetBrushOrg& Lib "GDI" (ByVal hDC%, ByVal X%, ByVal Y%)

Description   Sets the origin of the currently selected brush in the specified device context. Refer to "Brushes," earlier in this chapter.

Use with VB	Be sure to reset the DC's brush origin to 0,0 when finished. This may be done explicitly, or when the original DC is restored using the **RestoreDC** function.

Parameter	Type/Description
hDC	**Integer**—Handle to a device context.
X,Y	**Integers**—New position of the brush origin in device coordinates. These may be between 0 and 7 (inclusive).

Return Value	**Long**—The previous brush origin. The low word of the result contains the X coordinate in device coordinates. The high word contains the Y coordinate.
Comments	You must use the **UnrealizeObject** function on the brush before calling this function. Do not use on brushes obtained using the **GetStockObject** function.

■ SetMetaFileBits, SetMetaFileBitsBetter

VB Declaration	Declare Function SetMetaFileBits% Lib "GDI" (ByVal hMem%) Declare Function ⇔ SetMetaFileBitsBetter% Lib "GDI" (ByVal hmf%)
Description	Creates a metafile using the bits contained in the specified global memory handle (as created using the **GetMetaFileBits** function). This function is often used to create a metafile after reading raw metafile data from disk that had originally been obtained using the **GetMetaFileBits** function. **SetMetaFileBitsBetter** returns a metafile handle that is owned by GDI instead of the application, making it usable by applications that support object linking and embedding (OLE). It may be necessary to use this function when dealing with VB custom controls that support OLE and metafiles.
Use with VB	No problem.

Parameter	Type/Description
hMF	**Integer**—Handle to a global memory handle. This handle will no longer be valid after this function is called (and must not be freed by the programmer).

Return Value	**Integer**—A global metafile handle on success, zero otherwise.
Comments	Refer to Chapter 12 for information on using global memory handles.

■ SetPixel

VB Declaration	Declare Function SetPixel& Lib "GDI" (ByVal hDC%, ByVal X%, ByVal Y%, ByVal ⇔ crColor&)
Description	Sets the RGB value of a pixel in the specified device context.

Use with VB   No problem.

Parameter	Type/Description
hDC	**Integer**—Handle to a device context.
X,Y	**Integers**—Point to set in logical coordinates.
crColor	**Long**—New RGB color for the specified pixel.

Return Value   **Long**—The actual RGB color of the point. This will differ from **crColor** if the device does not support the exact color specified. It will return -1 if the point cannot be set (for example, if the point is outside of the clipping region for the device context).

■ SetPolyFillMode

VB Declaration   `Declare Function SetPolyFillMode% Lib "GDI" (ByVal hDC%, ByVal nPolyFillMode%)`

Description   Sets the filling mode for polygons. Refer to Figure 7.7 for a description of the two filling modes.

Use with VB   No problem.

Parameter	Type/Description
hDC	**Integer**—Handle to a device context.
nPolyFillMode	**Integer**—One of the following constants: **ALTERNATE**: Alternates filling. **WINDING**: Fills based on drawing direction. Refer to Figure 7.7 for details.

Return Value   **Integer**—The previous polygon filling mode on success. Zero on error.

■ SetROP2

VB Declaration   `Declare Function SetROP2% Lib "GDI" (ByVal hDC%, ByVal nDrawMode%)`

Description   Sets the drawing mode for the specified device context. This is identical to the VB **DrawMode** property.

Use with VB   This function sets the **DrawMode** property when used with the device context for a VB form or picture control.

Parameter	Type/Description
hDC	**Integer**—Handle to a device context.
nDrawMode	**Integer**—New drawing mode for the device context. Refer to Table 7.8 in the function reference entry for the **GetROP2** function for legal values.

Return Value   **Integer**—The previous drawing mode.

Comments   Drawing modes apply to raster devices only.

■ UnrealizeObject

VB Declaration   Declare Function UnrealizeObject% Lib "GDI" (ByVal hObject%)

Description   This function must be called for a brush object before selecting it into a device context if the brush origin is to be changed using the **SetBrushOrg** function. Refer to "Brushes," earlier in this chapter. This function may also be used with logical palettes as described in Chapter 16.

Use with VB   No problem.

Parameter	Type/Description
hObject	**Integer**—Handle to a brush or logical palette.

Return Value   **Integer**—TRUE (nonzero) on success, zero otherwise.

8

Bitmaps, Icons, and Raster Operations

T HIS CHAPTER DESCRIBES THE WINDOWS API FUNCTIONS THAT DEAL WITH image areas on raster devices, specifically the use of bitmaps and icons. Techniques for using raster operations to combine bitmaps or merge a bitmap onto an existing image are described along with a summary of the available raster operations. The chapter includes an example project called Puzzle, which implements a scrambled tiling game with any bitmap. Puzzle illustrates the creation of bitmaps, how they may be copied and stretched, and the use of device-independent bitmaps. A sample program that allows you to view the stock bitmaps and icons included in Windows is also provided.

Bitmaps

All Windows display screens and a great many printers are *raster devices*. On a raster device, an image is made up of multiple scan lines and individual pixels may be accessed. Windows also supports nonraster devices such as plotters, but most of the operations described in this chapter will not work with those devices. The **GetDeviceCaps** API function described in Chapter 4 may be used to determine which raster operations a device supports.

A bitmap is a set of data that represents an image in a form compatible with a raster device. Under Windows, this set of data is contained in a Windows object that is called a bitmap object. In order to understand the different types of bitmaps and how they are used, it is necessary to examine how raster devices represent pixels.

Displaying Pixels

A pixel is the smallest unit that can be displayed by a raster device. On a monochrome display, a pixel can be represented by a single bit of data. Typically a monochrome display will consist of a single array of bytes where each bit represents one pixel. Bits that are set to 1 will usually be displayed in white; bits that are set to 0 will be black. An example of a monochrome bitmap is shown in Figure 8.1.

On a color device, each pixel requires multiple bits. Table 8.1 shows the number of bits per pixel and number of colors available on various Windows devices.

Color Planes and Device Palettes

A color on a video display is generated by combining shading of the colors red, green, and blue. The total number of possible colors depends on the number of shades of each of those primary colors. On a 24-bit color device, each primary color has eight bits. The total number of possible colors is thus $2^8 * 2^8 * 2^8$ or 16,777,216.

Figure 8.1
A monochrome
bitmap

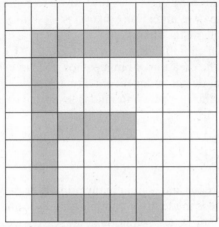

```
11111111
10000011
10111111
10111111
10000111
10111111
10111111
10000011
```

Image: each square represents one pixel   Image data = one bit per pixel

Table 8.1   **Color Support in Windows**

Bits per Pixel	Number of Colors	Typical Device
1	2	Monochrome graphics
4	16	Standard VGA
8	256	256-color VGA
16	32,768	32k-color super VGA
24	2^{24}	True 24-bit color devices

On a true 24-bit color device, each pixel has 24 bits, thus the device can display all 16,777,216 colors simultaneously. The disadvantage of this technique is that it requires huge amounts of memory. For example, a 1024×768 pixel 24-bit display requires 1024 * 768 * 3 = 2.36 megabytes of video memory! One common compromise is to use a 15-bit color card that provides 32,768 colors. In this case each of the primary colors uses five bits to provide 32 shades.

Though these cards are becoming increasingly common, most people still use standard or super VGA cards that use either four or eight bits per pixel. These cards are known as palette-based devices. The contents of the pixel do not directly determine the shadings of the primary colors that determine the pixel color. Instead, the pixel value is an index into an array of 24-bit values on the video card itself. Each entry in this palette array defines the color to use for the specified pixel value. This makes it possible for a device to select from millions of possible colors, even though it can display only a limited number of those colors simultaneously. Figure 8.2 illustrates this technique for a 16-color (four bits per pixel) device. In this example, the indicated pixel has the value of 3. This causes the color in the fourth entry in the palette to be used to determine the final color.

Figure 8.2
Palette-based
devices

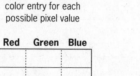

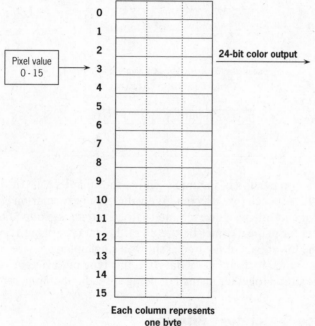

Windows also defines an object known as a *logical palette*. Logical palettes are described in further detail in Chapter 16.

The bits that are used for each pixel may be configured in a number of different ways depending on the device. For example, in a VGA card the bits are divided into four different planes. Each plane is an array of bits in a particular color. Figure 8.3 illustrates a four-bit pixel in both four-plane and four-bit configurations.

Figure 8.3

Four-plane versus four-bit device configurations

This diagram shows a scan line made up of four pixels with the values 0, 5, 10, and 15 on a four-plane device and on a four-bits-per-pixel device.

Four pixels (0, 5, 10, 15) on a four-plane device

Each column represents one bit

| 0 | 1 | 0 | 1 | **Plane 0** |

| 0 | 0 | 1 | 1 | **Plane 1** |

| 0 | 1 | 0 | 1 | **Plane 2** |

| 0 | 0 | 1 | 1 | **Plane 3** |

0   5   10   15

Four pixels (0, 5, 10, 15) on a single-plane device

Each cell describes a four-bit nibble.
Each pair of cells fills one byte.

0000	0101	1010	1111
0	**5**	**10**	**15**

The top portion of Figure 8.3 shows four planes, each of which contains a single bit for each pixel. To read the value of a particular pixel, you read one bit from each plane. However, internally, the data is grouped by plane—all of the data for plane 0 comes before all of the data for plane 1, and so on.

The lower part of Figure 8.3 shows a single plane device where each pixel is represented by four bits of data. On this type of device, all of the data for a pixel is stored together instead of being spread out among four planes.

Device-Dependent Bitmaps

A bitmap has already been defined as an object in Windows that holds an image. When the internal format of the image depends on the configuration of the device on which it is used, the bitmap is referred to as a *device-dependent bitmap*. All bitmaps in Windows are device-dependent unless noted otherwise. Generally speaking, a bitmap can only be used with devices that have the same internal configuration. The exception is the monochrome bitmap, which is compatible with all devices.

Windows requires that the data within a bitmap be aligned on integer (16-bit) boundaries. Figure 8.4 shows the internal data format of a monochrome bitmap. This is the required format for data buffers used to set or retrieve bitmap data, and more important, it is the data format used for monochrome data within icon- and device-independent bitmap files.

Figure 8.4

Monochrome bitmap data format

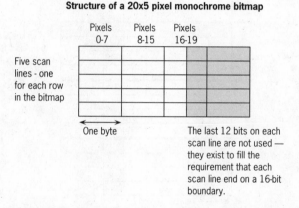

Structure of a 20x5 pixel monochrome bitmap

Each pixel requires one bit of data; thus eight pixels are grouped together in a single byte. Figure 8.4 shows a bitmap that is 20 pixels across and 5 pixels high. Figure 8.4 also illustrates the requirement that Windows imposes on monochrome bitmaps that each horizontal scan line lie on a 16-bit boundary.

Figure 8.5 shows the internal data format for a 16-color four-plane device-dependent bitmap.

In Figure 8.5 you can see how all of the data for a given scan line is grouped together. This corresponds closely to the bitmap format shown in the upper part of Figure 8.3. Once again there is a 16-bit boundary requirement.

It is not safe under Windows to make any assumptions regarding the internal data format of a color device-dependent bitmap. This is because each video device may define its own internal format for these bitmaps. Figure 8.5 is presented only as an example for clarification.

Table 8.2 lists functions used to create and load device-dependent bitmaps.

Figure 8.5

Four-plane bitmap
data format

**Structure of a 20x4 pixel 16-color device-dependent bitmap
(typical VGA format)**

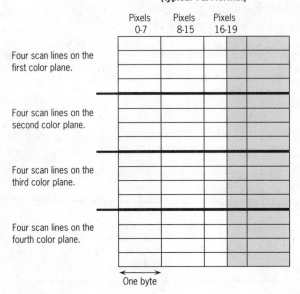

Pixels
0-7

Pixels
8-15

Pixels
16-19

Four scan lines on the
first color plane.

Four scan lines on the
second color plane.

Four scan lines on the
third color plane.

Four scan lines on the
fourth color plane.

The last 12 bits on each
scan line are not used —
they exist to fill the
requirement that each
scan line end on a 16-bit
boundary.

One byte

Table 8.2   Device-Dependent Bitmap Functions

Function	Description
CreateBitmap	Creates a bitmap and optionally initializes bitmap data.
CreateBitmapIndirect	Creates a bitmap based on a **BITMAP** data structure.
CreateCompatibleBitmap	Creates a bitmap that is compatible with a specified device context.
CreateDiscardableBitmap	Creates a bitmap that may be discarded by Windows if necessary.
GetBitmapBits	Retrieves the image data of a bitmap.
GetBitmapDimension GetBitmapDimensionEx	Retrieves the dimensions of a bitmap.
LoadBitmap	Loads a bitmap from a resource file or loads a stock system bitmap.
SetBitmapBits	Sets the bitmap image from a data buffer.
SetBitmapDimension SetBitmapDimensionEx	Sets the dimension of a bitmap.

Using Bitmaps

Bitmaps are GDI objects, and, like other GDI objects, a bitmap may be selected into a device context; however, it may only be selected into a memory device context. There is a logical reason for this. A bitmap represents the image area of a device. A display screen or printer already has an image area defined—it is the physical screen or page. A memory device context simulates a device in memory. The memory device context provides the interface to access the simulated device. The bitmap provides a block of memory that represents the device surface. It is always necessary to select a bitmap into a memory device context before drawing into it—if you wish to actually generate an image. Otherwise the drawing operations will have no image space to draw on.

When you no longer need a bitmap, it is important to delete it using the **DeleteObject** API function to free the system resources and memory that it occupies. Windows provides a number of functions to transfer images on a device, or from one device to another. These functions are described in Table 8.3.

Table 8.3   Bitmap Transfer Functions

Function	Description
BitBlt	Bit block transfer. Transfers an image area from one area to another.
PatBlt	Pattern block transfer. Fills an image area based on a specified pattern (as represented by a brush).
GetStretchBltMode	Determines the mechanism by which Windows deletes lines or pixels when stretching takes place.
SetStretchBltMode	Sets the mechanism by which Windows deletes lines or pixels when stretching takes place.
StretchBlt	Stretch block transfer. Transfers an image area from one area to another, stretching it in the process.

Since bitmaps are device-dependent objects, it is usually not possible to use these functions to transfer an image between devices that are not compatible with each other. In other words, it is rarely possible to use **BitBlt** to transfer an image directly from the display surface onto a printer. Windows supports device-independent bitmaps that can be used for interdevice transfers. They are described later in this chapter.

You can use the **BitBlt** function to move images around the screen or to stretch bitmap images.

In order to copy a bitmap to the display surface, you must first select it into a memory device context that is compatible with the display. You can then use the **BitBlt** or **StretchBlt** function to copy the image from the memory DC to the display DC. The Puzzle example program in this chapter shows how this is done.

Color Conversions

For accurate color conversions when transferring images between devices, it is necessary to use device-independent bitmaps. However, the **BitBlt** and **StretchBlt** functions do support conversions to and from monochrome bitmaps. To do this they use the foreground color, which is set by the **SetText-Color** function described in Chapter 10, and the background color, which is set by the **SetBkColor** function described in Chapter 7.

When converting from color to monochrome, all pixels that match the current background color are set to white, and all other pixels are set to black.

When converting from monochrome to color, white pixels are set to the current background color and black pixels are set to the foreground color.

Using Bitmaps with Visual Basic

As GDI objects, bitmaps can be used with Visual Basic in much the same way as the drawing objects described in Chapter 7. As before, be sure to restore a VB device context to its original state when you are finished using it.

The form and picture control **Picture** and **Image** properties return bitmaps that may be used with Windows API functions. The Puzzle example program takes advantage of this to store a bitmap in a picture control, which it can then access when needed.

Device-Independent Bitmaps

Device-independent bitmaps (DIBs) are used to hold images that are compatible with any raster device. They accomplish this by providing a standard format for the bitmap data and by including within the DIB the definitions of the colors represented by that data. DIBs may be defined as having two colors (monochrome), 16 colors, or 256 colors, or they may provide true 24-bit color support.

Device-independent bitmaps actually consist of two separate data structures followed by the actual data. The **BITMAPINFOHEADER** structure defines the size and type of the DIB. It also indicates the type of compression in effect and the number of colors.

The **BITMAPINFO** structure consists of the **BITMAPINFOHEADER** structure followed by a color table. The number of entries in the color table matches the number of colors supported by the DIB unless the DIB is a 24-bit color bitmap, in which case the color table is not present.

The data area follows the **BITMAPINFO** structure in memory. The number of bits for each pixel depends on the color configuration for the DIB. For two-, 16-, and 256-color DIBs, the pixel describes an index into the color table that contains the color for that pixel. For 24-bit color, each pixel consists of 24 bits (three bytes) that contain the actual RGB color to use.

The data for each scan line in a DIB must be aligned to a 32-bit boundary. Figure 8.6 shows the structure of a 16-color device-independent bitmap.

Figure 8.6

Structure of a device-independent bitmap

Structure of a 6x5 pixel 16-color device independent bitmap (DIB)

Color table for the DIB

Sixteen entries in the DIB color table.

Blue   Green   Red   Set to zero

Each column represents one byte

Data for the DIB

Five scan lines - one for each row in the bitmap

Pixels 0 & 1   Pixels 2 & 3   Pixels 4 & 5

Pix 0 | Pix 1

The last byte on each scan line are not used in this case—it exists to fill the requirement that each scan line end on a 32-bit boundary.

Each column represents one byte

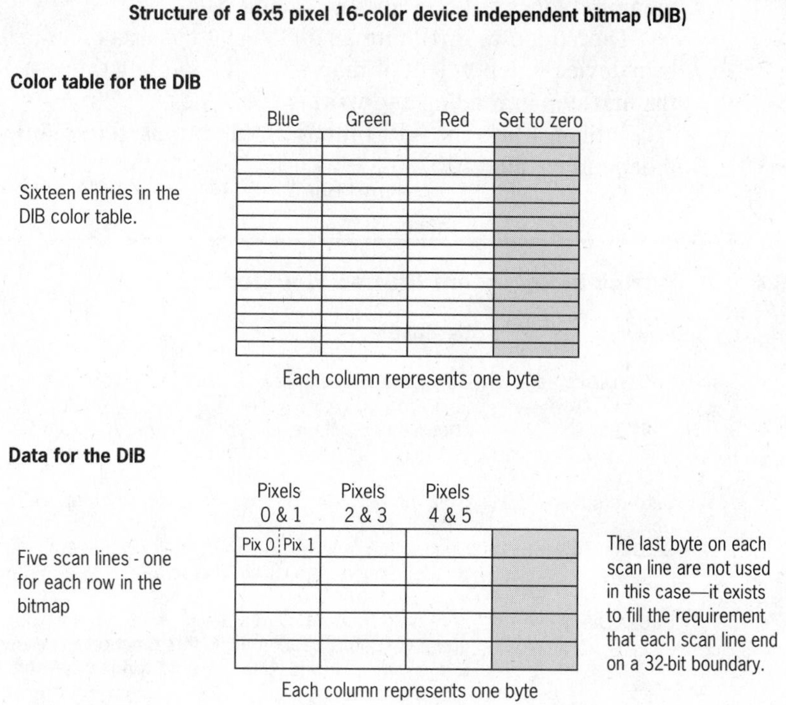

These structures are described in detail in Appendix B.

The color table represents the desired palette to use with this device-independent bitmap. Each entry in the DIB color table defines the ideal color to use for pixels that have the value corresponding to the position of the entry. Windows will choose the closest available color when copying the DIB to the device.

The data area is structured as a single plane bitmap with four bits per pixel. Note that unlike device-dependent bitmaps, DIBs require that scan lines end on 32-bit boundaries.

Several of the device-independent bitmap API functions allow you to keep only a portion of the bitmap data in memory at once. In these cases, the function allows you to specify the first horizontal line and the total number of lines in the DIB data array. These lines, which consist of a row of pixels the width of the DIB, are often referred to as scan lines.

Device-independent bitmaps are contained in memory buffers—they are not GDI resources. A few API functions call for an object known as a *packed DIB*. This is simply a DIB contained within a global memory block. Global memory blocks are described in Chapter 12.

The Windows BMP bitmap file format consists of a file header followed by a device-independent bitmap, so understanding the structure of a DIB is the first step in reading and writing these files.

Table 8.4 lists the API functions that are used to manipulate device-independent bitmaps.

Table 8.4   Device-Independent Bitmap Functions

Function	Description
CreateDIBitmap	Creates a device-dependent bitmap based on a DIB.
GetDIBits	Loads a device-independent bitmap with data from a device-dependent bitmap.
SetDIBits	Sets the image in a device-dependent bitmap with data from a DIB.
SetDIBitsToDevice	Sends data from a DIB directly to a device. This can be used to transfer data directly from a DIB to the screen or to a printer.
StretchDIBits	Sets data from a DIB to a device context, stretching the image as requested. Some devices allow this function to be used to set data directly to the output device. Use the **GetDeviceCaps** function to determine if this is the case.

Icons and Cursors

An icon is a small bitmap that has the unique capability of allowing any pixel to be not only one of the bitmap colors, but also the screen or inverted screen color. Icons in Windows 3.*x* are generally 32×32 pixels in size. Other sizes are supported in Windows, though not by Visual Basic.

An icon actually contains two separate bitmaps. The first bitmap may be monochrome or color and contains an image that will be combined with the display image using the exclusive-OR operation. It is referred to as the XOR bitmap. The second bitmap is a monochrome bitmap called the AND bitmap, which contains a mask that will be ANDed with the display image before it is combined with the XOR bitmap. Figure 8.7 shows how the two bitmaps in an icon combine to form an image when the bitmap is drawn.

Figure 8.7
Structure and use of icons

Illustration of a 3x3 pixel segment of a 16-color icon.

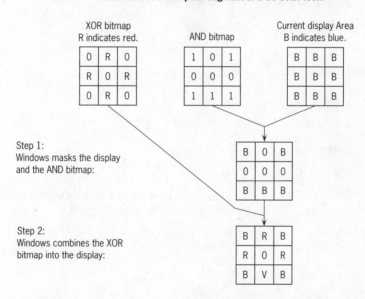

The AND bitmap is used to determine what parts of the display should be masked out before applying the icon. Note how the lower center square is affected. The AND bitmap did not mask out the display pixel, thus the XOR operation caused the red pixel in the XOR bitmap to be combined with the blue pixel on the display leading to the result V (violet).

In Figure 8.7, first, the AND bitmap is combined with the current display area. Display pixels that correspond to a zero in the AND bitmap are cleared—which means that the final image will be identical to the value of the pixel in the XOR bitmap. Display pixels that correspond to a one in the AND bitmap are kept and exclusive ORed with the XOR bitmap to produce the final image.

Icons are GDI objects and should be destroyed using the **DestroyIcon** API function when they are no longer needed. Do not destroy stock system icons retrieved using the **LoadIcon** API function.

A cursor is internally identical to an icon except that the XOR bitmap is always a monochrome bitmap. The cursor also contains two fields that define the "hot-spot"—the point on the cursor that represents its exact location.

Table 8.5 lists the API functions that are used to work with icons and to create cursors. API functions that describe how cursors are used are discussed in Chapter 5.

Table 8.5 **Icon and Cursor API Functions**

Function	Description
CopyCursor	Copies a cursor.
CopyIcon	Copies an icon.
CreateCursor	Creates a cursor.
CreateIcon	Creates an icon.
DestroyIcon	Destroys an icon.
DrawIcon	Draws an icon.
LoadIcon	Loads an icon from a resource file, or loads a stock system icon. Resource files are described in Chapter 12.
OpenIcon	Restores a minimized application. Refer to the **ShowWindow** function in Chapter 4 for details.

Raster Operations

When you consider transferring a bitmap onto a device context, you might think of the simple case where the bitmap is simply copied to the destination. The value of each bit on the destination device context is replaced by the corresponding bit in the source bitmap.

Windows actually provides 255 different ways in which the bits on the destination device context may be set; the simple copy described above is one of them. The destination DC bit values are determined by a Boolean equation that combines the source bitmap, the currently selected brush, and the current value of the destination. These equations are known as raster operation codes or raster-ops for short. (Chapter 7 described the 16 ROP2 line drawing raster-ops.)

The equation that determines the new value of the pixel has three possible operands, each with a single letter code:

D = Destination—the value of the bit in the destination bitmap.

S = Source—the value of the bit in the source bitmap that corresponds to a bit in the destination bitmap.

P = Pattern—the value of the bit in a pattern determined by the currently selected brush.

There are four Boolean operations that can be applied to these operands, each with a single letter code in lowercase:

a = AND operation

n = NOT operation (inverts the bit)

o = OR operation

x = XOR operation (exclusive OR)

The equation is written in reverse polish notation (RPN). This means that it is read from left to right, each operation affecting the operand to its left. Consider the following example:

```
DPSaxn
```

In this example, the source bitmap is ANDed with the current pattern. The result is then XORed with the destination bitmap. The result of that operation is inverted. The result of this final operation is set into the destination.

Using Raster-Ops

The most common raster operations are those used to copy one image to another or to exclusive OR one image by another. The advantage of the exclusive OR operation is that it is reversible—repeating the operation causes the original image to be restored.

Occasionally, a more complex series of raster operations may be used to good effect. For example, Windows provides no good way to extract the XOR and AND masks from an icon handle. The following steps can be used to generate those masks:

1. Create a 32×32 bitmap compatible with the display.

2. Use the **PatBlt** function to set this bitmap to black.

3. Draw the icon onto this bitmap, which contains the XOR bitmap. The **GetDIBits** function can be used to retrieve the mask in DIB format.

4. Create a second 32×32 bitmap compatible with the display.

5. Use the **PatBlt** function to set this bitmap to white.

6. Draw the icon onto this second bitmap.

7. Draw the XOR bitmap onto this second bitmap using the XOR operation by using the SRCINVERT raster-op. After this operation the bits determined only by the icon will be black, the bits that are influenced by the display will be white.

8. Use the **BitBlt** function to convert this bitmap into a monochrome bitmap. This will be the mask.

Keep in mind that the bitmaps need to be selected into memory device contexts before the **BitBlt** and **PatBlt** operations can be performed.

With clever application of Boolean algebra, it is possible to convert colors, merge pictures into each other, and otherwise achieve a great many effects, some of which have no practical use whatsoever.

See Appendix G for a list of raster operations available under Windows.

Example: StockBMs—A Stock Bitmap and Icon Viewer

StockBMs is a program that allows you to view the stock bitmaps and icons provided by Windows. It also demonstrates the loading and display of bitmaps and icons.

Figure 8.8 shows the runtime screen of the StockBMs program.

Figure 8.8
StockBMSs program screen

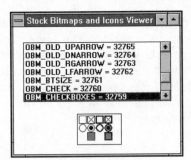

Using StockBMs

The StockBMs screen shown in Figure 8.8 contains only two controls. A list box is loaded with the constant definitions for the Windows stock bitmaps and icons. Selecting an entry in the list box causes the corresponding icon or bitmap to be loaded and displayed in the single picture control.

Project Description

The StockBMs project includes four files. STOCKBMS.FRM is the only form used in the program. STOCKBMS.BAS is the only module in the program and contains the constant type and global definitions. APIDECS.BAS is the type-safe API declaration file provided with this book. APIGUIDE.BAS contains the declarations for the APIGUIDE.DLL dynamic link library.

Listing 8.1 shows the project file for the StockBMs program.

Listing 8.1   Project Listing File STOCKBMS.MAK

```
STOCKBMS.FRM
STOCKBMS.BAS
APIDECS.BAS
APIGUIDE.BAS
ProjWinSize=175,439,248,215
ProjWinShow=2
```

Form Description

Listing 8.2 contains the header from file STOCKBMS.FRM that describes the control setup for the form.

Listing 8.2   STOCKBMS.FRM Header

```
VERSION 2.00
Begin Form StockBMS
    Caption         =    "Stock Bitmaps and Icons Viewer"
    Height          =    3390
    Left            =    1035
    LinkMode        =    1  'Source
    LinkTopic       =    "Form1"
    ScaleHeight     =    2985
    ScaleWidth      =    4065
    Top             =    1140
    Width           =    4185
    Begin PictureBox Picture1
```

Listing 8.2   STOCKBMS.FRM Header (Continued)

```
        Height       =   735
        Left         =   1560
        ScaleHeight  =   705
        ScaleWidth   =   1065
        TabIndex     =   1
        Top          =   2040
        Width        =   1095
    End
    Begin ListBox List1
        Height       =   1395
        Left         =   240
        TabIndex     =   0
        Top          =   360
        Width        =   3615
    End
End
```

StockBMs Listing

Module STOCKBMS.BAS contains the constant declarations and global variables used by the program.

Listing 8.3   Module STOCKBMS.BAS

```
' StockBMs program example


'-------------------------------------------------
'
'         Global Constants
'

Global Const CBM_INIT = &H4&     ' initialize bitmap
Global Const DIB_RGB_COLORS = 0 ' color table in RGBTriples
Global Const DIB_PAL_COLORS = 1 ' color table in palette indices

Global Const OBM_CLOSE = 32754
Global Const OBM_UPARROW = 32753
Global Const OBM_DNARROW = 32752
Global Const OBM_RGARROW = 32751
Global Const OBM_LFARROW = 32750
Global Const OBM_REDUCE = 32749
Global Const OBM_ZOOM = 32748
Global Const OBM_RESTORE = 32747
Global Const OBM_REDUCED = 32746
```

Listing 8.3   Module STOCKBMS.BAS (Continued)

```
Global Const OBM_ZOOMD = 32745
Global Const OBM_RESTORED = 32744
Global Const OBM_UPARROWD = 32743
Global Const OBM_DNARROWD = 32742
Global Const OBM_RGARROWD = 32741
Global Const OBM_LFARROWD = 32740
Global Const OBM_MNARROW = 32739
Global Const OBM_COMBO = 32738
Global Const OBM_UPARROWI = 32737
Global Const OBM_DNARROWI = 32736
Global Const OBM_RGARROWI = 32735
Global Const OBM_LFARROWI = 32734
Global Const OBM_OLD_CLOSE = 32767
Global Const OBM_SIZE = 32766
Global Const OBM_OLD_UPARROW = 32765
Global Const OBM_OLD_DNARROW = 32764
Global Const OBM_OLD_RGARROW = 32763
Global Const OBM_OLD_LFARROW = 32762
Global Const OBM_BTSIZE = 32761
Global Const OBM_CHECK = 32760
Global Const OBM_CHECKBOXES = 32759
Global Const OBM_BTNCORNERS = 32758
Global Const OBM_OLD_REDUCE = 32757
Global Const OBM_OLD_ZOOM = 32756
Global Const OBM_OLD_RESTORE = 32755
Global Const OIC_SAMPLE = 32512
Global Const OIC_HAND = 32513
Global Const OIC_QUES = 32514
Global Const OIC_BANG = 32515
Global Const OIC_NOTE = 32516
Global Const SRCCOPY = &HCC0020
Global Const SRCPAINT = &HEE0086
Global Const SRCAND = &H8800C6
Global Const SRCINVERT = &H660046
Global Const SRCERASE = &H440328
Global Const NOTSRCCOPY = &H330008
Global Const NOTSRCERASE = &H1100A6
Global Const MERGECOPY = &HC000CA
Global Const MERGEPAINT = &HBB0226
Global Const PATCOPY = &HF00021
Global Const PATPAINT = &HFB0A09
Global Const PATINVERT = &H5A0049
Global Const DSTINVERT = &H550009
Global Const BLACKNESS = &H42&
Global Const WHITENESS = &HFF0062
Global Const BLACKONWHITE = 1
Global Const WHITEONBLACK = 2
Global Const COLORONCOLOR = 3
```

Listing 8.3 Module STOCKBMS.BAS (Continued)

```
Global Const BI_RGB = 0&
Global Const BI_RLE8 = 1&
Global Const BI_RLE4 = 2&
Global Const TRANSPARENT = 1
Global Const OPAQUE = 2
```

Listing 8.4 Program Listing for STOCKBMS.FRM

```
'
'   Initialize the list box
'
Sub Form_Load ()
    ' Load the listbox with entries for each stock
    ' bitmap and icon
    List1.AddItem "OBM_CLOSE = 32754"
    List1.AddItem "OBM_UPARROW = 32753"
    List1.AddItem "OBM_DNARROW = 32752"
    List1.AddItem "OBM_RGARROW = 32751"
    List1.AddItem "OBM_LFARROW = 32750"
    List1.AddItem "OBM_REDUCE = 32749"
    List1.AddItem "OBM_ZOOM = 32748"
    List1.AddItem "OBM_RESTORE = 32747"
    List1.AddItem "OBM_REDUCED = 32746"
    List1.AddItem "OBM_ZOOMD = 32745"
    List1.AddItem "OBM_RESTORED = 32744"
    List1.AddItem "OBM_UPARROWD = 32743"
    List1.AddItem "OBM_DNARROWD = 32742"
    List1.AddItem "OBM_RGARROWD = 32741"
    List1.AddItem "OBM_LFARROWD = 32740"
    List1.AddItem "OBM_MNARROW = 32739"
    List1.AddItem "OBM_COMBO = 32738"
    List1.AddItem "OBM_UPARROWI = 32737"
    List1.AddItem "OBM_DNARROWI = 32736"
    List1.AddItem "OBM_RGARROWI = 32735"
    List1.AddItem "OBM_LFARROWI = 32734"
    List1.AddItem "OBM_OLD_CLOSE = 32767"
    List1.AddItem "OBM_SIZE = 32766"
    List1.AddItem "OBM_OLD_UPARROW = 32765"
    List1.AddItem "OBM_OLD_DNARROW = 32764"
    List1.AddItem "OBM_OLD_RGARROW = 32763"
    List1.AddItem "OBM_OLD_LFARROW = 32762"
    List1.AddItem "OBM_BTSIZE = 32761"
    List1.AddItem "OBM_CHECK = 32760"
    List1.AddItem "OBM_CHECKBOXES = 32759"
    List1.AddItem "OBM_BTNCORNERS = 32758"
    List1.AddItem "OBM_OLD_REDUCE = 32757"
```

Listing 8.4   Program Listing for STOCKBMS.FRM (Continued)

```
        List1.AddItem "OBM_OLD_ZOOM = 32756"
        List1.AddItem "OBM_OLD_RESTORE = 32755"
        List1.AddItem "OIC_SAMPLE = 32512"
        List1.AddItem "OIC_HAND = 32513"
        List1.AddItem "OIC_QUES = 32514"
        List1.AddItem "OIC_BANG = 32515"
        List1.AddItem "OIC_NOTE = 32516"
End Sub


'
'   Paints the stock icon or bitmap in picture1
'
'
'   Retrieve a stock bitmap or icon for the selected list
'   box entry. Draws the bitmap or icon on the picture
'   control.
'
Sub ShowObject ()
        Dim ShadowDC%
        Dim isbm%
        Dim param$
        Dim idlong&
        Dim objhandle%, oldobject%
        Dim bm As BITMAP

        ' Be sure there is a valid entry
        If List1.Listindex < 0 Then Exit Sub

        picture1.Cls     ' Clear the picture control
        param$ = List1.Text
        ' Find out if it's a bitmap or an icon
        If Left$(param$, 3) = "OBM" Then isbm% = -1

        ' Extract the id value to use
        idlong& = Val(Mid$(param$, InStr(param$, "=") + 1))

        If isbm% Then     ' It's a stock bitmap

            ' Create a memory device context compatible with
            ' the picture control
            ShadowDC% = CreateCompatibleDC%(picture1.hDC)

            ' Load the bitmap
            objhandle% = LoadBitmapBynum(0, idlong&)

            ' Retrieve the height and width of the bitmap
            di% = GetObjectAPI(objhandle%, 10, agGetAddressForObject&(bm))
```

Listing 8.4   Program Listing for STOCKBMS.FRM (Continued)

```
                    ' Select the bitmap into the memory DC, keeping
                    ' a handle to the prior bitmap.
                    oldobject% = SelectObject(ShadowDC%, objhandle%)

                    ' BitBlt the bitmap into the picture control,
                    ' offset by 2 pixels from the upper left corner
                    ' (just to make it look better)
                    di% = BitBlt(picture1.hDC, 2, 2, bm.bmWidth,bm.bmHeight, ShadowDC%, ⇔
                    0, 0, SRCCOPY)

                    ' Select the bitmap OUT of the memory DC
                    di% = SelectObject(ShadowDC%, oldobject%)
                    ' and delete it (yes - even though they are system
                    ' bitmaps - this doesn't destroy them, just releases
                    ' your private copy of the bitmap.
                    di% = DeleteObject(objhandle%)

                    ' Finally, delete the memory DC
                    di% = DeleteDC%(ShadowDC%)
                Else    ' It's an icon - a much easier process
                    ' Get the stock icon
                    objhandle% = LoadIconBynum(0, idlong&)

                    ' Draw it directly onto the picture control
                    di% = DrawIcon%(picture1.hDC, 2, 2, objhandle%)

                    ' Don't destroy system icons!
                    End If
            End Sub

            '
            '   Just display the current object
            '
            Sub List1_Click ()
                ShowObject
            End Sub

            '
            '   When redrawing the picture control, show the currently
            '   selected object (if any)
            '
            Sub Picture1_Paint ()
                ShowObject
            End Sub
```

Example: Puzzle—A Tiled Bitmap Puzzle Game

Puzzle is a simulation of a scrambled tile puzzle game. A bitmap is broken up into 25 tiles, which are then scrambled. One of the tiles is removed. It is up to the player to re-create the original bitmap by sliding the tiles one at a time into the empty space.

This program demonstrates use of device-dependent bitmaps, device-independent bitmaps, bitmap transfer and scaling, and creation of pattern brushes. It also uses a variety of device context and rectangle functions introduced in previous chapters.

Using Puzzle

The Puzzle application is extremely simple to use. When the program is loaded, it displays a scrambled version of a default bitmap (the arches bitmap provided by Windows). One of the squares in the 5x5 grid is black to indicate that it is empty. Clicking with the mouse on any of the tiles next to the empty square causes that tile to be moved into the empty square. The purpose of the game is to unscramble the image.

A menu bar shows three options. The Scramble menu option can be used to rescramble the image tiles. The Load menu option brings up a load bitmap form that allows you to load a new bitmap to descramble. The bitmap is scaled to fill the entire puzzle screen. The Empty menu option allows you to specify the look of the empty square. It can be black (the default), white, or a random color brush pattern.

Figure 8.9 shows the runtime screen of the Puzzle program.

Figure 8.9

The runtime Puzzle form

Project Description

The Puzzle project includes five files. PUZZLE.FRM is the main puzzle form used in the program. PUZZLE2.FRM is used to load new bitmap files and is a fairly typical example of a file load form. PUZZLE.BAS is the only module in the program and contains the constant type and global definitions. APIDECS.BAS is the type-safe API declaration file provided with this book. APIGUIDE.BAS contains the declarations for the APIGUIDE.DLL dynamic link library.

Listing 8.5 shows the project file for the Puzzle program.

Listing 8.5   **Project Listing File PUZZLE.MAK**

```
PUZZLE.FRM
PUZZLE.BAS
APIDECS.BAS
APIGUIDE.BAS
PUZZLE2.FRM
ProjWinSize=178,372,248,215
ProjWinShow=2
```

Description of PUZZLE.FRM

Listing 8.6 contains the header from file PUZZLE.FRM that describes the control setup for the form. Figure 8.10 shows the design time view of the Puzzle form. The picture control on the left is **Picture1**; the one on the right is **Picture2**. Their location and size are not critical, as the program resizes them as needed.

Listing 8.6   **PUZZLE.FRM Header**

```
VERSION 2.00
Begin Form Puzzle
    Caption       =   "Puzzle"
    Height        =   4335
    Left          =   1035
    LinkMode      =   1  'Source
    LinkTopic     =   "Form1"
    ScaleHeight   =   3645
    ScaleWidth    =   3735
    Top           =   1140
    Width         =   3855
```

Figure 8.10

Design time view of
PUZZLE.FRM

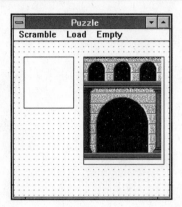

The file PUZZLE.FRX is the binary part of the PUZZLE.FRM file. It contains the default image used in the puzzle, in this case the ARCHES.BMP bitmap provided with Microsoft Windows. You can delete the line

```
Picture = Puzzle.FRX:0000
```

from the listing if you wish, in which case you should open the form in design mode and a default bitmap of your choice into the **Picture2** control.

```
Begin PictureBox Picture2
    Height          =   2535
    Left            =   1680
    Picture         =   PUZZLE.FRX:0000
    ScaleHeight     =   2505
    ScaleWidth      =   1905
    TabIndex        =   1
    Top             =   360
    Visible         =   0    'False
    Width           =   1935
End
Begin PictureBox Picture1
    Height          =   1215
    Left            =   240
    ScaleHeight     =   79
    ScaleMode       =   3    'Pixel
    ScaleWidth      =   79
    TabIndex        =   0
    Top             =   360
    Width           =   1215
End
Begin Menu MenuScramble
    Caption         =   "Scramble"
End
```

```
   Begin Menu MenuLoad
      Caption        =  "Load"
   End
   Begin Menu MenuEmptyCaption
      Caption        =  "Empty"
      Begin Menu MenuEmpty
         Caption      =  "Black"
         Checked      =  -1   'True
         Index        =  0
      End
      Begin Menu MenuEmpty
         Caption      =  "White"
         Index        =  1
      End
      Begin Menu MenuEmpty
         Caption      =  "Random"
         Index        =  2
      End
   End
End
```

Description of PUZZLE2.FRM

Listing 8.7 contains the header from file PUZZLE2.FRM that describes the
control setup for the form. This is a typical file load dialog box. Figure 8.11
shows the runtime view of this form.

Listing 8.7   **PUZZLE2.FRM Header**

```
VERSION 2.00
Begin Form Puzzle2
   Caption        =   "Load Bitmap"
   Height         =   2970
   Left           =   2925
   LinkMode       =   1   'Source
   LinkTopic      =   "Form1"
   ScaleHeight    =   2565
   ScaleWidth     =   5475
   Top            =   2490
   Width          =   5595
   Begin CommandButton CmdCancel
      Caption      =   "Cancel"
      Height       =   375
      Left         =   4200
      TabIndex     =   4
      Top          =   2040
      Width        =   1095
   End
```

Listing 8.7   PUZZLE2.FRM Header (Continued)

```
Begin CommandButton CmdLoad
    Caption        =   "Load"
    Height         =   375
    Left           =   2880
    TabIndex       =   3
    Top            =   2040
    Width          =   1095
End
Begin DirListBox Dir1
    Height         =   1815
    Left           =   120
    TabIndex       =   1
    Top            =   600
    Width          =   2535
End
Begin FileListBox File1
    Height         =   1785
    Left           =   2880
    Pattern        =   "*.bmp"
    TabIndex       =   2
    Top            =   120
    Width          =   2415
End
Begin DriveListBox Drive1
    Height         =   1530
    Left           =   120
    TabIndex       =   0
    Top            =   120
    Width          =   2535
End
End
```

Figure 8.11

Runtime view of
PUZZLE2.FRM

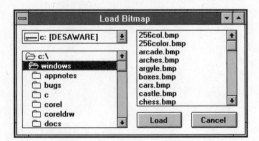

Puzzle Listing

Module PUZZLE.BAS contains the constant declarations and global variables used by the program.

Listing 8.8   Module PUZZLE.BAS

```
' Puzzle program example


'--------------------------------------------------
'
'          Global Constants
'

Global Const CBM_INIT = &H4&      '  initialize bitmap
Global Const DIB_RGB_COLORS = 0 '  color table in RGBTriples
Global Const DIB_PAL_COLORS = 1 '  color table in palette indices

Global Const SRCCOPY = &HCC0020
Global Const SRCPAINT = &HEE0086
Global Const SRCAND = &H8800C6
Global Const SRCINVERT = &H660046
Global Const SRCERASE = &H440328
Global Const NOTSRCCOPY = &H330008
Global Const NOTSRCERASE = &H1100A6
Global Const MERGECOPY = &HC000CA
Global Const MERGEPAINT = &HBB0226
Global Const PATCOPY = &HF00021
Global Const PATPAINT = &HFB0A09
Global Const PATINVERT = &H5A0049
Global Const DSTINVERT = &H550009
Global Const BLACKNESS = &H42&
Global Const WHITENESS = &HFF0062
Global Const BLACKONWHITE = 1
Global Const WHITEONBLACK = 2
Global Const COLORONCOLOR = 3
Global Const BI_RGB = 0&
Global Const BI_RLE8 = 1&
Global Const BI_RLE4 = 2&
Global Const TRANSPARENT = 1
Global Const OPAQUE = 2


'--------------------------------------------------
'
'          Global Variables
'
' Bitmap segment location in each puzzle area
```

Listing 8.8   **Module PUZZLE.BAS (Continued)**

```
' This represents a 5x5 square array
' The index represents the position on picture1
' The entry for each index indicates the number of the
' tile in the bitmap to place in position index.
Global Position%(24)

Global PuzzleRect As RECT

Global ShadowDC%
Global BMinfo As BITMAP

Global DestRects(24) As RECT
Global SourceRects(24) As RECT

' A flag set by the Puzzle2 form to let the Puzzle form
' know that a new bitmap was loaded.
Global DoTheUpdate%

' A random brush used for the empty square
Global EmptySquareBrush%

' The mode of the empty square.
' 0 = black, 1 = white, 2 = use EmptySquareBrush
Global EmptySquareMode%
```

Listing 8.9   **PUZZLE.FRM**

```
'
'    Sets the picture1 control to the visible form area
'    Also creates a compatible bitmap to work with
'    Call this any time the size of the form changes
'
Sub SetPuzzleSize ()
    Dim rc As RECT

    Picture1.BorderStyle = 0
    Picture1.left = 0
    Picture1.top = 0
    GetClientRect Puzzle.Hwnd, rc

    ' Actually, we need not subtract off rc.left and rc.top
    ' below as these fields are always 0 after a call to
    ' GetClientRect
    ' Note the conversion to twips in order to set the
```

Listing 8.9   PUZZLE.FRM (Continued)

```
        ' picture size using the VB properties
        ' We could have used the MoveWindow API call or Visual Basic Move method as ⇔
        well.
        Picture1.width = agXPixelsToTwips&(rc.right - rc.left)
        Picture1.height = agYPixelsToTwips&(rc.bottom - rc.top)

        ' This line is actually not necessary - we could
        ' have just used a copy of rc because we just set
        ' the client area to that specified by rc!
        GetClientRect agGetControlHwnd(Picture1), PuzzleRect

        ' Create a compatible memory DC for Picture1
        If ShadowDC% Then di% = DeleteDC%(ShadowDC%)
        ShadowDC% = CreateCompatibleDC%(Picture1.hDC)


End Sub

'
' Initialization routine
'
Sub Form_Load ()
    Randomize
    SetPuzzleSize    ' Set the size of the puzzle window
    CalcRects        ' Calculate the window tiles
    Scramble         ' Scramble them
    CreateEmptyBrush    ' Create a random brush for the
                        ' empty square.
End Sub

'
'   Clean up by deleting GDI objects that are no longer
'   needed.
'
Sub Form_Unload (Cancel As Integer)
    If ShadowDC% Then di% = DeleteDC%(ShadowDC%)
    If EmptySquareBrush% Then di% = DeleteObject(EmptySquareBrush%)


End Sub

'
'   Scramble the puzzle array
'
Sub Scramble ()
    Dim x%, newpos%, hold%
```

Listing 8.9   PUZZLE.FRM (Continued)

```
' Initialize the positions
For x% = 0 To 24
    Position%(x%) = x%
Next x%
' Now scramble them
For x% = 0 To 24
    ' For each source position, choose a random
    ' location and swap the two values.
    ' This is a simple and effective technique to
    ' randomize an array of numbers.
    newpos% = Int(Rnd * 25)
    hold% = Position(x%)
    Position(x%) = Position(newpos%)
    Position(newpos%) = hold%
Next x%
End Sub


'
'   Update the picture with rectangles based on the
'   puzzle array
'
Sub DoUpdate
Dim x%

    For x% = 0 To 24
        UpdateOne x%
    Next x%
End Sub


'
'   Calculate all source and destination rectangles
'   Call this whenever the form size changes or the
'   image bitmap is changed.
'
Sub CalcRects ()
    Dim x%, Y%, pos%

    Dim bmsegwidth%, bmsegheight%
    Dim picsegwidth%, picsegheight%

    ' Find the approx. height and width of each tile on
    ' the puzzle screen.
    picsegwidth% = (PuzzleRect.right - PuzzleRect.left) / 5
    picsegheight% = (PuzzleRect.bottom - PuzzleRect.top)/ 5

    ' Get information on the bitmap in picture2
    ' This loads the BITMAP structure bmInfo with
```

Listing 8.9 PUZZLE.FRM (Continued)

```
' information on the bitmap.
di% = GetObjectAPI(Picture2.picture, 10,agGetAddressForObject&(bmInfo))

bmsegwidth% = bmInfo.bmWidth / 5
bmsegheight% = bmInfo.bmHeight / 5

' Fill in the rectangle description for each
' rectangle on the destination DC
For Y% = 0 To 4
    For x% = 0 To 4
        pos% = Y% * 5 + x%
        DestRects(pos%).top = Y% * picsegheight%
        DestRects(pos%).bottom = (Y% + 1) *picsegheight%
        DestRects(pos%).left = x% * picsegwidth%
        DestRects(pos%).right = (x% + 1) * picsegwidth%
    Next x%
Next Y%

' Fill in the rectangle description for each rectangle
' on the source bitmap
For Y% = 0 To 4
    For x% = 0 To 4
        pos% = Y% * 5 + x%
        SourceRects(pos%).top = Y% * bmsegheight%
        SourceRects(pos%).bottom = (Y% + 1) *bmsegheight%
        SourceRects(pos%).left = x% * bmsegwidth%
        SourceRects(pos%).right = (x% + 1) *bmsegwidth%
        ' Make sure the rectangle does not exceed the
        ' source area for the bitmap or StretchBlt will
        ' fail
        If x% = 4 Then SourceRects(pos%).right =bmInfo.bmWidth
        If Y% = 4 Then SourceRects(pos%).bottom =bmInfo.bmHeight
    Next x%
Next Y%

End Sub

'
'   When the form is resized, call SetPuzzleSize to
'   adjust the size of the picture window and rescale
'   the image.
'
Sub Form_Resize ()
    SetPuzzleSize     ' Set the size of the puzzle window
    CalcRects         ' And recalculate the tiles
    Picture1.Refresh    ' Update the picture control
End Sub
```

| Listing 8.9 | **PUZZLE.FRM (Continued)** |

```
'
'   Paint picture1 by calling the full puzzle Update
'   routine
'
Sub Picture1_Paint ()
    DoUpdate
End Sub


'
'   Clicking on a tile next to the empty tile causes that
'   tile to slide into the empty space.
'
Sub Picture1_MouseDown (Button As Integer, Shift As Integer, x As Single, Y As⇔
Single)
    Dim pt As POINTAPI
    Dim u%
    Dim xpos%, ypos%
    Dim bxpos%, bypos%
    Dim dx%, dy%, tval%, hidden%

    pt.x = x     ' Picture1 scalemode is pixels
    pt.Y = Y

    ' Find the location of the black square
    ' Tile 24 in the bitmap is the missing piece.
    For hidden% = 0 To 24
        If Position%(hidden%) = 24 Then Exit For
    Next hidden%

    For u% = 0 To 24
        ' Find out which rectangle in the DestRects array
        ' contains the point specified by the mouse click.
        If PtInRect(DestRects(u%), agPOINTAPItoLong(pt)) Then
            Exit For
        End If
    Next u%
    ' Now find the X and Y coordinates for the mouse click
    ' and for the hidden tile.
    xpos% = u% Mod 5
    ypos% = Int(u% / 5)
    bxpos% = hidden% Mod 5
    bypos% = Int(hidden% / 5)

    ' The tile can slide into the empty square if it is
    ' one away from the empty square on the horizontal
    ' or vertical axis (but not both).
    dx% = Abs(xpos% - bxpos%)
```

Listing 8.9   PUZZLE.FRM (Continued)

```
        dy% = Abs(ypos% - bypos%)
        If (dx% = 1 And dy% = Ø) Or (dx% = Ø And dy% = 1) Then
            tval% = Position%(u%)
            ' So simply swap this tile with the hidden one
            Position%(u%) = Position%(hidden%)
            Position%(hidden%) = tval%
            ' And update both these tiles
            UpdateOne u%
            UpdateOne hidden%

        End If
End Sub


'
'   Copies a single tile from the picture2 bitmap to the
'   appropriate space in the picture1 destination.
'   x% is the position on the puzzle to update
'
Sub UpdateOne (x%)
    Dim oldbm%, pos%, oldbrush%
    ' Temporary variables for copying
    Dim sx%, sy%, sw%, sh%, dx%, dy%, dw%, dh%

    ' Select the bitmap into the ShadowDC
    oldbm% = SelectObject(ShadowDC%, Picture2.picture)
    ' Select the random brush we created into the
    ' picture DC
    If EmptySquareBrush% <> Ø Then oldbrush% = SelectObject(Picture1.hDC, ⇔
    EmptySquareBrush%)

    ' Get the position in the bitmap.
    ' Remember, Position 24 is the empty square
    pos% = Position%(x%)

    ' Calculate the rectangle on the puzzle display being
    ' updated
    dx% = DestRects(x%).left
    dy% = DestRects(x%).top
    dw% = DestRects(x%).right - dx%
    dh% = DestRects(x%).bottom - dy%

    ' The bitmap locations are based on x% - the source
    ' location in the bitmap
    sx% = SourceRects(pos%).left
    sy% = SourceRects(pos%).top
    sw% = SourceRects(pos%).right - sx%
```

Listing 8.9   PUZZLE.FRM (Continued)

```
        sh% = SourceRects(pos%).bottom - sy%

        ' Now do the transfer
        ' Transfer all tiles from the source except for tile
        ' number 24 which is the black one.
        If pos% <> 24 Then
            di% = StretchBlt(Picture1.hDC, dx%, dy%, dw%, dh%, ShadowDC%, ⇔
            sx%, sy%, sw%, sh%, SRCCOPY)
        Else  ' Tile #24 is empty - use EmptySquareMode% to
              ' determine what type of square to set.
            Select Case EmptySquareMode%
                Case 0
                    di% = PatBlt(Picture1.hDC, dx%, dy%, dw%, dh%, BLACKNESS)
                Case 1
                    di% = PatBlt(Picture1.hDC, dx%, dy%, dw%, dh%, WHITENESS)
                Case 2
                    di% = PatBlt(Picture1.hDC, dx%, dy%, dw%, dh%, PATCOPY)
            End Select
        End If

        ' Select the bitmap out of the shadow DC
        di% = SelectObject(ShadowDC%, oldbm%)
        ' And select the brush back to the original one
        If EmptySquareBrush% <> 0 Then di% = SelectObject(Picture1.hDC, oldbrush%)
    End Sub

    '
    '   Rescramble the bitmap image
    '
    Sub MenuScramble_Click ()
        Scramble
        DoUpdate  ' Redraw the puzzle window
    End Sub

    '
    '   Bring up the file load dialog box to load a new
    '   bitmap into the puzzle.
    '
    Sub MenuLoad_Click ()
        DoTheUpdate = 0 ' Preset the update flag to false
        Puzzle2.Show 1  ' Show the file load form modal
        If DoTheUpdate Then ' A valid bitmap was loaded
            CalcRects    ' Recalculate the tiles
            Scramble     ' And refresh the image
        End If

    End Sub
```

Function **CreateEmptyBrush** is one of the most important functions in this book and is worthy of further review. The function begins by creating a device-independent bitmap (DIB). A DIB is not a GDI object—in other words, there is no window handle to a DIB. A DIB is simply a set of data structures in memory that meets the specification for a device-independent bitmap. Most of the DIB functions divide the DIB into two parts. The header information (BITMAPINFO data structure) contains the definition of the DIB and the color table. The bitmap data itself is kept in a separate data array.

The **CreateEmptyBrush** creates a DIB by first defining and initializing a **BITMAPINFOHEADER** structure to the desired values. This structure is copied into a **BITMAPINFO** structure along with a desired color table. Finally, a separate block of memory (string **da**) is loaded with bitmap data—in this case a random pattern.

At this point the DIB is complete. It consists of structure **bi** containing the header and string **da** containing the bitmap data.

Unlike a DIB, a regular (device-dependent) bitmap is a GDI object and thus has a window handle. A device-dependent bitmap can be created easily from a valid DIB using the **CreateDIBitmap** function as shown, and this bitmap can in turn be used to create a brush.

The principles shown here can be applied to all DIB and bitmap operations.

```
'   Creates a brush to use for the empty square
'   This function demonstrates the creation of device
'   independent bitmaps, converting DIBs to a device
'   dependent bitmap and finally converting a DDB into a
'   brush.
'
Sub CreateEmptyBrush ()
    Dim compbitmap%
    Dim bih As BITMAPINFOHEADER
    Dim bi As BITMAPINFO
    ReDim colarray&(16)
    Dim x%
    Dim da As String * 32 ' Each byte contains 2 x 4bit pixels
    Dim buf$
    Dim bufstart&, sourceaddr&
    Dim oldbm%


    ' Prepare the bitmap information header
    bih.biSize = 40      ' 40 bytes in this structure
    bih.biWidth = 8      ' 8x8 -we'll be creating a brush
    bih.biHeight = 8     ' from this bitmap
    bih.biPlanes = 1     ' DIBs always 1 plane
    bih.biBitCount = 4   ' 16 colors, 4 bits/color
```

```
bih.biCompression = BI_RGB    ' no compression
bih.biSizeImage = 0           ' Not needed on BI_RGB
bih.biXPelsPerMeter = 0       ' Not used
bih.biYPelsPerMeter = 0       ' Not used
bih.biClrUsed = 16            ' All colors used
bih.biClrImportant = 0        ' All colors important


' Now fill the color array
For x% = 0 To 15
    colarray&(x%) = QBColor(x%)
Next x%

' Now we need to set the data array - for now, we're
' just going to put in random pixel data
For x% = 1 To 32
    ' Note how we pack two nibbles
    Mid$(da, x%, 1) = Chr$(Int(Rnd * 16) + Int(Rnd * 16) * 16)
Next x%

' Now we load the BITMAPINFO structure bi
LSet bi.bmiHeader = bih
' Now copy the color array into the BITMAPINFO
' bi.bmiColors string which begins 40 characters after
' the start of the structure.
' Refer to Appendix A for information on the subtleties
' of extracting addresses for strings in a structure.
bufstart& = agGetAddressForObject(bi) + 40

' Get the address of the start of the colarray color
' array
sourceaddr& = agGetAddressForLong(colarray&(0))
' And copy the 64 bytes
agCopyDataBynum sourceaddr&, bufstart&, 64

' Now create the bitmap
compbitmap% = CreateDIBitmap(Puzzle.hDC, bih, CBM_INIT, da, bi,⇔
DIB_RGB_COLORS)


' Now create a brush from this bitmap
EmptySquareBrush% = CreatePatternBrush(compbitmap%)

' And delete the source bitmap
di% = DeleteObject%(compbitmap%)

End Sub


'
'   Choose the color for the empty square
```

```
'
Sub MenuEmpty_Click (Index As Integer)
    Dim x%
    MenuEmpty(EmptySquareMode%).Checked = 0
    MenuEmpty(Index).Checked = -1
    EmptySquareMode% = Index
    DoUpdate
End Sub
```

Listing 8.10   PUZZLE2.FRM

```
Sub Dir1_Change ()
    File1.path = Dir1.path
End Sub

Sub Drive1_Change ()
    Dir1.path = Drive1.Drive
End Sub

'   Loads the bitmap file specified in the file box
'   into bitmap 2 and reinitializes.
'
Sub LoadBitmapFile ()
    Dim fname$
    If File1.filename <> "" Then
        fname$ = File1.path
        If fname$ <> "\" Then fname$ = fname$ + "\"
        fname$ = fname$ + File1.filename
        Puzzle.Picture2.Picture = LoadPicture(fname$)
        DoTheUpdate% = -1
    End If

    Puzzle2.Hide    ' And exit this form

End Sub

'
'   Load the selected file
'
Sub CmdLoad_Click ()
    LoadBitmapFile
End Sub

'
'   Load the selected file
'
Sub File1_DblClick ()
    LoadBitmapFile
End Sub
```

Listing 8.10   PUZZLE2.FRM (Continued)

```
'
'   Hide the form and return control to the Puzzle form
'
Sub CmdCancel_Click ()
    Puzzle2.Hide
End Sub
```

Suggestions for Improvements

There are a number of ways to improve the puzzle application. Here are
some suggestions that you may wish to consider:

- Detect the winning condition automatically (hint: it can be determined
  by looking at the contents of the **Position** array).

- Add lines to mark the tile borders. What line raster operation (ROP2)
  would produce the best effect?

- Add a form that allows you to edit an 8x8 pixel bitmap that will be used to
  create the brush pattern (instead of the random data used in the example).

Function Reference

This section contains an alphabetical reference for the functions described in this chapter.

■ BitBlt

VB Declaration   `Declare Function BitBlt% Lib "GDI" (ByVal hDestDC%, ByVal X%, ByVal Y%, ⇔`
`ByVal nWidth%, ByVal nHeight%,ByVal hSrcDC%, ByVal XSrc%, ByVal YSrc%, ⇔`
`ByVal dwRop&)`

Description   Copies a bitmap from one device context to another. The source and destination DCs must be compatible with one another as described in the chapter text.

Use with VB   Refer to "Using Bitmaps with Visual Basic," earlier in this chapter.

Parameter	Type/Description
hDestDC	**Integer**—Destination device context.
X%, Y%	**Integers**—Point describing the upper left corner of the destination rectangle within the destination DC. This is specified in logical coordinates of the destination DC.
nWidth, nHeight	**Integers**—Width and height of the image being transferred.
hSrcDC	**Integer**—Source device context. If the raster operation does not specify a source, this should be 0.
XSrc, YSrc	**Integers**—Point describing the upper left corner of the source rectangle within the source DC. This is specified in logical coordinates of the source DC.
dwRop	**Long**—Raster operation to use during the transfer. Refer to "Raster Operations," earlier in this chapter.

Return Value   Integer—TRUE (nonzero) on success, zero otherwise.

Comments   If the mapping modes of the destination and source DCs are such that the size in pixels of the rectangle must be changed during the transfer, this function will call the **StretchBlt** function to perform the transfer. Conversions between monochrome and color bitmaps are discussed in "Color Conversions," earlier in this chapter.

■ CopyCursor

VB Declaration   `Declare Function CopyCursor% Lib "User" (ByVal hinst%, ByVal hcur%)`

Description   Makes a copy of the specified cursor. The copy will belong to the specified application instance.

Use with VB   No problem. Use **agGetInstance** in APIGUIDE.DLL to obtain the instance of your VB application.

Parameter	Type/Description
hInst	**Integer**—Handle of the instance that will own the new cursor.
hicon	**Integer**—Handle of the cursor to copy.

Return Value   **Integer**—Handle of the new cursor.

Comments   When you load a cursor from a DLL or instance, that cursor can only be used as long as the DLL or instance remains loaded. This function allows you to make a copy of a cursor that belongs to your application. This cursor must be destroyed when no longer needed, using the **DestroyCursor** API function to free up the syst

◼ CopyIcon

VB Declaration   `Declare Function CopyIcon% Lib "User" (ByVal hinst%, ByVal hicon%)`

Description   Makes a copy of the specified icon. The copy will belong to the specified application instance.

Use with VB   No problem. Use **agGetInstance** in APIGUIDE.DLL to obtain the instance of your VB application.

Parameter	Type/Description
hInst	**Integer**—Handle of the instance that will own the new icon.
hicon	**Integer**—Handle of the icon to copy.

Return Value   **Integer**—Handle of the new icon.

Comments   When you load an icon from a DLL or instance, that icon can only be used as long as the DLL or instance remains loaded. This function allows you to make a copy of an icon that belongs to your application. This icon must be destroyed when it's no longer needed using the **DestroyIcon** API function to free up the system resources used.

◼ CreateBitmap, CreateBitmapBynum, CreateBitmapBystring

VB Declaration   `Declare Function CreateBitmap% Lib "GDI" (ByVal nWidth%,ByVal nHeight%, ⇔`
`ByVal nPlanes%, ByVal nBitCount%,ByVal lpBits As Any)`

`Declare Function CreateBitmapBynum% Lib "GDI" Alias"CreateBitmap" (ByVal ⇔`
`nWidth%, ByVal nHeight%, ByValnPlanes%, ByVal nBitCount%, ByVal lpBits&)`

`Declare Function CreateBitmapBystring% Lib "GDI" Alias"CreateBitmap" (ByVal ⇔`
`nWidth%, ByVal nHeight%, ByValnPlanes%, ByVal nBitCount%, ByVal lpBits$)`

Description   Creates a device-dependent bitmap. **CreateBitmapBynum** and **CreateBitmapBystring** are type-safe declarations for the function.

Use with VB   Refer to "Using Bitmaps with Visual Basic," earlier in this chapter.

Parameter	Type/Description
nWidth	**Integer**—Width of the bitmap in pixels.
nHeight	**Integer**—Height of the bitmap in pixels.
nPlanes	**Integer**—Number of color planes.
nBitCount	**Integer**—Number of bits per pixel.
lpBits	**String** or **Long**—Pointer to data to load into the bitmap. May be zero to leave the bitmap uninitialized. The format of this data must match that required by the device.

Return Value   **Integer**—The bitmap handle on success, zero on failure.

Comments   Use the **DeleteObject** function to free the memory and resources used by the bitmap when it is no longer needed. Refer to "Using Bitmaps," earlier in this chapter.

■ CreateBitmapIndirect

VB Declaration   `Declare Function CreateBitmapIndirect% Lib "GDI" (lpBitmap As BITMAP)`

Description   Creates a device-dependent bitmap.

Comments   Refer to "Using Bitmaps with Visual Basic," earlier in this chapter.

Parameter	Type/Description
lpBitmap	**BITMAP**—Structure describing a logical bitmap. Refer to Appendix B for further information.

Return Value   **Integer**—The bitmap handle on success, zero on failure.

Comments   Use the **DeleteObject** function to free the memory and resources used by the bitmap when it is no longer needed. Refer to "Using Bitmaps" earlier in this chapter.

When using a **BITMAP** structure obtained using the **GetObject** API function, keep in mind that **GetObject** does not retrieve bitmap data—only the size and configuration of the bitmap.

■ CreateCompatibleBitmap

VB Declaration   `Declare Function CreateCompatibleBitmap% Lib "GDI" (ByValhDC%, ByVal ⇔`
`nWidth%, ByVal nHeight%)`

Description   Creates a device-dependent bitmap that is compatible with the specified device context.

Use with VB   Refer to "Using Bitmaps with Visual Basic," earlier in this chapter.

Parameter	Type/Description
hDC	**Integer**—Handle to a device context.
nWidth	**Integer**—Width of the bitmap in pixels.
nHeight	**Integer**—Height of the bitmap in pixels.

Return Value	**Integer**—The bitmap handle on success, zero on failure.
Comments	Memory device contexts are compatible with both color and monochrome bitmaps. This function creates a bitmap that is compatible with the one currently selected into **hDC**. The default bitmap for a memory device context is monochrome. Use the **DeleteObject** function to free the memory and resources used by the bitmap when it is no longer needed. Refer to "Using Bitmaps," earlier in this chapter.

■ CreateCursor, CreateCursorBynum, CreateCursorBystring

VB Declaration
```
Declare Function CreateCursor% Lib "User" (ByVal hInstance%, ByVal ⇔
nXhotspot%, ByVal nYhotspot%, ByVal nWidth%, ByVal nHeight%, ByVal ⇔
lpANDbitPlane As Any, ByVal lpXORbitPlane As Any)

Declare Function CreateCursorBynum% Lib "User" Alias "CreateCursor" (ByVal ⇔
hInstance%, ByVal nXhotspot%,ByVal nYhotspot%, ByVal nWidth%, ByVal ⇔
nHeight%, ByVal lpANDbitPlane&, ByVal lpXORbitPlane&)

Declare Function CreateCursorBystring% Lib "User" Alias"CreateCursor" ⇔
(ByVal hInstance%, ByVal nXhotspot%, ByVal nYhotspot%, ByVal nWidth%, ByVal ⇔
nHeight%, ByVal lpANDbitPlane$, ByVal lpXORbitPlane$)
```

Description   Creates a cursor. Refer to "Icons and Cursors," earlier in this chapter, for information on how cursors and icons are created from two mask arrays.

Use with VB   Visual Basic provides very limited support for cursors. Refer to "Icons and Cursors," earlier in this chapter.

Parameter	Type/Description
hInstance	**Integer**—The handle of the application instance that will own the cursor. Use the **agGetInstance** function described in Appendix A to obtain the instance to the current application.
nXhotspot, nYhotspot	**Integers**—The X,Y coordinate within the cursor image that represents the exact cursor location.
nWidth	**Integer**—The width of the cursor image in pixels. Use the **GetSystemMetrics** function to determine the correct number for a particular device. Use 32 for VGA.
nHeight	**Integer**—The height of the cursor image in pixels. Use the **GetSystemMetrics** function to determine the correct number for a particular device. Use 32 for VGA.
lpANDbitPlane	**Long** or **String**—Pointer to the data for the AND bitmap. Refer to "Icons and Cursors," earlier in this chapter.
lpXORbitPlane	**Long** or **String**—Pointer to the data for the XOR bitmap. Refer to "Icons and Cursors," earlier in this chapter.

Return Value   **Integer**—A handle to the cursor on success, zero on error.

Comments	Use the **DestroyCursor** function to free the memory and resources used by the cursor when it is no longer needed.

■ CreateDIBitmap, CreateDIBitmapBynum

VB Declaration	Declare Function CreateDIBitmap% Lib "GDI" (ByVal hDC%,lpInfoHeader As ⇔ BITMAPINFOHEADER, ByVal dwUsage&,ByVal lpInitBits$, lpInitInfo As ⇔ BITMAPINFO, ByValwUsage%) Declare Function CreateDIBitmapBynum% Lib "GDI" Alias"CreateDIBitmap" ⇔ (ByVal hDC%, lpInfoHeader As BITMAPINFOHEADER, ByVal dwUsage&, ByVal ⇔ lpInitBits&, lpInitInfo As BITMAPINFO, ByVal wUsage%)
Description	Creates a device-dependent bitmap based on a device-independent bitmap. **CreateDIBitmapBynum** accepts a long pointer to the initialized data.
Use with VB	Refer to "Using Bitmaps with Visual Basic," earlier in this chapter.

Parameter	Type/Description
hDC	**Integer**—A handle to a device context defining the configuration of the device-dependent bitmap that is being created.
lpInfoHeader	**BITMAPINFOHEADER**—Structure that describes the format of the DIB. Refer to Appendix B for information on this structure.
dwUsage	**Long**—Zero if the bitmap data should not be initialized. **CBM_INIT** to initialize the bitmap according to the **lpInitBits** and **lpInitInfo** parameters.
lpInitBits	**String** or **Long**—A pointer to bitmap data in DIB format as specified by **lpInitInfo.**
lpInitInfo	**BITMAPINFO**—Structure that describes the format and colors of the **lpInitBits** DIB. Refer to Appendix B for information on this structure.
wUsage	**Integer**—One of the following two constants: **DIB_PAL_COLORS**: color table is relative to the currently selected palette. **DIB_RGB_COLORS**: color table contains RGB colors.

Return Value	**Integer**—The bitmap handle on success, zero on failure.
Comments	Use the **DeleteObject** function to free the memory and resources used by the bitmap when it is no longer needed. Refer to "Using Bitmaps," earlier in this chapter.

CreateDiscardableBitmap

VB Declaration
```
Declare Function CreateDiscardableBitmap% Lib "GDI" (ByVal hDC%, ByVal ⟺
nWidth%, ByVal nHeight%)
```

Description

Creates a device-dependent bitmap that is compatible with the specified device context. Windows may discard the memory used by this bitmap when it is not selected into a device context, in which case the **SelectObject** function will return zero when attempting to select the bitmap.

Use with VB

Discardable bitmaps are frequently used when you wish to use several large bitmaps that are easy to obtain and remain unchanged by the program. Windows can discard these bitmaps if it needs additional memory for an operation. When the **SelectObject** function returns zero, your application knows that the bitmap has been discarded and that it is necessary to reload the bitmap from disk, or otherwise recreate it.

Parameter	Type/Description
hDC	**Integer**—Handle to a device context.
nWidth	**Integer**—Width of the bitmap in pixels.
nHeight	**Integer**—Height of the bitmap in pixels.

Return Value

Integer—The bitmap handle on success, zero on failure.

Comments

Memory device contexts are compatible with both color and monochrome bitmaps. This function creates a bitmap that is compatible with the one currently selected into **hDC**. The default bitmap for a memory device context is monochrome.

Use the **DeleteObject** function to free the memory and resources used by the bitmap when it is no longer needed. **DeleteObject** must be called even if the bitmap has been discarded by Windows. Refer to "Using Bitmaps," earlier in this chapter.

CreateIcon, CreateIconBynum, CreateIconBystring

VB Declaration
```
Declare Function CreateIcon% Lib "User" (ByVal hInstance%, ByVal nWidth%, ⟺
ByVal nHeight%, ByVal nPlanes%, ByVal nBitsPixel%, ByVal lpANDbits As ⟺
Any,ByVal lpXORbits As Any)

Declare Function CreateIconBynum% Lib "User" Alias "CreateIcon" (ByVal ⟺
hInstance%, ByVal nWidth%, ByVal nHeight%, ByVal nPlanes%, ByVal ⟺
nBitsPixel%, ByVal lpANDbits&, ByVal lpXORbits&)

Declare Function CreateIconBystring% Lib "User" Alias"CreateIcon" (ByVal ⟺
hInstance%, ByVal nWidth%, ByValnHeight%, ByVal nPlanes%, ByVal ⟺
nBitsPixel%, ByVallpANDbits$, ByVal lpXORbits$)
```

Description

Creates an icon. Refer to the chapter text for information on how cursors and icons are created from two mask arrays.

Use with VB   Refer to "Icons and Cursors," earlier in this chapter, for information on using icons with Visual Basic.

Parameter	Type/Description
hInstance	**Integer**—The handle of the application instance that will own the icon. You may use the **agGetInstanceHandle** function provided in APIGUIDE.DLL to obtain the instance handle for the current application.
nWidth	**Integer**—The width of the icon image in pixels. Use the **GetSystem-Metrics** function to determine the correct number for a particular device. Use 32 for VGA.
nHeight	**Integer**—The height of the icon image in pixels. Use the **GetSystem-Metrics** function to determine the correct number for a particular device. Use 32 for VGA.
nPlanes	**Integer**—Number of color planes in the **lpXORbitPlane** data array.
nBitsPixel	**Integer**—Number of bits per pixel in the **lpXORbitPlane** data array.
lpANDbitPlane	**Long** or **String**—Pointer to the data for the AND bitmap. (Refer to "Icons and Cursors," earlier in this chapter.)
lpXORbitPlane	**Long** or **String**—Pointer to the data for the XOR bitmap. (Refer to "Icons and Cursors," earlier in this chapter.)

Return Value   **Integer**—A handle to the icon on success, zero on error.

Comments   Use the **DestroyIcon** function to free the memory and resources used by the icon when it is no longer needed.

■ DestroyIcon

VB Declaration   `Declare Function DestroyIcon% Lib "User" (ByVal hIcon%)`

Description   Destroys an icon created with the **CreateIcon** or **LoadIcon** API function.

Use with VB   No problem.

Parameter	Type/Description
hIcon	**Integer**—Handle to an icon.

Return Value   **Integer**—TRUE (nonzero) on success, zero otherwise.

■ DrawIcon

VB Declaration   `Declare Function DrawIcon% Lib "USER" (ByVal hDC%, ByVal X%, ByVal Y%, ⇔`
`ByVal hIcon%)`

Description   Draws an icon.

Use with VB	No problem.

Parameter	Type/Description
hDC	**Integer**—A handle to a device context on which to draw the icon.
X,Y	**Integers**—Point in logical coordinates specifying the location for the upper left corner of the icon.
hIcon	**Integer**—A handle to the icon to draw.

Return Value **Integer**—TRUE (nonzero) on success, zero otherwise.

■ ExtractIcon

VB Declaration
```
Declare Function ExtractIcon% Lib "shell.dll" (ByVal hinst%, ByVal ⇔
lpszExeName$, ByVal iIcon%)
```

Description This function can be used to determine if there are any icons in an executable file or dynamic link library and to extract those icons. Chapter 12 goes into further detail on the mechanisms by which icon resources are placed into executable and DLL files. This function requires use of the SHELL.DLL dynamic link library that is part of Windows 3.1.

Use with VB No problem.

Parameter	Type/Description
hinst	**Integer**—The instance handle of this program. Use the **agGetInstanceHandle** function in APIGUIDE.DLL to obtain the instance handle of a VB application.
lpszExeName	**String**—The full name of the program from which to extract an icon.
iIcon	**Integer**—The index number of the icon to retrieve. May be –1 to determine the number of icons in the file.

Return Value **Integer**—A handle to an icon on success, zero on error. If **iIcon** is –1, this will be the total number of icons in the file.

■ GetBitmapBits, GetBitmapBitsBynum, GetBitmapBitsBystring

VB Declaration
```
Declare Function GetBitmapBits& Lib "GDI" (ByVal hBitmap%, ByVal dwCount&, ⇔
ByVal lpBits As Any)

Declare Function GetBitmapBitsBynum& Lib "GDI" Alias "GetBitmapBits" (ByVal ⇔
hBitmap%, ByVal dwCount&, ByVal lpBits&)

Declare Function GetBitmapBitsBystring& Lib "GDI" Alias"GetBitmapBits" ⇔
(ByVal hBitmap%, ByVal dwCount&, ByVal lpBits$)
```

Description Copies bits from a bitmap into a buffer. **GetBitmapBitsBynum** and **GetBitmapBitsBystring** are type-safe declarations for this function.

Use with VB	No problem.

Parameter	Type/Description
hBitmap	**Integer**—Handle to a bitmap.
dwCount	**Long**—Number of bytes to copy. Set to zero to retrieve the number of bytes in the bitmap.
lpBits	**String** or **Long**—Pointer to a buffer to hold the bitmap bits. Be sure the buffer has been preinitialized to at least **dwCount** bytes.

Return Value   **Integer**—The number of bytes in the bitmap on success, zero otherwise.

Comments   Refer to "Device-Dependent Bitmaps," earlier in this chapter, for the required format for a device-dependent bitmap data area.

■ GetBitmapDimension

VB Declaration   `Declare Function GetBitmapDimension& Lib "GDI" (ByValhBitmap%)`

Description   Retrieves the width and height of a bitmap as set by the **SetBitmapDimension** or **SetBitmapDimensionEx** function.

Use with VB   No problem.

Parameter	Type/Description
hBitmap	**Integer**—Handle to a bitmap.

Return Value   **Long**—Low word contains the bitmap width, high word contains the bitmap height. Dimensions are in tenths of a millimeter.

Comments   Refer to the **SetBitmapDimension** or **SetBitmapDimensionEx** function for further information.

■ GetBitmapDimensionEx

VB Declaration   `Declare Function GetBitmapDimensionEx% Lib "GDI" (ByValhBitmap%, ⇔`
`lpDimension As SIZEAPI)`

Description   Retrieves the width and height of a bitmap as set by the **SetBitmapDimension** or **SetBitmapDimensionEx** function.

Use with VB   No problem.

Parameter	Type/Description
hBitmap	**Integer**—Handle to a bitmap.
lpDimension	**SIZEAPI**—Size structure to load with the dimensions of the bitmap as set by the **SetBitmapDimension** or **SetBitmapDimensionEx** function. Dimensions are in tenths of a millimeter.

Return Value   **Integer**—TRUE (nonzero) on success, zero otherwise.

Comments   Refer to the **SetBitmapDimension** or **SetBitmapDimensionEx** function for further information.

■ GetDIBits, GetDIBitsBynum

VB Declaration   Declare Function GetDIBits% Lib "GDI" (ByVal aHDC%, ByVal hBitmap%, ByVal ⇔
nStartScan%, ByVal nNumScans%,ByVal lpBits$, lpBI As BITMAPINFO, ByVal ⇔
wUsage%)

Declare Function GetDIBitsBynum% Lib "GDI" (ByVal aHDC%, ByVal hBitmap%, ⇔
ByVal nStartScan%, ByVal nNumScans%,ByVal lpBits&, lpBI As BITMAPINFO, ⇔
ByVal wUsage%)

Description   Copies bits from a bitmap into a device-independent bitmap. **GetDIBitsBynum** is a type-safe declaration for this function.

Use with VB   Refer to "Using Bitmaps with Visual Basic," earlier in this chapter.

Parameter	Type/Description
aHDC	**Integer**—A handle to a device context defining the configuration of the device-dependent bitmap **hBitmap**.
hBitmap	**Integer**—A handle to a source bitmap. This bitmap must not be selected into a device context.
nStartScan	**Integer**—The number of the first scan line to copy into the DIB.
cNumScans	**Integer**—The number of scan lines to copy.
lpBits	**String** or **Long**—A pointer to a buffer to load with the bitmap data in DIB format as specified by **lpBI**. If zero, **lpBI** is loaded with the information for the DIB, but no data is retrieved.
lpBI	**BITMAPINFO**—Structure that describes the format and colors of the **lpInitBits** DIB. Refer to Appendix B for information on this structure.
wUsage	**Integer**—One of the following two constants: **DIB_PAL_COLORS**: color table is relative to the currently selected palette. **DIB_RGB_COLORS**: color table contains RGB colors.

Return Value   **Integer**—The number of scan lines copied on success, zero on error.

■ GetStretchBltMode

VB Declaration   Declare Function GetStretchBltMode% Lib "GDI" (ByVal hDC%)

Description   Retrieves the current stretching mode for a device context.

Use with VB   No problem.

Parameter	Type/Description
hDC	**Integer**—A handle to a device context.

Return Value   Retrieves the current stretching mode.

Comments   Refer to the **SetStretchBltMode** API function for further information.

■ LoadBitmap, LoadBitmapBynum, LoadBitmapBystring

VB Declaration   Declare Function LoadBitmap% Lib "User" (ByVal hInstance%, ByVal ⇔
lpBitmapName As Any)

Declare Function LoadBitmapBynum% Lib "User" Alias "LoadBitmap" (ByVal ⇔
hInstance%, ByVal lpBitmapName&)

Declare Function LoadBitmapBystring% Lib "User" Alias"LoadBitmap" (ByVal ⇔
hInstance%, ByVal lpBitmapName$)

Description   Loads a bitmap from the specified module or application instance. **LoadBitmapBynum** and **Load-BitmapByString** are type-safe versions of the **LoadBitmap** function.

Use with VB   No problem.

Parameter	Type/Description
hInstance	**Instance**—Module handle for a dynamic link library, or instance handle that specifies the executable file that contains the bitmap.
lpBitmapName	**String** or **Long**—As a **String**, specifies the name of the bitmap resource to load. As a **Long**, specifies the resource ID to load or a constant representing one of the stock system bitmaps. When loading a stock system bitmap, the **hInstance** parameter should be set to 0. The constants are specified in the APICONST.TXT file with the **OBM_** prefix. For example, **OBM_REDUCE** refers to the down arrow bitmap that appears on the title bar to minimize a window. Refer to the APICONST.TXT file for a complete list of stock bitmaps. The sample program StockBMs can be used to view the stock system bitmaps and icons.

Return Value   **Integer**—A handle to the loaded bitmap.

Comments   You must use the **DeleteObject** function to delete bitmaps retrieved by this function even if they are stock system bitmaps.

■ LoadIcon, LoadIconBynum, LoadIconBystring

VB Declaration   Declare Function LoadIcon% Lib "User" (ByVal hInstance%, ByVal lpIconName ⇔
As Any)

Declare Function LoadIconBynum% Lib "User" Alias "LoadIcon" (ByVal ⇔
hInstance%, ByVal lpIconName&)

Declare Function LoadIconBystring% Lib "User" Alias"LoadIcon" (ByVal ⇔
hInstance%, ByVal lpIconName$)

Description   Loads an icon from the specified module or application instance. **LoadIconBynum** and **LoadIcon-ByString** are type-safe versions of the **LoadIcon** function.

Use with VB   No problem.

Parameter	Type/Description
hInstance	**Instance**—Module handle for a dynamic link library, or instance handle that specifies the executable file that contains the icon.
lpIconName	**String** or **Long**—As a **String**, specifies the name of the icon resource to load. As a **Long**, specifies the resource ID to load or a constant representing one of the stock system icons. When loading a stock system icon, the **hInstance** parameter should be set to 0. The constants are as follows: **IDI_APPLICATION**—Default icon for applications. **IDI_ASTERISK**—The letter 'i' in a filled circle. **IDI_EXCLAMATION**—Exclamation point in a circle. **IDI_HAND**—Stop sign. **IDI_QUESTION**—Question mark. The sample program StockBMs can be used to view the stock system bitmaps and icons.

Return Value   **Integer**—A handle to the loaded icon.

Comments   Do not destroy stock system icons or icons belonging to other applications. Be careful that **lpIconName** refers to an icon resource.

■ OpenIcon

VB Declaration   `Declare Function OpenIcon% Lib "User" (ByVal hWnd%)`

Description   Opens (restores) an iconized application. Equivalent to using the **ShowWindow** function with the **SW_SHOWNORMAL** flag.

Use with VB   Use the VB **WindowState** property on forms instead of this function.

Parameter	Type/Description
hWnd	**Integer**—Handle to a minimized window.

Return Value   **Integer**—TRUE (nonzero) on success, zero otherwise.

Comments   In terms of behavior, this function is probably a better fit for Chapter 4. Its name places it here.

■ PatBlt

VB Declaration   `Declare Function PatBlt% Lib "GDI" (ByVal hDC%, ByVal X%,ByVal Y%, ByVal ⇔ nWidth%, ByVal nHeight%, ByVal dwRop&)`

Description   Fills the specified device context with a pattern based on the currently selected brush.

Use with VB   No problem.

Parameter	Type/Description
hDC	**Integer**—Handle to a device context to draw on.
X%, Y%	**Integers**—Point describing the upper left corner of the destination rectangle within the destination DC in logical coordinates.
nWidth, nHeight	**Integers**—Width and height of the destination rectangle specified in logical units.
dwRop	**Long**—Raster operation to use during the transfer. Raster operations that refer to a source may not be used with this function. Refer to "Raster Operations," earlier in this chapter.

Return Value   **Integer**—TRUE (nonzero) on success, zero otherwise.

■ SetBitmapBits, SetBitmapBitsBynum, SetBitmapBitsBystring

VB Declaration   Declare Function SetBitmapBits& Lib "GDI" (ByVal hBitmap%, ByVal dwCount&, ⇔
ByVal lpBits As Any)

Declare Function SetBitmapBitsBynum& Lib "GDI" Alias "SetBitmapBits" (ByVal ⇔
hBitmap%, ByVal dwCount&, ByVal lpBits&)

Declare Function SetBitmapBitsBystring& Lib "GDI" Alias"SetBitmapBits" ⇔
(ByVal hBitmap%, ByVal dwCount&, ByVal lpBits$)

Description   Copies bits from a buffer into a bitmap. **SetBitmapBitsBynum** and **SetBitmapBitsBystring** are
type-safe declarations for this function.

Use with VB   No problem.

Parameter	Type/Description
hBitmap	**Integer**—Handle to a bitmap.
dwCount	**Long**—Number of bytes to copy.
lpBits	**String** or **Long**—Pointer to a buffer that contains the bitmap bits formatted correctly for the bitmap.

Return Value   **Integer**—The number of bytes copied on success, zero otherwise.

Comments   Refer to "Device-Dependent Bitmaps," earlier in this chapter, for the required format for a
device-dependent bitmap data area.

■ SetBitmapDimension

VB Declaration   Declare Function SetBitmapDimension& Lib "GDI" (ByValhBitmap%, ByVal X%, ⇔
ByVal Y%)

Description   Sets the width and height of a bitmap in tenths of a millimeter. This information is not used by Windows, but may be retrieved using the **GetBitmapDimension** and **GetBitmapDimensionEx** functions.

Use with VB   No problem.

Parameter	Type/Description
hBitmap	**Integer**—Handle to a bitmap.
X,Y	**Integers**—The width and height of the bitmap in tenths of a millimeter.

Return Value   **Long**—Low word contains the previous bitmap width, high word contains the previous bitmap height.

◼ SetBitmapDimensionEx

VB Declaration   `Declare Function SetBitmapDimensionEx% Lib "GDI" (ByValhBitmap%, ByVal nX%,` ⇔
`ByVal nY%, lpSize As SIZEAPI)`

Description   Sets the width and height of a bitmap in tenths of a millimeter. This information is not used by Windows, but may be retrieved using the **GetBitmapDimension** and **GetBitmapDimensionEx** functions.

Use with VB   No problem.

Parameter	Type/Description
hBitmap	**Integer**—Handle to a bitmap.
X,Y	**Integers**—The width and height of the bitmap in tenths of a millimeter.
lpSize	**SIZEAPI**—Structure to load with the previous bitmap dimensions.

Return Value   **Integer**—TRUE (nonzero) on success, zero otherwise.

◼ SetDIBits, SetDIBitsBynum

VB Declaration   `Declare Function SetDIBits% Lib "GDI" (ByVal aHDC%, ByValhBitmap%, ByVal` ⇔
`nStartScan%, ByVal nNumScans%, ByVallpBits$, lpBI As BITMAPINFO, ByVal wUsage%)`

`Declare Function SetDIBitsBynum% Lib "GDI" Alias "SetDIBits" (ByVal aHDC%,` ⇔
`ByVal hBitmap%, ByValnStartScan%, ByVal nNumScans%, ByVal lpBits&, lpBIAs` ⇔
`BITMAPINFO, ByVal wUsage%)`

Description   Copies bits from a device-independent bitmap into a device-dependent bitmap. **SetDIBitsBynum** is a type-safe declaration for this function.

Use with VB   Refer to "Using Bitmaps with Visual Basic," earlier in this chapter.

Parameter	Type/Description
aHDC	**Integer**—A handle to a device context defining the configuration of the device-dependent bitmap **hBitmap**.
hBitmap	**Integer**—A handle to a destination bitmap. This bitmap must not be selected into a device context.

Parameter	Type/Description
nStartScan	**Integer**—The number of the first scan line in the **lpBits** array.
cNumScans	**Integer**—The number of scan lines to copy.
lpBits	**String** or **Long**—A pointer to a buffer containing the bitmap data in DIB format as specified by **lpBI**.
lpBI	**BITMAPINFO**—Structure that describes the format and colors of the **lpBits** DIB. Refer to Appendix B for information on this structure.
wUsage	**Integer**—One of the following two constants: **DIB_PAL_COLORS**: color table is relative to the currently selected palette. **DIB_RGB_COLORS**: color table contains RGB colors.

Return Value   **Integer**—The number of scan lines copied on success, zero on error.

■ SetDIBitsToDevice, SetDIBitsToDeviceBynum

VB Declaration

```
Declare Function SetDIBitsToDevice% Lib "GDI" (ByVal hDC%, ByVal X%, ByVal ⇔
Y%, ByVal dX%, ByVal dY%, ByVal SrcX%, ByVal SrcY%, ByVal Scan%, ByVal ⇔
NumScans%, ByVal Bits$, BitsInfo As BITMAPINFO, ByVal wUsage%)

Declare Function SetDIBitsToDeviceBynum% Lib "GDI" Alias ⇔
"SetDIBitsToDevice" (ByVal hDC%, ByVal X%, ByVal Y%, ByVal dX%, ByVal dY%, ⇔
ByVal SrcX%, ByVal SrcY%, ByVal Scan%, ByVal NumScans%, ByVal Bits&,⇔
BitsInfo As BITMAPINFO, ByVal wUsage%)
```

Description   Copies all or part of a device-independent bitmap directly to a device. This function defines a destination rectangle on the device to receive the bitmap data. It also defines a source rectangle in the DIB from which to extract data. **SetDIBitsToDeviceBynum** is a type-safe declaration for this function.

Use with VB   Refer to "Using Bitmaps with Visual Basic," earlier in this chapter.

Parameter	Type/Description
aHDC	**Integer**—A handle to a device context to receive the bitmap data.
X,Y	**Integers**—Point in logical coordinates of the origin of the destination rectangle.
dX, dY	**Integers**—Width and height in device units of the destination rectangle.
SrcX, SrcY	**Integer**—Point in device coordinates of the origin of the source rectangle in the DIB.
Scan	**Integer**—The number of the first scan line in the **lpBits** array.
NumScans	**Integer**—The number of scan lines to copy.
Bits	**String** or **Long**—A pointer to a buffer containing the bitmap data in DIB format as specified by **BitsInfo**.

Parameter	Type/Description
BitsInfo	**BITMAPINFO**—Structure that describes the format and colors of the Bits DIB. Refer to Appendix B for information on this structure.
wUsage	**Integer**—One of the following two constants: **DIB_PAL_COLORS**: color table is relative to the currently selected palette. **DIB_RGB_COLORS**: color table contains RGB colors.

Return Value   **Integer**—The number of scan lines copied on success, zero on error.

■ SetStretchBltMode

VB Declaration   Declare Function SetStretchBltMode% Lib "GDI" (ByVal hDC%, ByVal ⇔ nStretchMode%)

Description   Specifies the stretching mode for the **StretchBlt** and **StretchDIBits** functions. The stretching mode determines how Windows handles scan lines that are eliminated during stretching.

Use with VB   It is recommended that you restore the original **StretchBlt** mode for VB forms and controls if you use this function during API drawing.

Parameter	Type/Description
hDC	**Integer**—Handle to a device context.
nStretchMode	**Integer**—The new stretching mode based on one of the following constants as defined in file APICONST.TXT **STRETCH_ANDSCANS**: (default) Eliminated lines are ANDed with the remaining lines. This mode is typically used with monochrome bitmaps that have a white background. **STRETCH_DELETESCANS**: Eliminated lines are simply removed. This mode is typically used with color bitmaps. **STRETCH_ORSCANS**: Eliminated lines are ORed with the remaining lines. This mode is typically used with monochrome bitmaps that have a black background.

Return Value   **Integer**—The value of the previous stretching mode.

Comments   As an example of the effect of stretching mode, consider what happens when a narrow black line on a white image is compressed. During the compression, pixels are removed from the image. In order to prevent the line from disappearing, it is necessary to AND pixels with a neighboring pixel before deleting them. This is accomplished with the **STRETCH_AND-SCANS** stretching mode.

■ StretchBlt

VB Declaration   Declare Function StretchBlt% Lib "GDI" (ByVal hDC%, ByVal X%, ByVal Y%, ⇔ ByVal nWidth%, ByVal nHeight%,ByVal hSrcDC%, ByVal XSrc%, ByVal YSrc%, ⇔ ByValnSrcWidth%, ByVal nSrcHeight%, ByVal dwRop&)

Description   Copies a bitmap from one device context to another. The source and destination DCs must be compatible with one another as described in "Device-Dependent Bitmaps," earlier in this chapter. This function defines a destination rectangle on the device context and a source rectangle within the bitmap. The source rectangle is stretched as needed to fit into the destination rectangle.

Use with VB   Refer to "Using Bitmaps with Visual Basic," earlier in this chapter.

Parameter	Type/Description
hDestDC	**Integer**—Destination device context.
X%, Y%	**Integers**—Point describing the upper left corner of the destination rectangle within the destination DC. This is specified in logical coordinates of the destination DC.
nWidth, nHeight	**Integers**—Width and height of the image being transferred in logical units (based on the destination DC).
hSrcDC	**Integer**—Source device context. If the raster operation does not specify a source, this should be 0.
XSrc, YSrc	**Integers**—Point describing the upper left corner of the source rectangle within the source DC. This is specified in logical coordinates of the source DC.
nSrcWidth, nSrcHeight	**Integers**—Width and height of the image being transferred in logical units (based on the source DC). If the sign of one of these parameters does not match the sign of the corresponding destination width parameter, the bitmap will be mirrored on the appropriate axis.
dwRop	**Long**—Raster operation to use during the transfer. Refer to "Raster Operations," earlier in this chapter. If a brush is part of the raster operation, the brush selected into the destination DC is used.

Return Value   **Integer**—TRUE (nonzero) on success, zero otherwise.

Comments   Use the **GetDeviceCaps** API function to determine if the device context can support this function.

■ StretchDIBits, StretchDIBitsBynum

VB Declaration
```
Declare Function StretchDIBits% Lib "GDI" (ByVal hDC%,ByVal X%, ByVal Y%, ⇔
ByVal dX%, ByVal dY%, ByVal SrcX%, ByVal SrcY%, ByVal wSrcWidth%, ByVal ⇔
wSrcHeight%, ByVal lpBits$, lpBitsInfo As BITMAPINFO, ByVal wUsage%, ByVal ⇔
dwRop&)

Declare Function StretchDIBitsBynum% Lib "GDI" Alias"StretchDIBits" (ByVal ⇔
hDC%, ByVal X%, ByVal Y%, ByVal dX%, ByVal dY%, ByVal SrcX%, ByVal SrcY%, ⇔
ByVal wSrcWidth%, ByVal wSrcHeight%, ByVal lpBits&,lpBitsInfo As ⇔
BITMAPINFO, ByVal wUsage%, ByVal dwRop&)
```

Description   Copies all or part of a device-independent bitmap directly to a device context. This function defines a destination rectangle on the device context to receive the bitmap data. It also defines a source rectangle in the DIB from which to extract data. The source rectangle is stretched as

needed to fit into the destination rectangle using the **StretchBlt** mode for the device context (as set by the **SetStretchBltMode** function).

StretchDIBitsBynum is a type-safe declaration for this function.

Use with VB   Refer to "Using Bitmaps with Visual Basic," earlier in this chapter.

Parameter	Type/Description
hDC	**Integer**—A handle to a device context to receive the bitmap data.
X,Y	**Integers**—Point in logical coordinates of the origin of the destination rectangle.
dX, dY	**Integers**—Width and height in logical units of the destination rectangle.
SrcX, SrcY	**Integers**—Point in device coordinates of the origin of the source rectangle in the DIB.
wSrcWidth, wSrcHeight	**Integers**—Width and height of the source rectangle in device coordinates.
lpBits	**String** or **Long**—A pointer to a buffer containing the bitmap data in DIB format as specified by **lpBI**.
lpBitsInfo	**BITMAPINFO**—Structure that describes the format and colors of the **lpBits** DIB. Refer to Appendix B for information on this structure.
wUsage	**Integer**—One of the following two constants: **DIB_PAL_COLORS**: color table is relative to the currently selected palette. **DIB_RGB_COLORS**: color table contains RGB colors.
dwRop	**Long**—Raster operation to use. Refer to "Raster Operations," earlier in this chapter.

Return Value   **Integer**—The number of scan lines copied on success, zero on error.

9

Working with Menus

MOST VISUAL BASIC APPLICATIONS USE MENUS TO ALLOW THE USER TO execute program commands. This chapter will show you how to use the Windows API functions to add to the menuing capabilities provided by Visual Basic. You will learn how to create custom checkmarks for checked menus, and how to use any bitmap as a menu entry in place of a string. You will also learn how to customize floating popup menus that can appear anywhere on the screen. The MenuLook sample program included in this chapter demonstrates these features and shows how you can use the Windows API functions to analyze the structure of an existing menu.

Inside the Menuing System

Before reviewing the Windows API functions that deal with menus, it is important for you to understand a bit about how menus work and how Visual Basic uses menus. The Windows API functions provide some powerful capabilities, but the Visual Basic environment imposes some strict requirements on their use in order to maintain compatibility.

How Windows Menus Work

Let's first examine how the Windows menuing system works outside of Visual Basic. Then you'll see how Visual Basic interacts with menus.

A menu is one of the few objects appearing on the screen that is not a window. This means that there is no window handle to a menu, nor does a menu have a window function. The appearance, visibility, and position of menus are handled entirely by the Windows environment.

There are two types of menus: top level menus and popup menus. A top level menu appears as a horizontal bar and may be assigned to a window. Once assigned, it will appear as the menu bar for the window. Popup menus appear as needed and disappear as soon as a selection is made, the Escape key is pressed, or the mouse is clicked outside of the menu.

Each entry in a menu has attributes as shown in Table 9.1.

Table 9.1   **Attributes of a Menu Entry**

Attribute	Description
Bitmap	Bitmap to display instead of a string for a menu entry.
Checked Unchecked	An entry can be checked or unchecked. A space to the left of the entry name (or string) displays a symbol to indicate if the entry is checked or unchecked. The default is nothing when unchecked and a check mark when checked, but any bitmap can be defined for either state.

Table 9.1   Attributes of a Menu Entry (Continued)

Attribute	Description
Checkmark symbol	Bitmaps to use for the checked and unchecked state for a menu entry. The default is no mark for the unchecked state, and a check mark for the checked state.
Enabled Disabled Grayed	If a menu entry is enabled, the user can click on that entry. When disabled, clicks on the entry are ignored. When grayed, the entry is disabled and appears in a gray color: it is not available to the user at that time.
Highlight	Top level menus only—the entry appears highlighted (inverted).
Menu ID (command)	Every entry other than separators and popup menus has a menu ID. This is a 16-bit integer that is sent to the window function of the menu's window when that entry is selected. Menu IDs need not be unique (that is, more than one entry may share the same menu ID).
MenuBreak MenuBarBreak	Specifies that an entry is the start of a new column (for popup menus) or line (for top level menus). With **MenuBarBreak**, a vertical separator line appears between the two columns.
OwnerDraw	Allows total customization of the appearance of a menu. Not supported by Visual Basic.
Popup	If an entry has a popup menu assigned, selecting the entry will cause that popup menu to appear. Popup entries generally have a string attribute assigned as well.
Position	The position of the entry in the menu. Positions are numbered from zero, with entry zero being the left entry (for top level menus) or top entry (for popup menus).
Separator	A special menu entry that appears as a separator line between entries. It is always disabled.
String (name)	The text string displayed for the entry. Also referred to as the name of the entry.

In Windows, a menu is built by first creating a top level menu and the associated popup menus. In most cases, each of the top level menu entries has a popup menu attached. Each entry has attributes set as needed. If an entry does not have a popup menu attached, it is assigned a menu ID attribute. Once the menu is built, it is assigned to a window and appears as a menu bar. Menus may also be loaded as resources from an executable module.

Consider what happens when the user clicks in a menu. Clicks inside of a disabled entry (such as a separator or disabled command) are ignored. Clicks inside of an entry that has a popup menu attached cause the popup menu to be displayed, from which the user may then select an entry.

When a user clicks on an enabled entry that does not have a popup menu attached, Windows sends a **WM_COMMAND** message to the window that contains the menu. This message contains the menu ID of the menu entry. Figure 9.1 illustrates the operation of menus under Windows.

Figure 9.1

The Windows menuing system

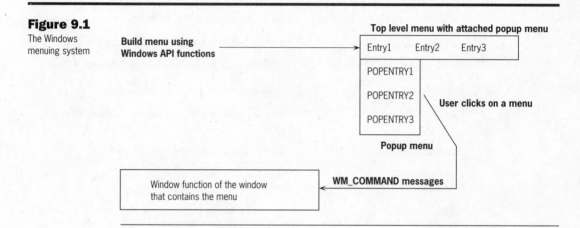

Each of the three entries in the popup menu has a menu ID that is sent as one of the parameters with the **WM_COMMAND** message. This allows the window function for the window owning the menu to determine which menu entry has been selected. The program can then take whatever action is appropriate for that menu selection.

Table 9.2 lists the API functions that deal with menus.

Table 9.2   **Menu API Functions**

Function	Description
AppendMenu	Adds an entry to a menu.
CheckMenuItem	Checks or unchecks a menu entry.
CreateMenu	Creates an empty top level menu.
CreatePopupMenu	Creates an empty popup menu.
DeleteMenu	Deletes a menu entry.
DestroyMenu	Destroys a menu.
DrawMenuBar	Updates (redraws) a menu.

Table 9.2   **Menu API Functions (Continued)**

Function	Description
EnableMenuItem	Enables, disables, or grays a menu entry.
GetMenu	Retrieves a handle to the menu for a window.
GetMenuCheckMarkDimensions	Determines the size of a menu checkmark symbol.
GetMenuItemCount	Determines the number of entries in a menu.
GetMenuItemID	Determines the menu ID of a menu entry.
GetMenuState	Retrieves information about the attributes of a menu entry.
GetMenuString	Retrieves the string (name) of a menu entry.
GetSubMenu	Retrieves a handle to the popup menu attached to a specified menu entry.
GetSystemMenu	Retrieves a handle to the system popup menu (referred to as the control menu in VB). This is the menu that appears when the **ControlBox** property for a form is set to TRUE.
HiliteMenuItem	Sets the highlight attribute for a top level menu entry.
InsertMenu	Inserts a menu entry into a menu.
IsMenu	Determines if a handle is not a menu handle.
LoadMenu	Loads a menu resource.
LoadMenuIndirect	Creates a menu from a data structure.
ModifyMenu	Changes the attributes of a menu entry.
RemoveMenu	Removes a menu entry. If the entry has a popup menu attached, the popup is not destroyed (unlike the case with **DeleteMenu**).
SetMenu	Sets the menu for a window.
SetMenuItemBitmaps	Sets the symbols to use to indicate the checked or unchecked state of a menu entry.
TrackPopupMenu	Brings up a popup menu anywhere on the screen.

How Visual Basic Menus Work

The Visual Basic environment includes a sophisticated menu design window that is used to create menus for Visual Basic programs. When you design a menu using the Visual Basic menu design window, you are not actually creating a Windows menu—at least not directly. The VB menu designer actually creates an internal VB menu object. VB uses this object to create the actual menu using Windows API functions. VB sets some of the attributes of the menu according to the properties you specify. Other attributes are assigned based on an internal scheme. Table 9.3 shows how VB menu control properties correspond to the Windows menu attributes.

Table 9.3   **VB Menu Properties and Corresponding Attributes**

Visual Basic Property	Windows Menu Attribute
Caption	String (name).
CtlName	No equivalent.
Index	No equivalent.
Tag	No equivalent.
Checked	Checked.
Enabled/Disabled	Enabled/Grayed. There is no VB equivalent to the Disabled but Ungrayed state.
Parent	No direct equivalent. This is the handle of the window that contains the menu.
Visible	Not an attribute. Visual Basic deletes any entries or menus that are not visible.

Some of the menu attributes have no equivalent in a VB property. Table 9.4 indicates the degree of VB compatibility of these attributes.

VB menu controls manipulate the actual menu in many ways. It is important to be aware of this situation when changing menus directly. The most important fact to keep in mind when modifying menus directly through API functions is that changes to the menus do not affect the VB menu controls.

Figure 9.2 shows the flow of control in the Visual Basic menuing system. Note how the VB menu controls set the structure of the menu, but that the menu has no corresponding arrow to set the contents of the VB menu controls. The Windows API functions bypass the VB menu controls and operate directly on the menu.

The impact of the structure of the menuing system on the programmer depends on the attributes and properties in question.

Figure 9.2

Visual Basic
menuing system

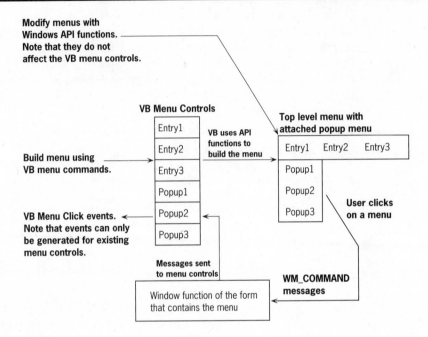

Modify menus with
Windows API functions.
Note that they do not
affect the VB menu controls.

VB Menu Controls

| Entry1 |
| Entry2 |
| Entry3 |
| Popup1 |
| Popup2 |
| Popup3 |

Build menu using
VB menu commands.

VB uses API
functions to
build the menu

VB Menu Click events.
Note that events can only
be generated for existing
menu controls.

**Top level menu with
attached popup menu**

| Entry1 | Entry2 | Entry3 |
| Popup1 |
| Popup2 |
| Popup3 |

User clicks
on a menu

Messages sent
to menu controls

Window function of the form
that contains the menu

**WM_COMMAND
messages**

Table 9.4 **Menu Attributes without Corresponding VB Properties**

Windows Menu Attribute	Visual Basic Equivalent
Separator	Caption property = "-".
Bitmap	No equivalent.
Checkmark Symbol	No equivalent.
Menu ID	Chosen internally by VB. User cannot set.
MenuBreak, MenuBarBreak	No equivalent.
Popup	Level in the menu design window.
Position	Position in menu design window.

The Caption, Checked, and Enabled Properties

If you change the string attribute of a menu entry, the menu will display the new string but the VB **Caption** property for that menu entry will *not* reflect the new string. This applies to the **Enabled** and **Checked** properties as well. Note that if you use an API function to change the menu entry string or the enabled or checked state, the menu will work as you specify. It will display the new string and it will be checked or enabled as you specify, so in this sense these API changes are compatible with VB. However, if you choose to use the API functions to change these attributes you must avoid using the equivalent VB property to read the current state of the menu (you may use it to set the state of the menu, as setting the property will immediately update the menu to the new state).

In general, it is recommended that you use the VB property to set these three attributes.

The Visible Property—Adding and Deleting Menu Entries

It is important to be aware that hiding a menu entry does not "hide" the entry—it actually deletes it from the menu. This affects the position attribute of all menu entries below the one that was hidden. By the same token, VB assumes that menu entries are where it expects them to be. If you start adding and deleting entries directly, you can cause Visual Basic to lose track of where menu entries are located, in which case changes to properties of a menu entry will actually affect the wrong menu entry.

As a result, you should not use API functions to add or delete menu entries on any menu in the VB menu structure. You may use these API functions if you are creating a custom menu that is compatible with the VB menu structure, as described in the next section.

The correct way to add or delete entries is to use a Visual Basic menu control array, then modify each menu entry as needed using properties or API functions.

The Menu ID Attribute and Ensuring Compatibility of Menu Entries to VB

Figure 9.2 shows how the **WM_COMMAND** messages from the menu are sent to the VB menu controls for processing. When a VB menu control receives a **WM_COMMAND** message that corresponds to its own menu ID, it generates a **Click** event.

Since a Visual Basic program cannot intercept windows messages directly, this imposes the requirement that every menu entry have a VB control. Note that VB controls only look at the menu ID for the **WM_COMMAND** message, so the reverse is not true—each VB control may have more than one menu entry.

From a practical point of view, this means that you may create popup menus at will, assign them to entries or use them as tracked popup menus, and reassign menu IDs as you wish as long as you make certain that the menu ID for each entry has a corresponding VB menu control. When a menu structure created or modified with API functions meets this condition, it is referred to in this book as a *compatible* menu structure.

Using the Menu API Functions with VB

This section describes a number of practical applications for the Windows menu API functions and how to safely use them with Visual Basic. Most of these examples are further illustrated in the MenuLook example program included in this chapter.

Creating Custom Checkmark Symbols

The space to the left of the menu entry text, or caption, is reserved for checkmarks. Normally, the space is empty when unchecked and displays a checkmark when the entry has been checked. Visual Basic is fully compatible with custom checkmarks; thus you could substitute another symbol such as a + or – for the standard √ symbol as needed by your application.

A custom checkmark must be the same size as the original checkmark. These dimensions may be obtained using the **GetMenuCheckMarkDimensions** API function. You may specify bitmaps for both the unchecked and checked state, and the bitmaps may be used on more than one menu entry. Note, however, that it is the programmer's responsibility to destroy the bitmap when it is no longer needed or before the program terminates.

Using Bitmaps to Customize Menus

You may replace the name (caption) of any menu entry with the bitmap of your choice. The menu entry will automatically be sized to hold the bitmap and will display color bitmaps in full color depending on the characteristics of the display. This is useful for any case where you would like to use a picture in a menu entry instead of a text string—for example, you could allow your user to choose among hatched brushes by displaying the available hatching patterns in the menu.

One subtle use of this capability is to employ different fonts or text styles in menus. All you need to do is draw text onto a bitmap using the desired font or style. This bitmap may then be used as a menu entry.

Use the **ModifyMenu** API function to change a menu entry into a bitmap. Note that this will have no effect on the **Caption** property for the menu entry, which will continue to return the previous caption. Setting the **Caption** property will, however, remove the bitmap and replace it with the specified string.

It is important that menu entry bitmaps be preserved during the existence of the menu. VB modifies the bitmap accessed by the **Image** property of controls, so it is not appropriate to use the bitmap returned by the **Image** property of a control as a menu entry bitmap. One may, however, use the **Picture** property as long as the bitmap is left unchanged while it is in use. The MenuLook application solves this problem by drawing into a picture control that has the **AutoRedraw** property set to TRUE, and then making a copy of the image bitmap.

Bitmaps may be shared by menu entries, and should be deleted when the application exits in order to release the associated Windows resources. Chapter 8 discusses bitmaps in greater depth.

Tracked Popup Menus

Visual Basic 3.0 provides direct support for floating popup menus to appear anywhere on the screen using the **PopupMenu** command. The **TrackPopupMenu** API function can also be used to create popup menus that need to be customized or used with previous version of Visual Basic. The only requirement is that this popup menu contain entries that have menu IDs that correspond to Visual Basic menu controls. One way to do this is to create a popup menu using the VB menu design tools, and simply hide it by setting the caption property of the top level menu for that popup to "" (note that this is *not* the same as setting the **Visible** property to zero, an action that destroys the menu). You can then use the **GetSubMenu** command to obtain a handle to the popup menu to use with **TrackPopupMenu**. Alternatively, you may create a new popup menu that is compatible with the VB menu structure.

The MenuLook application shows how to hide a top level entry and use its popup menu for a tracked popup. Note that even when a top level caption is set to the null string, it takes up space on the menu bar, so it is advisable to disable the menu entry as well.

Creating a Pool of VB Menu Controls

If you expect to do a lot of menu customization or use many tracked popup menus, you will probably need a pool of menu controls to use in order to obtain menu IDs that will generate click events. The easiest way to do this is as follows:

1. Set the last entry on your top level menu to have no caption and set the **Enabled** property to zero.

2. Create under this entry a popup menu with a single entry by creating an entry indented one level in the menu design window. Make this entry a control array by setting the value of the **Index** property to 0.

Now, any time you need a VB menu control to use in another menu entry, simply create a new entry in the control array using the Visual Basic **Load** command. Because the top level entry for the control array is effectively hidden, you need not worry about the user seeing all of the menu entries you are creating in the control array. Meanwhile, new entries you create may use those menu IDs safely and will trigger **Click** events in the control array when selected.

Menus, System Menus, and Subclassing

The subclassing technique allows you to interpret Windows messages going to a form. It can detect the WM_COMMAND Windows message directly, eliminating the need to ensure compatibility with a Visual Basic menu structure when using menu API functions. It also allows you to intercept the WM_SYS-COMMAND message, which makes it practical to customize an application's system menu. Refer to the Message Handling section in Chapter 17 for more information on subclassing.

Obtaining Information about the VB Menu Structure

It is remarkably easy to obtain information about the existing VB menu structure. The **GetMenu** API function retrieves a menu handle to the top level menu for a form. The **GetSubMenu** function can then be used to obtain handles to the popup menus that it contains.

Additional API functions may be used to retrieve values of the various menu properties. The MenuLook example program shows how you may obtain a complete description of the menu structure.

Example: MenuLook—A Menu Structure Viewer

MenuLook is a program that allows you to view the structure of the Visual Basic menu and shows how a menu may be modified. It also demonstrates many of the techniques for modifying menus described in this chapter.

Figure 9.3 shows the design time screen of the MenuLook program. Figures 9.4 through 9.6 show the menus.

Using MenuLook

The MenuLook screen shown in Figure 9.3 demonstrates a variety of menu control techniques. Refer to Figure 9.4 for a view of the menu analysis screen.

The List1 list box is loaded with an analysis of the existing menu structure when the Analyze command button is selected.

Figure 9.3

MenuLook design time screen

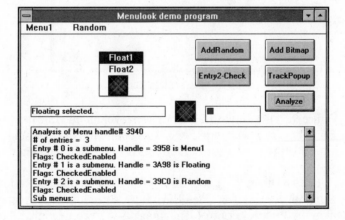

Figure 9.4

MenuLook program screen: Tracked popup and menu analysis

The menu analysis shown in Figure 9.4 displays the handle of each menu and a description of each menu entry. When an entry is a submenu, its handle is displayed along with its name. Handles are always displayed in hexadecimal; all other numbers are in decimal. Each submenu is analyzed in turn, with each menu entry shown along with its menu ID.

The AddBitmap command button adds a bitmap entry into the Floating top level menu. The bitmap used is obtained from the **Picture** property in the **Picture1** control.

When you click anywhere on the form that is not part of a control, the Floating top level menu is hidden by setting the caption to the empty string. The normal appearance of the menu bar can be seen in Figure 9.5. The program then takes a handle to the submenu for the Floating top level menu and displays it as a tracked popup menu at the cursor location. This will also take place when you select the TrackPopup command button.

Figure 9.5

MenuLook program screen: Menu1 and custom checkmarks

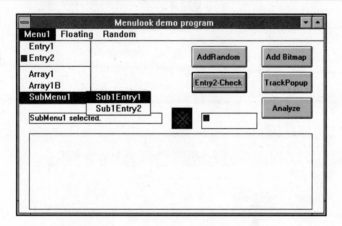

Figure 9.5 also shows the Menu1 top level menu after the Entry2-Check command button has been pressed. This command draws a small red rectangle in the **Picture2** control and then sets it as the new checkmark for the Entry1 menu entry as shown.

Figure 9.6 shows the effect on the Random menu of selecting the **AddRandom** control five times. Each time, a random set of rectangles is drawn in the **Picture2** control. The image is then copied into a bitmap that is added to the Random top level menu.

Project Description

The MenuLook project includes four files. MENULOOK.FRM is the only form used in the program. MENULOOK.BAS is the only module in the program and contains the constant type and global definitions. APIDECS.BAS is the type-safe API declaration file provided with this book. APIGUIDE.BAS contains the declarations for the APIGUIDE.DLL dynamic link library.

Figure 9.6

MenuLook program
screen: Custom
bitmap menu and
menu analysis

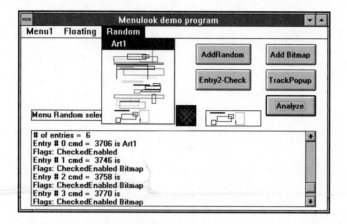

Listing 9.1 shows the project file for the StockBMs program.

Listing 9.1   Project Listing File MENULOOK.MAK

```
MENULOOK.FRM
MENULOOK.BAS
APIDECS.BAS
APIGUIDE.BAS
ProjWinSize=175,439,248,215
ProjWinShow=2
```

Form Description

Listing 9.2 contains the header from file MENULOOK.FRM that describes
the control setup for the form.

Listing 9.2   MENULOOK.FRM Header

```
VERSION 2.00
Begin Form Menulook
    Caption        =    "Menulook demo program"
    Height         =    4710
    Left           =    1035
    LinkMode       =    1  'Source
    LinkTopic      =    "Form1"
```

Listing 9.2   MENULOOK.FRM Header (Continued)

```
ScaleHeight    =    4020
ScaleWidth     =    7365
Top            =    1140
Width          =    7485
Begin ListBox List1
    Height         =    1785
    Left           =    240
    TabIndex       =    0
    Top            =    2160
    Width          =    6855
End
Begin PictureBox Picture2
    AutoRedraw     =    -1   'True
    Height         =    375
    Left           =    4440
    ScaleHeight    =    345
    ScaleWidth     =    1305
    TabIndex       =    6
    Top            =    1680
    Width          =    1335
End
```

File MENULOOK.FRX is the binary file for this form. It contains the definition of the **Picture** property for control Picture1. You may remove the line

```
Picture = MENULOOK.FRX:0000
```

in which case you should load a small bitmap into the control's **Picture** property in Visual Basic design mode. The sample program uses the bitmap AR-GYLE.BMP, which is provided with Windows 3.1.

```
Begin PictureBox Picture1
    Height         =    495
    Left           =    3720
    Picture        =    MENULOOK.FRX:0000
    ScaleHeight    =    465
    ScaleWidth     =    465
    TabIndex       =    5
    Top            =    1560
    Width          =    495
End
Begin CommandButton CmdAnalyze
    Caption        =    "Analyze"
    Height         =    495
    Left           =    5880
    TabIndex       =    1
    Top            =    1320
    Width          =    1215
```

```
End
Begin CommandButton CmdTrack
   Caption          =    "TrackPopup"
   Height           =    495
   Left             =    5880
   TabIndex         =    2
   Top              =    720
   Width            =    1215
End
Begin CommandButton CmdEntry2Chk
   Caption          =    "Entry2-Check"
   Height           =    495
   Left             =    4200
   TabIndex         =    8
   Top              =    720
   Width            =    1335
End
Begin CommandButton CmdAddBitmap
   Caption          =    "Add Bitmap"
   Height           =    495
   Left             =    5880
   TabIndex         =    4
   Top              =    120
   Width            =    1215
End
Begin CommandButton CmdAddRandom
   Caption          =    "AddRandom"
   Height           =    495
   Left             =    4200
   TabIndex         =    7
   Top              =    120
   Width            =    1335
End
Begin Label Label1
   BorderStyle      =    1    'Fixed Single
   Height           =    255
   Left             =    240
   TabIndex         =    3
   Top              =    1680
   Width            =    3255
End
Begin Menu MenuTop
   Caption          =    "Menu1"
   Begin Menu MenuEntry1
      Caption          =    "Entry1"
   End
   Begin Menu MenuEntry2
      Caption          =    "Entry2"
   End
   Begin Menu MenuEntry3
      Caption          =    "-"
   End
```

```
Begin Menu MenuArray1
    Caption        =   "Array1"
    Index          =   0
End
Begin Menu MenuArray1
    Caption        =   "Array1B"
    Index          =   1
End
Begin Menu MenuSubMenu1
    Caption        =   "SubMenu1"
    Begin Menu MenuSub1Entry1
        Caption    =   "Sub1Entry1"
    End
    Begin Menu MenuSub1Entry2
        Caption    =   "Sub1Entry2"
    End
End
End
Begin Menu MenuFloat
    Caption        =   "Floating"
    Begin Menu MenuFloat1
        Caption    =   "Float1"
        Index      =   0
    End
    Begin Menu MenuFloat1
        Caption    =   "Float2"
        Index      =   1
    End
End
Begin Menu MenuRandomTop
    Caption        =   "Random"
    Begin Menu MenuArt
        Caption    =   "Art1"
        Index      =   0
    End
End
End
End
```

MenuLook Listings

Module MENULOOK.BAS contains the constant declarations and global variables used by the program.

Listing 9.3   Module MENULOOK.BAS

```
' MenuLook program example
```

Listing 9.3   Module MENULOOK.BAS (Continued)

```
'-----------------------------------------------------


'       Global Constants

Global Const WM_USER = &H400

Global Const LB_RESETCONTENT = (WM_USER + 5)
Global Const MF_INSERT = &H0
Global Const MF_CHANGE = &H80
Global Const MF_APPEND = &H100
Global Const MF_DELETE = &H200
Global Const MF_REMOVE = &H1000
Global Const MF_BYCOMMAND = &H0
Global Const MF_BYPOSITION = &H400
Global Const MF_SEPARATOR = &H800
Global Const MF_ENABLED = &H0
Global Const MF_GRAYED = &H1
Global Const MF_DISABLED = &H2
Global Const MF_UNCHECKED = &H0
Global Const MF_CHECKED = &H8
Global Const MF_USECHECKBITMAPS = &H200
Global Const MF_STRING = &H0
Global Const MF_BITMAP = &H4
Global Const MF_OWNERDRAW = &H100
Global Const MF_POPUP = &H10
Global Const MF_MENUBARBREAK = &H20
Global Const MF_MENUBREAK = &H40
Global Const MF_UNHILITE = &H0
Global Const MF_HILITE = &H80
Global Const MF_SYSMENU = &H2000
Global Const MF_HELP = &H4000
Global Const MF_MOUSESELECT = &H8000
Global Const MF_END = &H80
Global Const TPM_LEFTBUTTON = &H0
Global Const TPM_RIGHTBUTTON = &H2
Global Const TPM_LEFTALIGN = &H0
Global Const TPM_CENTERALIGN = &H4
Global Const TPM_RIGHTALIGN = &H8
Global Const SRCCOPY = &HCC0020
Global Const SRCPAINT = &HEE0086
Global Const SRCAND = &H8800C6
Global Const SRCINVERT = &H660046
Global Const SRCERASE = &H440328
Global Const NOTSRCCOPY = &H330008
Global Const NOTSRCERASE = &H1100A6
Global Const MERGECOPY = &HC000CA
Global Const MERGEPAINT = &HBB0226
```

Listing 9.3 **Module MENULOOK.BAS (Continued)**

```
Global Const PATCOPY = &HF00021
Global Const PATPAINT = &HFB0A09
Global Const PATINVERT = &H5A0049
Global Const DSTINVERT = &H550009
Global Const BLACKNESS = &H42&
Global Const WHITENESS = &HFF0062

' Bitmap to use for checkmark on entry one menu
Global NewCheck%

Global B
MHandles%(32)
```

The ViewMenu function has the ability to add to the **List1** list box a description of the menu whose handle is passed to it as a parameter. It shows how to obtain the number of menu entries in a menu, and how to obtain information about each menu entry including the menu ID and state information. This function makes a list of all popup menus attached to this menu, and after completing the description of each entry proceeds to recursively call itself for each popup submenu.

Listing 9.4 **Program File MENULOOK.FRM**

```
'
'    This function loads into list1 an analysis of the
'    specified menu
'
Sub ViewMenu (ByVal menuhnd%)
    Dim menulen%
    Dim thismenu%
    Dim menuid%, db%
    Dim menuflags%
    Dim flagstring$
    Dim menustring As String * 128

    ' This routine can analyze up to 32 popup sub-menus
    ' for each menu. We keep track of them here so that
    ' we can recursively analyze the popups after we
    ' analyze the main menu.
    ReDim trackpopups%(32)

    Dim currentpopup%

    currentpopup% = 0
```

Listing 9.4   **Program File MENULOOK.FRM (Continued)**

```
List1.AddItem "Analysis of Menu handle# " +Hex$(menuhnd%)

' Find out how many entries are in the menu.
menulen% = GetMenuItemCount%(menuhnd%)
List1.AddItem "# of entries = " + Str$(menulen%)

For thismenu% = 0 To menulen% - 1
    ' Get the ID for this menu
    ' It's a command ID, -1 for a popup, 0 for a
    ' separator
    menuid% = GetMenuItemID%(menuhnd%, thismenu%)
    Select Case menuid%
        Case 0  ' It's a separator
            List1.AddItem "Entry #" + Str$(thismenu%)+ "is a separator"
        Case -1 ' It's a popup menu
            ' Save it in the list of popups
            trackpopups%(currentpopup%) = thismenu%
            currentpopup% = currentpopup% + 1
            ' And report that it's here
            db% = GetMenuString(menuhnd%, thismenu%,menustring$, ⇔
            Len(menustring)+1 MF_BYPOSITION)
            menuflags% = GetMenuState(menuhnd%,thismenu%, MF_BYPOSITION)
            List1.AddItem "Entry #" + Str$(thismenu%)+ " is a submenu. ⇔
            Handle = " + Hex$(GetSubMenu%(menuhnd%,thismenu%)) + " is " ⇔
            +Left$(menustring$, db%)
            List1.AddItem "Flags: " + GetFlagString$(menuflags%)

        Case Else ' A regular entry
            db% = GetMenuString(menuhnd%, menuid%, menustring$, ⇔
            Len(menustring)+1, MF_BYCOMMAND)
            List1.AddItem "Entry #" + Str$(thismenu%) + " cmd = " + ⇔
            Str$(menuid%) + " is " + Left$(menustring$, db%)
            menuflags% = GetMenuState(menuhnd%, menuid%, MF_BYCOMMAND)
            List1.AddItem "Flags: " + GetFlagString$(menuflags%)
    End Select
Next thismenu%
If currentpopup% > 0 Then
    ' At least one popup was found
    List1.AddItem "Sub menus:"
    For thismenu% = 0 To currentpopup% - 1
        menuid% = trackpopups%(thismenu%)
        ' Recursively analyze the popup menu.
        ViewMenu GetSubMenu(menuhnd%, menuid%)
    Next thismenu%
End If
```

Listing 9.4   Program File MENULOOK.FRM (Continued)

```
End Sub

'
'     Gets a string containing a description of the flags
'     set for this menu item.
'
Function GetFlagString$ (menuflags%)
    Dim f$
    If (menuflags% And MF_CHECKED) <> Ø Then
        f$ = f$ + "checked "
    Else
        f$ = f$ + "Unchecked"
    End If
    If (menuflags% And MF_DISABLED) <> Ø Then
        f$ = f$ + "Disabled "
    Else
        f$ = f$ + "Enabled "
    End If
    If (menuflags% And MF_GRAYED) <> Ø Then f$ = f$ +"Grayed "
    If (menuflags% And MF_BITMAP) <> Ø Then f$ = f$ +"Bitmap "
    If (menuflags% And MF_MENUBARBREAK) <> Ø Then f$ = f$+ "Bar-break "
    If (menuflags% And MF_MENUBREAK) <> Ø Then f$ = f$ +"Break "
    If (menuflags% And MF_SEPARATOR) <> Ø Then f$ = f$ +"Separator "
    GetFlagString$ = f$
End Function
```

When using a bitmap in a menu entry it is important that the bitmap not be destroyed while the menu is using it. The MenuLook program uses the **Picture2** control as a source for images. However, we cannot simply use the bitmap property returned by the **Image** property of the control—that bitmap changes as the application executes. This function makes a copy of the **Picture2** bitmap. The techniques shown here are based on the information in Chapter 8.

```
'     This function makes a copy of the Image property bitmap
'     and returns a handle to that bitmap
'
Function CopyPicture2Image% ()
    Dim bm As BITMAP
    Dim newbm%
    Dim tdc%, oldbm%

    ' First get the information about the image bitmap
    di% = GetObjectAPI(Picture2.image, Len(bm), agGetAddressForObject&(bm))
    bm.bmBits = Ø
    ' Create a new bitmap with the same structure and size
    ' of the image bitmap
```

```
            newbm% = CreateBitmapIndirect(bm)

            ' Create a temporary memory device context to use
            tdc% = CreateCompatibleDC(Picture2.hDC)
            ' Select in the newly created bitmap
            oldbm% = SelectObject(tdc%, newbm%)

            ' Now copy the bitmap from the persistent bitmap in
            ' picture 2 (note that picture2 has AutoRedraw set TRUE
            di% = BitBlt(tdc%, 0, 0, bm.bmWidth, bm.bmHeight,Picture2.hDC, 0, 0, ⇔
            SRCCOPY)
            ' Select out the bitmap and delete the memory DC
            oldbm% = SelectObject(tdc%, oldbm%)
            di% = DeleteDC%(tdc%)

            ' And return the new bitmap
            CopyPicture2Image% = newbm%
        End Function
```

The **GetNewCheck** function uses the same principles as the **CopyPicture2Image** function except that it demonstrates how to obtain the checkmark dimensions and copy a bitmap of that size only. The checkmark created by this routine is a magenta-filled rectangle two pixels smaller than the checkmark dimension (on each side).

```
        '
        ' Create a custom bitmap checkmark and return a
        ' handle to that bitmap.
        '
        Function GetNewCheck% ()
            Dim bm As BITMAP
            Dim pt As POINTAPI
            Dim newbm%
            Dim tdc%, oldbm%
            Dim markdims&
            Dim br%, oldbrush%

            ' Find out how big the checkmark should be.
            markdims& = GetMenuCheckMarkDimensions()
            agDWORDto2Integers markdims&, pt.x, pt.y

            ' And create a magenta brush (the check mark will be
            ' a magenta filled rectangle
            br% = CreateSolidBrush(QBColor(5))

            Picture2.Cls
            oldbrush% = SelectObject(Picture2.hDC, br%)
            ' Draw the rectangle.
            di% = Rectangle(Picture2.hDC, 2, 2, pt.x - 2, pt.y - 2)
            di% = SelectObject(Picture2.hDC, oldbrush%)
            di% = DeleteObject(br%) ' Dump the brush.
```

```
' Create a compatible bitmap of the right size
di% = GetObjectAPI(Picture2.image, 14, agGetAddressForObject&(bm))
bm.bmBits = 0
bm.bmWidth = pt.x
bm.bmHeight = pt.y
newbm% = CreateBitmapIndirect(bm)
' And create a memory device context to use
tdc% = CreateCompatibleDC(Picture2.hDC)
oldbm% = SelectObject(tdc%, newbm%)
' Copy in the new check mark
di% = BitBlt(tdc%, 0, 0, pt.x, pt.y, Picture2.hDC, 0, 0, SRCCOPY)
oldbm% = SelectObject(tdc%, oldbm%)
di% = DeleteDC%(tdc%)
GetNewCheck% = newbm%

End Function
```

The **CmdAddRandom_Click** function demonstrates several important techniques. First, it shows how to obtain the handle to the form's top level menu and how to obtain one of the popup menus that belong to the top level menu entries. This technique is repeated throughout the application.

Next, the function creates a menu to modify by using standard Visual Basic menu control array techniques. This ensures that a VB menu control is assigned to the entry that is to be modified. The **GetMenuItemID** API function is used to obtain the menu ID for the new menu entry. This menu ID is used later when calling the **ModifyMenu** command to make sure that all **WM_COMMAND** messages from the modified menu entry will continue to go to the VB menu control.

Last, the function demonstrates use of the **ModifyMenu** API function to change the new menu entry into a bitmap.

For this program, a number of random rectangles are drawn into an empty bitmap (the **Picture2**) control for use as a menu entry bitmap. Note how a copy of the picture control's bitmap is used. The bitmap is stored in a global array for destruction when the form is unloaded.

```
' This command creates a random bitmap and loads it into
' the Random popup menu.
'
Sub CmdAddRandom_Click ()
    Dim topmenuhnd%
    Dim floatmenu%
    Dim menuid%
    Dim newmenupos%
    Dim pw!, ph!
    Dim x%
    Dim newbm%

    ' First get the width and height of the picture2
```

```
            ' control
            pw! = Picture2.Scalewidth
            ph! = Picture2.Scaleheight
            ' Get a handle to the Random popup menu
            topmenuhnd% = GetMenu%(Menulook.hWnd)
            floatmenu% = GetSubMenu%(topmenuhnd%, 2)
            ' Find out how many menu items are already in the popup
            newmenupos% = GetMenuItemCount%(floatmenu%)

            ' Load a VB menu entry at that position
            Load MenuArt(newmenupos%)
            ' And get the Menu ID for that entry
            menuid% = GetMenuItemID%(floatmenu%, newmenupos%)

            ' Draw some stuff on picture2
            Picture2.Cls
            For x% = 0 To 5 ' Random rectangles
                Picture2.Line (Rnd * pw!, Rnd * ph!)-(Rnd * pw!,Rnd * ph!), QBColor⇔
                (CInt(Rnd * 15)), B
            Next x%
            ' Get a bitmap that is a copy of the picture2 control
            newbm% = CopyPicture2Image%()
            For x% = 0 To 32
                If BMHandles%(x%) = 0 Then Exit For
            Next x%
            If x% = 32 Then ' No room to store the bitmap handle
                di% = DeleteObject(newbm%)
                Exit Sub
            End If
            BMHandles(x%) = newbm%
            ' And place that bitmap in the menu
            di% = ModifyMenuBynum(floatmenu%, newmenupos%,MF_BITMAP Or ⇔
            MF_BYPOSITION, menuid%, newbm%)

End Sub
```

The **CmdAnalyze_Click** function obtains a handle to the top level menu for a form, then calls the **ViewMenu** command to display the structure of the menu in the **List1** control. **ViewMenu** is recursive, so this single call will cause the entire menu structure to be displayed.

```
'
'   Get the form's menu and analyze it.
'
Sub CmdAnalyze_Click ()
    Dim menuhnd%

    ' Clear the list box (see chapter 19)
    dl& = SendMessage(agGetControlHwnd%(List1),LB_RESETCONTENT, 0, 0&)
    ' Get a handle to the top level menu for this window
    menuhnd% = GetMenu%(Menulook.hWnd)
```

```
      ' And analyze it
      ViewMenu menuhnd%
End Sub


'
'
```

The **CmdAddBitmap_Click** function is similar to the **CmdAdd-Random_Click** function. We can safely use the **Picture1** control's **Picture** property because that bitmap remains unchanged through the life of the program. Try clearing it while the program is running and see what happens.

```
' This command adds the bitmap that is in the Picture1
' control to the Floating menu.
'
Sub CmdAddBitmap_Click ()
    Dim topmenuhnd%
    Dim floatmenu%
    Dim menuid%

    ' Get a handle to the top level menu
    topmenuhnd% = GetMenu%(Menulook.hWnd)
    ' And get a handle to the Floating popup menu.
    floatmenu% = GetSubMenu%(topmenuhnd%, 1)
    ' If 3rd (bitmap) entry is already loaded, exit now
    ' (we only load the bitmap once)
    If GetMenuItemCount%(floatmenu%) >= 3 Then Exit Sub

    ' First, add a menu entry under VB - this provides us
    ' with a menu entry that can be replaced with a bitmap,
    ' but whose menu ID will be the same (so it will work
    ' properly
    Load MenuFloat1(2)
    ' Now get the ID of that entry
    menuid% = GetMenuItemID%(floatmenu%, 2)
    ' And replace it with a bitmap.
    di% = ModifyMenuBynum(floatmenu%, 2, MF_BITMAP OrMF_BYPOSITION, ⟺
    menuid%, picture1.picture)

End Sub
```

The **CmdEntry2Chk_Click** function obtains a new bitmap for use as a checkmark by calling the **GetNewCheck** function. In this case the unchecked state is left at its default (nothing shown); however, it is possible to set a checkmark for both the checked and unchecked states. A handle to the bitmap is stored for destruction when the form is unloaded.

```
'
' Create a box checkmark bitmap for the Entry2 menu
'
Sub CmdEntry2Chk_Click ()
```

```
    Dim topmenuhnd%
    Dim floatmenu%
    Dim oldbkcolor&

    ' Get the new checkmark bitmap
    NewCheck% = GetNewCheck%()
    ' Get a handle to the top level menu
    topmenuhnd% = GetMenu%(Menulook.hWnd)
    ' Get a handle to the first popup
    floatmenu% = GetSubMenu%(topmenuhnd%, 0)
    ' And set the new check bitmap for the first (entry1)
    ' menu item
    di% = SetMenuItemBitmaps(floatmenu%, 1, MF_BYPOSITION, 0, NewCheck%)
    ' Check the entry
    MenuEntry2.Checked = -1
    ' Remind the user to look at it.
    MsgBox "Look at the Menu1 - Entry2 menu"
End Sub
```

The **CmdTrack_Click** function demonstrates two techniques. First it shows how to temporarily hide a menu by setting the caption to the empty string. In practice you would probably want to disable the menu entry as well, and to position it to the right of all other menus. Even when hidden, the menu takes up space. Keep in mind that you cannot hide the menu by setting the menu control's **Visible** property to FALSE—that causes the menu entry and associated popup to be destroyed.

Second, this function demonstrates how to bring up a tracked popup menu at the cursor position.

```
'   Hides the Floating menu entry in the caption,
'   and turns it into a tracked popup menu
'
Sub CmdTrack_Click ()
    Dim topmenuhnd%
    Dim floatmenu%
    Dim oldcap$
    Dim pt As POINTAPI

    ' Get a handle to the popup menu
    topmenuhnd% = GetMenu%(Menulook.hWnd)
    floatmenu% = GetSubMenu%(topmenuhnd%, 1)

    ' Hide the menu entry by clearing the string
    ' temporarily. Note, don't make it invisible or the
    ' menu will go away!
    oldcap$ = MenuFloat.caption
    MenuFloat.caption = ""
    ' Find where the mouse cursor is and place the
    ' popup at that point
    GetCursorPos pt
```

```
        di% = TrackPopupMenuBynum(floatmenu%, TPM_CENTERALIGN, pt.x, pt.y, 0, ⟺
        Menulook. hWnd,0&)
        ' Restore the original popup name
        MenuFloat.caption = oldcap$
End Sub


'
' Let the system know this menu has been clicked'
'
Sub MenuFloat_Click ()
        Label1.caption = "Floating selected."

End Sub
```

The following menu functions are self-explanatory. All they do is set the **Label1** caption with a message to the effect that the menu has been clicked. This is to help see what is happening with the tracked popup menus and the bitmap menus. Several of the menu **Click** functions also toggle the checked state when clicked.

```
'
' Let the system know this menu has been clicked'
'
Sub MenuEntry1_Click ()
        ' Check or uncheck the menu each time it is clicked
        Label1.caption = "Entry1 selected."
        MenuEntry1.Checked = Not MenuEntry1.Checked
End Sub


'
' Let the system know this menu has been clicked'
'
Sub MenuEntry2_Click ()
        ' Check or uncheck the menu each time it is clicked
        MenuEntry2.Checked = Not MenuEntry2.Checked
        Label1.caption = "Entry2 selected."

End Sub


'
' Let the system know this menu has been clicked
'
Sub MenuArray1_Click (Index As Integer)
        Label1.caption = "Array1(" + Str$(Index) + ")selected."

End Sub

'' Let the system know this menu has been clicked'
'
Sub MenuFloat1_Click (Index As Integer)
        Label1.caption = "Float1(" + Str$(Index) + ")selected."
```

```
End Sub


' Let the system know this menu has been clicked'
'
Sub MenuSub1Entry1_Click ()
    Label1.caption = "Sub1Entry1 selected."

End Sub

'
' Let the system know this menu has been clicked'
'
Sub MenuSub1Entry2_Click ()
    Label1.caption = "Sub1Entry2 selected."

End Sub

'
' Let the system know this menu has been clicked'
'
Sub MenuSubMenu1_Click ()
    Label1.caption = "SubMenu1 selected."

End Sub

'
' Let the system know this menu has been clicked'
'
Sub MenuTop_Click ()
    Label1.caption = "MenuTop selected."

End Sub

'
' Let the system know this menu has been clicked'
'
Sub MenuArt_Click (Index As Integer)
    Label1.caption = "Menu Random Art (" + Str$(Index) + ") selected."

End Sub

'
' Let the system know this menu has been clicked'
'
Sub MenuRandomTop_Click ()
    Label1.caption = "Menu Random selected."

End Sub

'
'
```

The **Form_Unload** function deletes the bitmaps that have been created by this application. The bitmaps in menus are not automatically deleted when the application is closed.

```
Sub Form_Unload (Cancel As Integer)
    Dim x%
    ' If a new check bitmap was set, we need to destroy it
    ' otherwise the resources used by the bitmap will not
    ' be freed.
    If NewCheck% <> 0 Then
        di% = DeleteObject(NewCheck%)
    End If
    ' The same applies to the random menu bitmaps
    For x% = 0 To 32
        If BMHandles%(x%) <> 0 Then
            di% = DeleteObject(BMHandles%(x%))
        End If
    Next x%

End Sub


'


Sub Form_MouseUp (Button As Integer, Shift As Integer, x As Single, y As ⇔
Single)
    ' Clicking anywhere on the form triggers the CmdTrack button
    CmdTrack.Value = -1
End Sub


'
' Clicking anywhere on the form triggers the CmdTrack command
' button.
'
Sub Form_Load ()
    Print "Click anywhere on the form to"
    Print "bring up a tracked popup menu"
    Randomize
End Sub
```

Function Reference

This section contains an alphabetical reference for the functions described in this chapter.

■ AppendMenu, AppendMenuByNum, AppendMenuByString

VB Declaration

```
Declare Function AppendMenu% Lib "User" (ByVal hMenu%,ByVal wFlags%, ByVal ⇔
wIDNewItem%, ByVal lpNewItem As Any)

Declare Function AppendMenuByNum% Lib "User" Alias"AppendMenu" (ByVal ⇔
hMenu%, ByVal wFlags%, ByValwIDNewItem%, ByVal lpNewItem&)

Declare Function AppendMenuByString% Lib "User" Alias"AppendMenu" (ByVal ⇔
hMenu%, ByVal wFlags%, ByValwIDNewItem%, ByVal lpNewItem$)
```

Description

This function adds a menu entry to the specified menu.

Use with VB

Refer to "How Visual Basic Menus Work," earlier in this chapter. Many of the changes made by this function will work, but will not be reflected by the VB menu object. The command ID added must be recognized by the VB menu system.

Parameter	Type/Description
hMenu	**Integer**—Handle to a menu.
wFlags	**Integer**—A combination of flags defined by constants in the file API-CONST.TXT. Refer to Table 9.7 under the description for the **ModifyMenu** function for a list of the constants permitted.
wIDNewItem	**Integer**—The new command ID for the specified menu entry. If the **MF_POPUP** flag is specified in parameter **wFlags**, this should be a handle to a popup menu.
lpNewItem	**String** or **Long**—If flag **MF_STRING** is set in parameter **wFlags**, this is the string to set into the menu. If flag **MF_BITMAP** is set, this is a long variable that contains a bitmap handle in the low 16 bits.

Return Value

Integer—TRUE (nonzero) on success, zero otherwise.

Comments

Refer to the comments for the **ModifyMenu** function for more information.

■ CheckMenuItem

VB Declaration:

```
Declare Function CheckMenuItem% Lib "User" (ByVal hMenu%,ByVal ⇔
wIDCheckItem%, ByVal wCheck%)
```

Description

Checks or unchecks the specified menu entry.

Use with VB Refer to "How Visual Basic Menus Work," earlier in this chapter. Changes made by this function will work, but will not be reflected by the VB menu **Checked** property.

Parameter	Type/Description
hMenu	**Integer**—Handle to a menu.
wIDCheckItem	**Integer**—Identifier of the menu entry to check or uncheck. If the **MF_BYCOMMAND** flag is set in the **wCheck** parameter, this parameter refers to the command ID of the menu entry to change. If the **MF_BYPOSITION** flag is set, this parameter refers to the position of the entry in the menu (the first entry is zero).
wCheck	**Integer**—A combination of flags defined by constants in the file API-CONST.TXT. Refer to Table 9.6 under the description of the **Modify-Menu** function for a list of menu constants. Only the following constants may be specified for this function: **MF_BYCOMMAND**, **MF_BYPOSITION, MF_CHECKED, MF_UNCHECKED**.

Return Value **Integer**—**MF_CHECKED** if the previous state of the entry was checked, **MF_UNCHECKED** if it was unchecked. -1 if the menu entry does not exist.

■ CreateMenu

VB Declaration `Declare Function CreateMenu% Lib "User" ()`

Description Creates an empty top level menu. The **AppendMenu** or **InsertMenu** function may be used to add entries into the window. The **SetMenu** command may be used to set this menu as the menu for a window.

Use with VB Refer to "How Visual Basic Menus Work," earlier in this chapter. The use of this function to create alternate VB menus is not recommended. Command IDs used in this window must match those of existing VB menu controls.

Return Value **Integer**—A handle to a menu on success, zero on error.

Comments This menu will be deleted automatically only if this menu is assigned to a window using the **Set-Menu** command. Otherwise, it is the programmer's responsibility to destroy the handle returned by this function using the **DestroyMenu** function.

■ CreatePopupMenu

VB Declaration `Declare Function CreatePopupMenu% Lib "User" ()`

Description Creates an empty popup menu. The **AppendMenu** or **InsertMenu** function may be used to add entries into the window and to add the popup to an existing menu.

Use with VB Refer to "How Visual Basic Menus Work," earlier in this chapter. The use of this function to create alternate VB menus is not recommended, except when creating menus for the **TrackPopupMenu** function. Command IDs used in this window must match those of existing VB menu controls.

Return Value **Integer**—A handle to a menu on success, zero on error.

Comments   This popup menu will be deleted automatically only if it is part of a higher level menu. Otherwise, it is the programmer's responsibility to destroy the handle returned by this function using the **DestroyMenu** function.

■ DeleteMenu

VB Declaration   `Declare Function DeleteMenu% Lib "User" (ByVal hMenu%,ByVal nPosition%, ⇔`
`ByVal wFlags%)`

Description   Deletes the specified menu entry.

Use with VB   Refer to "How Visual Basic Menus Work," earlier in this chapter. It is strongly recommended that you use the VB menu **Visible** property to delete entries from a menu. Use of this function will cause the **Visible** property for other menu entries in the specified menu to affect the wrong menu entry.

Parameter	Type/Description
hMenu	**Integer**—Handle to a menu.
nPosition	**Integer**—Identifier of the menu entry to delete. If the **MF_BYCOM-MAND** flag is set in the **wFlags** parameter, this parameter refers to the command ID of the menu entry to change. If the **MF_BYPOSI-TION** flag is set, this parameter refers to the position of the entry in the menu (the first entry is zero).
wFlags	**Integer**—**MF_BYCOMMAND** or **MF_BYPOSITION** as specified for the **nPosition** parameter.

Return Value   **Integer**—TRUE (nonzero) on success, zero otherwise.

Comments   If the entry has a popup menu attached, the popup menu is destroyed. Use the **RemoveMenu** API function to remove a popup menu entry without destroying the popup menu.

■ DestroyMenu

VB Declaration   `Declare Function DestroyMenu% Lib "User" (ByVal hMenu%)`

Description   Destroys the specified menu. Note that menus that are part of another menu or assigned directly to a window are automatically destroyed when the window is destroyed.

Use with VB   Refer to "How Visual Basic Menus Work," earlier in this chapter. This function is generally used on menus that were created with the **CreateMenu** and **CreatePopupMenu** functions.

Return Value   **Integer**—TRUE (nonzero) on success, zero otherwise.

■ DrawMenuBar

VB Declaration   `Declare Sub DrawMenuBar Lib "User" (ByVal hWnd%)`

Description   Redraws the menu for the specified window. Use this when using API functions to change the contents of a window's menu.

Use with VB   No problem, though it should rarely be necessary to use this function because you should not use API functions to change the top level menu of a window.

Parameter	Type/Description
hWnd	**Integer**—A handle to the window whose menu bar is to be redrawn.

Return Value   **Integer**—TRUE (nonzero) on success, zero otherwise.

■ EnableMenuItem

VB Declaration   `Declare Function EnableMenuItem% Lib "User" (ByVal hMenu%, ByVal ⇔`
`wIDEnableItem%, ByVal wEnable%)`

Description   Enables or disables the specified menu entry.

Use with VB   Refer to "How Visual Basic Menus Work," earlier in this chapter. Changes made by this function will work, but will not be reflected by the VB menu **Enabled** property.

Parameter	Type/Description
hMenu	**Integer**—Handle to a menu
wIDEnableItem	**Integer**—Identifier of the menu entry to enable, disable, or set to gray. If the **MF_BYCOMMAND** flag is set in the **wCheck** parameter, this parameter refers to the command ID of the menu entry to change. If the **MF_BYPOSITION** flag is set, this parameter refers to the position of the entry in the menu (the first entry is zero).
wEnable	**Integer**—A combination of flags defined by constants in the file API-CONST.TXT. Refer to Table 9.6 under the description for the **ModifyMenu** function for a list of menu constants. Only the following constants may be specified for this function: **MF_BYCOMMAND, MF_BYPOSITION, MF_ENABLED, MF_DISABLED**, and **MF_GRAYED**.

Return Value   **Integer**—0 if the previous state of the entry was disabled, 1 if it was enabled. -1 if the menu entry does not exist.

Comments   If the entry specified has a popup menu attached, the entire popup menu is affected.

■ GetMenu

VB Declaration `Declare Function GetMenu% Lib "User" (ByVal hWnd%)`

Description Retrieves the handle of the menu for a window.

Use with VB No problem.

Parameter	Type/Description
hWnd	**Integer**—A handle to a window. With VB, this should be a form handle.

Return Value **Integer**—The handle of the menu attached to the specified window if one exists, zero otherwise.

■ GetMenuCheckMarkDimensions

VB Declaration `Declare Function GetMenuCheckMarkDimensions& Lib "User" ()`

Description Returns the dimensions of a checkmark for a menu. Refer to the description for the **SetMenu-ItemBitmaps** for further information on use of this function.

Use with VB No problem.

Return Value **Long**—The high word (16 bits) contains the height of the menu checkmark in pixels; the low word contains the width. You can use the **agDWORDto2Integers** function to divide the result into two integers.

■ GetMenuItemCount

VB Declaration `Declare Function GetMenuItemCount% Lib "User" (ByValhMenu%)`

Description Returns the number of entries in a menu.

Use with VB No problem.

Parameter	Type/Description
hMenu	**Integer**—A handle to a menu.

Return Value **Integer**—The number of entries in the menu; -1 on error.

■ GetMenuItemID

VB Declaration `Declare Function GetMenuItemID% Lib "User" (ByVal hMenu%,ByVal nPos%)`

Description Returns the menu ID of the entry at the specified position in a menu.

Use with VB   No problem.

Parameter	Type/Description
hMenu	**Integer**—A handle to a menu.
nPos	**Integer**—The position of the entry in the menu. The first entry is number zero.

Return Value   **Integer**—The menu ID for the specified entry; -1 if the entry is a popup menu, 0 if the specified entry is a separator.

■ GetMenuState

VB Declaration   `Declare Function GetMenuState% Lib "User" (ByVal hMenu%,ByVal wId%, ByVal ⇔ wFlags%)`

Description   Retrieves information about the state of the specified menu entry.

Use with VB   Refer to "How Visual Basic Menus Work," earlier in this chapter.

Parameter	Type/Description
hMenu	**Integer**—Handle to a menu.
wId	**Integer**—Identifier of the menu entry for which to obtain the current state. If the **MF_BYCOMMAND** flag is set in the **wCheck** parameter, this parameter refers to the command ID of the menu entry. If the **MF_BYPOSITION** flag is set, this parameter refers to the position of the entry in the menu (the first entry is zero).
wFlags	**Integer**—The constant **MF_BYCOMMAND** or **MF_BYPOSITION** as specified in the **wId** parameter.

Return Value   **Integer**—A combination of flags defined by constants in the file APICONST.TXT as shown in Table 9.5.

Table 9.5   **Menu Constants for GetMenuState**

Constant	Description
MF_BITMAP	Menu entry is a bitmap.
MF_CHECKED	Menu entry is checked.
MF_DISABLED	Menu entry is disabled
MF_GRAYED	Menu entry is gray and disabled.
MF_MENUBARBREAK	A bar break is specified for this entry. Refer to Table 9.6 under the **ModifyMenu** command for details.

Table 9.5   **Menu Constants for GetMenuState (Continued)**

Constant	Description
MF_MENUBREAK	A menu break is specified for this entry. Refer to Table 9.6 under the **ModifyMenu** command for details.
MF_SEPARATOR	Menu entry is a separator.

■ GetMenuString

VB Declaration   `Declare Function GetMenuString% Lib "User" (ByVal hMenu%,ByVal wIDItem%, ⇔`
                       `ByVal lpString$, ByVal nMaxCount%,ByVal wFlag%)`

Description   Retrieves the string for a specified menu entry.

Use with VB   Refer to "How Visual Basic Menus Work," earlier in this chapter.

Parameter	Type/Description
hMenu	Integer—Handle to a menu.
wIDItem	Integer—Identifier of the menu entry to retrieve. If the **MF_BY-COMMAND** flag is set in the **wCheck** parameter, this parameter refers to the command ID of the menu entry. If the **MF_BYPOSITION** flag is set, this parameter refers to the position of the entry in the menu (the first entry is zero).
lpString	String—A preinitialized string buffer to load with the string for the menu entry.
nMaxCount	Integer—The maximum number of characters to load into **lpString** + 1.
wFlags	Integer—The constant **MF_BYCOMMAND** or **MF_BYPOSITION** as specified in the **wId** parameter.

Return Value   Integer—The length of the string returned in **lpString** (not including the null terminating character).

■ GetSubMenu

VB Declaration: `Declare Function GetSubMenu% Lib "User" (ByVal hMenu%,ByVal nPos%)`

Description   Retrieves the handle of a popup menu that is located at the specified position in a menu.

Use with VB   No problem.

Parameter	Type/Description
hMenu	Integer—A handle to a menu.
nPos	Integer—The position of the entry in the menu. The first entry is number zero.

Return Value   **Integer**—The handle of the popup menu at the specified position if one exists, zero otherwise.

■ GetSystemMenu

VB Declaration   `Declare Function GetSystemMenu% Lib "User" (ByVal hWnd%,ByVal bRevert%)`

Description   Retrieves the handle to the system menu for the specified window. This is referred to in VB as the control menu (the menu that appears when you click on the control box that exists on a form if the **ControlBox** property is TRUE).

Use with VB   System menus send WM_SYSCOMMAND messages to a window rather than WM_COM-MAND messages. This means that they are not compatible with VB menu control objects. Thus while you can change entries in the system menu if you wish, you cannot add new entries that will receive click events unless you use a subclassing tool, such as Desware's SpyWorks-VB. This command is most frequently used to remove entries from the system menu that you do not wish to make available to the user.

Parameter	Type/Description
hWnd	**Integer**—A handle to a window.
bRevert	**Integer**—Set TRUE to restore the original system menu.

Return Value   **Integer**—A handle to the system menu on success, zero otherwise. No meaning if **bRevert** is TRUE.

■ HiliteMenuItem

VB Declaration   `Declare Function HiliteMenuItem% Lib "User" (ByVal hWnd%,ByVal hMenu%, ↩`
`ByVal wIDHiliteItem%, ByVal wHilite%)`

Description   Controls the highlight on a top level menu entry.

Use with VB   Refer to "How Visual Basic Menus Work," earlier in this chapter.

Parameter	Type/Description
hWnd	**Integer**—A handle to a window that has a top level menu.
hMenu	**Integer**—Handle to the top level menu for window **hWnd**.
wIDHiliteItem	**Integer**—Identifier of the menu entry to highlight or unhighlight. If the **MF_BYCOMMAND** flag is set in the **wHilite** parameter, this parameter refers to the command ID of the menu entry to change. If the **MF_BYPOSITION** flag is set, this parameter refers to the position of the entry in the menu (the first entry is zero).
wHilite	**Integer**—A combination of flags defined by constants in the file API-CONST.TXT. Include **MF_BYCOMMAND** or **MF_BYPOSITION** to indicate the entry to change. Include **MF_HILITE** to set the highlight, or **MF_UNHILITE** to remove the highlight.

Return Value   **Integer**—TRUE (nonzero) on success, zero otherwise.

■ InsertMenu, InsertMenuByNum, InsertMenuByString

VB Declaration
```
Declare Function InsertMenu% Lib "User" (ByVal hMenu%,ByVal nPosition%, ⇔
ByVal wFlags%, ByVal wIDNewItem%,ByVal lpNewItem As Any)

Declare Function InsertMenuBynum% Lib "User" Alias"InsertMenu" (ByVal ⇔
hMenu%, ByVal nPosition%, ByValwFlags%, ByVal wIDNewItem%, ByVal lpNewItem&)

Declare Function InsertMenuBystring% Lib "User" Alias "InsertMenu" (ByVal ⇔
hMenu%, ByVal nPosition%, ByVal wFlags%, ByVal wIDNewItem%, ByVal lpNewItem$)
```

Description
This function inserts a menu entry at the specified location in a menu, moving other entries down as needed.

Use with VB
Refer to "How Visual Basic Menus Work," earlier in this chapter. Many of the changes made by this function will work but will not be reflected by the VB menu object. The command ID added must be recognized by the VB menu system.

Parameter	Type/Description
hMenu	**Integer**—Handle to a menu.
nPosition	**Integer**—Identifier to the menu entry specifying the insertion point of the new entry. If the **MF_BYCOMMAND** flag is set in the **wFlags** parameter, this parameter refers to the command ID of the menu entry to change. If the **MF_BYPOSITION** flag is set, this parameter refers to the position of the entry in the menu (the first entry is zero).
wFlags	**Integer**—A combination of flags defined by constants in the file API-CONST.TXT. Refer to Table 9.6 under the description for the **ModifyMenu** function for a list of the constants permitted.
wIDNewItem	**Integer**—The new command ID for the specified menu entry. If the **MF_POPUP** flag is specified in parameter **wFlags**, this should be a handle to a popup menu.
lpNewItem	**String** or **Long**—If flag **MF_STRING** is set in parameter **wFlags**, this is the string to set into the menu. If flag **MF_BITMAP** is set, this is a long variable that contains a bitmap handle in the low 16 bits.

Return Value
Integer—TRUE (nonzero) on success, zero otherwise.

Comments
Refer to the comments for the **ModifyMenu** function for more information.

■ IsMenu

VB Declaration
```
Declare Function IsMenu% Lib "User" (ByVal hMenu%)
```

Description
Determines if a handle is not a handle to a menu.

Use with VB　No problem.

Parameter	Type/Description
hMenu	**Integer**—The menu handle to test.

Return Value　**Integer**—FALSE (zero) if the handle is not a menu handle. If TRUE, the handle may be a menu.

■ LoadMenu

VB Declaration　`Declare Function LoadMenu% Lib "User" (ByVal hInstance%,ByVal lpString$)`

Description　Loads a menu from the specified module or application instance.

Use with VB　Because of the inability of VB to handle menus that are not compatible with existing VB menus, use of this function is not recommended.

Parameter	Type/Description
hInstance	**Instance**—Module handle for a dynamic link library, or instance handle that specifies the executable file that contains the menu resource.
lpString	**String** or **Long**—As a **String**, specifies the name of the menu resource to load. As a **Long**, specifies the menu ID to load. You will need to create a type declaration that accepts a **Long** parameter for **lpString** to use the menu ID form of this function.

Return Value　**Integer**—A handle to the loaded menu; zero on error.

Comments　If the menu is not assigned to a window, it will be necessary to use the **DestroyMenu** function to destroy the menu before the application closes.

■ LoadMenuIndirect

VB Declaration　`Declare Function LoadMenuIndirect% Lib "User"(lpMenuTemplate As ⇔`
`MENUITEMTEMPLATEHEADER)`

Description　Loads a menu based on a memory block containing **MENUITEMTEMPLATE** data structures.

Use with VB　Refer to the description of the **LoadMenu** function.

Parameter	Type/Description
lpMenuTemplate	**MENUITEMTEMPLATEHEADER**—This header structure should be followed in memory by one or more **MENUITEMTEMPLATE** data structures. Refer to Appendix B for a description of these data structures.

Return Value　**Integer**—A handle to the loaded menu; zero on error.

Comments　If the menu is not assigned to a window, it will be necessary to use the **DestroyMenu** function to destroy the menu before the application closes.

■ ModifyMenu, ModifyMenuBynum, ModifyMenuBystring

VB Declaration   Declare Function ModifyMenu% Lib "User" (ByVal hMenu%,ByVal nPosition%, ⇔
ByVal wFlags%, ByVal wIDNewItem%,ByVal lpString As Any)

Declare Function ModifyMenuBynum% Lib "User" Alias "ModifyMenu" (ByVal ⇔
hMenu%, ByVal nPosition%, ByValwFlags%, ByVal wIDNewItem%, ByVal lpString&)

Declare Function ModifyMenuBystring% Lib "User" Alias"ModifyMenu" (ByVal ⇔
hMenu%, ByVal nPosition%, ByValwFlags%, ByVal wIDNewItem%, ByVal lpString$)

Description   This function can be used to change a menu entry.

Use with VB   Refer to "How Visual Basic Menus Work," earlier in this chapter. Many of the changes made by this function will work, but will not be reflected by the VB menu object.

Parameter	Type/Description
hMenu	**Integer**—Handle to a menu.
nPosition	**Integer**—Identifier to the menu entry to change. If the **MF_BY-COMMAND** flag is set in the **wFlags** parameter, this parameter refers to the command ID of the menu entry to change. If the **MF_BYPOSITION** flag is set, this parameter refers to the position of the entry in the menu (the first entry is zero).
wFlags	**Integer**—A combination of flags defined by constants in the file API-CONST.TXT. Refer to Table 9.6 for a list of the constants permitted.
wIDNewItem	**Integer**—The new command ID for the specified menu entry. If the **MF_POPUP** flag is specified in parameter **wFlags**, this should be a handle to a popup menu.
lpString	**String** or **Long**—If flag **MF_STRING** is set in parameter **wFlags**, this is the string to set into the menu. If flag **MF_BITMAP** is set, this is a long variable that contains a bitmap handle in the low 16 bits.

Return Value   Integer—TRUE (nonzero) on success; zero otherwise.

Table 9.6   Constant Menu Flag Definitions

Constant	Description
MF_BITMAP	Menu entry is a bitmap. This bitmap must not be deleted once set into the menu, so the value returned by the VB **Image** property should not be used.
MF_BYCOMMAND	The menu entry is specified by the command ID of the menu.
MF_BYPOSITION	The menu entry is specified by the position of the entry in the menu. Zero specifies the first entry in the menu.

Table 9.6 **Constant Menu Flag Definitions (Continued)**

Constant	Description
MF_CHECKED	Checks the specified menu entry. Not compatible with the VB **Checked** property.
MF_DISABLED	Disables the specified menu entry. Not compatible with the VB **Enabled** property.
MF_ENABLED	Enables the specified menu entry. Not compatible with the VB **Enabled** property.
MF_GRAYED	Disables the specified menu entry and draws it in light gray. Not compatible with the VB **Enabled** property.
MF_MENUBARBREAK	On popup menus, places the specified entry on a new column with a vertical bar separating the columns.
MF_MENUBREAK	On popup menus, places the specified entry on a new column. On top level menus, places the entry on a new line.
MF_OWNERDRAW	Creates an owner draw menu (one in which your program is responsible for drawing each menu entry). Not compatible with VB.
MF_POPUP	Places a popup menu at the specified entry. This may be used to create submenus and popup menus.
MF_SEPARATOR	Places a separator line at the specified entry.
MF_STRING	Places a string at the specified entry. Not compatible with the VB **Caption** property.
MF_UNCHECKED	Checks the specified menu entry. Not compatible with the VB **Checked** property.

Comments The following combinations of flags are not allowed: **MF_BYCOMMAND** and **MF_BYPOSITION**; **MF_CHECKED** and **MF_UNCHECKED**; **MF_MENUBARBREAK** and **MF_MENUBREAK**; **MF_DISABLED**, **MF_ENABLED**, and **MF_GRAYED**; **MF_BITMAP**, **MF_STRING**, **MF_OWNERDRAW**, and **MF_SEPARATOR**.

The **DrawMenuBar** function may need to be called to update the menu after using this function.

■ RemoveMenu

VB Declaration
```
Declare Function RemoveMenu% Lib "User" (ByVal hMenu%,ByVal nPosition%, ⇔
ByVal wFlags%)
```

Description Removes the specified menu entry. If the removed entry is a popup menu, this function does not destroy the popup menu. You should first use the **GetSubMenu** function to obtain the handle of the popup menu.

Use with VB   Refer to "How Visual Basic Menus Work," earlier in this chapter. It is strongly recommended that you use the VB menu **Visible** property to delete entries from a menu instead of this function. Use of this function will cause the **Visible** property for other menu entries in the specified menu to affect the wrong menu entry.

Parameter	Type/Description
hMenu	**Integer**—Handle to a menu.
nPosition	**Integer**—Identifier of the menu entry to remove. If the **MF_BY-COMMAND** flag is set in the **wFlags** parameter, this parameter refers to the command ID of the menu entry to change. If the **MF_BYPOSITION** flag is set, this parameter refers to the position of the entry in the menu (the first entry is zero).
wFlags	**Integer**—**MF_BYCOMMAND** or **MF_BYPOSITION** as specified for the **nPosition** parameter.

Return Value   Integer—TRUE (nonzero) on success, zero otherwise.

■ SetMenu

VB Declaration   `Declare Function SetMenu% Lib "User" (ByVal hWnd%, ByVal hMenu%)`

Description   Sets the menu for a window.

Use with VB   Refer to "How Visual Basic Menus Work," earlier in this chapter. This function is not recommended for use with VB. If used, care must be taken that the command IDs in the new menu are compatible with the original VB window. Only form windows should be specified with this function.

Parameter	Type/Description
hWnd	**Integer**—A handle to a window.
hMenu	**Integer**—A handle to the new menu for the window. If zero, any existing menu for the window is removed.

Return Value   **Integer**—TRUE (nonzero) on success; zero otherwise.

Comments   The previous menu for the window is not destroyed by this function.

■ SetMenuItemBitmaps

VB Declaration   `Declare Function SetMenuItemBitmaps% Lib "User" (ByValhMenu%, ByVal ⇔`
`nPosition%, ByVal wFlags%, ByVal hBitmapUnchecked%, ByVal hBitmapChecked%)`

Description   Sets the bitmaps to use for the specified menu entry in place of the standard checkmark. The bitmaps must be the correct size for menu checkmarks as obtained by the **GetMenuCheckMarkDimensions** function.

Use with VB   No known problems.

Parameter	Type/Description
hMenu	**Integer**—Handle to a menu.
nPosition	**Integer**—Identifier of the menu entry for which to set the bitmaps. If the **MF_BYCOMMAND** flag is set in the **wFlags** parameter, this parameter refers to the command ID of the menu entry to change. If the **MF_BYPOSITION** flag is set, this parameter refers to the position of the entry in the menu (the first entry is zero).
wFlags	**Integer**—**MF_BYCOMMAND** or **MF_BYPOSITION** as specified for the **nPosition** parameter.
hBitmapUnchecked	**Integer**—A handle to the bitmap to display when the specified entry is unchecked. If zero, no checkmark will appear when the entry is unchecked.
hBitmapChecked	**Integer**—A handle to the bitmap to display when the specified entry is checked. If zero, the default window's checkmark will be displayed when the entry is checked.

Return Value   **Integer**—TRUE (nonzero) on success; zero otherwise.

Comments   The bitmap used may be shared by multiple entries. The bitmap must be destroyed by the application when it is no longer needed, as it is not destroyed automatically by Windows.

■ TrackPopupMenu, TrackPopupMenuBynum

VB Declaration
```
Declare Function TrackPopupMenu% Lib "User" (ByVal hMenu%, ByVal wFlags%, ⇔
ByVal x%, ByVal y%, ByVal nReserved%, ByVal hWnd%, lpRect As Any)

Declare Function TrackPopupMenuBynum% Lib "User" Alias"TrackPopupMenu" ⇔
(ByVal hMenu%, ByVal wFlags%, ByValx%, ByVal y%, ByVal nReserved%, ByVal ⇔
hWnd%, ByVallpRect&)
```

Description   Displays a popup menu anywhere on the screen.

Use with VB   Although Visual Basic 3.0 provides direct support for tracked popup menus, this function remains useful for customized menus and use with earlier versions of Visual Basic. Refer to "How Visual Basic Menus Work," earlier in this chapter. You may use a VB popup menu or create one yourself, in which case be careful that the command IDs in the menu match those expected by Visual Basic.

Parameter	Type/Description
hMenu	**Integer**—A handle to a popup menu.
wFlags	**Integer**—A combination of position flags and mouse tracking flags as shown in Table 9.7.
x,y	**Integers**—A point specifying the location of the popup menu in screen coordinates.
nReserved	**Integer**—Not used; set to zero.

Parameter	Type/Description
hWnd	**Integer**—A handle of the window to receive the popup menu commands. You should use the window handle of the form that has a menu that accepts the same set of command IDs as the popup menu.
lpRect	**RECT** or **Long**—A rectangle defining an area on the screen. Mouse clicks outside of this area will cause the popup window to close. Use the **Long** version set to zero to close the menu any time the mouse is clicked outside of the menu.

Return Value   **Integer**—TRUE (nonzero) on success, zero otherwise.

Table 9.7   **Position and Mouse Tracking Flags**

Position Flags	Description
TPM_CENTERALIGN	The menu is horizontally centered at the specified position.
TPM_LEFTALIGN	The left side of the menu is placed at the horizontal x coordinate.
TPM_RIGHTALIGN	The right side of the menu is placed at the horizontal x coordinate.

Mouse Tracking Flags	Description
TPM_LEFTBUTTON	Normal operation with the left mouse button.
TPM_RIGHTBUTTON	The menu tracks the right mouse button.

10

Text and Fonts

FONT AND TEXT MANIPULATION IS ONE OF THE MOST COMPLEX PARTS OF the Windows system. With the arrival of TrueType scalable font technology in Windows 3.1, it is safe to say that the complexity has increased even more. Fortunately, you do not need to be an expert to use this technology effectively in Visual Basic.

This chapter will focus on two areas: First, the chapter includes a brief overview of fonts in general, and Windows font technology in particular. A sample program, FontView, shows how to select and use a font, and how to obtain information about a font. Second, the chapter describes the use of the powerful Windows API text output functions. A sample program, TextDemo, illustrates the use of some of these functions.

If you are planning to write a complete WYSIWYG word processor in Visual Basic (which *is* possible), or other application that requires an in-depth understanding of the internal functioning of scalable fonts, you are advised to seek out additional sources. It is possible to find entire books that deal with the problems of handling fonts, text output, typesetting, and performing WYSIWYG ("What you see is what you get") text editing.

A Note on the Chapter Structure

Throughout this book, the chapters are structured to present background information on the subject first, followed by example code and then a reference section. Detailed information on function parameters and data structures has been left to the function reference and Appendix B (which contains a reference for the data structures used by the Windows API).

Fonts have numerous attributes, many of which are too complex to explain in a few words or even sentences. These attributes are used in many cases as function parameters or as fields in data structures. In order to bring all of the information on these attributes to one place, and eliminate the necessity of attempting to define them for each function, all of the parameters and data structure fields are defined later in this chapter in the section titled "Font Parameters." The function reference and data structure reference will refer to this section rather than attempt to describe each parameter.

Using Fonts

This section describes the attributes and characteristics of fonts. It also lists the fields to the Windows API font data structures, such as **LOGFONT** and **TEXT-METRIC**, and parameters to the font API functions, such as **CreateFont**.

Introduction to Fonts

A font describes the way a text string will appear on a device. Figure 10.1 shows how the choice of font can affect the appearance of the uppercase letter A.

Figure 10.1
The letter A in
different fonts

As you can see, the fonts can vary a great deal. Some are simple line characters. Some are highly decorative. They vary in size and in weight. For example, a bold font is considered to have a heavier weight than a normal or light font.

You might be wondering what the "snowflake" symbol is doing in the middle of the array of A's. One of the attributes of a font is the character set used. Character sets, which define the symbols used for each ASCII value, are described in Chapter 5. The letter A has the ASCII value of 65. The snowflake symbol just happens to be assigned to ASCII value 65 for the character set in that particular font.

A number of fonts will be installed on any given Windows system. Windows automatically installs a dozen or so standard fonts, but there are literally hundreds of fonts available that may be installed on a system. In the world of traditional typography, a font is called a typeface. Fonts are typically known by their typeface name and attributes; for example, *Courier Bold 12 point* is a commonly used fixed pitch font. The types and attributes of fonts will be covered through the course of this chapter.

Consider the case of a standard word processor document that uses several fonts. What happens when the document is transferred to another system that does not have the same fonts installed? If the document required that the exact font be present, it would be virtually impossible to transfer documents from one system to another.

One solution would be to include the font information in the document. Unfortunately, not only does this approach increase the size of each document, but in many cases it violates the copyright restrictions on the font. Windows does support this approach by supporting embedded fonts; however, for most cases Windows provides a much more flexible and powerful solution.

Windows avoids the problem that results when a font makes a document device-specific in much the same way as it provides other device-independent drawing capabilities. Instead of specifying an actual physical font, the programmer specifies an entity known as a *logical font*. A logical font can be thought of as the font that is ideal for a particular task. For example, the original manuscript for this book used a Courier font that is readable and makes it easy to calculate word counts. All of the fonts requested by a document are logical fonts rather than specific physical fonts.

Windows takes the requested logical font information and maps it into a physical font by finding the physical font that most closely matches the requested logical font. This mapping process is described later in this chapter.

It is important to recognize that each change in characteristic defines a different font. For example, say you have a normal Helvetica font such as that provided with Windows. The italicized version of that font is in fact a different font, even though only one attribute (italics) has changed. The same applies to other characteristics such as normal versus bold, normal versus underlined, and so on. And, with nonscalable fonts, each character size demands a different font.

In many cases, Windows can synthesize one font out of another. For example, Windows can usually do a good job of creating an underlined font out of a normal font, so you rarely need to purchase separate underlined fonts. In other cases, there is a significant drop in quality. For example, when Windows scales a raster font from a small size to a very large one, the result can be truly ugly because slight imperfections in a letter's form become pronounced as the letter increases in size.

Understanding Font Attributes

Before considering the font function parameters and data structure fields, it is important to understand some of the basic characteristics and dimensions of fonts, and to define some of the terms that are used in describing these attributes.

Font Technology

Windows uses a number of different font technologies, each with different advantages and disadvantages:

- *Raster fonts.* A raster font is defined as a series of character bitmaps. Whenever a character needs to be displayed, the bitmap for that character is copied to the device. A raster font is usually defined for a particular device and resolution. The primary advantage of raster fonts is that the font can be optimized to look good on the device for which it was designed. The disadvantage is that the font is not easily scalable—you need a separate set of character bitmaps for each font size you wish to use. Although Windows can scale raster fonts to create a synthesized font in a different size, the results are often of very poor quality.

- *Vector (or stroke) fonts.* These fonts are made up of graphic elements represented by GDI function calls. Because the vectors can be described mathematically (by numbers), they can be scaled through a fairly wide range while maintaining a reasonable quality. They have been superseded by TrueType fonts and are thus rarely used.

■ *Scalable fonts*. With scalable fonts, the lines describing the character are defined mathematically using vectors and curves. There are several add-on packages to Windows that provide scalable font technology, but this chapter will deal exclusively with the TrueType scaling technology included with Windows 3.1. The primary advantage of scalable fonts is their flexibility—these fonts may be scaled to virtually any size with little loss of quality. There are two disadvantages. First, at small sizes scalable fonts rarely look as good as a well-designed raster font. Second, scalable fonts are more complex and somewhat slower to draw than corresponding raster fonts.

Windows also differentiates between Windows fonts and device fonts. A *Windows font* is part of the Windows environment and may be used on the display and in most cases on the device. A *device font* is optimized for a particular device and may not be displayed on the screen. When drawing on the screen using a logical font that specifies a device font, Windows will display the closest available match to the requested font from those that it can display.

Font Pitch

Both raster and scalable fonts may be of either fixed pitch or variable pitch. In a *fixed pitch* font, the width of each character cell is equal—this means that the distance between any two characters is the same. In a *variable pitch* font, the spacing varies depending on the character. A narrow character such as the letter I will take up less space than a wide character such as W. Variable pitch fonts are also known as proportionally spaced fonts.

Font Dimensions

A character has a certain width and height. Sounds simple, doesn't it? If only it were so. The simple character cell actually has a great many attributes and characteristics. Table 10.1 and Figure 10.2 illustrate the parts of a character cell and define the terms used to describe them.

Table 10.2 and Figure 10.3 define the dimensions used for character cells and those used to determine character spacing both vertically and horizontally.

Spacing for variable pitch fonts varies for each character in the font. It is possible for part of one character to overhang or underhang another character. In order to provide this capability, Windows defines three width parameters for TrueType fonts. These are referred to as the A-B-C dimensions for the font. The B dimension defines the width of the glyph. The A dimension represents the distance from the left edge of the character cell to the left of the glyph. This may be a negative number, in which case the glyph will partially overlap the previous character. The C dimension describes the distance from the right edge of the character cell to the right of the glyph. This number may also be negative. Figure 10.4 illustrates the use of the A-B-C dimensions.

Figure 10.2
Parts of a
character cell

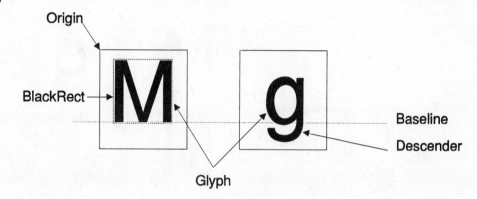

Table 10.1 **Parts of a Character Cell**

Font Attribute	Description
Baseline	An imaginary line within a character cell that indicates the base of a character. See Descender.
BlackRect	The smallest rectangle that fully encloses the character symbol (or glyph).
Cell	A rectangular cell that contains the glyph.
Cell Origin	The upper-left corner of the character cell.
Descender	The part of the character that drops beneath the baseline.
Glyph	The actual character symbol.

Windows provides a number of API functions to determine character spacing, as shown in Table 10.3. The space taken up by one or more characters is called the *extent* of the text. When two characters are printed near each other, the distance between them depends not only on the size of the character itself, but also on the two characters involved. A font may dictate that two characters be placed closer to each other than normal in order to provide a more pleasing look. The process of adjusting character position is known as *kerning*.

Figure 10.3
Character cell
dimensions

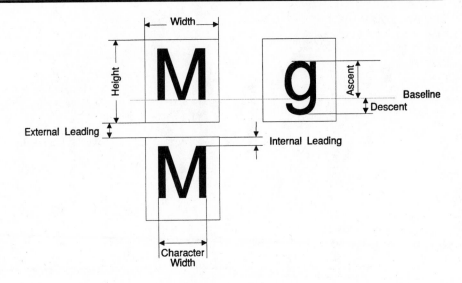

Figure 10.4
A-B-C dimensions

The A and C dimensions represent space added to the text position before drawing the next character. If they are negative, underhangs and overhangs are allowed as seen here. Note how the top of the f overhangs the next letter.

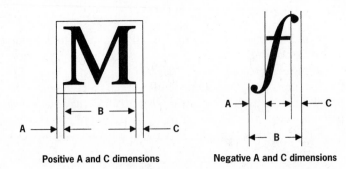

Positive A and C dimensions   Negative A and C dimensions

 **Using Fonts**

For this reason, it is not possible to determine the space required by a string of text by simply adding up the character spacing. You must call one of the extent calculation functions and specify the entire string for which extents are needed.

Table 10.2   **Character Cell Dimensions**

Font Attribute	Description
A-B-C	Character spacing for TrueType fonts. Refer to Figure 10.4.
Ascent	The height that a character rises above the baseline. The ascent for a font is usually defined by the letter M.
Average character width	The average width of the character (glyph) within the character cell.
Character width	The actual width of a character. This can vary with variable width fonts. For TrueType fonts, use the A-B-C dimensions.
Descent	The distance that a character descender drops below the baseline.
External leading	The recommended vertical spacing between character cells. (It's called leading because in the old days a typesetter adjusted the space between the lines by inserting slugs of lead.)
Height	The height of a character cell.
Internal leading	The distance from the baseline to the top of the character cell. This area may be used by the character.
Maximum character width	The width of the widest character in the font. With fixed pitch fonts, all characters have the same width.
Width	The width of a character cell.

Table 10.3   **Font Extent Functions**

Function	Description
GetCharABCWidths	Retrieves the A-B-C dimensions for one or more characters in a TrueType font.
GetCharWidth	Retrieves the widths of one or more characters in a font.
GetTabbedTextExtent	Retrieves the width and height of a text string as it will appear on a device. This function takes tabs into account.

Table 10.3   **Font Extent Functions (Continued)**

Function	Description
GetTextCharacterExtra	Retrieves the amount of extra intercharacter spacing used by Windows when drawing text. This is usually zero.
GetTextExtent GetTextExtentPoint	Retrieves the width and height of a text string as it will appear on a device.
SetTextCharacterExtra	Sets the amount of extra intercharacter spacing used by Windows when drawing text.

Font Families

A family describes a general class of fonts. Figure 10.5 shows the font families that are used by Windows. Every font should fall into one of these categories.

Figure 10.5
Windows font
families

Decorative: Any decorative fonts used for special applications

Modern: Fixed pitch font where the stroke width of the font is constant.

Roman: Proportionally spaced font with serifs. The stroke width may vary.

Script: Proportionally spaced font that looks like handwriting. The stroke width may vary.

Swiss: Proportionally spaced font without serifs. The stroke width may vary.

The decorative family is used for special applications. For example, an elegant "antique styled" invitation could be created using an decorative gothic font. This is the catch-all family that describes any font that does not fall into one of the other categories.

Modern fonts are the simplest family of fonts. They use constant width lines and may or may not have *serifs*, the small decorative lines or hooks that appear at the ends of the lines. For example, the bottom of the two vertical strokes on the M character have tiny horizontal serifs. Typewriter style fonts such as Courier and other fixed pitch fonts fall into this category.

Roman fonts are probably the most commonly used fonts for general text applications. The line or stroke width may vary as can be seen in the legs of the letter M for this family. These fonts also have serifs.

Script fonts are fonts that are designed to look like handwriting. These fonts are often used to provide a handwritten or personalized look.

Swiss fonts are similar to Roman fonts except that they do not have the serifs (thus these are often referred to as *sans serif* fonts). These fonts are frequently used for headlines or captions in a document, or to provide a modern look.

In Windows, the term *family* is used to describe classifications of fonts and the term *typeface* or *facename* is used to identify a set of fonts that shares a common character set and design but varies in attributes such as size, weight, slant, and so on. The term *family* in the world outside of Windows typically refers to the typeface of the font. For example, in Windows, a Helvetica bold 10 point font and Helvetica normal 12 point font have the same typeface (Helvetica) and are part of the Swiss family. A commercial font package or printer may refer to these fonts as belonging to the Helvetica font family.

Character Set

Figure 10.1 showed the effect that character set has on a font and introduced the idea that fonts may have different character sets. (Refer to Chapter 5 for an in-depth explanation of character sets.) Windows defines three standard character sets for fonts:

- ANSI_CHARSET is the standard Windows character set.

- SYMBOL_CHARSET is a symbol character set in which each ASCII value represents an arbitrary symbol. Note that each symbol font will probably have different sets of symbols.

- OEM_CHARSET is the OEM character set. This set is system-dependent.

When Windows chooses a physical font based on a requested logical font, it gives highest priority to obtaining the requested character set.

Weight, Italics, and Underlines

Table 10.4 describes additional font attributes that are commonly used.

Table 10.4   Other Font Attributes

Attribute	Description
Aspect Ratio	Each raster font is designed for a specific display aspect ratio. Displaying the font on a device with a different aspect ratio will cause it to appear taller or shorter than it should be.
Escapement	The rotation of the font.
FaceName	Also knows as the "Typeface" of the font, the name of the font. Each font has a name which is usually copyrighted. For example, the most common Swiss family sans serif font is referred to as HELV, Ariel, Universe, Helvetica, Swiss, and other names, depending on who created the font.
Italic	The font is italicized (slanted).
Quality	Some fonts are defined as draft or proof (letter) quality. This is especially common for dot-matrix printer fonts.
StrikeOut	The font has a horizontal line through each character.
Underlined	The font is underlined.
Weight	Specifies how dark the font looks. A light font will appear light with thin character strokes. A heavy font will appear darker. The terms Normal and Bold are generally used to describe two commonly defined standard weights for a font. The Windows font functions define weight as a number from 100 to 900, where 400 is normal and 700 is bold.

TrueType fonts may define additional styles (OUTLINE, for example).

Working with Fonts

Windows provides a number of functions to create and manipulate fonts.

Creating Logical Fonts

Before drawing text under Windows, it is necessary to request a font to use by specifying a logical font. A logical font is a Windows GDI object that defines the attributes for the desired font. Table 10.5 shows the functions used to create a logical font.

The API **DeleteObject** function can be used to delete a logical font.

Table 10.5   **Font Creation Functions**

Function	Description
CreateFont	Creates a logical font according to a specified set of attribute values.
CreateFontIndirect	Creates a logical font based on attribute values specified in a **LOGFONT** data structure.

GDI Font Mapping

When an application requests a particular font from Windows, it provides a logical font that Windows uses to select a physical font. If the exact physical font requested does not exist, the Windows Graphics Device Interface (GDI) will choose or synthesize a font to use in its place. This process of mapping a logical to a physical font involves looking at attributes according to a set priority. Each attribute is assigned a penalty value. GDI examines each available physical font and scores each attribute according to how closely it matches the requested value. The physical font with the lowest penalty value is actually selected.

The order of priorities for attributes is listed in Table 10.6. In most cases, it is possible to specify a "don't care" value for an attribute, in which case GDI does not consider that particular attribute.

Table 10.6   **Attribute Priorities**

Attribute	Comments
Character set	The most important attribute for font mapping.
Pitch	Variable pitch fonts are highly penalized if a fixed pitch font is requested as the application may not be able to handle variable width fonts.
Family	The family of the font (See Figure 10.5).
FaceName	The name of the typeface of the font.
Height	GDI will never choose a font with a greater height than requested.
Width	GDI will never choose a font that is wider than requested.
Weight	GDI will always prefer an actual bold font to a synthesized bold font.
Slant	GDI will always prefer an actual italic font over a synthesized italic font.
Underline	GDI will always prefer an actual underline font over a synthesized underline font.
StrikeOut	GDI will always prefer an actual strikeout font over a synthesized strikeout font.

Scalable fonts can be scaled to match the requested font size.

Windows provides several API functions that allow you to influence the mapping process. These are shown in Table 10.7.

Table 10.7　GDI Mapping Control Functions

Function	Description
SetMapperFlags	Allows you to specify whether or not font mapping should take the device aspect ratio into account. Not used for TrueType fonts.
GetAspectRatioFilter GetAspectRatioFilterEx	Determines the aspect ratio to be used when mapping fonts.
GetRasterizerCaps	Determines if TrueType fonts are installed in the system.

Windows performs mapping to obtain a physical font when the logical font is selected into a device context using the **SelectObject** API function. As with all GDI drawing objects, be sure to select the font out of the device context and select the original font back into the DC before deleting the font or the device context.

Font Information Functions

Table 10.8 lists the API functions that may be used to retrieve information about a font.

Table 10.8　Font Information Functions

Function	Description
EnumFontFamilies	Enumerates available fonts from a specified family. Requires use of the CBK.VBX custom control.
EnumFonts	Enumerates fonts for a specified device. Requires use of the CBK.VBX custom control. **EnumFontFamilies** is preferred for Windows 3.1 and later.
GetFontData	Extracts font data that can be embedded in an application.
GetGlyphOutline	Retrieves information about the glyph of a TrueType font.
GetOutlineTextMetrics	Retrieves information about a TrueType font.

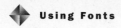

Table 10.8 **Font Information Functions (Continued)**

Function	Description
GetTextFace	Retrieves the face (font name) of the font selected into a device context.
GetTextMetrics	Retrieves information about the font selected into a device context.

Adding and Removing Fonts

In order to use a font, the font must be installed in the Windows system. This is generally accomplished using the control panel application provided with Windows (program CONTROL.EXE).

It is possible to add or remove fonts from the Windows system using the functions listed in Table 10.9. Fonts can be contained in any executable file including dynamic link libraries. They may also be kept in a special font resource file identified with the extension .FON, .FOT, or .FOR (for FONt, FOntTruetype, and FOntReadonly respectively). TrueType font files cannot directly be loaded by Windows, so an interface resource file must be created using the **CreateScalableFontResource** API function.

Table 10.9 **Font Resource Functions**

Function	Description
AddFontResource	Adds a font resource to Windows. It may then be used by any application.
CreateScalableFontResource	Creates a font resource file for a TrueType font.
RemoveFontResource	Removes a font resource from Windows.

Font Parameters Used in Functions and Data Structures

The font attributes described to this point are used by the programmer in two ways. Information functions return structures that contain fields that indicate the state of a font attribute. The **CreateFont** function and **LOGFONT** data structure contain fields that specify the attributes for a logical font. This section lists the common parameters and structure data fields that correspond to these attributes.

The LOGFONT Structure Fields and CreateFont Function Parameters

The following fields are used in the **LOGFONT** and **NEWLOGFONT** data structures and the **CreateFont** API function. They are used to specify the attributes of a logical font. GDI uses the information in this structure to choose a physical font.

All units are in the logical units of the device context for the logical font. All parameters are integers unless otherwise specified (for the **CreateFont** structure) or as defined in the **LOGFONT** data structure. Note that in a data structure a single byte is defined as a fixed width character string of length one, whereas on a function call the integer data type is used.

- **lfCharSet.** Specifies the character set (see Chapter 5). The following constants define character sets:
  ANSI_CHARSET: The Windows character set.
  DEFAULT_CHARSET: Use any character set.
  SYMBOL_CHARSET: Symbol character set.
  OEM_CHARSET: System-dependent character set.

- **lfClipPrecision**. Defines the precision for clipping the font when a character is partly outside of the clipping region. Defined by the **CLIP_???_PRE-CIS** constants in file APICONST.TXT. Default is specified by the constant **CLIP_DEFAULT_PRECIS**.

- **lfEscapement**. Defines the angle for drawing text by specifying the angle between the font baseline and the X axis in one-tenth degree increments. If Y increases in the downward direction, this angle is measured from the baseline up. Otherwise it is measured from the baseline down.

- **lfFaceName**. String: Specifies the name of the typeface. If NULL, GDI attempts to select the default device typeface.

- **lfFullName**. String: The full face name and style name for a TrueType font. Used only in the **NEWLOGFONT** structure.

- **lfHeight, lfWidth**. The height and width of the font in logical units. Refers to the cell dimensions if positive, character (glyph) dimensions if negative. Refers to average character width for variable pitch fonts. GDI will always choose a physical font with dimensions equal to or smaller than those specified if such a font is available.

- **lfItalic**. Nonzero to specify an italic font.

- **lfOrientation**. Part of the **LOGFONT** structure; it is not used.

- **lfOutPrecision**. Provides guidelines to GDI to use for matching the font. Defined by the **OUT_???_PRECIS** constants in file APICONST.TXT. Default is specified by the constant **OUT_DEFAULT_PRECIS**. The

OUT_TT_ONLY_PRECIS constant can be used to request only True-Type fonts.

- **lfPitchAndFamily**. Integer: A combination of the pitch and family. Pitch and family are specified by constants that are ORed together. The pitch constants are:

  DEFAULT_PITCH: Use the default for the system.

  FIXED_PITCH: Request a fixed pitch font. GDI will never return a variable pitch font if this is specified unless there are no fixed pitch fonts in the requested character set.

  VARIABLE_PITCH: Request a variable pitch font.

  The family is specified by the constants **FF_DECORATIVE, FF_MODERN, FF_ROMAN, FF_SCRIPT, FF_SWISS**, or **FF_DONTCARE** if any family is acceptable.

- **lfQuality**. One of the following constants:
  DEFAULT_QUALITY: Don't care.
  DRAFT_QUALITY: Request a draft quality font.
  PROOF_QUALITY: Request a proof quality font.

- **lfStrikeOut**. Nonzero to specify a strike-out font.

- **lfStyle**. String: The style of a TrueType font. TrueType fonts may define unique styles such as OUTLINE. This string allows you to determine the style of a TrueType font.

- **lfUnderline**. Nonzero to specify an underline font.

- **lfWeight**. The character weight ranging from 100 to 900. Example values are 100 for light, 400 for normal, 700 for bold. Refer to the **FW_???** constants for a complete list of values.

The TEXTMETRIC and NEWTEXTMETRIC Structure Fields

The following fields are used in the **TEXTMETRIC** and **NEWTEXTMETRIC** data structures. These structures return the attributes of an actual physical font selected into a device context. All units specified are in logical units of the device context unless specified otherwise. Most of these attributes are defined earlier in this chapter.

- **ntmAvgWidth**. The average character width for a TrueType font given in EM logical units. The EM is the approximate width of the letter M in that font.

- **ntmCellHeight**. The height of a TrueType character cell given in EM logical units.

- **ntmFlags**. Specifies font style using the constants **NTM_REGULAR**, **NTM_BOLD**, and **NTM_ITALIC**. This is only used for TrueType fonts.

- **ntmSizeEM**. Specifies the EM square size of the font. It represents the logical units in which a TrueType font was laid out. The EM is the approximate width of the letter M in that font.

- **tmAscent**. The ascent of the character cell.

- **tmAveCharWidth**. The average width of the characters in the font. For ANSI fonts, only letters and the space character are used.

- **tmBreakChar**. The character used to define word breaks when text is justified. Usually the space character.

- **tmCharSet**. Specifies the character set for the font.

- **tmDefaultChar**. The ASCII value of the character that will be displayed whenever a character that is not defined for the font is requested.

- **tmDescent**. The descent of the character cell.

- **tmDigitizedAspectX, tmDigitizedAspectY**. The horizontal and vertical aspect ratio for which the font was designed.

- **tmExternalLeading**. The external leading dimension of the character cell.

- **tmFirstChar**. The ASCII value of the first character defined for the font (not all fonts define all 255 ASCII characters).

- **tmHeight**. The height of a character cell.

- **tmInternalLeading**. The internal leading dimension of the character cell.

- **tmItalic**. TRUE if this is an italic font.

- **tmLastChar**. The ASCII value of the last character defined for the font.

- **tmMaxCharWidth**. Specifies the width of the widest character in the font. This refers to the B spacing of the character for TrueType fonts.

- **tmOverhang**. This attribute is used when GDI synthesizes fonts that require a change in the intercharacter spacing. For example, when GDI synthesizes an italic or bold font, this represents the change in spacing. When you have a character in a normal font next to one in an italic font, this can be used to calculate the spacing between the two.

- **tmPitchAndFamily**. The pitch is defined by constants **FF_DECORA-TIVE**, **FF_MODERN**, **FF_ROMAN**, **FF_SCRIPT**, and **FF_SWISS** in the same manner as the **lfPitchAndFamily** attribute described in the previous section. **FF_DONTCARE** indicates the font is not assigned to a family. Four constants define the bit flags for the pitch as follows:

TMPF_FIXED_PITCH: This is a fixed pitch font. (Note that experimentation seems to indicate that a font is fixed pitch when this bit is zero, not one. Refer to the code for the FontView application.)

TMPF_VECTOR: This is a vector or TrueType font.

TMPF_TRUETYPE: This is a TrueType font.

TMPF_DEVICE: This is a device font.

These bits may be combined; for example, a TrueType fixed pitch font would have the **TMPF_TRUETYPE** and **TMPF_FIXED_PITCH** flag bits set.

- **tmStruckOut**. TRUE if this is a strikeout font.

- **tmUnderlined**. TRUE if this is an underlined font.

- **tmWeight**. See the lfWeight attribute in the previous section.

TrueType Specification

This overview of font technology and the font API functions should prove adequate for most VB applications. The TrueType font specification is available directly from Microsoft for those who wish to explore the internals of font technology, use embedded fonts in their applications, or use some of the advanced TrueType API functions.

Drawing Text

Windows provides a number of powerful text drawing functions, all of which are compatible with Visual Basic.

The Process of Drawing Text

The most important thing to realize about text output under Windows is that the process is identical to any other graphic output. This can be seen in Table 10.10, which compares the process of drawing a rectangle with that of drawing a line of text.

There are two differences between the actual drawing of the rectangle and the drawing of the text. First, unlike the rectangle, you do not always know how much space is needed to contain a particular block of text. Second, the rectangle origin is always aligned at a rectangle corner (upper left or upper right depending on the coordinate system). With text, you have a number of alignment options depending on the output function used.

Table 10.10   Comparison of Graphics versus Text Output

Drawing a Rectangle	Drawing Text
Obtain a device context to draw into.	Same.
Obtain a pen to draw with.	Obtain a font to draw with.
Select the pen into the device context.	Select the font into the device context.
Decide where to place the rectangle.	Decide the starting point for the text.
Draw the rectangle.	Draw the text.
Restore the original pen into the device context.	Restore the original font into the device context.
Free GDI objects as needed (pen, device context).	Free GDI objects as needed (font, device context).

Text Extents and Alignment

Text extents refer to the size that a particular block of text will take up on the output device. This size is influenced by many factors including the font, the text to be displayed, and the coordinate system of the device context. Windows provides a number of functions to help calculate text extents as shown in Table 10.3. When drawing text, it is common to calculate the extent of a block of text before drawing it, and use that value to determine the location of the next block of text. For more complex situations where multiple fonts are combined on a line, you may need to use the text metrics for the font to calculate the spacing between individual characters.

In most cases you also have control over the alignment of text output. The first alignment issue relates to what part of text the drawing coordinate applies to. If you are trying to fit text into a particular rectangle, you will probably want the origin to refer to the upper-left or lower-left corner of the character cell depending on the coordinate system in use. If, however, you are combining several fonts on a line, you will probably want to align all of the characters to a single baseline, thus the drawing coordinate should be aligned to the font baseline.

A formatting rectangle is used by some of the text drawing functions. This allows you to specify a rectangle in which the text will be drawn, and provides the ability to specify additional formatting options. These include left, center, and right alignment for a line, automatic word breaks at rectangle boundaries, and more. Table 10.11 lists the text output API functions and their supporting functions, along with some additional text manipulation routines.

Table 10.11   **Text Output and Support Functions**

Function	Description
AnsiLower, AnsiLowerBuff	Convert text to lowercase.
AnsiUpper, AnsiUpperBuff	Convert text to uppercase.
DrawText	The most powerful text output function with formatting. Includes tabbing, automatic word wrap, and more.
ExtTextOut	An extended text output function that provides the ability to specify the exact location of every character.
GetTextAlign	Retrieves the current text alignment.
GetTextColor	Retrieves the current text drawing color.
GrayString	A function to draw gray strings. This is most frequently used to draw text on disabled controls.
IsCharAlpha	Determines if a character is a letter.
IsCharAlphaNumeric	Determines if a character is a letter or number.
IsCharLower	Determines if a character is lowercase.
IsCharUpper	Determines if a character is uppercase.
SetTextAlign	Sets the text alignment.
SetTextColor	Sets the drawing color for text.
SetTextJustification	Supports text justification while drawing text.
TabbedTextOut	Text output function that supports user-definable tab stops.
TextOut	The most basic text output function.

Example Program: FontView

FontView is a program that allows you to modify the attributes of a logical font, then display the resulting font using a user-defined text sample. It then allows you to view text metric information about the actual physical font selected.

Using FontView

The FontView runtime screen is shown in Figure 10.6. The list box is loaded with the available font typeface names. The Height and Width text boxes specify the requested font width and height in pixels. The font returned will not be larger than these dimensions, even if GDI needs to select a different typeface in order to meet these requirements.

Figure 10.6
FontView program
screen

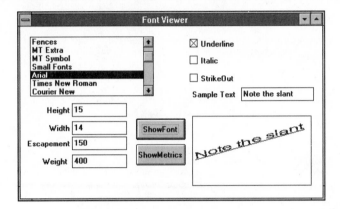

The Escapement text box allows you to specify the angle of the text drawing in tenths of a degree. The Underline, Italic, and StrikeOut check boxes are self-explanatory. The Sample Text text box allows you to specify the text to display.

The ShowFont command button causes the logical font to be selected into the picture control and the sample text drawn. The ShowMetrics command button brings up a message box that displays information about the physical font that was actually selected as shown in Figure 10.7.

Figure 10.7
FontView program
screen: Viewing text
metrics

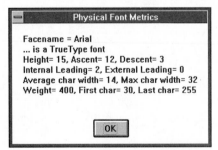

Project Description

The FontView project includes four files. FONTVIEW.FRM is the only form used in the program. FONTVIEW.BAS is the only module in the program and contains the constant type and global definitions. APIDECS.BAS is the type-safe API declaration file provided with this book. APIGUIDE.BAS contains the declarations for the APIGUIDE.DLL dynamic link library.

Listing 10.1 shows the project file for the FontView program.

Listing 10.1　Project Listing File FONTVIEW.MAK

```
FONTVIEW.FRM
FONTVIEW.BAS
APIDECS.BAS
APIGUIDE.BAS
ProjWinSize=175,438,248,215
ProjWinShow=2
```

Form Description

Listing 10.2 contains the header from file FONTVIEW.FRM that describes the control setup for the form.

Listing 10.2　FONTVIEW.FRM Header

```
VERSION 2.00
Begin Form Form1
    Caption        =    "Font Viewer"
    Height         =    4425
    Left           =    1035
    LinkMode       =    1  'Source
    LinkTopic      =    "Form1"
    ScaleHeight    =    4020
    ScaleWidth     =    7365
    Top            =    1140
    Width          =    7485
    Begin TextBox TxtWeight
        Height         =    315
        Left           =    1260
        TabIndex       =    8
        Text           =    "400"
        Top            =    2880
        Width          =    1335
    End
```

Listing 10.2   FONTVIEW.FRM Header (Continued)

```
Begin CommandButton CmdShowMetrics
    Caption        =    "ShowMetrics"
    Height         =    495
    Left           =    2820
    TabIndex       =    16
    Top            =    2760
    Width          =    1215
End
Begin TextBox TxtEscapement
    Height         =    315
    Left           =    1260
    TabIndex       =    6
    Text           =    "0"
    Top            =    2520
    Width          =    1335
End
Begin CommandButton CmdShowFont
    Caption        =    "ShowFont"
    Height         =    495
    Left           =    2820
    TabIndex       =    13
    Top            =    2160
    Width          =    1215
End
Begin TextBox TxtWidth
    Height         =    315
    Left           =    1260
    TabIndex       =    4
    Text           =    "10"
    Top            =    2160
    Width          =    1335
End
```

The sample text appears in the **PicText** control when the ShowFont command button is clicked.

```
Begin PictureBox PicText
    Height         =    1635
    Left           =    4200
    ScaleHeight    =    1605
    ScaleWidth     =    2865
    TabIndex       =    9
    Top            =    2100
    Width          =    2895
End
```

```
Begin TextBox TxtHeight
   Height          =    315
   Left            =    1260
   TabIndex        =    1
   Text            =    "10"
   Top             =    1800
   Width           =    1335
End
Begin TextBox TxtSample
   Height          =    315
   Left            =    5400
   TabIndex        =    14
   Text            =    "ABC"
   Top             =    1440
   Width           =    1755
End
Begin CheckBox ChkStrikeout
   Caption         =    "StrikeOut"
   Height          =    375
   Left            =    4140
   TabIndex        =    12
   Top             =    1020
   Width           =    1575
End
Begin CheckBox ChkItalic
   Caption         =    "Italic"
   Height          =    375
   Left            =    4140
   TabIndex        =    11
   Top             =    600
   Width           =    1575
End
Begin CheckBox ChkUnderline
   Caption         =    "Underline"
   Height          =    315
   Left            =    4140
   TabIndex        =    10
   Top             =    240
   Width           =    1635
End
Begin ListBox FontList
   Height          =    1395
   Left            =    240
   Sorted          =    -1   'True
   TabIndex        =    0
   Top             =    240
   Width           =    3015
End
Begin Label Label4
   Alignment       =    1    'Right Justify
```

```
            Caption         =    "Weight"
            Height          =    315
            Left            =    120
            TabIndex        =    7
            Top             =    2940
            Width           =    1035
         End
         Begin Label Label3
            Alignment       =    1  'Right Justify
            Caption         =    "Escapement"
            Height          =    315
            Left            =    60
            TabIndex        =    5
            Top             =    2580
            Width           =    1155
         End
         Begin Label Label2
            Alignment       =    1  'Right Justify
            Caption         =    "Width"
            Height          =    255
            Left            =    540
            TabIndex        =    3
            Top             =    2220
            Width           =    675
         End
         Begin Label Label1
            Alignment       =    1  'Right Justify
            Caption         =    "Height"
            Height          =    255
            Left            =    540
            TabIndex        =    2
            Top             =    1860
            Width           =    675
         End
         Begin Label Label5
            Caption         =    "Sample Text"
            Height          =    255
            Left            =    4200
            TabIndex        =    15
            Top             =    1500
            Width           =    1095
         End
      End
End
```

FontView Listings

Module FONTVIEW.BAS contains the constant declarations and global variables used by the program.

Listing 10.3   Module FONTVIEW.BAS

```
' FontView program example


Global Const OUT_DEFAULT_PRECIS = 0
Global Const OUT_STRING_PRECIS = 1
Global Const OUT_CHARACTER_PRECIS = 2
Global Const OUT_STROKE_PRECIS = 3
Global Const OUT_TT_PRECIS = 4
Global Const OUT_DEVICE_PRECIS = 5
Global Const OUT_RASTER_PRECIS = 6
Global Const OUT_TT_ONLY_PRECIS = 7
Global Const CLIP_DEFAULT_PRECIS = 0
Global Const CLIP_CHARACTER_PRECIS = 1
Global Const CLIP_STROKE_PRECIS = 2
Global Const CLIP_LH_ANGLES = &H10
Global Const CLIP_TT_ALWAYS = &H20
Global Const CLIP_EMBEDDED = &H80
Global Const DEFAULT_QUALITY = 0
Global Const DRAFT_QUALITY = 1
Global Const PROOF_QUALITY = 2
Global Const DEFAULT_PITCH = 0
Global Const FIXED_PITCH = 1
Global Const VARIABLE_PITCH = 2
Global Const TMPF_FIXED_PITCH = 1
Global Const TMPF_VECTOR = 2
Global Const TMPF_DEVICE = 8
Global Const TMPF_TRUETYPE = 4
Global Const ANSI_CHARSET = 0
Global Const ANSI_CHARSET = 1
Global Const SYMBOL_CHARSET = 2
Global Const SHIFTJIS_CHARSET = 128
Global Const OEM_CHARSET = 255
Global Const NTM_REGULAR = &H40&
Global Const NTM_BOLD = &H20&
Global Const NTM_ITALIC = &H1&
Global Const LF_FULLFACESIZE = 64
Global Const RASTER_FONTTYPE = 1
Global Const DEVICE_FONTTYPE = 2
Global Const TRUETYPE_FONTTYPE = 4
Global Const FF_DONTCARE = 0
Global Const FF_ROMAN = 16
Global Const FF_SWISS = 32
Global Const FF_MODERN = 48
Global Const FF_SCRIPT = 64
Global Const FF_DECORATIVE = 80
Global Const FW_DONTCARE = 0
Global Const FW_THIN = 100
```

Listing 10.3 Module FONTVIEW.BAS (Continued)

```
Global Const FW_EXTRALIGHT = 200
Global Const FW_LIGHT = 300
Global Const FW_NORMAL = 400
Global Const FW_MEDIUM = 500
Global Const FW_SEMIBOLD = 600
Global Const FW_BOLD = 700
Global Const FW_EXTRABOLD = 800
Global Const FW_HEAVY = 900
Global Const FW_ULTRALIGHT = FW_EXTRALIGHT
Global Const FW_REGULAR = FW_NORMAL
Global Const FW_DEMIBOLD = FW_SEMIBOLD
Global Const FW_ULTRABOLD = FW_EXTRABOLD
Global Const FW_BLACK = FW_HEAVY

' Global Variables

Global FontToUse% ' The font in use
```

Listing 10.4 Form Listing FONTVIEW.FRM

```
Sub Form_Load ()
    Dim x%
    Dim a$
    Screen.MousePointer = 11
    For x% = 1 To Screen.FontCount
        a$ = Screen.Fonts(x%)
        If a$ <> "" Then FontList.AddItem a$
    Next x%
    Screen.MousePointer = 0
End Sub
```

This function shows how you can create a logical font by filling in entries in a **LOGFONT** data structure. This example does not cover all of the fields—you might want to experiment with some of the others such as precision and font family. The **SelectObject** API function causes Windows to find a physical font that is as close as possible to the logical font you specified.

```
' Creates a logical font based on the various control
' settings. Then displays a sample string in that font.
'
Sub CmdShowFont_Click ()
    Dim lf As LOGFONT
    Dim oldhdc%
    Dim rc As RECT
    PicText.Cls
```

```
    If FontToUse% <> Ø Then di% = DeleteObject(FontToUse%)
    lf.lfHeight = Val(TxtHeight.Text)
    lf.lfWidth = Val(TxtWidth.Text)
    lf.lfEscapement = Val(TxtEscapement.Text)
    lf.lfWeight = Val(TxtWeight.Text)
    If (ChkItalic.Value = 1) Then lf.lfItalic = Chr$(1)
    If (ChkUnderline.Value = 1) Then lf.lfUnderline = Chr$(1)
    If (ChkStrikeout.Value = 1) Then lf.lfStrikeOut = Chr$(1)
    lf.lfOutPrecision = Chr$(OUT_CHARACTER_PRECIS)
    lf.lfClipPrecision = Chr$(CLIP_CHARACTER_PRECIS)
    lf.lfQuality = Chr$(DEFAULT_QUALITY)
    lf.lfPitchAndFamily = Chr$(DEFAULT_PITCH Or FF_DONTCARE)
    lf.lfCharSet = Chr$(DEFAULT_CHARSET)
    lf.lfFaceName = FontList.Text + Chr$(Ø)
    FontToUse% = CreateFontIndirect(lf)
    If FontToUse% = Ø Then Exit Sub
    oldhdc% = SelectObject(PicText.hDC, FontToUse%)

    ' Get the client rectangle in order to place the
    ' text midway down the box
    GetClientRect agGetControlHwnd(PicText), rc
    di% = TextOut(PicText.hDC, 1, rc.bottom / 2, (TxtSample.Text),⇔
    Len(TxtSample.Text))
    di% = SelectObject(PicText.hDC, oldhdc%)
End Sub
```

The **GetTextMetrics** function retrieves information about a physical font. The message box brought up by this function presents the text metrics that can be compared with the requested logical font.

```
' Display the text metrics for the physical font.
'
Sub CmdShowMetrics_Click ()
    Dim tm As TEXTMETRIC
    Dim r$
    Dim crlf$
    Dim oldfont%
    Dim tbuf As String * 80
    crlf$ = Chr$(13) + Chr$(10)
    If FontToUse% = Ø Then
        MsgBox "Font not yet selected"
        Exit Sub
    End If
    oldfont% = SelectObject(PicText.hDC, FontToUse%)
    di% = GetTextMetrics(PicText.hDC, tm)
    di% = GetTextFace(PicText.hDC, 79, tbuf)
    ' Add to r$ only the part up to the null terminator
    r$ = "Facename = " + agGetStringFromLPSTR$(tbuf) +crlf$
    If (Asc(tm.tmPitchAndFamily) And TMPF_TRUETYPE) <> ØThen r$ = r$ + "... ⇔
    is a TrueType font" + crlf$
    If (Asc(tm.tmPitchAndFamily) And TMPF_DEVICE) <> Ø Then r$ = r$ + "... ⇔
    is a Device font" + crlf$
```

```
        r$ = r$ + "Height=" + Str$(tm.tmHeight) + ", Ascent=" + Str$(tm.tmAscent) ⇔
        + ", Descent=" +Str$(tm.tmDescent) + crlf$
        r$ = r$ + "Internal Leading=" +Str$(tm.tmInternalLeading) + ", External⇔
        Leading=" + Str$(tm.tmExternalLeading) + crlf$
        r$ = r$ + "Average char width=" + Str$(tm.tmAveCharWidth) + ", Max char ⇔
        width=" +Str$(tm.tmMaxCharWidth) + crlf$
        r$ = r$ + "Weight=" + Str$(tm.tmWeight) + ", Firstchar=" + ⇔
        Str$(Asc(tm.tmFirstChar)) + ", Lastchar=" + Str$(Asc(tm.tmLastChar)) + crlf$

        MsgBox r$, Ø, "Physical Font Metrics"
        di% = SelectObject(PicText.hDC, oldfont%)
    End Sub

    Sub Form_Unload (Cancel As Integer)
        ' Be sure to clean up GDI objects when leaving the program
        If FontToUse% <> Ø Then di% = DeleteObject(FontToUse%)
    End Sub
```

Example Program: TextDemo

TextDemo shows several techniques relating to drawing text and demonstrates use of two of the text output functions.

Using TextDemo

Figure 10.8 shows the TextDemo program in action. The list box is loaded with the typeface names of the available screen fonts. The lower picture box shows a text string using the default font for the control scaled to different sizes. Contrast this with the screen shown in Figure 10.9, which shows the scaling for a TrueType font.

Figure 10.8
TextDemo program screen: Non-TrueType font

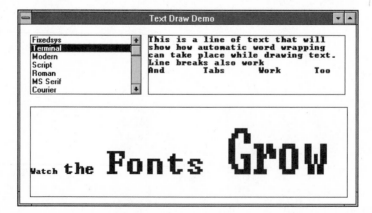

Figure 10.9

TextDemo program screen: TrueType font

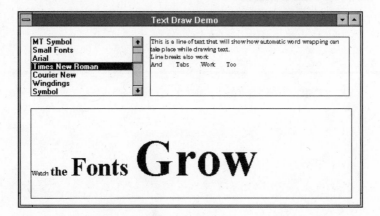

The picture box at the upper right in Figure 10.9 shows a text string displayed using automatic word wrapping. It also demonstrates the use of tab stops.

The only user control for this program is the selection of the typeface to display.

Project Description

The TextDemo project includes four files. TEXTDEMO.FRM is the only form used in the program. TEXTDEMO.BAS is the only module in the program and contains the constant type and global definitions. APIDECS.BAS is the type-safe API declaration file provided with this book. APIGUIDE.BAS contains the declarations for the APIGUIDE.DLL dynamic link library.

Listing 10.5 shows the project file for the FontView program.

Listing 10.5 **Project Listing File TEXTDEMO.MAK**

```
TEXTDEMO.FRM
TEXTDEMO.BAS
APIDECS.BAS
APIGUIDE.BAS
ProjWinSize=175,439,248,215
ProjWinShow=2
```

Form Description

Listing 10.6 contains the header from file TEXTDEMO.FRM that describes the control setup for the form.

Listing 10.6   TEXTDEMO.FRM Header

```
VERSION 2.00
Begin Form TextDemo
    Caption        =   "Text Draw Demo"
    Height         =   4590
    Left           =   1035
    LinkMode       =   1  'Source
    LinkTopic      =   "Form1"
    ScaleHeight    =   4185
    ScaleWidth     =   8190
    Top            =   1140
    Width          =   8310
    Begin PictureBox PicText
        Height         =   2115
        Left           =   240
        ScaleHeight    =   2085
        ScaleWidth     =   7725
        TabIndex       =   1
        Top            =   1920
        Width          =   7755
    End
    Begin PictureBox PicFrame
        Height         =   1395
        Left           =   3120
        ScaleHeight    =   1365
        ScaleWidth     =   4785
        TabIndex       =   2
        Top            =   240
        Width          =   4815
    End
    Begin ListBox FontList
        Height         =   1395
        Left           =   240
        Sorted         =   -1  'True
        TabIndex       =   0
        Top            =   240
        Width          =   2715
    End
End
```

TextDemo Listings

Module TEXTDEMO.BAS contains the constant declarations and global
variables used by the program.

Listing 10.7   **Module TEXTDEMO.BAS**

```
' TextDemo program example

Global Const OEM_FIXED_FONT = 10
Global Const ANSI_FIXED_FONT = 11
Global Const ANSI_VAR_FONT = 12
Global Const SYSTEM_FONT = 13
Global Const DEVICE_DEFAULT_FONT = 14
Global Const DEFAULT_PALETTE = 15
Global Const SYSTEM_FIXED_FONT = 16

Global Const OUT_DEFAULT_PRECIS = 0
Global Const OUT_STRING_PRECIS = 1
Global Const OUT_CHARACTER_PRECIS = 2
Global Const OUT_STROKE_PRECIS = 3
Global Const OUT_TT_PRECIS = 4
Global Const OUT_DEVICE_PRECIS = 5
Global Const OUT_RASTER_PRECIS = 6
Global Const OUT_TT_ONLY_PRECIS = 7
Global Const CLIP_DEFAULT_PRECIS = 0
Global Const CLIP_CHARACTER_PRECIS = 1
Global Const CLIP_STROKE_PRECIS = 2
Global Const CLIP_LH_ANGLES = &H10
Global Const CLIP_TT_ALWAYS = &H20
Global Const CLIP_EMBEDDED = &H80
Global Const DEFAULT_QUALITY = 0
Global Const DRAFT_QUALITY = 1
Global Const PROOF_QUALITY = 2
Global Const DEFAULT_PITCH = 0
Global Const FIXED_PITCH = 1
Global Const VARIABLE_PITCH = 2
Global Const TMPF_FIXED_PITCH = 1
Global Const TMPF_VECTOR = 2
Global Const TMPF_DEVICE = 8
Global Const TMPF_TRUETYPE = 4
Global Const ANSI_CHARSET = 0
Global Const ANSI_CHARSET = 1
Global Const SYMBOL_CHARSET = 2
Global Const SHIFTJIS_CHARSET = 128
Global Const OEM_CHARSET = 255
Global Const NTM_REGULAR = &H40&
Global Const NTM_BOLD = &H20&
Global Const NTM_ITALIC = &H1&
```

Listing 10.7   Module TEXTDEMO.BAS (Continued)

```
Global Const LF_FULLFACESIZE = 64
Global Const RASTER_FONTTYPE = 1
Global Const DEVICE_FONTTYPE = 2
Global Const TRUETYPE_FONTTYPE = 4
Global Const FF_DONTCARE = 0
Global Const FF_ROMAN = 16
Global Const FF_SWISS = 32
Global Const FF_MODERN = 48
Global Const FF_SCRIPT = 64
Global Const FF_DECORATIVE = 80
Global Const FW_DONTCARE = 0
Global Const FW_THIN = 100
Global Const FW_EXTRALIGHT = 200
Global Const FW_LIGHT = 300
Global Const FW_NORMAL = 400
Global Const FW_MEDIUM = 500
Global Const FW_SEMIBOLD = 600
Global Const FW_BOLD = 700
Global Const FW_EXTRABOLD = 800
Global Const FW_HEAVY = 900
Global Const FW_ULTRALIGHT = FW_EXTRALIGHT
Global Const FW_REGULAR = FW_NORMAL
Global Const FW_DEMIBOLD = FW_SEMIBOLD
Global Const FW_ULTRABOLD = FW_EXTRABOLD
Global Const FW_BLACK = FW_HEAVY

Global Const TA_NOUPDATECP = 0
Global Const TA_UPDATECP = 1
Global Const TA_LEFT = 0
Global Const TA_RIGHT = 2
Global Const TA_CENTER = 6
Global Const TA_TOP = 0
Global Const TA_BOTTOM = 8
Global Const TA_BASELINE = 24

Global Const DT_TOP = &H0
Global Const DT_LEFT = &H0
Global Const DT_CENTER = &H1
Global Const DT_RIGHT = &H2
Global Const DT_VCENTER = &H4
Global Const DT_BOTTOM = &H8
Global Const DT_WORDBREAK = &H10
Global Const DT_SINGLELINE = &H20
Global Const DT_EXPANDTABS = &H40
Global Const DT_TABSTOP = &H80
Global Const DT_NOCLIP = &H100
Global Const DT_EXTERNALLEADING = &H200
Global Const DT_CALCRECT = &H400
```

Listing 10.7 **Module TEXTDEMO.BAS (Continued)**

```
Global Const DT_NOPREFIX = &H800
Global Const DT_INTERNAL = &H1000
```

Listing 10.8 **Form Listing TEXTDEMO.FRM**

```
'   Load the font list dialog box with the available fonts
'
Sub Form_Load ()
    Dim x%
    Dim a$
    Screen.MousePointer = 11
    For x% = 1 To Screen.FontCount
        a$ = Screen.Fonts(x%)
        If a$ <> "" Then FontList.AddItem a$
    Next x%
    Screen.MousePointer = 0
    FontList.ListIndex = 0
End Sub



' Redraw the demo pictures in the new font
'
Sub FontList_Click ()
    PicText.FontName = FontList.text
    PicFrame.FontName = FontList.text
    PicText.Refresh
    PicFrame.Refresh
End Sub
```

The following function illustrates several interesting techniques. First, it shows how to obtain the default font for a device context by temporarily selecting into the context a temporary stock font. This can be especially useful for printer devices if you wish to determine the default font for a printer DC.

Next, the function shows how the **LOGFONT** structure obtained can be modified in order to change selected attributes, in this case the size of the font. The **CreateFontIndirect** function may then be used to request the modified font.

This function also demonstrates use of GDI's text alignment capabilities to have the coordinate refer to the text block's baseline instead of the top or bottom of the character cell.

Finally, the function shows how you may use the current position for the device context to allow text output without having to calculate the extents manually for each text block.

```
'   Draw a multiple font demo in the picture control
'
Sub PicText_Paint ()
    ReDim demo$(4)
    Dim lf As LOGFONT
    Dim oldfont%, newfont%
    Dim rc As RECT
    Dim vpos%
    Dim alignorig%
    Dim todraw%

    demo$(1) = "Watch "
    demo$(2) = "the "
    demo$(3) = "Fonts "
    demo$(4) = "Grow "

    ' Get the dimensions of the control
    GetClientRect agGetControlHwnd%(PicText), rc

    ' We get the current logical font by selecting in
    ' temporarily a stock font
    oldfont% = SelectObject%(PicText.hDC,GetStockObject(SYSTEM_FONT))
    di% = GetObjectAPI%(oldfont%, 50, agGetAddressForObject&(lf))
    ' Restore the original font
    di% = SelectObject%(PicText.hDC, oldfont%)


    ' Reset current position and alignment
    ' Be sure to keep the original alignment
    ' Since we're changing font sizes, align to the
    ' baseline
    ' To make life easier, we use the current position
    alignorig% = SetTextAlign%(PicText.hDC, TA_LEFT Or TA_BASELINE ⇔
    Or TA_UPDATECP)

    ' Draw the text about 3/4 of the way down.
    vpos% = rc.bottom - rc.bottom / 4
    dl& = MoveTo(PicText.hDC, 0, vpos%)

    ' Draw the first word
    di% = TextOut%(PicText.hDC, 0, 0, demo$(1), Len(demo$(1)))

    ' Now start drawing the rest of the words
    For todraw% = 2 To 4
        ' Debug.Print lf.lfHeight
        lf.lfHeight = lf.lfHeight * 2
        newfont% = CreateFontIndirect%(lf)
        oldfont% = SelectObject%(PicText.hDC, newfont%)
```

```
        di% = TextOut%(PicText.hDC, 0, 0, demo$(todraw%),Len(demo$(todraw%)))
        newfont% = SelectObject%(PicText.hDC, oldfont%)
        di% = DeleteObject%(newfont%)
    Next todraw%

        di% = SetTextAlign%(PicText.hDC, alignorig%)

End Sub
```

This function demonstrates how the **DrawText** API function can perform complex text formatting including word wrapping and handling of line breaks. It then follows with a demonstration of tab expansion to a tab interval that the user can set.

```
'   Use of DrawText to do some powerful text drawing
'
Sub PicFrame_PAINT ()
    Dim demo$
    Dim rc As RECT
    Dim atab$
    Dim heightused%
    Dim crlf$

    atab$ = Chr$(9)
    crlf$ = Chr$(13) + Chr$(10)

    demo$ = "This is a line of text that will show how "
    demo$ = demo$ + "automatic word wrapping can take place while drawing text."
    demo$ = demo$ + crlf$ + "Line breaks also work"

    demo2$ = "And" + atab$ + "Tabs" + atab$ + "Work" + atab$ + "Too" + atab$

    ' Get the dimensions of the control
    GetClientRect agGetControlHwnd%(PicFrame), rc


    heightused% = DrawText(PicFrame.hDC, demo$, -1, rc,DT_WORDBREAK)

    rc.top = heightused%

    ' Tabs are set 10 characters apart (based on averagechar width)
    heightused% = DrawText(PicFrame.hDC, demo2$, -1, rc,DT_EXPANDTABS ↩
    Or DT_TABSTOP Or &HA00)


End Sub
```

Function Reference

This section contains an alphabetical reference for the functions described in this chapter.

■ AddFontResource, AddFontResourceByname, AddFontResourceBynum

VB Declaration　
```
Declare Function AddFontResource% Lib "GDI" (ByVal pFilename As Any)

Declare Function AddFontResourceByname% Lib "GDI" Alias AddFontResource" ⇔
(ByVal lpFilename$)

Declare Function AddFontResourceByHandle% Lib "GDI" Alias "AddFontResource" ⇔
(ByVal lpFilename&)
```

Description　Adds a font resource to the Windows system. Once added, a font is accessible by any application.

Use with VB　No problem.

Parameter	Type/Description
lpFileName	**String** or **Long**—As a **String**, the DOS file name of a font resource file. As a **Long**, the low order 16 bits contain a handle to a loaded module that contains a font resource.

Return Value　**Integer**—The number of fonts added.

Comments　You must call the following API function after adding a resource:
```
di% = SendMessageBynum(HWND_BROADCAST, WM_FONTCHANGE,0,0)
```
where **HWND_BROADCAST** and **WM_FONTCHANGE** use the values from file APICONST-.TXT. This informs all Windows applications that a change to the font list has occurred.

■ AnsiLower, AnsiLowerBuff

VB Declaration　
```
Declare Function AnsiLower& Lib "User" (ByVal lpString$)

Declare Function AnsiLowerBuff% Lib "User" (ByVallpString$, ByVal aWORD%)
```

Description　Converts a string or buffer to lowercase.

Use with VB　No problem.

Parameter	Type/Description
lpString	**String**—String or buffer to convert.
aWord	**Integer**—The number of characters to convert.

Return Value　**Integer**—The length of the converted string.

■ AnsiUpper, AnsiUpperBuff

VB Declaration   Declare Function AnsiUpper& Lib "User" (ByVal lpString$)

Declare Function AnsiUpperBuff% Lib "User" (ByVallpString$, ByVal aWORD%)

Description   Converts a string or buffer to uppercase.

Use with VB   No problem.

Parameter	Type/Description
lpString	**String**—String or buffer to convert.
aWord	**Integer**—The number of characters to convert.

Return Value   **Integer**—The length of the converted string.

■ CreateFont

VB Declaration   Declare Function CreateFont% Lib "GDI" (ByVal H%, ByVal W%, ByVal E%, ByVal ⇔ O%, ByVal W%, ByVal I%,ByVal U%, ByVal S%, ByVal C%, ByVal OP%, ByVal CP%, ⇔ ByVal Q%, ByVal PAF%, ByVal F$)

Description   Creates a logical font with the attributes specified.

Use with VB   No problem, though the Visual Basic font properties are quite effective at selecting fonts.
The parameters are described in detail earlier in this chapter. The declaration here uses single characters due to the limited line length. The letters correspond to parameters as follows:

Declaration parameter	Attribute (corresponds to a field in the LOGFONT data structure)
H	lfHeight
W	lfWidth
E	lfEscapement
O	lfOrientation
W	lfWeight
I	lfItalic
U	lfUnderline
S	lfStrikeOut
C	lfCharSet
OP	lfOutputPrecision
CP	lfClipPrecision
Q	lfQuality
PAF	lfPitchAndFamily
F$	lfFaceName

Return Value   Integer—A handle to a logical font on success, zero otherwise.

■ CreateFontIndirect

VB Declaration   `Declare Function CreateFontIndirect% Lib "GDI" (lpLogFont As LOGFONT)`

Description   Creates a logical font with the attributes specified.

Use with VB   No problem, though the Visual Basic font properties are quite effective at selecting fonts.

Parameter	Type/Description
lpLogFont	**LOGFONT**—A **LOGFONT** structure defining the requested attributes for the logical font.

Return Value   Integer—A handle to a logical font on success, zero otherwise.

■ CreateScalableFontResource

VB Declaration   `Declare Function CreateScalableFontResource% Lib "GDI" (ByVal fHidden%, ⇔`
`ByVal lpszResourceFile$, ByVal lpszFontFile$, ByVal lpszCurrentPath$)`

Description   Creates a resource file for a TrueType font so that it may be added into Windows using the **Add-FontResource** API function. The font information is not itself copied into the font resource file; instead, the resource file contains the name of the TrueType file to use.

Use with VB   No problem.

Parameter	Type/Description
fHidden	**Integer**—Zero to create a normal font resource, one to create a read only font resource that can be embedded in a document.
lpszResourceFile	**String**—The name of the resource file to create. Use the .FOT extension for normal files, .FOR for read only files.
lpszFontFile	**String**—The DOS file name of the TrueType font file. If this contains a full path, the font file will be expected to be at that location and the **lpszCurrentPath** parameter is not used. If this contains a name and extension only, the font file is assumed to currently be at the location specified by the **lpszCurrentPath** parameter, and that the font will be copied into the Windows SYSTEM directory before the **AddFontResource** function is called.
lpszCurrentPath	**String**—As described under the **lpszFontFile** parameter.

Return Value   Integer—TRUE (nonzero) on success, zero otherwise.

■ DrawText

VB Declaration   `Declare Function DrawText% Lib "User" (ByVal hDC%, ByVallpStr$, ByVal ⇔`
`nCount%, lpRect As RECT, ByVal wFormat%)`

Description	Draws text into the specified rectangle.
Use with VB	No problem.

Parameter	Type/Description
hDC	**Integer**—A handle to a device context on which to draw.
lpStr	**String**—The text string to draw.
nCount	**Integer**—The number of characters to draw. If the entire string is to be drawn (up to the null terminator), this may be set to -1.
lpRect	**RECT**—The formatting rectangle to use for drawing.
wFormat	**Integer**—An array of flag bits that determines how the drawing will be performed. Refer to the list of constants in Table 10.12.

Return Value	**Integer**—The height of the text drawn.

Table 10.12   Text Drawing Flags

Flag Constant	Description
DT_BOTTOM	**DT_SINGLE** must also be specified. Aligns text with the bottom of the formatting rectangle.
DT_CALCRECT	Calculates the formatting rectangle as follows: On multiline drawing, the bottom of the rectangle is extended as needed to hold the text. On single line drawing the right of the rectangle is extended. No text is drawn. The rectangle specified by the **lpRect** parameter is loaded with the calculated values.
DT_CENTER	Text is centered horizontally.
DT_EXPANDTABS	Tabs are expanded when text is drawn. The default tab spacing is eight characters; however, this may be changed using the **DT_TABSTOP** flag.
DT_EXTERNALLEADING	Use the external leading attribute of the current font when calculating the line height.
DT_LEFT	Text is left-aligned.
DT_NOCLIP	Draws without clipping to the specified rectangle.
DT_NOPREFIX	Normally, this function assumes that the & character indicates that the next character should be underlined. This flag turns off this behavior.
DT_RIGHT	Text is right-aligned.
DT_SINGELINE	Draws a single line only.
DT_TABSTOP	Specifies the new tab spacing in the high eight bits of this integer.

Table 10.12   Text Drawing Flags (Continued)

Flag Constant	Description
DT_TOP	**DT_SINGLE** must also be specified. Aligns text with the top of the formatting rectangle.
DT_VCENTER	**DT_SINGLE** must also be specified. Aligns text with at the center of the formatting rectangle.
DT_WORDBREAK	Performs word wrapping. Starts a new line whenever a word would exceed the rectangle boundary or a carriage return linefeed sequence is met. Has no effect if the **TA_UPDATECP** flag has been set using the **SetTextAlign** function.

■ EnumFontFamilies, EnumFontFamiliesBynum

VB Declaration   Declare Function EnumFontFamilies% Lib "GDI" (ByVal hDC%,ByVal ⇔
lpszFamily$, ByVal lpFontFunc&, ByVal lpData&)

Declare Function EnumFontFamiliesBynum% Lib "GDI" Alias"EnumFontFamilies" ⇔
(ByVal hDC%, ByVal lpszFamily&,ByVal lpFontFunc&, ByVal lpData&)

Description   Enumerates the available fonts for a given device.

Use with VB   Requires the CBK.VBX custom control provided with this book.

Parameter	Type/Description
hDC	**Integer**—Handle to a device context.
lpszFamily	**String** or **Long**—The family of the fonts to be enumerated. As a **Long**, specify NULL to enumerate one font from each available font family.
lpObjectFunc	**Long**—Pointer to function to call for each font. Use the **ProcAddress** property of the CBK.VBX custom control to obtain a function pointer for callbacks.
lpData	**Long**—Value that is passed to the **EnumFontFamilies** event of the CBK.VBX custom control during enumeration.

Return Value   **Integer**—The last value returned by the callback function.

Comments   Refer to Appendix A for details on using the CBK.VBX custom control with enumeration functions. This function supersedes the **EnumFonts** API function due to its ability to handle True-Type font style descriptions.

Only actual existing fonts are enumerated. Fonts that may be synthesized by GDI are not included.

■ EnumFonts, EnumFontsBynum

VB Declaration Declare Function EnumFonts% Lib "GDI" (ByVal hDC%, ByVal lpFacename$, ByVal ⇔ lpFontFunc&, ByVal lpData&)

Declare Function EnumFontsBynum% Lib "GDI" Alias "EnumFonts" (ByVal hDC%, ⇔ ByVal lpFacename&, ByVallpFontFunc&, ByVal lpData&)

Description Enumerates the available fonts for a given device.

Use with VB Requires the CBK.VBX custom control provided with this book.

Parameter	Type/Description
hDC	**Integer**—Handle to a device context.
lpFaceName	**String** or **Long**—The font name (or typeface name) of the fonts to be enumerated. As a **Long**, specify NULL to enumerate one font from each available typeface.
lpFontFunc	**Long**—Pointer to function to call for each font. Use the **ProcAddress** property of the CBK.VBX custom control to obtain a function pointer for callbacks.
lpData	**Long**—Value that is passed to the **EnumFonts** event of the CBK.VBX custom control during enumeration.

Return Value **Integer**—The last value returned by the callback function.

Comments Refer to Appendix A for details on using the CBK.VBX custom control with enumeration functions. This function is superseded by the **EnumFont** families API function.
Only actual existing fonts are enumerated. Fonts that may be synthesized by GDI are not included.

■ ExtTextOut, ExtTextOutBynum, ExtTextOutByrect

VB Declaration Declare Function ExtTextOut% Lib "GDI" (ByVal hDC%, ByVal X%, ByVal Y%, ⇔ ByVal wOptions%, lpRect As Any,ByVal lpString$, ByVal nCount%, lpDx As Any)

Declare Function ExtTextOutBynum% Lib "GDI" Alias "ExtTextOut" (ByVal ⇔ hDC%, ByVal X%, ByVal Y%, ByValwOptions%, ByVal lpRect&, ByVal lpString$, ⇔ ByValnCount%, ByVal lpDx&)

Declare Function ExtTextOutByrect% Lib "GDI" Alias "ExtTextOut" (ByVal hDC%, ⇔ ByVal X%, ByVal Y%, ByVal wOptions%, lpRect as RECT, ByVal lpString$, ⇔ ByValnCount%, ByVal lpDx&)

Description Extended text drawing function. Refer also to the **SetTextAlign** function.

Use with VB   No problem.

Parameter	Type/Description
hDC	**Integer**—A handle to a device context.
X, Y	**Integer**—Point in logical coordinates specifying the starting position for drawing.
wOptions	**Integer**—Any combination of the following flag constants: **ETO_CLIPPED**: Clips text output to the specified rectangle. **ETO_OPAQUE**: Fills the rectangle with the current background color before drawing the text.
lpRect	**RECT** or **Long**—A rectangle to use for formatting the text. May specify the **Long** value zero to draw text without using a rectangular region.
lpString	**String**—The string to draw.
nCount	**Integer**—The number of characters in the string to draw.
lpDx	**Long**—If not zero, this is a pointer to an array of integers describing the spacing between each pair of characters in logical units. The first entry is the space between the first and second character, and so on. If zero, the function uses the default spacing for the font. Chapter 3 discusses techniques for passing pointers to arrays to a DLL function.

Return Value   Integer—TRUE (nonzero) on success, zero otherwise.

■ GetAspectRatioFilter, GetAspectRatioFilterEx

VB Declaration   `Declare Function GetAspectRatioFilter& Lib "GDI" (ByValhDC%)`

`Declare Function GetAspectRatioFilterEx% Lib "GDI" (ByVal hDC%, lpAspectRatio ⇔ As SIZEAPI)`

Description   The **SetMapperFlags** function can be used to request that Windows select only raster fonts that match the current aspect ratio of a device. This function can be used to determine the aspect ratio that is being used for this selection process.

Use with VB   No problem.

Parameter	Type/Description
hDC	**Integer**—A handle to a device context.
lpAspectRatio	**SIZEAPI**—A structure to load with the aspect ratio.

Return Value   **GetAspectRatioFilter**: **Long**—The low 16 bits contain the horizontal aspect, the high 16 bits contain the vertical aspect. **GetAspectRatioFilterEx** returns TRUE (nonzero) on success, zero otherwise.

GetCharABCWidths

VB Declaration   Declare Function GetCharABCWidths Lib "GDI" (ByVal hDC%,ByVal uFirstChar%, ⇔
ByVal uLastChar%, lpabc As ABC)

Description   Retrieves the A-B-C dimensions of one or more characters in a TrueType font.

Use with VB   No problem.

Parameter	Type/Description
hDC	**Integer**—A handle to a device context.
uFirstChar	**Integer**—The ASCII value of the first character for which to obtain A-B-C dimensions.
uLastChar	**Integer**—The ASCII value of the last character for which to obtain A-B-C dimensions.
lpABC	**ABC**—The first entry in an array of ABC structures to fill with the dimensions of the characters specified. This array must be long enough to hold the dimensions of all of the characters requested.

Return Value   **Integer**—TRUE (nonzero) on success, zero otherwise.

Comments   Use the **GetCharWidth** function for non-TrueType fonts.

GetCharWidth

VB Declaration   Declare Function GetCharWidth% Lib "GDI" (ByVal hDC%, ByVal wFirstChar%, ⇔
ByVal wLastChar%, lpBuffer%)

Description   Retrieves the widths of one or more characters in a non-TrueType font.

Use with VB   No problem.

Parameter	Type/Description
hDC	**Integer**—A handle to a device context.
wFirstChar	**Integer**—The ASCII value of the first character for which to obtain the width.
wLastChar	**Integer**—The ASCII value of the last character for which to obtain the width.
lpBuffer	**Integer**—The first entry in an array of integers to fill with the widths of the characters specified. This array must be long enough to hold the dimensions of all of the characters requested.

Return Value   **Integer**—TRUE (nonzero) on success, zero otherwise.

Comments   Use the **GetCharABCWidths** function for TrueType fonts.

◼ GetFontData

VB Declaration   Declare Function GetFontData& Lib "GDI" (ByVal hDC%, ByVal dwTable&, ByVal ⇔
dwOffset&, ByVal lpvBuffer$,ByVal cbData&)

Description   Retrieves the data for a scalable font file. This data may then be used to embed font information
into a document. This can be useful in cases where a document requires a specific font that is not
commonly available on systems and wishes to include the font information with the document.

   A full discussion of font embedding is beyond the scope of this book. Refer to the TrueType
Fonts specification published by Microsoft for further information.

Use with VB   Untested.

◼ GetGlyphOutline

VB Declaration   Declare Function GetGlyphOutline& Lib "GDI" (ByVal hDC%,ByVal uChar%, ⇔
ByVal fuFormat%, lpgm As GLYPHMETRICS,ByVal cbBuffer&, lppt As POINTAPI, ⇔
lpmat2 As MAT2)

Description   Retrieves information about the curves that make up a character in a TrueType font. It is primarily useful for converting text into curves or manipulating fonts (tasks for which a programmer
would require advanced references on font technology anyway). Refer to the TrueType Font
specification published by Microsoft for further information on this function.

◼ GetOutlineTextMetrics

VB Declaration   Declare Function GetOutlineTextMetrics& Lib "GDI" (ByValhDC%, ByVal cbData%, ⇔
lpOTM As OUTLINETEXTMETRIC)

Description   Retrieves detailed information about the internal characteristics of a TrueType font. Refer to the
TrueType Font specification published by Microsoft for further information on this function.

◼ GetRasterizerCaps

VB Declaration   Declare Function GetRasterizerCaps% Lib "GDI" (lpraststatAs RASTERIZERSTATUS, ⇔
ByVal cb%)

Description   Retrieves information about the ability of the system to support scalable fonts. This can be used
to determine if TrueType fonts are enabled for the system.

Use with VB   No problem.

Parameter	Type/Description
lprasstat	**RASTERIZERSTATUS**—A structure to load with the rasterizer in-formation. Refer to Appendix B for further information.
cb	**Integer**—The number of bytes to copy into the structure.

Return Value   **Integer**—TRUE (nonzero) on success, zero otherwise.

Comments   For Windows 3.1, the size of the structure is six bytes and is contained in the first integer in the RASTERIZERSTATUS structure.

■ GetTabbedTextExtent

VB Declaration   `Declare Function GetTabbedTextExtent& Lib "GDI" (ByValhDC%, ByVal lpString$, ⇔ ByVal nCount%, ByVal nTabPositions%, lpnTabStopPositions%)`

Description   Determines the extents of a string taking tab expansion into account. Refer also to the **Tabbed-TextOut** function.

Use with VB   No problem.

Parameter	Type/Description
hDC	**Integer**—A handle to a device context.
lpString	**String**—The string to calculate.
nCount	**Integer**—The number of characters in the string.
nTabPositions	**Integer**—The number of tabs in the **lpnTabStopPositions** array. If zero, the **lpnTabStopPositions** should also be NULL (you will need to create a declaration where this parameter is declared as **ByVal nTabPositions&**) in which case tabs will be set to a default eight character spacing based on the average character width of the current font. If **nTabPositions** is one, tab spacing will be according to the first entry in the **lpnTabStopPositions** array.
lpnTabStopPositions	**Integer**—The first element in an array of tab stop positions specified in device coordinates in ascending order.

Return Value   **Long**—The low 16 bits contain the text width in logical coordinates in the device context. The high 16 bits contain the text height.

Comments   The clipping region is not taken into account during this calculation.

■ GetTextAlign

VB Declaration   `Declare Function GetTextAlign% Lib "GDI" (ByVal hDC%)`

Description   Retrieves the current text alignment flags for a device context.

Use with VB   No problem.

Parameter	Type/Description
hDC	**Integer**—A handle to a device context.

Return Value   **Integer**—The current text alignment flags.

Comments   Refer to the description of the **SetTextAlign** function for information on text alignment flags.

GetTextCharacterExtra

VB Declaration   Declare Function GetTextCharacterExtra% Lib "GDI" (ByValhDC%)

Description   Retrieves the current value of the extra character spacing. Refer to the **SetTextCharacterExtra** function for further information.

Use with VB   No problem.

Parameter	Type/Description
hDC	**Integer**—A handle to a device context.

Return Value   **Integer**—The extra space between characters added when Windows draws text.

GetTextColor

VB Declaration   Declare Function GetTextColor& Lib "GDI" (ByVal hDC%)

Description   Retrieves the current text color. This is also known as the foreground color.

Use with VB   Be sure to restore the original text color for VB forms and controls if you change this setting.

Parameter	Type/Description
hDC	**Integer**—A handle to a device context.

Return Value   **Long**—The current RGB color setting for the text color.

GetTextExtent, GetTextExtentPoint

VB Declaration   Declare Function GetTextExtent& Lib "GDI" (ByVal hDC%, ByVal lpString$, ⇔
ByVal nCount%)

Declare Function GetTextExtentPoint% Lib "GDI" (ByVal hDC%, ByVal lpString$, ⇔
ByVal lpString%, lpSize As SIZEAPI)

Description   Determines the extents of a string.

Use with VB   No problem.

Parameter	Type/Description
hDC	**Integer**—A handle to a device context.
lpString	**String**—The string to calculate.
nCount	**Integer**—The number of characters in the string.
lpSize	**POINTAPI**—Point to load with the horizontal and vertical text extents for the **GetTextExtentPoint** function.

Return Value	**GetTextExtent—Long:** The low 16 bits contain the text width in logical coordinates in the device context. The high 16 bits contain the text height.
	GetTextExtentPoint returns an **Integer**—TRUE (nonzero) on success, zero otherwise.
Comments	The clipping region is not taken into account during this calculation.

■ GetTextFace

VB Declaration	`Declare Function GetTextFace% Lib "GDI" (ByVal hDC%, ByVal nCount%, ByVal ⇔ lpFacename$)`
Description	Retrieves the name of the typeface for a font.
Use with VB	No problem. This is similar to reading the VB FontName property.

Parameter	Type/Description
hDC	**Integer**—A handle to a device context.
nCount	**Integer**—The size of the **lpFacename** property.
lpFacename	**String**—A string to load with the typeface name of the currently selected font. This buffer must be preinitialized to at least **nCount+1** characters.

Return Value	**Integer**—The number of bytes loaded into the buffer.

■ GetTextMetrics

VB Declaration	`Declare Function GetTextMetrics% Lib "GDI" (ByVal hDC%, lpMetrics As TEXTMETRIC)`
Description	Retrieves information about the physical font selected for a device context.
Use with VB	No problem.

Parameter	Type/Description
hDC	**Integer**—A handle to a device context.
lpMetrics	**TEXTMETRIC**—A structure to fill with the metrics of the physical font. Refer to the TEXTMETRIC and NEWTEXTMETRIC structure fields, earlier in this chapter.

Return Value	**Integer**—TRUE (nonzero) on success, zero otherwise.

■ GrayString, GrayStringBystring

VB Declaration   Declare Function GrayString% Lib "User" (ByVal hDC%, ByVal lpOuputFunc&, ⇔
ByVal lpData&, ByVal nCount%,ByVal X%, ByVal Y%, ByVal nWidth%, ByVal nHeight%)

Declare Function GrayStringBystring% Lib "User" Alias"GrayString" (ByVal ⇔
hDC%, ByVal lpOuputFunc&, ByVallpData$, ByVal nCount%, ByVal X%, ByVal Y%, ⇔
ByValnWidth%, ByVal nHeight%)

Description   Draws a "grayed" string like that used by Windows to indicate the disabled state. This function
uses the current font, but ignores the background and text color.

Use with VB   No problem.

Parameter	Type/Description
hDC	**Integer**—A handle to a device context.
lpOutputFunc	**Long**—A pointer to a function to output the text. Normally use zero to use the **TextOut** function. Otherwise this may be a procedure address as returned by the **ProcAddress** property of the CBK custom control. Refer to Appendix A for further details.
lpData	**String** or **Long**—As a string (when **lpOutputFunc** is NULL), this is the string to gray. Otherwise it is a long variable that will be passed to the **GrayString** event of the CBK control.
nCount	**Integer**—The number of characters to print. If zero and **lpData** is a string, this calculates the length of the string.
X,Y	**Integers**—The X,Y coordinates of the rectangle that bounds the string.
nWidth	**Integer**—The width of the rectangle that bounds the string.
nHeight	**Integer**—The height of the rectangle that bounds the string.

Return Value   **Integer**—TRUE (nonzero) on success, zero if the **TextOut** function or the CBK text drawing
event returns zero.

■ IsCharAlpha

VB Declaration   Declare Function IsCharAlpha% Lib "User" (ByVal cChar%)

Description   Determines if a character is a letter as defined by the language that is currently in use.

Use with VB   No problem.

Parameter	Type/Description
cChar	**Integer**—The ASCII value of the character. The VB **ASC** function returns this value for the first character in a string.

Return Value   **Integer**—TRUE (nonzero) if the character is a letter, zero otherwise.

◼ IsCharAlphaNumeric

VB Declaration   Declare Function IsCharAlphaNumeric% Lib "User" (ByValcChar%)

Description   Determines if a character is alphanumeric (character or numeral) as defined by the language that is currently in use.

Use with VB   No problem.

Parameter	Type/Description
cChar	**Integer**—The ASCII value of the character. The VB **ASC** function returns this value for the first character in a string.

Return Value   **Integer**—TRUE (nonzero) if the character is alphanumeric, zero otherwise.

◼ IsCharLower

VB Declaration   Declare Function IsCharLower% Lib "User" (ByVal cChar%)

Description   Determines if a character is lowercase as defined by the language that is currently in use.

Use with VB   No problem.

Parameter	Type/Description
cChar	**Integer**— The ASCII value of the character. The VB **ASC** function returns this value for the first character in a string.

Return Value   **Integer**—TRUE (nonzero) if the character is lowercase, zero otherwise.

◼ IsCharUpper

VB Declaration   Declare Function IsCharUpper% Lib "User" (ByVal cChar%)

Description   Determines if a character is uppercase as defined by the language that is currently in use.

Use with VB   No problem.

Parameter	Type/Description
cChar	**Integer**—The ASCII value of the character. The VB **ASC** function returns this value for the first character in a string.

Return Value   **Integer**—TRUE (nonzero) if the character is uppercase, zero otherwise.

■ RemoveFontResource, RemoveFontResourceByname, RemoveFontResourceBynum

VB Declaration Declare Function RemoveFontResource% Lib "GDI" (ByVallpFilename As Any)

Declare Function RemoveFontResourceBynum% Lib "GDI" Alias "RemoveFont ⇔ Resource" (ByVal lpFilename&)

Declare Function RemoveFontResourceBystring% Lib "GDI"Alias "RemoveFont ⇔ Resource" (ByVal lpFilename$)

Description Removes a font resource to the Windows system. The font will not be removed immediately if it is currently in use by another application.

Use with VB No problem.

Parameter	Type/Description
lpFileName	**String** or **Long**—As a **String**, the DOS file name of a font resource file. As a **Long**, the low order 16 bits contain a handle to a loaded module that contains a font resource.

Return Value **Integer**—The number of fonts removed.

Comments You must call the following API function after removing a resource:

di% = SendMessageBynum(HWND_BROADCAST, WM_FONTCHANGE,0,0)

where **HWND_BROADCAST** and **WM_FONTCHANGE** use the values from file APICONST-.TXT. This informs all Windows applications that a change to the font list has occurred.

■ SetMapperFlags

VB Declaration Declare Function SetMapperFlags& Lib "GDI" (ByVal hDC%,ByVal dwFlag&)

Description When Windows is mapping fonts, this function may be used to select raster fonts that match the aspect ratio of the device. Not used for TrueType fonts. Refer to function **GetAspectRatioFilter** for further information.

Use with VB No known problem.

Parameter	Type/Description
hDC	**Integer**—A handle to a device context.
dwFlags	**Long**—Use the constant **ASPECT_FILTERING** to request that GDI select fonts that match the aspect ratio of the device.

Return Value **Long**—The previous value of the font mapping flag.

■ SetTextAlign

VB Declaration   `Declare Function SetTextAlign% Lib "GDI" (ByVal hDC%, ByVal wFlags%)`

Description   Sets the text alignment and specifies the use of the device context current position during text output.

Use with VB   Be sure to restore the original alignment to any VB form or control that you modify. You can obtain the existing alignment using the **GetTextAlign** function.

The alignment specified here is used in the **TextOut**, **ExtTextOut**, and **TabbedTextOut** functions.

Parameter	Type/Description
hDC	**Integer**—A handle to a device context.
wFlags	**Integer**—An ORed combination of one flag constant from each of the following categories:

Horizontal Alignment Flags:
TA_CENTER: Center the text within the bounding rectangle.
TA_LEFT: Left-align the text within the bounding rectangle. This is the default.
TA_RIGHT: Right-align the text within the bounding rectangle.

Vertical Alignment Flags:
Define the meaning of the Y parameter of the text output functions.
TA_BASELINE: The Y parameter specifies placement of the baseline of the font.
TA_BOTTOM: The Y parameter specifies the placement of the bottom of the bounding rectangle.
TA_TOP: The Y parameter specifies the placement of the top of the bounding rectangle. This is the default.

Current Position:
TA_NOUPDATECP: Text output functions do not use the device context's current drawing position.
TA_UPDATECP: Text output functions use the device's current position. The output function updates the current position after drawing. The X and Y parameters of the text output functions are ignored—drawing begins instead at the current position.

Return Value   **Integer**—The previous text alignment flags.

■ SetTextCharacterExtra

VB Declaration   `Declare Function SetTextCharacterExtra% Lib "GDI" (ByVal hDC%, ⇔`
`ByVal nCharExtra%)`

Description   Specifies the extra spacing to insert between characters when drawing text.

Use with VB	Be sure to restore the original character spacing for a VB form or control if you change this setting.

Parameter	Type/Description
hDC	**Integer**—A handle to a device context.
nCharExtra	**Integer**—The extra space to add between characters specified in logical coordinates in the device context.

Return Value	**Integer**—The previous extra spacing for this device context.

■ SetTextColor

VB Declaration	`Declare Function SetTextColor& Lib "GDI" (ByVal hDC%, ByVal crColor&)`
Description	Sets the current text color. This is also known as the foreground color.
Use with VB	Be sure to restore the original text color for VB forms and controls if you change this setting.

Parameter	Type/Description
hDC	**Integer**—A handle to a device context.
crColor	**Long**—The new text color.

Return Value	**Long**—The previous RGB color setting for the text color.

■ SetTextJustification

VB Declaration	`Declare Function SetTextJustification% Lib "GDI" (ByValhDC%, ByVal nBreak⇔ Extra%, ByVal nBreakCount%)`
Description	This function is used to justify lines by specifying the extra space that a line should take. The extra space is divided among the break characters in the line. The break character is defined by the font but is usually the space character. You can use the **GetTextMetrics** function to determine the break character for a font. The normal sequence of operations when you wish to justify text is as follows:

1. Calculate the extent of the string using the **GetTextExtent** API function.

2. Determine how much space (in logical coordinates) to add to the line in order to justify it. This is typically the right margin minus the horizontal extent of the text.

3. Count the number of break characters in the line of text.

4. Call the **SetTextJustification** function using the extra space and number of break characters as parameters.

5. Call the text-drawing function.

   This function maintains an error term internally to correct for round-off errors during justification. This allows you to distribute the extra spacing between different parts of a line (if the line

contains several fonts) by breaking the line into segments and calling this function for each segment. This error term must be cleared for a new line by calling the function with a zero value for the **nBreakExtra** and **nBreakCount** parameters.

Use with VB   No problem—but be sure to clear the error term for a VB form or control if you use this function.

Parameter	Type/Description
hDC	**Integer**—A handle to a device context.
nBreakExtra	**Integer**—The amount of extra space to add to the string when drawing.
nBreakCount	**Integer**—The number of break characters in which to distribute the extra space.

Return Value   **Integer**—TRUE (nonzero) on success, zero otherwise.

■ TabbedTextOut

VB Declaration
```
Declare Function TabbedTextOut& Lib "User" (ByVal hDC%,ByVal X%, ByVal Y%, ⇔
ByVal lpString$, ByVal nCount%,ByVal nTabPositions%, lpnTabStopPositions%, ⇔
ByVal nTabOrigin%)
```

Description   Text-drawing function that supports tabs. Refer also to the **SetTextAlign** function.

Use with VB   No problem.

Parameter	Type/Description
hDC	**Integer**—A handle to a device context.
X, Y	**Integer**—Point in logical coordinates specifying the starting position for drawing.
lpString	**String**—The string to draw.
nCount	**Integer**—The number of characters in the string to draw.
nTabPositions	**Integer**—The number of tabs in the **lpnTabStopPositions** array. If zero, the **lpnTabStopPositions** should also be NULL (you will need to create a declaration where this parameter is declared as **ByVal nTabPositions&**) in which case tabs will be set to a default eight character spacing based on the average character width of the current font. If **nTabPositions** is one, tab spacing will be according to the first entry in the **lpnTabStopPositions** array.
lpnTabStopPositions	**Integer**—The first element in an array of tab stop positions specified in device coordinates in ascending order.
nTabOrigin	**Integer**—Specifies the origin to use for tabbing. This is useful if you call the function several times for the same line and wish to maintain the same tab origin.

Return Value   **Integer**—TRUE (nonzero) on success, zero otherwise.

■ TextOut

VB Declaration   `Declare Function TextOut% Lib "GDI" (ByVal hDC%, ByVal X%, ByVal Y%, ⇔`
`ByVal lpString$, ByVal nCount%)`

Description   Text-drawing function. Refer also to the **SetTextAlign** function.

Use with VB   No problem.

Parameter	Type/Description
hDC	**Integer**—A handle to a device context.
X, Y	**Integer**—Point in logical coordinates specifying the starting position for drawing.
lpString	**String**—The string to draw.
nCount	**Integer**—The number of characters in the string to draw.

Return Value   **Integer**—TRUE (nonzero) on success, zero otherwise.

11

Printing

THE WINDOWS API PROVIDES AN EXTREMELY POWERFUL AND FLEXIBLE interface to printers and other output devices. It offers many printing features that can be extremely useful to the Visual Basic programmer. These include the ability to print a bitmap, to abort a print operation, and to switch between portrait and landscape orientation within a document. Those features, and more, are discussed in this chapter and demonstrated in the PicPrint sample program.

The Windows API is so flexible, however, that some of its features are beyond the scope of this book. For example, an in-depth discussion of relative kerning of device fonts is probably of interest only to those writing their own high-end desktop publishing applications.

Printing in Windows

Before going into detail on how to perform certain printing tasks under Visual Basic, it is important to discuss how printing works in the Windows environment.

Printer Device Contexts

A printer device context can be used in exactly the same way as any other device context. This means that all of the graphic functions described in previous chapters work the same way for printers as they do for display devices. This device independence is one of the powerful features that Windows provides. It is possible to create a drawing function that accepts a device context as a parameter. The function will draw on either the screen or the printer depending on the device context used.

Drivers, Devices, and Ports

Every printer in the Windows system has three characteristics: the driver name, the device name, and the output port. The translation of GDI graphics calls to printer output data is performed by a special dynamic link library known as a printer driver. Every printer must have a printer driver DLL to work under Windows.

Some printer drivers support more than one printer. For example, a single PostScript driver can support dozens of different PostScript printers. The HP PCL5 driver, for example, handles the LaserJet III and IIIP and understands the features supported by both. The device name is used by the driver to determine which printer it is dealing with.

The output name or port name describes where the printer output should go. This is typically the printer port name (LPT1:, LPT2:) or the name of a file for redirecting the output to disk.

All three of these parameters are needed to create a printer device context using the **CreateDC** API function.

The Default Printer and Others

The WIN.INI initialization file contains information describing the printers connected to the system and which one is the default printer. Visual Basic supports only the default printer, but the API functions can access any printer in the system. Chapter 13 describes how initialization files can be accessed.

The default printer settings for a driver are kept in the WIN.INI initialization file. These settings may be modified using the control panel application (CONTROL.EXE). The format for the WIN.INI file can be found in the retail Windows package and in the WIN.INI file itself. Generally, a printer entry consists of a driver name, device name, and the output port.

As you will see, it is possible to set these parameters directly using the printer configuration functions and to keep application-specific printer configuration information in a private initialization file.

Printer Configuration

Each printer driver provides a setup dialog box that allows the user to configure the printer. The three functions **DeviceCapabilities**, **DeviceMode**, and **ExtDeviceMode** are included in most printer drivers to support configuration of printers under program control. Because these functions are in the driver DLL, it is difficult to access them from Visual Basic. This is because direct access to the functions would require a separate **Declare** statement for every possible printer driver, each one with an aliased function name to prevent errors due to duplicate function definitions. The APIGUIDE.DLL dynamic link library provided with this book includes the interface functions **agDeviceCapabilities**, **agDeviceMode**, and **agExtDeviceMode**, which provide easy access to the driver functions in any printer driver. The features provided by these functions include:

- The ability to determine the capabilities of a printer.

- The ability to retrieve the current settings of the printer.

- The ability to temporarily change the printer configuration without affecting other applications. This may be accomplished under program control or via the printer setup dialog box.

- The ability to modify the default printer settings, and to keep a copy of the printer settings in a private initialization file so that you can preserve a printer configuration required for a particular application.

Many of these techniques are demonstrated in the PicPrint example program and are described in detail in the reference section of this chapter.

The Printing Sequence

Once a device context has been obtained for a printer, there are several steps that need to be performed before drawing begins. Consider the differences between a printer and a screen display.

A screen has a single drawing area, which can be erased. A printer page cannot be erased, but you can print multiple pages. Applications share the display by drawing into windows that are owned by the application. This approach is clearly not applicable to printers where it is necessary to keep all of the pages grouped by application and by document. A printer needs a mechanism for controlling paging and for managing documents so that applications do not conflict with each other.

Figure 11.1 illustrates the sequence used in printing under Windows. Note that the actual drawing commands are identical to those used for display devices.

Figure 11.1

Print operation
sequence under
Windows

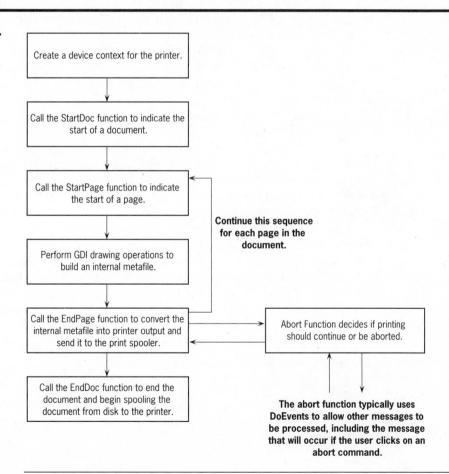

Windows deals with printing on both a page and document level. On the document level, the **StartDoc** API function informs Windows that you are beginning a document. Windows will make sure that all pages in a document are printed together. Without this capability, if more than one application was printing it would be possible for pages from different applications to be mixed with each other during printing. The **EndDoc** API function informs Windows that the document is complete. If the Windows print manager PRINTMAN.EXE is in use, the **EndDoc** function informs the print manager that it may begin to spool data from the disk to the printer.

The **StartPage** and **EndPage** API functions bracket the graphics operations on a page. There is one interesting subtlety to printing that has a significant impact on the ability to abort printing operations. When you perform a graphics operation to a display device, the operation takes place immediately. This is possible because the entire screen is available to a display device context at all times. A printer device driver, on the other hand, generally needs to prepare the entire page in memory before sending it to the printer. Once a page is printed, no further printing to that page is possible.

A printer device context must accumulate all of the information required to print a page before it actually begins to send output to the printer. As a result, all graphic operations to a printer are in fact stored in a metafile until the **EndPage** API function is executed. At that time, the metafile is played onto the printer and the graphic operations are converted into output data in the format or language expected by the printer.

Windows also supports a technique known as *banding*, which allows you to print under limited memory situations by dividing the print area into bands. The internal metafile is played onto each band, which is output in turn. This technique was used frequently in earlier versions of Windows, and in fact was often implemented manually by programmers. Version 3.0 significantly improved the performance of printers, mostly by providing sufficient memory to hold entire pages of data in memory when necessary. In addition, many printers now support advanced page description languages that accept graphics information, eliminating the need to draw all of the graphics into memory before sending it to the printer. As a result, banding is rarely handled on the programmer's level. This book assumes that you will draw graphics on a page level and allow Windows to perform any internal banding if necessary.

Aborting the Print Operation

Windows builds an internal metafile for printing, which is played back as needed during the **EndPage** function. Building a metafile—a process which is little more than recording GDI graphics functions—is a very fast operation. Converting the graphics into the format required for the printer may be extremely time-consuming. As a result, the **EndPage** function can take a very long time to finish.

In order to make it possible to abort a print operation in progress, Windows allows you to specify a special abort function using the **SetAbortProc** API function. This function is called by Windows during execution of the **EndPage** function. The abort function returns a value indicating whether printing should continue. Visual Basic does not directly support function callbacks of this type; however, this book provides the CBK.VBX custom control, which can be used to trigger an event whenever the abort function is called.

One technique that is frequently used is the creation of a dialog box that has a button for aborting the print job. The abort function periodically allows events to be processed, so a button click can be detected. The PicPrint example program demonstrates this technique.

Printing and Visual Basic

The Windows API functions are generally compatible with Visual Basic. There are, however, areas where conflicts can occur that should be avoided.

Compatibility Issues

Visual Basic provides an object called the *printer object* that supports printing to the default Windows printer. The printer object provides access to the printer device context via the **hDC** property, which may be used as a parameter to most API graphics functions. This provides the first and most common level of API support for printing.

Additional capability may be provided but that requires the programmer to use only the API printing functions. Even though Visual Basic provides **NewPage** and **EndDoc** methods for the printer object device context, you should not attempt to mix the Windows API printer control functions with those methods. In other words, the **StartDoc**, **StartPage**, **EndPage**, and **End-DocAPI** API functions should not be used on the printer object or the device context, nor should the **SetAbortProc** function be used to attempt to create a printer abort capability to the printer object. The reason for this is that the Visual Basic methods do not correspond directly to the API functions.

In practice, you can mix these function with some success; however, you should be careful to perform error trapping because various printer errors are likely to occur. An example of this is abort print processing. You can use the techniques shown here to abort printing into the VB printer object, but you are likely to get a printer error during the next **NewPage** or **EndDoc** method. No harm will be done, however, so feel free to experiment.

Driver Quirks

One of the great strengths of Windows is its ability to provide device-independent output. In theory, once you have written a printer output routine that works with one printer, it will work perfectly with all printers.

In practice, this is not always the case. Each printer has its own printer driver, and some printer drivers can be extremely sophisticated. Each one is therefore prone to its own set of potential bugs or features.

To create a robust printing application using API calls, there are a number of steps you can take. First, before performing raster operations, verify that the printer has in fact implemented the appropriate commands. The **GetDevice-Caps** function described in Chapter 6 allows you to obtain information on the features supported by the device. This include the device's ability to support **Bit-Blt** transfers or device-independent bitmap (DIB) functions. You can also determine if the printer can transfer bitmaps over 64k in size. If not, you may find it necessary to divide the bitmap into smaller segments for transfer.

You may create memory device contexts that are compatible with a printer. These device contexts use the same printer driver and thus have the same feature set as the actual printer device context.

Another consideration is the actual printable area on the page (most laser printers cannot print all the way to the edge of the paper). The GETPHYSPAGESIZE and GETPRINTINGOFFSET Escape functions allow you to determine the actual printable area if necessary. Most drivers set the device context coordinate system to the printable area rather than the upper-left corner of the sheet of paper, so you should rarely need to perform this calculation yourself.

Printer Settings and the DEVMODE Structure

There are hundreds of printers available that work with Windows, each of which has its own unique features. It is the responsibility of the printer driver to support these features and provide a way for a Windows application to modify them. This is accomplished primarily via the **ExtDeviceMode** function and a special data structure known as the **DEVMODE** structure.

It is possible to use the **DEVMODE** structure to change the printer configuration during printing by using the **ResetDC** function between pages. This function also works on the Visual Basic printer object.

The definition of the **DEVMODE** structure appears in Listing 11.1. It is important to keep in mind that in addition to the standard fields defined in the listing, each printer driver may define its own private data area. The fields in this private data area are not accessible to the programmer, but it is necessary to allocate sufficient buffer space to include this data area when using the **ExtDeviceMode** function.

Listing 11.1   DEVMODE Structure

```
Type DEVMODE      ' 68 Bytes
    dmDeviceName As String *32
    dmSpecVersion As Integer
    dmDriverVersion As Integer
    dmSize As Integer
    dmDriverExtra As Integer
    dmFields As Long
    dmOrientation As Integer
    dmPaperSize As Integer
    dmPaperLength As Integer
    dmPaperWidth As Integer
    dmScale As Integer
    dmCopies As Integer
    dmDefaultSource As Integer
    dmPrintQuality As Integer
    dmColor As Integer
    dmDuplex As Integer
    dmYResolution As Integer
    dmTTOption As Integer
End Type
```

Table 11.1 describes the fields of the **DEVMODE** structure. Not all fields apply to every printer. You can use the **dmFields** field to determine which fields in a particular structure are valid.

Table 11.1   DEVMODE Structure Fields

Field	Description
dmDeviceName	The device name. Many printer drivers support more than one printer. This string identifies the printer in use.
dmSpecVersion	The **DEVMODE** version. &H30A for Windows 3.1.
dmDriverVersion	The version of the printer driver.
dmSize	The total size of the **DEVMODE** structure not including the private data area.
dmDriverExtra	The size of the private data area of the **DEVMODE** structure.
dmFields	Specifies which entries in the DEVMODE structure are valid. Refer to the APICONST.TXT field for a list of flag constants with the prefix DM_

Table 11.1   DEVMODE Structure Fields (Continued)

Field	Description
dmOrientation	One of the following two constants: **DMORIENT_PORTRAIT** for portrait mode, or **DMORIENT_LANDSCAPE** for landscape mode.
dmPaperSize	Specifies the current paper size. If zero, the **dmPaperLength** and **dmPaperWidth** fields are used to set the paper size. Otherwise, this field refers to one of the constant values as defined in file APICONST.TXT with the prefix DMPAPER_.
dmPaperLength	The paper length measured in tenths of a millimeter. This field takes precedence over the **dmPaperSize** field.
dmPaperWidth	The paper width measured in tenths of a millimeter. This field takes precedence over the **dmPaperSize** field.
dmScale	Scales the page size by a factor of X/100. For example, if the paper size is 8 1/2 × 11 and the **dmScale** is 4, the application will see a page size of 34 × 44. All output will be scaled to fit on the paper.
dmCopies	Specifies the number of copies to print.
dmDefaultSource	Some printers support several paper sources. Each of these sources is called a bin. This field specifies the bin to use. Refer to the constants in file APICONST.TXT that begin with the prefix DMBIN_ for a list of standard bins.
dmPrintQuality	Specifies the print quality to use for printers that support multiple resolutions. These may be specified by the constants in file APICONST.TXT that begin with the prefix DMRES_. If the **dmYResolution** field is not zero, this field contains the horizontal resolution in dots per inch and the **dmYResolution** field contains the vertical resolution in dots per inch.
dmColor	One of the following constants: **DMCOLOR_COLOR** for color printers, **DMCOLOR_MONOCHROME** for monochrome printers.
dmYResolution	Refer to the description of the **dmPrintQuality** field.
dmTTOption	Specifies how to print TrueType fonts. It is one of the following constants: **DMTT_BITMAP**: Prints TrueType fonts as graphics. This is used for most dot matrix printers. **DMTT_DOWNLOAD**: Downloads TrueType fonts to the printer. This is used for most PCL (LaserJet-compatible) printers. **DMTT_SUBDEV**: Uses a device font if available. This is used for most PostScript printers.

Printer Escapes

It would probably take dozens of functions to support every possible printer capability. Instead of adding these rarely used device control functions to the API, Microsoft created a special function called the **Escape** function for specialized device access. The **Escape** function defines dozens of possible device control operations, not all of which are supported by every device. This function works with any device—not just printers, so several of the device control operations apply to other devices such as plotters or the display screen. This function is defined below.

■ Escape, EscapeBynum, EscapeBystring

VB Declaration
```
Declare Function Escape% Lib "GDI" (ByVal hDC%, ByVal nEscape%, ByVal ⇔
nCount%, lpInData As Any, lpOutData As Any)

Declare Function EscapeBynum% Lib "GDI" Alias "Escape" (ByVal hDC%, ByVal ⇔
nEscape%, ByVal nCount%, ByVal lpInData&, ByVal lpOutData&)

Declare Function EscapeBystring% Lib "GDI" Alias "Escape" (ByVal hDC%, ByVal ⇔
nEscape%, ByVal nCount%,ByVal lpInData$, ByVal lpOutData$)
```

Description A flexible device control function.

Use with VB Depends on the **nEscape** parameter.

Parameter	Type/Description
hDC	**Integer**—A handle to a device context.
nEscape	**Integer**—The number of the escape as defined by a constant in file APICONST.TXT. This determines the operation that will take place. Table 11.2 describes the available escape operations.
nCount	**Integer**—The size of the input structure pointed to by the **lpInData** parameter.
lpInData	**Varies**—Input data. Refer to Table 11.2 for details.
lpOutData	**Varies**—Output data. Refer to Table 11.2 for details.

Return Value **Integer**—Depends on the **nEscape** parameter. Unless otherwise specified in Table 11.2, the return is greater than zero on success, zero if the Escape is not implemented, and a negative number on error based on the following constants:

SP_ERROR: General error
SP_OUTOFDISK: Insufficient disk space for the operation
SP_OUTOFMEMORY: Insufficient memory for the operation
SP_USERABORT: The user aborted the operation

Escape Function Operations

Table 11.2 briefly describes the available escapes. Many of the escapes dupli-cate functionality provided by the **ExtDeviceMode** or other API functions. The **ExtDeviceMode** function is the preferred method for setting the printer configuration on programs written for Windows 3.1 or greater.

Not all devices support all of these escapes. Fortunately, the **QUE-RYESCSUPPORT** escape is provided to help determine if an escape is sup-ported for a particular device.

Many of the escape operations duplicate functionality that is now provided by other functions, especially the **ExtDeviceMode** and **DeviceCapabilities** functions. It is highly recommended that you use the new functions unless it is absolutely necessary to preserve compatibility with earlier versions of Windows.

All escapes use the **hDC** parameter to specify the device context and the **nEscape** parameter to specify the escape operation. All other function parame-ters should be set to zero unless otherwise specified. If the **lpInData** parameter is specified, the **nCount** parameter should be set to the size of the structure to which it points unless otherwise specified.

Table 11.2	Escape Function Operations	
nEscape Operation Constant	**Description**
ABORTDOC	Same as the **AbortDoc** API function.
BANDINFO	This escape is used to support a technique known as banding where a page is divided into bands of text and graphic informa-tion. **lpInData** and **lpoutData** point to a BANDINFO structure.
BEGIN_PATH	Specifies the beginning of a path for a PostScript device.
CLIP_TO_PATH	**lpInData** points to an integer with one of the following values: 0 to save the current clipping region, 1 to restore the previous clip-ping region, 2 to set a clipping region, 3 to exclude a clipping re-gion. Returns zero on error. This function is used only by PostScript devices.
DEVICEDATA	See the **PASSTHROUGH** escape.
DRAFTMODE	**lpInData** points to an integer containing 0 to turn draft mode off, 1 to turn it on.
DRAWPATTERNRECT	Provides the ability to draw a gray pattern in block graphics on the text band of a LaserJet-compatible printer.
ENABLEDUPLEX	**lpInData** points to an integer containing 0 for single-sided print-ing, 1 for double-sided printing with a vertical binding, 2 for dou-ble-sided printing with a horizontal binding.

Table 11.2   Escape Function Operations (Continued)

nEscape Operation Constant	Description
ENABLEPAIRKERNING	**lpInData** points to an integer containing 0 to disable kerning by the printer driver, 1 to enable it.
ENABLERELATIVEWIDTHS	**lpInData** points to an integer containing 0 to disable relative widths, 1 to enable it. When relative widths are enabled, a character may not always be specified in integral device units, so the extent of a string may not equal the sum of the character extents.
ENDDOC	Same as the **EndDoc** API function.
END_PATH	Specifies the end of a path for PostScript printers.
ENUMPAPERBINS	**lpInData** points to an integer containing the number of bins. **lpOutData** points to an integer array to load with bin information. This is identical to the **DeviceCapabilities** function with the **DC_BINS** operation specified.
ENUMPAPERMETRICS	**lpInData** points to an integer containing 0 to return the number of **RECT** structures needed for this function, 1 to load the paper metrics. **lpOutData** is the address of the first element in an array of **RECT** structures to load with page sizes. This is identical to the **DeviceCapabilities** function with the **DC_PAPERSIZE** operation specified.
EPSPRINTING	**lpInData** points to an integer containing 0 to disable PostScript graphics by preventing output of the header control section, 1 to enable PostScript graphics.
EXT_DEVICE_CAPS	**lpInData** points to an integer containing a raster capability index as specified in Table 11.3. This table also describes the **lpOutData** parameter. This escape is used only on PostScript devices.
EXTTEXTOUT	Obsolete. Use the **ExtTextOut** API function instead.
FLUSHOUTPUT	Clears the printer output buffer.
GETCOLORTABLE	**lpInData** points to an integer containing an index into the device color table. **lpOutData** points to a 32-bit value to load with the RGB color for the specified entry.
GETEXTENDEDTEXTMETRICS	This escape loads **lpOutData** with extended metrics on a device physical font. This escape is only needed for advanced word processing applications.
GETEXTENTTABLE	This escape loads **lpOutData** with extents for a device physical font. This escape is only needed for advanced word processing applications.
GETFACENAME	**lpOutData** points to a 60-character buffer that will be loaded with the face name of the physical font.

Table 11.2   Escape Function Operations (Continued)

nEscape Operation Constant	Description
GETPAIRKERNDATA	This escape loads **lpOutData** with detailed kerning information for a device physical font. This escape is only needed for advanced word processing applications.
GETPHYSPAGESIZE	**lpOutData** points to a **POINTAPI** structure with the physical page size in device units based on the current orientation.
GETPRINTINGOFFSET	**lpOutData** points to a **POINTAPI** structure that is loaded with the offset from the upper-left corner of the page in device units.
GETSCALINGFACTOR	lpOutData points to a **POINTAPI** structure that is loaded with the X and Y scaling coordinates in powers of two (for example, -X = 3 implies a scaling factor of 8).
GETSETPAPERBINS	**lpInData** and **lpOutData** point to a 12-byte structure. The first two integers contain the bin number and the number of bins available. Either of the two parameters may be NULL. If **lpInData** is specified, the bin number field in the structure it refers to is used to set the current bin number. If **lpOutData** is specified, the bin number and bin count fields in the structure it points to are set according to the device configuration before this function was called.
GETSETPAPERMETRICS	**lpInData** and **lpOutData** point to **RECT** structures containing the imaged area to set or retrieve. The **DeviceCapabilities** and **ExtDeviceMode** functions make this escape obsolete.
GETSETPRINTORIENT	**lpInData** points to a 20-byte structure. The first 32-bit LONG value contains the orientation. If **lpInData** is NULL, the Escape function will return the current orientation. The **DeviceCapabilities** and **ExtDeviceMode** functions make this escape obsolete.
GETSETSCREENPARAMS	**lpInData** and **lpOutData** point to a two-integer structure. The first interger contains the halftone screen frequency in degrees. The second contains the dots per inch of the screen.
GETTRACKKERNTABLE	This escape loads **lpOutData** with detailed kerning information for a device physical font. This escape is only needed for advanced word processing applications.
GETVECTORBRUSHSIZE	**lpInData** points to a **LOGBRUSH** structure. **lpOutData** points to a **POINTAPI** structure whose y field is loaded with the width of the pen in device units. This is especially useful for plotters.
GETVECTORPENSIZE	**lpInData** points to a **LOGPEN** structure. **lpOutData** points to a **POINTAPI** structure whose y field is loaded with the width of the pen in device units. This is especially useful for plotters as it allows you to determine the actual width of a line.

Table 11.2	**Escape Function Operations (Continued)**

nEscape Operation Constant	Description
MOUSETRAILS	**lpInData** points to an integer describing the number of cursors to display as a trail. -3 enables trails but does not update WIN-.INI, -2 disables trails but does not update WIN.INI, -1 enables trails based on the entry in WIN.INI, 0 disables mouse trails, 1-7 sets the trail size. This Escape only applies to display devices.
NEWFRAME	Identical to the **EndPage** API function.
NEXTBAND	This escape is used to support a technique known as banding where a page is divided into bands of text and graphic information. **lpOutData** points to a RECT structure that describes the banding rectangle to use.
PASSTHROUGH	**lpInData** points to a structure. The first 16 bits indicate the number of bytes of data to send to the device. The remaining data is sent directly to the device. This function bypasses the normal printer driver operations and may interfere with its correct operation.
POSTSCRIPT_DATA	Same as **PASSTHROUGH**.
POSTSCRIPT_IGNORE	**lpOutData** points to an integer which, when nonzero, turns off PostScript device output.
QUERYESCSUPPORT	**lpInData** points to an integer containing an escape operation constant. The function returns 0 if the escape is not implemented, nonzero otherwise. For **DRAWPATTERNRECT**, 2 indicates implementation for the HP IIP printer.
RESTORE_CTM	Restores a saved transformation matrix for a PostScript printer. Refer to the PostScript language definition for further information.
SAVE_CTM	Saves the current transformation matrix for a PostScript printer.
SELECTPAPERSOURCE	Obsolete. Use the **DeviceCapabilities** API function.
SETABORTPROC	**lpInData** points to the abort function to use for this device context. Refer to the description for the **SetAbortProc** function for further information.
SETALLJUSTVALUES	Obsolete. Use the **ExtTextOut** function for justified text output.
SET_ARC_DIRECTION	**lpInData** points to an integer which is set to 1 to change the arc drawing direction to clockwise from counter-clockwise (the default). It is designed primarily for PostScript devices.
SET_BACKGROUND_COLOR	**lpInData** and **lpOutData** point to 32-bit RGB colors for the background color of the device. **lpInData** specifies a new background color, **lpOutData** retrieves the current background color. The default is white.

Table 11.2   Escape Function Operations (Continued)

nEscape Operation Constant	Description
SET_BOUNDS	**lpInData** points to a **RECT** that contains the bounds of the image that is to be drawn. This should be called before the **StartDoc** function is called.
SET_CLIP_BOX	**lpInData** points to a **RECT** containing the clipping rectangle to set (the previous clipping rectangle is saved). If zero, the previously saved clipping rectangle is restored.
SETCOLORTABLE	**lpInData** points to a structure with an integer index value followed by a 32-bit RGB color value. **lpOutData** points to a 32-bit RGB color value. The entry specified by the index is loaded with the RGB color value in the **lpInData** structure. The actual color used is returned in the **lpOutData** structure. This function does not work with EGA, VGA, or devices with fixed color tables.
SETCOPYCOUNT	**lpInData** points to an integer containing the number of copies requested. **lpOutData** points to an integer that is loaded with the actual number of copies. The **ExtDeviceMode** function is a preferred way to set copies.
SETKERNTRACK	This escape supports a kerning capability that is only needed for advanced word processing applications.
SETLINECAP	**lpInData** points to an integer specifying how the ends of lines are drawn. -1 for the default, 0 for an endpoint that does not pass the end of the segment, 1 for a rounded endpoint whose diameter is the width of the line, 2 for a square endpoint that passes the end of the segment by one-half the line width.
SETLINEJOIN	**lpInData** points to an integer specifying how the ends of intersecting lines are joined. -1 for the default, 0 for a mitered join (the outer ends of the lines are extended until they join), 1 for a rounded join (a semicircle is drawn between the outer ends of the lines), 2 for a squared join (a line is drawn between the outer ends of the lines).
SETMITERLIMIT	**lpInData** and **lpOutData** point to integers that specify the miter limit. Refer to your printer page description language for further information.
SET_POLY_MODE	**lpInData** points to an integer specifying the polygon mode. This determines the meaning of a point when using the GDI polygon functions. The return value is the previous setting. It's 0 if the requested polygon mode is not supported. Legal settings include: 1—the standard; 2—every four points define Bezier spline curves, which are generated using a mathematical Bezier formula; 3—every two points specify line coordinate pairs; 4—every two points specify a vertical or horizontal line segment. This function is used only on PostScript devices.

Table 11.2 **Escape Function Operations (Continued)**

nEscape Operation Constant	Description
SET_SCREEN_ANGLE	**lpInData** points to an integer specifying the screen angle in tenths of a degree. This is used during color separation.
SET_SPREAD	**lpInData** points to an integer describing the number of pixels that nonwhite graphic objects are expanded. This is used for spot color separation.
STARTDOC	See the **StartDoc** API function.
TRANSFORM_CTM	**lpInData** points to a 3×3 array of **Long** variables that describe the transformation matrix for this postscript device. Refer to your PostScript language documentation for details.

Table 11.3 **EXT_DEVICE_CAPS Operations**

EXT_DEVICE_CAPS Index	Description
R2_CAPS	**lpOutData** points to a 32-bit value indicating which binary raster operations the device supports. Refer to the **SetROP2** function in Chapter 7 for a list of binary raster operations.
PATTERN_CAPS	**lpOutData** points to a 32-bit value that is loaded with the maximum width and height of the device pattern brush in the low and high 16-bit words, respectively.
PATH_CAPS	**lpOutData** points to a 32-bit value that is loaded with the path capabilities of the device. Refer to the constants in file APICONST.TXT with the PATH_ prefix.
POLYGON_CAPS	**lpOutData** points to a 32-bit value that is loaded with the maximum number of polygon points supported by the device.
PATTERN_COLOR_CAPS	**lpOutData** points to a 32-bit value that is set to 1 if the device can convert monochrome bitmaps to color.
R2_TEXT_CAPS	**lpOutData** points to a 32-bit value indicating in the low 16 bits which binary raster operations the device can use on text. Refer to the **SetROP2** function in Chapter 7 for a list of binary raster operations. The high 16 bits contain a combination of the flags **RASTER_TEXT**, **DEVICE_TEXT**, and **VECTOR_TEXT** to indicate what type of text the raster operations work on.
POLYMODE_CAPS	**lpOutData** points to a 32-bit value that is loaded with either or both of the constants **PM_POLYSCANLINE** and **PM_BEZIER** to indicate the type of polygon mode supported.

Example: PicPrint—Prints a Bitmap and Shows Printer Configuration

PicPrint is a program that demonstrates a number of the techniques described in this chapter. It illustrates a method for printing a bitmap to a printer that will work successfully with most printers and accurately preserves the color of the bitmap. It shows how to read the printer configuration information and change it temporarily during printing.

Using PicPrint

The PicPrint screen has a single picture control, which holds the bitmap to print. Figure 11.2 shows the PicPrint program in action. The ExtDevMode menu command reads the current configuration for the printer, brings up the printer setup dialog box, and then displays a message box showing a number of the attributes of the printer configuration. Figures 11.3 and 11.4 illustrate this sequence.

Figure 11.2

PicPrint main program screen

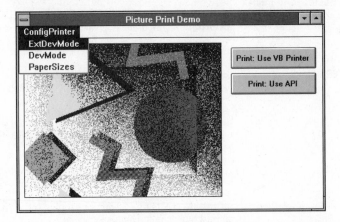

The DeviceMode menu entry uses the **DeviceMode** API function to bring up the printer setup dialog box. Note that changes to this box will affect the default configuration for the default printer and modify the WIN.INI file accordingly. You may wish to back up your WIN.INI file before running this part of the program.

The PaperSizes menu command shows how to use the **DeviceCapabilities** function to obtain the names of the papers supported by this printer. Figure 11.5 shows the paper names message box.

Figure 11.3
Printer setup
dialog box

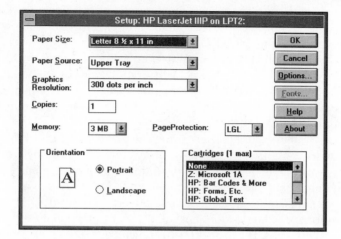

Figure 11.4
DEVMODE
configuration
message box

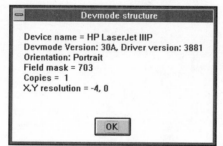

Figure 11.5
Paper names
message box

Note that not all of these functions are supported by every print driver. You may wish to temporarily load a LaserJet or PostScript driver to demonstrate these functions. You can install a printer using the Windows control panel application (CONTROL.EXE).

The two command buttons shown in Figure 11.2 print the bitmap in the picture control. The bitmap is actually printed twice on the same page: One version is a direct unscaled copy, the other stretches the bitmap to fill the rest of the page. The API printing function also shows how to temporarily set the printer into landscape mode.

You will find that in some cases when you click on the abort printing button shown in Figure 11.6, there is a delay before the printing is actually canceled—depending on the size of the bitmap being printed and the speed of the system this could be several minutes. During the end of page processing, the internal metafile is played back, producing a series of GDI graphic calls to the printer. Windows does not call the abort function during individual GDI graphic calls. The **StretchDIBits** function is extremely slow in this application and an abort command received while this function is in progress will not be processed until it is complete.

Figure 11.6
AbortForm design time screen

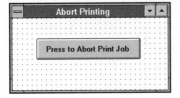

Project Description

The PicPrint project includes six files. PICPRINT.FRM is the main form used in the program. The ABORTFOR.FRM is used to allow the user to abort printing. PICPRINT.BAS is the only module in the program and contains the constant type and global definitions and some program code. APIDECS.BAS is the type-safe API declaration file provided with this book. APIGUIDE-.BAS contains the declarations for the APIGUIDE.DLL dynamic link library. CBK.VBX is the generic callback custom control included on the program disk of this book which enables use of callback functions with Visual Basic. This custom control is described in detail in Appendix A.

Listing 11.2 shows the project file for the PicPrint program.

Listing 11.2   Project Listing File PICPRINT.MAK

```
PICPRINT.FRM
CBK.VBX
PICPRINT.BAS
APIDECS.BAS
APIGUIDE.BAS
ABORTFOR.FRM
ProjWinSize=175,439,248,215
ProjWinShow=2
```

PicPrint Form Description

Listing 11.3 contains the header from file PICPRINT.FRM that describes the control setup for the form.

Listing 11.3   PICPRINT.FRM Header

```
VERSION 2.00
Begin Form Picprint
   Caption        =   "Picture Print Demo"
   Height         =   4710
   Left           =   1320
   LinkMode       =   1  'Source
   LinkTopic      =   "Form1"
   ScaleHeight    =   4020
   ScaleWidth     =   7365
   Top            =   1410
   Width          =   7485
   Begin ccCallback Callback1
      Left             =   5760
      Top              =   1680
      Type             =   1  'AbortProc
   End
   Begin CommandButton CmdPrintAPI
      Caption          =   "Print: Use API"
      Height           =   495
      Left             =   5160
      TabIndex         =   2
      Top              =   840
      Width            =   2055
   End
   Begin CommandButton CmdPrint
      Caption          =   "Print: Use VB Printer"
```

Listing 11.3   PICPRINT.FRM Header (Continued)

```
    Height         =    495
    Left           =    5160
    TabIndex       =    1
    Top            =    240
    Width          =    2055
End
```

File PICPRINT.FRX is the binary file for this form. It contains the definition of the **Picture** property for control **Picture1**. You may remove the line

```
Picture = PICPRINT.FRX:0000
```

in which case you should load a bitmap into the control's **Picture** property in Visual Basic design mode. The sample program uses the bitmap PARTY.BMP, which is provided with Windows 3.1.

```
Begin PictureBox Picture1
    AutoRedraw     =    -1    'True
    Height         =    3615
    Left           =    120
    Picture        =    PICPRINT.FRX:0000
    ScaleHeight    =    3585
    ScaleWidth     =    4785
    TabIndex       =    0
    Top            =    120
    Width          =    4815
End
Begin Menu MenuConfigPrinter
    Caption        =    "ConfigPrinter"
    Begin Menu MenuExtDevMode
        Caption        =    "ExtDevMode"
    End
    Begin Menu MenuDevMode
        Caption        =    "DevMode"
    End
    Begin Menu MenuPaperSizes
        Caption        =    "PaperSizes"
    End
End
End
```

AbortForm Form Description

Listing 11.4 contains the header from file ABORTFOR.FRM that describes the control setup for the form.

Listing 11.4   ABORTFOR.FRM Header

```
VERSION 2.00
Begin Form AbortForm
    Caption          =    "Abort Printing"
    Height           =    2100
    Left             =    2175
    LinkMode         =    1  'Source
    LinkTopic        =    "Form1"
    ScaleHeight      =    1695
    ScaleWidth       =    3795
    Top              =    1995
    Visible          =    0  'False
    Width            =    3915
    Begin CommandButton CmdAbort
        Caption      =    "Press to Abort Print Job"
        Height       =    495
        Left         =    600
        TabIndex     =    0
        Top          =    480
        Width        =    2535
    End
End
```

PicPrint Listings

Module PICPRINT.BAS contains the constant declarations and global variables used by the program.

Listing 11.5   Module PICPRINT.BAS

```
' PicPrint program example


' Global constants

Global Const SRCCOPY = &HCC0020
Global Const SRCPAINT = &HEE0086
Global Const SRCAND = &H8800C6
Global Const SRCINVERT = &H660046
Global Const SRCERASE = &H440328
Global Const NOTSRCCOPY = &H330008
Global Const NOTSRCERASE = &H1100A6
Global Const MERGECOPY = &HC000CA
Global Const MERGEPAINT = &HBB0226
Global Const PATCOPY = &HF00021
Global Const PATPAINT = &HFB0A09
```

Listing 11.5   Module PICPRINT.BAS (Continued)

```
Global Const PATINVERT = &H5A0049
Global Const DSTINVERT = &H550009
Global Const BLACKNESS = &H42&
Global Const WHITENESS = &HFF0062
Global Const BLACKONWHITE = 1
Global Const WHITEONBLACK = 2
Global Const COLORONCOLOR = 3
Global Const NEWFRAME = 1
Global Const ABORTDOCCONST = 2
Global Const NEXTBAND = 3
Global Const SETCOLORTABLE = 4
Global Const GETCOLORTABLE = 5
Global Const FLUSHOUTPUT = 6
Global Const DRAFTMODE = 7
Global Const QUERYESCSUPPORT = 8
Global Const SETABORTPROCCONST = 9
Global Const STARTDOCCONST = 10
Global Const ENDDOCAPICONST = 11
Global Const GETPHYSPAGESIZE = 12
Global Const GETPRINTINGOFFSET = 13
Global Const GETSCALINGFACTOR = 14
Global Const MFCOMMENT = 15
Global Const GETPENWIDTH = 16
Global Const SETCOPYCOUNT = 17
Global Const SELECTPAPERSOURCE = 18
Global Const DEVICEDATA = 19
Global Const PASSTHROUGH = 19
Global Const GETTECHNOLGY = 20
Global Const GETTECHNOLOGY = 20
Global Const SETENDCAP = 21
Global Const SETLINEJOIN = 22
Global Const SETMITERLIMIT = 23
Global Const BANDINFO = 24
Global Const DRAWPATTERNRECT = 25
Global Const GETVECTORPENSIZE = 26
Global Const GETVECTORBRUSHSIZE = 27
Global Const ENABLEDUPLEX = 28
Global Const GETSETPAPERBINS = 29
Global Const GETSETPRINTORIENT = 30
Global Const ENUMPAPERBINS = 31
Global Const SETDIBSCALING = 32
Global Const EPSPRINTING = 33
Global Const ENUMPAPERMETRICS = 34
Global Const GETSETPAPERMETRICS = 35
Global Const POSTSCRIPT_DATA = 37
Global Const POSTSCRIPT_IGNORE = 38
Global Const GETEXTENDEDTEXTMETRICS = 256
Global Const GETEXTENTTABLE = 257
```

Listing 11.5   Module PICPRINT.BAS (Continued)

```
Global Const GETPAIRKERNTABLE = 258
Global Const GETTRACKKERNTABLE = 259
Global Const EXTTEXTOUTCONST = 512
Global Const ENABLERELATIVEWIDTHS = 768
Global Const ENABLEPAIRKERNING = 769
Global Const SETKERNTRACK = 770
Global Const SETALLJUSTVALUES = 771
Global Const SETCHARSET = 772
Global Const STRETCHBLTCONST = 2048
Global Const BEGIN_PATH = 4096
Global Const CLIP_TO_PATH = 4097
Global Const END_PATH = 4098
Global Const EXT_DEVICE_CAPS = 4099
Global Const RESTORE_CTM = 4100
Global Const SAVE_CTM = 4101
Global Const DM_ORIENTATION = &H1&
Global Const DM_PAPERSIZE = &H2&
Global Const DM_PAPERLENGTH = &H4&
Global Const DM_PAPERWIDTH = &H8&
Global Const DM_SCALE = &H10&
Global Const DM_COPIES = &H100&
Global Const DM_DEFAULTSOURCE = &H200&
Global Const DM_PRINTQUALITY = &H400&
Global Const DM_COLOR = &H800&
Global Const DM_DUPLEX = &H1000&
Global Const DM_YRESOLUTION = &H2000&
Global Const DM_TTOPTION = &H4000&
Global Const DMORIENT_PORTRAIT = 1
Global Const DMORIENT_LANDSCAPE = 2
Global Const DMPAPER_LETTER = 1
Global Const DMPAPER_LETTERSMALL = 2
Global Const DMPAPER_TABLOID = 3
Global Const DMPAPER_LEDGER = 4
Global Const DMPAPER_LEGAL = 5
Global Const DMPAPER_STATEMENT = 6
Global Const DMPAPER_EXECUTIVE = 7
Global Const DMPAPER_A3 = 8
Global Const DMPAPER_A4 = 9
Global Const DMPAPER_A4SMALL = 10
Global Const DMPAPER_A5 = 11
Global Const DMPAPER_B4 = 12
Global Const DMPAPER_B5 = 13
Global Const DMPAPER_FOLIO = 14
Global Const DMPAPER_QUARTO = 15
Global Const DMPAPER_10X14 = 16
Global Const DMPAPER_11X17 = 17
Global Const DMPAPER_NOTE = 18
Global Const DMPAPER_ENV_9 = 19
```

Listing 11.5   Module PICPRINT.BAS (Continued)

```
Global Const DMPAPER_ENV_10 = 20
Global Const DMPAPER_ENV_11 = 21
Global Const DMPAPER_ENV_12 = 22
Global Const DMPAPER_ENV_14 = 23
Global Const DMPAPER_CSHEET = 24
Global Const DMPAPER_DSHEET = 25
Global Const DMPAPER_ESHEET = 26
Global Const DMPAPER_ENV_DL = 27
Global Const DMPAPER_ENV_C5 = 28
Global Const DMPAPER_ENV_C3 = 29
Global Const DMPAPER_ENV_C4 = 30
Global Const DMPAPER_ENV_C6 = 31
Global Const DMPAPER_ENV_C65 = 32
Global Const DMPAPER_ENV_B4 = 33
Global Const DMPAPER_ENV_B5 = 34
Global Const DMPAPER_ENV_B6 = 35
Global Const DMPAPER_ENV_ITALY = 36
Global Const DMPAPER_ENV_MONARCH = 37
Global Const DMPAPER_ENV_PERSONAL = 38
Global Const DMPAPER_FANFOLD_US = 39
Global Const DMPAPER_FANFOLD_STD_GERMAN = 40
Global Const DMPAPER_FANFOLD_LGL_GERMAN = 41
Global Const DMPAPER_USER = 256
Global Const DMBIN_UPPER = 1
Global Const DMBIN_ONLYONE = 1
Global Const DMBIN_LOWER = 2
Global Const DMBIN_MIDDLE = 3
Global Const DMBIN_MANUAL = 4
Global Const DMBIN_ENVELOPE = 5
Global Const DMBIN_ENVMANUAL = 6
Global Const DMBIN_AUTO = 7
Global Const DMBIN_TRACTOR = 8
Global Const DMBIN_SMALLFMT = 9
Global Const DMBIN_LARGEFMT = 10
Global Const DMBIN_LARGECAPACITY = 11
Global Const DMBIN_CASSETTE = 14
Global Const DMBIN_USER = 256
Global Const DMRES_DRAFT = -1
Global Const DMRES_LOW = -2
Global Const DMRES_MEDIUM = -3
Global Const DMRES_HIGH = -4
Global Const DMCOLOR_MONOCHROME = 1
Global Const DMCOLOR_COLOR = 2
Global Const DMDUP_SIMPLEX = 1
Global Const DMDUP_VERTICAL = 2
Global Const DMDUP_HORIZONTAL = 3
Global Const DMTT_BITMAP = 1
Global Const DMTT_DOWNLOAD = 2
```

Listing 11.5 Module PICPRINT.BAS (Continued)

```
Global Const DMTT_SUBDEV = 3
Global Const DM_UPDATE = 1
Global Const DM_COPY = 2
Global Const DM_PROMPT = 4
Global Const DM_MODIFY = 8
Global Const DM_IN_BUFFER = 8
Global Const DM_IN_PROMPT = 4
Global Const DM_OUT_BUFFER = 2
Global Const DM_OUT_DEFAULT = 1
Global Const DC_FIELDS = 1
Global Const DC_PAPERS = 2
Global Const DC_PAPERSIZE = 3
Global Const DC_MINEXTENT = 4
Global Const DC_MAXEXTENT = 5
Global Const DC_BINS = 6
Global Const DC_DUPLEX = 7
Global Const DC_SIZE = 8
Global Const DC_EXTRA = 9
Global Const DC_VERSION = 10
Global Const DC_DRIVER = 11
Global Const DC_BINNAMES = 12
Global Const DC_ENUMRESOLUTIONS = 13
Global Const DC_FILEDEPENDENCIES = 14
Global Const DC_TRUETYPE = 15
Global Const DC_PAPERNAMES = 16
Global Const DC_ORIENTATION = 17
Global Const DC_COPIES = 18
Global Const DCTT_BITMAP = &H1&
Global Const DCTT_DOWNLOAD = &H2&
Global Const DCTT_SUBDEV = &H4&
Global Const SP_NOTREPORTED = &H4000
Global Const SP_ERROR = (-1)
Global Const SP_APPABORT = (-2)
Global Const SP_USERABORT = (-3)
Global Const SP_OUTOFDISK = (-4)
Global Const SP_OUTOFMEMORY = (-5)
Global Const PR_JOBSTATUS = &H0
Global Const DRIVERVERSION = 0
Global Const TECHNOLOGY = 2
Global Const HORZSIZE = 4
Global Const VERTSIZE = 6
Global Const HORZRES = 8
Global Const VERTRES = 10
Global Const BITSPIXEL = 12
Global Const PLANES = 14
Global Const NUMBRUSHES = 16
Global Const NUMPENS = 18
Global Const NUMMARKERS = 20
```

Listing 11.5 Module PICPRINT.BAS (Continued)

```
Global Const NUMFONTS = 22
Global Const NUMCOLORS = 24
Global Const PDEVICESIZE = 26
Global Const CURVECAPS = 28
Global Const LINECAPS = 30
Global Const POLYGONALCAPS = 32
Global Const TEXTCAPS = 34
Global Const CLIPCAPS = 36
Global Const RASTERCAPS = 38
Global Const ASPECTX = 40
Global Const ASPECTY = 42
Global Const ASPECTXY = 44
Global Const LOGPIXELSX = 88
Global Const LOGPIXELSY = 90
Global Const SIZEPALETTE = 104
Global Const NUMRESERVED = 106
Global Const COLORRES = 108
Global Const RC_BITBLT = 1
Global Const RC_BANDING = 2
Global Const RC_SCALING = 4
Global Const RC_BITMAP64 = 8
Global Const RC_GDI20_OUTPUT = &H10
Global Const RC_DI_BITMAP = &H80
Global Const RC_PALETTE = &H100
Global Const RC_DIBTODEV = &H200
Global Const RC_BIGFONT = &H400
Global Const RC_STRETCHBLT = &H800
Global Const RC_FLOODFILL = &H1000
Global Const RC_STRETCHDIB = &H2000
Global Const GMEM_FIXED = &H0
Global Const GMEM_MOVEABLE = &H2
Global Const GMEM_NOCOMPACT = &H10
Global Const GMEM_NODISCARD = &H20
Global Const GMEM_ZEROINIT = &H40
Global Const GMEM_MODIFY = &H80
Global Const GMEM_DISCARDABLE = &H100
Global Const GMEM_NOT_BANKED = &H1000
Global Const GMEM_SHARE = &H2000
Global Const GMEM_DDESHARE = &H2000
Global Const GMEM_NOTIFY = &H4000
Global Const GMEM_LOWER = GMEM_NOT_BANKED
Global Const DIB_RGB_COLORS = 0
Global Const DIB_PAL_COLORS = 1

' Global variables
Global AbortPrinting%
```

Function **GetDefPrinter$** can be used to extract the definition of the default printer from the WIN.INI initialization file. The **GetDeviceDriver$**, **GetDeviceName$**, and **GetDeviceOutput$** functions divide this string into its driver, description, and output port components.

Listing 11.6   **Form Listing PICPRINT.FRM**

```
'    This function retrieves the definition of the default
'    printer on this system
'
Function GetDefPrinter$ ()
    Dim def$

    def$ = String$(128, 0)
    di% = GetProfileString%("WINDOWS", "DEVICE", "", ⇔
    def$, 127)
    def$ = agGetStringFromLPSTR$(def$)
    GetDefPrinter$ = def$

End Function


'    Retrieves the name portion of a device string
'
Function GetDeviceName$ (dev$)
    Dim npos%
    npos% = InStr(dev$, ",")
    GetDeviceName$ = Left$(dev$, npos% - 1)
End Function


'    This function returns the driver module name
'
Function GetDeviceDriver$ (dev$)
    Dim firstpos%, nextpos%
    firstpos% = InStr(dev$, ",")
    nextpos% = InStr(firstpos% + 1, dev$, ",")
    GetDeviceDriver$ = Mid$(dev$, firstpos% + 1, ⇔
    nextpos% - firstpos% - 1)
End Function


'    Returns the output destination for the specified device
'
Function GetDeviceOutput$ (dev$)
    Dim firstpos%, nextpos%
    firstpos% = InStr(dev$, ",")
    nextpos% = InStr(firstpos% + 1, dev$, ",")
    GetDeviceOutput$ = Mid$(dev$, nextpos% + 1)
End Function
```

The **MenuExtDevMode_Click** function demonstrates a number of important techniques. First, it shows how to load a device driver dynamic link library using the **LoadLibrary** API function. This process is described in further detail in Chapter 12.

The function then uses the **agExtDeviceMode** function in the APIGUIDE-.DLL dynamic link library to obtain the required size of the **DEVMODE** data structure including the private data area for this driver. It then uses the **String$** function to allocate string buffers of the required length. The **agGetAddressFor-VBString** function is used to obtain the address of the string buffer. These strings may move in memory, so be sure to obtain the address again if operations occur that can move string memory (these include all string operations).

Once the buffers are loaded, the data is copied into **DEVMODE** data structures, which can be easily accessed under program control in BASIC.

It is important to free the library when it is no longer needed. Windows maintains a count of how many applications are using the library, so it will not actually be freed until it is no longer needed.

```
'  Demonstration of the Extended Device Mode function
'
Sub MenuExtDevMode_Click ()
    Dim dev$, devname$, devoutput$
    Dim dm As DEVMODE, dmout As DEVMODE
    Dim libhnd%
    Dim bufsize%
    Dim dminstring$, dmoutstring$
    Dim dminaddr&, dmoutaddr&

    dev$ = GetDefPrinter$() ' Get default printer info
    If dev$ = "" Then Exit Sub
    devname$ = GetDeviceName$(dev$)
    devoutput$ = GetDeviceOutput$(dev$)

    ' Load the device driver library - exit if unavailable
    libhnd% = LoadLibrary(GetDeviceDriver$(dev$) + ".drv")
    If libhnd% = Ø Then Exit Sub

    bufsize% = agExtDeviceMode%(hWnd, libhnd%, Ø, ⟺
    devname$, devoutput$, agGetAddressForObject(dm), Ø, Ø)
    dminstring$ = String$(bufsize%, Ø)
    dmoutstring$ = String$(bufsize%, Ø)
    dminaddr& = agGetAddressForVBString&(dminstring$)
    dmoutaddr& = agGetAddressForVBString&(dmoutstring$)

    ' The output DEVMODE structure will reflect any changes
    ' made by the printer setup dialog box.
    ' Note that no changes will be made to the default
    ' printer settings!
    di% = agExtDeviceMode(hWnd, libhnd%, dmoutaddr&, ⟺
    devname$, devoutput$, dminaddr&, Ø, DM_IN_BUFFER ⟺
```

```
    Or DM_IN_PROMPT Or DM_OUT_BUFFER)
    ' Copy the data buffer into the DEVMODE structure
    agCopyDataBynum dmoutaddr&, ⇔
    agGetAddressForObject&(dmout), 68
    ShowDevMode dmout
    FreeLibrary (libhnd%)
End Sub
```

The **ShowDevMode** function displays a number of the fields from the **DEVMODE** data structure for the printer.

```
' Shows information about the current device mode
'
Sub ShowDevMode (dm As DEVMODE)
    Dim crlf$
    Dim a$

    crlf$ = Chr$(13) + Chr$(10)
    a$ = "Device name = " + ⇔
    agGetStringFromLPSTR$(dm.dmDeviceName) + crlf$
    a$ = a$ + "Devmode Version: " + ⇔
    Hex$(dm.dmSpecVersion) + ", Driver version: " + ⇔
    Hex$(dm.dmDriverVersion) + crlf$
    a$ = a$ + "Orientation: "
    If dm.dmOrientation = DMORIENT_PORTRAIT Then a$ = a$ ⇔
    + "Portrait" Else a$ = a$ + "Landscape"
    a$ = a$ + crlf$
    a$ = a$ + "Field mask = " + Hex$(dm.dmFields) + crlf$
    a$ = a$ + "Copies = " + Str$(dm.dmCopies) + crlf$
    If dm.dmFields And DM_YRESOLUTION <> 0 Then
        a$ = a$ + "X,Y resolution = " + ⇔
    Str$(dm.dmPrintQuality) + "," + ⇔
    Str$(dm.dmYResolution) + crlf$
    End If
    MsgBox a$, 0, "Devmode structure"
End Sub
```

This function demonstrates how the **agDeviceCapabilities** function can be used to obtain a list of paper names for a printer. This technique can be used to obtain other information as well, as described in the reference section for this function.

Note the use of a preallocated string variable to simulate a fixed length string array.

```
'   This function shows how to use the agDeviceCapabilities
'   function to find out how many paper names the device
'   supports. This technique can be used for any
'   device capability
'
Sub MenuPaperSizes_Click ()
    Dim dev$, devname$, devoutput$
    Dim libhnd%
```

```
    Dim papercount%
    Dim papername$
    Dim a$, crlf$, tname$
    Dim x%

    crlf$ = Chr$(13) + Chr$(10)

    dev$ = GetDefPrinter$() ' Get default printer info
    If dev$ = "" Then Exit Sub
    devname$ = GetDeviceName$(dev$)
    devoutput$ = GetDeviceOutput$(dev$)

    ' Load the device driver library - exit if unavailable
    libhnd% = LoadLibrary(GetDeviceDriver$(dev$) + ".drv")
    If libhnd% = 0 Then Exit Sub

    ' Find out how many paper names there are
    papercount% = agDeviceCapabilities(libhnd%, ⇔
    devname$, devoutput$, DC_PAPERNAMES, 0, 0)
    If papercount% = 0 Then
        MsgBox "No paper names available", 0, ⇔
        "Paper name capability"
        Exit Sub
    End If

    ' Now dimension the string large enough to hold them
    ' all
    papername$ = String$(64 * papercount%, 0)
    di% = agDeviceCapabilities(libhnd%, devname$, ⇔
    devoutput$, DC_PAPERNAMES, ⇔
    agGetAddressForVBString&(papername$), 0)

    ' Now display the results
    For x% = 1 To papercount%
        tname$ = Mid$(papername$, (x% - 1) * 64 + 1)
        a$ = a$ + agGetStringFromLPSTR$(tname$) + crlf$
    Next x%
    MsgBox a$, 0, "Paper Names for Default Printer"
    FreeLibrary (libhnd%)
End Sub
```

The **PrintBitmap** function prints the bitmap in the picture property of the **Picture1** control twice. The first time it is printed at 1:1 scale using the **SetDIBits-ToDevice** function. Next the function calculates how much space is left on the page and scales the bitmap to fill that space using the **StretchDIBits** function.

This function uses the techniques introduced in Chapter 8 for determining the size of a bitmap and for copying a bitmap into a device-independent bitmap. The function also uses the **GetDeviceCaps** function to find out if the printer driver supports the device-independent bitmap functions.

Device-independent bitmaps are the best way to print due to their ability to correctly handle color conversions. If a printer driver does not handle DIBs, it is still possible to print (at least in monochrome) using the following technique:

1. Create a memory device context compatible with the printer.

2. Create a memory device context compatible with the screen.

3. Select into the printer memory device context a monochrome bitmap the size of the area to print.

4. Select into the screen device context the bitmap that you wish to print.

5. Use the **BitBlt** or **StretchBlt** API function to copy the bitmap from the screen memory device context to the printer memory device context. (Refer to the reference section for these functions for information on using the Foreground and Background colors to handle color conversions.)

6. Use the **BitBlt** or **StretchBlt** API function to copy the image from the printer memory device context to the printer device context.

7. Finally, be sure to delete any device contexts or bitmaps that are no longer needed.

If memory is limited, or if the printer driver cannot support bitmaps larger than 64k (as determined by the **GetDeviceCaps** function), you can use a smaller intermediate bitmap and transfer the image in segments. If the source bitmap is monochrome, you may be able to select it directly into the printer memory device context for transfer to the printer.

This function also uses the global memory allocation functions to create a buffer for the device-independent bitmap data. This is used instead of a Visual Basic string in order to make certain that the function can handle bitmaps greater than 64k in size. Global memory functions are described in detail in Chapter 12.

The following function demonstrates how the **ExtDeviceMode** function may be used to set the configuration of a printer without affecting other applications. In this case the printer is set into landscape mode before printing.

```
'    Prints the bitmap in the picture1 control to the
'    printer context specified.
'
Sub PrintBitmap (hdc%)
    Dim bi As BITMAPINFO
    Dim dctemp%, dctemp2%
    Dim msg$
    Dim bufsize&
    Dim bm As BITMAP
```

```
Dim ghnd%
Dim gptr&
Dim xpix%, ypix%
Dim doscale%
Dim uy%, ux%

' Create a temporary memory DC and select into it
' the background picture of the picture1 control.
dctemp% = CreateCompatibleDC(picture1.hdc)

' Get the size of the picture bitmap
di% = GetObjectAPI%(picture1.picture, 14, ⇔
agGetAddressForObject(bm))

' Can this printer handle the DIB?
If (GetDeviceCaps(dctemp%, RASTERCAPS)) And ⇔
RC_DIBTODEV = 0 Then
    msg$ = "This device does not support DIBs" + ⇔
    crlf$ + "See source code for further info"
    MsgBox msg$, 0, "No DIB support"
End If

' Fill the BITMAPINFO for the desired DIB
bi.bmiHeader.biSize = 40
bi.bmiHeader.biWidth = bm.bmWidth
bi.bmiHeader.biHeight = bm.bmHeight
bi.bmiHeader.biPlanes = 1
bi.bmiHeader.biBitCount = 4
bi.bmiHeader.biCompression = BI_RGB
' Now calculate the data buffer size needed
bufsize& = bi.bmiHeader.biWidth

' Figure out the number of bytes based on the
' number of pixels in each byte. In this case we
' really don't need all this code because this example
' always uses a 16 color DIB, but the code is shown
' here for your future reference
Select Case bi.bmiHeader.biBitCount
    Case 1
        bufsize& = (bufsize& + 7) / 8
    Case 4
        bufsize& = (bufsize& + 1) / 2
    Case 24
        bufsize& = bufsize& * 3
End Select
' And make sure it aligns on a long boundary
bufsize& = ((bufsize& + 3) / 4) * 4
' And multiply by the # of scan lines
bufsize& = bufsize& * bi.bmiHeader.biHeight

' Now allocate a buffer to hold the data
```

```
' We use the global memory pool because this buffer
' could easily be above 64k bytes.
ghnd% = GlobalAlloc(GMEM_MOVEABLE, bufsize&)
gptr& = GlobalLock&(ghnd%)

di% = GetDIBitsBynum%(dctemp%, picture1.picture, 0, ⇔
bm.bmHeight, gptr&, bi, DIB_RGBCOLORS)
di% = SetDIBitsToDeviceBynum(hdc%, 0, 0, bm.bmWidth, ⇔
bm.bmHeight, 0, 0, 0, bm.bmHeight, gptr&, bi, ⇔
DIB_RGB_COLORS)

' Now see if we can also print a scaled version
xpix% = GetDeviceCaps(hdc%, HORZRES)
' We subtract off the size of the bitmap already
' printed, plus some extra space
ypix% = GetDeviceCaps(hdc%, VERTRES) - (bm.bmHeight ⇔
+ 50)

' Find out the largest multiplier we can use and still
' fit on the page
doscale% = xpix% / bm.bmWidth
If (ypix% / bm.bmHeight < doscale%) Then doscale% = ⇔
ypix% / bm.bmHeight
If doscale% > 1 Then
    ux% = bm.bmWidth * doscale%
    uy% = bm.bmHeight * doscale%
    ' Show how this is offset a bit so that we don't
    ' print over the 1:1 scaled bitmap
    di% = StretchDIBitsBynum(hdc%, 0, bm.bmHeight + ⇔
    50, ux%, uy%, 0, 0, bm.bmWidth, bm.bmHeight, ⇔
    gptr&, bi, DIB_RGB_COLORS, SRCCOPY)
End If
' Dump the global memory block
di% = GlobalUnlock(ghnd%)
di% = GlobalFree(ghnd%)
di% = DeleteDC%(dctemp%)

End Sub


' Printing using the VB printer object
'
Sub CmdPrint_Click ()
    Dim oldcursor%
    oldcursor% = Screen.MousePointer
    Screen.MousePointer = 11
    PrintBitmap CInt(printer.hdc)
    printer.NewPage
    printer.EndDoc
    Screen.MousePointer = oldcursor%
End Sub
```

This function shows how an abort function can be defined when printing using the API functions. In this case, the abort function box is set to the system modal state to prevent input to other applications as well as this one during the printing operation. This is not necessary, but if you do not do this you should be careful to disable any forms in your application that could interfere with the print process or cause reentrancy problems.

```
' This function shows how you can use the API to obtain
'   a printer device context for printing.
'   Note how this function also switches to print in
'   landscape mode without changing the default printer
'   configuration.
'
Sub CmdPrintAPI_Click ()
    Dim dev$, devname$, devoutput$
    Dim dm As DEVMODE, dmout As DEVMODE
    Dim libhnd%
    Dim bufsize%
    Dim dminstring$, dmoutstring$
    Dim dminaddr&, dmoutaddr&
    Dim prhdc%
    Dim dinfo As DOCINFO
    Dim docname$
    Dim oldcursor%

    dev$ = GetDefPrinter$() ' Get default printer info
    If dev$ = "" Then Exit Sub
    devname$ = GetDeviceName$(dev$)
    devoutput$ = GetDeviceOutput$(dev$)

    ' Load the device driver library - exit if unavailable
    libhnd% = LoadLibrary(GetDeviceDriver$(dev$) + ".drv")
    If libhnd% = 0 Then GoTo cleanup2

    ' Get a copy of the DEVMODE structure for this printer
    ' First find out how big the DEVMODE structure is
    bufsize% = agExtDeviceMode%(hWnd, libhnd%, 0, devname$, devoutput$, ⇔
    agGetAddressForObject(dm), 0, 0)
    ' Allocate a buffer of that size and get a pointer to it
    dminstring$ = String$(bufsize%, 0)
    dminaddr& = agGetAddressForVBString&(dminstring$)
    dmoutstring$ = String$(bufsize%, 0)
    dmoutaddr& = agGetAddressForVBString&(dmoutstring$)

    ' Get the input DEVMODE structure
    di% = agExtDeviceMode(hWnd, libhnd%, dmoutaddr&, devname$, devoutput$, ⇔
    dminaddr&, 0, DM_OUT_BUFFER)

    ' Copy the data buffer into the DEVMODE structure
    agCopyDataBynum dmoutaddr&, agGetAddressForObject&(dm), 68
    ' Set the orientation, and set the dmField flag so that
```

```
' the function will know that it is valid.
dm.dmOrientation = DMORIENT_LANDSCAPE
dm.dmFields = dm.dmFields Or DM_ORIENTATION

' We now have a DC to the default printer
' This DC is also initialized to landscape mode
prhdc% = CreateDC%(GetDeviceDriver$(dev$) + ".drv", ⇔
devname$, devoutput$, agGetAddressForObject&(dm))
If prhdc% = 0 Then GoTo cleanup2

' The DOCINFO structure is the information that the
' print manager will show. This also gives you the
' opportunity of dumping output to a file.
docname$ = "Sample Document"
dinfo.cbSize = 10
dinfo.lpszDocName = agGetAddressForLPSTR&(docname$)
dinfo.lpszOutput = 0

' We set up the abort procedure here
AbortPrinting% = 0
di% = SetAbortProc(prhdc%, Callback1.ProcAddress)

' And show the abort form which will be system modal
AbortForm.Show
BringWindowToTop AbortForm.hWnd
AbortForm.Refresh
di% = SetSysModalWindow(AbortForm.hWnd)

' The usual print sequence here
di% = StartDoc(prhdc%, dinfo)
di% = StartPage(prhdc%)
PrintBitmap prhdc%

' The system will spend a long time in the EndPage
' function, but it will periodically call the Abort
' procedure which in turn triggers the Callback1
' AbortProc event.
di% = EndPage(prhdc%)
If di% >= 0 Then di% = EndDocAPI(prhdc%)

' You must unload it (not hide it) so that the
' system modal state will be released.
Unload AbortForm

cleanup2:
    If prhdc% <> 0 Then di% = DeleteDC%(prhdc%)
    If libhnd% <> 0 Then FreeLibrary libhnd%


End Sub
```

This event is triggered every time the abort function is called by Windows during page processing. The function calls the **DoEvents** function to allow system messages to be processed in the Abort dialog box (without it, a mouse click on the abort button would never be processed).

The following function looks at the **AbortPrinting** flag to determine if the user canceled the print operation. The **retval** parameter is set to 0 to terminate printing.

```
' This function is called during the EndPage API function
' to allow the user to abort printing
'
Sub Callback1_AbortProc (hPr As Integer, code As Integer, ⇔
retval As Integer)
    ' We must allow events to take place, otherwise the
    ' user button press on the abortform form will never
    ' be detected!
    di% = DoEvents()
    If code = SP_OUTOFDISK Or AbortPrinting% Then
        retval = 0
        Exit Sub
    End If
    retval = -1
End Sub
```

The **DeviceMode** API function, accessible through the **agDeviceMode** interface function in APIGUIDE.DLL, is extremely limited as compared to the **ExtDeviceMode** function. It brings up the printer setup dialog box for the specified printer, but all changes are made directly to the WIN.INI initialization file.

```
Sub MenuDevMode_Click ()
    Dim dev$, devname$, devoutput$
    Dim libhnd%

    dev$ = GetDefPrinter$() ' Get default printer info
    If dev$ = "" Then Exit Sub
    devname$ = GetDeviceName$(dev$)
    devoutput$ = GetDeviceOutput$(dev$)

    ' Load the device driver library - exit if unavailable
    libhnd% = LoadLibrary(GetDeviceDriver$(dev$) + ".drv")
    If libhnd% = 0 Then Exit Sub

    ' WARNING - this allows change of the default printer
    ' settings!
    di% = agDeviceMode(hWnd, libhnd%, devname$, devoutput$)

    FreeLibrary (libhnd%)

End Sub
```

Clicking on the abort button causes a global variable to be set to indicate to the abort function that printing should be aborted.

Listing 11.7   Form Listing ABORTFOR.FRM

```
Sub CmdAbort_Click ()
    AbortPrinting = -1
End Sub
```

Reference for APIGUIDE.DLL Functions

Windows defines three API functions that are used for printer configuration: **DeviceCapabilities**, **DeviceMode**, and **ExtDeviceMode**. Unlike most API functions, these functions are part of the individual printer driver—not part of the normal Windows environment. Each printer driver is required to implement at least the **DeviceMode** function, and most now implement the others.

Unfortunately, Visual Basic does not provide a general way to access functions in a printer driver directly. It is possible to use a separate **Declare** statement for each printer driver, but this approach is inflexible and consumes a great deal of code.

In order to provide access to these three functions, the APIGUIDE.DLL dynamic link library provided with this book includes interface functions that allow access to these three API functions.

Most of the functions in APIGUIDE.DLL are documented in Appendix A, but these three are so closely tied to printing that they are described here instead.

■ agDeviceCapabilities

VB Declaration

```
Declare Function agDeviceCapabilities& Lib "Apiguide.dll" (ByVal hlib%, ⇔
ByVal lpszDevice$, ByVal lpszPort$, ByVal fwCapability%, ByVal lpszOutput&, ⇔
ByVal lpdm&)
```

Description This function allows you to obtain information about the capabilities of a device.

Use with VB No problem.

Parameter	Type/Description
hlib	**Integer**—The module handle of the loaded device driver. Refer to the description of the **LoadLibrary** API function in Chapter 12 for further information.
lpszDevice	**String**—The device name. Refer to "Drivers, Devices, and Ports" earlier in this chapter.
lpszPort	**String**—The destination for device output. Refer to "Drivers, Devices, and Ports" earlier in this chapter.
fwCapability	**Integer**—The capability to test. Refer to Table 11.4 for a list of possible values.

Parameter	Type/Description
lpszOutput&	**Long**—A pointer to a buffer to load with the capabilities data. The contents of this buffer for each value of **fwCapability** is described in Table 11.4. The table also describes those cases when this parameter should be set to zero.
lpdm	**Long**—The address of a **DEVMODE** structure or zero. If present, this function will retrieve information based on the settings of this structure. If zero, this function will retrieve information based on the default values for the printer driver.

Return Value   **Long**—Depends on the value of the **fwCapabilities** parameter. Refer to Table 11.4 for details. The function will return -1 if the function fails or if the printer driver does not support this function.

Table 11.4   Device Capabilities Constants

fwCapabilities	Description
DC_BINNAMES	If **lpszOutput** is zero, return the number of bins supported by the printer. Otherwise, **lpszOutput** should point to a buffer of at least (24* # of bins) bytes. Each 24 bytes will be loaded with the null terminated name of a paper bin.
DC_BINS	If **lpszOutput** is zero, return the number of bins supported by the printer. Otherwise, **lpszOutput** is a pointer to an integer array of at least (# of bins) entries. The values correspond to the **DMBIN_???** constants defined for the **DEVMODE** structure.
DC_COPIES	Returns the maximum number of copies the printer can print.
DC_DRIVER	Returns the version number of the printer driver.
DC_DUPLEX	Returns 1 if the printer can print on both sides of a page at once, zero otherwise.
DC_ENUMRESOLUTIONS	If **lpszOutput** is zero, returns the number of printer resolutions supported by the printer. Otherwise, **lpszOutput** is a pointer to a **Long** array of at least (2 * # of resolutions) entries. Each pair of entries reflects a horizontal and vertical resolution in dots per inch.
DC_EXTRA	Returns the number of device-specific bytes appended to the **DEVMODE** structure for this device.
DC_FIELDS	Returns the value of the **dmFields** field for the device's default **DEVMODE** data structure.
DC_FILEDEPENDENCIES	If **lpszOutput** is zero, returns the number of files required by the printer driver. Otherwise, **lpszOutput** should point to a buffer of at least (64* # of files) bytes. Each 64 bytes will be loaded with the null terminated name of a required file.

Table 11.4   Device Capabilities Constants (Continued)

fwCapabilities	Description
DC_MAXEXTENT	Returns **Long** value containing the maximum length and width of paper supported by the printer. The low word contains the width value. These are the maximum values of the **dmPaperWidth** and **dmPaperLength DEVMODE** fields.
DC_MINEXTENT	Returns **Long** value containing the minimum length and width of paper supported by the printer. The low word contains the width value. These are the minimum values of the **dmPaperWidth** and **dmPaperLength DEVMODE** fields.
DC_ORIENTATION	Returns the rotation in degrees between landscape mode and portrait mode. Zero indicates that the driver does not support landscape mode. 90 is common for laser printers, 270 for dot matrix printers.
DC_PAPERNAMES	If **lpszOutput** is zero, returns the number of paper sizes supported by the printer driver. Otherwise, **lpszOutput** should point to a buffer of at least (64* # of paper sizes) bytes. Each 64 bytes will be loaded with the null terminated name of a supported paper size.
DC_PAPERS	If **lpszOutput** is zero, returns the number of paper sizes supported by the printer. Otherwise, **lpszOutput** is a pointer to an integer array of at least (# of paper sizes) entries. The values correspond to the **DMPAPER_???** constants defined for the **DEVMODE** structure.
DC_PAPERSIZE	**lpszOutput** is a pointer to an array of POINTAPI structures which are loaded with the dimensions of supported paper sizes in tenths of a millimeter. Sizes are always returned for portrait mode regardless of the current printer configuration.
DC_SIZE	Returns the total size of the printer **DEVMODE** data structure.
DC_TRUETYPE	One of the following constants: **DCTT_BITMAP**: Device can print TrueType fonts as graphics. **DCTT_DOWNLOAD**: Device can download TrueType fonts. **DCTT_SUBDEV**: Device can substitute built-in fonts that are compatible with corresponding TrueType fonts.
DC_VERSION	Returns the version of the specification for the device driver.

Note on use of **lpszOutput**: In many cases this function returns a list of names; for example, when the **fwCapabilities** flag is **DC_PAPERNAMES** a list of names of supported paper sizes is obtained. In these cases the **lpszOutput** buffer should be a string variable preallocated to the length specified in Table 11.4. The function will load the buffer with all of the names, with each name taking the specified fixed space in the string. It is then possible to extract each entry using the **Mid$** function. The PicPrint sample program shows how this is done for paper names, but the technique is identical for other capabilities.

In some cases **lpszOutput** needs to point to a numeric array. This address may be obtained by using the **agGetAddressForInteger** or **agGetAddressForLong** API function using the first entry in a numeric array as the object parameter.

■ agDeviceMode

VB Declaration

```
Declare Function agDeviceMode% Lib "Apiguide.dll" (ByVal hWnd%, ByVal ⇔
hModule%, ByVal lpszDevice$, ByVal lpszOutput$)
```

Description

This function accesses the printer setup dialog box in the print driver. Any changes made to the printer configuration will affect the default settings for the printer.

Use with VB

No problem.

Parameter	Type/Description
hWnd	**Integer**—A handle to the parent window for the dialog box. This will typically be the current active form.
hModule	**Integer**—The module handle of the loaded device driver. Refer to the description of the **LoadLibrary** API function in Chapter 12 for further information.
lpszDevice	**String**—The device name. Refer to "Drivers, Devices, and Ports," earlier in this chapter.
lpszOutput	**String**—The destination for device output. Refer to "Drivers, Devices, and Ports," earlier in this chapter.

Return Value

Integer—If the function cannot be accessed, –1, zero otherwise.

■ agExtDeviceMode

VB Declaration

```
Declare Function agExtDeviceMode% Lib "Apiguide.dll" (ByVal hWnd%, ByVal ⇔
hDriver%, ByVal lpdmOutput&, ByVal lpszDevice$, ByVal lpszPort$, ByVal ⇔
lpdmInput&, ByVal lpszProfile&, ByVal fwMode%)
```

Description

This is a flexible printer configuration control function that replaced the **DeviceMode** function in version 2.0 of Windows. It defines two **DEVMODE** data structures: one for input and one for output. The **fwMode** field determines how these data structures are used.

This function allows you to bring up the printer settings dialog box to change the settings in these data structures. The **DEVMODE** structure can then be used during the creation of a device context to change the printer setting for a single application, or even to change printer settings during the course of printing a document.

Use with VB

This function may be used with the Visual Basic printer object to change some settings while printing (for example, to switch between portrait and landscape mode).

Refer to "Printer Settings and the DEVMODE Structure," earlier in this chaper, for important information on using the **DEVMODE** structure with Visual Basic.

Parameter	Type/Description
hWnd	**Integer**—A handle to the parent window for the dialog box. This will typically be the current active form.
hDriver	**Integer**—The module handle of the loaded device driver. Refer to the description of the **LoadLibrary** API function in Chapter 12 for further information.

Parameter	Type/Description
lpdmOutput	**Long**—Pointer to a **DEVMODE** data structure for the device. Refer to Table 11.5 for further information. Note that this pointer must refer to a buffer that is large enough to include the private printer driver data as well as the standard **DEVMODE** structure.
lpszDevice	**String**—The device name. Refer to "Drivers, Devices, and Ports," earlier in this chapter.
lpszPort	**String**—The destination for device output. Refer to "Drivers, Devices, and Ports," earlier in this chapter.
lpdmInput	**Long**—Pointer to a **DEVMODE** data structure for the device. Refer to Table 11.5 for further information.
lpszProfile	**Long**—When zero, all access to and from the initialization file goes to WIN.INI. Otherwise, this may be a pointer to a null terminated string that specifies the name of the private initialization file to use for printer settings. This allows you to save printer settings for your application in a private profile file.
fwMode	**Integer**—Mode flags that determine the operation of this function as shown in Table 11.5.

Return Value   **Integer**—Depends on the value of the **fwMode** field as follows:

If **fwMode** is zero, this function returns the size of the **DEVMODE** structure for this device. Note that this structure may be larger than the size specified in the type definition file API-TYPES.TXT.

If **fwMode** has the **DM_IN_PROMPT** constant flag set, the printer settings dialog box will appear. In this case, the return value will be the constant **IDOK** or **IDCANCEL** depending on which button the user presses to close the dialog box.

In all other cases, this function returns **IDOK** on success. For all cases, this function returns a negative value on error.

Comments   The buffers pointed to by the **lpdmInput** and **lpdmOutput** parameters must be the size required by the printer driver. This may be obtained by calling this function with the **fwMode** parameter set to zero.

The best way to handle this is to determine the necessary buffer size and then initialize a string to that size using the Visual Basic **String$** function. The **agCopyData** or API **hmemcpy** function may be used to copy the first 68 bytes of the buffer to and from a **DEVMODE** structure so that it may be easily modified by the program.

Table 11.5 describes the four flag constants that control operation of this function. These constants may be combined together using the OR operator.

Table 11.5 **ExtDeviceMode Operating Modes**

Constant Flag	Operation
None	**lpdmInput** is not used; **lpdmOutput** may be zero. The function returns the required size of the **DEVMODE** structures referenced by these two parameters.
DM_IN_BUFFER	The **DEVMODE** structure referenced by the **lpdmInput** buffer will be used to set the printer driver. Only those fields that are specified by the **dmFields** field of the structure will be used. The settings specified by the **lpdmInput** buffer when this flag is set will effect the printer driver or the **lpdmOutput** buffer depending on the settings of the other flags. For example: Setting the **DM_IN_BUFFER** and **DM_OUT_DEFAULT** flags lets you use the **lpdmInput** buffer to set the configuration of the default printer.
DM_IN_PROMPT	The printer setup dialog box is displayed allowing the user to specify printer settings for output.
DM_OUT_BUFFER	Causes the printer settings to be output to the buffer referred to by the **lpdmOutput** parameter. These settings will be determined by the two input flags and may thus reflect the original input structure, the current printer settings, and any user modifications entered through the printer setup dialog box. If this flag is not specified, the **lpdmOutput** parameter may be set to zero.
DM_OUT_DEFAULT	Causes the printer settings to be output to a Windows initialization file. If the **lpszProfile** parameter is zero, the printer settings in the WIN.INI file will be set. Otherwise, the function will write the settings to the specified private initialization file.

Reference for API Functions

This section contains an alphabetical reference for the functions described in this chapter.

■ AbortDoc

VB Declaration   Declare Function AbortDoc% Lib "GDI" (ByVal hDC%)

Description   Aborts printing of a document. All output since the last call to the **StartDoc** function is canceled. If the print manager is in use, no part of the document will print; otherwise it is possible that part of the document will already have been printed.

Use with VB   If you use this function with the printer device context referred to by the **hDC** property of the printer object, it will work. You may, however, receive a printer error if you call the **EndDoc** method afterward.

It is strongly recommended that you trap printer errors when combining API printer functions with VB printer methods.

Parameter	Type/Description
hDC	**Integer**—Handle to a device context

Return Value   **Integer**—TRUE (nonzero) on success, zero otherwise.

■ EndDocAPI

VB Declaration   `Declare Function EndDocAPI% Lib "GDI" Alias "EndDoc" (ByVal hDC%)`

Description   This function is used to end a successful print job. If the print spooler is in use, this will cause the print job to begin printing.

Use with VB   When using the Visual Basic printer object, you should use the **EndDoc** method instead of this function.

Parameter	Type/Description
hDC	**Integer**—Handle to a device context.

Return Value   **Integer**—TRUE (nonzero) on success, zero otherwise.

■ EndPage

VB Declaration   `Declare Function EndPage% Lib "GDI" (ByVal hDC%)`

Description   This function is used to complete printing on a page and prepare the device context for printing on the next page.

Use with VB   When using the Visual Basic Printer object, you should use the **NewPage** method instead of this function.

Parameter	Type/Description
hDC	**Integer**—Handle to a device context.

Return Value   **Integer**—Value >= zero on success. One of the negative constants specified in Table 11.6 on error. These constants are defined in file APICONST.TXT.

Table 11.6   Printer Error Values

Constant Value	Description
SP_ERROR	General printer error.
SP_APPABORT	The printing was aborted using the application's abort procedure.

Table 11.6 **Printer Error Values (Continued)**

Constant Value	Description
SP_USERABORT	The printing was aborted by the user via the print manager application (PRINTMAN.EXE).
SP_OUTOFDISK	There is insufficient disk space for this print job. When using the spooler, the entire print job is saved on disk before printing begins.
SP_OUTOFMEMORY	There is insufficient memory for printing.

Comments   This function may take a very long time to execute, depending on the complexity of the drawing that is taking place. In order to allow the user to abort the printing operation, this function calls the abort procedure specified by the **SetAbortProc** API call periodically during its operation.

■ Escape

See "Printer Escapes" earlier in this chapter.

■ ResetDC

VB Declaration   `Declare Function ResetDC% Lib "GDI" (ByVal hDC%, lpdm As DEVMODE)`

Description   This function resets a device context according to the **DEVMODE** structure provided. This allows you to change the configuration of the printer during printing. For example, you can change a single page in a document to landscape mode using this function. You may use the **agExtDevice-Mode** function to obtain the default **DEVMODE** structure for a device.

Use with VB   Experimentation indicates that this function can be used successfully on the device context returned by the **hDC** property of the Visual Basic Printer object.

Parameter	Type/Description
hDC	**Integer**—A handle to a device context.
lpdm	**DEVMODE**—A **DEVMODE** structure containing the new settings to use for this device context.

Return Value   **Integer**—hDC on success, zero on error.

Comments   Be sure to set the **dmFields** field of **lpdm** correctly. Refer to "Printer Settings and the DEVMODE Structure," earlier in this chapter.

■ SetAbortProc

VB Declaration   `Declare Function SetAbortProc% Lib "GDI" (ByVal hDC%, ByVal abrtprc&)`

Description   It is possible to provide Windows with a function to call during extended print operations. This function is known as an abort function. The result of the abort function informs Windows whether it should continue the print operation or abort it.

The **SetAbortProc** function specifies the address of the abort function to Windows. Since Visual Basic does not support function addresses, it is necessary to use the **CBK.VBX** generic callback custom control provided with this book in order to use this function.

Use with VB   Use of this function with the Visual Basic printer object may interfere with the normal VB print mechanism. It has been demonstrated to work, but will lead to printer errors which must be trapped on the next occurrence of the **Printer.NewPage** method. It is recommended that you thoroughly test code that attempts to install an abort function for the Visual Basic Printer object.

There are no problems using this function when you print to a device context that you create.

Parameter	Type/Description
hDC	**Integer**—A handle to a device context.
abrtprt	**Long**—The address of an abort function. This can be obtained from the **ProcAddress** property of the CBK.VBX custom control.

Return Value   **Integer**—TRUE (nonzero) on success, zero otherwise.

Comments   Refer to Appendix A for details on using the CBK.VBX custom control.

■ StartDoc

VB Declaration   `Declare Function StartDoc% Lib "GDI" (ByVal hDC%, lpdi As DOCINFO)`

Description   This function begins a print job.

Use with VB   When using the Visual Basic Printer object, do not use this function.

Parameter	Type/Description
hDC	**Integer**—Handle to a device context.
lpdi	**DOCINFO**—A structure defining a document. A description of this structure follows.

Return Value   **Integer**—Value >= zero on success, the constant **SP_ERROR** on error.

Comments   The **DOCINFO** structure is defined as follows:

```
Type DOCINFO    ' 10 Bytes
    cbSize As Integer
    lpszDocName As Long
    lpszOutput As Long
End Type
```

The structure fields are defined as follows:

Field	Type/Description
cbSize	**Integer**—The size of the structure, currently ten bytes.
lpszDocName	**Long**—Pointer to a string containing the name of the document. This document name will be shown by the print manager application.
lpszOutput	**Long**—Pointer to a string containing the name of an output file if you wish to redirect printer output to a disk file. Set to zero to send the output to the device.

The **agGetAddressForLPSTR** function may be used to obtain a pointer for a string. Refer to Appendix A for details.

■ StartPage

VB Declaration `Declare Function StartPage% Lib "GDI" (ByVal hDC%)`

Description This function is called before printing into a new page. Use with VB. When using the Visual Basic printer object, do not use this function.

Parameter	Type/Description
hDC	**Integer**—Handle to a device context.

Return Value **Integer**—Value > = zero on success, negative on error.

12

Memory, Task, and Resource Management

Global Memory

Resources

Task and Module Functions

Function Reference

THIS CHAPTER COVERS THE IMPORTANT SUBJECTS OF MEMORY, DATA, and the ownership of memory and data objects under Windows. Ownership in this case addresses the fact that in a multitasking system such as Windows, which has many programs running at the same time, there must be a method to associate different data objects with particular programs.

First, the issue of memory buffers and Windows global memory will be addressed. Small code fragments that illustrate how global memory can be used with Visual Basic are presented. The techniques shown are especially useful for allocating and using buffers that are greater than 64k in size.

Next, the concept of resources will be introduced. Although many resource functions for particular Windows objects have already been demonstrated, this chapter will explain more thoroughly why resources exist and how they may be used.

Finally, the Windows module and task management system will be described, accompanied by a sample application called EXECDEMO, which shows how to launch a shell program and wait for it to complete before continuing to execute the original application.

Global Memory

Many of the Windows API functions require the use of memory buffers. These blocks of memory may vary from short buffers for strings to extremely large buffers for device-independent bitmaps.

Using Visual Basic Strings as Buffers

Most of the examples in this book use Visual Basic strings to provide temporary buffers. This is by far the easiest way to obtain a temporary memory buffer in Visual Basic due to their ease of allocation. A string buffer of a specified length can be created in two ways. First, by creating a fixed length string using

```
Dim FixedSample As String * N
```

where N is the length of the string. Second, by using the Visual Basic **String$** function on a variable-length string variable as follows:

```
Dim VarSample As String
VarSample = String$(N,0)
```

where N is the number of bytes in the string.

The API functions that require pointers to buffers expect 32-bit address parameters. The address of a string can be obtained in two ways. The easiest is to use the **agGetAddressForLPSTR** or **agGetAddressForVBString** functions provided in the APIGUIDE.DLL dynamic link library. These functions are described in detail in Appendix A.

It is also possible to use the **AnsiNext** API function, described in Chapter 16, as follows:

```
Address32bit& = AnsiNext(vbstring$) - 1
```

However, this solution will not work successfully on character sets that use more than one byte per character (such as Japanese character sets).

You should be aware of two problems that may result from using VB strings as buffers. The first is that Visual Basic strings can move in memory. Consider this code fragment:

```
Dim tbuf$
Dim otherstring$
Dim StringAddress&, StringAddress2&
tbuf$ = String$(128,0)      ' Allocate a 128 character buffer
StringAddress& = agGetAddressForVBString(tbuf$)
' Perform other string operations such as this one
otherstring$ = String$(512,0)
' The location of tbuf$ in memory may have changed due
' to the use of other string operations. Thus you may
' not call a Windows API function using StringAddress&
' as a parameter.
'
StringAddress2& = agGetAddressForVBString(tbuf$)
' StringAddress2& may not be equal to StringAddress1&
```

Because string operations can cause strings to move in memory, it is necessary to obtain the string address before each use of the string buffer by an API call. This is not a particularly serious problem as the address calculation function is very fast and easy to use, but it is a factor that a programmer must be aware of.

The other more serious problem with using Visual Basic strings as buffers is that VB strings are limited to somewhat less than 64k bytes in length. In many cases you may wish to use objects such as device-independent bitmaps that are larger than 64k in size, or to create huge buffers for text.

The Windows API provides all of the tools you need to allocate buffers that are greater than 64k in size and to avoid buffer movement problems by locking blocks of memory in place for as long as necessary. It also provides the ability to create discardable memory buffers that Windows can discard automatically when it runs short on memory. These are useful for blocks of data that do not need to be modified and that you would like to hold in memory in order to improve performance, but could re-create or reload from disk if necessary.

The Windows Global Memory Heap

All of the free memory that is available to Windows applications is kept in a pool of memory called the *global memory heap*. A heap is a way of organizing memory so that arbitrarily sized blocks can be allocated as needed. When a block is no longer needed it can be freed and reclaimed by the heap to be allocated later.

Memory in this case does not refer just to physical memory, but also to Windows virtual memory. Refer to your Microsoft Windows users guide for an in-depth discussion of virtual memory and the types of memory available under Windows.

The main point to remember here is that the amount of memory available in the global heap is frequently larger than the amount of physical RAM installed in your system.

Global Memory Handles

Global memory blocks are Windows objects, and as such they have handles associated with them. You obtain a handle to a memory block using the **GlobalAlloc** API function. This function provides you with a number of options that specify the type of memory block. The complete list of memory block types is included in the function reference for the **GlobalAlloc** function; however, only a few are of use to the Visual Basic programmer:

- *Fixed memory blocks*. These memory blocks are fixed in memory. This means that once you obtain an address pointer to allocated memory, it is guaranteed not to change.

- *Moveable memory blocks*. These memory blocks are allowed to move in memory as long as they are not explicitly locked. This is the preferred type of memory block to use, as it provides Windows with the most flexibility in terms of managing memory in all memory modes.

- *Discardable memory blocks*. These memory blocks may be discarded if Windows needs additional memory. A mechanism exists by which an application can determine if the memory block has been discarded. This kind of memory block is commonly used for resources and other data that is not changed by the application.

Other types of global memory blocks are used for dynamic data exchange or sharing of memory blocks between applications. There are a number of techniques that are available for using global memory to share data among applications, but the advent of dynamic data exchange and OLE (object linking and embedding) makes these largely unnecessary. In all cases this chapter presents the correct and legal way to work with global memory and avoids techniques that may not be compatible with future versions of Windows.

Global Memory Pointers

Once you have allocated a global memory block, you can use the **GlobalLock** function to obtain the 32-bit address of the memory block. This function also locks moveable memory blocks in memory so that the returned address is guaranteed to remain valid until the memory block is explicitly unlocked using the **GlobalUnlock** function. Each memory block has a lock count. **GlobalLock** increments the lock count and **GlobalUnlock** decrements it. You should be careful to match every **GlobalLock** function with a **GlobalUnlock** function. Attempting to free a locked memory object can cause an unrecoverable application error under Windows 3.0.

The sequence of operations for using global memory blocks is as follows:

1. Allocate the global memory block using the **GlobalAlloc** function.

2. Obtain an address for the global memory block using the **GlobalLock** function.

3. Use the memory as desired.

4. Unlock the memory block using the **GlobalUnlock** function.

5. Repeat steps 2-4 as needed. The **GlobalReAlloc** function may be used to change the size of the global memory block.

6. Use the **GlobalFree** function to free the global memory block when it is no longer needed.

Global memory blocks allocated in the manner described here belong to the calling application. This means that they will be automatically freed when the application terminates. Nevertheless, it is good programming practice to explicitly free any memory blocks that your program uses. Table 12.1 lists the most commonly used global memory API functions.

Table 12.1   Global Memory API Functions

Function	Description
GlobalAlloc	Allocates a global memory block.
GlobalFlags	Determines the type and state of a global memory block.
GlobalFree	Frees a global memory block.
GlobalLock	Locks a global memory block in memory and retrieves a 32-bit address pointer to the locked memory.
GlobalReAlloc	Changes the size of a global memory block.

Table 12.1	**Global Memory API Functions (Continued)**
GlobalSize	Determines the size of a global memory block.
GlobalUnlock	Unlocks a global memory block.

Controlling the Global Memory Heap

The Windows global heap is not only used by applications, but also by dynamic link libraries and device drivers. As a result, the Windows API contains many functions to control the operation of the global heap that relate to virtual memory, shared memory blocks for dynamic data exchange, private local heaps, and so on, and are not generally applicable to the Visual Basic programmer. These functions are listed in Table 12.2 and described briefly in the function reference section.

Table 12.2	**Global Heap Control Functions**	
	Function	**Description**
	GlobalCompact	Compacts the global heap.
	GlobalFix	Prevents a global block from moving in memory.
	GlobalHandle	Retrieves a global handle for a given selector.
	GlobalLRUNewest	Reduces the likelihood of a global memory block being discarded.
	GlobalLRUOldest	Increases the likelihood of a global memory block being discarded.
	GlobalUnfix	Cancels a **GlobalFix** operation.

Using Global Memory Blocks from Visual Basic

Using global memory from Visual Basic requires a good understanding of the use of 32-bit addresses, especially for accessing huge memory blocks (those that are greater than 64k in size).

Accessing Small Memory Blocks

Copying data to and from small memory blocks—those that are under 64k— is easy. The **agCopyData** and **agCopyDataBynum** API functions provided in the APIGUIDE.DLL dynamic link library can be used to copy one block of memory to another given 32-bit **Long** parameters containing the addresses of the memory blocks. The address of the global memory block can be obtained using the **GlobalLock** function. The address of any Visual Basic string, variable, or data structure can be obtained using functions in the APIGUIDE-.DLL library.

Listing 12.1 demonstrates access to global memory blocks that are below 64k in size. In this case, the global memory block is being used to hold a copy of a **TEXTMETRIC** data structure. The **GlobalAlloc** function is used to allocate the global memory buffer. It returns a 16-bit integer handle to the memory buffer, which is stored in a global variable **Glblhnd%**. Note how the result of this function is always checked to make sure that an error did not occur.

Listing 12.1   Accessing Small Memory Blocks

```
Sub Under64KAlloc ()
Dim temptm As TEXTMETRIC
Dim Glbladdr&

' The TEXTMETRIC structure is 31 bytes
Glblhnd% = GlobalAlloc(GMEM_ZEROINIT Or GMEM_MOVEABLE, 31&)

If Glblhnd% = 0 Then
    ' Perform appropriate error handling here. Do not
    ' continue to the next line!
End If

Glbladdr& = GlobalLock(Glblhnd%)

agCopyDataBynum agGetAddressForObject(temptm), Glbladdr&, 31&

' Now you can perform any operations on the text metric
' structure When done, copy the data back.

agCopyDataBynum Glbladdr&, agGetAddressForObject(temptm), 31&

di% = GlobalUnlock(Glblhnd%)

'The memory block is still available.

End Sub
```

Listing 12.2 shows how a function can later access the global variable **Glblhnd%** to access the block of global memory. It is good practice to check the result after locking the memory with **GlobalLock**. In this example, the function should always return a valid address. If it returns zero, you can assume a serious error has occurred and terminate the application as quickly as possible. In practice this should never happen.

However, if the memory block had been defined as discardable by specifying the **GMEM_DISCARDABLE** flag to the **GlobalAlloc** function, a return value of zero for the **GlobalLock** function would indicate to the program that the memory block has been discarded by Windows. In this case the global handle remains valid. You have two choices as to how to proceed. You could just free the handle using the **GlobalFree** function and reallocate a new buffer. Or, you could use the **GlobalReAlloc** function to reallocate the global memory block.

Listing 12.2   **Accessing Glblhnd%**

```
Sub Under64KFree ()
Dim temptm As TEXTMETRIC
Dim Glbladdr&

' The TEXTMETRIC structure is 31 bytes

If Glblhnd% = 0 Then
    ' The buffer does not exist, don't continue
    ' Do appropriate error handling.
    Exit Sub
End If


Glbladdr& = GlobalLock(Glblhnd%)


If Glbladdr& = 0 Then
    'This should only occur on either a major error, or
    ' if the memory block was discardable and has been
    ' discarded
End If


agCopyDataBynum agGetAddressForObject(temptm), Glbladdr&,31&

' Now you can perform any operations on the text metric

di% = GlobalUnlock(Glblhnd%)
' Now free the memory block
' This also clears the Glblhnd% variable
Glblhnd% = GlobalFree(Glblhnd%)


End Sub
```

The last line in the function shows how you can free the memory block when it is no longer needed. Note how the **GlblHnd%** variable is set back to zero (which is the result after a successful **GlobalFree** operation). This is important in order to prevent other functions from trying to access a freed memory block.

Note also how each **GlobalLock** function is balanced with a matching **GlobalUnlock** operation.

Structure of Huge Memory

A memory block that is greater than 64k in size is referred to as a huge memory block. While the general approach described for small memory buffers is the same for blocks of memory greater than 64k in size, there are several crucial differences. In order to understand why these exist, it is necessary to learn a bit about how memory is structured and addressed under Windows.

Even though Windows can now run on 32-bit microprocessors such as the 80386 and 80486 processors, it is still a 16-bit operating environment. A 16-bit integer can reference up to 64k of memory, so the system memory is divided into segments of up to 64k each. This means that each 32-bit address is actually divided into two parts. The high 16 bits are the segment and the low 16 bits are the offset into the segment.

If you are familiar with programming under DOS, you may be accustomed to performing address calculations manually, based on the assumption that each number in the segment represents a 16-byte paragraph. Thus you might use &H0010:0000 to access memory at location &H0000:0100. You might also be accustomed to calculating offsets in blocks of memory greater in size than 64k by adding the appropriate values to the segment and offset parts of the address. But remember this rule: *Under Windows you must never perform manual address operations that affect the segment value.*

Windows runs in the protected mode. This means that the high order 16 bits of the address are actually a selector that identifies a segment in memory. This selector uses an internal memory mapping table to determine where in virtual memory the segment actually lies. You must never perform a calculation on a selector or change it directly.

Under Windows, any calculations within a 64k buffer can be performed directly. For example, to access the 16,823th byte in a buffer, you can simply add 16,823 to the **Long** variable containing the address. Global memory buffers always start at offset zero, so you need not worry about errors unless you exceed the length of the buffer as created with the **GlobalAlloc** buffer.

The situation is different for buffers greater than 64k. Consider the case of accessing the 78,959th byte in a huge memory buffer. If Windows used a flat memory scheme you could simply add 78,959 to the long address variable, as shown in the flat memory model illustration in Figure 12.1. However, Windows actually uses a tiled segmented memory model to allocate huge memory blocks that are greater than 64k in size, as shown in the segmented memory model illustration in Figure 12.1.

Figure 12.1	Flat Memory Model			Segmented Memory Model		
Structure of memory blocks greater than 64k	Hex	Decimal		Hex	Decimal	
	10FD:0000	85016064	64k	10FD:0000	85016064	64k
	10FD:FFFF	85081599		10FD:FFFF	85081599	
	10FE:0000	85081600	64k	1101:0000	85278208	64k
	10FE:FFFF	85147135		1101:FFFF	85343743	
	10FF:0000	85147136	64k	1105:0000	85540352	64k
	10FF:FFFF	85212671		1105:FFFF	85605887	
	1100:0000	85212672	64k	1109:0000	85802496	64k
	1100:FFFF	85278207		1109:FFFF	85868031	
	1101:0000	85278208	64k	110D:0000	86064640	64k
	1101:FFFF	85343743		110D:FFFF	86130175	
			WRONG			RIGHT

Figure 12.1 shows the start and end addresses of individual 64k memory blocks in a flat memory model system and in the Windows segmented memory model. The addresses are shown first in hexadecimal and then in decimal to show how the selector number changes along with the decimal number. It is clear from this that under a segmented model, simply adding an offset beyond a 64k boundary is certain to cause you to access an invalid or incorrect memory location.

In order to calculate memory positions in a huge memory block, you must use the **agHugeOffset** function contained in APIGUIDE.DLL and described in Appendix A. This function takes a buffer address and an offset and returns the correct 32-bit address for the desired location.

Accessing Huge Memory Blocks

In order to copy data to and from huge memory buffers, the function performing the transfer must know how to do the correct memory calculation for huge memory blocks. The Windows API includes the function **hmemcpy**, which performs this task. This function can, of course, also be used for buffers that are smaller than 64k in size. The Windows API also includes functions **hread** and **hwrite** that can read and write huge buffers to and from disk. Those functions are described in Chapter 13.

Listing 12.3 illustrates one application of huge global memory heaps. In this case the program is using a huge memory buffer to hold up to 1,000 fixed strings of 256 bytes each. This code shows how the buffer is allocated and how you can use the **agHugeOffset** function to calculate the address offset of any string in the buffer. The **hmemcpy** function is used to copy data to and from the buffer.

Listing 12.3   A Huge Global Memory Array

```
Sub Over64KArray ()
Dim GlblAddr&, GlblAddr2&
Dim tstring As String * 256

Glblhnd% = GlobalAlloc(GMEM_ZEROINIT Or GMEM_MOVEABLE, CLng(1000 * 256))

If Glblhnd% = 0 Then
    ' Perform appropriate error handling here. Do not
    ' continue to the next line!
End If

GlblAddr& = GlobalLock(Glblhnd%)

' Here's how you retrieve one of the 256 byte strings
' from the huge memory block -
' In this case, the 500th entry

GlblAddr2& = agHugeOffset(GlblAddr&, CLng(500 * 256))

' Now extract the string
hmemcpyBynum agGetAddressForLPSTR(tstring), GlblAddr2&, 256

di% = GlobalUnlock(Glblhnd%)

'The memory block is still available.

End Sub
```

This approach is even more powerful when you consider that the size of this huge memory block may be changed using the **GlobalReAlloc** function as needed. Thus it is very easy to implement a huge array whose length can be changed under program control.

In order to help prevent errors in accessing memory, Windows provides a number of functions to test and access memory addresses. These functions are shown in Table 12.3.

Table 12.3   Memory Access Functions

Function	Description
hmemcpy	Copies a huge memory block.
IsBadHugeReadPtr	Determines if a block of huge memory is valid and readable.

Table 12.3	**Memory Access Functions (Continued)**	
	Function	**Description**
	IsBadHugeWritePtr	Determines if a block of huge memory is valid and writable.
	IsBadReadPtr	Determines if a block of memory is valid and readable.
	IsBadStringPtr	Determines if a block of memory is valid, can be read and written, and is a null terminated string.
	IsBadWritePtr	Determines if a block of memory is valid and writable.

Windows 3.1 provides additional functions for analyzing the global memory heap. However, these are not normally used in the course of programming and are unlikely to be of use to the Visual Basic programmer, and thus are not covered in this book.

Resources

Resources provide a mechanism for including various objects and data in an executable file. Unfortunately, many of the features built into Windows for handling resources are not compatible with Visual Basic. In order to understand both the features and limitations of the resource mechanism, it is first necessary to understand what resources are and how they work with regular Windows applications.

Resources and Windows Applications

Some of the objects that are used under Windows can have a great deal of data associated with them. Consider, for example, the case of a font.

A font has associated with it all the data in the **TEXTMETRIC** structure introduced in Chapter 10. It also contains all the information needed to actually draw each character, and the spacing information needed to draw a text string. This can easily total thousands of bytes of data.

Icons are another example of an object that requires a fair amount of data. On a 16-color VGA monitor, the typical 32×32 pixel icon requires 512 bytes for one device-independent bitmap, an additional 128 bytes for the monochrome mask, and additional space for the icon header information.

Other objects that can take large amounts of data are bitmaps, strings, and cursors.

In many cases, it is desirable to include one or more of these objects in an executable file. This poses an interesting problem. In C or Pascal it is possible to hard code the data—to create static data structures that have the binary data defined. But this approach is tricky. First, it can be excruciatingly difficult to program. Imagine writing out the pattern for a bitmap in hexadecimal! Second, this approach makes it extremely difficult to change the object, a problem if you need to support several languages in your program for use in foreign countries.

Windows solves this problem through a mechanism called Windows resources. A resource is a block of data that represents a Windows object such as a cursor, icon, bitmap, font, or string. Each Windows executable file contains a resource table that lists the resources in the file. The Windows API contains functions that allow you to load these resources.

Each resource is created using an appropriate tool. Icons, bitmaps, and cursors are created with specialized image drawing programs. The Iconwrks program provided with Visual Basic is an example of an icon editor. Strings are created using a text editor. Fonts are created using special font editing programs.

Once the data for each object is created, a special tool known as a resource compiler combines the objects into a single resource file. The resource editor can then be used to insert the resource file into an executable file. Figure 12.2 illustrates the sequence of operations needed to add resources to an executable file.

The resource compiler makes use of a special resource definition file that lists the resources to include. It can also be used to define dialog boxes, menus, and even user-defined resources.

You might consider the entire concept of resources to be an incredibly powerful and flexible equivalent to the BASIC "Data" statement, except that you can save not only strings, but virtually any type of data object. Once resources are included in an executable file, they can be loaded by the application as needed.

One of the powerful subtleties of this approach becomes clear when you consider the fact that any application can load the resources contained in *any* executable file, including dynamic link libraries. For example, it is possible to create a dynamic link library that has no functions or program code at all—only hundreds of icon resources that are available to any application.

One of the other advantages of the Windows resource mechanism is that resources are loaded only as needed. Not only that, but Windows can discard them if necessary and reload them automatically when they are again required.

Resources and Visual Basic

There is both good news and bad news regarding the use of resources under Visual Basic. The bad news is that the normal resource mechanism defined in the previous section is not fully compatible with Visual Basic. Because Visual Basic applications are not true Windows executable files, it is not possible to add a Windows resource file to a Visual Basic .EXE file.

Figure 12.2

Compiling resources

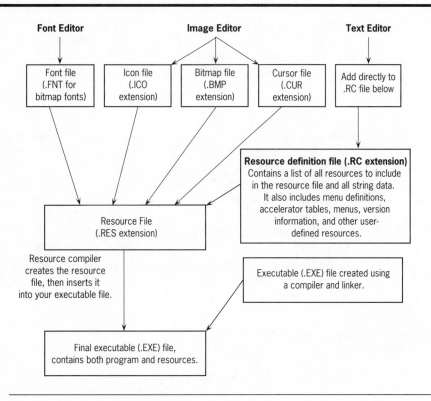

In addition, most of the resource tools required to create and compile Windows resources are not included with Visual Basic. These include the font editor, image editor, cursor editor and, of course, the resource compiler itself.

The good news is many of the objects that resources were designed to handle can be easily saved in a Visual Basic executable file using features that are built into the environment. Bitmaps and icons can be stored in the **Picture** property of the picture control. Menus are handled automatically using the menu design system. Dialog boxes are not needed in the Visual Basic form-based environment.

In addition, the resource API functions are generally compatible with Visual Basic, thus your VB application can easily access resources in dynamic link libraries or executable files.

There are several approaches you can take to use resources under Visual Basic. The most common use will be to take advantage of the standard "stock" (built-in) Windows resources such as icons or bitmaps. The **StockBms** sample application described in Chapter 8 shows how this is accomplished.

Another approach is to create your own executable files that contain resources. To do this you will need a set of resource development tools that are capable of creating executable files containing resources, and the appropriate object generation or editing programs. These are available from a number of vendors including Microsoft and Borland.

A third approach is to extract resources from existing executable files. The Windows API provides a powerful set of functions for loading or directly reading resources from an executable file if you know that it is there—in other words, if you know the name or identifier of the resource. It also provides the **ExtractIcon** function that allows you to rapidly scan through any icon resources in a file. Unfortunately, it does not provide strong support for obtaining a list of nonicon resources.

There are two ways to obtain such a list. The hard way is to read the executable file and look in its internal resource table. This involves a good understanding of the data format of both the executable file and the resources themselves, and is beyond the scope of this book. The easy way is to obtain a program that is capable of reading the resources in a file (a resource decompiler). You may wish to check public domain and shareware libraries for low-cost or free software that can perform this task.

Resource API Functions

Every resource must have a unique identifier, which can take two forms: a string or an integer. As a string, for example, an icon resource can have the name "Icon1". You would pass the string "Icon1" to the resource API functions when you wish to access or load this icon.

In order to save space, however, most resources are identified by an integer. Most of the resource API functions expect the resource identifier to be a 32-bit **Long** parameter. If the high-order 16 bits are zero, the function assumes that the low-order 16 bits contain the integer identifier. Otherwise the function assumes that the parameter is a 32-bit pointer to a null terminated string containing the name of the resource.

The API definitions in the declaration file APIDECS.BAS included with this book generally provide two declarations for accessing resources: one accepting a **Long** parameter, the other accepting a string parameter.

Most of the resource access functions that a Visual Basic programmer would use are defined in the chapters that describe the associated Windows object. For example, the **LoadBitmap** API function used to load bitmap resources is described in Chapter 8 with the other bitmap functions.

The resource API functions described in Table 12.4 are thus rarely used in Visual Basic. They are presented here mostly for the sake of completeness. These functions are used internally by Windows to implement specific resource functions such as **LoadBitmap** and **LoadIcon**. They are made available through the Windows API primarily in order to support user-defined resources. Refer to the function reference for an outline of how they are used.

Table 12.4   **General Resource Functions**

Function	Description
AccessResource	Used to read a resource from a file using DOS file I/O.
AllocResource	Allocates memory for a resource.
FindResource	Finds a resource in an executable file.
FreeResource	Frees a resource.
LoadResource	Loads a resource into memory.
LoadString	Loads a string resource.
LockResource	Obtains a pointer to a resource in memory.
SizeOfResource	Determines the size of a resource.

The general sequence of operations is as follows:

1. Use the **FindResource** function to obtain a resource information handle.

2. Use the **LoadResource** function to obtain a handle to the resource and to load the resource.

3. Use the **LockResource** function to lock the resource and obtain a pointer to the resource data.

4. Use the **GlobalUnlock** function to unlock the resource.

5. Use the **FreeResource** function to free the memory used by the resource and the resource handle.

The **AllocResource**, **SizeOfResource**, and **AccessResource** functions can be used to manually allocate a resource memory block and read the resource directly. **LoadResource** calls these functions and is easier to use.

Task and Module Functions

Windows provides a number of functions that can be used to work with tasks and modules. These functions allow you to launch applications, and to obtain information about running applications.

Three terms used in Windows that tend to cause a great deal of confusion are *modules*, *instances*, and *tasks*. Once you understand the differences between them, you will find the API functions relating to tasks and modules quite easy to grasp.

Modules

The term *module* refers to any Windows executable file or dynamic link library. In the case of dynamic link libraries, the module might be a function library, a device driver, a Visual Basic custom control, a font resource file, or other types of DLLs.

A module is loaded by Windows using the **LoadLibrary** or **LoadModule** function, though a user might load a module using other techniques; for example, an application module may be loaded using the program manager or file manager. Many dynamic link library modules are loaded automatically by applications as needed.

Each module has a 16-bit handle that identifies the module. Application modules may have more than one handle associated with them (see "Instances," below).

Windows keeps track of how many applications are using a module at once. This usage count is used by Windows to determine when a module can actually be unloaded. Dynamic link libraries are frequently used by several applications at once. Even an application module may be shared by multiple instances of an application. This occurs when you run more than one copy of the same program.

Table 12.5 lists the API functions that can be used to load, unload, and obtain information about modules.

Table 12.5 **Module Functions**

Function	Description
FreeLibrary	Frees a loaded dynamic link library module by decrementing the usage count for the module. Once the usage count is zero, the library is freed.
FreeModule	Frees a loaded module by decrementing the usage count for the module. Once the usage count is zero, the library is freed. **FreeLibrary** should be used for DLLs.
GetModuleFileName	Retrieves the file name for a module.
GetModuleHandle	Retrieves the handle to a loaded module given the module file name.
GetModuleUsage	Determines the usage count for a module.

Table 12.5	Module Functions (Continued)	
GetProcAddress	Retrieves the address of a function in a module. Under VB this may be used to determine if a function is present in a module, but there is no mechanism for actually calling the function.	
LoadLibrary	Loads a dynamic link library module.	
LoadModule	Loads an application module or starts a new instance of a Windows application.	

Instances

The term *instance* refers to a Windows application. Each Windows application that is running has a unique instance handle that identifies that application. This handle can also be used to identify the module.

If you have two instances of the same application running at the same time, each will have a unique instance handle, but both handles will refer to the same module because the two instances share one module.

Because instance handles also refer to the application module, all functions that accept module handles as parameters also accept instance handles. One way of demonstrating this is to run two copies of a Windows program using the Visual Basic **Shell** command. This function returns the instance handle of the newly launched program instance (note that the original VB 1.0 documentation stated incorrectly that this function returns a task handle). Next, use the **GetModuleUsage** API function to show that the usage count for the application's module is now two. Finally, use the **GetModuleFilename** function to demonstrate that the name of the module for both instances is the same. The ExecDemo example program in this chapter demonstrates how you can launch applications in this manner.

The most significant difference between a program instance and a dynamic link library is that a program instance has a main window and is capable of processing Windows messages.

Tasks

The term *task* refers to a running application under Windows. A task and an instance are very similar. Each instance represents a unique task and has its own task identification handle. The task handle and instance handle are not the same, however. A task handle can only be used by API functions that expect task handles as parameters. From the programmer's point of view, the task handle is rarely used. Table 12.6 lists the API functions that use tasks.

Table 12.6   **Task API Functions**

Function	Description
FindExecutable	Finds the executable program for the specified file. Refer to the function reference for a complete description of file associations and use of this function.
GetCurrentTask	Retrieves the handle of the currently running task.
GetNumTasks	Retrieves the number of tasks currently running in the system.
GetWindowTask	Retrieves the task handle for the specified Window.
IsTask	Determines if a handle is a valid task handle.
ShellExecute	Used to open or print a file based on the type of file. Refer to the function reference for a complete description of file associations and use of this function.
WinExec	Runs an application. Identical to the Visual Basic **Shell** function.

Example: ExecDemo—A Program Launcher

ExecDemo is a simple program that demonstrates how you can launch an application, wait for the shelled application to close, and then continue the original application.

Figure 12.3 shows the runtime screen of the ExecDemo program.

Figure 12.3
EXECDEMO.FRM
runtime screen

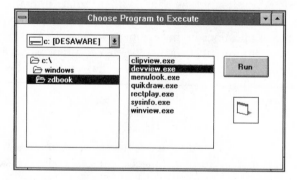

Using ExecDemo

The ExecDemo screen contains the standard drive, directory, and file controls configured to allow you to select an executable file (with a .EXE extension). If the executable file contains at least one icon resource, the first icon in the file is displayed in the **Picture1** control.

Selecting the Run button or double clicking on the file box causes the specified program to be executed.

Project Description

The ExecDemo project includes three files. EXECDEMO.FRM is the only form used in the program. APIDECS.BAS is the type-safe API declaration file provided with this book. APIGUIDE.BAS contains the declarations for the APIGUIDE.DLL dynamic link library.

Listing 12.4   **Project Listing File EXECDEMO.MAK**

```
EXECDEMO.FRM
APIDECS.BAS
APIGUIDE.BAS
ProjWinSize=175,439,248,215
ProjWinShow=2
```

Form Description

Listing 12.5 contains the header from file PALTEST.FRM that describes the control setup for the form.

Listing 12.5   **Form Description for File EXECDEMO.FRM**

```
VERSION 2.00
Begin Form ExecDemo
    Caption        =   "Choose Program to Execute"
    Height         =   3765
    Left           =   1035
    LinkMode       =   1  'Source
    LinkTopic      =   "Form1"
    ScaleHeight    =   3360
    ScaleWidth     =   6480
    Top            =   1140
    Width          =   6600
    Begin PictureBox Picture1
        Height         =   615
```

Listing 12.5   Form Description for File PALTEST.FRM (Continued)

```
        Left            =   5280
        ScaleHeight     =   585
        ScaleWidth      =   585
        TabIndex        =   4
        Top             =   1680
        Width           =   615
    End
    Begin CommandButton CmdRun
        Caption         =   "Run"
        Height          =   495
        Left            =   5040
        TabIndex        =   3
        Top             =   720
        Width           =   1095
    End
    Begin FileListBox File1
        Height          =   2175
        Left            =   2760
        Pattern         =   "*.exe"
        TabIndex        =   2
        Top             =   720
        Width           =   2055
    End
    Begin DirListBox Dir1
        Height          =   2175
        Left            =   240
        TabIndex        =   1
        Top             =   720
        Width           =   2295
    End
    Begin DriveListBox Drive1
        Height          =   315
        Left            =   240
        TabIndex        =   0
        Top             =   240
        Width           =   2295
    End
End
```

ExecDemo Listings

The **Drive1_Change**, **Dir1_Change**, and **File1_DblClick** functions use the standard Visual Basic file control techniques described in the Visual Basic manuals.

Listing 12.6   Form Listing EXECDEMO.FRM

```
Sub Drive1_Change ()
    Dir1.Path = Drive1.Drive
End Sub

Sub Dir1_Change ()
    File1.Path = Dir1.Path
    File1.SetFocus
End Sub

Sub File1_DblClick ()
    CmdRun.Value = -1    ' Trigger the 'run' button

End Sub
```

The **ExtractIcon** function can be used to extract an icon resource from a Windows executable file. The icon is drawn onto the **Picture** control using the techniques described in Chapter 8.

```
'
'   When you click on the file box, the first icon in the
'   specified executable file is displayed in the picture1
'   control.
'
Sub File1_Click ()
    Dim hicon%
    Dim execname$

    execname$ = GetExecName$()
    hicon% = ExtractIcon(agGetInstance%(), execname$, 0)

    ' Draw the first icon for the executable file into
    ' the picture1 control.
    Picture1.Cls

    If (hicon%) Then
        di% = DrawIcon%(Picture1.hDC, 0, 0, hicon%)
    End If

End Sub

'
' Retrieves the executable file name string
'
Function GetExecName$ ()
    GetExecName$ = File1.Path + "\" + File1.Filename
End Function
```

Once the shelled application is launched, the ExecDemo program disables and minimizes itself. The DoEvents loop allows other programs in the system to run while this application keeps checking the instance handle of the shelled application.

As long as the instance handle returned by the Visual Basic **Shell** function is valid, the **GetModuleUsage** function will return a result greater than zero. When the shelled application is closed, the **DoEvents** loop will end and the ExecDemo program will restore its window and reenable the Run command button.

```
'
' Run the application, minimize this application until
'    the task is completed.
'
Sub CmdRun_Click ()
    Dim hinstance%
    CmdRun.Enabled = 0
    ExecDemo.WindowState = 1

    hinstance% = Shell(GetExecName$(), 1)
    Do
        di% = DoEvents()
    Loop While GetModuleUsage%(hinstance%) <> 0

    CmdRun.Enabled = -1
    ExecDemo.WindowState = 0

End Sub
```

Function Reference

This section contains an alphabetical reference for the functions described in this chapter.

■ AccessResource

VB Declaration `Declare Function AccessResource% Lib "Kernel" (ByVal hInstance%, ByVal ⇔ hResInfo%)`

Description This function returns an MS-DOS file handle that is set to read a resource in the specified module.

Use with VB This function requires a knowledge of the internal format of a Windows resource.

Parameter	Type/Description
hInstance	**Integer**—A handle to a loaded executable module that contains the desired resource.
hResInfo	**Integer**—A handle to a resource as returned by the **FindResource** function.

Return Value **Integer**—An MS-DOS file handle on success, -1 on error.

Comments Refer to Chapter 13 for information on use of file handles under Visual Basic. Be sure to close the file handle when it is no longer needed.

■ AllocResource

VB Declaration `Declare Function AllocResource% Lib "Kernel" (ByVal hInstance%, ByVal ⇔ hResInfo%, ByVal dwSize&)`

Description Allocates global memory to hold a resource.

Use with VB Used only for low level resource access.

Parameter	Type/Description
hInstance	**Integer**—A handle to a loaded executable module that contains the desired resource.
hResInfo	**Integer**—A handle to a resource as returned by the **FindResource** function.
dwSize	**Long**—The size of the buffer to allocate in bytes. Zero to use the actual size of the resource.

Return Value **Integer**—A global handle on success, zero on error.

Comments The global memory object may be locked and data read into the resulting buffer. A file handle to the resource file can be obtained using the **AccessResource** function.

■ FindExecutable

VB Declaration   `Declare Function FindExecutable% Lib "shell.dll" (ByVal lpszFile$, ⇔`
`ByVal lpszDir$, ByVal lpszResult$)`

Description   Finds the file name of the program that is associated with a specified file. The Windows registration editor (REGEDIT.EXE) can be used to associate types of files with particular applications. Associations may also be set by editing the WIN.INI file. For example, text files that have the extension .TXT are typically associated with the Windows Notepad (NOTEPAD.EXE). Selecting any file with the .TXT extension in the file manager causes the file manager to load it into Notepad.

Use with VB   This function requires that the SHELL.DLL dynamic link library be present on your system. This DLL is distributed with Windows 3.1.

Parameter	Type/Description
lpszFile	**String**—A program name or a file name for which to find an associated program.
lpszDir	**String**—The full path of the default directory to use.
lpszResult	**String**—A string buffer to load with the name of the executable program found for **lpszFile**. This string should be preallocated to be larger than the maximum expected file name length (typically 128 characters).

Return Value   **Integer**—Greater than 32 on success. Refer to Table 12.8 for a list of error codes.

Table 12.8   FindExecutable and ShellExecute Error Codes

Error Value	Description
0	Insufficient system memory or corrupt program file.
2	File not found.
3	Invalid path.
5	Sharing or protection error.
6	Separate data segments are required for each task.
8	Insufficient memory to run the program.
10	Incorrect Windows version.
11	Invalid program file.
12	Program file requires a different operating system.
13	Program requires MS-DOS 4.0.

Table 12.8 **FindExecutable and ShellExecute Error Codes (Continued)**

Error Value	Description
14	Unknown program file type.
15	Windows program does not support protected memory mode.
16	Invalid use of data segments when loading a second instance of a program.
19	Attempt to run a compressed program file.
20	Invalid dynamic link library.
21	Program requires Windows 32-bit extensions.

■ FindResource, FindResourceByname, FindResourceBynum

VB Declaration
```
Declare Function FindResource% Lib "Kernel" (ByVal hInstance%, ByVal lpName$, ⇔
ByVal lpType As Any)

Declare Function FindResourceByname% Lib "Kernel" Alias"FindResource" (ByVal ⇔
hInstance%, ByVal lpName$, ByVal lpType$)

Declare Function FindResourceBynum% Lib "Kernel" Alias "FindResource" (ByVal ⇔
hInstance%, ByVal lpName$, ByVal lpType&)
```

Description   Finds the specified resource in an executable file and returns a resource handle that can be used by other functions to actually load the resource.

Use with VB   Subject to the limitations on resources described earlier in this chapter.

Parameter	Type/Description
hInstance	**Integer**—A handle to a loaded executable module that contains the desired resource.
lpName	**String** or **Long**—The identifier of the requested resource. Resources are identified either by a name (contained in a string) or an integer. If using a string and the first character is the # symbol, the string specifies an integer ID in string format (for example, #56 finds resource number 56).
lpType	**String** or **Long**—The name of the resource or one of the predefined resource types as specified by the constants having the RT_ prefix in the APICONST.TXT file.

Return Value   **Integer**—A special handle to the resource that can be used by other resource functions to access the resource.

Comments   Use the **LoadCursor**, **LoadIcon**, and **LoadString** functions to load cursors, icons, and strings. It is recommended that you use the **LoadBitmap** function to load bitmaps instead of doing it manually using this function and the **LoadResource** function.

■ FreeLibrary

VB Declaration   `Declare Sub FreeLibrary Lib "Kernel" (ByVal hLibModule%)`

Description   Frees the specified dynamic link library that has been loaded using the **LoadLibrary** API function.

Use with VB   This function should be used only to free DLLs that were explicitly loaded by your application. Each call to LoadLibrary should be balanced with a matching FreeLibrary call.

Parameter	Type/Description
hLibModule	**Integer**—A handle to a library module.

■ FreeModule

VB Declaration   `Declare Sub FreeModule Lib "Kernel" (ByVal hModule%)`

Description   Frees the specified module that has been loaded using the **LoadModule** API function.

Use with VB   LoadModule is typically used to load an executable module. Freeing an executable module is very dangerous, as it frees the module without terminating the application. As a result, this function has little practical use to the VB programmer.

Parameter	Type/Description
hModule	**Integer**—A handle to a module.

■ FreeResource

VB Declaration   `Declare Function FreeResource% Lib "Kernel" (ByVal hResData%)`

Description   Frees the specified resource. This should be used for resources loaded with the **LoadResource** function. Each time **LoadResource** is called, a lock count is incremented. It is decremented by this function and the resource is actually freed only when the lock count reaches zero.

Use with VB   Subject to the limitations on resources described earlier in this chapter.

Parameter	Type/Description
hResData	**Integer**—A handle to a resource as returned by the **LoadResource** function.

Return Value   **Integer**—Zero on success, nonzero on error.

■ GetCurrentTask

VB Declaration `Declare Function GetCurrentTask% Lib "Kernel" ()`

Description Retrieves the task handle for the currently running task.

Use with VB No problem.

Return Value **Integer**—A handle to the current task.

■ GetModuleFileName

VB Declaration `Declare Function GetModuleFileName% Lib "Kernel" (ByVal hModule%, ByVal ⇔`
`lpFilename$, ByVal nSize%)`

Description Retrieves the full path name of a loaded module.

Use with VB · No problems.

Parameter	Type/Description
hModule	**Integer**—A handle to a module. This can be a DLL module or the instance handle of an application.
lpFileName	**String**—String buffer to load with the null terminated path name to the file from which module **hModule** was loaded. This string should be preallocated to be at least **nSize+1** characters long.
nSize	**Integer**—The maximum number of characters to load into buffer **lpFileName**.

Return Value **Integer**—The actual number of bytes copied into **lpFileName** on success, zero on error.

■ GetModuleHandle

VB Declaration `Declare Function GetModuleHandle% Lib "Kernel" (ByVal lpModuleName$)`

Description Retrieves the module handle for an application or dynamic link library.

Use with VB No problem.

Parameter	Type/Description
lpModuleName	**String**—The name of the module. This is usually the same as the name of the module's file name. For example, the NOTEPAD.EXE program has the module file name of NOTEPAD.

Return Value **Integer**—The module handle on success, zero on error.

▓ GetModuleUsage

VB Declaration   `Declare Function GetModuleUsage% Lib "Kernel" (ByVal hModule%)`

Description   Windows maintains a usage count that keeps track of how many times a module has been loaded. When an application that has loaded a module frees it, the usage count is reduced by one. Modules with a usage count of zero are automatically freed by Windows. This function determines the current usage count of a module.

Use with VB   No problem.

Parameter	Type/Description
hModule	**Integer**—A handle to a module.

Return Value   **Integer**—The usage count of the module. Zero if the module handle is no longer valid.

▓ GetNumTasks

VB Declaration   `Declare Function GetNumTasks% Lib "Kernel" ()`

Description   Retrieves the number of tasks running in the system.

Use with VB   No problem.

Return Value   **Integer**—The number of tasks running.

▓ GetProcAddress

VB Declaration   `Declare Function GetProcAddress& Lib "Kernel" (ByVal hModule%, ByVal ⇔`
`lpProcName$)`

Description   Retrieves the address of a function in an executable module.

Use with VB   Visual Basic does not provide a mechanism for calling a function based on the address returned by this function. However, this function can be used to determine if a function is present in a module.

Parameter	Type/Description
hModule	**Integer**—A handle to a module.
lpProcName	**String**—The name of the function.

Return Value   **Long**—The address of the function, zero on error.

▓ GetWindowTask

VB Declaration   `Declare Function GetWindowTask% Lib "User" (ByVal hWnd%)`

Description   Retrieves the handle of the task that owns the specified window.

Use with VB	No problem.

Parameter	Type/Description
hWnd	**Integer**—A handle to a window.

Return Value	**Integer**—Determines the task handle of the application that owns the specified window.
Comments	Once you have obtained a task handle for a window, you can use the **IsTask** API function to determine when the application owning the window closes.

■ GlobalAlloc

VB Declaration	`Declare Function GlobalAlloc% Lib "Kernel" (ByVal wFlags%, ByVal dwBytes&)`
Description	Allocates a block of global memory.
Use with VB	Refer to "Using Global Memory Blocks from Visual Basic," earlier in this chapter.

Parameter	Type/Description
wFlags	**Integer**—Constant flags that specify the type of memory to allocate as described in Table 12.9.
dwBytes	**Long**—The size of the memory block.

Return Value	**Integer**—A handle to the global memory on success, zero on error.
Comments	Refer to the **GlobalLock**, **GlobalUnlock**, and **GlobalFree** functions for further information. Table 12.9 lists the constants defined in file APICONST.TXT that are used with global memory functions. These flags may be combined unless otherwise specified.

Table 12.9	Global Memory Flags

Flag Constant	Description
GMEM_DDESHARE	Specifies a shareable block of memory. Used only to create blocks of memory to transfer using DDE, this flag is not typically used by VB programmers.
GMEM_DISCARDABLE	This memory block may be discarded if Windows needs additional memory. You can determine if a memory block has been discarded by using the **GlobalFlags** function, or by interrogating the result of the **GlobalLock** function.
GMEM_FIXED	Creates a memory block that is fixed in memory. It is preferred to use the **GMEM_MOVEABLE** flag instead.
GMEM_MODIFY	Used only by the **GlobalReAlloc** function. Refer to the comments section for that function for details.

Table 12.9   **Global Memory Flags (Continued)**

Flag Constant	Description
GMEM_MOVEABLE	Creates a block of memory that may be moved by Windows if necessary. This is the preferred flag to use.
GMEM_NOCOMPACT	Prevents memory from being moved or discarded during a memory allocation. This is unlikely to be of use to VB programmers.
GMEM_NODISCARD	Prevents memory from being discarded during a memory allocation. This is unlikely to be of use to VB programmers.
GMEM_NOTBANKED	In versions of Windows prior to 3.1, this flag forced the memory block to be loaded in the lower 640k of memory.
GMEM_NOTIFY	This flag should not be used by Visual Basic programs.
GMEM_ZEROINIT	Fills the memory buffer with zeros during allocation.

The **GMEM_FIXED** and **GMEM_MOVEABLE** flags may not be combined.

GlobalCompact

VB Declaration   `Declare Function GlobalCompact& Lib "Kernel" (ByVal dwMinFree&)`

Description   This function can be used to determine if a block of memory of the specified size can be allocated by Windows. The function assumes that it can move, free, and discard memory blocks as allowed in order to fulfill the request.

Use with VB   No problem.

Parameter	Type/Description
dwMinFree	**Long**—The size of the memory block requested. Zero to determine the largest available memory block.

Return Value   **Long**—The size of the block that can actually be allocated (less than or equal to **dwMinFree**).

GlobalFix

VB Declaration   `Declare Sub GlobalFix Lib "Kernel" (ByVal hMem%)`

Description   Locks a moveable memory block so that it may not move. Each call to **GlobalFix** for a particular memory block should be balanced with a call to the **GlobalUnfix** function.

Use with VB   This function interferes with Windows normal memory management and should not be used.

Parameter	Type/Description
hMem	**Integer**—A handle to a global memory block.

■ GlobalFlags

VB Declaration   `Declare Function GlobalFlags% Lib "Kernel" (ByVal hMem%)`

Description   Retrieves the global memory flags for a memory block.

Use with VB   No problem.

Parameter	Type/Description
hMem	**Integer**—A handle to a global memory block.

Return Value   **Integer**—The low eight bits of the integer contain the current lock count for the memory block. Flag bits set as specified by the following constants:
GMEM_DISCARDABLE: The memory block is discardable.
GMEM_DISCARDED: The memory block has been discarded.

■ GlobalFree

VB Declaration   `Declare Function GlobalFree% Lib "Kernel" (ByVal hMem%)`

Description   Frees the specified global memory block. After calling this function, handle **hMem** will no longer be valid. Be sure that the memory block is not locked when this function is called.

Use with VB   No problem.

Parameter	Type/Description
hMem	**Integer**—A handle to a global memory block.

Return Value   **Integer**—Zero on success, **hMem** on error.

■ GlobalHandle

VB Declaration   `Declare Function GlobalHandle& Lib "Kernel" (ByVal wMem%)`

Description   Determines the memory handle for a memory block given a selector.

Use with VB   No problem.

Parameter	Type/Description
wMem	**Integer**—A memory selector. This is the high 16 bits of a 32-bit address.

Return Value   **Long**—The low 16 bits contain the global memory handle on success and the high-order word contains **wMem**. The result is zero if the selector is invalid.

■ GlobalLock

VB Declaration   Declare Function GlobalLock& Lib "Kernel" (ByVal hMem%)

Description   Locks the specified memory block in memory and returns an address value that points to the beginning of the memory block. The address will remain valid until the memory block is unlocked using the **GlobalUnlock** function. Windows maintains a lock count for each memory object. Each call to this function should have a matching call to **GlobalUnlock**.

Use with VB   No problem.

Parameter	Type/Description
hMem	Integer—A handle to a global memory block.

Return Value   **Long**—The address of the memory block on success. Zero if an error occurred or if this is a discardable block that has been discarded.

■ GlobalLRUNewest

VB Declaration   Declare Function GlobalLRUNewest% Lib "Kernel" (ByVal hMem%)

Description   Windows determines the next memory block to discard based on a least recently used scheme. This function moves the specified discardable memory block to the newest position on the list, making it the least likely to be discarded if Windows needs to discard memory.

Use with VB   No problem.

Parameter	Type/Description
hMem	Integer—A handle to a discardable global memory block.

Return Value   **Integer**—Zero if **hMem** is not a valid handle.

■ GlobalLRUOldest

VB Declaration   Declare Function GlobalLRUOldest% Lib "Kernel" (ByVal hMem%)

Description   Windows determines the next memory block to discard based on a least recently used scheme. This function moves the specified discardable memory block to the oldest position on the list, making it the most likely to be discarded if Windows needs to discard memory.

Use with VB   No problem.

Parameter	Type/Description
hMem	Integer—A handle to a discardable global memory block.

Return Value   **Integer**—Zero if **hMem** is not a valid handle.

◼ GlobalReAlloc

VB Declaration   `Declare Function GlobalReAlloc% Lib "Kernel" (ByVal hMem%, ByVal dwBytes&, ⇔`
`ByVal wFlags%)`

Description   Changes the size of a block of global memory.

Use with VB   Refer to "Using Global Memory Blocks from Visual Basic," earlier in this chapter.

Parameter	Type/Description
hMem	**Integer**—A handle to a global memory block.
dwBytes	**Long**—The size of the memory block. Zero to discard a memory block if it is discardable and not locked.
wFlags	**Integer**—Constant flags that specify the type of memory to allocate as described in Table 12.9 under the description of the **GlobalAlloc** function. Only the **GMEM_DISCARDABLE, GMEM_MODIFY, GMEM_MOVEABLE, GMEM_NODISCARD**, and **GMEM_ZEROINIT** flags may be used.

Return Value   **Integer**—A handle to the global memory block on success, zero on error or if the request cannot be fulfilled.

Comments   Note that the handle returned may not be the same as the **hMem** parameter. Programs should take this into account. If an error occurs, the global handle referenced by the **hMem** parameter remains valid.
   The **GMEM_MODIFY** flag causes the **GMEM_MOVEABLE** flag to change a fixed memory block into a moveable memory block. If **GMEM_MODIFY** is not specified the **GMEM_MOVEABLE** flag allows the memory block to be moved to fulfill the request even if the memory block is fixed. **GMEM_MODIFY** may not be used with **GMEM_NODISCARD** or **GMEM_ZEROINIT**.

◼ GlobalSize

VB Declaration   `Declare Function GlobalSize& Lib "Kernel" (ByVal hMem%)`

Description   Returns the minimum size of the specified global memory block. This value may be larger than the size of the block when it was allocated.

Use with VB   No problem.

Parameter	Type/Description
hMem	**Integer**—A handle to a global memory block.

Return Value   **Long**—The size of the memory block on success, zero on error or if the memory block has been discarded.

■ GlobalUnfix

VB Declaration   Declare Function GlobalUnfix% Lib "Kernel" (ByVal hMem%)

Description   Unlocks a moveable memory block so that it can move after it has been locked by a call to the **GlobalFix** function.

Use with VB   This function interferes with Windows's normal memory management and should not be used.

Parameter	Type/Description
hMem	Integer—A handle to a global memory block.

■ GlobalUnlock

VB Declaration   Declare Function GlobalUnlock% Lib "Kernel" (ByVal hMem%)

Description   Unlocks the specified memory block that had been previously locked using the **GlobalLock** function.

Use with VB   No problem.

Parameter	Type/Description
hMem	**Integer**—A handle to a global memory block.

Return Value   **Integer**—Zero if a moveable memory block has had its lock count reduced to zero. Nonzero otherwise.

Comments   Be careful that the number of **GlobalUnlock** calls matches the number of **GlobalLock** calls. Attempting to unlock a memory block that had not been locked can lead to an unrecoverable application error under Windows 3.0.

■ hmemcpy, hmemcpyBynum

VB Declaration   Declare Sub hmemcpy Lib "Kernel" (hpvDest As Any, hpvSource As Any, ByVal ⇔ cbCopy&)
Declare Sub hmemcpyBynum Lib "Kernel" Alias "hmemcpy" (ByVal hpvDest&, ByVal ⇔ hpvSource&, ByVal cbCopy&)

Description   Copies one block of memory to another. Correctly handles transfers greater than 64k in size.

Use with VB   Refer to "Structure of Huge Memory," earlier in this chapter, for information on creating and using huge memory blocks.

Parameter	Type/Description
hpvDest	**Long** or **Structure**—The destination address.
hpvSource	**Long** or **Structure**—The source address.
cbCopy	**Long**—The number of bytes to copy.

Comments　　It is usually easier to use the **hmemcpyBynum** function to pass long addresses that are obtained using the **agGetAddressForObject** and **agGetAddressForLPSTR** functions.

■ IsBadHugeReadPtr

VB Declaration　`Declare Function IsBadHugeReadPtr% Lib "Kernel" (ByVal lp&, ByVal cb&)`

Description　　Checks to make sure that the specified block of huge memory is valid and can be read.

Use with VB　　No problem.

Parameter	Type/Description
lp	**Long**—Address of the start of a huge memory block.
cb	**Long**—The length of the huge memory block.

Return Value　　**Integer**—TRUE (nonzero) if the specified memory block is invalid and not readable by this application.

■ IsBadHugeWritePtr

VB Declaration　`Declare Function IsBadHugeWritePtr% Lib "Kernel" (ByVal lp&, ByVal cb&)`

Description　　Checks to make sure that the specified block of huge memory is valid. and can be written to. Code segments are an example of a memory block that is readable but not writeable.

Use with VB　　No problem.

Parameter	Type/Description
lp	**Long**—Address of the start of a huge memory block.
cb	**Long**—The length of the huge memory block.

Return Value　　**Integer**—TRUE (nonzero) if the specified memory block is invalid and not writable by this application.

■ IsBadReadPtr

VB Declaration　`Declare Function IsBadReadPtr% Lib "Kernel" (ByVal lp&, ByVal cb%)`

Description　　Checks to make sure that the specified block of memory is valid and can be read.

Use with VB　　No problem.

Parameter	Type/Description
lp	**Long**—Address of the start of a memory block.
cb	**Integer**—The length of the memory block.

Return Value　　**Integer**—TRUE (nonzero) if the specified memory block is invalid and not readable by this application.

■ IsBadStringPtr

VB Declaration   `Declare Function IsBadStringPtr% Lib "Kernel" (ByVal lpsz&, ByVal cb%)`

Description   Checks to make sure that the specified block of memory is valid and contains a valid null terminated string.

Use with VB   No problem.

Parameter	Type/Description
lp	**Long**—Address of the start of a memory block.
cb	**Integer**—The maximum length of the string.

Return Value   **Integer**—TRUE (nonzero) if the specified memory block is invalid and does not contain a null terminated string.

■ IsBadWritePtr

VB Declaration   `Declare Function IsBadWritePtr% Lib "Kernel" (ByVal lp&, ByVal cb%)`

Description   Checks to make sure that the specified block of memory is valid and can be written to. Code segments are an example of a memory block that is readable but not writeable.

Use with VB   No problem.

Parameter	Type/Description
lp	**Long**—Address of the start of a memory block.
cb	**Integer**—The length of the memory block.

Return Value   **Integer**—TRUE (nonzero) if the specified memory block is invalid and not writable by this application.

■ IsTask

VB Declaration   `Declare Function IsTask% Lib "Kernel" (ByVal htask%)`

Description   Determines if a handle represents a valid task.

Use with VB   No problem.

Parameter	Type/Description
htask	**Integer**—A handle to a task.

Return Value   **Integer**—TRUE (nonzero) if the task handle is valid.

Comments   This function can be used to detect when a task terminates.

■ LockResource

VB Declaration   `Declare Function LockResource& Lib "Kernel" (ByValhResData%)`

Description   Locks the specified resource. The function returns a 32-bit pointer to the data for the resource. This should be used for resources loaded with the **LoadResource** function.

Use with VB   Subject to the limitations on resources described earlier in this chapter.

Parameter	Type/Description
hResData	**Integer**—A handle to a resource as returned by the LoadResource function.

Return Value   **Long**—A 32-bit pointer value on success, zero on error.

Comments   After accessing the data in the resource, the resource should be unlocked using the **GlobalUn-lock** function.

■ ShellExecute, ShellExecuteBynum

VB Declaration   `Declare Function ShellExecute% Lib "shell.dll" (ByVal hwnd%, ByVal ⇔`
`lpszOp$, ByVal lpszFile$, ByVal spszParams$, ByVal lpszDir$, ByVal fsShowCmd%)`

`Declare Function ShellExecuteBynum% Lib "shell.dll" Alias "ShellExecute" ⇔`
`(ByVal hwnd%, ByVal lpszOp&,ByVal lpszFile$, ByVal spszParams&, ByVal ⇔`
`lpszDir$, ByVal fsShowCmd%)`

Description   Finds the file name of the program that is associated with a specified file and either runs the program for the file or prints the file. The Windows registration editor (REGEDIT.EXE) can be used to associate types of files with particular applications. Associations may also be set by editing the WIN.INI file. For example, text files that have the extension .TXT are typically associated with the Windows Notepad (NOTEPAD.EXE). Specifying any file with the .TXT extension to this function will either launch the Notepad program using the file name as a parameter, or will print the specified file.

Use with VB   This function requires that the SHELL.DLL dynamic link library be present on your system. This DLL is distributed with Windows 3.1.

Parameter	Type/Description
hwnd	**Integer**—A handle to a window. Sometimes it is necessary for a Windows application to show a message box before it has created its own main window. If this occurs, the window specified by this parameter will be used as the parent window of the message box. Under Visual Basic you would usually use the window handle of the active form for this parameter.
lpszOp	**String** or **Long**—The string "Open" to open the **lpszFile** document or "Print" to print it. This may be zero to default to "Open".
lpszFile	**String**—A program name or the name of a file to print or open using the associated program.

Parameter	Type/Description
lpszParams	**String** or **Long**—A string containing parameters to pass to the executable file if **lpszFile** is an executable file. Zero if **lpszFile** refers to a document file or if no parameters are used.
lpszDir	**String**—The full path of the default directory to use.
fsShowCmd	**Integer**—A constant value specifying how to show the launched program. This matches the **nCmdShow** parameter to the **ShowWindow** API function described in Chapter 4.

Return Value **Integer**—Greater than 32 on success. Refer to Table 12.8 under the description of the **FindExecutable** function for a list of error codes.

■ SizeOfResource

VB Declaration `Declare Function SizeofResource% Lib "Kernel" (ByVal hInstance%, ByVal ⇔ hResInfo%)`

Description Determines the size of a resource.

Use with VB Subject to the limitations on resources described earlier in this chapter.

Parameter	Type/Description
hInstance	**Integer**—A handle to a loaded executable module that contains the desired resource.
hResInfo	**Integer**—A handle to a resource as returned by the **FindResource** function.

Return Value **Long**—The size of the resource, zero if the resource is not found.

■ WinExec

VB Declaration `Declare Function WinExec% Lib "Kernel" (ByVal lpCmdLine$, ByVal nCmdShow%)`

Description Runs the specified program.

Use with VB This function is essentially identical to the Visual Basic **Shell** command. Refer to the description for the **LoadModule** and **ShellExecute** functions for information on other methods for launching applications.

Parameter	Type/Description
lpCmdFile	**String**—Contains the command line to execute.
fuCmdShow	**Integer**—A constant value specifying how to show the launched program. This matches the **nCmdShow** parameter to the **ShowWindow** API function described in Chapter 4.

Return Value   **Integer**—Module handle for the executed application – value > 32 on success. Refer to Table 12.8 under the description of the **FindExecutable** function for a list of error codes.

Comments   Refer to the description of the **LoadLibrary** function for a description of the order in which directories are searched for the specified program file.

13

File Operations

V ISUAL BASIC PROVIDES A NUMBER OF FUNCTIONS FOR MANIPULATING and accessing files. This chapter demonstrates the use of initialization files—both the Windows file WIN.INI and application-specific files. Version stamping, a feature new in Windows 3.1, is introduced along with the functions required to access the version information contained in a file.

This chapter also describes general-purpose file operations, including those necessary to read and write to huge memory blocks (greater than 64k in size). The LZEXPAND.DLL library included with Windows 3.1 is described along with techniques to use it to decompress files or to copy files in general.

Finally, FileDemo, an example program that illustrates many of the techniques introduced in this chapter, is presented.

Initialization Files

Windows provides the capability for applications to easily save initialization or status information in standard format text files known as initialization files. The best known of these is the WIN.INI initialization file. This file is used by Windows to save system settings such as font and device information, and by some applications to save their own initialization data. Windows allows each application to create and maintain its own initialization files as well.

Initialization files, or profile files as they are sometimes called, have a standard format. This format is described in detail in the file WININI.WRI that was placed in your Windows directory when you installed Windows. This file also includes example settings for file WIN.INI.

Each initialization file is divided into sections. Each section is marked by the name of the section in brackets, as shown here:

```
[section name]
```

Within the section, entries are formed of two parts separated by an equal sign. The first part is called the *key name* or *entry name*. The second part is the string for that key. This is the format of an entry:

```
keyname=string for this key
```

For example, the WIN.INI file has a section for various sounds that the system will play during certain events. The default "beep" sound is specified using the **SystemDefault** key. The string defined for that entry is the name of a sound file, in this case ding.wav, followed by a description of the entry as shown here.

```
[sounds]
 SystemDefault=ding.wav, Default Beep
```

Visual Basic programs can easily use the initialization file functions both to support private initialization files and to read or set entries in the WIN.INI file. The available API functions are shown in Table 13.1.

Table 13.1   **Initialization File Functions**

Function	Description
GetProfileInt	Retrieves an integer setting from the WIN.INI initialization file.
GetProfileString	Retrieves a string from the WIN.INI initialization file.
GetPrivateProfileInt	Retrieves an integer setting from a private initialization file.
GetPrivateProfileString	Retrieves a string from a private initialization file.
WritePrivateProfileString	Sets a string into a private initialization file.
WriteProfileString	Sets a string into the WIN.INI initialization file.

The WIN.INI initialization file contains configuration information that is used by Windows and is accessible to many files. If you change an entry in WIN.INI that is not unique to your application, it is important to notify the other applications in the system that WIN.INI has changed. This can be accomplished by posting a WM_WININICHANGE message to all applications as follows:

```
di% = PostMessageBystring(HWND_BROADCAST, WM_WININICHANGE, 0, sectionname$)
```

where *sectionname$* is the name of the section that was changed.

Version Stamping

In the DOS world, software upgrades have not been much of a problem. When upgrading the DOS operating system, the upgrade generally included new copies of all of the files required by the system. When upgrading an application, the application had its own set of files, so one rarely needed to be concerned that something loaded by one application might affect another.

With Windows, the situation is more complex. For one thing, the Windows environment contains literally hundreds of files. In addition, many files under Windows can be shared among applications. Consider the following situation: You have an application that uses a particular dynamic link library or custom control. You then purchase a second application that uses the same DLL or custom control. When installing the second application, how can you be certain that the version of the DLL or control provided is in fact the latest version of the file? Perhaps that second application has been sitting on the shelf for a while—or perhaps its vendor never bothered to update those files, figuring that as long as they worked with their software there would be no problem.

If the second application simply copies over its version of the DLL or controls, there is a chance that the first application, which may depend on some new feature or fix in the newer version of those files, will stop working properly.

Windows 3.1 solved this problem through a technique called *version stamping*. A special version resource was defined that can be examined by an installation program to determine which version of the file is the latest. Version stamping may also be used to verify that the new file matches the target operating system, that it supports the correct language for the version of Windows running, and so on.

Version Stamping and Visual Basic

If this idea sounds exciting, don't get too enthusiastic. Visual Basic unfortunately does not support version stamping for executable VB applications. Nevertheless, it is important for VB programmers to understand how version stamping works because the many dynamic link libraries and custom controls that are typically used by Visual Basic programs do support version stamping—assuming the add-on vendor takes advantage of this technology.

Version stamps are created using a resource compiler in much the same way as any other resource, and cannot be created from within Visual Basic. They can, however, be read and used by an installation program to make sure that only the latest versions of files are installed on a system.

All of the version functions described here require that the dynamic link library VER.DLL be present on your system. This dynamic link library is provided with Windows 3.1 and many other applications. It is not included with this book.

The functions listed in Table 13.2 are used to support version resources and to aid in the installation of files based on their version stamp.

Table 13.2   **Version Control API Functions**

Function	Description
GetFileResource	May be used to load a version resource. **GetFileVersionInfo** is preferred, however.
GetFileResourceSize	May be used to determine the size of a version resource. **GetFileVersionInfoSize** is preferred, however.
GetFileVersionInfo	Loads a version information resource block.

Table 13.2	**Version Control API Functions (Continued)**

Function	Description
GetFileVersionInfoSize	Determines the size of a version information resource block.
VerFindFile	Determines the recommended destination directory in which to install a file.
VerInstallFile	A powerful function for installing a file onto a system. Supports expansion of compressed files and version checking.
VerLanguageName	Determines the text name of a language based on a standard language code.
VerQueryValue	Determines the value of a version attribute for a file.

The Version Data Structures

The version stamp for a file can have many different components depending on the file. Three of these are commonly used by installing programs and are used in virtually all programs that use version stamping. The first component is a data structure known as the **FIXEDFILEINFO** structure. It contains numeric version information and flags defining the type of the file. The second component defines the language and code page translations that exist in the version resource. The third component consists of one or more strings called StringFileInfo attributes.

The FIXEDFILEINFO Structure

The **FIXEDFILEINFO** data structure is present in every file that has a version stamp. It is defined below.

VB Declaration

```
Type FIXEDFILEINFO ' 52 Bytes
     dwSignature As Long
     dwStrucVersion As Long
     dwFileVersionMS As Long
     dwFileVersionLS As Long
     dwProductVersionMS As Long
     dwProductVersionLS As Long
     dwFileFlagsMask As Long
     dwFileFlags As Long
     dwFileOS As Long
     dwFileType As Long
     dwFileSubtype As Long
     dwFileDateMS As Long
     dwFileDateLS As Long
End Type
```

Field	Type/Description
dwSignature	**Long**—Always contains &HFEEF04BD.
dwStrucVersion	**Long**—The version of this structure. Will be greater than 29.
dwFileVersionMS	**Long**—The high 32 bits of the file version number.
dwFileVersionLS	**Long**—The low 32 bits of the file version number.
dwProductVersionMS	**Long**—The high 32 bits of the product version number.
dwProductVersionLS	**Long**—The low 32 bits of the product version number.
dwFileFlagsMask	**Long**—Any combination of the constants in Table 13.3. The presence of a flag in this parameter indicates that the value of the **dwFileFlags** parameter for that bit is valid.
dwFileFlags	**Long**—Any combination of the constants in Table 13.3.
dwFileOS	**Long**—One of the constants defined in Table 13.4 to specify the operating system for which this file was designed.
dwFileType	**Long**—One of the constants defined in Table 13.5 to specify the type of file.
dwFileSubtype	**Long**—One of the constants defined in the APICONST-.TXT file that begin with the VFT2_ prefix.
dwFileDataMS	**Long**—The high 32 bits that specify the date and time of the file's creation. The Microsoft resource compiler does not set this value.
dwFileDataLS	**Long**—The low 32 bits that specify the date and time of the file's creation. The Microsoft resource compiler does not set this value.

Version numbers are typically 64 bits long to allow for numeric comparisons of versions. However, the internal structure of these numbers deserves further clarification.

On the most significant 32 bits, the high 16 bits comprise the major revision number, and the low 16 bits comprise the minor revision number. Thus Windows 3.10 will have &H0003000A in its major version number. The 3 in the high-order word indicates version 3, and the hexadecimal A represents the number 10 for a minor revision number of .10. This technique is used on the lower 32 bits to allow even finer resolution of versions, but these numbers are typically used only in a development environment and are rarely used by either application programmers or users.

Table 13.3 lists the flags that are used in the **dwFileFlags** parameter to specify general information about the file.

Table 13.3   **Version File Flags**

Constants	Description
VS_FF_DEBUG	This file contains debugging information.
VS_FF_INFOINFERRED	The version resource for this file is dynamically allocated and some of the blocks in the resource may be incorrect.
VS_FF_PATCHED	This file has been patched. it may differ from the original file that has the same version number.
VS_FF_PRERELEASE	This is a prerelease version of the file.
VS_FF_PRIVATEBUILD	This version of the file is built specially as defined by the Private-Build StringFileInfo string.
VS_FF_SPECIALBUILD	This version of the file is built specially as defined by the Special-Build StringFileInfo string.

Table 13.4 lists the constants that are used in the **dwFileType** parameter to specify the file type.

Table 13.4   **Version File Operating System Types**

Constant	Target Operating System for This File
VOS_UNKNOWN	Undefined or unknown.
VOS_DOS	MS-DOS.
VOS_NT	Windows NT.
VOS_WINDOWS16	16-bit Windows (includes Windows 3.0 and 3.1).
VOS_WINDOWS32	32-bit Windows.
VOS_DOS_WINDOWS16	16-bit Windows (includes Windows 3.0 and 3.1) running under MS-DOS.
VOS_DOS_WINDOWS32	32-bit Windows running under MS-DOS.
VOS_NT_WINDOWS32	32-bit Windows running under Windows NT.

Table 13.5 lists the constants that are used in the **dwFileOS** parameter to specify the target operating system for the file.

Table 13.5 **Version File Types**

Constant	Type of File
VFT_UNKNOWN	Unknown.
VFT_APP	Application.
VFT_DLL	Dynamic link library. This includes most Visual Basic custom controls.
VFT_DRV	Driver. The type is specified by the **dwFileSubType** parameter.
VFT_FONT	Font. The type is specified by the **dwFileSubType** parameter.
VFT_VXD	Virtual device driver.
VFT_STATIC_LIB	A static link library.

The Translation Table

The translation table in a version stamp defines the language and code page combinations that are included in the version stamp. It takes the form of an array of integer pairs. The first integer is the language code as listed in Table 13.14 under the description of the **VerLanguageName** API function later in this chapter. The second integer defines the character set or code page to use for that language.

It is perhaps an indication of how new this feature is, that the language and code page definitions are not followed consistently by every application. For this reason, it is important to look at the translation table if one exists. You need accurate language and code page information to access the **String-FileInfo** strings that are defined in the next section.

If a translation table is not defined, the most common language/code combinations are &H040904E4, indicating U.S. English and the standard multilingual Windows character set, and &H04090000, which indicates U.S. English and the seven-bit ASCII character set. Table 13.6 lists the available character set identifiers.

Table 13.6 **Windows Character Sets**

Identifier Value	Character Set
0	Seven-bit ASCII
&H3A4	Windows—Japan
&H3B5	Windows—Korea

Table 13.6   **Windows Character Sets (Continued)**

Identifier Value	Character Set
&H3B6	Windows—Taiwan
&H4B0	Unicode
&H4E2	Windows—Latin (Eastern Europe)
&H4E3	Windows—Cyrillic
&H4E4	Windows—Multilingual (U.S. Standard)
&H4E5	Windows—Greek
&H4E6	Windows—Turkish
&H4E7	Windows—Hebrew
&H4E8	Windows—Arabic

The FileDemo example program illustrates how the translation table for a version resource can be read, and shows how to find the U.S. English entry in the table.

StringFileInfo Data

The **StringFileInfo** entries in a version resource are strings that describe certain characteristics of the file. A file may contain unique strings for each language supported, thus the language/code page information is used to access this data as well. Refer to the description of the **VerQueryValue** function for further information on retrieving these values.

The standard **StringFileInfo** strings are listed in Table 13.7. Not all of the strings defined are present in every file.

Table 13.7   **Version StringFileInfo Data Names**

StringFileInfo Name	Description
Comments	General comments.
CompanyName	The name of the company.
FileDescription	A description of the file.
FileVersion	The version of the file in string form.

Table 13.7   Version StringFileInfo Data Names (Continued)

StringFileInfo Name	Description
InternalName	The internal module or application name.
LegalCopyright	A copyright notice.
LegalTrademarks	Trademark notices.
OriginalFilename	The original name of the file. Useful in determining if the file has been renamed.
PrivateBuild	A description of this build if the **VS_FF_PRIVATEBUILD** flag was set in the **dwFileFlags** field of the **FIXEDFILEINFO** structure.
ProductName	The name of the product to which this file belongs.
ProductVersion	The version of the product to which this file belongs.
SpecialBuild	A description of this build if the **VS_FF_SPECIALBUILD** flag was set in the **dwFileFlags** field of the **FIXEDFILEINFO** structure.

File and Directory Operations

Windows provides a set of API functions for file operations. These functions are fully compatible with Visual Basic, and in many cases duplicate functionality that is provided by Visual Basic.

There are two areas where the Windows file operations can be especially useful to the Visual Basic programmer. One is in the use of the **OpenFile** function—a powerful function for creating and manipulating files. The second involves use of the Windows file access functions that are capable of reading and writing blocks of data greater than 64k in size.

Table 13.8 lists the Windows API functions related to file and directory operations.

Table 13.8   File and Directory API Functions

Function	Description
GetDriveType	Determines the type of a specified disk drive.
GetSystemDirectory	Retrieves the path of the Windows system directory.
GetTempDrive	Retrieves the letter of the first hard drive on the system.

Table 13.8   File and Directory API Functions (Continued)

Function	Description
GetTempFileName	Retrieves the name of a unique temporary file.
GetWindowsDirectory	Retrieves the path of the Windows directory.
hread	Reads from a file (supports transfers greater than 64k).
hwrite	Writes to a file (supports transfers greater than 64k).
lclose	Closes a file.
lcreat	Creates a file.
llseek	Seeks to a position in a file.
lopen	Opens a file.
lread	Reads from a file.
lwrite	Writes to a file.
OpenFile	Flexible file open function.
SetHandleCount	Sets the maximum number of file handles for an application.
WNetAddConnection	Redirects a drive or port to a network.
WNetCancelConnection	Cancels a network redirection.
WNetGetConnection	Retrieves information about a network redirection.

The OpenFile Function and the OFSTRUCT Structure

The **OpenFile** function is capable of a number of file-related operations including:

- Creating files.
- Deleting files.
- Testing if a file exists.
- Searching for a file.
- Controlling access to a file.

OpenFile is described in detail in the function reference section of this chapter. It uses a structure known as the **OFSTRUCT** structure which contains information about the file including an error code describing the results of the **OpenFile** operation. **OFSTRUCT** is defined here:

VB Declaration

```
Type OFSTRUCT  '136 Bytes
cBytes As String * 1
fFixedDisk As String * 1
nErrCode As Integer
reserved As String * 4
szPathName As String * 128
End Type
```

Description

The **OFSTRUCT** structure is used by the **OpenFile** function and other API functions that access files.

Field	Type/Description
cBytes	**String**—Use the **Asc** function to obtain the number of bytes in this structure (it is 136 in the current version of Windows).
fFixedDisk	**String**—The value of this byte will be nonzero if the file is on a fixed disk.
nErrCode	**Integer**—An error code as shown in Table 13.9.
szPathName	**String**—The full path name of the file. This string uses the OEM character set (see Chapter 5 for further information on character sets).

The **nErrCode** field of this structure describes the error of the most recent **OpenFile** call if the function returns an error status.

Table 13.9   **OFSTRUCT Error Codes**

Value in Hexadecimal	Description
1	Invalid function.
2	File not found.
3	Path not found.
4	No file handle available.
5	Access denied.
7	DOS memory corrupted.
6	Handle is invalid.
8	Insufficient memory for the operation.
9	Invalid block.
A	Illegal environment.

Table 13.9　OFSTRUCT Error Codes (Continued)

Value in Hexadecimal	Description
B	Invalid format.
C	Invalid access.
D	Invalid data.
F	Invalid drive.
10	Invalid current directory.
11	Device is different.
12	No more files.
13	Write protect error.
14	Illegal unit.
15	Drive not ready.
16	Invalid command.
17	CRC validation error.
18	Invalid length.
19	Seek error.
1A	Disk is not MS-DOS compatible.
1B	Sector not found.
1C	Out of paper.
1D	Write fault.
1E	Read fault.
1F	General failure of the drive.
20	Sharing violation.
21	File lock violation.
22	Incorrect disk.
23	No file control block available.
24	Sharing buffer exceeded.
32	Device not supported.
33	Remote device unavailable.
34	Duplicate name.
35	Bad network path.
36	Network is busy.
37	Illegal device.
38	Too many commands.
39	Hardware error on the network adapter.

Table 13.9 **OFSTRUCT Error Codes (Continued)**

Value in Hexadecimal	Description
3A	Network response error.
3B	Other network error.
3C	Remote adapter error.
3D	Full print queue.
3E	Print spooler full.
3F	Print canceled.
40	Deleted netname.
41	Network access denied.
42	Invalid device type.
43	Invalid network name.
44	Too many names.
45	Too many sessions.
46	Sharing paused.
47	Request not accepted.
48	Redirection paused.
50	File exists.
51	Duplicate file control block.
52	Cannot make.
53	Interrupt 24 failure.
54	Out of structures.
55	Already assigned.
56	Invalid password.
57	Invalid parameter.
58	Network write fault.

File Access Functions

Generally, the file access functions for creating, deleting, opening, closing, and reading and writing files duplicate functionality already present in Visual Basic. The **hread** and **hwrite** API functions are useful for reading and writing to files in two situations: when over 64k of data needs to be transferred, or when data is being transferred to or from a memory block that crosses a segment boundary. Chapter 12 discusses issues relating to use of huge memory blocks.

When a file is opened from Visual Basic using a Visual Basic file number, that file number will have a corresponding DOS file handle that can be determined using the Visual Basic **FileAttr** function. The file handles used by the API file access functions are standard DOS integer file handles. You must use the **FileAttr** function to use API file access functions on files opened from Visual Basic. You cannot use the Visual Basic file functions on files opened using API functions because there is no way to manually associate a Visual Basic file number with a DOS file handle.

Since the Visual Basic file numbers do draw upon the DOS pool of file handles, the **SetHandleCount** function can be used to increase the number of files that can be open at a time, even if only the Visual Basic file functions are used.

The Windows API also provides functions for performing redirection of a device to a network.

Compressed File Operations

One of the new features for Windows 3.1 is support for expansion of compressed files. These functions, listed in Table 13.10, are designed for use by installation programs and require that files be compressed by the Microsoft COMPRESS.EXE program. This program is included in the professional version of Visual Basic.

These functions require that the LZEXPAND.DLL dynamic link library be present on your system.

Table 13.10 **File Expansion Functions**

Function	Description
CopyLZFile	Copies a file. Used when copying multiple files.
LZClose	Closes a compressed file.
LZCopy	Copies a single file.
LZDone	Ends a multiple-file copy operation and frees the associated buffers.
LZInit	Initializes the internal data buffers required for use with compressed files.
LZOpenFile	Opens or performs other operations on compressed files. Similar to the **OpenFile** API function except that it is compatible with compressed files.
LZRead	Reads and decompresses data from a compressed file.
LZSeek	Seeks to a new position in a compressed file.
LZStart	Allocates buffers that are needed for the **LZCopy** function.

The decompression library provides several techniques for reading from and copying compressed files. In most cases, these techniques involve use of special file handles that access internal buffers used to decompress the file. Up to 16 of these handles may be open at once.

The decompression functions can determine if a file is compressed. If the file is not compressed, the functions call the appropriate standard API functions to perform the requested operation. This means that you may use these functions to copy uncompressed files as well.

Copying a Single File

A single file can be copied using the **LZCopy** function as follows:

1. Open the source file and destination file using the **LZOpenFile** function.

2. Copy the source to the destination using the **LZCopy** function.

3. Close the source and destination file using the **LZClose** function.

Copying Multiple Files

Decompressing files requires the LZEXPAND.DLL dynamic link library to allocate a number of internal buffers. Performance can be improved by allocating them once for a group of files instead of allocating and deallocating them for each file. Use the following sequence of operations for copying multiple consecutive files:

1. Use the **LZStart** function to allocate the internal buffers used for decompressing files.

2. Open the source and destination files using the **LZOpenFile** function.

3. Copy the file using the **CopyLZFile** function.

4. Close the source and destination files using the **LZClose** function.

5. Repeat steps 2-5 for each file to be copied.

6. Use the **LZDone** function to free the internal buffers used for decompressing files.

Reading Data from a Compressed File

It is possible to read decompressed data from a compressed file as follows:

1. Open the file that you want to read using the **LZOpenFile** function. Or you can open the file with the normal **OpenFile** function and then use the **LZInit** function to obtain a compressed file handle for that file.

2. You may use the **GetExpandedName** function to determine the original name of a compressed file.

3. The **LZRead** function may be used to read from the file. The **LZSeek** function may be used to set the current position in the file.

4. Use the **LZClose** function to close the file handle.

Example: FileDemo—Initialization File and Version Stamping Program

FileDemo is a program that demonstrates how to access initialization files from Visual Basic, and how to read the version stamping information for those files that have it.

Using FileDemo

The FileDemo screen shown in Figure 13.1 allows you to select an executable file, DLL, or custom control and determine the version information for that file. The menu also allows you to invoke commands to display the current environment for the task, and the entries under the devices section of the WIN.-INI file as shown in Figure 13.2.

Figure 13.1
FileDemo runtime screen

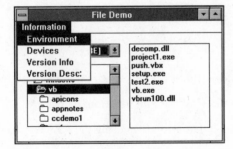

Figure 13.2
Entries under the Devices section in WIN.INI

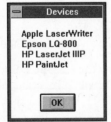

Version information is obtained in two parts. The Version Info menu command accesses the **FIXEDFILEINFO** structure in the file's version resource to show the type of the file and the file and product version numbers as shown in Figure 13.3. The Version Desc menu command accesses the **StringFileInfo** strings in the version resource to obtain the company, file description, and copyright notice for the file as shown in Figure 13.4. The figures show the information retrieved for the Microsoft CARDFILE.EXE application.

Figure 13.3
File version
information

Fixed Version Info

File Version 3.10
Product Version 3.10
File type is: application

OK

Figure 13.4
File version strings

Fixed Version Info

Company: Microsoft Corporation
File Desc: Windows Cardfile application file
Copyright: Copyright © Microsoft Corp. 1991-1992

OK

Project Description

The FileDemo project includes four files. FILEDEMO.FRM is the only form used in the program. FILEDEMO.BAS is the only module in the program and contains the constant type and global definitions. APIDECS.BAS is the type-safe API declaration file provided with this book. APIGUIDE.BAS contains the declarations for the APIGUIDE.DLL dynamic link library.

Listing 13.1 shows the project file for the FILEDEMO program.

Listing 13.1   Project Listing File FILEDEMO.MAK

```
FILEDEMO.FRM
FILEDEMO.BAS
APIDECS.BAS
```

Listing 13.1   Project Listing File FILEDEMO.MAK (Continued)

```
APIGUIDE.BAS
ProjWinSize=179,502,248,215
ProjWinShow=2
Title="FILEDEMO"
```

Form Description

Listing 13.2 contains the header from file FILEDEMO.FRM that describes
the control setup for the form.

Listing 13.2   FILEDEMO.FRM Header

```
VERSION 2.00
Begin Form FileDemo
   Caption         =   "File Demo"
   Height          =   3210
   Left            =   1035
   LinkMode        =   1  'Source
   LinkTopic       =   "Form1"
   ScaleHeight     =   2520
   ScaleWidth      =   4980
   Top             =   1140
   Width           =   5100
   Begin DirListBox Dir1
      Height           =   1455
      Left             =   240
      TabIndex         =   1
      Top              =   720
      Width            =   2295
   End
   Begin FileListBox File1
      Height           =   1980
      Left             =   2760
      Pattern          =   "*.exe;*.dll;*.vbx"
      TabIndex         =   2
      Top              =   240
      Width            =   1935
   End
   Begin DriveListBox Drive1
      Height           =   315
      Left             =   240
      TabIndex         =   0
      Top              =   240
      Width            =   2295
   End
```

Listing 13.2   FILEDEMO.FRM Header (Continued)

```
   Begin Menu MenuInformation
      Caption        =   "Information"
      Begin Menu MenuEnvironment
         Caption        =   "Environment"
      End
      Begin Menu MenuDevices
         Caption        =   "Devices"
      End
      Begin Menu MenuVersionInfo
         Caption        =   "Version Info"
      End
      Begin Menu MenuVersionDesc
         Caption        =   "Version Desc:"
      End
   End
End
```

FileDemo Listings

Module FILEDEMO.BAS contains the constant declarations and global variables used by the program.

Listing 13.3   Module FILEDEMO.BAS

```
' FileDemo program example


'
'   Global Variables
'
Global verbuf$      ' Version buffer
Global Filename$    ' Current file to examine
```

The **ShowDosEnvironment** function shows how you can obtain the value for any DOS environment variable, using API functions. In practice, the Visual Basic **Environ$** function is a more practical solution.

The DOS environment contains the environment strings separated by NULL characters with two consecutive NULL characters marking the end of the last string.

The trick here is to use the **lstrcpy** API function (described in Chapter 16) to copy each string from the memory block address returned by the **GetDos-Environment** function. This function copies the string including the null terminator. After each string is copied, the address variable **envaddr&** is positioned at the start of the next string. Once an empty string is obtained, the function knows that all strings have been copied.

Listing 13.4   **Form Listing FILEDEMO.FRM**

```
'
'   Shows information on the DOS environment
'
Sub ShowDosEnvironment ()
    Dim envstring As String * 256
    Dim envaddr&
    Dim res$
    Dim curpos%
    Dim crlf$

    crlf$ = Chr$(13) + Chr$(10)

    envaddr& = GetDosEnvironment()
    dl& = lstrcpy(envstring, envaddr&)
    Do While (Asc(envstring) <> 0)
        curpos% = InStr(envstring, Chr$(0))
        res$ = res$ + Left$(envstring, curpos% - 1) + crlf$
        envaddr& = envaddr& + curpos%
        dl& = lstrcpy(envstring, envaddr&)
    Loop
    MsgBox res$, 0, "Environment"

End Sub
```

This function shows how the **GetProfileString** function is used to obtain a list of the key names for a section in the WIN.INI file. If a string was specified instead of the zero for the second parameter, the function would fill the buffer with the entire value of the specified key string.

Private initialization files can be accessed using the **GetPrivateProfile-String** function, which works the same way.

```
'
'   Lists all devices in the WIN.INI file
'
Sub ShowDevices ()
    Dim devstring As String * 4096
    Dim startpos%, endpos%
    Dim crlf$
    Dim res$

    crlf$ = Chr$(13) + Chr$(10)

    di% = GetProfileString("devices", 0&, "", devstring, 4095)
```

```
        startpos% = 1
        Do While (Asc(Mid$(devstring, startpos%, 1)) <> 0)
            endpos% = InStr(startpos%, devstring, Chr$(0))
            res$ = res$ + Mid$(devstring, startpos%, endpos% - startpos%) + crlf$
            startpos% = endpos% + 1
        Loop
        MsgBox res$, 0, "Devices"
End Sub
```

The File_Click function demonstrates how the version resource information is loaded into a Visual Basic string buffer. Note how the **GetFileVersion-InfoSize** function is used to determine the required size for the string buffer.

```
Sub File1_Click ()
    Dim fressize&
    Dim freshnd&

    ' Build the file name
    If Right$(Dir1.Path, 1) = "\" Then
        Filename$ = Dir1.Path + File1.Filename
    Else
        Filename$ = Dir1.Path + "\" + File1.Filename
    End If

    ' Determine if version information is present, and
    ' if so how large a buffer is needed to hold it.
    fressize& = GetFileVersionInfoSize(Filename$, freshnd&)
    If fressize& = 0 Then
        verbuf$ = ""
        Exit Sub
    End If
    ' Version info is unlikely to ever be greater than 64k
    ' but check anyway. If it was larger than 64k, we would
    ' need to allocate a huge buffer instead.  Note, we
    ' are only using an approximation to 64k here to take
    ' into account the VB string overhead.
    If fressize& > 64000 Then fressize& = 64000
    verbuf$ = String$(CInt(fressize&) + 1, Chr$(0))
    ' Load the string with the version information

    di% = GetFileVersionInfo(Filename$, freshnd&, fressize&, ⇔
    agGetAddressForVBString&(verbuf$))
    ' The menu commands will use the information
    ' in this global version buffer.

    If di% = 0 Then verbuf$ = ""    ' Error occurred
End Sub
```

The **ShowVersionInfo** function demonstrates how a **FIXEDFILEINFO** block is loaded from the version resource string. The version resource string

verbuf$ is loaded by the **File1_Click** function each time a file is selected. It
will be empty if the file has no version information.

```
'
' Show information from the fixed version info for the
'   current file.
'
Sub ShowVersionInfo ()
    Dim ffi As FIXEDFILEINFO
    Dim ffiaddr&, fiilen%
    Dim res$, crlf$

    crlf$ = Chr$(13) + Chr$(10)

    If verbuf$ = "" Then
        MsgBox "No version information available for this file"
        Exit Sub
    End If

    di% = VerQueryValue(agGetAddressForVBString (verbuf$), "\", fiiaddr&, ⇔
    fiilen%)
    If di% = 0 Then
        MsgBox "No fixed version information in this file"
        Exit Sub
    End If

    ' Copy the fixed file info into the structure
    agCopyDataBynum fiiaddr&, agGetAddressForObject& (ffi), 52

    ' Now build the output report
    res$ = "File Version " + CalcVersion$(ffi.dwFileVersionMS) + crlf$
    res$ = res$ + "Product Version " + CalcVersion$(ffi.dwProductVersionMS) + ⇔
    crlf$
    res$ = res$ + "File type is: "
    Select Case ffi.dwFileType
        Case VFT_UNKNOWN
                    res$ = res$ + "unknown"
        Case VFT_APP
                    res$ = res$ + "application"
        Case VFT_DLL
                    res$ = res$ + "dynamic link library"
        Case VFT_DRV
                    res$ = res$ + "device driver"
        Case VFT_FONT
                    res$ = res$ + "Font resource"
        Case VFT_VXD
                    res$ = res$ + "virtual device"
        Case VFT_STATIC_LIB
                    res$ = res$ + "static link library"
    End Select
    res$ = res$ + crlf$
```

```
        MsgBox res$, 0, "Fixed Version Info"

End Sub


    '
    '   Breaks a 32 bit version into major and minor revs, then
    '   then returns the string representation.
    '
Function CalcVersion$ (vernum&)
    Dim major%, minor%
    major% = CInt(vernum& / &H10000)
    minor% = CInt(vernum& And &HFFFF&)
    CalcVersion$ = Str$(major%) + "." + LTrim$(Str$(minor%))
End Function
```

The **ShowDescInfo** and **GetInfoString** functions work together to obtain string information from the version resource for a file. Only a few of the strings are examined by these functions, but they can be easily extended to read all of the file version information using the same techniques.

The **GetInfoString** function first retrieves the translation array for the version resource, then demonstrates how you can look for the U.S. English entry in the table. It then builds the eight-character hexadecimal string required by the **VerQueryValue** function to obtain **StringFileInfo** strings.

The **VerQueryValue** function sets the value of a long address and integer variables with the address and size of the string respectively, if it is found. The string is then copied into a Visual Basic string for display in a message box.

```
    '
    ' This function shows how to obtain other information about
    ' a file.
    '
Sub ShowDescInfo ()
    Dim res$, crlf$

    crlf$ = Chr$(13) + Chr$(10)

    If verbuf$ = "" Then
        MsgBox "No version information available for this file"
        Exit Sub
    End If

    res$ = "Company: " + GetInfoString$("CompanyName") + crlf$
    res$ = res$ + "File Desc: " + GetInfoString$("FileDescription") + crlf$
    res$ = res$ + "Copyright: " + GetInfoString$("LegalCopyright") + crlf$

    MsgBox res$, 0, "Fixed Version Info"
```

```
End Sub

Function GetInfoString$ (stringtoget$)
    Dim tbuf$
    Dim nullpos%
    Dim xlatelang%
    Dim xlatecode%
    Dim numentries%
    Dim fiilen%, fiiaddr&
    Dim xlatestring$

    di% = VerQueryValue(agGetAddressForVBString(verbuf$), ⇔
    "\VarFileInfo\Translation", fiiaddr&, fiilen%)
    If (di% <> 0) Then ' Translation table exists
        numentries% = fiilen% / 4
        xlateval& = 0
        For x% = 1 To numentries%
            ' Copy the 4 byte translation entry for the first
            agCopyDataBynum fiiaddr&, agGetAddressForObject(xlatelang%), 2
            agCopyDataBynum fiiaddr& + 2, agGetAddressForObject(xlatecode%), 2
            ' Exit if U.S. English was found
            If xlatelang% = &H409 Then Exit For
            fiiaddr& = fiiaddr& + 4
        Next x%
    Else
        ' No translation table - Assume standard ASCII
        xlatelang% = &H409
        xlatecode% = 0
    End If

    xlatestring$ = Hex$(xlatecode%)
    ' Make sure hex string is 4 chars long
    While Len(xlatestring$) < 4
        xlatestring$ = "0" + xlatestring$
    Wend
    xlatestring$ = Hex$(xlatelang%) + xlatestring$
    ' Make sure hex string is 8 chars long
    While Len(xlatestring$) < 8
        xlatestring$ = "0" + xlatestring$
    Wend

    di% = VerQueryValue(agGetAddressForVBString(verbuf$), "\StringFileInfo\" ⇔
    + xlatestring$ + "\" + stringtoget$, fiiaddr&, fiilen%)
    If di% = 0 Then
        GetInfoString$ = "Unavailable"
        Exit Function
    End If

    tbuf$ = String$(fiilen% + 1, Chr$(0))

    ' Copy the structure info into the string
    agCopyDataBynum fiiaddr&, agGetAddressForVBString&(tbuf$), fiilen%
```

```
    nullpos% = InStr(tbuf$, Chr$(Ø))
    If (nullpos% > 1) Then
        GetInfoString$ = Left$(tbuf$, nullpos% - 1)
    Else
        GetInfoString$ = "None"
    End If

End Function

Sub MenuVersionInfo_Click ()
    ShowVersionInfo
End Sub

Sub MenuVersionDesc_Click ()
    ShowDescInfo
End Sub

Sub MenuEnvironment_Click ()
    ShowDosEnvironment
End Sub

Sub MenuDevices_Click ()
    ShowDevices
End Sub

Sub Drive1_Change ()
    Dir1.Path = drive1.drive
End Sub

Sub Dir1_Change ()
    File1.Path = Dir1.Path
End Sub
```

Function Reference

This section contains an alphabetical reference for the functions described in this chapter.

▮ CopyLZFile

VB Declaration   `Declare Function CopyLZFile& Lib "lzexpand" (ByVal hfSource%, ByVal hfDest%)`

Description   This function is identical to the **LZCopy** function except that it is designed for use in copying multiple files. Before using this function to copy files, you must call the **LZStart** function. When all files have been copied, the **LZDone** function should be called to release the internal buffers used for decompressing files.

Refer to the description of the **LZCopy** function for further details on using this function. This function requires that the LZEXPAND.DLL dynamic link library provided with Windows 3.1 be present on your system.

▮ GetDOSEnvironment

VB Declaration   `Declare Function GetDOSEnvironment& Lib "Kernel" ()`

Description   Retrieves an address pointer to the current environment string settings for a task. Each environment string is separated by a NULL character, and the last string is terminated with two NULL characters.

Use with VB   No problem.

Return Value   **Long**—Address of the environment block.

Comments   Refer to the FileDemo example program in this chapter for an illustration of the use of this function.

▮ GetDriveType

VB Declaration   `Declare Function GetDriveType% Lib "Kernel" (ByVal nDrive%)`

Description   Determines the type of the specified drive.

Use with VB   No problem.

Parameter	Type/Description
nDrive	**Integer**—The number of the drive to examine. Drive A is zero, B is one, and so on.

Return Value   **Integer**—Zero if the drive type cannot be determined. One of the following constants otherwise:
DRIVE_REMOVABLE: It is a removable disk drive (such as a floppy disk).
DRIVE_FIXED: It is a fixed disk drive.
DRIVE_REMOTE: It is a remote drive (such as a network server).

■ GetExpandedName

VB Declaration   Declare Function GetExpandedName% Lib "lzexpand" (ByVal lpszSource$, ByVal ⇔
lpszBuffer$)

Description   Retrieves the full name of a compressed file. The file must have been compressed using the
COMPRESS.EXE program using the /r option.

Use with VB   Refer to "Compressed File Operations," earlier in this chapter. This function requires that the
LZEXPAND.DLL library distributed with Windows 3.1 be present.

Parameter	Type/Description
lpszSource	**String**—The name of the compressed file.
lpszBuffer	**String**—A buffer to load with the full name of the file.

Return Value   **Integer**—A positive integer greater than zero on success, negative on error.

■ GetFileResource

VB Declaration   Declare Function GetFileResource% Lib "ver.dll" (ByVal lpszFileName$, ByVal ⇔
lpszResType&, ByVal lpszResID&, ByVal dwFileOffset&, ByVal dwResLen&, ByVal ⇔
lpvData&)

Description   Retrieves a resource into a buffer. This is typically used for version resources.

Use with VB   Not recommended. The **GetFileVersionInfo** function is easier to use. This function requires that
the VER.DLL library distributed with Windows 3.1 be present. Refer to "Version Stamping,"
earlier in this chapter, for additional information.

Parameter	Type/Description
lpszFileName	**String**—The name of the module that contains the resource.
lpszResType	**Long**—The type of resource. Typically **VS_FILE_INFO** for version information.
lpszResID	**Long**—The identifier of the resource to load. This is **VS_VERSION_INFO** for version information.
dwFileOffset	**Long**—A long variable. If zero, the **lpszResType** and **lpszResID** parameters are used to determine the location of the resource in the file. Otherwise, this parameter specifies the offset of the specified resource in bytes from the beginning of the module file and the **lpszResType** and **lpszResID** parameters are ignored.
dwResLen	**Long**—The size, in bytes, of the buffer specified by the **lpvData** parameter. The **GetFileResourceSize** function may be used to determine the required buffer size to hold the entire resource.
lpvData	**Long**—The address of the memory block or buffer to load with the resource.

Return Value   **Integer**—TRUE (nonzero) on success, zero otherwise.

■ GetFileResourceSize

VB Declaration   Declare Function GetFileResourceSize& Lib "ver.dll" (ByVal lpszFileName$, ⇔
ByVal lpszResType&, ByVal lpszResID&, dwFileOffset&)

Description   Determines the size of a resource in a module. This is typically used for version resources.

Use with VB   Not recommended. The **GetFileVersionInfoSize** function is easier to use. This function requires that the VER.DLL library distributed with Windows 3.1 be present. Refer to "Version Stamping," earlier in this chapter, for additional information.

Parameter	Type/Description
lpszFileName	**String**—The name of the module that contains the resource.
lpszResType	**Long**—The type of resource. Typically **VS_FILE_INFO** for version information.
lpszResID	**Long**—The identifier of the resource to load. This is **VS_VERSION_INFO** for version information.
dwFileOffset	**Long**—A long variable that will be loaded with the offset of the specified resource in bytes from the beginning of the module file.

Return Value   **Long**—The size of the resource in bytes, zero on error.

■ GetFileVersionInfo

VB Declaration   Declare Function GetFileVersionInfo% Lib "ver.dll" (ByVal lpszFileName$, ⇔
ByVal handle&, ByVal cbBuf&, ByVal lpvData&)

Description   Retrieves the file version information from a module that supports version stamping.

Use with VB   This function requires that the VER.DLL library distributed with Windows 3.1 be present. Refer to "Version Stamping," earlier in this chapter, for additional information.

Parameter	Type/Description
lpszFileName	**String**—The name of the module file from which to load version information.
handle	**Long**—The handle returned by the **GetFileVersionInfoSize** buffer. May be zero to search for version information in the file.
cbBuf	**Long**—The size of the **lpvData** buffer.
lpvData	**Long**—The address of a buffer to load with version information. This buffer must be at least **cbBuf** bytes long.

Return Value   **Integer**—TRUE (nonzero) on success, zero otherwise.

Comments   The **VerQueryValue** API function can be used to extract data from the resource buffer loaded by this function.

■ GetFileVersionInfoSize

VB Declaration `Declare Function GetFileVersionInfoSize% Lib "ver.dll" (ByVal lpszFile ⇔ Name$, lpdwHandle&)`

Description Retrieves the size of the buffer required to hold the file version information for a module that supports version stamping.

Use with VB This function requires that the VER.DLL library distributed with Windows 3.1 be present. Refer to "Version Stamping," earlier in this chapter, for additional information.

Parameter	Type/Description
lpszFileName	**String**—The name of the module file from which to load version information.
lpdwHandle	**Long**—A long variable to load with the required buffer size for the version resource information for the specified file.

Return Value **Integer**—TRUE (nonzero) on success, zero otherwise. Zero is also returned if the file does not support version stamping.

■ GetPrivateProfileInt

VB Declaration `Declare Function GetPrivateProfileInt% Lib "Kernel" (ByVal lpApplication ⇔ Name$, ByVal lpKeyName$, ByVal nDefault%, ByVal lpFileName$)`

Description Retrieves an integer value for the specified entry in an initialization file.

Use with VB No problem.

Parameter	Type/Description
lpApplicationName	**String**—The section to search for the entry. This string is not case-sensitive.
lpKeyName	**String**—The key name or entry to retrieve. This string is not case-sensitive.
nDefault	**Integer**—The default value to return if the specified entry is not found.
lpFileName	**String**—The name of the private initialization file. If a full path name is not specified, Windows will search for the file in the Windows directory.

Return Value **Integer**—The value of the entry found, or the default value if the specified entry is not found. If the number found is not a legal integer, the function will return that portion that is legal. For example, the entry xyz=55zz will cause 55 to be returned.

This function also understands hexadecimal numbers in standard C format: A hex number will be prefixed by the characters 0x, thus 0x55ab would be equivalent to &H55AB in Visual Basic.

GetPrivateProfileString

VB Declaration　`Declare Function GetPrivateProfileString% Lib "Kernel" (ByVal lpApplication⇔`
`Name$, ByVal lpKeyName As Any, ByVal lpDefault$, ByVal lpReturnedString$, ⇔`
`ByVal nSize%, ByVal lpFileName$)`

Description　Retrieves the string for the specified entry in an initialization file.

Use with VB　No problem.

Parameter	Type/Description
lpApplicationName	**String**—The section to search for the entry. This string is not case-sensitive.
lpKeyName	**String** or **Long**—The key name or entry to retrieve. This string is not case-sensitive. If zero, the **lpReturnedString** buffer will be loaded with a list of all of the keys for the specified section. This parameter has no type checking, so be sure to use a string or long variable as a parameter to prevent errors.
lpszDefault	**String**—The default value to return if the specified entry is not found. This may be the empty string (`""`).
lpReturnedString	**String**—A string buffer preallocated to at least **nSize** bytes in length.
nSize	**Integer**—The maximum number of characters to load into the **lpszReturnedString** buffer.
lpFileName	**String**—The name of the private initialization file. If a full path name is not specified, Windows will search for the file in the Windows directory.

Return Value　**Integer**—The number of bytes copied into the **lpReturnedString** buffer not counting the terminating NULL character.

Comments　If the **lpKeyName** parameter is zero, the **lpReturnedString** buffer will be loaded with a list of all of the keys for the specified section. Each key will be terminated with a NULL character, with the final key being terminated with two NULL characters.

GetProfileInt

VB Declaration　`Declare Function GetProfileInt% Lib "Kernel" (ByVal lpAppName$, ByVal ⇔`
`lpKeyName$, ByVal nDefault%)`

Description　Retrieves an integer value for the specified entry in the WIN.INI initialization file.

Use with VB　No problem.

Parameter	Type/Description
lpApplicationName	**String**—The section to search for the entry. This string is not case-sensitive.

Parameter	Type/Description
lpKeyName	**String**—The key name or entry to retrieve. This string is not case-sensitive.
nDefault	**Integer**—The default value to return if the specified entry is not found.

Return Value **Integer**—The value of the entry found, or the default value if the specified entry is not found. If the number found is not a legal integer, the function will return that portion that is legal. For example, the entry xyz=55zz will cause 55 to be returned.

This function also understands hexadecimal numbers in standard C format: A hex number will be prefixed by the characters 0x, thus 0x55ab would be equivalent to &H55AB in Visual Basic.

■ GetProfileString

VB Declaration
```
Declare Function GetProfileString% Lib "Kernel" (ByVal lpAppName$, ByVal ⇔
lpKeyName As Any, ByVal lpDefault$, ByVal lpReturnedString$, ByVal nSize%)
```

Description Retrieves the string for the specified entry in the WIN.INI initialization file.

Use with VB No problem.

Parameter	Type/Description
lpApplicationName	**String**—The section to search for the entry. This string is not case-sensitive.
lpKeyName	**String** or **Long**—The key name or entry to retrieve. This string is not case sensitive. If zero, the **lpReturnedString** buffer will be loaded with a list of all of the keys for the specified section. This parameter has no type checking, so be sure to use a string or long variable as a parameter to prevent errors.
lpszDefault	**String**—The default value to return if the specified entry is not found. This may be the empty string ("").
lpReturnedString	**String**—A string buffer preallocated to at least **nSize** bytes in length.
nSize	**Integer**—The maximum number of characters to load into the **lpszReturnedString** buffer.

Return Value **Integer**—The number of bytes copied into the **lpReturnedString** buffer not counting the terminating NULL character.

Comments If the **lpKeyName** parameter is zero, the **lpReturnedString** buffer will be loaded with a list of all of the keys for the specified section. Each key will be terminated with a NULL character, with the final key being terminated with two NULL characters.

■ GetSystemDirectory

VB Declaration   `Declare Function GetSystemDirectory% Lib "Kernel" (ByVal lpBuffer$, ⇔`
`ByVal nSize%) .`

Description   This function retrieves the full path name of the Windows system directory. This is the directory that contains all of the system files. Microsoft is beginning to standardize on placing Visual Basic custom control files in this directory as well. Generally, you should avoid creating files in this directory.

Use with VB   No problem.

Parameter	Type/Description
lpBuffer	**String**—A string buffer to load with the system directory name. It should be preallocated to at least **nSize+1** characters long. You should usually allocate at least 144 characters for this buffer.
nSize	**Integer**—The maximum length of the **lpBuffer** string.

Return Value   **Integer**—The length of the string copied into **lpBuffer**. Zero on error.

■ GetTempDrive

VB Declaration   `Declare Function GetTempDrive% Lib "Kernel" (ByVal cDriveLetter%)`

Description   Retrieves the letter of a disk drive that may be used for temporary files. Note that this function does not take into account a temporary drive setting specified by the TEMP or TMP environment variables. If a hard drive is available, this function will return the letter of the first hard drive in the system.

Use with VB   No problem.

Parameter	Type/Description
cDriveLetter	**Integer**—Not used.

Return Value   **Integer**—The low-order byte contains the drive letter. In Visual Basic, the drive letter in string form may be obtained as follows:

`drivename$ = Chr$(GetTempDrive%(0) And &H00FF)`

■ GetTempFileName

VB Declaration   `Declare Function GetTempFileName% Lib "Kernel" (ByVal cDriveLetter%, ⇔`
`ByVal lpPrefixString$, ByVal wUnique%, ByVal lpTempFileName$)`

Description   This function obtains the name of a temporary file that can be used by an application.

Use with VB	No problem.

Parameter	Type/Description
cDriveLetter	**Integer**—The letter of the drive to use for temporary files. If zero, the first hard drive will be used. In either case, the drive will be over-ridden if a TEMP environment variable is defined that specifies a drive letter. Use the Visual Basic **Asc** function to set this parameter as follows: `GetTempFileName(Asc("c"),....`
lpPrefixString	**String**—The file name prefix to use. You should limit this to less than eight characters so that there will be room for the function to append the integer according to the **wUnique** parameter.
wUnique	**Integer**—A number to append to the prefix string. If zero, this function will generate a file name using a random number. It will then see if a file by that name exists. If it does, the function will increment the number and continue with the attempt until a unique file name is generated. The file will remain on the drive with a length of zero bytes.
lpTempFileName	**String**—A buffer to load with the new temporary file name. This buffer should be at least 144 characters long.

Return Value	**Integer**—The value of the **wUnique** number actually used to generate the file name. If the **wUnique** parameter was not zero, this will be the value of the parameter.
Comments	File names always use the OEM character set. Refer to Chapter 5 for information on use of character sets under Windows. Temporary files are not automatically deleted by Windows.

■ GetWindowsDirectory

VB Declaration	`Declare Function GetWindowsDirectory% Lib "Kernel" (ByVal lpBuffer$, ⇔` `ByVal nSize%)`
Description	This function retrieves the full path name of the Windows directory. This is the directory that contains most Windows application files and initialization files.
Use with VB	No problem.

Parameter	Type/Description
lpBuffer	**String**—A string buffer to load with the Windows directory name. It should be preallocated to at least **nSize+1** characters long. You should usually allocate at least 144 characters for this buffer.
nSize	**Integer**—The maximum length of the **lpBuffer** string.

Return Value	**Integer**—The length of the string copied into **lpBuffer**. Zero on error.

■ hread

VB Declaration   Declare Function hread& Lib "Kernel" Alias "_hread" (ByVal hf%, ByVal ⇔ hpvBuffer&, ByVal cbBuffer&)

Description   Reads data from a file into a memory buffer. This function is capable of transferring blocks greater than 64k in size and blocks that cross segment boundaries. Allocation and use of huge (greater than 64k) memory blocks is described in Chapter 12.

Use with VB   No problem.

Parameter	Type/Description
hf	**Integer**—A DOS file handle. The DOS file handle for a Visual Basic file number can be obtained using the Visual Basic **FileAttr** function.
hpvBuffer	**Long**—Pointer to a block of memory into which data is read.
cbBuffer	**Long**—Number of bytes to read.

Return Value   **Long**—The number of bytes read, -1 on error. If this number is less than **cbBuffer**, the end of the file has been reached.

■ hwrite

VB Declaration   Declare Function hwrite& Lib "Kernel" Alias "_hwrite" (ByVal hf%, ByVal ⇔ hpvBuffer&, ByVal cbBuffer&)

Description   Writes data to a file from a memory buffer. This function is capable of transferring blocks greater than 64k in size and blocks that cross segment boundaries. Allocation and use of huge (greater than 64k) memory blocks is described in Chapter 12.

Use with VB   No problem.

Parameter	Type/Description
hf	**Integer**—A DOS file handle. The DOS file handle for a Visual Basic file number can be obtained by using the Visual Basic **File-Attr** function.
hpvBuffer	**Long**—Pointer to a block of memory to write to the file.
cbBuffer	**Long**—Number of bytes to write.

Return Value   **Long**—The number of bytes written, -1 on error.

■ lclose

VB Declaration   Declare Function lclose% Lib "Kernel" Alias "_lclose" (ByVal hFile%)

Description   Closes the specified file.

| **Use with VB** | Identical to the Visual Basic **Close** command. It is generally better to use **Close** because it supports Visual Basic error handling. |

Parameter	Type/Description
hFile	**Integer**—A DOS file handle. The DOS file handle for a Visual Basic file number can be obtained by using the Visual Basic **File-Attr** function.

Return Value   **Integer**—Zero on success, **HFILE_ERROR** on error.

■ lcreat

VB Declaration
```
Declare Function lcreat% Lib "Kernel" Alias "_lcreat" (ByVal lpPathName$, ⇔
ByVal iAttribute%)
```

Description   Creates a file. If the file already exists, it is truncated to a length of zero and opened for reading and writing.

Use with VB   This function duplicates functionality available in the Visual Basic **Open** statement.

Parameter	Type/Description
lpPathName	**String**—The name of the file to create.
iAttribute	**Integer**—One of the following values: 0: File can be read or written. 1: Create a read-only file. 2: Create a hidden file. 3: Create a system file.

Return Value   **Integer**—A DOS file handle to the open file on success, **HFILE_ERROR** on error.

Comments   This function can open files that have already been opened by other applications, so use it with caution.

■ llseek

VB Declaration
```
Declare Function llseek& Lib "Kernel" Alias "_llseek" (ByVal hFile%, ByVal ⇔
lOffset&, ByVal iOrigin%)
```

Description   Sets the current position for reading or writing in a file.

Use with VB   This function duplicates the functionality of the Visual Basic **Seek** statement. Note that this function may produce unexpected results if you attempt to use it on files opened in Visual Basic in modes other than binary mode.

Parameter	Type/Description
hFile	**Integer**—A DOS file handle. The DOS file handle for a Visual Basic file number can be obtained using the Visual Basic **FileAttr** function.
lOffset	**Long**—The offset in bytes.

Parameter	Type/Description
iOrigin	**Integer**—One of the following values: 0: **lOffset** specifies the new position as an offset from the start of the file. 1: **lOffset** specifies the new position as an offset from the current position. 2: **lOffset** specifies the new position as an offset from the end of the file.

Return Value   **Long**—The new position as an offset in bytes from the start of the file.

■ lopen

VB Declaration
```
Declare Function lopen% Lib "Kernel" Alias "_lopen" (ByVal lpPathName$, ByVal ⇔
iReadWrite%)
```

Description   Opens the specified file in binary mode.

Use with VB   The Visual Basic **Open** command is recommended due to its flexibility and compatibility with the Visual Basic error handler.

Parameter	Type/Description
lpPathName	**String**—The name of the file to open.
iReadWrite	**Integer**—A combination of the access mode and share mode constants as follows: *Access Mode* **READ**: File is open for reading. **READ_WRITE**: File is open for reading and writing. **WRITE**: File is open for writing. *Share Mode* **OF_SHARE_COMPAT, OF_SHARE_DENY_NONE, OF_-SHARE_DENY_READ, OF_SHARE_DENY_WRITE, OF_-SHARE_EXCLUSIVE**, as defined in Table 13.12 later in this chapter.

Return Value   **Integer**—A DOS file handle to the open file on success, **HFILE_ERROR** on error.

■ lread

VB Declaration
```
Declare Function lread% Lib "Kernel" Alias "_lread" (ByVal hFile%, ByVal ⇔
lpBuffer$, ByVal wBytes%)
```

Description   Reads data from a file into a memory buffer.

Use with VB   No problem, but the Visual Basic file functions are more flexible.

Parameter	Type/Description
hf	**Integer**—A DOS file handle. The DOS file handle for a Visual Basic file number can be obtained using the Visual Basic **FileAttr** function.
hpvBuffer	**Long**—Pointer to a block of memory into which data is read.
wBytes	**Integer**—Number of bytes to read.

Return Value   **Integer**—The number of bytes read, -1 on error. If this number is less than **cbBuffer**, the end of the file has been reached.

■ lwrite

VB Declaration   ```
Declare Function lwrite% Lib "Kernel" Alias "_lwrite" (ByVal hFile%, ⇔
ByVal lpBuffer$, ByVal wBytes%)
```

**Description**     Writes data to a file from a memory buffer.

**Use with VB**     No problem, but the Visual Basic file functions are more flexible.

| Parameter | Type/Description |
|---|---|
| hf | **Integer**—A DOS file handle. The DOS file handle for a Visual Basic file number can be obtained by using the Visual Basic **FileAttr** function. |
| hpvBuffer | **Long**—Pointer to a block of memory to write to the file. |
| wBytes | **Integer**—Number of bytes to write. |

**Return Value**     **Integer**—The number of bytes written, -1 on error.

# ■ LZClose

**VB Declaration**     ```
Declare Sub LZClose Lib "lzexpand" (ByVal hf%)
```

Description   Closes a file opened by the **LZOpenFile** or **LZInit** functions.

Use with VB   No problem. This function requires that the LZEXPAND.DLL dynamic link library provided with Windows 3.1 be present on your system.

Parameter	Type/Description
hf	**Integer**—A file handle.

■ LZCopy

VB Declaration   ```
Declare Function LZCopy& Lib "lzexpand" (ByVal hfSource%, ByVal hfDest%)
```

**Description**     Copies a file. If the source file is compressed, it will be decompressed during the copy process.
```

Use with VB

No problem. This function requires that the LZEXPAND.DLL dynamic link library provided with Windows 3.1 be present on your system.

Parameter	Type/Description
hfSource	**Integer**—A handle to the source file. This handle is provided by the **LZOpenFile** function.
hfDest	**Integer**—A handle to the destination file. This handle is provided by the **LZOpenFile** function.

Return Value

Long—The size of the destination files in bytes on success. A constant smaller than zero on error as shown in Table 13.11.

Table 13.11   **LZCopy Error Codes**

Error Code Constant	Description
LZERROR_BADINHANDLE	**hfSource** is invalid.
LZERROR_BADOUTHANDLE	**hfDest** is invalid.
LZERROR_GLOBALLOC	Insufficient memory for the internal decompression buffers.
LZERROR_GLOBLOCK	The handles to the internal decompression buffers are not valid.
LZERROR_READ	Invalid source file format.
LZERROR_UNKNOWNALG	The decompression DLL does not recognize the compression algorithm used by the source file.
LZERROR_WRITE	Error writing the output file. This is typically caused by insufficient disk space.

■ LZDone

VB Declaration   `Declare Sub LZDone Lib "lzexpand" ()`

Description

Use after a multiple file copy operation to release the internal decompression buffers. Refer to "Compressed File Operations," earlier in this chapter, for further information.

Use with VB

This function requires that the LZEXPAND.DLL dynamic link library provided with Windows 3.1 be present on your system.

■ LZInit

VB Declaration   `Declare Function LZInit% Lib "lzexpand" (ByVal hfSrc%)`

Description   This function initializes the internal buffers required to decompress a file given an open file handle to that file.

Use with VB   No problem. This function requires that the LZEXPAND.DLL dynamic link library provided with Windows 3.1 be present on your system.

Parameter	Type/Description
hfSrc	**Integer**—A handle to a file.

Return Value   **Integer**—A handle to the file. If the file is not compressed, this will be the same as **hfSrc**. If the file is compressed, this will be a special file handle compatible with the **LZCopy**, **CopyLZFiles**, **LZRead**, and **LZSeek** functions. On error, this function will return one of the error constants listed in Table 13.11.

■ LZOpenFile

VB Declaration   `Declare Function LZOpenFile% Lib "lzexpand" (ByVal lpszFile$, lpof As ⇔`
`OFSTRUCT, ByVal style%)`

Description   This function performs a number of different file operations and is compatible with compressed files. If the file is not compressed, this function simply calls the normal **OpenFile** function. Refer to "File and Directory Operations," earlier in this chapter.

Use with VB   No problem. This function requires that the LZEXPAND.DLL dynamic link library provided with Windows 3.1 be present on your system.

Parameter	Type/Description
lpszFile	**String**—The name of the file to open.
lpof	**OFSTRUCT**—**OFSTRUCT** structure to fill with data including information about the file and results of the operation.
Style	**Integer**—A combination of flag constants specifying the operation to perform as described in Table 13.12 under the description of the **OpenFile** function.

Return Value   **Integer**—A normal DOS file handle as described under the description of the **OpenFile** function if the file is successful and the style is not **OF_READ**. If the style parameter is **OF_READ** and the file is compressed, this function returns a special file handle that may be used by the **LZCopy**, **CopyLZFiles**, **LZRead**, and **LZSeek** functions.

Comments   Refer to the comments for the **OpenFile** function later in this section.

■ LZRead

VB Declaration   `Declare Function LZRead% Lib "lzexpand" (ByVal hf%, ByVal lpvBuf&, ByVal cb%)`

Description   Reads data from a file into a memory buffer. If **hf%** is a handle to a compressed file opened by the **LZOpenFile** or **LZInit** functions, this function will decompress the data as it is read.

Use with VB	No problem.

Parameter	Type/Description
hf	**Integer**—A file handle. This can be a DOS file handle or a special compressed file handle.
lpvBuf	**Long**—Pointer to a block of memory into which data is read.
cb	**Integer**—Number of bytes to read.

Return Value	**Integer**—The number of bytes read. If this number is less than **cbBuffer**, the end of the file has been reached. On error, this function will return one of the error constants listed in Table 13.11.

■ LZSeek

VB Declaration	Declare Function LZSeek& Lib "lzexpand" (ByVal hf%, ByVal lOffset&, ByVal ⇔ nOrigin%)
Description	Sets the current position for reading or writing in a file. If **hf%** is a handle to a compressed file opened by the **LZOpenFile** or **LZInit** function, this function will seek based on the decompressed version of the file.
Use with VB	No problem.

Parameter	Type/Description
hf	**Integer**—A handle to the file. This can be a DOS file handle or a special compressed file handle.
lOffset	**Long**—The offset in bytes.
iOrigin	**Integer**—One of the following values: 0: **lOffset** specifies the new position as an offset from the start of the file. 1: **lOffset** specifies the new position as an offset from the current position. 2: **lOffset** specifies the new position as an offset from the end of the file.

Return Value	**Long**—The new position as an offset in bytes from the start of the file. On error, this function will return one of the error constants listed in Table 13.11.

■ LZStart

VB Declaration	Declare Function LZStart% Lib "lzexpand" ()
Description	Use before a multiple file copy operation to allocate the internal decompression buffers. Refer to "Compressed File Operations," earlier in this chapter, for further information.
Use with VB	This function requires that the LZEXPAND.DLL dynamic link library provided with Windows 3.1 be present on your system.

OpenFile

VB Declaration   `Declare Function OpenFile% Lib "Kernel" (ByVal lpFileName$, lpReOpenBuff ⇔`
`As OFSTRUCT, ByVal wStyle%)`

Description   This function performs a number of different file operations. Refer to "File and Directory Operations," earlier in this chapter.

Use with VB   No problem.

Parameter	Type/Description
lpFileName	**String**—The name of the file to open.
lpReOpenBuff	**OFSTRUCT**—**OFSTRUCT** structure to fill with data including information about the file and results of the operation.
wStyle	**Integer**—A combination of flag constants specifying the operation to perform as described in Table 13.12.

Return Value   **Integer**—An MS-DOS file handle on success. Note that the file handle is not necessarily valid; for example, if the **OF_EXIST** flag is specified, the file is closed before the function returns, but the handle that was used when it was open is nevertheless returned. The function returns a negative number on error, in which case the **nErrCode** of the **OFSTRUCT** structure specified by **lpReOpenBuff** is set to the error that occurred. Errors are listed in Table 13.9 earlier in this chapter.

Comments   If the file name is specified without a full path name, or the **OF_SEARCH** flag is specified, the file will be searched for in the following locations:

1. The current directory.

2. The Windows directory.

3. The Windows system directory.

4. The directory containing the executable file for the current application.

5. Directories specified in the PATH environment variable.

6. Directories mapped into the network.

Table 13.12   OpenFile API Function Styles

wStyle Constant	Description
OF_CANCEL	If **OF_PROMPT** is specified, a cancel button will appear in the dialog box.
OF_CREATE	Creates the specified file. Truncates it to zero length if it already exists.
OF_DELETE	Deletes the specified file.

Table 13.12   OpenFile API Function Styles (Continued)

wStyle Constant	Description
OF_EXIST	Determines if a file exists by attempting to open the file. If the file exists, it is closed. The function will return the file handle used when the file was opened if the file exists, but the handle will not be valid. A negative number will be returned if the file does not exist.
OF_PARSE	Fills the **lpReOpenBuff** structure, but performs no other operation.
OF_PROMPT	If the file does not exist, a message box appears requesting the user to insert a diskette containing the file into drive A.
OF_READ	File is opened for reading only.
OF_READWRITE	File is opened for reading and writing.
OF_REOPEN	Opens the file specified in the **lpReOpenBuff** structure rather than using the **lpFileName** parameter.
OF_SEARCH	Forces Windows to search for the file even if a path is specified.
OF_SHARE_COMPAT	File can be opened multiple times by multiple applications.
OF_SHARE_DENY_NONE	File can be opened for reading or writing by other programs.
OF_SHARE_DENY_READ	Other programs may not read the file.
OF_SHARE_DENY_WRITE	Other programs may read, but may not write to this file.
OF_SHARE_EXCLUSIVE	No other program may open this file.
OF_VERIFY	Returns HFILE_ERROR if the time and date of the file specified by the lpFileName$ parameter does not match that specified by the lpReOpenBuff parameter.
OF_WRITE	File is opened for writing only.

■ SetHandleCount

VB Declaration   `Declare Function SetHandleCount% Lib "Kernel" (ByVal wNumber%)`

Description   Visual Basic, like other Windows applications, is limited in the number of files that it can open simultaneously. The default maximum is 20 file handles, but the limit can be increased by this function.

Use with VB   No problem. This function can be used to increase the maximum number of files that can be opened simultaneously by a Visual Basic Program.

Parameter	Type/Description
wNumber	**Integer**—The new limit on the number of file handles that can be used by the application. This may not be greater than 255.

Return Value **Integer**—The number of file handles available to an application after this function is called.

■ VerFindFile

VB Declaration
```
Declare Function VerFindFile% Lib "ver.dll" (ByVal fl%, ByVal FileName$, ⇔
ByVal WinDir&, ByVal AppDir$, ByVal CurrDir$, CurDirLen%, ByVal DestDir$, ⇔
DestDirLen%)
```

Description This function is used to determine where a file should be installed.

Use with VB Refer to "Version Stamping," earlier in this chapter. This function requires that the VER.DLL library distributed with Windows 3.1 be present.

Parameter	Type/Description
fl	**Integer**—Currently only **VFFF_ISSHAREDFILE** is defined to indicate that the file can be shared by multiple applications. If this flag is specified, this function will recommend that the file be installed in the Windows or system directory. If this parameter is zero, the function will recommend that the file be installed in the application directory.
Filename	**String**—The name of the file to be installed. This string should not include the path of the file.
WinDir	**Long**—Zero.
AppDir	**String**—The full path name of the directory in which the application and all its related files are being installed.
CurrDir	**String**—A buffer to load with the directory containing the existing version of the file. If a version of the file is not already present, the buffer will be loaded with the directory of the source file. Must be allocated to be at least 260 bytes long.
CurrDirLen	**Integer**—The length of the **CurrDir** buffer. This variable will be set to the actual number of characters loaded to the buffer.
DestDir	**String**—A buffer to load with the directory in which the new file should be installed. Must be allocated to be at least 260 bytes long.
DestDirLen	**Integer**—The length of the DestDir buffer. This variable will be set to the actual number of characters loaded to the buffer.

Return Value **Integer**—One of the following values:
VFF_CURNEDEST: Indicates that the existing version of the file is not in the directory specified by **DestDir**, which is where this function recommends that the new version be installed.
VFF_FILEINUSE: Indicates that the existing file is currently in use and that it may not be deleted at this time.
VFF_BUFFTOOSMALL: Indicates that one or both of the **DestDir** or **CurrDir** buffers are too small to hold the directory name.

■ VerInstallFile

VB Declaration   Declare Function VerInstallFile& Lib "ver.dll" (ByVal fl%, ByVal SrcFile$, ⇔
ByVal DstFile$, ByVal SrcDir$, ByVal DstDir$, ByVal CurrDir$, ByVal TmpFile$, ⇔
TmpFileLen%)

Description   This function is used to install a file. It uses the information provided by the **VerFindFile** function to determine where a file should be installed. The function works by first comparing the version stamps of the two files. If the source file is a newer and compatible version, the source file is copied to a temporary file in the destination directory, decompressing the file if it is compressed. Then the existing version of the file is deleted and the temporary file is renamed to match the destination file name.

   If the versions are not compatible, the temporary file may still exist in the destination directory. At that time you have the option of either deleting the temporary file, or installing the file with the **VIFF_FORCEINSTALL** flag set to force the installation.

Use with VB   Refer to "Version Stamping," earlier in this chapter. This function requires that the VER.DLL library distributed with Windows 3.1 be present.

Parameter	Type/Description
fl	**Integer**—A combination of the following constant values: **VIFF_FORCEINSTALL**: Forces installation of the source file without version checking. **VIFF_DONTDELETEOLD**: Does not delete the existing version of the file if it is not in the destination directory. If it is in the destination directory, it will be overwritten by the new file.
SrcFile	**String**—The name of the file to install. This should not include the path name for the file.
DestFile	**String**—The name that should be given to the file once it is installed. This is usually the same as **SrcFile**.
SrcDir	**String**—The source directory from which the new version of the file is copied.
DstDir	**String**—The directory in which to install the new version of the file. The **DestDir** buffer returned by the **VerFindFile** function is typically used for this parameter.
CurrDir	**String**—The directory that contains the current version of the file. The **CurrDir** buffer returned by the **VerFindFile** function is typically used for this parameter. If the string is empty, no previous version of the file exists on the system.
TmpFile	**String**—A buffer to load with the name of a temporary copy of the source file. Must be allocated to be at least 260 bytes long.
TmpFileLen	**Integer**—The length of the **TmpFile** buffer. This variable will be set to the actual number of characters loaded to the buffer including the terminating NULL character. If **VIFF_FORCEINSTALL** is specified and **TmpFileLen** is not zero, the temporary file will be renamed to the name specified in the **SrcFile** parameter.

Return Value   **Long**—An integer that contains a combination of one or more of the constants listed in Table 13.13.

Table 13.13   VerInstallFile Result Constants

Constant	Description
VIF_TEMPFILE	A temporary file that is a copy of the new file is present in the destination directory and needs to be deleted.
VIF_MISMATCH	The existing file differs from the new file in one or more version attributes. Can be overridden by specifying **VIFF_FORCEIN-STALL** in the **fl** parameter.
VIF_SRCOLD	The new version of the file is older than the existing file based on the version stamping of the files. Can be overridden by specifying **VIFF_FORCEINSTALL** in the **fl** parameter.
VIF_DIFFLANG	The new version of the file has a different language or code page value from the existing file. Can be overridden by specifying **VIFF_FORCEINSTALL** in the **fl** parameter.
VIF_DIFFCODEPG	The new version of the file needs a code page that is not present on the version of Windows now running. Can be overridden by specifying **VIFF_FORCEINSTALL** in the **fl** parameter.
VIF_DIFFTYPE	The new version of the file differs in type, subtype, or target operating system from the existing version. Can be overridden by specifying **VIFF_FORCEINSTALL** in the **fl** parameter.
VIF_WRITEPROT	The preexisting file is write-protected.
VIF_FILEINUSE	The existing file is in use.
VIF_OUTOFSPACE	There is insufficient disk space on the destination drive.
VIF_ACCESSVIOLATION	Operation failed due to an access violation.
VIF_SHARINGVIOLATION	Operation failed due to a sharing violation.
VIF_CANNOTCREATE	The temporary file could not be created.
VIF_CANNOTDELETE	The existing version of the file could not be deleted.
VIF_CANNOTRENAME	The temporary file could not be renamed to the name of the existing file. The existing file has already been deleted.
VIF_OUTOFMEMORY	Operation failed due to lack of memory.
VIF_CANNOTREADDISK	The source file could not be read.
VIF_CANNOTREADDEST	The existing destination file cannot be read (thus version information can not be checked).
VIF_BUFFTOOSMALL	The **TmpFileLen** parameter is too small to hold the name of the temporary file.

■ VerLanguageName

VB Declaration   `Declare Function VerLanguageName% Lib "ver.dll" (ByVal Lang%, ByVal ⇔`
`lpszLang$, ByVal cbLang%)`

Description   This function retrieves the name of a language based on the 16-bit language code. Language codes are used in the version resource for a file to determine the language for which the file was written. Table 13.14 lists the language codes supported by Windows.

Use with VB   Refer to "Version Stamping," earlier in this chapter. This function requires that the VER.DLL library distributed with Windows 3.1 be present.

Parameter	Type/Description
Lang	**Integer**—The language ID.
lpszLang	**String**—A buffer to load with the text name of the specified language. This buffer should be preallocated to at least **cbLang+1** bytes.
cbLang	**Integer**—The length of the **lpszLang** buffer.

Return Value   **Integer**— The number of characters loaded into the **lpszLang** buffer, zero on error.

Table 13.14   **Language Codes Supported by Windows**

Language Value	Language
&H401	Arabic
&H402	Bulgarian
&H403	Catalan
&H404	Traditional Chinese
&H405	Czech
&H406	Danish
&H407	German
&H408	Greek
&H409	U.S. English
&H40A	Castilian Spanish
&H40B	Finnish
&H40C	French
&H40D	Hebrew

Table 13.14   Language Codes Supported by Windows (Continued)

Language Value	Language
&H40E	Hungarian
&H40F	Icelandic
&H410	Italian
&H411	Japanese
&H412	Korean
&H413	Dutch
&H414	Norwegian—Bokmål
&H415	Polish
&H416	Brazilian Portugese
&H417	Rhaeto-Romanic
&H418	Romanian
&H419	Russian
&H41A	Croato-Serbian (Latin)
&H41B	Slóvak
&H41C	Albanian
&H41D	Swedish
&H41E	Thai
&H41F	Turkish
&H420	Urdu
&H421	Bahasa
&H804	Simplified Chinese
&H807	Swiss German
&H809	U.K. English
&H80A	Mexican Spanish
&H80C	Belgian French

Table 13.14   Language Codes Supported by Windows (Continued)

Language Value	Language
&H810	Swiss Italian
&H813	Belgian Dutch
&H814	Norwegian—Nynorsk
&H816	Portugese
&H81A	Serbo-Croatian (Cyrillic)
&HC0C	Canadian French
&H100C	Swiss French

■ VerQueryValue

VB Declaration   Declare Function VerQueryValue% Lib "ver.dll" (ByVal lpvBlock&, ByVal ⇔
SubBlock$, lpBuffer&, lpcb%)

Description   This function is used to retrieve information from the version resource. Before calling this function, the version resource information must be retrieved using the **GetFileVersionInfo** structure. This function examines the resource information and copies the requested data into a buffer.

Use with VB   Refer to "Version Stamping," earlier in this chapter. This function requires that the VER.DLL library distributed with Windows 3.1 be present.

Parameter	Type/Description
lpvBlock	**Long**—The address of a block of memory containing version information data as retrieved by the **GetFileVersionInfo** function.
SubBlock	**String**—One of the following: **"\"**: to retrieve the **FIXEDFILEINFO** structure for this file. **"\VarFileInfo\Translation"**: to retrieve the translation table for this file. **"\StringFileInfo\...."**: to retrieve string information for a file. Refer to the Comments section for a full description.
lpBuffer&	**Long**—The address of the buffer to load with the requested version information. This should be preallocated to at least **lpcb** bytes long.
lpcb	**Short**—The length, in bytes, of the **lpBuffer** buffer.

Return Value   **Integer**—TRUE (nonzero) on success, zero if the requested information does not exist or **lpvBlock** is not valid version information.

Comments   When the **SubBlock** parameter is **"\VarFileInfo\Translation"**, the buffer will be loaded with an integer array. Each pair of integers represents a language and code page pair describing available

string information. The **StringFileInfo** string data is retrieved by specifying a string with three parts as follows:

`"\StringFileInfo\`*languagecodepage*`\`*stringname*`"`

languagecodepage is an eight-character hex number in string form. If the language code page entry in the translation table is &H04090000, then this string should be **"04090000"**. *stringname* is a string name from those listed in Table 13.6 in "Version Stamping," earlier in this chapter. An example of this parameter would be:

`"\StringFileInfo\04090000\CompanyName"`

■ WNetAddConnection

VB Declaration
```
Declare Function WNetAddConnection% Lib "User" (ByVal lpszNetPath$, ⇔
ByVal lpszPassword$, ByVal lpszLocalName$)
```

Description   This function redirects a port or disk drive to a network server or device.

Use with VB   No known problems.

Parameter	Type/Description
lpszNetPath	**String**—The name of the network device or server.
lpszPassword	**String**—Any required network password.
lpszLocalName	**String**—The local device or drive name. This can be drives A-Z, or LPT1 through LPT3.

Return Value   **Integer**—Refer to the constants beginning with the prefix WN_ in the APICONST.TXT file provided with this book.

■ WNetCancelConnection

VB Declaration
```
Declare Function WNetCancelConnection% Lib "User" (ByVal lpszName$, ⇔
ByVal fForce%)
```

Description   This function cancels the redirection of a port or disk drive to a network server or device.

Use with VB   No known problems.

Parameter	Type/Description
lpszName	**String**—The local device or drive name for which redirection is to be canceled. This can be drives A-Z, or LPT1 through LPT3.
fForce	**Integer**—If TRUE (nonzero), the redirection is ended even if there are open files or print jobs in progress. If zero, the redirection will not be canceled if there are any open files across the network or print jobs in progress, and the **WN_OPEN_FILES** error will be returned.

Return Value   **Integer**—Refer to the constants beginning with the prefix WN_ in the APICONST.TXT file provided with this book.

■ **WNetGetConnection**

VB Declaration   `Declare Function WNetGetConnection% Lib "User" (ByVal lpszLocalName$, ⇔`
`ByVal lpszRemoteName$, cbRemoteName%)`

Description   This function retrieves information about the redirection of a port or disk drive to a network server or device.

Use with VB   No known problems.

Parameter	Type/Description
lpszLocalName	**String**—The local device or drive name. This can be drives A-Z, or LPT1 through LPT3.
lpszRemoteName	**String**—This buffer will be loaded with the name of the network device or server that is associated with the redirected device or drive specified by **lpszLocalName**. This buffer should be preallocated to be at least **cbRemoteName** bytes long.
cbRemoteName	**Integer**—The length of the **lpszRemoteName** buffer. After the function is called, this variable is set to the number of characters actually copied to the **lpszRemoteName** buffer.

Return Value   **Integer**—Refer to the constants beginning with the prefix WN_ in the APICONST.TXT file provided with this book.

■ **WritePrivateProfileString, WritePrivateProfileStringBynum**

VB Declaration   `Declare Function WritePrivateProfileString% Lib "Kernel" (ByVal lpApplication ⇔`
`Name$, ByVal lpKeyName As Any, ByVal lpString$, ByVal lplFileName$)`

`Declare Function WritePrivateProfileStringBynum% Lib "Kernel" Alias "Write ⇔`
`PrivateProfileString" (ByVal lpApplicationName$, ByVal lpKeyName&, ByVal ⇔`
`lpString&, ByVal lplFileName$)`

Description   Sets a string in the specified section of a private initialization file.

Use with VB   No problem.

Parameter	Type/Description
lpApplicationName	**String**—The section in which to write the new string. This string is not case-sensitive.
lpKeyName	**String** or **Long**—The key name or entry to set. This string is not case-sensitive. Zero to delete all of the keys for this section.
lpString	**String** or **Long**—The value to write for this key. Zero to delete the existing string for this key.
lpFileName	**String**—The name of the private initialization file. If a full path name is not specified, Windows will search for the file in the Windows directory. If the file is not found, this function will create the file.

Return Value   Integer—TRUE (nonzero) on success, zero otherwise.

■ WriteProfileString, WriteProfileStringBynum

VB Declaration
```
Declare Function WriteProfileString% Lib "Kernel" (ByVal lpApplicationName$, ⇔
ByVal lpKeyName$, ByVal lpString$)

Declare Function WriteProfileStringBynum% Lib "Kernel" Alias "WriteProfile ⇔
String" (ByVal lpApplicationName&, ByVal lpKeyName&, ByVal lpString&)
```

Description   Sets a string in the specified section of the WIN.INI initialization file.

Use with VB   No problem. Keep in mind that changes to the WIN.INI file may affect other applications. If you are modifying a section that is used by other programs, be sure to send the WM_WININI-CHANGE message to all windows as described in "Initialization Files," earlier in this chapter.

Parameter	Type/Description
lpApplicationName	**String**—The section in which to write the new string. The section will be created if it does not yet exist. This string is not case-sensitive.
lpKeyName	**String** or **Long**—The key name or entry to set. This string is not case-sensitive. Zero to delete all of the keys for this section.
lpString	**String** or **Long**—The value to write for this key. Zero to delete the existing string for this key.

Return Value   Integer—TRUE (nonzero) on success, zero otherwise.

14

Serial
Communications

AN EARLY CRITICISM OF VISUAL BASIC WAS ITS LACK OF GOOD SUPPORT for serial communications. While Visual Basic does allow you to open a serial port as a device using the **Open** statement, it does not provide a good event-driven serial interface. Even Quick Basic, with its **On Com** command, seems on the surface to provide better support for serial communications than Visual Basic.

The truth of the matter is that every copy of Visual Basic comes with a powerful, fully interrupt-driven, serial communication driver that allows you to define almost every aspect of the communications protocol from the size of the internal transmit/receive buffers, to the character to use for Xon-Xoff flow control. The trick, as usual, involves using the Windows API—in this case to access the serial port driver that is built into Windows.

The professional version of Visual Basic includes the MSCOMM.VBX custom control, which provides easy access to most of the features in the Windows serial communication driver. The information in this chapter will help you understand the MSCOMM.VBX control should you choose to use it instead of directly accessing the driver.

For those readers who find the previous paragraphs somewhat cryptic, this chapter begins with a brief introduction to serial communications that will also serve to define the terms used. A description of the serial communications API functions and data structures follows. The chapter concludes with an example program that shows how to use the Windows API to implement a simple terminal program.

Introduction to Serial Communications

On a serial port, the eight bits of a data byte are sent through the port a single bit at a time. This contrasts with a parallel port (such as the PC printer ports) in which each data bit has a separate wire. Parallel ports tend to support much higher data rates than serial ports; however, serial ports are uniquely qualified for tasks where the number of wires is limited, such as communicating through phone lines using a modem.

This chapter will not attempt to provide a comprehensive review of serial communications. Fortunately, there are a great many books available on the subject. For now, this chapter assumes that you know how to hook up your modem or serial port correctly. Wiring a serial port can sometimes seem like a black art. Fortunately, in the PC world, most of the complexity is hidden due to a relatively high degree of standardization. In most cases you can purchase a modem or modem card and plug it in as instructed and actually have it work correctly the first time.

Serial Data Format

It has already been mentioned that data is transferred through a serial port one bit at a time. There are a number of other attributes that affect the serial data format. Generally, two devices must use the same data format in order to transfer data successfully. Incompatible formats are usually indicated by the appearance of "garbage" characters.

All of the attributes that follow can be set for a serial port using Windows API functions.

Data Rate

The first, and perhaps most important, parameter to set is the data transfer rate. The most common PC data rates are 1200, 2400, and 9600 bits per second. You may occasionally hear the term "baud" rate to refer to the data rate. During the time of more primitive computers (say, 10 years ago), these were one and the same—each signal transition on the modem corresponded to a single bit of data. Today's modems use sophisticated mathematics to cram multiple bits into each analog signal transition (baud), so a 9600-bit-per-second modem is not, in fact, a 9600-baud modem. However, since the two terms are frequently interchanged, this distinction is only of real use to modem designers and purists.

Data Bits

Because the bits in a data byte are sent in sequence, one way to increase the effective data rate is to reduce the number of bits sent. Seven bits are sufficient to represent the entire ASCII character set, thus it is possible to configure the serial port to transfer only seven data bits.

Most online services and BBSes now use eight bits in order to support binary transfers as well as text transfers.

Parity Bits

A serial port can be configured to add an extra bit known as a parity bit after the data bits. A parity bit is used to detect errors that may occur during the data transfer. The most common parity configurations are odd, even, and none. Even parity indicates that the sum of the data bits plus the parity bit will always be even. For example, if the data bits are 10110110, the sum of the bits is 5. If even parity is specified, the parity bit will be 1 to bring the total to 6. Odd parity works the same way except that it guarantees that the sum of the bits will be odd.

Today's high-speed modems frequently incorporate more advanced error detection and correction schemes than is possible with simple parity bits. Also, most binary transfers use error-detecting protocols such as X-modem. Thus most online services today specify no parity bit.

Stop Bits

Stop bits are extra bits that are appended to the end of each data character to inform the receiving serial port that the end of a byte has been reached and to allow it to complete character processing. A serial port may be configured for 1, 1.5, or 2 stop bits. Most online services today specify a single stop bit.

The RS-232 Standard

The PC serial ports are sometimes referred to as RS-232 communications ports. RS-232-C is an industry standard published by the Electronics Industries Association that defines the mechanical and electrical characteristics of a serial port. The standard actually defines 21 different signals that can be used on a serial link. Unfortunately, very few devices implement all of these signals—thus the fact that two devices support RS-232-C does not guarantee that they will actually be able to communicate with each other. A serial link can be established with as few as three signals (send, receive, and signal ground). This chapter will focus on those signals supported by the Windows driver—which will be adequate for all but the most specialized tasks.

DTE and DCE

Each serial data link must obviously have two sides. The RS-232 standard defines the characteristics of the two devices. The computer side is referred to as the DTE device, for Data Terminal Equipment. This recalls the days when actual serial terminals would be used instead of PCs with terminal programs. The modem side is referred to as the DCE device, or Data Communication Equipment.

Figure 14.1 illustrates the signal lines typically used for PC communication along with the direction of the data flow. For example, the TxD (transmit data) signal is shown as transferring data from the DTE to the DCE, in other words, from the computer to the modem.

The signals are typically referred to by their two- or three-letter acronym. I have tried to avoid using acronyms in this book with the exception of a few of the most common, but in the world of serial communications the fact is that the acronyms are used more often than the full-signal name. This convention is followed here, and the text will therefore usually refer to the RTS signal rather than the Request to Send signal, and so on for the other signals.

In some cases the device you wish to connect to your PC might be configured internally as a DTE device. Or you may wish to transfer data between two computers, both of which are connected as DTE devices. Obviously, there will be a conflict if they are connected directly, as both devices will try to send data on the same signal line. The solution is to connect them using a special cable known as a *null modem*, which swaps signal lines in such a way that the two DTE devices each think that the other is a DCE device. Null modem cables are available at most computer stores.

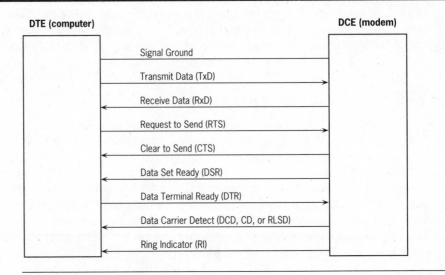

Figure 14.1
RS-232 signals

DTE (computer) — DCE (modem)

Signal Ground
Transmit Data (TxD)
Receive Data (RxD)
Request to Send (RTS)
Clear to Send (CTS)
Data Set Ready (DSR)
Data Terminal Ready (DTR)
Data Carrier Detect (DCD, CD, or RLSD)
Ring Indicator (RI)

For the balance of this discussion, the typical PC computer-to-modem connection will be assumed, so the DTE will be referred to as the computer and the DCE as the modem.

Data Signals
The transmit data and receive data lines are the signals used to transfer data between the computer and the modem.

RTS and CTS
The Request to Send (RTS) signal line is sent from the computer to the modem to indicate that it wishes to send data to the modem. If the modem is able to receive the data, it will send the Clear to Send (CTS) signal to the computer. The Windows serial driver allows you to specify the maximum time that the system should wait for the CTS response to the RTS signal. This pair of lines is sometimes used for flow control as described later in this chapter.

DTR and DSR
The Data Terminal Ready (DTR) signal line is sent from the computer to the modem to indicate that it is ready to begin a communications session. The modem will generally use this as a signal to initialize itself. It will then send the Data Set Ready (DSR) signal back to the computer. The Windows serial driver allows you to specify the maximum time that the system should wait for the DSR response to the DTR signal. This pair of lines is sometimes used for flow control as described later in this chapter.

RI and DCD

The Ring Indicator signal (RI) is sent from the modem to the computer to indicate that the line is ringing. The Data Carrier Detect (DCD or CD) signal is sent from the modem to the computer to indicate that connection has been established with another modem and that communication is now possible. This signal is also known as the Receive Line Signal Detect, or RLSD signal.

Connect Sequence

Table 14.1 illustrates the typical sequence in which signals are asserted during the establishment of a communications session. The first column indicates the operation of the terminal program. The second column indicates the operation of the serial driver, and the third column indicates the operation of the modem. This table should be read from top to bottom to show the sequence of operations.

It is important to realize that the scenario shown in Table 14.1 is only one possible sequence. Many serial ports do not use all of the signal lines.

Table 14.1   **Connect Sequence**

Terminal Program	Serial Driver	Modem
Start the program.		
	Send DTR to the modem.	
		Modem is initialized. Send DSR to the computer.
	Send RTS to the modem.	
		Send CTS to the computer.
Program sends initialization commands to the modem. Program instructs the modem to dial.		
		Ring indication is sent to the computer. Once communication is established, the Carrier Detect (CD) signal is sent to the computer.
	Software is notified that connection is established.	
Data transfer commences.		

Flow Control

There will be times during a communication session when a device is unable to receive more data. This typically occurs when the internal communications buffer has been filled with data and the application software has not had a chance to retrieve it. In order to prevent data from disappearing, there needs to be a flow control mechanism to inform the other device that it must hold off sending more data.

There are two types of flow control. Hardware flow control uses either the RTS and CTS signals or the DSR and DTR signals. For example, RTS and CTS hardware flow control works as follows: When the computer wants the modem to stop sending data, it turns off the request to send signal. It turns RTS back on when the application has cleared enough space in the receive buffer to allow further data to be received. Hardware flow control is typically used when connecting a computer to a serial device other than a modem (such as a printer) that supports or requires hardware flow control. The Windows serial driver provides a great deal of flexibility in defining the characteristics of the hardware flow control.

Software flow control is typically used with modems. With this type of flow control, the device that can no longer receive data sends a special character called an X-Off (Xoff) character to the other device to inform it to stop sending data. Once it can receive data again, it sends the X-On (Xon) character.

Windows allows you to define the Xoff and Xon characters, but in most cases you will use the standards of ^Q (ASCII code 17 decimal) as the Xon character and ^S (ASCII code 19 decimal) as the Xoff character.

When the Xoff character is sent, the serial driver stops further transmission until the Xon character is sent. This is because many drivers resume transmission on receipt of any character regardless of which character is defined as the Xon character.

The Windows Serial Communications Driver

Windows includes a high-quality serial communications driver that is highly configurable. This section describes the driver and its associated data structures.

Architecture of a Serial Driver

At first look, serial communication seems simple. Send a character to the modem when you have data to send, and read characters from the modem when you are ready to receive data.

There is one large problem with this simplistic approach, and it relates to time. If you depend on the application program to process each character, it is almost impossible to process the characters in the time given. Consider the problem of transferring a 1,000-character block of text:

At 1200 baud, 1,000 characters will take about nine seconds to send. This is not bad, but if you depend on the application to send each character individually you will be wasting most of that time waiting for the serial port to be ready to process the next character. This is the situation in fact when you send data to the comm port using the Visual Basic **Print** statement to send data to a port opened with the Visual Basic **Open** statement.

But imagine trying to receive data even at 2400 baud. Each character must be received and processed by the application in about 4 milliseconds. A Windows task switch takes longer than that—so any characters received when your application is not active are likely to be lost. It is possible that on a fast 486 PC it would be possible to write a tight Visual Basic loop that could monitor the serial port and read received data into a buffer, but even if you could do this, your program would not have time to perform any other operations, and the rest of the system would likely be frozen. At 14,400 baud, where a character is received approximately every 500 microseconds, all bets are off.

In order to make serial communications possible, Windows implements an interrupt-driven driver with user-definable input and output buffers. Each time a character is received, it causes a low-level hardware interrupt. The serial driver immediately takes control and places the character in an input data buffer. It then returns control to whatever application was running. If the input buffer is getting full, the driver uses the currently defined flow control scheme to inform the other device that it should stop sending data.

A similar process works for sending data. The application places data to send in an output buffer. Each time the serial port hardware sends a character a low-level hardware interrupt occurs. If another character is present in the output buffer, the serial driver sends the character to the serial port for output. Figure 14.2 illustrates this process.

All aspects of the serial driver are user-definable, including the sizes of the input and output buffers and the limits that determine when flow control commands should be used to suspend data transfers.

Using the Serial Driver

Using a serial port under MS-DOS is essentially a two-step process. First the port is configured to the desired speed, parity, and flow control protocol. Next, data is read and written to the port.

Access to the serial ports is slightly more complex under Windows. There are two reasons for this. The first is due to the fact that Windows is a multitasking operating environment. There needs to be a mechanism to make certain that only one application has access to the serial port at any one time. The second reason relates to the fact that the Windows serial driver provides a number of advanced capabilities in terms of event detection and error handling.

Figure 14.2
Serial driver
architecture

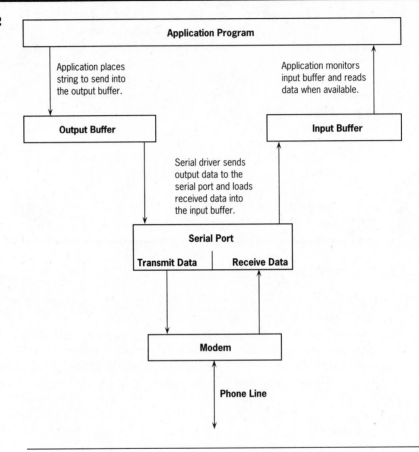

Serial communications under Windows is a four-step process:

1. Open a serial port for communications using the **OpenComm** function. This informs Windows that the application requires the serial port and locks all other applications from using the port.

2. Configure the serial port.

3. Transfer data to and from the serial port.

4. When the port is no longer needed, release the serial port using the **CloseComm** API function so that it will be available to other applications.

Serial Driver Events

Under Visual Basic, the term *event* is used to describe something that occurs in the system that can cause a Visual Basic event subroutine to be executed. When discussing serial communications, the term event is also used, in this case to describe something that occurs during the communication process. This type of event, however, is not the same thing as a Visual Basic event in that no program code is executed when it occurs.

The serial driver maintains a 16-bit integer known as an event mask. Each bit in this integer represents whether the event has occurred. Events that can be detected include the receipt of a character, the receipt of a particular character, transitions on the signal lines, parity errors, and so on. Refer to the function reference for the **SetCommEventMask** API function for a complete list. Your program can determine which of these events should be detected.

When an event has been detected, it is necessary to use the **GetComm-EventMask** API function to determine which event has occurred and to clear that event so that the next occurrence of the event may be detected. Under Windows 3.0, it was necessary to poll the event mask to determine if an event had occurred. Windows 3.1 has added a notification capability by which Windows can send a message to a window when an event occurs. The CBK.VBX custom control provided with this book can be used to generate Visual Basic events when this type of notification occurs. Refer to the description of the **EnableCommNotification** API function in the function reference for this chapter for further details.

The Windows serial driver also allows you to specify one character that will trigger an event when it is received. This is frequently chosen to be a break character such as ^C or ^X. When the character is received, it sets the bit in the event mask immediately, regardless of how many characters are ahead of it in the receive buffer. This allows your program to provide an "abort" character which can be used to interrupt or cancel the current operation.

The "Break" State

The Windows serial driver provides the ability to set a serial port into a "Break" state. This causes the port to stop sending characters and causes a break in the carrier signal. This technique was commonly used in the past to provide signaling between devices, but is rarely used now. If you do use this capability, refer to the documentation of the devices that you are using to determine the maximum time that a break can take without ending the communications link.

The Communications Driver and Parallel Ports

The communications API functions described here may also be used to access the parallel ports. A data transfer through the parallel port using this method is not interrupt-driven and does not use buffering. This capability is rarely used because the most common parallel device is the printer, and

Windows provides excellent support for it using the printer drivers. Other parallel devices generally come with their own drivers, thus once again this technique is not necessary. This chapter therefore focuses exclusively on the use of the communications functions to access the serial comm ports.

Configuring Serial Ports and the Device Control Block

The serial ports and serial communications driver are configured with the help of a data structure known as a *Device Control Block* or DCB. This structure is defined as follows:

```
Type DCB    '25 Bytes
    Id As String * 1
    BaudRate As Integer
    ByteSize As String * 1
    Parity As String * 1
    StopBits As String * 1
    RlsTimeout As Integer
    CtsTimeout As Integer
    DsrTimeout As Integer
    Bits1 As String * 1
    Bits2 As String * 1
    XonChar As String * 1
    XoffChar As String * 1
    XonLim As Integer
    XoffLim As Integer
    PeChar As String * 1
    EofChar As String * 1
    EvtChar As String * 1
    TxDelay As Integer
End Type
```

You may have noticed the extensive use of single-character strings to hold single-byte data in this structure. Even though it is defined as a string, in many cases the data contained in the field is an eight-bit numeric value. For example, the **ByteSize** field, which defines the number of bits in a character, contains a value ranging from four to eight. In this case you may set the value of the field using the VB **Chr$** function as shown in the following example:

```
Dim dcb1 As DCB
dcb1.ByteSize = Chr$(8)
```

You would retrieve the value using the **Asc** function as follows:

```
sizeofbyte% = Asc(dcb1.ByteSize)
```

Table 14.2 describes the fields of the DCB structure.

Table 14.2   The DCB Structure

Field	Type/Description
Id	**String**—Identifies the comm port. This value is set by the driver.
BaudRate	**Integer**—The data transfer rate in bits per second.
ByteSize	**String**—The number of bits in a character. This can be a value from four to eight, and is typically eight.
Parity	**String**—One of the following constants:
	EVENPARITY: sets even parity.
	MARKPARITY: sets mark parity—seldom used.
	NOPARITY: no parity checking. This is the most common setting.
	ODDPARITY: odd parity.
	SPACEPARITY: space parity.
StopBits	**String**—One of the following constants specifying the number of stop bits to append to the character:
	ONESTOPBIT: 1
	ONE5STOPBITS: 1.5
	TWOSTOPBITS: 2
RlsTimeout	**Integer**—The maximum time in milliseconds that the system will wait for a carrier to be detected as indicated by the Carrier Detect (CD, or RLSD) signal without indicating an error status.
CtsTimeout	**Integer**—The maximum time in milliseconds that the system will wait for a CTS signal without indicating an error status.
DsrTimeout	**Integer**—The maximum time in milliseconds that the system will wait for a DSR signal without indicating an error status.
Bits1	**String**—See Table 14.3.
Bits2	**String**—See Table 14.4.
XonChar	**String**—The character to use as the Xon character when using software flow control. This character is typically ^Q (ASCII value 17).
XoffChar	**String**—The character to use as the Xoff character when using software flow control. This character is typically ^S (ASCII value 19).
XonLim	**Integer**—Specifies when the Xon character will be sent to resume flow. The Xon character will be sent when the number of characters in the receive buffer drops below this value.

Table 14.2   The DCB Structure (Continued)

Field	Type/Description
XoffLim	**Integer**—Specifies when the Xoff character will be sent to pause data flow. The Xoff character will be sent when the number of characters in the receive buffer exceeds this value.
PeChar	**String**—Specifies the character that will be placed in the receive buffer in place of any character received with a parity error.
EofChar	**String**—Specifies the character that is used to indicate the end of a data stream.
EvtChar	**String**—Specifies a character to use to indicate an event. This is often set to ^C (ASCII value 3) to allow the software to easily detect when a user wants to cancel an operation. The event is indicated as soon as the character is received, regardless of how many characters are ahead of it in the receive buffer.
TxDelay	**Integer**—Not implemented.

The **Bits1** and **Bits2** fields each contain eight flag bits that are used to control various aspects of the serial driver. Refer to Chapter 3 for information on testing and setting bitfields.

Table 14.3   Bits1 DCB Field

Bit #	Name	Description
0	fBinary	1 indicates binary mode. In binary mode the **EofChar** character has no effect. Otherwise it indicates the end of a data stream.
1	fRtsDisable	1 indicates that the RTS signal is not used. Otherwise RTS is sent when the serial port is opened, and cleared when the serial port is closed.
2	fParity	1 turns on parity checking.
3	fOutxCtsFlow	1 indicates that the CTS signal is used for hardware flow control on output. Transmission is suspended any time the CTS signal is not present.
4	fOutxDsrFlow	1 indicates that the DSR signal is used for hardware flow control on output. Transmission is suspended any time the DSR signal is not present.
5-6		Not used.
7	fDtrDisable	1 indicates that the DSR signal is not used. Otherwise DTR is sent when the serial port is opened, and cleared when the serial port is closed.

Table 14.4   Bits2 DCB Field

Bit #	Name	Description
0	fOutX	1 indicates that Xon/Xoff software flow control is used for transmission. Sending is paused when the Xoff character is received and resumes when the Xon character is received.
1	fInX	1 indicates that Xon/Xoff software flow control is used for receiving data. The Xoff character is sent when the number of bytes in the receive buffer exceeds the **XoffLim** field value. The Xon character is sent when the number of bytes in the receive buffer drops below the **XonLim** field value.
2	fPeChar	1 indicates that characters that have parity errors are to be replaced with the character specified in the **PeChar** field. The fParity bit in the **Bits1** field must be set for this to occur.
3	fNull	1 indicates that null characters (ASCII value 0) should be discarded.
4	fChEvt	1 indicates that receipt of the EvtChar character should trigger an event.
5	fDtrFlow	1 indicates that the DTR signal is used for hardware flow control on input. The DTR signal is cleared when the number of bytes in the receive buffer exceeds **XoffLim** characters and set when the number of bytes in the receive buffer falls below **XonLim** characters.
6	fRtsFlow	1 indicates that the RTS signal is used for hardware flow control on input. The RTS signal is cleared when the number of bytes in the receive buffer exceeds **XoffLim** characters and set when the number of bytes in the receive buffer falls below **XonLim** characters.

Obtaining Serial Port Status

Windows provides two functions for retrieving the status of a communications port. The **GetCommState** function retrieves the current configuration of a port by loading a device control block with the port configuration.

The **GetCommError** API function returns the value of the latest error flag if a communication error occurred. The list of errors detected is described in the function reference section for this function and in Table 14.9.

The **GetCommError** function also loads the current status of the device into the **COMSTAT** structure, which is defined here:

```
Type COMSTAT    '5 Bytes
    Bits As String * 1
    cbInQue As Integer
    cbOutQue As Integer
End Type
```

Field	Type/Description
Bits	**String**—Refer to Table 14.5.
cbInQue	**Integer**—The number of characters in the input buffer.
cbOutQue	**Integer**—The number of characters in the output buffer.

Table 14.5   **COMSTAT Bits Bitfield Definition**

Bit #	Name	Description
0	CSTF_CTSHOLD	Transmission is on hold pending receipt of the CTS signal.
1	CSTF_DSRHOLD	Transmission is on hold pending receipt of the DSR signal.
2	CSTF_RLSDHOLD	Transmission is on hold pending receipt of the RLSD (CD or carrier detect) signal.
3	CSTF_XOFFHOLD	Transmission is on hold pending receipt of an Xon character.
4	CSTF_XOFFSENT	Transmission is on hold because an Xoff character was sent. Transmission is always halted after an Xoff is sent as many systems interpret the receipt of any character after an Xoff as an instruction to resume transmission.
5	CSTF_EOF	An EOF character has been received.
6	CSTF_TXIM	A character is waiting to be transmitted.

The Serial Driver API Functions

Table 14.6 lists the API functions that are used with the Windows serial driver.

Table 14.6   **Serial Driver API Functions**

Function	Description
BuildCommDCB	Builds a device control block (DCB) based on a string containing an MS-DOS **Mode** command line.
ClearCommBreak	Takes a serial port out of the break state.
CloseComm	Closes a serial port and releases it for use by any application.
EnableCommNotification	Specifies the window to which Windows should send communications notification messages (WM_COMMNOTIFY). Use with the CBK.VBX custom control.

Table 14.6   **Serial Driver API Functions (Continued)**

Function	Description
EscapeCommFunction	Provides additional control of a serial port.
FlushComm	Clears the transmit or receive buffers of a serial port.
GetCommError	Retrieves the status of a serial port.
GetCommEventMask	Retrieves the event mask for a serial port.
GetCommState	Retrieves a device control block (DCB) for a serial port specifying the current configuration of the port.
OpenComm	Opens a serial port for communications and prevents other applications from accessing the port.
ReadComm	Reads data from a serial port.
SetCommBreak	Sets a serial port into the break state.
SetCommEventMask	Specifies which events on a serial port should be detected.
SetCommState	Configures a serial port according to the specified DCB.
TransmitCommChar	Transmits a single character through a serial port, bypassing the transmit buffer.
UngetCommChar	Puts a character back into the receive buffer of a serial port so that it will be the next character read.
WriteComm	Writes data to a serial port.

Example: CommDemo—A Simple Terminal Program

CommDemo is a very simple terminal program implemented entirely in Visual Basic using the communications API functions introduced in this chapter. Note that due to the use of the WM_COMMNOTIFY message in this program, this sample application requires Windows version 3.1 to run.

Using CommDemo

The CommDemo screen shown in Figure 14.3 illustrates a sample communication session. CommDemo provides only two menu commands: Configuration and Dial. The Configuration command may be used to select the communications port and the default baud rate as shown in Figure 14.4. The methods used to configure these two parameters are applicable to all other port configuration tasks, however, and demonstrate the principles involved.

Figure 14.3

CommDemo
communications
session

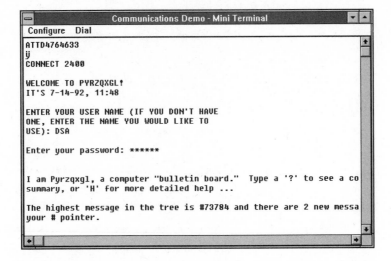

```
┌─────────────────────────────────────────────────────────┐
│ ─   Communications Demo - Mini Terminal        ▼  ▲      │
├─────────────────────────────────────────────────────────┤
│  Configure   Dial                                        │
├─────────────────────────────────────────────────────────┤
│ ATTD4764633                                           ↑  │
│ ÿ                                                        │
│ CONNECT 2400                                             │
│                                                          │
│ WELCOME TO PYRZQXGL!                                     │
│ IT'S 7-14-92, 11:48                                      │
│                                                          │
│ ENTER YOUR USER NAME (IF YOU DON'T HAVE                  │
│ ONE, ENTER THE NAME YOU WOULD LIKE TO                    │
│ USE): DSA                                                │
│                                                          │
│ Enter your password: ******                             │
│                                                          │
│                                                          │
│ I am Pyrzqxgl, a computer "bulletin board."  Type a '?' to see a co │
│ summary, or 'H' for more detailed help ...              │
│                                                          │
│ The highest message in the tree is #73784 and there are 2 new messa │
│ your # pointer.                                       ↓  │
│ ←│                                                    │→ │
└─────────────────────────────────────────────────────────┘
```

Figure 14.4

CommDemo
configuration form

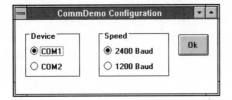

```
┌──────────────────────────────────────────┐
│ ─     CommDemo Configuration    ▼  ▲      │
├──────────────────────────────────────────┤
│  ┌─Device──┐   ┌─Speed──────┐            │
│  │ ◉ COM1  │   │ ◉ 2400 Baud│  ┌─────┐   │
│  │         │   │            │  │ Ok  │   │
│  │ ○ COM2  │   │ ○ 1200 Baud│  └─────┘   │
│  └─────────┘   └────────────┘            │
└──────────────────────────────────────────┘
```

The Dial command prompts for a number and will cause a modem that uses the industry standard AT command set to dial that number.

If your computer does not have serial port COM1 available, or if the port is in use by another device such as a mouse, CommDemo will notify you that it cannot open the port. When the prompt asking if the program should attempt to close the port and reopen it appears, you should answer "No," then use the Configure menu command to select COM2. If your computer uses COM3 or COM4, you will have ample motivation to examine the source code and extend the configuration form and the **OpenThePort** function to support those serial ports as well.

Project Description

The CommDemo project includes seven files. COMMDEMO.FRM contains a single text control and a single generic callback (CBK.VBX) control. These controls may be positioned anywhere on the screen, as the text control is automatically sized to fill the form and the CBK.VBX control is invisible at runtime.

COMMCFG.FRM is the configuration form for the serial port. It contains two sets of option buttons inside of frames as shown in Figure 14.4. COMMDEMO.BAS contains the constant type and global definitions. COMMUTIL.BAS is a code module that contains routines that configure the serial port and transfer data to and from the port. APIDECS.BAS is the type-safe API declaration file provided with this book. APIGUIDE.BAS contains the declarations for the APIGUIDE.DLL dynamic link library. CBK.VBX is the generic callback custom control that is used to detect communication events as indicated by receipt of the WM_COMMNOTIFY message to the control. This control is described further in Appendix A.

Listing 14.1 shows the project file for the CommDemo program.

Listing 14.1   Project Listing File COMMDEMO.MAK

```
COMMDEMO.FRM
CBK.VBX
COMMDEMO.BAS
APIDECS.BAS
APIGUIDE.BAS
COMMUTIL.BAS
COMMCFG.FRM
ProjWinSize=175,439,248,215
ProjWinShow=2
```

Form Description

Listing 14.2 contains the header from file COMMDEMO.FRM that describes the control setup for the form. Listing 14.3 contains the header from file COMMCFG.FRM that describes the control setup for the form.

Listing 14.2   COMMDEMO.FRM

```
VERSION 2.00
Begin Form CommDemo
   Caption        =   "Communications Demo - Mini **
     Terminal"
   Height         =   5595
   Left           =   915
   LinkMode       =   1   'Source
   LinkTopic      =   "Form1"
   ScaleHeight    =   4905
```

Listing 14.2   COMMDEMO.FRM (Continued)

```
    ScaleWidth      =    8400
    Top             =    1155
    Width           =    8520
    Begin TextBox TermText
        FontBold          =    0     'False
        FontItalic        =    0     'False
        FontName          =    "Fixedsys"
        FontSize          =    9
        FontStrikethru    =    0     'False
        FontUnderline     =    0     'False
        Height            =    4095
        Left              =    120
        MultiLine         =    -1    'True
        ScrollBars        =    3     'Both
        TabIndex          =    0
        Top               =    600
        Width             =    8175
    End
    Begin ccCallback Callback1
        Left            =    7800
        Top             =    120
    End
    Begin Menu MenuConfigure
        Caption         =    "Configure"
    End
    Begin Menu MenuDial
        Caption         =    "Dial"
    End
End
```

Listing 14.3   COMMCFG.FRM Header

```
VERSION 2.00
Begin Form Commcfg
    Caption         =    "CommDemo Configuration"
    Height          =    2145
    Left            =    1455
    LinkMode        =    1 'Source
    LinkTopic       =    "Form1"
    ScaleHeight     =    1740
    ScaleWidth      =    4905
    Top             =    1575
    Width           =    5025
    Begin CommandButton CmdOk
        Caption         =    "Ok"
```

Listing 14.3   COMMCFG.FRM Header (Continued)

```
        Height          =   495
        Left            =   3960
        TabIndex        =   6
        Top             =   360
        Width           =   735
     End
     Begin Frame Frame2
        Caption         =   "Speed"
        Height          =   1095
        Left            =   2040
        TabIndex        =   3
        Top             =   240
        Width           =   1695
        Begin OptionButton Option1200
           Caption      =   "1200 Baud"
           Height       =   255
           Left         =   120
           TabIndex     =   5
           Top          =   720
           Width        =   1215
        End
        Begin OptionButton Option2400
           Caption      =   "2400 Baud"
           Height       =   255
           Left         =   120
           TabIndex     =   4
           Top          =   360
           Value        =   -1   'True
           Width        =   1455
        End
     End
     Begin Frame Frame1
        Caption         =   "Device"
        Height          =   1095
        Left            =   240
        TabIndex        =   0
        Top             =   240
        Width           =   1335
        Begin OptionButton OptionCom2
           Caption      =   "COM2"
           Height       =   255
           Left         =   120
           TabIndex     =   2
           Top          =   720
           Width        =   975
        End
        Begin OptionButton OptionCom1
           Caption      =   "COM1"
```

Listing 14.3 COMMCFG.FRM Header (Continued)

```
            Height      =   255
            Left        =   120
            TabIndex    =   1
            Top         =   360
            Value       =   -1   'True
            Width       =   975
        End
    End
End
```

CommDemo Listings

Module COMMDEMO.BAS contains the constant declarations and global
variables used by the program.

Listing 14.4 Module COMMDEMO.BAS

```
' CommDemo program example


' Communication Constants
Global Const NOPARITY = 0
Global Const ODDPARITY = 1
Global Const EVENPARITY = 2
Global Const MARKPARITY = 3
Global Const SPACEPARITY = 4
Global Const ONESTOPBIT = 0
Global Const ONE5STOPBITS = 1
Global Const TWOSTOPBITS = 2
Global Const IGNORE = 0
Global Const INFINITE = &HFFFF
Global Const CE_RXOVER = &H1
Global Const CE_OVERRUN = &H2
Global Const CE_RXPARITY = &H4
Global Const CE_FRAME = &H8
Global Const CE_BREAK = &H10
Global Const CE_CTSTO = &H20
Global Const CE_DSRTO = &H40
Global Const CE_RLSDTO = &H80
Global Const CE_TXFULL = &H100
Global Const CE_PTO = &H200
Global Const CE_IOE = &H400
Global Const CE_DNS = &H800
Global Const CE_OOP = &H1000
Global Const CE_MODE = &H8000
```

Listing 14.4   Module COMMDEMO.BAS (Continued)

```
Global Const IE_BADID = (-1)
Global Const IE_OPEN = (-2)
Global Const IE_NOPEN = (-3)
Global Const IE_MEMORY = (-4)
Global Const IE_DEFAULT = (-5)
Global Const IE_HARDWARE = (-10)
Global Const IE_BYTESIZE = (-11)
Global Const IE_BAUDRATE = (-12)
Global Const EV_RXCHAR = &H1
Global Const EV_RXFLAG = &H2
Global Const EV_TXEMPTY = &H4
Global Const EV_CTS = &H8
Global Const EV_DSR = &H10
Global Const EV_RLSD = &H20
Global Const EV_BREAK = &H40
Global Const EV_ERR = &H80
Global Const EV_RING = &H100
Global Const EV_PERR = &H200
Global Const EV_CTSS = &H400
Global Const EV_DSRS = &H800
Global Const EV_RLSDS = &H1000
Global Const SETXOFF = 1
Global Const SETXON = 2
Global Const SETRTS = 3
Global Const CLRRTS = 4
Global Const SETDTR = 5
Global Const CLRDTR = 6
Global Const RESETDEV = 7
Global Const GETMAXLPT = 8
Global Const GETMAXCOM = 9
Global Const GETBASEIRQ = 10
Global Const CBR_110 = &HFF10
Global Const CBR_300 = &HFF11
Global Const CBR_600 = &HFF12
Global Const CBR_1200 = &HFF13
Global Const CBR_2400 = &HFF14
Global Const CBR_4800 = &HFF15
Global Const CBR_9600 = &HFF16
Global Const CBR_14400 = &HFF17
Global Const CBR_19200 = &HFF18
Global Const CBR_38400 = &HFF1B
Global Const CBR_56000 = &HFF1F
Global Const CBR_128000 = &HFF23
Global Const CBR_256000 = &HFF27
Global Const CN_RECEIVE = &H1
Global Const CN_TRANSMIT = &H2
Global Const CN_EVENT = &H4
Global Const CSTF_CTSHOLD = &H1
```

Listing 14.4   Module COMMDEMO.BAS (Continued)

```
Global Const CSTF_DSRHOLD = &H2
Global Const CSTF_RLSDHOLD = &H4
Global Const CSTF_XOFFHOLD = &H8
Global Const CSTF_XOFFSENT = &H10
Global Const CSTF_EOF = &H20
Global Const CSTF_TXIM = &H40
Global Const LPTx = &H80

' Application constants

' The size of the input and output buffers we will use
Global Const BufferSize% = 2048



' The port configuration for the demo

Global PortConfig As DCB

Global CommID%  ' Identifier of the open port. -1 on error
Global CommNum% ' Number of the com port currently open

Global Dialing% ' Currently dialing
```

The **OpenThePort** function is called when the program first loads or when the configuration form is used to switch to a different port. This function performs a number of tasks. First it opens the requested communications port if it is not already open, closing the previous one if necessary. If the requested port is already open, this function has no effect. If the port cannot be opened, the program provides the user with the option to try closing the port and reopening it. This will usually occur when working in the Visual Basic environment if the program was run and the form **Unload** event was not called. Since the comm port is closed during the **Unload** event, failure to call the event will lead to the port remaining open. This can be avoided by closing the program with the system menu Close command before using the Visual Basic End command (in the Run menu).

This function then retrieves the current setting for the communications port and sets the device control block to the requested parameters. It then configures the port using the modified DCB.

Next, event notification is turned on for characters and errors using the **SetCommEventMask** function. Finally, the **EnableCommNotification** API function is used to inform Windows that WM_COMMNOTIFY messages should be sent to the Callback1 control. Those messages will trigger **CommEvent** events in the Callback1 control.

Listing 14.5 Form Listing COMMUTIL.BAS

```
'   Open the port if it is not yet open
'
Sub OpenThePort ()
    Dim Commtouse%

    If CommCfg.OptionCom1.value Then Commtouse% = 1 Else Commtouse% = 2
    If CommNum% = Commtouse% Then Exit Sub ' Already open.
    If CommID% >= Ø Then ' Close the current port
        di% = CloseComm%(CommID%)
        CommID% = -1
    End If

    ' Open the serial port
    CommID% = OpenComm%("COM" + LTrim$(Str$(Commtouse%)), BufferSize%, ⇔
    BufferSize%)
    If CommID% < Ø Then ' An error occurred.
        ' You may wish to extend this to report the actual
        ' error that occurred.
        di% = MsgBox("Unable to open serial device" + Chr$(13) + Chr$(1Ø) + ⇔
        "Attempt to close, then reopen?", 4)
        If di% = 6 Then
            ' Try closing the requested port
            di% = CloseComm(Commtouse% - 1)
            ' Try again
            If di% = Ø Then ' The close was successful
                OpenThePort
                Exit Sub
            End If
        End If
        CommID% = -1
        CommNum% = -1
        Exit Sub
    End If
    CommNum% = Commtouse%

    ' Load the device configuration
    ' A real application would check the error status here.
    di% = GetCommState(CommID%, PortConfig)
    ' Now set other important settings
    PortConfig.ByteSize = Chr$(8)
    PortConfig.BaudRate = 24ØØ
    PortConfig.Parity = Chr$(Ø)
    PortConfig.StopBits = Chr$(Ø)
    PortConfig.Bits2 = Chr$(Asc(PortConfig.Bits2) Or &H13)
    PortConfig.XonChar = Chr$(17)
    PortConfig.XoffChar = Chr$(19)
    PortConfig.XonLim = 1ØØ
    PortConfig.XoffLim = BufferSize% - 1ØØ
```

Listing 14.5   Form Listing COMMUTIL.BAS (Continued)

```
        di% = SetCommState(PortConfig)

        dll& = SetCommEventMask(CommID%, EV_ERR)

        di% = EnableCommNotification(CommID%, CommDemo.Callback1.hWnd, 1, -1)
End Sub
```

The **SendChars** function is used to output characters to the serial port. First it uses the **GetCommError** function to find out how much space exists in the output buffer. This represents the largest string that may be sent in a single **Write-Comm** command. If the string does not fit into the buffer, there needs to be some mechanism to inform the calling function that part of the data was not sent. This function accomplishes this by changing the parameter string to contain only the data not sent. In this sample program, the parameter string is ignored by the calling function, so this type of error would not be handled correctly.

```
'
' Sends the characters specified.  Changes tosend$ to
' the characters that do not fit into the output buffer
'
Sub SendChars (tosend$)
    Dim csbuf As COMSTAT
    Dim outstring$

    If CommID% < Ø Then Exit Sub ' Make sure port is open

    ' Is there space for the data?

    di% = GetCommError(CommID%, csbuf)

    If BufferSize% - csbuf.cbOutQue < Len(tosend$) Then
        ' This is an error - a real application would somehow
        ' need to notify the calling function that it could
        ' only write part of the data so that the calling
        ' function would know what to do next.
        ' What we do is only write the portion of the string
        ' that fits, then change tosend$ to exclude the data
        ' written.
        outstring$ = Left$(tosend$, BufferSize% - csbuf.cbOutQue)
        tosend$ = Mid$(tosend$, BufferSize% - csbuf.cbOutQue + 1)
    Else
        outstring$ = tosend$
        tosend$ = ""
    End If

    ' A real application would check for an error here
```

```
    di% = WriteComm(CommID%, outstring$, Len(outstring$))
End Sub
```

The **GetChars$** function is used to read characters from the serial port. It does this by first determining how many characters are in the input buffer using the **GetCommError** function. If there is no data available, the function simply returns an empty string. Otherwise, it allocates a string of the required size and reads the data into that string.

The function then calls itself recursively. This is an important step because it is quite possible that characters were received between calls to the **GetCommError** function and the **ReadComm** function. If we were polling the serial port, this would not be a problem, as the extra characters would be picked up during the next **GetChars$** function call. However, this program is event-driven. It is therefore necessary that each call to **GetChars$** reduces the number of characters in the queue to below the number specified that triggers a Callback1 **CommEvent** event. This number, specified in the third parameter to the **EnableCommNotification** function in the **OpenThePort** function, is one—thus in this case the **GetChars$** function must empty the input buffer on each call. If it does not, no further input event will be triggered. Refer to the function reference for the **EnableCommNotification** function for further information.

In order to empty the input buffer, we simply keep calling the **GetChars$** function recursively until an empty string is returned. This is not the most elegant way of handling this situation, as it poses a risk of a stack overflow if a great deal of data is coming in very rapidly.

One method for avoiding this is to check the buffer size after the **Read-Comm** function call and to use a loop to build the input string. Another method would be to set a flag to indicate to the application that there is a possibility that more data is in the input buffer that will not trigger an input event. The application can examine the buffer later. Yet another technique involves allocating extra space in the string and attempting to read a larger string than you expect to need. The result of the **ReadComm** function can then be used to determine if there may be additional characters in the input buffer. If the number of bytes returned is smaller than the allocated string length, you know that the input buffer was emptied.

```
'
'   This function checks the input port and retrieves the
'   contents of the input buffer. Returns the empty string
'   if no characters were found.
'
Function GetChars$ ()
    Dim csbuf As COMSTAT
    Dim instring$
    Dim charsread%
```

```
        If CommID% < Ø Then Exit Function' Make sure port is open

        ' Is there space for the data?

        di% = GetCommError(CommID%, csbuf)

        If csbuf.cbInQue = Ø Then ' No characters found
            GetChars$ = ""
            Exit Function
        End If

        instring$ = String$(csbuf.cbInQue, Ø)

        ' A real application would check for an error here
        di% = ReadComm(CommID%, instring$, csbuf.cbInQue)

        charsread% = Abs(di%)
        If charsread% = csbuf.cbInQue Then instring$ = instring$ + GetChars$()

        GetChars$ = instring$

End Function
```

We preload the COMMCFG form in order to make it possible to examine the option button states for the configuration. It won't be shown until the appropriate menu command is invoked.

The TermText text control is moved to fill the client area of the form, global variables are initialized, and the default serial port is opened (if possible).

The **Unload** event is used to disable event notification and close the serial port.

Listing 14.6   Form Listing COMMDEMO.FRM

```
'
' We open the port and get things started here
'
Sub Form_Load ()
    ' We load the configuration form so that the default
    ' settings can be read by OpenThePort
    Load CommCfg
    TermText.Move Ø, Ø, ScaleWidth, ScaleHeight
    CommID% = -1
    CommNum% = -1
    OpenThePort
End Sub


'
' This routine performs necessary cleanup
```

Listing 14.6   Form Listing COMMDEMO.FRM (Continued)

```
Sub Form_Unload (Cancel As Integer)
    If CommID% <> -1 Then
        di% = EnableCommNotification(CommID%, 0, 0, 0)
        di% = CloseComm%(CommID%)
    End If
End Sub
```

The **Callback1_CommEvent** function is called when a communication error occurs or a character is received. The **GetCommError** function is called first to determine if an error occurred. If an error occurred during dialing, and the "CONNECT 1200" line is present in the TermText text control, the function has automatically dropped down to 1200 baud from 2400 baud. It is now necessary to drop the serial port to 1200 baud as well as shown.

Next the **GetChars$** function is used to read the input data. Any carriage return characters (chr$(13)) are converted to CR LF pairs so that the text control will see them as a line break. Extra line feed characters are ignored. You could choose to take the opposite approach and convert line feed characters into CR LF pairs and dump extra carriage returns.

The string is then appended to the end of the text box. The software checks to make sure that the text box is not too large (defined arbitrarily as 4k bytes). Once it exceeds the specified limit the first part of the text buffer is discarded.

```
Sub Callback1_CommEvent (DeviceID As Integer, NotifyStatus As Integer)
    Dim t$
    Dim textlen%
    Dim cstat As COMSTAT
    Dim crloc%
    Dim use$
    Dim cpos%


    If NotifyStatus And CN_EVENT Then
        di% = GetCommError(DeviceID, cstat)
        If di% <> 0 And Dialing% Then
            ' Check for connect fallback
            If InStr(TermText.Text, "CONNECT 1200") <> 0 Then
                PortConfig.BaudRate = 1200
                di% = SetCommState(PortConfig)
            End If
            Dialing% = 0
        Else
            MsgBox "Communication Error Occurred - " + Hex$(di%)
        End If
        ' Clear the error event mask
        dl& = GetCommEventMask(CommID%, EV_ERR)
    End If
```

```
t$ = GetChars$()
use$ = ""
If t$ <> "" Then
    ' Substitute the CR with a CRLF pair, dump the LF

    For cpos% = 1 To Len(t$)
        Select Case Asc(Mid$(t$, cpos%))
            Case 13
                use$ = use$ + Chr$(13) + Chr$(10)
            Case 10
                ' Dump the line feeds
            Case Else
                use$ = use$ + Mid$(t$, cpos%, 1)
        End Select
    Next cpos%
    TermText.selstart = Len(TermText.Text)
    TermText.sellength = 0
    TermText.seltext = use$

    If Len(TermText.Text) > 4096 Then
        TermText.Text = Right$(TermText.Text, 2048)
    End If
    TermText.selstart = Len(TermText.Text)


End If


End Sub
```

This simple function serves to intercept all character entry into the Term-Text text control. The characters are sent to the serial port instead. The modem will generally echo every character received, so the characters will ultimately appear on the text box. If you wanted a local echo you could set a flag variable that would prevent the **KeyAscii** parameter from being set to zero.

```
Sub TermText_KeyPress (KeyAscii As Integer)
    SendChars Chr$(KeyAscii)
    KeyAscii = 0
End Sub
```

The **MenuDial_Click** function is an extremely simple dialing routine. It takes whatever string is entered using the Visual Basic **InputBox$** function and appends it to the modem dial command (ATTD = Command, set touch tone, dial). The dialing flag is set so that the program knows to look for the possibilities of a baud rate fallback when connection is made.

```
Sub MenuDial_Click ()
    Dim dnum$
    TermText.Text = ""
    dnum$ = InputBox$("Enter number to dial", "Dialer")
    SendChars "ATTD" + dnum$ + Chr$(13)
    Dialing% = -1
End Sub
```

The **Form_Resize** event adjusts the size of the text control to fill the client area of the form. The **MenuConfigure_Click** function brings up the COMMCFG form as a modal dialog box.

```
Sub Form_Resize ()
    TermText.Move Ø, Ø, ScaleWidth, ScaleHeight
End Sub

Sub MenuConfigure_Click ()
    CommCfg.Show 1
End Sub
```

This next function takes advantage of the fact that the PortConfig global device control block is always valid. This means that the configuration can be easily changed simply by modifying the DCB and setting it to the device using the **SetCommState** function.

The **OpenThePort** function has no effect if the port is unchanged, so it may be safely called. This port can easily be extended to handle additional data rates or ports.

Listing 14.7   Form Listing COMMCFG.FRM

```
' The port to use and configuration may have changed
'
Sub CmdOk_Click ()
    Dim baudtouse%

    OpenThePort

    ' Now make any configuration changes
    If Option1200.Value = TRUE Then baudtouse% = 1200 Else baudtouse% = 2400
    If PortConfig.BaudRate <> baudtouse% Then
        PortConfig.BaudRate = baudtouse%
        If (CommID% >= Ø) Then di% = SetCommState(PortConfig)
    End If
    Commcfg.Hide

End Sub
```

Function Reference

This section contains an alphabetical reference for the functions described in this chapter.

■ BuildCommDCB

VB Declaration   `Declare Function BuildCommDCB% Lib "User" (ByVal lpDef$, lpDCB As DCB)`

Description   This function loads a device control block with settings according to a string similar to that used by the MS-DOS **Mode** command parameters. This can be used to initialize a DCB that may then be used to configure a serial port using the **SetCommState** function. This function does not itself configure the port.

Use with VB   No problem.

Parameter	Type/Description
lpDef	**String**—A string defining the port characteristics. This string is identical to the compact form of the MS-DOS **Mode** command for configuring serial ports as described in the Comments section below.
lpDCB	**DCB**—A device control block to load based on the lpDef string.

Return Value   **Integer**—Zero if the string was successfully translated and the DCB loaded. -1 on error.

Comments   This function uses a subset of the **Mode** parameter string for serial ports. The string should take the form:

`COMm:b[,p[,d[,s]]]`

m is the port number and b is a two-digit code for the baud rate (11=110 baud, 15=150 baud, 30=300 baud, 60=600 baud, 12=1200 baud, 24=2400 baud, 48=4800 baud, 96=9600 baud, 19=19200 baud). p is a letter indicating the parity (n=none, e=even (the default), o=odd, m=mark, s=space). d is the number of bits per character from 5 to 8 (default is 7). s is the number of stop bits (1, 1.5, or 2—default is 1 except for 110 baud for which it is 2).

The baud rate is required, but the other parameters are optional, though each one requires that those that precede it be present. The **BuildCommDCB** function demands that the **lpDef** parameter follow this format exactly—it is less tolerant of variations than the MS-DOS **mode** command.

A DCB built with this function will have flow control disabled. If flow control is desired, the appropriate DCB fields should be set before configuring the port.

■ ClearCommBreak

VB Declaration   `Declare Function ClearCommBreak% Lib "User" (ByVal nCid%)`

Description   Takes the specified serial port out of the break state.

Use with VB   No problem.

Parameter	Type/Description
nCid	**Integer**—The handle to the open serial port. This handle is returned by the **OpenComm** function.

Return Value   **Integer**—Zero on success. A value less than zero if the **nCid** parameter is not valid.

■ CloseComm

VB Declaration   `Declare Function CloseComm% Lib "User" (ByVal nCid%)`

Description   Closes the specified serial port and makes it available to other applications.

Use with VB   No problem.

Parameter	Type/Description
nCid	**Integer**—The handle to the open serial port. This handle is returned by the **OpenComm** function.

Return Value   **Integer**—Zero on success, negative value on error.

Comments   Any characters that remain in the transmit buffer are sent before the port is actually closed.

■ EnableCommNotification

VB Declaration   `Declare Function EnableCommNotification% Lib "User" (ByVal idComDev%, ByVal ⇔ hWnd%, ByVal cbWriteNotify%, ByVal cbOutQueue%)`

Description   This function is used to inform Windows that WM_COMMNOTIFY messages should be sent to a specified window. This message is used to notify the application that a communication event has occurred.

Use with VB   Although Visual Basic does not directly support Windows messages, the window handle of a CBK.VBX custom control may be used for this function, in which case the control will produce a **CommEvent** event whenever the WM_COMMNOTIFY message is received.

Parameter	Type/Description
idComDev	**Integer**—The handle to the open serial port. This handle is returned by the **OpenComm** function.
hWnd	**Integer**—A handle to a window which will receive WM_COMMNO-TIFY messages. This should be retrieved from the **hWnd** property of the CBK.VBX custom control that is to trigger **CommEvent** events.

cbWriteNotify	**Integer**—Specifies the number of bytes in the input buffer that will trigger a WM_COMMNOTIFY message. The message will be sent when the number of bytes in the input buffer exceeds this number. -1 disables input buffer notification.
cbOutQueue	**Integer**—Specifies the number of bytes in the output buffer that will trigger a WM_COMMNOTIFY message. The message will be sent when the number of bytes in the output buffer falls below this number. -1 disables output buffer notification.

Return Value   **Integer**—TRUE (nonzero) on success, zero otherwise.

Comments   Once an input or output buffer notification is received, the condition that caused the event must be removed before another notification will be generated. For example: If the **cbWriteNotify** parameter is set to 100, the event will be triggered when the number of bytes in the buffer exceeds 100, and will not occur again until the byte count falls below 100, and then exceeds 100 again. This capability is only implemented in Windows version 3.1 or higher.

The **CommEvent** event of the CBK.VBX custom control has two parameters:

DeviceID—Integer: Identifies the communications device that caused the event.

NotifyStatus—Integer: Contains one or more of the following flag constants:

CN_EVENT: An event occurred that was enabled with the **SetCommEventMask** API function. Use the **GetCommEventMask** function to determine the specific event that occurred.

CN_RECEIVE: The input buffer contains at least **cbWriteNotify** characters as specified by the **EnableCommNotification** function.

CN_TRANSMIT: The output buffer contains less than **cbOutQueue** characters as specified by the **EnableCommNotification** function.

■ EscapeCommFunction

VB Declaration   `Declare Function EscapeCommFunction% Lib "User" (ByVal nCid%, ByVal nFunc%)`

Description   This function provides additional functionality for a serial port.

Use with VB   No problem.

Parameter	Type/Description
nCid	**Integer**—The handle to the open serial port. This handle is returned by the **OpenComm** function.
nFunc	**Integer**—A constant describing the function to perform as follows: **CLRDTR**: Clears the DTR signal. **CLRRTS**: Clears the RTS signal. **GETMAXCOM**: Returns the identifier of the highest available comm port. Zero corresponds to COM0, one to COM1, and so on. **GETMAXLPT**: Returns the identifier of the highest available parallel port. &H80 corresponds to LPT1, &H81 to LPT2, and so on. **RESETDEV**: Resets a device on a printer port. Has no effect on a serial port. **SETDTR**: Sets the DTR signal. **SETRTS**: Sets the RTS signal.

Parameter	Type/Description
nFunc (continued)	**SETXOFF**: Causes the port to behave as if an Xoff character has been received. **SETXON**: Causes the port to behave as if an Xon character has been received.

Return Value   **Integer**—Zero on success, a result smaller than zero on error. As specified by the parameter description when **GETMAXCOM** and **GETMAXLPT** are specified.

■ FlushComm

VB Declaration   `Declare Function FlushComm% Lib "User" (ByVal nCid%, ByVal nQueue%)`

Description   Clears the input or output buffers for a serial device.

Use with VB   No problem.

Parameter	Type/Description
nCid	**Integer**—The handle to the open serial port. This handle is returned by the **OpenComm** function.
nQueue	**Integer**—Zero to clear the output buffer, one to clear the input buffer.

Return Value   **Integer**—Zero on success. Less than zero if **nCid** or **nQueue** is not valid. A positive value indicates an error as described for the return value of the **GetCommError** function.

■ GetCommError

VB Declaration   `Declare Function GetCommError% Lib "User" (ByVal nCid%, lpStat As COMSTAT)`

Description   Determines the latest status and error results for the specified communications port. This function also clears the error status so that the port may resume operation.

Use with VB   No problem.

Parameter	Type/Description
nCid	**Integer**—The handle to the open serial port. This handle is returned by the **OpenComm** function.
lpStat	**COMSTAT**—A **COMSTAT** structure that will be loaded with the current communications status. See "Obtaining Serial Port Status," earlier in this chapter.

Return Value   **Integer**—An error value that is specified by a combination of one or more of the constants listed in Table 14.9.

Table 14.9 **Communication Error Flags**

Constant	Description
CE_BREAK	A break condition was detected on the line.
CE_CTSTO	Timeout occurred while waiting for the CTS signal.
CE_DNS	Parallel device was not selected.
CE_DSRTO	Timeout occurred while waiting for the DSR signal.
CE_FRAME	A framing error occurred. This occurs when synchronization fails on a serial link.
CE_IOE	I/O error on a parallel device.
CE_MODE	A requested device mode is not available.
CE_OOP	Out of paper on a parallel device.
CE_OVERRUN	A character was received before a prior character was read causing that prior character to be lost.
CE_PTO	Timeout on parallel device.
CE_RLSDTO	Timeout waiting for CD (RLSD) signal.
CE_RXOVER	Input buffer overflow. This occurs when the buffer is full, or if a character is received after an EOF (end of file) character was received if EOF characters are being detected on the device.
CE_RXPARITY	Parity error occurred on input.
CE_TXFULL	Indicates an attempt to write a character to the output buffer when it is full.

■ GetCommEventMask

VB Declaration   `Declare Function GetCommEventMask% Lib "User" (ByVal nCid%, ByVal nEvtMask%)`

Description   Retrieves the event mask for a device and clears the current event status. Refer to "Serial Driver Events," earlier in this chapter, for further information on this function.

Use with VB   No problem.

Parameter	Type/Description
nCid	Integer—The handle to the open serial port. This handle is returned by the **OpenComm** function.
nEvtMask	Integer—Bitfield indicating which event bits to clear in the current event status. The bits of this mask are defined in Table 14.10 below.

Return Value　　Integer—The current event status. Refer to Table 14.10 for a definition of this bitfield.

Comments　　Only events that were enabled using the **SetCommEventMask** function will be detected.

　　　　　　Table 14.10 provides the meaning of each bit in the event mask. Each constant defines a mask for a single bit. The **SetCommEventMask** function uses the event mask to define which events are to be detected. The **GetCommEventMask** function uses the event mask to determine which events have occurred and to specify which events are to be cleared.

Table 14.10　　**Event Mask Bit Definitions**

Constant Name	Description
EV_BREAK	A break condition was detected during input.
EV_CTS	The CTS signal changed state.
EV_CTSS	Indicates the current state of the CTS signal.
EV_DSR	The DSR signal changed state.
EV_ERR	A serial device error occurred. This includes framing errors, overruns, and parity errors.
EV_PERR	A parallel device error occurred.
EV_RING	A ring signal was detected.
EV_RLSD	The RLSD (carrier detect or CD) signal changed state.
EV_RLSDS	Indicates the current state of the RLSD signal.
EV_RXCHAR	A character was received.
EV_RXFLAG	The event character was received.
EV_TXEMPTY	The last character in the output buffer was sent.

■ GetCommState

VB Declaration　　`Declare Function GetCommState% Lib "User" (ByVal nCid%, lpDCB as DCB)`

Description　　Retrieves the current configuration of a device.

Use with VB　　No problem.

Parameter	Type/Description
nCid	**Integer**—The handle to the open serial port. This handle is returned by the **OpenComm** function.
lpDCB	**DCB**—A device control block to load with the device configuration.

Return Value   **Integer**—Zero on success, less than zero on error.

■ OpenComm

VB Declaration   `Declare Function OpenComm% Lib "User" (ByVal lpComName$, ByVal wInQueue%, ⇔`
`ByVal wOutQueue%)`

Description   Opens a device for communication.

Use with VB   No problem.

Parameter	Type/Description
lpComName	**String**—The name of the port to open. This will be in the form COM*x* or LPT*x* where *x* is the number of the device.
wInQueue	**Integer**—The size of the input buffer in bytes.
wOutQueue	**Integer**—The size of the output buffer in bytes.

Return Value   **Integer**—A handle to the device on success. A negative number on error as shown by the constants in Table 14.11.

Table 14.11   **OpenComm Function Error Constants**

Constant	Description
IE_BADID	Invalid device identifier.
IE_BAUDRATE	Invalid baud rate.
IE_BYTESIZE	The byte size is invalid.
IE_DEFAULT	The default parameters are invalid.
IE_HARDWARE	The device is not available.
IE_MEMORY	Insufficient memory for the input and output buffers.
IE_NOPEN	The device cannot be opened.
IE_OPEN	The device is already open.

■ ReadComm

VB Declaration   `Declare Function ReadComm% Lib "User" (ByVal nCid%, ByVal lpBuf$, ByVal nSize%)`

Description   Reads information from a communications device.

Use with VB   No problem.

Parameter	Type/Description
nCid	**Integer**—The handle to the open serial port. This handle is returned by the **OpenComm** function.
lpBuf	**String**—A string to load with the input data. This string should be preallocated to at least **nSize** bytes.
nSize	**Integer**—The maximum number of bytes to read.

Return Value   **Integer**—The number of characters actually read. If an error occurred, the number will be negative and the absolute value of the result will reflect the number of characters read.

Comments   When an error occurs you must use the **GetCommError** function to determine what the error was and clear the error state. This should also be done if the result is zero just in case an error occurred while the input buffer was empty.

■ SetCommBreak

VB Declaration   `Declare Function SetCommBreak% Lib "User" (ByVal nCid%)`

Description   Places the specified serial port into the break state.

Use with VB   No problem.

Parameter	Type/Description
nCid	**Integer**—The handle to the open serial port. This handle is returned by the **OpenComm** function.

Return Value   **Integer**—Zero on success. A value less than zero if the **nCid** parameter is not valid.

■ SetCommEventMask

VB Declaration   `Declare Function SetCommEventMask& Lib "User" (ByVal nCid%, ByVal nEvtMask%)`

Description   Sets the event mask for a device. Only the events specified by this mask are detected.

Use with VB   No problem.

Parameter	Type/Description
nCid	**Integer**—The handle to the open serial port. This handle is returned by the **OpenComm** function.
nEvtMask	**Integer**—Bitfield indicating which events to detect. The bits of this mask are defined in Table 14.10 earlier.

Return Value   **Long**—The address of an integer that contains the current event status. This can be copied into an integer using the **agCopyData** function defined in the APIGUIDE.DLL dynamic link library. Refer to Table 14.10 for a definition of this bitfield.

■ SetCommState

VB Declaration Declare Function SetCommState% Lib "User" (lpDCB as DCB)

Description Sets the current configuration of a device.

Use with VB No problem.

Parameter	Type/Description
lpDCB	**DCB**—A device control block that defines the new configuration of a device. The device to configure is specified by the Id field of the DCB structure.

Return Value **Integer**—Zero on success, less than zero on error.

■ TransmitCommChar

VB Declaration Declare Function TransmitCommChar% Lib "User" (ByVal nCid%, ByVal cChar%)

Description Sends a character by placing it at the front of the output buffer. This character will be sent before any characters currently present in the output buffer. This function will return an error if it is called again before the previous character is sent.

Use with VB No problem.

Parameter	Type/Description
nCid	**Integer**—The handle to the open serial port. This handle is returned by the **OpenComm** function.
cChar	**Integer**—The ASCII value of the character to transmit. This value may be obtained using the Visual Basic **Asc** function.

Return Value **Integer**—Zero on success, negative value on error.

■ UngetCommChar

VB Declaration Declare Function UngetCommChar% Lib "User" (ByVal nCid%, ByVal cChar%)

Description Replaces a character back into the input buffer. This is used when the program retrieves a character and determines that it should not be processed right away. The character will be the first one read on the next read operation.

Use with VB No problem.

Parameter	Type/Description
nCid	**Integer**—The handle to the open serial port. This handle is returned by the **OpenComm** function.

Parameter	Type/Description
cChar	**Integer**—The ASCII value of the character to place back in the input buffer. This value may be obtained using the Visual Basic **Asc** function.

Return Value   **Integer**—Zero on success, negative value on error.

Comments   The character placed in the input buffer must be read before this function can be called again.

■ WriteComm

VB Declaration   `Declare Function WriteComm% Lib "User" (ByVal nCid%, ByVal lpBuf$, ByVal nSize%)`

Description   Writes data to a communication device.

Use with VB   No problem.

Parameter	Type/Description
nCid	**Integer**—The handle to the open serial port. This handle is returned by the **OpenComm** function.
lpBuf	**String**—A string to write to the output buffer.
nSize	**Integer**—The number of characters in **lpBuf** to write.

Return Value   **Integer**—The number of characters actually written. If an error occurred, the number will be negative and the absolute value of the result will reflect the number of characters written.

Comments   When an error occurs you must use the **GetCommError** function to determine what the error was and clear the error state. Use the **GetCommError** function to make certain that there is sufficient space in the output buffer for the string. Data written when insufficient space remains will overwrite data already in the buffer.

For serial devices, under no circumstances should the number of characters to write exceed the size of the output buffer as defined with the **OpenComm** function.

The Clipboard, Sound Drivers, and Other Topics

Clipboard Operations

Sound Capabilities and Multimedia

Scroll Bars, Port I/O, and Online Help

Function Reference

T HIS CHAPTER COVERS A NUMBER OF TOPICS THAT, WHILE IMPORTANT, DO not quite justify a chapter of their own.

First, this chapter will introduce the Windows API functions that work with Visual Basic's clipboard and describe how you can go beyond Visual Basic's clipboard support in your application.

A brief introduction to the Windows multimedia interface follows, along with a description of the built-in sound capabilities. Sample code and directions for further study are included.

Other subjects that will be reviewed are the Windows API scroll bar functions, port input/output, and online help.

Clipboard Operations

The Windows clipboard is an object that can hold various other objects and transfer them among applications. Typical uses for the clipboard include copying text from one document to another in a word processor, copying a chart from a spreadsheet to a word processor, copying images between applications, and more. While this description sounds simple, there is a surprising amount of complexity and flexibility behind it. The Windows API clipboard functions provide the tools for the Visual Basic programmer to work with the clipboard.

How the Clipboard Works

If all the clipboard did was hold data objects that were used by a single application, the clipboard would be very simple. Each application could have its own clipboard, and one would never need to worry about the ownership of clipboard objects.

Since the clipboard can be used to transfer objects among applications, it must be a shared resource. Only one application may use the clipboard at a time. The **OpenClipboard** function is used to open the clipboard and assign it to a window. This reserves the clipboard for use by the application until the **CloseClipboard** function is called.

The clipboard contains either bitmap handles, palette handles, or global memory handles. All of these objects are usually owned by an application. This means that they can only be used by that application, and are deleted automatically when the application terminates. Clearly there would be a problem if these objects were simply placed into the clipboard. As soon as the application that created the object terminated, the clipboard would find itself holding a handle to an object that no longer exists! This is a sure path to various system errors, including general protection faults.

In order to make an object shareable among applications, Windows changes the ownership of the object when it is placed into the clipboard. Each object in the clipboard is owned by the clipboard. This means that once an object is placed into the clipboard, the handle to that object must never be used again by the application. It also means that any handle retrieved by an application from the clipboard may be examined, but must not be modified in any way.

The clipboard is capable of holding many different types of objects and more than one object at one time. In general, when an application places data into the clipboard it will place it in several different formats. For example, an Excel chart may be placed into a clipboard in an internal Excel graphics format, a metafile picture format, and a bitmap format. In addition, a text format object containing a description of the object may be included and link information used for object linking and embedding. All of these formats are a representation of the same data object, though the accuracy of each rendition varies. In this case the internal Excel format graph contains far more data than the bitmap, which in turn is far more accurate than the text description of the graph.

Clipboard Formats

Each clipboard format has an integer identifier. A number of formats are predefined by Windows. These are listed in Table 15.1. Each format is identified by a constant defined with the CF_ prefix in file APICONST.TXT.

Table 15.1   **Standard Clipboard Formats**

Identifier Constant	Description of the Clipboard Data for This Format
CF_BITMAP	A bitmap handle.
CF_DIB	A global memory block containing a device-independent bitmap.
CF_DIF	A global memory block containing data in data interchange format (DIF).
CF_DSPBITMAP	A bitmap that represents a private data format.
CF_DSPMETAFILEPICT	A global memory block containing a **METAFILEPICT** structure describing a metafile that represents a private data format.
CF_DSPTEXT	A global memory block containing text that represents a private data format.
CF_METAFILEPICT	A global memory block containing a **METAFILEPICT** structure describing a metafile.
CF_OEMTEXT	A global memory block containing text in the OEM character set. Each line is separated by a carriage return line feed (CR LF) pair. The end of the text is marked by a null character.
CF_OWNERDISPLAY	The clipboard data is in a private format that can be displayed only by the owner of the clipboard data.

Table 15.1	Standard Clipboard Formats (Continued)
Identifier Constant	**Description of the Clipboard Data for This Format**
CF_PALETTE	A handle to a palette. See Chapter 16 for further information on palettes.
CF_RIFF	A global handle containing data in resource interchange file format (RIFF).
CF_SYLK	A global handle containing data in Microsoft Symbolic Link format (SYLK).
CF_TEXT	A global memory block containing text. Each line is separated by a carriage return line feed (CR LF) pair. The end of the text is marked by a null character.
CF_TIFF	A global memory block containing an image in tagged image file format (TIFF).
CF_WAVE	A global memory block containing sound data. This must be a subset of the RIFF format.

All of these formats can be used from Visual Basic except for **CF_OWNER-DISPLAY**. This is because Visual Basic does not provide access to the Windows messages that supply the notification necessary for displaying and destroying these objects.

It is also possible to define private formats using the **RegisterClipboardFormat** function. A private format should not contain memory handles or object handles that need to be destroyed, as Windows has no way of knowing how to destroy them when the clipboard object is deleted.

You will generally want to use the format that contains the most information about the object in the clipboard. **EnumClipboardFormats** can be used to determine which data formats are present in the clipboard. Listing 15.1 shows the Visual Basic code that may be used to retrieve a list of available clipboard formats and display them in a list box.

The function begins by clearing the list box and opening the clipboard. If the clipboard can't be opened, the function exits; otherwise, it proceeds to list the clipboard formats in order. The most accurate formats (those containing the most information about the object) will be listed first.

Listing 15.1   Enumerating Clipboard Formats

```
Sub DisplayFormats ()
    Dim cfname$
    Dim cfnum%
    Dim cnum%
```

Listing 15.1   Enumerating Clipboard Formats (Continued)

```
cfname$ = String$(256, 0)
' Clear the clipboard
While list1.listcount <> 0
    list1.RemoveItem 0
Wend

cnum% = OpenClipboard%(hWnd)
if cnum%=0 then Exit Sub
Do
    cfnum% = EnumClipboardFormats%(cfnum%)
    Select Case cfnum%
        Case 1
            cfname$ = "CF_TEXT"
        Case 2
            cfname$ = "CF_BITMAP"
        Case 3
            cfname$ = "CF_METAFILEPICT"
        Case 4
            cfname$ = "CF_SYLK"
        Case 5
            cfname$ = "CF_DIF"
        Case 6
            cfname$ = "CF_TIFF"
        Case 7
            cfname$ = "CF_OEMTEXT"
        Case 8
            cfname$ = "CF_DIB"
        Case 9
            cfname$ = "CF_PALETTE"
        Case &H80
            cfname$ = "CF_OWNERDISPLAY"
        Case &H81
            cfname$ = "CF_DSPTEXT"
        Case &H82
            cfname$ = "CF_DSPBITMAP"
        Case &H83
            cfname$ = "CF_DSPMETAFILEPICT"
        Case Else
            di% = GetClipboardFormatName%(cfnum%, cfname$, 255)
    End Select

    list1.AddItem cfname$
Loop While cfnum% <> 0
di% = CloseClipboard()


End Sub
```

Accessing the Clipboard

Accessing the clipboard from the Windows API is a very straightforward process:

1. Open the clipboard using the **OpenClipboard** function. Be sure to check the result of this function to make certain that the clipboard is available to the application.

2. To retrieve data from the clipboard, use the **GetClipboardData** function. Remember, the handle returned by this function is owned by the clipboard and may be examined, but must not be modified or kept by the application. If you lock a global memory handle returned by this function, be sure to unlock it before closing the clipboard.

3. To set data into the clipboard, set the handle or bitmap into the clipboard using the **SetClipboardData** function. Once a handle is set into the clipboard, it must not be used again by the application in any way.

4. Close the clipboard using the **CloseClipboard** function.

Table 15.2 lists the Windows API functions used to access the clipboard.

Table 15.2 **Clipboard API Functions**

Function	Description
CloseClipboard	Closes the clipboard.
CountClipboardFormats	Determines how many formats are present in the cli board.
EmptyClipboard	Clears all objects from the clipboard.
EnumClipboardFormats	Used to determine the data formats available in the clipboard.
GetClipboardData	Used to extract data from the clipboard.
GetClipboardFormatName	Determines the name of a nonstandard clipboard format.
GetClipboardOwner	Determines which window owns the clipboard. This is most frequently used for **CF_OWNERDISPLAY** formats, which are not supported by VB.
GetOpenClipboardWindow	Determines which window has opened the clipboard.
GetPriorityClipboardFormat	Used to determine the presence of a format according to an application-defined priority.
IsClipboardFormatAvailable	Determines if a specified clipboard format is present in the clipboard.
OpenClipboard	Opens the clipboard.

Table 15.2   **Clipboard API Functions (Continued)**

Function	Description
RegisterClipboardFormat	Registers a private format.
SetClipboardData	Sets data into the clipboard.

Use with VB

The Windows clipboard functions are fully compatible with Visual Basic. In cases where you are dealing with text, metafiles, bitmaps, or palettes, you will probably want to use the Visual Basic clipboard objects instead of API functions. They take care of all of the overhead of opening the clipboard, setting the text into a global memory handle or making a copy of the image data, and setting it into the clipboard.

Because the Visual Basic clipboard commands open and close the clipboard themselves, they cannot be used when the clipboard has been opened by an application using the API functions. It is necessary therefore to close the clipboard before attempting to access the clipboard using VB commands.

Most clipboard formats use global memory blocks to hold the data (see Chapter 12). It is important to remember that once a memory handle is transferred to the clipboard, the application may no longer use it and should not free it. Memory blocks retrieved from the clipboard should not be modified. These blocks are typically either examined or their data is copied into a new global memory block or Visual Basic string buffer.

Windows actually provides additional clipboard capabilities including formats that are drawn by the application, and a viewer chain by which applications can be notified whenever the clipboard changes. These tasks cannot be performed directly from Visual Basic, but can be implemented using subclassing techniques as described in the Message Handling section in Chapter 17.

Sound Capabilities and Multimedia

Multimedia technology has exploded onto the computer scene in the past year, so it is no surprise that Windows 3.1 has extensive support for multimedia and sound. This support takes two forms. First, there is the original sound-generating capability that has been part of Windows since it was first created. This consists of a set of sound functions that reflect traditional synthesizer technology. It provides for multiple voices, sound generation based on notes and frequency, and support for noise sources.

This type of sound support is gradually being replaced by the second form—the Microsoft multimedia extensions, an updated version of which is included as part of Windows 3.1.

Multimedia

The Windows 3.1 multimedia extensions support a large number of devices. The audio devices include the ability to play and record digitized sound files (.WAV extensions), and to access MIDI-based devices. MIDI is a computer interface that is used by most medium to high-end sound equipment including keyboards, sequencers, drum machines, mixers, and so on. Support is also provided for playing compact disc audio, video discs, and animation players.

When we refer to multimedia extensions, we are really referring to another API that defines functions used to access various devices. The functions for the multimedia API are contained in a dynamic link library called MMSYSTEM.DLL. Like the regular API functions, the multimedia functions can be accessed directly from Visual Basic once you have defined the appropriate function declarations.

This book includes three files that contain the function, type, and constant declarations for the multimedia API. File MMDECS.BAS contains the type and function declarations. File MMCONST.TXT contains definitions for the global constants. The program APICONS provided with this book (and described in detail in Chapter 19) can be used to extract constants from the MMCONST.TXT file into the clipboard for inclusion in your programs.

The easiest way to access multimedia devices is to use the Visual Basic multimedia MCI control that is provided with the professional version of Visual Basic. If you wish to use the multimedia API directly, you will need to obtain a copy of the *Windows Multimedia Programmer's Reference* or an equivalent reference. That document, along with the declaration files provided with this book, should provide you with enough information to use the multimedia API effectively.

In addition to low-level API functions, the multimedia extensions define a string-based interface, where you can send control strings to a device. Listing 15.2 presents a Visual Basic function **SendMMString** that sends a command string to the multimedia driver. It returns an empty string on success, or an error message if an error occurs.

Listing 15.2   Function mciSendString

```
' The following declaration for function mciSendString
' can be found in file MMCONST.TXT.

Declare Function mciSendStringAny& Lib "MMSYSTEM.DLL"  ⇔
```

Listing 15.2   Function mciSendString (Continued)

```
            Alias "mciSendString" (ByVal lpstrCommand$, ByVal ⇔
            lpstrReturnString As Any, ByVal uReturnLength%, ⇔
            ByVal hwndCallback%)

Function SendMMString$ (cmdstring$)
    Dim res%
    Dim errstring As String * 128

    ' Send the command string.
    res% = mciSendStringAny&(cmdstring$, Ø&, Ø, Ø)

    ' On success, just return an empty string
    If res% = Ø Then
        SendMMString$ = ""
        Exit Function
    End If

    ' On error, return the error description
    res% = mciGetErrorString(res%, errstring, ⇔
     Len(errstring) - 1)
    If res% <> Ø Then
        SendMMString$ = errstring
    Else
        SendMMString$ = "Unknown error"
    End If
End Function
```

Listing 15.3 presents function PlayWAV$, which can be used to play a digitized sound file (.WAV file). It is followed by a command button function, which can be used to play the standard TADA.WAV file that is included with Windows 3.1.

Listing 15.3   Function PlayWAV$

```
Function PlayWAV$ (wavename$)
    Dim e$, e2$
    ' Open the audio waveform player. All you need to
    ' do is provide the name of a .WAV file.  The Windows
    ' SYSTEM.INI initialization file associates the .WAV
    ' extension to the sound driver you currently have
    ' installed.  This needs to be the full pathname to
    ' the .WAV file.
    e$ = SendMMString$("Open " + wavename$)
    If e$ <> "" Then
        PlayWAV$ = e$
```

Listing 15.3   Function PlayWAV$ (Continued)

```
        Exit Function
    End If

    ' Tell the system to wait until the file has been
    ' played. Otherwise, you would need to poll the
    ' status to make sure that the sound was complete
    ' before closing the file.
    e$ = SendMMString$("Play " + wavename$ + " wait")

    ' Close the file when done.
    e2$ = SendMMString$("Close " + wavename$)
    PlayWAV$ = e$ & e2$

End Function


' The Command2_Click function shows how function
' PlayWAV$ is called.

Sub Command2_Click ()
    Dim e$
    e$ = PlayWAV$("\windows\tada.wav")
    If e$ <> "" Then MsgBox e$
End Sub
```

The **MessageBeep** function defined in the function reference of this chapter can be used to play the standard sounds defined under the **[sounds]** section of the WIN.INI file. These sounds are also defined by .WAV sound files.

Windows Sound Driver

Windows 3.0 provided a set of functions for accessing sound devices that are still available for driving the PC speaker. These functions assume that the sound device is made up of one or more voice queues, each of which has space for a certain number of notes. To use these functions, follow this sequence:

1. Open the sound driver using the **OpenSound** function.

2. Set the size of the voice queue using the **SetVoiceQueueSize** function.

3. Set the tempo for playing notes using the **SetVoiceAccent** function.

4. Set notes into the voice queue using the **SetVoiceNote** function.

5. Start the sound playing using the **StartSound** function.

6. You can stop the sound from playing using the **StopSound** function.

7. When finished with the sound driver, use the **CloseSound** function to release the driver resources.

The Windows API defines additional functions that allow you to create noises and the sounds of different frequencies, choose sound waveform envelopes, and so on. Some of these are not supported with the standard sound driver, and as these functions have been declared to be obsolete for version 3.1 of Windows, it is unlikely that they will be supported by future sound drivers. They should, however, be safe to use for generating sounds on the PC speaker.

Listing 15.4 demonstrates how sounds can be generated using the API sound functions. The **PlaySounds** function generates random notes from the PC speaker. The **PlaySiren** function demonstrates how a siren sound effect can be generated. Variable **soundstat%** is a global variable that is used to indicate that the sound driver is open.

Listing 15.4   Sample Sound Routine

```
Sub PlaySounds ()
    Dim note%, duration%

    If soundstat% = 0 Then soundstat% = OpenSound%()
    di% = SetVoiceQueueSize(1, 1024)
    Do
        note% = Int(Rnd * 84 + 1)
        duration% = 2 ^ Int(Rnd * 4)
        di% = SetVoiceNote%(1, note%, duration%, 1)
    Loop While di% = 0

    di% = StartSound%()

End Sub

Sub PlaySiren ()
    Dim soundval&
    Dim freq%
    Dim duration%
    Dim offset%

    If soundstat% = 0 Then soundstat% = OpenSound%()
    di% = SetVoiceQueueSize(1, 1000)
    di% = SetVoiceAccent(1, 120, 255, 1, 0)
    freq% = 800
    duration% = 10
    offset% = 5

    Do
        ' Note how the high word contains the frequency
```

Listing 15.4   **Sample Sound Routine (Continued)**

```
            soundval& = CLng(freq%) * &H10000
            di% = SetVoiceSound(1, soundval&, duration%)
            freq% = freq% + offset%
            If freq% >= 1000 Then offset% = -5
            If freq% <= 800 Then offset% = 5

        Loop While di% = 0

        di% = StartSound%()


End Sub
```

The following function, triggered by a command button, stops the sound and closes the sound driver.

```
Sub Command3_Click ()
    If soundstat% <> 0 Then
        di% = StopSound()
        CloseSound
        soundstat% = 0
    End If
End Sub
```

Table 15.3 lists the sound functions that are built into the Windows API.

Table 15.3   **PC Speaker Sound Functions**

Function	Description
CloseSound	Closes the sound driver.
CountVoiceNotes	Determines the number of notes in the queue.
GetThresholdEvent	Returns a flag that indicates when the number of notes in the queue has dropped below the threshold level.
GetThresholdStatus	Determines in which voice queues the number of notes has fallen below the queue's threshold level.
MessageBeep	Sounds a beep signal. This is typically used to indicate a warning or notice to the user when a message box appears.
OpenSound	Opens the sound driver.
SetSoundNoise	Generates a noise from the speaker.
SetVoiceAccent	Specifies the tempo, volume, and pitch for a voice.

Table 15.3   **PC Speaker Sound Functions (Continued)**

Function	Description
SetVoiceNote	Adds a note to the voice queue.
SetVoiceQueueSize	Sets the size of a voice queue.
SetVoiceSound	Adds a sound to the voice queue.
SetVoiceThreshold	Sets the threshold level for the voice queue.
StartSound	Starts playing the voice queue.
StopSound	Stops the voice queue from playing.
SyncAllVoices	Used to synchronize voices. The PC speaker only has one voice, so this is fairly useless.

Scroll Bars, Port I/O, and Online Help

This section briefly describes the use of scroll bars, port I/O, and online help under Visual Basic.

Scroll Bars

The Visual Basic scroll bar controls are subclassed from the standard Windows scroll bar. Visual Basic does, however, provide its own access to the scroll bar attributes using Visual Basic properties. As a result, it is inadvisable to access a Visual Basic scroll bar directly from the Windows API. Only one API function can be used safely with a Visual Basic scroll bar: the **EnableScrollBar** function, which provides you with the ability to disable one or both of the scroll bar arrows individually. The other scroll bar API functions are described briefly in the function reference section, but should be used with caution, as they can interfere with the correct operation of the Visual Basic scroll bar properties. Table 15.4 lists the Windows API functions that work with scroll bars.

Port I/O

Visual Basic lacks the port input and output functions that are common in most versions of BASIC. The Windows API does not provide this capability either.

The APIGUIDE.DLL dynamic link library included with this book provides a number of functions, listed in Table 15.5, that give you direct access to the system I/O ports. These functions should be used with caution. You should avoid directly accessing devices that Windows provides access to (such as disk drives, video devices, sound cards, and so on). These functions are frequently used to access specialized hardware such as instrumentation controllers that do not have Windows drivers available.

Refer to Appendix A for details on using these functions.

Table 15.4   **Windows API Scroll Bar Functions**

Function	Description
EnableScrollBar	Enables or disables one or both arrows on a scroll bar.
GetScrollPos	Retrieves the current position of the scroll bar indicator.
GetScrollRange	Retrieves the minimum and maximum positions of the scroll bar indicator.
SetScrollPos	Sets the current position of the scroll bar indicator.
SetScrollRange	Sets the minimum and maximum positions of the scroll bar indicator.

Table 15.5   **I/O Functions**

Function	Description
agInp	Inputs a byte from an I/O port.
agInw	Inputs a 16-bit integer from an I/O port.
agOutp	Outputs a byte to an I/O port.
agOutw	Outputs a 16-bit integer to an I/O port.

Online Help

The Windows API provides the **WinHelp** function for accessing online help. This function accepts a context identifier as an integer to provide online help. This means that you can assign each form a context number so that when help is requested the help topic for that form appears.

The catch here is that you must already have a help file in the necessary format. Help files are built using a program called a help compiler. The help compiler and specifications for generating help files are available from Microsoft and are also part of the professional version of Visual Basic.

Function Reference

This section contains an alphabetical reference for the functions described in this chapter. For information on multimedia functions, refer to the *Multimedia Programmer's Reference* available from Microsoft, or other reference material that describes the Microsoft multimedia extensions. Declarations for the multimedia extensions can be found in files MMCONST.TXT, MMDECS-.TXT, and MMTYPES.TXT on the disk provided with this book.

■ CloseClipboard

VB Declaration `Declare Function CloseClipboard% Lib "User" ()`

Description Closes the clipboard so that it may be accessed by other applications. An application should close the clipboard as soon as it has finished using it.

Use with VB No problem.

Return Value **Integer**—TRUE (nonzero) on success, zero otherwise.

■ CloseSound

VB Declaration `Declare Sub CloseSound Lib "Sound" ()`

Description Closes the sound driver.

Use with VB No problem.

■ CountClipboardFormats

VB Declaration `Declare Function CountClipboardFormats% Lib "User" ()`

Description Determines the number of clipboard formats present in the clipboard.

Use with VB No problem.

Return Value **Integer**—The number of clipboard formats currently in the clipboard.

■ CountVoiceNotes

VB Declaration `Declare Function CountVoiceNotes% Lib "Sound" (ByVal nVoice%)`

Description Determines the number of notes in a voice queue.

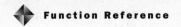

Use with VB	No problem.	
	Parameter	**Type/Description**
	nVoice	**Integer**—The number of the voice queue (starting from 1). The PC speaker driver has only one voice.

Return Value   **Integer**—The number of notes in the queue.

Comments   Only notes placed in the queue using the **SetVoiceNotes** function are included in the result.

■ EmptyClipboard

VB Declaration   `Declare Function EmptyClipboard% Lib "User" ()`

Description   Clears the contents of the clipboard. The clipboard must be opened by the application using the **OpenClipboard** function before calling this function.

Use with VB   No problem. Use the Visual Basic **Clipboard.Clear** command for the same result.

Return Value   **Integer**—TRUE (nonzero) on success, zero otherwise.

■ EnableScrollBar

VB Declaration   `Declare Function EnableScrollBar% Lib "User" (ByVal hWnd%, ByVal fnSBFlags%, ↔`
`ByVal fuArrowFlags%)`

Description   Allows you to enable or disable one or both of the arrows of a scroll bar.

Use with VB	No known problems.	
	Parameter	**Type/Description**
	hWnd	**Integer**—A handle to a window. This can be the window handle of a form that has a vertical or horizontal scroll bar, or the window handle of the scroll bar as retrieved using the **agGetControlHwnd** function.
	fnSBflags	**Integer**—A constant as described in Table 15.6.
	fuArrowFlags	**Integer**—One of the following constants defined in APICONST.TXT: **ESB_ENABLE_BOTH**: Enable both arrows. **ESB_DISABLE_LTUP**: Disable the left or up arrow. **ESB_DISABLE_RTDN**: Disable the right or down arrow. **ESB_DISABLE_BOTH**: Disable both arrows.

Return Value   **Integer**—TRUE (nonzero) if the arrows are changed as specified, zero if no change took place or an error occurred.

Comments   A Windows scroll bar API function can affect both scroll bars that are part of a form and scroll bars that are controls. The constants shown in Table 15.6 are used to specify which controls are affected by the API functions.

Table 15.6   **Scroll Bar Selection Constants**

Constant Value	Scroll Bar Affected by the Function
SB_BOTH	The horizontal and vertical scroll bars of a form. The **hWnd** parameter is the window handle of the form that contains the scroll bars.
SB_CTL	The scroll bar is a control. The **hWnd** parameter is the window handle of the scroll bar control.
SB_HORZ	The horizontal scroll bar of a form. The **hWnd** parameter is the window handle of the form that contains the scroll bar.
SB_VERT	The vertical scroll bar of a form. The **hWnd** parameter is the window handle of the form that contains the scroll bar.

■ EnumClipboardFormats

VB Declaration   `Declare Function EnumClipboardFormats% Lib "User" (ByVal wFormat%)`

Description   Enumerates the formats currently present in the clipboard. The clipboard must be opened by the application using the **OpenClipboard** function before calling this function.

Use with VB   No problem.

Parameter	Type/Description
wFormat	Integer—Zero to retrieve the value of the first format in the clipboard. Specify a clipboard format ID to retrieve the clipboard format that follows it in the list.

Return Value   Integer—The clipboard format identifier.

Comments   Formats are retrieved in the same order as that used during pasting. The formats are provided in the order of those that contain the most information to those that contain the least.

■ GetClipboardData

VB Declaration   `Declare Function GetClipboardData% Lib "User" (ByVal wFormat%)`

Description   Retrieves data from the clipboard. The clipboard must be opened by the application using the **OpenClipboard** function before calling this function.

Use with VB   No problem.

Parameter	Type/Description
wFormat	Integer—The identifier of the clipboard format of the data to retrieve. Refer to Table 15.1 in "Clipboard Operations," earlier in this chapter, for a list of standard clipboard formats.

Return Value **Integer**—A global memory handle to a memory block containing the data in the requested format. Zero on failure. Refer to Chapter 12 for information on using global memory blocks.

Comments The application should not free the memory handle returned by this function.

■ GetClipboardFormatName

VB Declaration `Declare Function GetClipboardFormatName% Lib "User" (ByVal wFormat%, ⇔`
`ByVal lpString$, ByVal nMaxCount%)`

Description Retrieves the name of the specified clipboard format given the identifier of the format. This function does not retrieve a name for the standard clipboard formats such as **CF_TEXT**, **CF_BIT-MAP**, and so on.

Use with VB No problem.

Parameter	Type/Description
wFormat	**Integer**—The identifier of a clipboard format.
lpString	**String**—A string that will be loaded with the format name. This string must be preallocated to at least **nMaxCount+1** characters.
nMaxCount	**Integer**—The maximum length of the string to retrieve.

Return Value **Integer**—The number of characters retrieved, zero on error.

■ GetClipboardOwner

VB Declaration `Declare Function GetClipboardOwner% Lib "User" ()`

Description Determines which window currently owns the clipboard.

Use with VB No problem.

Return Value **Integer**—A handle to the window that owns the clipboard. Zero on error or if the clipboard is not owned.

Comments It is possible for the clipboard data to have no owner, for example, if an application sets data into the clipboard and then terminates.

■ GetOpenClipboardWindow

VB Declaration `Declare Function GetOpenClipboardWindow% Lib "User" ()`

Description Determines which window has opened the clipboard.

Use with VB No problem.

Return Value **Integer**—The window handle of the window that has opened the clipboard. Zero if the clipboard is not open.

■ GetPriorityClipboardFormat

VB Declaration   Declare Function GetPriorityClipboardFormat% Lib "User" (lpPriority⇔
List%, ByVal nCount%)

Description   This function is used to retrieve the first clipboard format in a list that is present in the clipboard.
An application can create an integer array containing the identifiers of clipboard formats in an
order that the application would prefer to access the data. This function checks the array against
the available clipboard formats and returns the value of the first clipboard format from the list
that is available in the clipboard.

Use with VB   No problem.

Parameter	Type/Description
lpPriorityList	**Integer**—The first entry in an integer array containing the identifiers of clipboard formats in priority order.
nCount	**Integer**—The number of entries in the **lpPriorityList** array.

Return Value   **Integer**—The identifier of the first clipboard format found. Zero if the clipboard is empty. -1 if the
clipboard contains data but the formats do not match those requested in the **lpPriorityList** array.

■ GetScrollPos

VB Declaration   Declare Function GetScrollPos% Lib "User" (ByVal hWnd%, ByVal nBar%)

Description   Retrieves the current indicator position of the scroll bar.

Use with VB   The position returned uses the internal range of the scroll bar, which is not compatible with a VB
scroll bar's **Min**, **Max**, and **Value** properties.

Parameter	Type/Description
hWnd	**Integer**—A handle to a window. This can be the window handle of a form that has a vertical or horizontal scroll bar, or the window handle of the scroll bar as retrieved using the **agGetControlHwnd** function.
nBar	**Integer**—A constant as described in Table 15.6 under the **Enable-ScrollBar** function.

Return Value   **Integer**—The current position of the scroll bar indicator. Zero on error.

■ GetScrollRange

VB Declaration   Declare Sub GetScrollRange Lib "User" (ByVal hWnd%, ByVal nBar%, ⇔
lpMinPos%, lpMaxPos%)

Description   Retrieves the current minimum and maximum indicator positions of a scroll bar.

Use with VB   The values returned reflect the internal range of the scroll bar, which is not compatible with a VB scroll bar's **Min**, **Max**, and **Value** properties.

Parameter	Type/Description
hWnd	**Integer**—A handle to a window. This can be the window handle of a form that has a vertical or horizontal scroll bar, or the window handle of the scroll bar as retrieved using the **agGetControlHwnd** function.
nBar	**Integer**—A constant as described in Table 15.6 under the **Enable-ScrollBar** function.
lpMinPos%	**Integer**—An integer variable to set with the minimum indicator position.
lpMaxPos%	**Integer**—An integer variable to set with the maximum indicator position.

■ GetThresholdEvent

VB Declaration   `Declare Function GetThresholdEvent& Lib "Sound" ()`

Description   This function returns the address of an integer indicating which queues have dropped below the threshold level specified by the **SetThresholdEvent** function.

Use with VB   No problem. You will need to copy the data into an integer using the **agCopyData** function.

Return Value   **Long**—The address of an integer indicating the threshold event that occurred.

■ GetThresholdStatus

VB Declaration   `Declare Function GetThresholdStatus% Lib "Sound" ()`

Description   This function returns an integer flag indicating which queues have dropped below the threshold level specified by the **SetThresholdEvent** function.

Use with VB   No problem.

Return Value   **Integer**—Each voice queue has a bit assigned to it (voice queue 1 is bit 0). The bit will be set if the number of notes in the voice queue is less than the specified threshold for that queue.

■ IsClipboardFormatAvailable

VB Declaration   `Declare Function IsClipboardFormatAvailable% Lib "User" (ByVal wFormat%)`

Description   Determines if clipboard data is available in a requested format.

Use with VB   No problem. The Visual Basic **Clipboard.GetFormat** command is a subset of this function.

Parameter	Type/Description
wFormat	**Integer**—The identifier of the format that is being requested.

Return Value   Integer—TRUE (nonzero) if data exists in the clipboard in the specified format, zero otherwise.

■ MessageBeep

VB Declaration   `Declare Sub MessageBeep Lib "User" (ByVal wType%)`

Description   Causes a sound waveform to be played. The waveform depends on the type specified by the function and the waveform assigned to that type in the **[sounds]** section of the WIN.INI initialization file. If one or more system sounds are disabled via the Control panel (CONTROL.EXE) application, those sounds will not be played.

Use with VB   No problem.

Parameter	Type/Description
wType	**Integer**—1 to play a beep sound through the computer speaker. The following constants specify other sounds: **MB_ICONASTERISK**: The sound specified by the **SystemAsterisk** entry in WIN.INI. **MB_ICONEXCLAMATION**: The sound specified by the **SystemExclamation** entry in WIN.INI. **MB_ICONHAND**: The sound specified by the **SystemHand** entry in WIN.INI. **MB_ICONQUESTION**: The sound specified by the **SystemQuestion** entry in WIN.INI. **MB_OK**: The sound specified by the **SystemDefault** entry in WIN.INI.

Comments   This function returns immediately. The sound is played asynchronously in the background as the program continues to run.

■ OpenClipboard

VB Declaration   `Declare Function OpenClipboard% Lib "User" (ByVal hWnd%)`

Description   Opens the clipboard. Only one window may have the clipboard open at a time.

Use with VB   No problem.

Parameter	Type/Description
hWnd	**Integer**—A handle to a window. This will typically be a form.

Return Value   Integer—TRUE (nonzero) on success, zero if the clipboard is already open by another application.

■ OpenSound

VB Declaration   `Declare Function OpenSound% Lib "Sound" ()`

Description   Opens the sound driver for use by the application.

Use with VB	No problem.
Return Value	**Integer**—The number of voices available on success. Negative constant **S_SERDVNA** if the sound driver is already open or **S_SEROFM** if there is inadequate memory available to open the sound driver.

■ RegisterClipboardFormat

VB Declaration	`Declare Function RegisterClipboardFormat% Lib "User" (ByVal lpString$)`
Description	Defines a new clipboard format.
Use with VB	This function makes it possible for VB applications to create their own private clipboard formats.

Parameter	Type/Description
lpString	**String**—The name of the clipboard format to register.

Return Value	**Integer**—The identifier of the clipboard format.
Comments	Once a clipboard format is registered, the same identifier will be returned by this function each time the function is called with the name of the format. This applies even if the format is registered by a different application, so applications may share a clipboard format.

■ SetClipboardData

VB Declaration	`Declare Function SetClipboardData% Lib "User" (ByVal wFormat%, ByVal hMem%)`
Description	Sets data into the clipboard. The clipboard must be opened by the current application using the **OpenClipboard** function.
Use with VB	No problem.

Parameter	Type/Description
wFormat	**Integer**—The identifier of the clipboard format of the **hMem** memory block. Refer to Table 15.1 in "Clipboard Operations," earlier in this chapter, for a list of standard clipboard formats.
hMem	**Integer**—A global memory handle to a memory block containing data in the format specified by **wFormat**. If the format is **CF_BITMAP**, this value is a bitmap handle. If the format is **CF_PALETTE**, this value is a palette handle.

Return Value	**Integer**—**hMem** on success, zero on error.
Comments	Once the handle specified by **hMem** is placed in the clipboard, it is kept by the clipboard and should no longer be used by the application. Refer to Chapter 12 for information on using global memory handles and Chapter 8 for information on using bitmap handles. Palette handles are discussed in Chapter 16.

■ SetScrollPos

VB Declaration Declare Function SetScrollPos% Lib "User" (ByVal hWnd%, ByVal nBar%, ⇔
ByVal nPos%, ByVal bRedraw%)

Description Sets the current indicator position of the scroll bar.

Use with VB Changing the internal position of a scroll bar may interfere with the proper operation of the Visual Basic scroll bars. Use the scroll bar **Value** property instead.

Parameter	Type/Description
hWnd	**Integer**—A handle to a window. This can be the window handle of a form that has a vertical or horizontal scroll bar, or the window handle of the scroll bar as retrieved using the **agGetControlHwnd** function.
nBar	**Integer**—A constant as described in Table 15.6 under the **Enable-ScrollBar** function.
nPos	**Integer**—The new position of the scroll bar indicator.
bRedraw	**Integer**—TRUE (nonzero) to redraw the scroll bar.

Return Value **Integer**—The current position of the scroll bar indicator. Zero on error.

■ SetScrollRange

VB Declaration Declare Sub SetScrollRange Lib "User" (ByVal hWnd%, ByVal nBar%, ⇔
ByVal nMinPos%, ByVal nMaxPos%, ByVal bRedraw%)

Description Sets the current minimum and maximum indicator positions of a scroll bar.

Use with VB Changing the internal range of a scroll bar will interfere with the proper operation of the Visual Basic scroll bars. Use the scroll bar **Min** and **Max** properties instead.

Parameter	Type/Description
hWnd	**Integer**—A handle to a window. This can be the window handle of a form that has a vertical or horizontal scroll bar, or the window handle of the scroll bar as retrieved using the **agGetControlHwnd** function.
nBar	**Integer**—A constant as described in Table 15.6 under the **Enable-ScrollBar** function.
nMinPos%	**Integer**—The new minimum indicator position.
nMaxPos%	**Integer**—The new maximum indicator position.
bRedraw	**Integer**—TRUE (nonzero) to redraw the scroll bar.

■ SetSoundNoise

VB Declaration Declare Function SetSoundNoise% Lib "Sound" (ByVal nSource%, ByVal nDuration%)

Description   Generates a specified noise.

Use with VB   No problem, though this function is not supported by all devices.

Parameter	Type/Description
nSource	**Integer**—A constant value defining the type of noise to generate: **S_PERIOD512**: High pitch noise. **S_PERIOD1024**: Medium pitch noise. **S_PERIOD2048**: Low pitch noise. **S_PERIODVOICE**: Source frequency determined from voice #3. **S_WHITE512**: High pitch white noise. **S_WHITE1024**: Medium pitch white noise. **S_WHITE2048**: Low pitch white noise. **S_WHITEVOICE**: White noise based on voice #3.
nDuration	**Integer**—The duration of the noise measured in clock ticks. Refer to "System and Time Functions," in Chapter 5 for information on system timing.

Return Value   **Integer**—Zero on success, the constant **S_SERDSR** on error.

■ SetVoiceAccent

VB Declaration   `Declare Function SetVoiceAccent% Lib "Sound" (ByVal nVoice%, ByVal ⇔ nTempo%, ByVal nVolume%, ByVal nMode%, ByVal nPitch%)`

Description   Used to set the tempo, volume, and pitch of a voice.

Use with VB   No problem.

Parameter	Type/Description
nVoice	**Integer**—The number of the voice queue (starting from 1). The PC speaker driver has only one voice.
nTempo	**Integer**—The number of quarter notes/second played. May range from 32 to 255 (default is 120).
nVolume	**Integer**—An integer indicating the volume ranging from 0 to 255.
nMode	**Integer**—One of the following constants: **S_LEGATO**: Notes are blended. **S_NORMAL**: Notes are stopped before the next note begins. **S_STACCATO**: Notes play for only part of the note period.
nPitch	**Integer**—A pitch to add to each note value using modulo 84 arithmetic before it is played. This can be a value from 0 to 83.

Return Value   **Integer**—Zero on success, one of the following constants on error:
       S_SERDMD: Invalid mode.
       S_SERDTP: Invalid tempo.
       S_SERDVL: Invalid volume.
       S_SERQFUL: Queue is full.

■ SetVoiceNote

VB Declaration   `Declare Function SetVoiceNote% Lib "Sound" (ByVal nVoice%, ByVal nValue%, ⇔`
`ByVal nLength%, ByVal nCdots%)`

Description   Adds a note into the voice queue.

Use with VB   No problem.

Parameter	Type/Description
nVoice	**Integer**—The number of the voice queue (starting from 1). The PC speaker driver has only one voice.
nValue	**Integer**—The number of the note (1–84).
nLength	**Integer**—The length of the note: 1/**nLength** where **nLength** is 1, 2, 4, 8, 16, and so on.
nCdots	**Integer**—The duration of the note. This parameter seems to have no effect on the PC speaker sound driver.

Return Value   **Integer**—Zero on success, one of the following constants on error:
S_SERDCC: Invalid **nCdots** parameter.
S_SERDLND: Invalid length.
S_SERDNT: Invalid note.
S_SERQFUL: Queue is full.

■ SetVoiceQueueSize

VB Declaration   `Declare Function SetVoiceQueueSize% Lib "Sound" (ByVal nVoice%, ByVal nBytes%)`

Description   Sets the size of a voice queue in bytes. Each note requires approximately six bytes. This function may not be called while sounds are playing.

Use with VB   No problem.

Parameter	Type/Description
nVoice	**Integer**—The number of the voice queue (starting from 1). The PC speaker driver has only one voice.
nBytes	**Integer**—The size of the voice queue.

Return Value   **Integer**—Zero on success, one of the following constants on error:
S_SERMACT: Sound is currently playing.
S_SEROFM: Insufficient memory.

■ SetVoiceSound

VB Declaration   `Declare Function SetVoiceSound% Lib "Sound" (ByVal nVoice%, ByVal ⇔`
`lFrequency&, ByVal nDuration%)`

Description	Adds a sound into the voice queue.
Use with VB	No problem.

Parameter	Type/Description
nVoice	**Integer**—The number of the voice queue (starting from 1). The PC speaker driver has only one voice.
lFrequency	**Long**—The frequency of the sound. The high word contains the whole frequency, the low word contains the fractional frequency.
nDuration	**Integer**—The duration of the sound measured in clock ticks. Refer to "System and Time Functions" in Chapter 5 for information on system timing.

Return Value   **Integer**—Zero on success, one of the following constants on error:
  S_SERMACT: Sound is currently playing.
  S_SEROFM: Insufficient memory.

■ SetVoiceThreshold

VB Declaration   `Declare Function SetVoiceThreshold% Lib "Sound" (ByVal nVoice%, ByVal nNotes%)`

Description   Sets a threshold for a voice queue. This value is used by the **GetThresholdStatus** and **GetThresholdEvent** functions to determine when the number of notes in the queue drops below the threshold value.

Use with VB   No problem.

Parameter	Type/Description
nVoice	**Integer**—The number of the voice queue (starting from 1). The PC speaker driver has only one voice.
nNotes	**Integer**—The threshold value.

Return Value   **Integer**—Zero on success, 1 on error.

■ StartSound

VB Declaration   `Declare Function StartSound% Lib "Sound" ()`

Description   Starts playing the sounds queued in the voice queues. This function may be called again to replay the current contents of the queue. This allows a voice queue to be played continuously by retriggering the sound using this function.

Use with VB   No problem.

Return Value   **Integer**—Not used.

■ StopSound

VB Declaration Declare Function StopSound% Lib "Sound" ()

Description Stops all sound playing and clears the contents of the voice queues.

Use with VB No problem.

Return Value Integer—Not used.

■ SyncAllVoices

VB Declaration Declare Function SyncAllVoices% Lib "Sound" ()

Description A sync mark is placed in each voice queue. When a sync mark is reached in the course of playing a voice queue, playing on that voice is paused until the sync mark is reached on all of the voice queues.

Use with VB No problem, but keep in mind that the PC speaker driver supports only one voice queue.

Return Value Integer—Zero on success, **S_SERQFUL** if the queue is full.

■ WaitSoundState

VB Declaration Declare Function WaitSoundState% Lib "Sound" (ByVal nState%)

Description This function does not return until a specified driver state has been reached.

Use with VB No problem.

Parameter	Type/Description
nState	Integer—One of the following constants defining the state to wait for: **S_ALLTHRESHOLD**: All voice queues have fewer notes in their queue than the current threshold. **S_QUEUEEMPTY**: All voice queues are empty and sound has stopped. **S_THRESHOLD**: Any voice queue reaches its threshold value.

Return Value Integer—If **nState** is **S_THRESHOLD**, this will be the number of the voice that has reached the threshold. In all other cases, zero on success or the **S_SERDST** constant on error.

■ WinHelp, WinHelpBynum

VB Declaration Declare Function WinHelp% Lib "User" (ByVal hWnd%, ByVal lpHelpFile$, ByVal ⇔ wCommand%, dwData As Any)

Declare Function WinHelpBynum% Lib "User" Alias "WinHelp" (ByVal hWnd%, ByVal ⇔ lpHelpFile$, ByVal wCommand%, ByVal dwData&)

Description   These functions bring up the Windows help application with the specified help file and context. Function **WinHelpBynum** is used to allow the **dwData** parameter to be zero.

Use with VB   No problem.

Parameter	Type/Description
hWnd	**Integer**—The handle of the window that has requested help. This will typically be the main form for the application. Before this form is closed, the **WinHelp** function should be called using the **HELP_QUIT** parameter so that Windows will know that this application no longer needs the help application.
lpHelpFile	**String**—The name of the help file including the path if needed. The file name may be followed by a > symbol and the name of a secondary window in which to display the requested topic. Refer to the help file documentation provided with the help compiler for an explanation of secondary windows.
wCommand	**Integer**—The command to perform as listed in Table 15.7.
dwData	**Long**—Depends on the **wCommand** parameter as shown in Table 15.7.

Return Value   **Integer**—TRUE (nonzero) on success, zero otherwise.

Comments   This table describes the commands available to the **WinHelp** function. The **dwData** parameter should be zero (and the **WinHelpBynum** function used) unless noted otherwise.

For an explanation of some of the terms used here including contexts, topics, keys, and so on, refer to your help compiler documentation.

Table 15.7   WinHelp Function Commands

Command Constant	Description
HELP_CONTEXT	Invokes help for a topic. **dwData** contains the context number of the topic.
HELP_CONTENTS	Invokes the help topic defined as containing the contents of the help file.
HELP_SETCONTENTS	**dwData** contains the context number of the topic that should be set to be the new contents topic of the help file.
HELP_CONTEXTPOPUP	**dwData** contains the context number of the topic that should be displayed in a popup window.
HELP_KEY	**dwData** contains the address of a string containing a keyword to search for. If no match exists or multiple matches exist, the Search dialog box for the help file will be displayed. You should use the **agGetAddressForLPSTR** function to obtain an address for a string, or create a new aliased declaration for this function in which **dwData** is defined: **ByVal dwData$**.

Table 15.7   **WinHelp Function Commands (Continued)**

Command Constant	Description
HELP_PARTIALKEY	**dwData** contains the address of a string containing part of a keyword to search for. If no match exists or multiple matches exist, the Search dialog box for the help file will be displayed. A pointer to an empty string will cause the Search dialog box to always be displayed. You should use the **agGetAddressForLPSTR** function to obtain an address for a string, or create a new aliased declaration for this function in which **dwData** is defined: **ByVal dwData$**.
HELP_MULTKEY	**dwData** contains a pointer to a **MULTIKEYHELP** structure that determines the topic to display. Refer to Appendix B for a description of this structure.
HELP_COMMAND	**dwData** contains the address of a string containing a help macro command to execute. Refer to the help application documentation for information on help macros. You should use the **agGetAddressForLPSTR** function to obtain an address for a string, or create a new aliased declaration for this function in which **dwData** is defined: **ByVal dwData$**.
HELP_SETWINPOS	**dwData** contains a pointer to a **HELPWININFO** structure that determines the size and position of the help application window. Refer to Appendix B for a description of this structure.
HELP_FORCEFILE	Forces the specified help file to be displayed. If it is already displayed, this command will have no effect.
HELP_HELPONHELP	Displays the help contents topic on using the help system. This topic is built into the help application.
HELP_QUIT	This command should be sent before the window that called the help application is closed. This informs the help application that it is no longer needed. If no other applications are using the help system, the help application is closed.

16

Advanced Topics

THIS CHAPTER BEGINS WITH A DISCUSSION OF THE INTERNAL ORGANIZATION of data inside of strings and structures. This section is meant to elaborate on the material on data types contained in Chapter 3. The Windows API string functions are reviewed as well.

Next, the subject of color palettes is discussed. Color palette support was limited under version 1.0 of Visual Basic but has been vastly improved for later versions. A sample program, PalTest, shows how to create and use palettes under Visual Basic version 2.0.

Message processing is then examined. Techniques for examining messages to a window are presented, along with the message processing techniques to take advantage of Windows' ability to select files in the Windows file manager, drag them to a VB control, and "drop" them. Sample code for dragging and dropping files is included.

The chapter concludes with a discussion of atoms and properties and a review of a few functions that don't quite seem to fit anywhere else.

Inside Strings and Structures

Chapter 3 discussed the use of Visual Basic data types as parameters to API functions and how Visual Basic structures can be created to match Windows data structures. This section shows how the data in several Visual Basic data types is organized in memory.

There are two situations where this information is used. First, there are cases where you may be reading raw data into a string buffer or global memory block that does not correspond to a structure. In most cases it will be a simple matter to copy the data from the buffer to a Visual Basic variable, but on occasion the numeric format of the data structure may not match the numeric format used on your PC. For example, you may notice this when you examine a data file from a system that is not based on 80x86 technology. There may also be cases where you wish to examine a particular byte in a numeric variable without first copying it into a variable of that type. In such cases, you will need to know how to determine which byte in memory corresponds to a particular byte in a numeric data type.

The other, more common, situation occurs when accessing fixed length strings inside of Visual Basic structures. These strings are not handled in the same way as regular string variables, and it is important to understand how to use them.

String Functions

The Windows API provides a number of functions to perform common string operations. These functions are rarely needed from within Visual Basic because Visual Basic provides a powerful set of string operations that are much easier to use and pose no risk of system errors caused by copying data into invalid memory addresses. These functions are summarized in Table 16.1.

Table 16.1 **Windows API String Functions**

Function	Description
AnsiNext	Finds the next character in a string.
AnsiPrev	Finds the previous character to a specified character in a string.
lstrcat	Appends (concatenates) one string to another.
lstrcmp	Compares two strings.
lstrcmpi	Compares two strings, ignoring their case.
lstrcpy	Copies one string to another.
lstrlen	Determines the length of a string.

Organization of Data in Variables

Ultimately, every variable is stored in memory that is a sequence of eight-bit bytes. The order in which the bytes of a numeric variable are placed in memory varies depending on the type of computer. Figure 16.1 illustrates the byte order used on 80x86-based computers and thus under Windows.

In Figure 16.1, you can see how the bytes of integer variables are swapped so that the low-order byte is at the lowest memory address. The same applies to both bytes and words in a long variable.

This information is also important when you refer to the address of a variable. The address of a variable in memory as returned by the **agGetAddressForObject** is the memory address of the lowest memory location that holds a byte from that variable.

Organization of Data in Structures

Variables inside of Visual Basic data structures appear in order in memory as shown in Figure 16.2. Note how fixed length strings take up a space equal to the allocated size of the string. Chapter 3 discusses the difference between fixed length and variable length strings with regard to data structures. To review, variable length strings should never be used in data structures that are meant to be passed to API functions because in a structure they take the form of a four-byte Visual Basic string handle (**HLSTR**). This handle is not recognized by any Windows function.

Figure 16.1

Byte ordering of numeric variables in memory

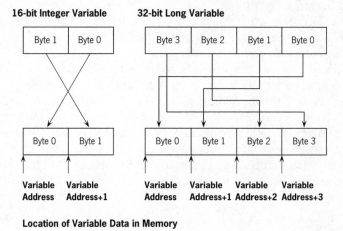

Location of Variable Data in Memory

Figure 16.2

Organization of a Visual Basic structure in memory

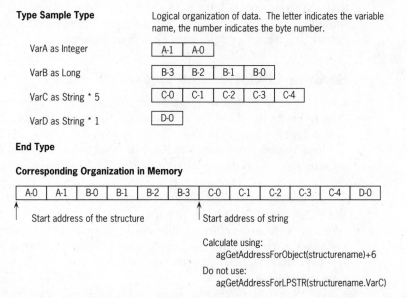

Calculate using:
    agGetAddressForObject(structurename)+6

Do not use:
    agGetAddressForLPSTR(structurename.VarC)

In many cases, it is necessary to obtain the address of a string for use in a Windows structure or API function call. When using a string that is not part of a structure, there are no problems. If you obtain the address of the string using **agGetAddressForLPSTR** or **agGetAddressForVBString**, you need not worry about the address of the string changing as long as you perform no other string operations.

However, when you access a string inside of a structure a problem occurs. When you use such a string as a parameter to a function, Visual Basic actually copies the contents of that string into a temporary buffer. The buffer is copied back into the structure before the function returns. This is necessary because of the way Visual Basic handles strings internally.

As a result, the address returned by a function such as **agGetAddressForLPSTR** or **AnsiNext** is the address of the temporary buffer, not the address of the string inside of the structure. Consequently, in order to obtain the address of a string inside of a structure you must calculate the address based on the address of the structure and your knowledge of the size of the variables inside the structure. The memory structure part of Figure 16.2 illustrates this technique.

Color Palettes

This section describes the use of the color palette API functions in the Windows API. There are limitations on using these functions with Visual Basic that will be described later in this chapter. Before reading further, you should thoroughly review Chapter 8, which introduces the concept of a palette and discusses device-independent bitmaps.

Hardware Palettes and Logical Palettes

Chapter 8 described how a graphics card can use a hardware palette or color table to map a limited range of pixel values into a much greater range of possible colors. For example, on an eight-bit-per-pixel VGA display, each pixel can have one of 256 possible values. The pixel value is used as an index into the hardware (or system) palette to determine the actual color to use. This color is a true 24-bit color and thus may be one of 16,777,216 possible colors.

At this time, the most common display devices are standard 16-color VGA, 256-color-based VGA or super VGA, 32,768-color "hicolor" graphic cards, and true 24-bit color graphic cards. Of these, only the 256-color devices use palettes. You can use the palette management routines with the other devices. Windows will provide you with the color you request even if the hardware is not using a palette.

Like other hardware resources such as the display and printer, Windows provides a device-independent mechanism for controlling the system palette and sharing it among applications. It does this using an object known as a logical palette. A logical palette describes the color table that an application would like to use—and the one that it would use if it had complete control over the system palette. It is possible for each window to use its own logical palette.

When an application wants to draw into a window using a color palette, it first informs Windows that it has a logical palette and requests that Windows set the logical palette into the system palette for the device. Windows will attempt to comply with the request. If there are free spaces in the hardware color table that are not used by other logical palettes, the request will be filled exactly and colors drawn into the window will be displayed exactly as requested.

But what happens if other windows on the screen have requested color palettes that are significantly different from the one requested by the new window? First, Windows will attempt to fill the request by sharing system palette entries; for example, if two logical palettes request the same shade of red, the entry for that color in both logical palettes will be matched with the same system palette entry. Second, Windows will give priority to the active window. Thus the colors in the active window will always match the request, but colors in inactive windows will be displayed using the closest available colors in the current hardware palette.

Drawing with Palettes

The GDI drawing objects can be created with a particular color. If you are not using color palettes, the color specified will be a 24-bit RGB color. When drawing with that object, Windows will actually use the color in the first 20 entries in the system palette that most closely matches the requested color. Windows reserves the first 20 entries in the system palette to provide a selection of default colors that will always be available no matter which logical palettes are selected.

If you are using color palettes, you can create GDI objects using palette-relative indexes. Colors in Windows require only 24 bits, but are always contained in 32-bit parameters. The high byte, which is unused for RGB colors (and must be set to zero), is used to indicate the type of color format. If bit zero of that high byte is 1, the lower three bytes represent the index, or number of an entry in the logical palette. For example, if the third entry in a palette is red, color &H01000002& represents that color.

If bit one of the high byte in a color is 1, the lower three bytes represent a 24-bit RGB color in the palette. The difference between this and a standard RGB color is that standard RGB colors are matched only with the default system palette colors—the first 20 entries. When palette-relative RGB values are specified, Windows chooses the closest color in the logical palette.

For example, the following code can be used to create a brush that takes advantage of a logical palette:

```
newpen% = CreateSolidBrush(&H02000000 Or rgbcolor&)
```

where *rgbcolor* is the desired RGB color value. It is important to stress that if you do not set the palette relative bit in the high byte, the color of the new brush will be based only on the 20 reserved colors of the system palette—regardless of the color palette used by the device context that you are drawing into.

Color palettes work correctly even on devices that do not support hardware palettes. In that case, when a color is requested Windows always chooses the closest color that the device can actually display.

The above description for GDI object colors applies in part to device-independent bitmaps. The color tables in a DIB can be specified as true RGB colors or as palette-relative indexes.

When using a GDI object or DIB that specifies palette-relative colors it is essential to always select and realize the palette before drawing with that object or DIB. This process is described next.

Using Logical Palettes

There are two steps required to actually use a logical palette. First it is necessary to select the palette into a device context using the **SelectPalette** API function. This defines the palette to be used for all palette-relative drawing into a device context.

Consider this example: You create a logical palette that has the color red in its third entry. You then create a red pen as follows:

```
newpen=CreatePen(PS_SOLID, 1, &H01000002&)
```

This pen will always use the third entry in the currently selected palette. If you select a logical palette into a device context that had red in its third entry, then select and draw with this pen, the pen will draw in red. However, if you select a logical device into a device context that has blue as its third entry, then select and draw with this same pen, it will draw in blue.

If you were to create the pen using this code:

```
newpen=CreatePen(PS_SOLID, 1, &H020000FF&)
```

you will have created a pen that will use the entry in the currently selected logical palette that is closest to the color red, regardless of which palette is selected. If the high byte was zero, the pen would always use the red entry in the first 20 entries in the system palette.

The second step to drawing using palettes must take place immediately before drawing each time drawing is about to commence. This step is called *realizing* the palette and is done with the **RealizePalette** API function. This function informs Windows that drawing to a device context is about to begin and that it should determine which system palette entry is to be used for each entry in the logical palette.

One other factor needs to be considered when using logical palettes. As long as you are only using the standard system palette, you need not worry about other applications changing entries in the system palette that your

application is using. As soon as you use logical palettes, it is possible that when another application realizes its palette, it will affect system colors that your window is using. Windows sends two messages to manage use of color palettes. The **WM_QUERYNEWPALETTE** message is sent to a window before it becomes active to allow the application to invalidate its windows if any of the colors have been remapped since the last time its palette has been realized. This makes it possible for Windows to make certain that the active window is always accurately represented. The **WM_PALETTECHANGED** message is sent to all top level windows when any application changes the system palette by realizing its palette. This makes sure that nonactive windows are given the most accurate possible color rendering given the current state of the system palette.

Visual Basic version 1.0 did not provide any mechanism for intercepting these two messages, thus it did not provide enough support to use color palettes effectively. Later versions of Visual Basic provide support for color palettes as described in the next section.

Table 16.2 lists the Windows API palette functions and briefly describes their use.

Table 16.2 **Palette API Functions**

Function	Description
AnimatePalette	Substitutes colors in a logical palette with new colors and immediately maps them to the system palette. This can be used to provide fast color cycling.
CreatePalette	Creates a new logical palette.
GetNearestPaletteIndex	Determines the entry in a logical palette that most closely matches a specified RGB color.
GetPaletteEntries	Retrieves entries from a logical palette.
GetSystemPaletteEntries	Retrieves entries from the system palette.
GetSystemPaletteUse	Determines how the system palette is currently being used.
RealizePalette	Causes Windows to map entries in a logical palette into the system palette.
ResizePalette	Changes the size of a logical palette.
SelectPalette	Selects a palette to use during drawing to a device context.
SetPaletteEntries	Sets entries into a logical palette.

Table 16.2	**Palette API Functions (Continued)**

Function	Description
SetSystemPaletteUse	Can be used to free up 18 of the reserved system palette entries for use by logical palettes.
UpdateColors	Used to cause colors displayed in a window to be updated to the closest available system color when the system palette changes.

Using Palette Functions with Visual Basic

Visual Basic provides support for logical palettes in forms, picture controls, and many custom controls. A brief description of how Visual Basic handles palettes internally will provide insight into how you can take advantage of the Windows API palette functions.

When a Visual Basic form receives a **WM_PALETTECHANGED** message from Windows, it needs to update the colors displayed both in the form and in any child windows. In order to do this, it sends an internal Visual Basic message called **VBM_PALETTECHANGED** that has a value of &H101B to any controls that have registered themselves as both palette-aware and having a palette.

This means that in order for palettes to work with a control, two conditions must be met. First, the control must support color palettes and second, Visual Basic must be informed that the control has a palette assigned. There are two methods for accomplishing this.

The first method is the easiest and safest one and is documented in the Visual Basic manual. It consists of assigning a palette to a control by either assigning a device-independent bitmap to the **picture** property of the control, or by pasting a palette into a control using the clipboard. When a palette is assigned in this manner, the control notifies Visual Basic that it has a palette and the control is notified any time it needs to realize its palette to ensure color accuracy.

The second method consists of selecting and realizing the palette using Windows API functions before drawing. In this case it is necessary for the application to use the **agVBSetControlFlags** function in the APIGUIDE.DLL library to notify Visual Basic that a palette has been set. This function is described in Appendix A.

The Windows API can be used to create custom palettes that can be easily transferred into a VB control under program control. This technique is illustrated in the PalTest sample application that follows.

Example: PalTest—A Palette Demonstration Program

The PalTest program demonstrates the use of palettes to draw smooth color spectrums in a number of picture controls. Figure 16.3 shows the runtime screen for the program. Note that this program requires Visual Basic 2.0 to run, and will only run properly on a device that supports color palettes or true RGB color (32k or 24-bit).

Figure 16.3

PalTest program runtime screen

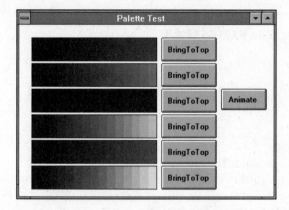

Using PalTest

The six picture controls shown in Figure 16.3 display color bar spectrums of red, green blue, yellow, violet, and gray in order from top to bottom. As provided, the bars are divided into 16 colors. You can increase the constant **PALENTRIES** defined in file PALTEST.BAS to provide a smoother gradient; however, this will lead to side effects on 256-color devices. Since the system palette only has 236 colors available, if the total number of colors requested exceeds 236 colors, some of the colors will not be matched correctly. This leads to some interesting effects. Visual Basic always gives priority to the active window, and then to the control on that window that is at the top of the Z-order. The BringToTop command buttons can be used to bring each picture control to the top of the Z-order, providing a demonstration of this feature.

It is also possible to define colors in a palette as reserved. This means that the logical palette entry will be assigned a system palette entry that cannot be used by any other logical palette. These entries can then be animated using the **AnimatePalette** API function, which is triggered in this case by the Animate command button.

Project Description

The PalTest project includes four files. PALTEST.FRM is the only form used in the program. PALTEST.BAS is the only module in the program and contains the constant type and global definitions. APIDECS.BAS is the type-safe API declaration file provided with this book. APIGUIDE.BAS contains the declarations for the APIGUIDE.DLL dynamic link library.

Listing 16.1 shows the project file for the PalTest program.

Listing 16.1   **Project Listing File PALTEST.MAK**

```
PALTEST.FRM
APIDECS.BAS
APIGUIDE.BAS
PALTEST.BAS
ProjWinSize=152,402,248,215
ProjWinShow=2
```

Listing 16.2 contains the header from file PALTEST.FRM that describes the control setup for the form. There are six picture control that are part of the **Picture1** control array. There are six corresponding command buttons that are part of the **BringToTop** control array.

Listing 16.2   **PALTEST.FRM Header**

```
VERSION 2.00
Begin Form PalTest
    BackColor       =   &H00FFFFFF&
    Caption         =   "Palette Test"
    Height          =   4425
    Left            =   1350
    LinkTopic       =   "Form1"
    ScaleHeight     =   4020
    ScaleWidth      =   6120
    Top             =   1365
    Width           =   6240
    Begin Timer Timer1
        Enabled     =   0       'False
        Interval    =   100
        Left        =   5160
        Top         =   2640
    End
    Begin CommandButton Command1
        Caption     =   "Animate"
        Height      =   495
```

Listing 16.2 PALTEST.FRM Header (Continued)

```
            Left         =    4860
            TabIndex     =    12
            Top          =    1500
            Width        =    1095
         End
         Begin CommandButton BringToTop
            Caption      =    "BringToTop"
            Height       =    555
            Index        =    5
            Left         =    3420
            TabIndex     =    11
            Top          =    3300
            Width        =    1335
         End
         Begin CommandButton BringToTop
            Caption      =    "BringToTop"
            Height       =    555
            Index        =    4
            Left         =    3420
            TabIndex     =    10
            Top          =    2700
            Width        =    1335
         End
         Begin CommandButton BringToTop
            Caption      =    "BringToTop"
            Height       =    555
            Index        =    3
            Left         =    3420
            TabIndex     =    9
            Top          =    2100
            Width        =    1335
         End
         Begin CommandButton BringToTop
            Caption      =    "BringToTop"
            Height       =    555
            Index        =    2
            Left         =    3420
            TabIndex     =    8
            Top          =    1500
            Width        =    1335
         End
         Begin CommandButton BringToTop
            Caption      =    "BringToTop"
            Height       =    555
            Index        =    1
            Left         =    3420
            TabIndex     =    7
            Top          =    900
```

Listing 16.2   PALTEST.FRM Header (Continued)

```
        Width           =   1335
    End
    Begin CommandButton BringToTop
        Caption         =   "BringToTop"
        Height          =   555
        Index           =   0
        Left            =   3420
        TabIndex        =   6
        Top             =   300
        Width           =   1335
    End
    Begin PictureBox Picture1
        Height          =   555
        Index           =   5
        Left            =   300
        ScaleHeight     =   525
        ScaleWidth      =   2985
        TabIndex        =   5
        Top             =   3300
        Width           =   3015
    End
    Begin PictureBox Picture1
        Height          =   555
        Index           =   4
        Left            =   300
        ScaleHeight     =   525
        ScaleWidth      =   2985
        TabIndex        =   4
        Top             =   2700
        Width           =   3015
    End
    Begin PictureBox Picture1
        Height          =   555
        Index           =   3
        Left            =   300
        ScaleHeight     =   525
        ScaleWidth      =   2985
        TabIndex        =   3
        Top             =   2100
        Width           =   3015
    End
    Begin PictureBox Picture1
        Height          =   555
        Index           =   2
        Left            =   300
        ScaleHeight     =   525
        ScaleWidth      =   2985
        TabIndex        =   2
```

Listing 16.2   PALTEST.FRM Header (Continued)

```
        Top             =   1500
        Width           =   3015
    End
    Begin PictureBox Picture1
        Height          =   555
        Index           =   1
        Left            =   300
        ScaleHeight     =   525
        ScaleWidth      =   2985
        TabIndex        =   1
        Top             =   900
        Width           =   3015
    End
    Begin PictureBox Picture1
        Height          =   555
        Index           =   0
        Left            =   300
        ScaleHeight     =   525
        ScaleWidth      =   2985
        TabIndex        =   0
        Top             =   300
        Width           =   3015
    End
End
```

PalTest Listings

Module PALTEST.BAS contains the constant declarations and global variables used by the program. It also contains most of the palette management and creation functions. The declarations section is shown in Listing 16.3.

Listing 16.3   Module PALTEST.BAS

```
' Project PalTest

' Module containing global constants and general purpose
' routines.


Option Explicit
Global Const PC_RESERVED = &H1
Global Const PC_EXPLICIT = &H2
Global Const PC_NOCOLLAPSE = &H4
Global Const DIB_RGB_COLORS = 0
```

Listing 16.3   Module PALTEST.BAS (Continued)

```
Global Const DIB_PAL_COLORS = 1
Global Const SYSPAL_STATIC = 1
Global Const SYSPAL_NOSTATIC = 2
Global Const CF_TEXT = 1
Global Const CF_BITMAP = 2
Global Const CF_METAFILEPICT = 3
Global Const CF_SYLK = 4
Global Const CF_DIF = 5
Global Const CF_TIFF = 6
Global Const CF_OEMTEXT = 7
Global Const CF_DIB = 8
Global Const CF_PALETTE = 9
Global Const CF_OWNERDISPLAY = &H80
Global Const CF_DSPTEXT = &H81
Global Const CF_DSPBITMAP = &H82
Global Const CF_DSPMETAFILEPICT = &H83
Global Const CF_PRIVATEFIRST = &H200
Global Const CF_PRIVATELAST = &H2FF


' Increase this number to 32 or 64 to see the effect of
' the Zorder on the palettes.

Global Const PALENTRIES = 15

'    This is similar to the LOGPALLETTE defined in
'    APIDECS.BAS, however instead of using a buffer, we
'    create a 64 entry palette for our use.

Type LOGPALETTE64
    palVersion As Integer
    palNumEntries As Integer
    palPalEntry(PALENTRIES) As PALETTEENTRY
End Type

' And create a type safe alias to create a palette that handles this structure
Declare Function CreatePalette64% Lib "GDI" Alias "CreatePalette" (lpLogPalette
As LOGPALETTE64)


' The six palettes that this program will use are defined here
Global UsePalettes%(6)
Global logPalettes(6) As LOGPALETTE64

' This is a message used within Visual Basic to retrieve
' the handle of a palette
Global Const VBM_GETPALETTE% = &H101C
```

As you can see, this program supports up to **PALENTRIES** colors in each palette. A **LOGPALETTE64** type structure is defined, as the standard **LOGPALETTE** structure defined in file APIDECS.BAS uses a string buffer to hold the palette entries. This technique simplifies the programming considerably. Also note how the **CreatePalette** function is aliased to create a type-safe definition for this type.

The **CreateAllPalettes** function creates the six palettes that are used for color gradients. This is accomplished by loading the colors into the logical palette structure array. Then the palettes are created using the **CreatePalette** function.

```
'   This function creates 6 palettes that are used by
'   the PalTest program
'
Sub CreateAllPalettes ()
    Dim entrynum%
    Dim oldmouseptr%
    Dim x%

    oldmouseptr% = Screen.MousePointer
    Screen.MousePointer = 11
    ' Initialize the logical palette
    For x% = 1 To 6
        logPalettes(x%).palVersion = &H300
        logPalettes(x%).palNumEntries = PALENTRIES
    Next x%

    ' Palette 1 will be red
    For entrynum% = 0 To PALENTRIES - 1
        logPalettes(1).palPalEntry(entrynum%).peRed = ↔
        Chr$((255 * entrynum%) / PALENTRIES)
        logPalettes(1).palPalEntry(entrynum%).peGreen = Chr$(0)
        logPalettes(1).palPalEntry(entrynum%).peBlue = Chr$(0)
        logPalettes(1).palPalEntry(entrynum%).peFlags = Chr$(0)
    Next entrynum%

    ' Palette 2 will be green
    For entrynum% = 0 To PALENTRIES - 1
        logPalettes(2).palPalEntry(entrynum%).peRed = Chr$(0)
        logPalettes(2).palPalEntry(entrynum%).peGreen = ↔
        Chr$((255 * entrynum%) / PALENTRIES)
        logPalettes(2).palPalEntry(entrynum%).peBlue = Chr$(0)
        logPalettes(2).palPalEntry(entrynum%).peFlags = Chr$(0)
    Next entrynum%

    ' Palette 3 will be blue and can be animated
    For entrynum% = 0 To PALENTRIES - 1
        logPalettes(3).palPalEntry(entrynum%).peRed = Chr$(0)
        logPalettes(3).palPalEntry(entrynum%).peGreen = Chr$(0)
        logPalettes(3).palPalEntry(entrynum%).peBlue = ↔
        Chr$((255 * entrynum%) / PALENTRIES)
        logPalettes(3).palPalEntry(entrynum%).peFlags = ↔
```

```
        Chr$(PC_RESERVED)
    Next entrynum%

    ' Palette 4 will be yellow
    For entrynum% = 0 To PALENTRIES - 1
        logPalettes(4).palPalEntry(entrynum%).peRed = ⇔
        Chr$((255 * entrynum%) / PALENTRIES)
        logPalettes(4).palPalEntry(entrynum%).peGreen = ⇔
        Chr$((255 * entrynum%) / PALENTRIES)
        logPalettes(4).palPalEntry(entrynum%).peBlue = Chr$(0)
        logPalettes(4).palPalEntry(entrynum%).peFlags = Chr$(0)
    Next entrynum%

    ' Palette 5 will be violet
    For entrynum% = 0 To PALENTRIES - 1
        logPalettes(5).palPalEntry(entrynum%).peRed = ⇔
        Chr$((255 * entrynum%) / PALENTRIES)
        logPalettes(5).palPalEntry(entrynum%).peGreen = ⇔
        Chr$(0)
        logPalettes(5).palPalEntry(entrynum%).peBlue = ⇔
        Chr$((255 * entrynum%) / PALENTRIES)
        logPalettes(5).palPalEntry(entrynum%).peFlags = Chr$(0)
    Next entrynum%

    ' Palette 6 will be gray
    For entrynum% = 0 To PALENTRIES - 1
        logPalettes(6).palPalEntry(entrynum%).peRed = ⇔
        Chr$((255 * entrynum%) / PALENTRIES)
        logPalettes(6).palPalEntry(entrynum%).peGreen = ⇔
        Chr$((255 * entrynum%) / PALENTRIES)
        logPalettes(6).palPalEntry(entrynum%).peBlue = ⇔
        Chr$((255 * entrynum%) / PALENTRIES)
        logPalettes(6).palPalEntry(entrynum%).peFlags = Chr$(0)
    Next entrynum%

    ' And create the palettes
    For x% = 1 To 6
   UsePalettes(x%) = CreatePalette64(logPalettes(x%))
    Next x%

    Screen.MousePointer = oldmouseptr%
End Sub
```

Animation is accomplished by using a palette that has had the **PC_RE-SERVED** flag set for the colors to be animated. In color animation, each entry in the logical palette is mapped to a reserved entry in the system palette. The **AnimatePalette** function causes a new set of colors to be immediately set into these reserved system palette entries. This causes the colors to switch immediately allowing very rapid color cycling without drawing.

This function also demonstrates use of the **VBM_GETPALETTE** Visual Basic message to retrieve a handle to the palette that being used by this control. This message has the value &H101C.

```
'
'   We're doing color animation on the third picture box
'   (that's blue)
'
Sub DoTheAnimate ()
    Dim entrynum%
    Dim usepal%
    Dim holdentry As PALETTEENTRY

    ' Get a handle to the control's palette
    usepal% = SendMessageByNum(PalTest.Picture1(2).hWnd, ⇔
    VBM_GETPALETTE, 0, 0)

    ' The following code simply loops the color values
    LSet holdentry = logPalettes(3).palPalEntry(0)
    For entrynum% = 0 To PALENTRIES - 2
       LSet logPalettes(3).palPalEntry(entrynum%) = ⇔
       logPalettes(3).palPalEntry(entrynum% + 1)
    Next entrynum%
    LSet logPalettes(3).palPalEntry(PALENTRIES - 1) = holdentry
    AnimatePalette usepal%, 0, PALENTRIES, ⇔
     logPalettes(3).palPalEntry(0)

End Sub
```

The **FillPicture** function draws the actual color gradient. The **GetPal-Color** function demonstrates how you can read the colors in a logical palette.

```
'   FillPicture draws a spectrum in the specified picture
'   control using the appropriate palette for that control
'
Sub FillPicture (picnum%)
    Dim totwidth&, startloc&, endloc&
    Dim pic As control
    Dim x&
    'Dim rc As RECT
    'Dim usebrush%
    'Dim t%

    Set pic = PalTest.Picture1(picnum%)

    totwidth& = pic.ScaleWidth
    For x& = 0 To PALENTRIES - 1
       ' We're using long arithmetic for speed. Note the
       ' ordering of operations to preserve precision
       startloc& = (totwidth& * x&) / PALENTRIES
       endloc& = (totwidth& * (x& + 1)) / PALENTRIES
```

```
           pic.Line (startloc&, Ø)-(endloc&, pic.ScaleHeight), ⇔
           GetPalColor(picnum%, (x&)), BF
      Next x&

End Sub


'   Gets the Long RGB color for a palette entry
'
Function GetPalColor& (picnum%, entry%)
    Dim res&
    Dim pe As PALETTEENTRY
    LSet pe = logPalettes(picnum% + 1).palPalEntry(entry%)
    ' We build a long value using this rather awkward
    ' shifting technique.
    ' We actually could save time by performing a raw
    ' memory copy from the pe object into a long variable.
    ' since they are the same format.
    res& = Asc(pe.peRed)
    res& = res& Or (Asc(pe.peGreen) * 256&)
    res& = res& Or (Asc(pe.peBlue) * 256& * 256&)
    GetPalColor& = res&
End Function
```

The form header and object descriptions for PALTEST.FRM can be found in Listing 16.2. The **BringToTop_Click** function brings the picture control corresponding to the selected command button to the top of the Z-order. This control will be given priority in setting its palette.

Listing 16.4   Form Listing PALTEST.FRM

```
'
Sub BringToTop_Click (Index As Integer)
    picture1(Index).ZOrder Ø
End Sub


'
' Toggle the color animation
'
Sub Command1_Click ()
    Timer1.Enabled = Not Timer1.Enabled
End Sub
```

This function demonstrates how you can use the clipboard to copy a newly created palette into a control. The Windows API functions that are used to copy a palette into the clipboard are described in the Clipboard section of Chapter 15.

```
'
' Load and create all of the palettes used by this program
'
Sub Form_Load ()
    Dim x%, h%

    CreateAllPalettes

    For x% = 0 To 5
        h% = OpenClipboard(paltest.hWnd)
        If h% = 0 Then
            MsgBox "Can't open clipboard"
            End
        End If
        h% = SetClipboardData(CF_PALETTE, UsePalettes%(x% + 1))
        h% = CloseClipboard()
        picture1(x%).Picture = Clipboard.GetData(CF_PALETTE)
    Next x%
    ' We put the palettes in the clipboard - that means we
    ' don't own them any more, so don't mess with them.


End Sub

Sub Picture1_Paint (Index As Integer)
    FillPicture Index
End Sub

'
'  Do the color animation
'
Sub Timer1_Timer ()
    DoTheAnimate
End Sub
```

Message Processing and File Dragging

Chapter 2 described how Windows processes messages by calling a window function that exists for each window. Each window has a queue of messages. Windows divides up processing time among the windows, thus each window has a chance to process the messages in its queue in turn.

An example of this is the mechanism by which a window is typically updated. When a function needs to redraw a window, it invalidates the area of the window using functions such as **InvalidateRect**, which are described in Chapter 4. Windows generates two messages: a **WM_ERASEBKGND** message to erase and a **WM_PAINT** message to paint the window, and places these messages in the message queue for the window. In due course, windows will process the messages for the window by calling the window function for that window with these messages as parameters. The window then performs the operation specified by the message.

When writing a Windows program in C, the programmer writes the window function and thus has access to all of the messages that a window receives. This allows for a great deal of flexibility in handling messages.

In Visual Basic, this message processing is by and large hidden from the programmer. The advantage of this is that it significantly simplifies the task of writing a Visual Basic program. The disadvantage is that some flexibility is lost. Only those messages that generate Visual Basic events are accessible to the programmer.

Visual Basic does provide a limited capability for intercepting the message stream as described in the next section.

Using PeekMessage

The **PeekMessage** function can be used to watch for the receipt of a message or group of messages to a window. If you are acquainted with this function through programming for Windows under C, be warned—the function does not behave as expected under Visual Basic. It does not yield to the system properly, and therefore must be used in conjunction with the Visual Basic **Do-Events** function. The safe way to intercept messages for a window is to use the following code loop:

```
Dim Message As MSG
Do
    gotone% = PeekMessage(Message, 0, firstmessage, lastmessage, PM_REMOVE ⇔
    Or PM_NOYIELD)
    di% = DoEvents()
Loop While -1
```

The **DoEvents** function is necessary due to the fact that the **PeekMessage** function does not yield. In this case the **PM_NOYIELD** flag is specified to prevent yielding to other applications, but in fact the function does not seem to yield even if this flag is not specified.

Before using this technique you should be warned: Microsoft has indicated that the **PeekMessage** function is incompatible with Visual Basic and should be avoided. The method described here seems to work under Visual Basic 1.0 through 3.0.

This approach is adequate for intercepting one or two messages, but poses its own problems. By intercepting the message queue early, the messages are not processed using the normal Windows processing system. This does not matter for messages such as the **WM_DROPFILES** message described in the next section, but may affect the operation of VB or the system when used with other messages. This method for intercepting messages is undocumented in Visual Basic and may not be compatible with future versions of VB. For full access to the message stream from Visual Basic including the ability to subclass controls as described in Chapter 2, you will need a third-party tool such as Desaware's SpyWorks package.

Table 16.3 lists the message processing functions that can be used successfully with Visual Basic.

Table 16.3   Message Processing Functions

Function	Description
GetMessageExtraInfo	Retrieves device-specified extra information about the most recent message.
GetMessagePos	Determines the position of the cursor at the time of the most recent message.
PeekMessage	Retrieves a message from the message queue for a window.

An example of where the **PeekMessage** function can be extremely useful to intercept messages is in supporting the file dragging capability provided by the Windows 3.1 file manager.

Dragging Files

Windows 3.1 added a dynamic link library named SHELL.DLL that supports the dragging and dropping of files from the Windows file manager. You can use this functionality to select one or more files in the file manager window, then drag the files to a window in your Visual Basic application. When the files are dropped in the window, you can retrieve the list of files and the location in the window where the files were dropped.

The functions used to implement this file dragging and dropping are listed in Table 16.4.

Table 16.4   File Dragging Functions

Function	Description
DragAcceptFiles	Informs the system that a specified window can accept files that are dropped from the file manager.
DragFinish	Used to release internal structures allocated during the file drop process.
DragQueryFile	Used to retrieve a list of files that were dropped on a window.

Table 16.4 **File Dragging Functions (Continued)**

Function	Description
DragQueryPoint	Used to determine the drop location for files that were dropped on a window.

Listing 16.5 demonstrates the use of these functions. You will need to create a form that contains a picture control named **picture1**, and a list control named **list1**. After calling the **SpyMessage** function, any time files are dragged from the file manager onto the **picture1** control, the names of those files will be added to the list box.

The **PM_REMOVE**, **PM_NOYIELD**, and **WM_DROPFILES** constants are defined in file APICONST.TXT.

Listing 16.5 **Using File Drag and Drop in Visual Basic**

```
Sub SpyMessage ()
    Dim DropMessage As MSG
    Dim gotone%
    Dim hdrop%
    Dim filename As String * 128
    Dim numfiles%
    Dim thisfile%

    ' Go into an infinite loop looking for the WM_DROPFILES
    ' messages
    DragAcceptFiles agGetControlHwnd(picture1), -1
    Do
        gotone% = PeekMessage(DropMessage, 0, WM_DROPFILES, WM_DROPFILES, ⇔
        PM_REMOVE Or PM_NOYIELD)

        If gotone Then ' Got a drop message
            ' Retrieve the handle to the internal dropfiles
            ' structure
            hdrop% = DropMessage.wParam

            ' Get the number of files
            numfiles% = DragQueryFile(hdrop%, -1, filename$, 127)

            For thisfile% = 1 To numfiles%
                di% = DragQueryFile(hdrop%, thisfile% - 1, filename$, 127)
                List1.AddItem filename$
            Next thisfile%
            ' Dispose of the hdrop% structure
            DragFinish (hdrop%)
```

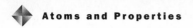

Atoms and Properties

Listing 16.5   Using File Drag and Drop in Visual Basic (Continued)

```
        End If
        di% = DoEvents()
    Loop While -1

End Sub
```

Atoms and Properties

You've seen that Windows makes extensive use of handles to identify objects. You've also seen that many objects, such as windows, can have data associated with them as attributes. It should be no surprise that Windows also provides the ability to use these techniques for user defined data.

This takes two forms. The Windows atom functions make it possible to assign a handle to any string. The Windows property functions make it possible to associate a handle with a window.

Atoms

An *atom* is a handle to a string. There are two types of atoms, local atoms and global atoms. A local atom is accessible only by the application that created it. A global atom is accessible by any application in the system.

An atom is created using the **AddAtom** or **GlobalAddAtom** function. These functions take a string as a parameter and return the integer atom value. The string may then be retrieved using the **GetAtomName** or **GlobalGetAtomName** function. If an attempt is made to create another atom using the same string, the same integer atom value will be returned—in other words, a given string can have only one atom value. Strings used in atoms are not case-sensitive.

The most common use for global atoms is to transfer data between applications. The dynamic data exchange (DDE) system uses them extensively. Otherwise they are not of much use to the Visual Basic programmer. Table 16.5 lists the local and global atom functions.

Table 16.5   Atom Functions

Function	Description
AddAtom	Creates an atom.
DeleteAtom	Deletes an atom.
FindAtom	Retrieves the atom number for a string.

Table 16.5   **Atom Functions (Continued)**

Function	Description
GetAtomName	Retrieves the string given an atom number.
GlobalAddAtom	Creates a global atom.
GlobalDeleteAtom	Deletes a global atom.
GlobalFindAtom	Retrieves the global atom number for a string.
GlobalGetAtomName	Retrieves the string given a global atom number.
InitAtomTable	Changes the size of a local atom hash table.

Property Functions

The term *property* under Windows does not refer to the properties that each Visual Basic control possesses. Property here refers to the ability to associate any integer data value with a window based on the name of the property. For example, you can create a property for a window named **PenToUse**, which has an integer handle to a pen object as its value. Once you have created the property, you can retrieve the pen handle at any time by referencing property **PenToUse**.

The name of the property can be specified using an atom instead of a string, in which case a global atom must be used.

Any application can access window properties, thus this is another mechanism that can be used to share data. However, be careful: An application can access the values of the property but should only use those handles that are legally accessible to it. GDI objects may be shared in this manner, but global memory blocks may not.

Another common use of properties is to identify a window as belonging to a common set of applications. For example, let's say you have created a series of programs. You would like to set things up so that if any one of these programs is opened, the other programs will be minimized.

Chapter 4 showed how you can enumerate windows to find out which applications are open. There also needs to be a way to identify which programs belong to that series of applications. You could examine the application name, but this works only if you know in advance the name of every program that you wish to belong to the series.

A better approach is to define a property; for example, you could define a property could be called **MinimizeOnRequest** for the main form of each program in the series. Now all you need to do is enumerate all of the top level windows and minimize any window that has the property **MinimizeOnRequest** defined. You could even get more sophisticated and base the operation on the value of the property; for example, you could define property **HandleOnRequest** for which the value 0 indicates no operation, 1 indicates to minimize the window, 2 indicates to redraw the window, and so on.

Properties for a window should be removed using the **RemoveProperty** function before a window is destroyed. One way to do this is to remove the properties for a form and any controls on that form during the form's **Unload** event.

The property functions are listed in Table 16.6.

Table 16.6 **Property Functions**

Function	Description
EnumProps	Enumerates all the properties for a window. This function requires use of the CBK.VBX custom control.
GetProp	Retrieves the value of a property.
RemoveProp	Removes a property.
SetProp	Creates a property.

Miscellaneous Functions

The functions described in this section simply don't seem to fit into a particular category. These functions are listed in Table 16.7.

Table 16.7 **Miscellaneous Functions**

Function	Description
GetDialogBaseUnits	Retrieves the average width and height of the system font.
MapDialogRect	Converts dialog base units into screen coordinates.
MulDiv	Many people find it astonishing that Windows does not make any use of floating point math. The **MulDiv** function is used to maintain precision during integer multiplication and division.
MessageBox	This function is an almost exact duplicate of the Visual Basic **MsgBox** function, so it is unlikely that you will ever need it.
wvsprintf	This function allows you to create a formatted string in a manner similar to the Visual Basic **Format** function.

The **GetDialogBaseUnits** and **MapDialogRect** functions use a dimension called *dialog base units*. Dialog boxes tend to use their own coordinate systems that are based on the default font for that dialog box. Normally, this would not be of any interest to the Visual Basic programmer, but several of the control messages that will be described in Part 3 of this book use dialog base units. For example, you can set tab stops in a list box based on these units.

Dialog base units specify a coordinate system within a dialog box. Each horizontal dialog unit is one-quarter of the width of the dialog box font. Thus if the font is eight pixels wide, the horizontal base unit will be two pixels. Each vertical dialog unit is one-eighth of the height of the dialog box font. Chapter 19 demonstrates how these units are used when setting tabs in a list box.

Function Reference

This section contains an alphabetical reference for the functions described in this chapter.

◼ AddAtom

VB Declaration   `Declare Function AddAtom% Lib "Kernel" (ByVal lpString$)`

Description   Adds an atom to the local atom table.

Use with VB   No problem.

Parameter	Type/Description
lpString	**String**—The string associated with the atom, also known as the name of the atom.

Return Value   **Integer**—The atom value on success, zero on error.

Comments   You should always check the result to make sure that the atom was allocated successfully. Also note that atoms are not case-sensitive.

◼ AnimatePalette

VB Declaration   `Declare Sub AnimatePalette Lib "GDI" (ByVal hPalette%, ByVal wStartIndex%, ⇔`
`ByVal wNumEntries%, lpPaletteColors As PALETTEENTRY)`

Description   This function replaces entries in a logical palette and immediately maps them to the system palette. This is typically used to produce rapid color cycling effects. The **PALETTEENTRY** structures for the logical palette entries that are being replaced must have the **PC_RESERVED** flag set to indicate that system palette entries for that entry will not be shared with other logical palettes. Refer to Appendix B for a description of the **PALETTEENTRY** structure.

Use with VB   No problem. To obtain a palette for a Visual Basic control, you will need to use the **VBM_GET-PALETTE** message as follows:

`pal% = SendMessageByNum(control.hWnd, VBM_GETPALETTE, 0, 0)`

where the **VBM_GETPALETTE** constant has the value &H101C.

Palettes set into controls using bitmaps will not have the **PC_RESERVED** flag set, so in most cases you will need to create your own palette or modify an existing palette and copy it into the Visual Basic control using the techniques demonstrated in the PalTest example program. Not compatible with VB 1.0.

Parameter	Type/Description
hPalette	**Integer**—A handle to a logical palette.
wStartIndex	**Integer**—The number of the first entry in the palette to change.

Parameter	Type/Description
wNumEntries	**Integer**—The number of entries to change. There must be at least this many entries in the **lpPaletteColors** array.
lpPaletteColors	**PALETTEENTRY**—The first entry in an array of **PALETTEENTRY** structures that will replace the current entries in the logical palette.

■ AnsiNext, AnsiNextBynum

VB Declaration   Declare Function AnsiNext& Lib "User" (ByVal lpString$)

Declare Function AnsiNextBynum& Lib "User" Alias "AnsiNext" (ByVal lpString&)

Description   Retrieves the address of the character in a string that follows the one pointed to by **lpString**. This function will correctly handle strings in character sets that use more than one byte per character (such as the Japanese character sets).

Use with VB   No problem. This function can be used in VB to obtain the address for a string. The Long address of a string will be **AnsiNext(thestring$)-1** for non-Japanese character sets. The function **agGetAddressForLPSTR()** provided in APIGUIDE.DLL performs this same task.

Parameter	Type/Description
lpString	**String** or **Long**—The string for which to find the second character or a Long address of a character in a string for which to find the succeeding character.

Return Value   **Long**—The address of the character following the character pointed to by parameter **lpString**.

■ AnsiPrev, AnsiPrevBynum

VB Declaration   Declare Function AnsiPrev& Lib "User" (ByVal lpString$, ByVal lpCurrent&)

Declare Function AnsiPrevBynum& Lib "User" Alias "AnsiPrev" (ByVal ⇔ lpString&, ByVal lpCurrent&)

Description   Retrieves the address of the character in a string that precedes the one pointed to by **lpString**. This function will correctly handle strings in character sets which use more than one byte per character (such as the Japanese character sets).

Use with VB   No problem.

Parameter	Type/Description
lpString	**String** or **Long**—A string or the address of the beginning of a string.
lpCurrent	**Long**—The address of a character within a string for which to find the preceding character.

Return Value   **Long**—The address of the character preceding the character pointed to by parameter **lpString**.

CreatePalette

VB Declaration   Declare Function CreatePalette% Lib "GDI" (lpLogPalette As LOGPALETTE)

Description   Creates a new logical palette.

Use with VB   No problem. Not compatible with VB 1.0.

Parameter	Type/Description
lpLogPalette	**LOGPALETTE**—A structure describing the logical palette to create. This structure is discussed in Appendix B.

Return Value   **Integer**—A handle to a newly created logical palette on success, zero on error.

Comments   A palette is a GDI object and thus should be deleted using the **DeleteObject** function once it is no longer needed.

DeleteAtom

VB Declaration   Declare Function DeleteAtom% Lib "Kernel" (ByVal nAtom%)

Description   Deletes the specified atom.

Use with VB   No problem.

Parameter	Type/Description
nAtom	**Integer**—The atom number to delete.

Return Value   **Integer**—Zero on success, the atom number on failure.

Comments   If the atom has been allocated multiple times, the atom will not actually be deleted until this function has been called the same number of times. Windows maintains a reference count for each atom.

DragAcceptFiles

VB Declaration   Declare Sub DragAcceptFiles Lib "shell.dll" (ByVal hwnd%, ByVal fAccept%)

Description   Specifies that a window can accept files dropped from the file manager.

Use with VB   Requires that a **PeekMessage** loop or other technique be used to intercept **WM_DROPFILES** messages for this window.

Parameter	Type/Description
hWnd	**Integer**—The handle of the window that will accept dropped files.
fAccept	**Integer**—TRUE (nonzero) for the window to accept dropped files. Zero to stop accepting dropped files.

Comments   Refer to "Message Processing and File Dragging" earlier in this chapter for further information.

■ DragFinish

VB Declaration   `Declare Sub DragFinish Lib "shell.dll" (ByVal hDrop%)`

Description   Use after processing the **WM_DROPFILES** message to free up the internal data structures used in transferring the file information to the application.

Use with VB   No problem.

Parameter	Type/Description
hDrop	**Integer**—A handle to an internal data structure provided by the **WM_DROPFILES** message.

Comments   Refer to "Message Processing and File Dragging" earlier in this chapter.

■ DragQueryFile

VB Declaration   `Declare Function DragQueryFile% Lib "shell.dll" (ByVal hDrop%, ByVal ⇔`
`iFile%, ByVal lpszFile$, ByVal cb%)`

Description   Retrieves information on the file or files dropped on a control using an internal data structure provided by the **WM_DROPFILES** message.

Use with VB   No problem.

Parameter	Type/Description
hDrop	**Integer**—A handle to an internal data structure provided by the **WM_DROPFILES** message.
iFile	**Integer**—The number of the file to retrieve. -1 to retrieve the number of files listed in the **hDrop** structure.
lpszFile	**String**—A string buffer to load with the name of the file that has been retrieved. It is possible to add a declaration in which this parameter is a **Long** variable and to use the value zero to obtain the number of characters for a file name. This string should be allocated to at least **cb+1** characters long.
cb	**Integer**—The maximum number of characters to load.

Return Value   **Integer**—The number of characters copied into the **lpszFile** string. If **iFile** is zero, returns the number of files available to query. If **iFile** is not zero and **lpString** is defined as a **Long** and set to zero, returns the length of the file name to be retrieved.

Comments   Refer to "Message Processing and File Dragging," earlier in this chapter.

■ DragQueryPoint

VB Declaration   `Declare Function DragQueryPoint% Lib "shell.dll" (ByVal hDrop%, lppt ⇔`
`As POINTAPI)`

Description	Retrieves information on the location in the window on which a file or files were dropped.
Use with VB	No problem.

Parameter	Type/Description
hDrop	**Integer**—A handle to an internal data structure provided by the **WM_DROPFILES** message.
lppt	**POINTAPI**—A **POINTAPI** structure to load with the location on which files were dropped. The coordinates are in window client coordinates.

Return Value	**Integer**—TRUE (nonzero) if the files were dropped on the window, zero otherwise.
Comments	Refer to "Message Processing and File Dragging" earlier in this chapter.

■ EnumProps

VB Declaration	`Declare Function EnumProps% Lib "User" (ByVal hWnd%, ByVal lpEnumFunc&)`
Description	Enumerates the properties of a window. This function requires use of the CBK.VBX custom control provided with this book. The **EnumProps** event of the CBK.VBX control will be triggered for each property. There are a number of restrictions on the operations that may be performed during the CBK.VBX **EnumProps** event. Refer to Appendix A for further information.
Use with VB	Requires use of the CBK.VBX custom control.

Parameter	Type/Description
hWnd	**Integer**—A handle of a window for which properties are to be enumerated.
lpEnumFunc	**Long**—A function address obtained using the **ProcAddress** property of the CBK.VBX custom control.

Return Value	**Integer**—-1 if there were no properties to be enumerated. Otherwise returns the last value set to the **retval** parameter of the CBK.VBX **EnumProps** event.

■ FindAtom

VB Declaration	`Declare Function FindAtom% Lib "Kernel" (ByVal lpString$)`
Description	Retrieves the atom number for a string.
Use with VB	No problem.

Parameter	Type/Description
lpString	**String**—The string to search for.

Return Value	**Integer**—The number of the atom for the string. Zero if there is no atom for the specified string.

GetAtomName

VB Declaration   Declare Function GetAtomName% Lib "Kernel" (ByVal nAtom%, ByVal lpBuffer$, ⇔
ByVal nSize%)

Description   Retrieves the string associated with an atom.

Use with VB   No problem.

Parameter	Type/Description
nAtom	**Integer**—An atom number.
lpBuffer	**String**—A string buffer to load with the string associated with an atom. This buffer should be preallocated to at least **nSize+1** characters long.
nSize	**Integer**—The maximum number of characters to load into the buffer.

Return Value   **Integer**—The number of characters loaded into the **lpBuffer** string.

GetDialogBaseUnits

VB Declaration   Declare Function GetDialogBaseUnits& Lib "User" ()

Description   Retrieves the average width and height of the system font. This value is used to determine the default base units of a dialog box.

Use with VB   No problem.

Return Value   **Long**—The low 16 bits contain the average width of the system font; the high 16 bits contain the average height.

Comments   The dialog base units are one-quarter of the average character width horizontally and one-eighth of the average character height vertically. When calculating a position in a dialog box, always multiply first. Thus to find the width of a control that is 25 dialog units wide, use (25 * low 16 bits of result) / 4.

GetMessageExtraInfo

VB Declaration   Declare Function GetMessageExtraInfo& Lib "User" ()

Description   After a **PeekMessage** call, retrieves information associated with the most recently processed messages. The information is dependent on the device, so this function is only of use if you have information about extra information provided by a driver.

Use with VB   No known problem, but rarely used (if ever) by VB programmers.

Return Value   **Long**—Defined by the driver.

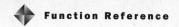

■ GetMessagePos

VB Declaration   Declare Function GetMessagePos& Lib "User" ()

Description   Retrieves the screen coordinates of the cursor at the time the most recent message was processed. This is typically used after a call to **PeekMessage**.

Use with VB   No problem.

Return Value   **Long**—The low word contains the horizontal position of the cursor in screen coordinates, the high word contains the vertical position.

■ GetNearestPaletteIndex

VB Declaration   Declare Function GetNearestPaletteIndex% Lib "GDI" (ByVal hPalette%, ⇔ ByVal crColor&)

Description   Retrieves the index into a logical palette of the color that most closely matches the requested color.

Use with VB   No problem.

Parameter	Type/Description
hPalette	**Integer**—A handle to a logical palette.
crColor	**Long**—The color to look for in the palette.

Return Value   **Integer**—The index to the entry that most closely matches this color.

■ GetPaletteEntries

VB Declaration   Declare Function GetPaletteEntries% Lib "GDI" (ByVal hPalette%, ByVal wStart ⇔ Index%, ByVal wNumEntries%, lpPaletteEntries As PALETTEENTRY)

Description   This function retrieves entries in a logical palette.

Use with VB   No problem.

Parameter	Type/Description
hPalette	**Integer**—A handle to a logical palette.
wStartIndex	**Integer**—The number of the first entry in the palette to retrieve.
wNumEntries	**Integer**—The number of entries to retrieve. There must be at least this many entries in the **lpPaletteColors** array.
lpPaletteColors	**PALETTEENTRY**—The first entry in an array of **PALETTEENTRY** structures that will be loaded with the current entries in the logical palette.

■ GetProp, GetPropBystring, GetPropBynum

VB Declaration   Declare Function GetProp% Lib "User" (ByVal hWnd%, ByVal lpString As Any)

Declare Function GetPropBystring% Lib "User" Alias "GetProp" (ByVal hWnd%, ⇔ ByVal lpString$)

Declare Function GetPropBynum% Lib "User" Alias "GetProp" (ByVal hWnd%, ByVal ⇔ lpString&)

Description   Retrieves the integer data handle for the specified property.

Use with VB   No problem.

Parameter	Type/Description
hWnd	**Integer**—A handle to a window.
lpString	**String** or **Long**—The name of the property or an atom to use as the name of the property. If it is an atom, it must be a global atom and the high word of the parameter must be zero.

Return Value   **Integer**—The 16-bit value or handle that was saved for the property using the **SetProp** function.

■ GetSystemPaletteEntries

VB Declaration   Declare Function GetSystemPaletteEntries% Lib "GDI" (ByVal hDC%, ByVal ⇔ wStartIndex%, ByVal wNumEntries%, lpPaletteEntries As PALETTEENTRY)

Description   This function retrieves entries in the system palette.

Use with VB   No problem.

Parameter	Type/Description
hDC	**Integer**—A handle to a device context for the device whose palette is being examined—usually the display.
wStartIndex	**Integer**—The number of the first entry in the system palette to retrieve.
wNumEntries	**Integer**—The number of entries to retrieve. There must be at least this many entries in the **lpPaletteColors** array.
lpPaletteColors	**PALETTEENTRY**—The first entry in an array of **PALETTEENTRY** structures that will be loaded with the current entries in the system palette.

Comments   Use the **GetDeviceCaps** API function described in Chapter 6 to determine if the device supports palettes before calling this function.

GetSystemPaletteUse

VB Declaration Declare Function GetSystemPaletteUse% Lib "GDI" (ByVal hDC%)

Description Determines if a device context has obtained access to the entire system palette including the 20 entries that are normally reserved.

Use with VB No problem.

Parameter	Type/Description
hDC	**Integer**—A handle to a device context for the device to check.

Return Value **Integer**—One of the two constants **SYSPAL_NOSTATIC** or **SYSPAL_STATIC**. These are described under the function reference entry for the **SetSystemPaletteUse** function.

Comments Use the **GetDeviceCaps** API function described in Chapter 6 to determine if the device supports palettes before calling this function. Refer to the description of the **SetSystemPaletteUse** function for further details.

GlobalAddAtom

VB Declaration Declare Function GlobalAddAtom% Lib "User" (ByVal lpString$)

Description Adds an atom to the global atom table.

Use with VB No problem.

Parameter	Type/Description
lpString	**String**—The string associated with the atom, also known as the name of the atom.

Return Value **Integer**—The atom value on success, zero on error.

Comments You should always check the result to make sure that the atom was allocated successfully. Also note that atoms are not case-sensitive.

GlobalDeleteAtom

VB Declaration Declare Function GlobalDeleteAtom% Lib "User" (ByVal nAtom%)

Description Deletes the specified global atom.

Use with VB No problem.

Parameter	Type/Description
nAtom	**Integer**—The atom number to delete.

Return Value **Integer**—Zero on success, the atom number on failure.

Comments   If the atom has been allocated multiple times, the atom will not actually be deleted until this function has been called the same number of times. Windows maintains a reference count for each atom.

■ GlobalFindAtom

VB Declaration   `Declare Function GlobalFindAtom% Lib "User" (ByVal lpString$)`

Description   Retrieves the global atom number for a string.

Use with VB   No problem.

Parameter	Type/Description
lpString	**String**—The string to search for.

Return Value   **Integer**—The number of the global atom for the string. Zero if there is no atom for the specified string.

■ GlobalGetAtomName

VB Declaration   `Declare Function GlobalGetAtomName% Lib "User" (ByVal nAtom%, ByVal ⇔`
`lpbuffer$, ByVal nSize%)`

Description   Retrieves the string associated with a global atom.

Use with VB   No problem.

Parameter	Type/Description
nAtom	**Integer**—An atom number.
lpBuffer	**String**—A string buffer to load with the string associated with a global atom. This buffer should be preallocated to at least **nSize+1** characters long.
nSize	**Integer**—The maximum number of characters to load into the buffer.

Return Value   **Integer**—The number of characters loaded into the **lpBuffer** string.

■ InitAtomTable

VB Declaration   `Declare Function InitAtomTable% Lib "Kernel" (ByVal nSize%)`

Description   Changes the size of the local atom table. This is a hash table used to identify atoms with strings. Increasing the size of this table can improve performance for applications that use large numbers of atoms.

Use with VB	No known problems. It is unclear what effect this function actually has on the size of the atom hash table for VB applications, but it seems to do no harm.

Parameter	Type/Description
nSize	**Integer**—The new size of the local atom hash table. The default size is 37.

Return Value **Integer**—TRUE (nonzero) on success, zero otherwise.

■ lstrcat

VB Declaration `Declare Function lstrcat& Lib "Kernel" (ByVal lpString1 As Any, ByVal ⇔ lpString2 As Any)`

Description Appends string **lpString2** to string **lpString1**.

Use with VB Works fine, but be sure that **lpString1** has been preallocated to a length adequate to hold the resulting string. The VB string operations are easier and safer to use.

Parameter	Type/Description
lpString1	**String** or **Long**—A string or address of a string buffer containing a NULL terminated string. This parameter is not type checked so be careful that only **String** or **Long** variables are used. The buffer referenced must be large enough to hold this string and **lpString2**.
lpString2	**String** or **Long**—A string or address of a string buffer containing a NULL terminated string to append to **lpString1**. This parameter is not type checked so be careful that only **String** or **Long** variables are used.

Return Value **Long**—The value of **lpString1** on success.

Comments This function does not handle huge (>64k) strings.

■ lstrcmp, lstrcmpi

VB Declaration `Declare Function lstrcmp% Lib "User" (ByVal lpString1 As Any, ByVal lpString2 ⇔ As Any)`

`Declare Function lstrcmpi% Lib "User" (ByVal lpString1 As Any, ByVal ⇔ lpString2 As Any)`

Description Compares string **lpString2** to string **lpString1**. **lstrcmpi** is not case-sensitive.

Use with VB No problem. The VB string comparison operations are easier to use.

Parameter	Type/Description
lpString1	**String** or **Long**—A string or address of a string buffer containing a NULL terminated string. This parameter is not type checked so be careful that only **String** or **Long** variables are used.

Parameter	Type/Description
lpString2	**String** or **Long**—A string or address of a string buffer containing a NULL terminated string to compare with **lpString1**. This parameter is not type checked so be careful that only **String** or **Long** variables are used.

Return Value **Integer**—A negative value if **lpString1** is less than **lpString2**, zero if the strings are equal, and a positive value if **lpString1** is greater than **lpString2**.

Comments This function does not handle huge strings.

■ lstrcpy

VB Declaration `Declare Function lstrcpy& Lib "Kernel" (ByVal lpString1 As Any, ByVal ⇔`
`lpString2 As Any)`

Description Copies string **lpString2** to string **lpString1**

Use with VB Works fine, but be sure that **lpString1** has been preallocated to be at least as long as string **lpString2**. The VB string operations are easier and safer to use.

Parameter	Type/Description
lpString1	**String** or **Long**—A string or address of a string buffer containing a NULL terminated string. This parameter is not type checked so be careful that only **String** or **Long** variables are used. The buffer referenced must be large enough to hold string **lpString2**.
lpString2	**String** or **Long**—A string or address of a string buffer containing a NULL terminated string to copy to **lpString1**. This parameter is not type checked so be careful that only **String** or **Long** variables are used.

Return Value **Long**—The value of **lpString1** on success.

Comments This function does not handle huge strings.

■ lstrlen

VB Declaration `Declare Function lstrlen% Lib "Kernel" (ByVal lpString As Any)`

Description Determines the length of **lpString**.

Use with VB Works fine, but the VB **Len** operation is easier to use.

Parameter	Type/Description
lpString	**String** or **Long**—A string or address of a string buffer containing a NULL terminated string. This parameter is not type checked so be careful that only **String** or **Long** variables are used.

Return Value	**Integer**—The length of string **lpString** on success.
Comments	This function does not handle huge strings.

■ MapDialogRect

VB Declaration   `Declare Sub MapDialogRect Lib "User" (ByVal hDlg%, lpRect As RECT)`

Description   Converts dialog base units into screen pixel coordinates.

Use with VB   Not particularly useful because dialog boxes are not easily created under Visual Basic.

Parameter	Type/Description
hDlg	**Integer**—A handle to a dialog box window.
lpRect	**RECT**—A rectangle that contains a rectangle to convert in dialog box unit coordinates. Upon return, this structure will contain the rectangle in screen coordinates.

■ MessageBox

VB Declaration   `Declare Function MessageBox% Lib "User" (ByVal hWnd%, ByVal lpText$, ⇔`
                     `ByVal lpCaption$, ByVal wType%)`

Description   Displays a message box.

Use with VB   Works, but the Visual Basic **MsgBox** function and statement are easier to use.

Parameter	Type/Description
hWnd	**Integer**—A handle to a window that will be the parent window of the message box. This will generally be the handle of the active form. Avoid using the window handle of a control.
lpText	**String**—The string containing the message to display. There is no automatic wraparound, but carriage return characters will cause line breaks. If the **MB_ICONHAND** and **MB_SYSTEMMODAL** flags are specified, the message box is limited to three lines.
lpCaption	**String**—The caption of the message box.
wType	**Integer**—The type of message box as described in Table 16.8.

Return Value   **Integer**—One of the following constants describing the button that was pressed: **IDABORT, IDCANCEL, IDIGNORE, IDNO, IDOK, IDRETRY**, and **IDYES**.

Table 16.8   **MsgBox Flags**

wType Constant	Description
MB_ABORTRETRYIGNORE	Message box contains Abort, Retry, and Ignore buttons.
MB_DEFBUTTON1 MB_DEFBUTTON2 MB_DEFBUTTON3	You may OR in one of these constants to set the default button for the message box.
MB_APPLMODAL MB_TASKMODAL MB_SYSTEMMODAL	You may OR in one of these constants to set the modality of the message box. Use **MB_TASKMODAL** only if there is no **hWnd** parameter available to make the message box modal. **MB_SYSTEM-MODAL** makes the message box system modal. Use the **MB_ICONHAND** flag to prevent any further messages from going to windows during the message box creation—this is designed for serious errors.
MB_ICONEXCLAMATION	Displays an exclamation point icon.
MB_ICONHAND	Displays a stop sign icon.
MB_ICONINFORMATION	Displays an icon showing a lowercase i in a circle.
MB_ICONQUESTION	Displays a question mark icon.
MB_OK	Message box contains a single OK button.
MB_OKCANCEL	Message box contains an OK and a Cancel button.
MB_RETRYCANCEL	Message box contains Retry and Cancel buttons.
MB_YESNO	Message box contains Yes and No buttons.
MB_YESNOCANCEL	Message box contains Yes, No, and Cancel buttons.

■ MulDiv

VB Declaration   Declare Function MulDiv% Lib "GDI" (ByVal nNumber%, ByVal nNumerator%, ⇔
ByVal nDenominator%)

Description   Multiplies two 16-bit integers, then divides the result by a 16-bit integer, rounding the result.

Use with VB   No problem.

Parameter	Type/Description
nNumber	**Integer**—First multiplicand.
nNumerator	**Integer**—Second multiplicand.
nDenominator	**Integer**—Divisor.

Return Value   **Integer**—(nNumber * nNumerator)/nDenominator.

■ PeekMessage

VB Declaration   `Declare Function PeekMessage% Lib "User" (lpMsg As MSG, ByVal hWnd%, ⇔`
`ByVal wMsgFilterMin%, ByVal wMsgFilterMax%, ByVal wRemoveMsg%)`

Description   This function is used to retrieve a message from the message queue of a window.

Use with VB   Refer to "Message Processing and File Dragging," earlier in this chapter, for information on message queues and using the **PeekMessage** function in Visual Basic. Microsoft has indicated that this message is incompatible with Visual Basic, but experimentation indicates that you may use it safely if you set both the **PM_REMOVE** and **PM_NOYIELD** flags in the **wRemoveMsg** field. However, this may not work on future versions of Visual Basic.

Parameter	Type/Description
lpMsg	**MSG**—A **MSG** structure that will be loaded with information about the current message. This structure is described in Appendix B.
hWnd	**Integer**—A handle to a window. Only messages to this window will be examined by this function. If this value is zero, messages to all of an application's windows will be examined.
wMsgFilterMin	**Integer**—Messages below this value will not be retrieved by this function.
wMsgFilterMax	**Integer**—Messages above this value will not be retrieved by this function.
wRemoveMsg	**Integer**—A combination of flags as described in the Comments section below.

Return Value   **Integer**—TRUE (nonzero) if a message is available to process. Zero if no message is available.

Comments   You should specify either the **PM_NOREMOVE** OR **PM_REMOVE** constant in the **wRemoveMsg** parameter. This tells the function whether to remove the message from the message queue or leave it for later processing. The **PM_NOYIELD** flag may be ORed in with the other flags to specify that this function should not yield to allow other applications to run.

Under Visual Basic, you will typically use the **PM_REMOVE OR PM_NOYIELD** combination in conjunction with the **DoEvents** function as shown in "Message Processing and File Dragging," earlier in this chapter. Use of this function in a manner other than that described in the chapter may lead to problems with the system including Windows freezing up.

■ RealizePalette

VB Declaration   `Declare Function RealizePalette% Lib "User" (ByVal hDC%)`

Description   Maps the entries in the logical palette selected into the specified device context into the system palette. This function should be called before drawing into the device context.

Use with VB   If you use the recommended technique for copying a palette into a VB control using the clipboard, you should not need to use this function. If you select the palette directly, you will need to use this function before drawing into the control. You must also use the **agVBSetControlFlags** function to inform Visual Basic that the control has a palette selected.

Parameter	Type/Description
hDC	**Integer**—A handle to a device context.

Return Value   **Integer**—The number of entries in the logical palette that were remapped to different system palette entries.

Comments   Refer to the description of the **SelectPalette** function for additional information on using this function. This function is not compatible with version 1.0 of Visual Basic.

■ RemoveProp, RemovePropBynum

VB Declaration
```
Declare Function RemoveProp% Lib "User" (ByVal hWnd%, ByVal lpString$)

Declare Function RemovePropBynum% Lib "User" Alias "RemoveProp" (ByVal ⇔
hWnd%, ByVal lpString$)
```

Description   Deletes (or removes) a property for a window.

Use with VB   No problem.

Parameter	Type/Description
hWnd	**Integer**—A handle to a window.
lpString	**String** or **Long**—The name of the property or an atom to use as the name of the property. If it is an atom, it must be a global atom and the high word of the parameter must be zero.

Return Value   **Integer**—The 16-bit value or handle that was saved for the property using the **SetProp** function on success, zero on error.

Comments   You must remove any properties before the window is destroyed. This is typically done before unloading a form or control, or in the **Unload** event for the form.

■ ResizePalette

VB Declaration
```
Declare Function ResizePalette% Lib "GDI" (ByVal hPalette%, ByVal ⇔
nNumEntries%)
```

Description   Changes the size of a logical palette.

Use with VB   No problem.

Parameter	Type/Description
hPalette	**Integer**—A handle to a logical palette.
nNumEntries	**Integer**—The number of entries in the palette after the function is called.

Return Value   **Integer**—TRUE (nonzero) on success, zero otherwise.

◼ SelectPalette

VB Declaration   `Declare Function SelectPalette% Lib "User" (ByVal hDC%, ByVal hPalette%, ⇔`
`ByVal bForceBackground%)`

Description   Selects the palette to use for a specified device context.

Use with VB   If you use the recommended technique for copying a palette into a VB control using the clipboard, you should not need to use this function.

        If you choose to use this function to select the palette directly, you will also need to use the **agVBSetControlFlags** function to inform Visual Basic that the control has a palette selected. You will need to select the palette and realize the palette using the **RealizePalette** function before drawing on the control.

        If you are subclassing an existing control, you should refer to the documentation on the **VBM_PALETTECHANGED** message in the *Control Development Guide* in the professional edition of Visual Basic.

Parameter	Type/Description
hDC	**Integer**—A handle to a device context.
hPalette	**Integer**—A handle to a palette to use when drawing into the device context.
bForceBackground	**Integer**—Normally zero. When TRUE, always forces this palette to be a background palette. Normally Windows makes sure that the active window is displayed as accurately as possible and gives its logical palette priority.

Return Value   **Integer**—A handle to the previous logical palette for this device context on success, zero otherwise.

Comments   Logical palettes may be used by more than one device context at a time. Changes to the palette will affect all device contexts that used that palette. This function is not compatible with version 1.0 of Visual Basic.

◼ SetPaletteEntries

VB Declaration   `Declare Function SetPaletteEntries% Lib "GDI" (ByVal hPalette%, ByVal ⇔`
`wStartIndex%, ByVal wNumEntries%, lpPaletteEntries As PALETTEENTRY)`

Description   This function sets entries in a logical palette.

Use with VB   No problem.

Parameter	Type/Description
hPalette	**Integer**—A handle to a logical palette.
wStartIndex	**Integer**—The number of the first entry in the palette to set.
wNumEntries	**Integer**—The number of entries to set. There must be at least this many entries in the **lpPaletteColors** array.
lpPaletteColors	**PALETTEENTRY**—The first entry in an array of **PALETTEEN-TRY** structures that will be set into the logical palette.

Comments   If a logical palette is in use when this function is called, the changes will not take place until the **RealizePalette** function is called.

■ SetProp, SetPropBynum

VB Declaration   `Declare Function SetProp% Lib "User" (ByVal hWnd%, ByVal lpString$, ⇔`
`ByVal hData%)`

`Declare Function SetPropBynum% Lib "User" Alias "SetProp" (ByVal hWnd%, ⇔`
`ByVal lpString&, ByVal hData%)`

Description   Sets the integer data handle for the specified property.

Use with VB   No problem.

Parameter	Type/Description
hWnd	**Integer**—A handle to a window.
lpString	**String** or **Long**—The name of the property or an atom to use as the name of the property. If it is an atom, it must be a global atom and the high word of the parameter must be zero.

Return Value   **Integer**—TRUE (nonzero) on success, zero otherwise.

Comments   You must remove any properties before the window is destroyed. This is typically done before unloading a form or control, or in the **Unload** event for the form.

■ SetSystemPaletteUse

VB Declaration   `Declare Function SetSystemPaletteUse% Lib "GDI" (ByVal hDC%, ByVal wUsage%)`

Description   Normally Windows reserves the first 20 entries of the system palette for default colors that will always be available to applications. This function allows an application to grab all but two of the system palette entries for use by a logical palette (only black and white remain reserved).

Use with VB   Avoid using this function. If you must use this function, you will need a subclassing tool capable of detecting the **WM_LOSTFOCUS** and **WM_DESTROY** Windows messages in order to know when to restore the normal state of the system palette. The Visual Basic **LostFocus** and **Unload** events are not appropriate for this task.

Parameter	Type/Description
hDC	**Integer**—A handle to a device context.
wUsage	**Integer**—One of the following constant values: **SYSPAL_NOSTATIC**: Device context will have access to all but two of the system palette entries (black and white). **SYSPAL_STATIC**: The system will reserve 20 entries for a default color palette that will not be changed when the logical palette for this device context is realized.

Return Value Integer—The previous **wUsage** value for this device context.

Comments Use the **GetDeviceCaps** API function described in Chapter 6 to determine if the device supports palettes before calling this function.

Any time this function is called, the following steps must be followed:

1. Use the **UnrealizeObject** function with the palette handle as a parameter to force Windows to completely remap the palette next time it is realized.

2. Realize the palette.

3. Use the **GetSysColor** function to retrieve the values for all system colors (see Chapter 5).

4. Use the **SetSysColors** function to set the system colors to values that are appropriate for a monochrome screen (use black and white only—see Chapter 5).

5. Send the **WM_SYSCOLORCHANGE** message to all top level windows using the **SendMessage** function (see Chapter 4).

When the window loses the focus or the application closes, you must follow the following steps to restore the prior system state:

1. Call the **SetSystemPaletteUse** function with the **wUsage** parameter set to **SYSPAL_-STATIC** to restore the default system palette.

2. Use the **UnrealizeObject** function with the palette handle as a parameter to force Windows to completely remap the palette next time it is realized (see Chapter 7).

3. Realize the palette.

4. Restore the system colors to their previous values using the **SetSysColors** function (see Chapter 5).

5. Send the **WM_SYSCOLORCHANGE** message to all top level windows using the **SendMessage** function (see Chapter 4).

■ UpdateColors

VB Declaration `Declare Function UpdateColors% Lib "GDI" (ByVal hDC%)`

Description This function updates the colors in a window by choosing the closest available system palette color. This is generally used when a window is not active and the system palette is changed by the realization of a logical palette by a different application.

Use with VB Compatible but not useful. Visual Basic 2.0 and 3.0 invalidate and redraw controls when the system palette is changed.

Parameter	Type/Description
hDC	Integer—A handle to a device context to update.

Return Value Integer—Not used.

Comments   Continuous use of this function can lead to a cumulative error in the color rendition of a window that will not be corrected until the window is redrawn. This is because each time the function is called, the new pixel color is based on the previous pixel color.

■ wvsprintf

VB Declaration   `Declare Function wvsprintf Lib "User" (ByVal lpszOutput$, ByVal lpszFormat$, ⇔`
`lpvArglist%)`

Description   This function is used to create a formatted string based on a list of numeric arguments. This function is similar to the C language **sprintf** function.

Use with VB   No problem.

Parameter	Type/Description
lpszOutput	**String**—A string buffer to load with the formatted output. Be sure to allocate a string that is long enough to contain any possible result.
lpszFormat	**String**—A format string as defined in the Comments section.
lpvArglist	**Integer**—The first entry in an integer array. The data required for formatting is read from the array. The array has enough entries to satisfy the requirements of the format string. Each **Integer** argument uses one entry in the array, each **Long** argument uses two entries in the array. The low word appears first in the array and is followed by the high word. If the **%s** is specified in the format string, two entries in the array are used to specify an address of a string, and the offset appears first in the array followed by the segment.

Return Value   **Integer**—The length of the **lpszOutput** string.

Comments   The format string is copied to the output string exactly except for specified arguments. Arguments are specified using a % character and take the following form:

`%[-][#][0][width][.precision]type`

where items in brackets are optional. **%%** produces a single % character in the output.
The available types are as follows:

Character Indicating Type	Type
c	A single character. If the value of the argument is zero, this argument is ignored.
d,i	A signed integer.
ld,li	A **Long** signed integer.
u	An unsigned integer.
lu	A **Long** unsigned integer.

Character Indicating Type	Type
x, X	A 16-bit hexadecimal number. X specifies uppercase, x specifies lowercase
lx,lX	A **Long** hexadecimal number. lX specifies uppercase, lx specifies lowercase.
s	A string.

The argument fields have the following meanings:

Optional Field	Description
[-]	The output value is left-aligned. The right is padded with spaces or zeros.
[#]	Hexadecimal values are preceded with 0x or 0X.
[0]	Pad the extra space in the output field with zeros instead of spaces.
[width]	A number specifying the minimum width that this argument will take in the output field.
[precision]	A number specifying the minimum number of digits to copy into the output field for this argument. The number will be padded on the left with zeros to match this value if the converted value has fewer digits than the precision.

General Windows Messages

Edit Control Messages

List Box, Combo Box, and Button Messages

3

Windows Messages

17

General Windows Messages

Message Handling

Messages That Are
Useful with Visual Basic

Message Reference

THIS CHAPTER DESCRIBES THE STANDARD MESSAGES DEFINED BY THE Windows operating system. It begins with a review of what messages are and how they are used. Messages that are useful under Visual Basic are described.

The chapter concludes with a reference section that describes most of the standard Windows messages that are likely to be used by even the most expert Visual Basic programmer using advanced subclassing techniques.

Message Handling

Under Windows, messages are used in two ways. First, they are sent by Windows to a window function to indicate that an event such as a mouse click or a keyboard press has occurred. A message can also be a notification by Windows of an internal event such as a change of focus. Finally, it can be a command from Windows that it is time for a window to perform some task such as erasing the background or painting the client area of the window.

Second, messages are often sent to a control or window to request it to perform a specified operation.

Windows Event Messages

Most Visual Basic events correspond to an internal Windows event; however, most Windows messages do not generate Visual Basic events. This is not surprising since there are dozens of Windows events, many of which are rarely used by programmers. Supporting all Windows messages under Visual Basic would lead to a significant increase in the complexity of Visual Basic and would certainly impair the language's performance.

This has one unfortunate side effect: There is no easy way for a Visual Basic programmer to detect the occurrence of a Windows message, though there are times when the ability to do so would be very helpful. One classic example is detection of mouse messages on a control, such as the command button, that does not support mouse events. Access to such messages would make it possible to detect a click with the right mouse button, or the presence of the cursor over the control for updating a status bar. Messages would also be helpful to detect a file drop when dragging files from the file manager (the **WM_DROPFILES** message described in Chapter 16), and the **WM_COMM-NOTIFY** message (described in Chapter 14).

If you had the ability to intercept and modify Windows messages arriving at a control, you could customize every aspect of the operation of that control. This technique, described in Chapter 2, is known as subclassing. Visual Basic provides limited capability for intercepting messages arriving at a window by using the **PeekMessage** function. An example of this technique is presented in the file dragging example in Chapter 16.

True subclassing cannot be accomplished directly in Visual Basic. There are two techniques for subclassing a Visual Basic window or control. The first is to create a dynamic link library using C or C++ and to have it subclass the control. The second is to use a third-party package such as Desaware's Spy-Works application, which subclasses Visual Basic windows and maps selected messages into Visual Basic events to allow the programmer to effectively subclass a form or control from within Visual Basic.

When subclassing a control, there are two ways to process each message that is received. You can allow the default processing for the message to continue and return the result of the default message, or you can handle the message directly. The reference section later in this chapter describes the values that must be returned when subclassing a message if default processing is not performed.

Messages That Perform Operations

There are a large number of messages that can be used to request a control to perform an operation. Examples of this include the **WM_COPY** message, which can be sent to some controls to instruct them to copy data into the clipboard. The **WM_REDRAW** message controls whether some controls update themselves each time they are changed.

These messages differ from event messages in that they are frequently sent to a control by applications, not just by Windows. They can also return values to an application, and can thus be used to retrieve information about a control. The following section describes in more detail how this type of message can be used.

Message Organization

Each message has a number. This integer is the message parameter to the window function for a form or control. The messages numbered from 1 to &H400 are standard Windows messages. Not every control processes all of these messages, but no control may redefine them.

The messages above &H400 are user-defined and their meaning depends on the class of the window. Thus &H401 is the **EM_SETSEL** message, which sets the start and end positions of a selection for an edit box. It is also the **LB_ADDSTRING** message, which is used to add a string to a list box. The message numbers are the same, but the operation depends on whether the control is a list box or edit control.

The Visual Basic text and list controls are subclassed off of standard Windows controls and thus respond correctly to most of the messages for these controls, as was described earlier in Chapter 2.

Keep in mind that each application may define its own messages. Only the standard Windows messages are described in this book.

Sending Messages

Messages can be sent using either the **SendMessage** or the **PostMessage** function. Both of these functions have additional type-safe aliases provided, as some messages use long parameters and others require string parameters. These functions are described in detail in Chapter 4.

The **SendMessage** function and its aliases are used to send a message by calling the Windows function for the window directly. The function does not return until the message has been completely processed. This function must be used for messages that return values.

The **PostMessage** function adds a message to the window queue for a window. The message will be processed during the normal course of event processing at some future time.

Message Parameters

Each message has two parameters, a 16-bit integer parameter and a 32-bit long parameter. The integer parameter is typically known as the **wParam** parameter, the long parameter as the **lParam** parameter.

The **lParam** parameter is frequently used to transfer two 16-bit integer parameters: one in the high 16-bit word and the other in the low 16-bit word.

You can create a 32-bit parameter from two 16-bit numbers in Visual Basic as follows:

```
Dim wordLow%, wordHigh%
Dim lParam&
lParam& = CLng(wordHigh%) * &H10000& Or wordLow%
```

The easiest way to extract two integers from a 32-bit long variable is to use the **agDwordTo2Integers** provided with the APIGUIDE.DLL dynamic link library that comes with this book. This is done as follows:

```
agDwordTo2Integers lParam&, wordLow%, wordHigh%
```

The reason for using this function instead of mathematic operations under Visual Basic is to avoid the problems of converting unsigned variables to Visual Basic signed integers. Refer to Chapter 3 for further information.

Messages That Return Values

The **SendMessage** returns a long value. Since this function calls a window function directly, it is possible for the window function to return a value that appears as the result of the **SendMessage** function. The meaning of this value depends on the message. For the purposes of the message reference in this book, unless a message is listed as providing a return value, the result of the **SendMessage** function has no meaning and should be ignored.

The WM_COMMAND Message

The **WM_COMMAND** message is somewhat unusual in that it actually reflects an entire set of messages. This message is used in two ways.

First, the **WM_COMMAND** message is sent to a window that owns a menu when a menu command occurs. This process is described at some length in Chapter 9.

Second, the **WM_COMMAND** message is sent by a control to its parent window when certain events occur. These are special messages known as notification messages. The low 16 bits of the **lParam** parameter contain the window handle of the control sending the notification and the high 16 bits contain the notification number. Notification messages are listed for each of the standard Windows controls in Chapters 18 and 19.

Messages That Are Useful with Visual Basic

This section contains a reference and examples of standard Windows messages that are useful under Visual Basic. Messages that are specific to text, list, combo, and other controls are discussed in Chapters 18 and 19.

The messages listed here have been tested under the standard Visual Basic controls. They are likely to work with most custom controls as well, especially if they are subclassed from standard Windows controls.

Table 17.1 summarizes the messages that are most useful under Visual Basic. The detailed descriptions of each function can be found in the message reference section of this chapter.

Table 16.1   Messages Useful under Visual Basic

Message	Control	Description
WM_CLEAR	Text, combo	Clears the selected text.
WM_CLOSE	Form	Closes the window or application.
WM_COPY	Text, combo	Copies the selected text into the clipboard.
WM_CUT	Text, combo	Cuts the selected text into the clipboard.

Table 16.1 **Messages Useful under Visual Basic (Continued)**

Message	Control	Description
WM_GETFONT	Most controls that show text	Retrieves a handle to the default logical font used by the control.
WM_PASTE	Text, combo	Pastes text from the clipboard into the control.
WM_SETFONT	Most controls that show text	Sets the default font that the control should use to display text.
WM_SETREDRAW	List, combo, text	Determines whether a control should update its display when the contents of the control are changed.
WM_SYSCOMMAND	Form	Can be used to execute system menu commands under program control.
WM_UNDO	Text	Reverses the effect of the most recent editing operation.

Message Reference

This section contains a list of the most frequently used Windows messages. Many of these messages are either not directly accessible or useful under Visual Basic, or duplicate functionality provided by a Windows API function or Visual Basic property. They are described briefly here for two reasons. First, you may have access to technology to subclass Visual Basic forms or controls, in which case this reference can be extremely useful for modifying the behavior of the subclassed control.

Second, these messages provide a great deal of insight to the internal workings of Windows and Visual Basic.

Many of the message descriptions include a section on their Use with Subclassing, which describes briefly the functionality that is available using subclassing technology. Subclassing is described further in "Windows Event Messages," earlier in this chapter, and in Chapter 2.

■ WM_ACTIVATE

VB Declaration   Global Const WM_ACTIVATE = &H6

Description   Sent to a window when it is activated or deactivated.

Use with VB   None. The Visual Basic **Activate** and **Deactivate** events are triggered by this message.

Parameter	Description
wParam	One of the following constants: **WA_INACTIVE**: Window is deactivated. **WA_ACTIVE**: Window is activated. **WA_CLICKACTIVE**: Window is activated after a mouse click.
lParam	High word: Nonzero if window is minimized. Low word: The handle of the window whose state is changing. May be zero.

■ WM_ACTIVATEAPP

VB Declaration   Global Const WM_ACTIVATEAPP = &H1C

Description   This message is sent to all top level windows of an application that is being activated or deactivated.

Use with VB   None.

**Use with
Subclassing**   Used to determine when a user is switching between applications.

Parameter	Description
wParam	TRUE (nonzero) if the application is being activated.
lParam	Low word: A task handle. If window is being activated, the task handle of the deactivated task. If window is being deactivated, the task handle of the task being activated.

■ WM_ASKCBFORMATNAME

VB Declaration   `Global Const WM_ASKCBFORMATNAME = &H30C`

Description   Sent to the clipboard owner when the clipboard contains data in the **CF_OWNERDISPLAY** format. The clipboard owner must copy the name of the format into the buffer pointed to by **lParam**.

Use with VB   None.

**Use with
Subclassing**   Makes possible use of the **CF_OWNERDISPLAY** format for VB applications.

Parameter	Description
wParam	The maximum number of bytes to copy.
lParam	The address of a buffer to load with the name of the buffer.

■ WM_CANCELMODE

VB Declaration   `Global Const WM_CANCELMODE = &H1F`

Description   Informs a window that a dialog box or message box is about to be displayed.

Use with VB   None.

**Use with
Subclassing**   Generally used to cancel modes such as the mouse capture. Return zero if this message is processed.

■ WM_CHAR

VB Declaration   `Global Const WM_CHAR = &H102`

Description   Sent to a window when a character is received.

Use with VB   None. This message triggers the Visual Basic **KeyPressed** event on controls that support it. Refer to "Keyboard Control" in Chapter 5 for further information.

Use with Subclassing Allows detection of keyboard input on controls that do not support the **KeyUp**, **KeyDown**, and **KeyPressed** events.

Parameter	Description
wParam	The virtual key number of the character.
lParam	Bits 0 - 15: The number of repetitions of the character received (used during auto repeat). Bits 16 - 23: The device scan code of the key pressed. Bit 24: 1 if it is an extended key such as a function key or numeric keypad entry. Bit 29: 1 if the Alt key was held down when the key was pressed. Bit 30: 1 if the key was down before this message was added to the queue. This is common during auto-repeat. Bit 31: 0 if the key is being pressed, 1 if released.

Comments The data in **lParam** only reflects the most recent key operation for this character and is rarely used.

■ WM_CHILDACTIVATE

VB Declaration `Global Const WM_CHILDACTIVATE = &H22`

Description This message is sent to Multiple Document Interface (MDI) controls when they are activated.

Use with VB None.

Use with Subclassing Return zero if this message is processed.

■ WM_CLEAR

VB Declaration `Global Const WM_CLEAR = &H303`

Description This message can be sent to a text box or combo box to clear the selected text.

Use with VB No problem. This is equivalent to the Visual Basic command:

`ctl.SelText = ""`

where ctl is the name of the control.

Parameter	Description
wParam	Not used—set to zero.
lParam	Not used—set to zero.

■ WM_CLOSE

VB Declaration   Global Const WM_CLOSE = &H10

Description   This message is sent to indicate that a request has been made to close a window or application.

Use with VB   Posting this message to a form or window is equivalent to invoking the Close command on the system menu for that form or window.

Use with Subclassing   If you prevent default processing for this message from taking place, you can cause the system menu Close command to be ignored. In that case return zero.

Parameter	Description
wParam	Not used—set to zero.
lParam	Not used—set to zero.

Comments   The following line of code demonstrates use of this message to close a form:

```
di% = PostMessage(hWnd, WM_CLOSE, 0, 0&)
```

■ WM_COMMAND

VB Declaration   Global Const WM_COMMAND &H111

Description   This message is sent to a window when a message command is invoked, or when a control sends a notification message to a window. It is described in more detail in "The WM_COMMAND Message," earlier in this chapter. This message can be used to simulate the sending of menu commands to a form.

Use with VB   No problem.

Use with Subclassing   This message could be used to detect and intercept menu commands to a form.

Parameter	Description
wParam	The menu command ID if this is a menu command.
lParam	Low 16 bits: The window handle of a control if this is a notification message. High 16 bits: The message number of the notification message. Notification messages for the various controls can be found in the message reference sections of Chapters 18 and 19.

■ WM_COMMNOTIFY

VB Declaration   `Global Const WM_COMMNOTIFY = &H44`

Description   This message is supported as the **CommEvent** Visual Basic event in the CBK.VBX control provided with this book. Refer to the description of the **EnableCommNotification** function in Chapter 14 and the description of the CBK.VBX control in Appendix B for further information.

Use with VB   None.

**Use with
Subclassing**   Handled by the CBK.VBX custom control.

Parameter	Description
wParam	Identifier of the comm device.
lParam	Low Word: Refer to the **NotifyStatus** event parameter to the **Comm-Event** event of the CBK.VBX custom control described in Appendix B and Chapter 14 as stated in the description above.

■ WM_COMPACTING

VB Declaration   `Global Const WM_COMPACTING = &H41`

Description   Sent to all top level windows when Windows is short on memory.

Use with VB   None.

**Use with
Subclassing**   Frequently used as a signal to an application to free up any memory that it can.

Parameter	Description
wParam	N where N/&HFFFF is the percentage of time being spent compact-ing memory.

■ WM_COPY

VB Declaration   `Global Const WM_COPY = &H301`

Description   This message can be sent to a text box or combo box to copy the selected text into the clipboard.

Use with VB   No problem. This is equivalent to the Visual Basic commands:

`Clipboard.SetText Text1.SelText`

Parameter	Description
wParam	Not used—set to zero.
lParam	Not used—set to zero.

■ WM_CREATE

VB Declaration   `Global Const WM_CREATE = &H1`

Description   Sent to a window as soon as it is created.

Use with VB   None.

Use with Subclassing   Return –1 to destroy the window, in which case the calling **CreateWindow** or **CreateWindowEx** function will return zero.

Parameter	Description
lParam	A pointer to a **CREATESTRUCT** data structure.

■ WM_CTLCOLOR

VB Declaration   `Global Const WM_CTLCOLOR = &H19`

Description   Sent by a standard Windows control to its parent window before the control is drawn.

Use with VB   None.

Use with Subclassing   Typically used to set the background or foreground color for the control; this message probably has no value under Visual Basic.

Parameter	Description
wParam	A device context for the control.
lParam	Low word: The control window handle. High word: The type of control. Refer to the constants with the **CTL-COLOR_** prefix.

Comments   Return a handle to a brush to use for background fill or zero to use the default brush.

■ WM_CUT

VB Declaration   `Global Const WM_CUT = &H300`

Description   This message can be sent to a text box or combo box to cut the selected text into the clipboard.

Use with VB   No problem. This is equivalent to the Visual Basic commands:

```
Clipboard.SetText Text1.SelText
Text1.SelText = ""
```

Parameter	Description
wParam	Not used—set to zero.
lParam	Not used—set to zero.

■ WM_DEADCHAR

VB Declaration   `Global Const WM_DEADCHAR = &H103`

Description   This is similar to the **WM_CHAR** message except that it indicates that a character is to be combined with another character: for example, the accent mark used on many non-English character sets. Refer to the **WM_CHAR** message for information on use with VB, subclassing, and parameters.

■ WM_DESTROY

VB Declaration   `Global Const WM_DESTROY = &H2`

Description   Sent to a window before it is destroyed, but after it has been hidden.

Use with VB   None—the Visual Basic **Unload** event is triggered by this message.

Use with Subclassing   A good opportunity to clean up any window properties.

Comments   A window's child windows still exist when this message is received.

■ WM_DEVMODECHANGE

VB Declaration   `Global Const WM_DEVMODECHANGE = &H1B`

Description   Sent to all top level windows when the default configuration of a device has been changed.

Use with VB   None.

Use with Subclassing   Detects changes caused by the **agDeviceMode** function. Refer to Chapter 11 for information on this function.

Parameter	Description
lParam	A string address containing the name of the device that has been reconfigured.

■ WM_ENABLE

VB Declaration Global Const WM_ENABLE = &HA

Description This message is sent to a window when it becomes enabled or disabled.

Use with VB None.

Parameter	Description
wParam	TRUE (nonzero) if the window is enabled.

Comments The **WS_DISABLED** style bit for the window is not yet changed when this message is received.

■ WM_ENDSESSION

VB Declaration Global Const WM_ENDSESSION = &H16

Description Sent to the main window of an application before a Windows session ends.

Use with VB None.

Use with Subclassing Can be used to perform cleanup operations before a Windows session ends.

Parameter	Description
wParam	TRUE (nonzero) if the session is ending.

■ WM_ENTERIDLE

VB Declaration Global Const WM_ENTERIDLE = &H121

Description This message is sent to a window when a dialog box or menu for that window is idle (waiting for user input).

Use with VB None.

Parameter	Description
wParam	The constant **MSGF_DIALOGBOX** if a dialog box is displayed, **MSGF_MENU** if a menu is displayed.
lParam	Low word: The dialog box handle, or handle of the window that owns the menu.

■ WM_ERASEBKGND

VB Declaration Global Const WM_ERASEBKGND = &H14

Description Sent to a window to inform it that it should erase its background.

Use with VB   None.

**Use with
Subclassing**   The default operation is to erase the window background. This message can be intercepted to create a custom background.

Parameter	Description
wParam	A device context for the window.

■ WM_FONTCHANGE

VB Declaration   Global Const WM_FONTCHANGE = &H1D

Description   This message is sent to all top level windows when the available system fonts change.

Use with VB   None.

**Use with
Subclassing**   If your application displays a list of available fonts, this serves as notification that the list should change. If a window is using a font that is no longer available, it may be necessary to redraw the window.

Parameter	Description
wParam	Not used—set to zero.
lParam	Not used—set to zero.

■ WM_GETFONT

VB Declaration   Global Const WM_GETFONT = &H31

Description   Retrieves the handle to the logical font used by a control. The logical font handle is in the low word of the result of the **SendMessage** function call. Logical fonts are described in Chapter 10.

Use with VB   Works with standard Visual Basic controls.

■ WM_GETMINMAXINFO

VB Declaration   Global Const WM_GETMINMAXINFO = &H24

Description   Sent to a window when Windows needs to determine the minimum or maximum sizes for the window.

Use with VB   None.

**Use with
Subclassing**   Can be used to change the default minimum or maximum sizes for a window.

Parameter	Description
wParam	Not used—set to zero

Parameter	Description
lParam	A pointer to a **MINMAXINFO** data structure as defined in the comments section below.

Comments   The MINMAXINFO is defined as follows:

```
Type MINMAXINFO
    ptReserved As POINTAPI
    ptMaxSize As POINTAPI
    ptMaxPosition As POINTAPI
    ptMinTrackSize As POINTAPI
    ptMaxTrackSize As POINTAPI
End Type
```

ptMaxSize specifies the maximum width and height of the window. **ptMaxPosition** specifies the maximum position of the upper left corner of the window. **ptMinTrackSize** and **ptMaxTrackSize** specify the minimum and maximum width and height of the window when sized by dragging the borders.

■ WM_GETTEXT

VB Declaration   Global Const WM_GETTEXT = &HD

Description   Sent to a window to retrieve the window text. Duplicates the functionality of the **GetWindowText** function.

Use with VB   No problem, but is rarely used due to the availability of the Visual Basic **Text** and **Caption** properties, and the **GetWindowText** function.

Parameter	Description
wParam	The size of the buffer.
lParam	An address of the buffer to load with the window text.

■ WM_GETTEXTLENGTH

VB Declaration   Global Const WM_GETTEXTLENGTH = &HE

Description   Sent to a window to retrieve the window text. Duplicates the functionality of the **GetWindowText-Length** function.

Use with VB   No problem, but is rarely used due to the availability of the Visual Basic **Text** and **Caption** properties, and the **GetWindowTextLength** function.

Parameter	Description
wParam	Not used—set to zero.
lParam	Not used—set to zero.

WM_HSCROLL

VB Declaration   Global Const WM_HSCROLL = &H114

Description   This message is sent to a window when the user clicks on the window's horizontal scroll bar. It is also sent in response to user clicks on a horizontal scroll control. Refer to the section on scroll bars in Chapter 15 for further information.

Use with VB   None.

Use with Subclassing   Can be used to change the behavior of the window or scroll control. For example, if you intercept this message and do not send it to the control, you can manually control the thumb position instead of letting the normal positioning take effect. This could allow you to simulate scrolling through ranges greater than 64k in size.

Parameter	Description
wParam	One of the following constants: **SB_ENDSCROLL**: End of dragging. **SB_LEFT**: Scroll all the way to the left. **SB_LINELEFT**: Scroll one unit to the left. **SB_LINERIGHT**: Scroll one unit to the right. **SB_PAGELEFT**: Scroll one page to the left. **SB_PAGERIGHT**: Scroll one page to the right. **SB_RIGHT**: Scroll all the way to the right. **SB_THUMBPOSITION**: The thumb was dragged and released at the position specified in the low word of **lParam**. The possible values depend on the minimum and maximum settings as set by **SetScrollRange**. **SB_THUMBTRACK**: The thumb is in the process of being dragged. The current thumb position is specified in the low word of **lParam**.
lParam	Low word: As specified in the description of **wParam**. Unused otherwise. High word: If the scroll bar is a control, this is the handle of the control window. Zero otherwise.

WM_ICONERASEBKGND

VB Declaration   Global Const WM_ICONERASEBKGND = &H27

Description   This message is sent to a minimized window before drawing the icon for the window if a class icon is defined.

Use with VB   None.

Use with Subclassing   The default processing for this message uses the background brush or pattern of the parent window. Return zero if you process this message.

Parameter	Description
wParam	The device context on which the icon will be drawn.

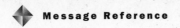

■ WM_INITMENU

VB Declaration   Global Const WM_INITMENU = &H116

Description   This message is sent to a window before its menu is displayed. Refer to Chapter 9 for more information on menus.

Use with VB   None.

Use with Subclassing   Typically used to change the menu before it is displayed in response to the current state of the system. Also used to detect when a pop-up menu is activated in order to update a status bar.

Parameter	Description
wParam	The handle of the menu.

■ WM_INITMENUPOPUP

VB Declaration   Global Const WM_INITMENUPOPUP = &H117

Description   This message is sent to a window before a pop-up menu is displayed. Refer to Chapter 9 for more information on menus.

Use with VB   None.

Use with Subclassing   Typically used to change the menu before it is displayed in response to the current state of the system. Also used to detect when a pop-up menu is activated in order to update a status bar.

Parameter	Description
wParam	Handle of the pop-up menu.
lParam	Low word: The index (position) of the pop-up menu in the top level menu. High word: TRUE (nonzero) if this is the system pop-up menu.

■ WM_KEYDOWN

VB Declaration   Global Const WM_KEYDOWN = &H100

Description   Sent to a window when a key is pressed that is not a system character. This message occurs when a window has the input focus and the Alt key is not pressed.

Use with VB   None. This messages triggers the Visual Basic **KeyDown** event on controls that support it. Refer to the discussion of keyboard control in Chapter 5 for further information.

**Use with
Subclassing**   Allows detection of keyboard input on controls that do not support the **KeyUp**, **KeyDown**, and **KeyPressed** events.

Parameter	Description
wParam	The virtual key number of the character.
lParam	Same as that defined for the **WM_CHAR** message except that bits 29 and 31 are always zero.

■ WM_KEYUP

VB Declaration   `Global Const WM_KEYUP = &H101`

Description   Sent to a window when a key is released that is not a system character. This message occurs when a window has the input focus and the Alt key is not pressed.

Use with VB   None. This messages triggers the Visual Basic **KeyUp** event on controls that support it. Refer to the discussion of keyboard control in Chapter 5 for further information.

**Use with
Subclassing**   Allows detection of keyboard input on controls that do not support the **KeyUp**, **KeyDown**, and **KeyPressed** events.

Parameter	Description
wParam	The virtual key number of the character.
lParam	Same as that defined for the **WM_CHAR** message except that bit 29 is always zero and bit 31 is always one.

■ WM_KILLFOCUS

VB Declaration   `Global Const WM_KILLFOCUS = &H8`

Description   This message is sent to a window before it loses the input focus.

Use with VB   None.

**Use with
Subclassing**   Frequently used to destroy the caret when custom carets are used. Refer to the discussion of caret control in Chapter 5 for further information.

Parameter	Description
lParam	Low word: The handle of the window gaining the focus. May be zero.

Comments   This differs from the Visual Basic **LostFocus** event, which actually occurs after the control has already lost the focus.

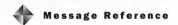

■ WM_LBUTTONDBLCLK

VB Declaration   Global Const WM_LBUTTONDBLCLK = &H203

Description   This message is sent to a window when the left mouse button is double clicked inside a window. The window must belong to a class that has the **CS_DBLCLKS** style set.

Use with VB   May be used to simulate a mouse action. For example, sending a **WM_LBUTTONDBLCLK** message to a control will cause the control to behave as if it had actually been double clicked. In order to use this successfully, you should simulate the entire sequence that is received by a control being double clicked. This consists of a **WM_LBUTTONDOWN** message followed by a **WM_LBUTTONDBLCLK** message and a **WM_LBUTTONUP** message.

Use with Subclassing   Very handy for detecting double clicks in controls that do not support the **DblClk** event.

Parameter	Description
wParam	A combination of one or more of the following constants indicating the state of the shift, control keys, and other mouse buttons: **MK_CONTROL**: The control key is pressed. **MK_LBUTTON**: The left mouse button is down. **MK_MBUTTON**: The middle mouse button is down. **MK_RBUTTON**: The right mouse button is down. **MK_SHIFT**: The shift key is down.
lParam	Low word: The X coordinate of the cursor in window client coordinates. High word: The Y coordinate of the cursor in window client coordinates.

■ WM_LBUTTONDOWN

VB Declaration   Global Const WM_LBUTTONDOWN = &H201

Description   This message is sent to a window when the left mouse button is pressed inside a window.

Use with VB   May be used to simulate a mouse action. For example, sending a **WM_LBUTTONDOWN** message to a button control followed by a **WM_LBUTTONUP** message will cause the control to behave as if it had actually been clicked.

Use with Subclassing   Useful for detecting mouse events in controls that do not support the **MouseDown** event.

Parameter	Description
wParam	A combination of one or more of the following constants: **MK_CONTROL**: The control key is pressed. **MK_MBUTTON**: The middle mouse button is down. **MK_RBUTTON**: The right mouse button is down. **MK_SHIFT**: The shift key is down.
lParam	Low word: The X coordinate of the cursor in window client coordinates. High word: The Y coordinate of the cursor in window client coordinates.

◼ WM_LBUTTONUP

VB Declaration   Global Const WM_LBUTTONUP = &H202

Description   This message is sent to a window when the left mouse button is released inside a window.

Use with VB   May be used to simulate a mouse action. For example, sending a **WM_LBUTTONDOWN** message to a button control followed by a **WM_LBUTTONUP** message will cause the control to behave as if it had actually been clicked.

Use with Subclassing   Useful for detecting mouse events in controls that do not support the **MouseUp** event.

Parameter	Description
wParam	Same as for the **WM_LBUTTONDOWN** message.
lParam	Same as for the **WM_LBUTTONDOWN** message.

◼ WM_MBUTTONDBLCLK

VB Declaration   Global Const WM_MBUTTONDBLCLK = &H209

Description   This message is sent to a window when the center mouse button is double clicked inside a window. The window must belong to a class that has the **CS_DBLCLKS** style set.

Use with VB   May be used to simulate a mouse action. For example, sending a **WM_MBUTTONDBLCLK** message to a control will cause the control to behave as if it had actually been double clicked with the middle mouse button. In order to use this successfully, you should simulate the entire sequence that is received by a control being double clicked. This consists of a **WM_MBUTTONDOWN** message followed by a **WM_MBUTTONDBLCLK** message and a **WM_MBUTTONUP** message.

Use with Subclassing   Useful for detecting double clicks in controls that do not support the **DblClk** event and for mouse buttons other than the left mouse button.

Parameter	Description
wParam	Same as for the **WM_LBUTTONDBLCLK** message.
lParam	Same as for the **WM_LBUTTONDBLCLK** message.

◼ WM_MBUTTONDOWN

VB Declaration   Global Const WM_MBUTTONDOWN = &H207

Description   This message is sent to a window when the center mouse button is pressed inside a window.

Use with VB   May be used to simulate a mouse action. For example, sending a **WM_MBUTTONDOWN** message to a control followed by a **WM_MBUTTONUP** message will cause the control to behave as if it had actually been clicked with the middle mouse button.

Use with Subclassing

Useful for detecting mouse events in controls that do not support the **MouseDown** event.

Parameter	Description
wParam	A combination of one or more of the following constants: **MK_CONTROL**: The control key is pressed. **MK_LBUTTON**: The left mouse button is down. **MK_RBUTTON**: The right mouse button is down. **MK_SHIFT**: The shift key is down.
lParam	Low word: The X coordinate of the cursor in window client coordinates. High word: The Y coordinate of the cursor in window client coordinates.

■ WM_MBUTTONUP

VB Declaration   `Global Const WM_MBUTTONUP = &H208`

Description   This message is sent to a window when the center mouse button is released inside a window.

Use with VB   May be used to simulate a mouse action. For example, sending a **WM_MBUTTONDOWN** message to a button control followed by a **WM_MBUTTONUP** message will cause the control to behave as if it had actually been clicked with the middle mouse button.

Use with Subclassing

Useful for detecting mouse events in controls that do not support the **MouseUp** event.

Parameter	Description
wParam	Same as for the **WM_MBUTTONDOWN** message.
lParam	Same as for the **WM_MBUTTONDOWN** message.

■ WM_MDIACTIVATE

VB Declaration   `Global Const WM_MDIACTIVATE = &H222`

Description   This message can be used to activate an MDI child window. It is also sent to MDI child windows when they are activated or deactivated. The active MDI child window is brought to the top of the display order and given the focus if the application is active.

Use with VB   This message must be sent to the MDIClient child window of an MDI form, not the form itself. Use the **GetWindow** function or hWnd property to find the window handle of this child window. Chapter 2 discusses the structure of MDI windows.

**Use with
Subclassing**　　Can be used to monitor the activation of MDI child windows. MDI forms are not part of Visual Basic 1.0.

Sending WM_MDIACTIVATE to the MDIClient Window

Parameter	Description
wParam	The handle of the window to activate.
lParam	Not used—set to zero.

WM_MDIACTIVE as Received by MDI Child Windows

Parameter	Description
wParam	TRUE (nonzer) if the window receiving this message is being activated. FALSE if it is being deactivated.
lParam	Low 16 bits: The window handle of the MDI child window being activated High 16 bits: The window handle of the MDI child window being deactivated.

■ WM_MDICASCADE

VB Declaration　　`Global Const WM_MDICASCADE = &H227`

Description　　This message can be used to cascade the MDI child windows on an MDI form.

Use with VB　　This message must be sent to the MDIClient child window of an MDI form, not the form itself. Use the **GetWindow** function to find the window handle of this child window. Chapter 2 discusses the structure of MDI windows.

　　The Visual Basic **Arrange** method provides this functionality and is easier to use. (MDI forms are not part of Visual Basic 1.0.)

**Use with
Subclassing**　　Not particularly useful.

Parameter	Description
wParam	The constant **MDITILE_SKIPDISABLED** may be specified to prevent the cascade of disabled MDI child windows.
lParam	Not used—set to zero.

■ WM_MDIGETACTIVE

VB Declaration　　`Global Const WM_MDIGETACTIVE = &H229`

Description　　This message can be used to retrieve the window handle of the currently active MDI child window.

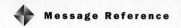

Use with VB   This message must be sent to the MDIClient child window of an MDI form, not the form itself. Use the **GetWindow** function to find the window handle of this child window. Chapter 2 discusses the structure of MDI windows. (MDI forms are not part of Visual Basic 1.0.)

Parameter	Description
wParam	Not used—set to zero.
lParam	Not used—set to zero.

Returns   **Long**—The low 16 bits contain the window handle of the active MDI child window. The high 16 bits is one if the MDI child window is maximized, zero otherwise.

■ WM_MDIICONARRANGE

VB Declaration   `Global Const WM_MDIICONARRANGE = &H228`

Description   This message can be used to arrange the icons of all minimized MDI child windows on the MDI form.

Use with VB   This message must be sent to the MDIClient child window of an MDI form, not the form itself. Use the **GetWindow** function to find the window handle of this child window. Chapter 2 discusses the structure of MDI windows.

The Visual Basic **Arrange** method provides this functionality and is easier to use. (MDI forms are not part of Visual Basic 1.0.)

Parameter	Description
wParam	Not used—set to zero.
lParam	Not used—set to zero.

■ WM_MDIMAXIMIZE

VB Declaration   `Global Const WM_MDIMAXIMIZE = &H225`

Description   This message can be used to maximize an MDI child window within an MDI form.

Use with VB   This message must be sent to the MDIClient child window of an MDI form, not the form itself. Use the **GetWindow** function to find the window handle of this child window. Chapter 2 discusses the structure of MDI windows. (MDI forms are not part of Visual Basic 1.0.)

Parameter	Description
wParam	The window handle of the MDI child window to maximize.
lParam	Not used—set to zero.

■ WM_MDINEXT

VB Declaration   `Global Const WM_MDINEXT = &H224`

Description   This message can be used to activate the next or previous MDI child window within an MDI form.

Use with VB   This message must be sent to the MDIClient child window of an MDI form, not the form itself. Use the **GetWindow** function to find the window handle of this child window. Chapter 2 discusses the structure of MDI windows. (MDI forms are not part of Visual Basic 1.0.)

Parameter	Description
wParam	The window handle of the active MDI child window.
lParam	Zero if the next MDI child window should be activated, nonzero if the previous MDI child window should be activated.

■ WM_MDIRESTORE

VB Declaration   Global Const WM_MDIRESTORE = &H223

Description   This message can be used to restore a minimized or maximized MDI child window to its previous state.

Use with VB   This message must be sent to the MDIClient child window of an MDI form, not the form itself. Use the **GetWindow** function to find the window handle of this child window. Chapter 2 discusses the structure of MDI windows. (MDI forms are not part of Visual Basic 1.0.)

Parameter	Description
wParam	The window handle of the MDI child window to restore.
lParam	Not used—set to zero.

■ WM_MDITILE

VB Declaration   Global Const WM_MDITILE = &H226

Description   This message can be used to tile MDI child windows within an MDI form.

Use with VB   This message must be sent to the MDIClient child window of an MDI form, not the form itself. Use the **GetWindow** function to find the window handle of this child window. Chapter 2 discusses the structure of MDI windows.
The Visual Basic **Arrange** method provides the same functionality and is easier to use. (MDI forms are not part of Visual Basic 1.0.)

Parameter	Description
wParam	One of the following flags: **MDITILE_HORIZONTAL**: Tiles windows horizontally. **MDITILE_SKIPDISABLED**: Prevents tiling of disabled windows. **MDITILE_VERTICAL**: Tiles windows vertically.
lParam	Not used—set to zero.

■ WM_MENUCHAR

VB Declaration Global Const WM_MENUCHAR = &H120

Description This message is sent to a window any time a character is entered while a menu is displayed and the character does not match a mnemonic (underlined) character for a menu entry. Refer to Chapter 9 for a detailed description of menus.

Use with VB None.

Use with Subclassing Typically used to allow mnemonic access to bitmap entries in a menu. Return one of the following values in the high order word: zero if the character should be discarded and a short beep sounded on the speaker, one if Windows should close the menu, and two if the item specified in the low order word should be selected.

Parameter	Description
wParam	The ASCII value of the character.
lParam	Low word: The constant **MF_POPUP** if the menu is a pop-up menu, **MF_SYSMENU** if the menu is a system menu. High word: The handle of the menu.

■ WM_MENUSELECT

VB Declaration Global Const WM_MENUSELECT = &H11F

Description This message is sent to a window when the user selects a menu entry. Refer to Chapter 9 for a detailed description of menus.

Use with VB None.

Use with Subclassing Typically used to update a status bar as the user selects different entries in a menu.

Parameter	Description
wParam	The command identifier of the menu entry, or a menu handle if the entry is a pop-up menu.
lParam	Low word: A menu entry flag made up of one or more of the **MF_** constants defined in Chapter 9. High word: If the **MF_SYSMENU** flag is specified in the low word, this is the handle of the system menu.

Comments When a menu is closed, wParam will be zero and the low word of lParam will be &HFFFF.

■ WM_MOUSEACTIVATE

VB Declaration Global Const WM_MOUSEACTIVATE = &H21

Description This message is sent to an inactive window when the user clicks a mouse button over the window.

Use with VB   None.

Use with Subclassing   Provides additional control over whether a window should be activated.

Parameter	Description
wParam	A handle to the top level window for the application of the window being activated.
lParam	Low word: A hit test code as defined in the return value of the **WM_NCHITTEST** message. High word: The value of the mouse message that caused this message.

Comments   The return value to this message is a constant that specifies the action to take as follows:
MA_ACTIVATE: The window is activated.
MA_NOACTIVATE: The window is not activated.
MA_ACTIVATEANDEAT: The window is activated and the mouse message that caused it is discarded.
MA_NOACTIVATEANDEAT: The window is not activated and the mouse message that caused it is discarded.

■ WM_MOUSEMOVE

VB Declaration   `Global Const WM_MOUSEMOVE = &H200`

Description   This message is sent to a window when the mouse moves over the window or when the window has set the capture for the mouse cursor.

Use with VB   None.

Use with Subclassing   Frequently used for detecting the positioning of the mouse over a control.

Parameter	Description
wParam	A combination of one or more of the following constants indicating the state of the shift, control keys, and other mouse buttons: **MK_CONTROL**: The control key is pressed. **MK_LBUTTON**: The left mouse button is down. **MK_MBUTTON**: The middle mouse button is down. **MK_RBUTTON**: The right mouse button is down. **MK_SHIFT**: The shift key is down.
lParam	Low word: The X coordinate of the cursor in window client coordinates. High word: The Y coordinate of the cursor in window client coordinates.

■ WM_MOVE

VB Declaration   `Global Const WM_MOVE = &H3`

Description   This message is sent to a window when it has been moved.

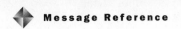

Parameter	Description
lParam	Low word: The X coordinate of the top left corner of the window. High word: The Y coordinate of the top left corner of the window. These values are in window client coordinates for child windows, and screen coordinates for pop-up and top-level windows.

Use with VB   None.

■ WM_NCCREATE

VB Declaration   `Global Const WM_NCCREATE = &H81`

Description   This is the first message sent to a window. This is the only time when the style of a window may be changed and guaranteed to take effect properly.

Use with VB   None.

Use with Subclassing   Difficult, as it is hard to obtain a handle for a newly created window to use in subclassing.

Parameter	Description
wParam	Not used—set to zero.
lParam	The address of the **CREATESTRUCT** structure for this window.

■ WM_NCHITTEST

VB Declaration   `Global Const WM_NCHITTEST = &H84`

Description   Used to determine what part of the nonclient area of a window contains the mouse cursor.

Use with VB   None.

Use with Subclassing   Usually used to examine the result after default processing occurs. The available areas are described by the constants beginning with the **HT** prefix in the file APICONST.TXT. These constants are self-explanatory.

Parameter	Description
wParam	Not used—set to zero.
lParam	Low word: The horizontal position of the cursor in screen coordinates. High word: The vertical position of the cursor in screen coordinates.

■ WM_PAINT

VB Declaration   `Global Const WM_PAINT = &HF`

Description   This message is sent to a window when it is time for the window to update its client area.

Use with VB	This message triggers the Visual Basic **Paint** event.
Use with Subclassing	This is sometimes used to perform additional drawing on the window after the default processing for painting the window is complete.

■ WM_PALETTECHANGED

VB Declaration	`Global Const WM_PALETTECHANGED = &H311`
Description	This message is sent to all top level windows when the system palette has been changed.
Use with VB	Refer to the discussion of color palettes in Chapter 16.
Use with Subclassing	A window that uses color palettes will typically either realize its own palette (unless **wParam** is the handle of this window), or call **UpdateWindows** to update its display on receipt of this message.

Parameter	Description
wParam	The handle of the window that caused the palette to change.

■ WM_PALETTEISCHANGING

VB Declaration	`Global Const WM_PALETTEISCHANGING = &H310`
Description	This message is sent to an application to notify it that the system palette may have been changed due to another window realizing its logical palette.
Use with VB	None.

Parameter	Description
wParam	The handle of the window that is about to realize its palette.

■ WM_PARENTNOTIFY

VB Declaration	`Global Const WM_PARENTNOTIFY = &H210`
Description	Notifies a parent window when certain events take place in a child window unless the **WS_EX_NO-PARENTNOTIFY** flag is set in the window's extended style.
Use with VB	None.

Parameter	Description
wParam	The number of the message that has been received by the child window. This will be **WM_CREATE, WM_DESTROY, WM_LBUT-TONDOWN, WM_MBUTTONDOWN,** or **WM_RBUTTONDOWN.**

lParam   Low word: The handle of the child window if **wParam** is **WM_CRE-ATE** or **WM_DESTROY**. Otherwise the X coordinate of the cursor. High word: The ID number of the child window if **wParam** is **WM_CREATE** or **WM_DESTROY**. Otherwise the Y coordinate of the cursor.

■ WM_PASTE

VB Declaration   Global Const WM_PASTE = &H302

Description   This message can be sent to a text box or combo box to paste the clipboard text into the control.

Use with VB   No problem. This is equivalent to the Visual Basic commands:

Text1.SelText = Clipboard.GetText

Parameter	Description
wParam	Not used—set to zero.
lParam	Not used—set to zero.

Comments   This function only has an effect if the clipboard contains text in the **CF_TEXT** format.

■ WM_POWER

VB Declaration   Global Const WM_POWER = &H48

Description   This message is sent to all top level windows to inform them that the system is entering or leaving a power conservation state. This is typically used only on battery operated computers. Not all portable computers support this message.

Use with VB   None.

Parameter	Description
wParam	One of the following constants: **PWR_SUSPENDREQUEST**: System is about to be suspended or placed in a power conservation mode. You can return constant **PWR_FAIL** to prevent the system from entering the suspended condition, and should return **PWR_OK** otherwise. **PWR_SUSPENDRESUME**: System is resuming normal operation. **PWR_CRITICALRESUME**: System is resuming operation but a **PWR_SUSPENDREQUEST** message had not been sent.

■ WM_QUERYDRAGICON

VB Declaration   Global Const WM_QUERYDRAGICON = &H37

Description   This message is sent to windows that do not have a class icon defined in order to display an icon.

Use with VB	None. Visual Basic draws the icon for a form on receipt of this message.
Use with Subclassing	Can be used to take over drawing of the form icon from VB when a form is minimized. To do so, do not allow default processing of the message. Return a cursor or icon handle in the low word of the result. The cursor or icon must be compatible with the display.

■ WM_QUERYENDSESSION

VB Declaration	Global Const WM_QUERYENDSESSION = &H11
Description	This message is sent to all top level windows to query if it is all right to end the Windows session.
Use with VB	None.
Use with Subclassing	Return TRUE if the application can be terminated, zero otherwise. A **WM_ENDSESSION** message will follow to inform the window if the Windows session is actually ending.

■ WM_QUERYNEWPALETTE

VB Declaration	Global Const WM_QUERYNEWPALETTE = &H30F
Description	This message is sent to a window that is about to receive the input focus to allow it to realize its logical palette.
Use with VB	Refer to the discussion of color palettes in Chapter 16.
Use with Subclassing	A window that uses color palettes will typically realize its own palette at this time.

■ WM_QUERYOPEN

VB Declaration	Global Const WM_QUERYOPEN = &H13
Description	This message is sent to a minimized window when the user has requested that the window be restored to its previous position and size.
Use with VB	None.
Use with Subclassing	Allows the program to determine if the window should actually be restored or not. Return TRUE if the window can be restored, zero otherwise. The default operation is to return TRUE.

■ WM_RBUTTONDBLCLK

VB Declaration   Global Const WM_RBUTTONDBLCLK = &H206

Description   This message is sent to a window when the right mouse button is double clicked inside a window. The window must belong to a class that has the **CS_DBLCLKS** style set.

Use with VB   May be used to simulate a mouse action. For example, sending a **WM_RBUTTONDBLCLK** message to a control will cause the control to behave as if it had actually been double clicked with the right mouse button. In order to use this successfully, you should simulate the entire sequence that is received by a control being double clicked. This consists of a **WM_RBUTTON-DOWN** message followed by a **WM_RBUTTONDBLCLK** message and a **WM_RBUTTONUP** message.

Use with Subclassing   Useful for detecting double clicks in controls that do not support the **DblClk** event and for mouse buttons other than the left mouse button.

Parameter	Description
wParam	Same as for the **WM_LBUTTONDBLCLK** message.
lParam	Same as for the **WM_LBUTTONDBLCLK** message.

■ WM_RBUTTONDOWN

VB Declaration   Global Const WM_RBUTTONDOWN = &H204

Description   This message is sent to a window when the right mouse button is pressed inside a window.

Use with VB   May be used to simulate a mouse action. For example, sending a **WM_RBUTTONDOWN** message to a control followed by a **WM_RBUTTONUP** message will cause the control to behave as if it had actually been clicked with the right mouse button.

Use with Subclassing   Useful for detecting mouse events in controls that do not support the **MouseDown** event.

Parameter	Description
wParam	A combination of one or more of the following constants: **MK_CONTROL**: The control key is pressed. **MK_LBUTTON**: The left mouse button is down. **MK_MBUTTON**: The center mouse button is down. **MK_SHIFT**: The shift key is down.
lParam	Low word: The X coordinate of the cursor in window client coordinates. High word: The Y coordinate of the cursor in window client coordinates.

■ WM_RBUTTONUP

VB Declaration   Global Const WM_RBUTTONUP = &H205

Description   This message is sent to a window when the right mouse button is released inside a window.

Use with VB   May be used to simulate a mouse action. For example, sending a **WM_RBUTTONDOWN** message to a button control followed by a **WM_RBUTTONUP** message will cause the control to behave as if it had actually been clicked with the right mouse button.

Use with Subclassing   Useful for detecting mouse events in controls that do not support the **MouseUp** event.

Parameter	Description
wParam	Same as for the **WM_MBUTTONDOWN** message.
lParam	Same as for the **WM_MBUTTONDOWN** message.

■ WM_SETCURSOR

VB Declaration   Global Const WM_SETCURSOR = &H20

Description   This message is sent to a window when the mouse is over the window, and no other window has the mouse capture.

Use with VB   None.

Use with Subclassing   Can be used to implement custom cursors in Visual Basic. Return TRUE if a cursor has been selected.

Parameter	Description
wParam	The handle of the window that contains the cursor.
lParam	Low word: A hit test code as defined by the return values of the **WM_NCHITTEST** message. High word: The number of the mouse message that caused this message.

■ WM_SETFOCUS

VB Declaration   Global Const WM_SETFOCUS = &H7

Description   This message is sent to a window after it receives the input focus.

Use with VB   None.

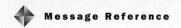

Use with
Subclassing   Frequently used to create the caret when custom carets are used. Refer to the discussion of caret control in Chapter 5 for further information.

Parameter	Description
lParam	Low word: The handle of the window losing the focus. May be zero.

◼ WM_SETFONT

VB Declaration   `Global Const WM_SETFONT = &H30`

Description   Sets a logical font as the font to be used in a control. Logical fonts are described in Chapter 10.

Use with VB   Works with standard Visual Basic controls; however, the standard Visual Basic font properties are a preferred way to select fonts.

Parameter	Description
wParam	A handle to a logical font to use in this control. Zero to select the default system font.
lParam	Low word: TRUE (nonzero) to redraw the control when the font is changed.

◼ WM_SETREDRAW

VB Declaration   `Global Const WM_SETREDRAW = &HB`

Description   This function controls the redraw operation on a control. Normally, each time a change is made to a control—for example, adding a string to a list box—the control is immediately updated to reflect the new state of the control. While this ensures that the current contents of a control are always displayed, it can slow down the process of changing a control when a large number of changes are to be processed at once. This message can be used to turn off the redraw state. This allows changes to be made to a control without updating the control display. Once the redraw state is reenabled, the control can be updated.

Use with VB   Extremely useful for text, combo box, and list box controls.

Parameter	Description
wParam	TRUE (nonzero) to turn redraw on, zero to turn it off.
lParam	Not used—set to zero.

Comments   To take advantage of this function you may need to perform the modifications using Windows messages as described in Chapters 18 and 19 due to the fact that most modifications performed with Visual Basic property access cause an immediate update regardless of the state of the **Redraw** flag.

Normally under Windows, setting the **Redraw** flag back to TRUE after making modifications does not update the control—an explicit redraw operation is necessary using either the VB **Refresh** command or the Windows **InvalidateRect** function. Visual Basic seems to detect the setting of the **Redraw** flag using this message to automatically update the display.

Listing 17.1 demonstrates use of the **WM_SETREDRAW** flag when performing list box modifications. This sample code is triggered by a command button named Command1 and assumes that a list box named List1 is present on the form. The **WM_SETREDRAW** and **LB_ADDSTRING** messages are defined in the file APICONST.TXT.

Listing 17.1   Using the Redraw Flag with a VB List Box

```
Sub Command1_Click ()
    Dim x%

    di& = SendMessageByNum(agGetControlHwnd%(list1), WM_SETREDRAW, 0, 0&)
    For x% = 1 To 20
        di& = SendMessageByString(agGetControlHwnd%( list1), LB_ADDSTRING, 0, ⇔
        "This is string " + Str$(x%))
        ' list1.AddItem "This is string " + Str$(x%)
    Next x%
    di& = SendMessageByNum(agGetControlHwnd%(list1), WM_SETREDRAW, 1, 0&)
    ' VB list box does a refresh on receipt of WM_SETREDRAW
    ' so the line below is not necessary
    ' list1.Refresh
End Sub
```

■ WM_SETTEXT

VB Declaration   `Global Const WM_SETTEXT = &HC`

Description   Sent to a window to set the window text. Duplicates the functionality of the **SetWindowText** function.

Use with VB   No problem, but is rarely used due to the availability of the Visual Basic **Text** and **Caption** properties, and the **SetWindowText** function.

Parameter	Description
lParam	The string to set into the control.

■ WM_SHOWWINDOW

VB Declaration   `Global Const WM_SHOWWINDOW = &H18`

Description   This message is sent to a window when it is hidden or displayed.

Use with VB   None.

Use with Subclassing   Can be used to determine a change in the display state of a window.

Parameter	Description
wParam	TRUE (nonzero) if the window is being shown, zero if it is being hidden.

Parameter	Description
lParam	One of the following constants: **SW_PARENTCLOSING**: Indicates that the parent window is being hidden or minimized. **SW_PARENTOPENING**: Indicates that the parent window is being displayed.

■ WM_SIZE

VB Declaration   `Global Const WM_SIZE = &H5`

Description   This message is sent to a window when its size has been changed.

Use with VB   This message is used to trigger the Visual Basic **Resize** event.

Use with Subclassing   This can be used to restrict a control to certain sizes by sending a **MoveWindow** API call during the event processing.

Parameter	Description
wParam	One of the following constants: **SIZE_MAXIMIZED**: The window is maximized. **SIZE_MINIMIZED**: The window is minimized. **SIZE_RESTORED**: The window is restored. **SIZE_MAXHIDE**: Another window is being maximized. **SIZE_MAXSHOW**: Another maximized window has been restored.
lParam	Low word: The new width of the window. High word: The new height of the window. These values are in window client coordinates for child windows, and screen coordinates for pop-up and top level windows.

■ WM_SPOOLERSTATUS

VB Declaration   `Global Const WM_SPOOLERSTATUS = &H2A`

Description   This message is sent to applications to inform them that a print job has been added or removed from the print queue.

Use with VB   None.

Parameter	Description
lParam	Low word: The number of jobs remaining in the queue.

■ WM_SYSCHAR

VB Declaration   `Global Const WM_SYSCHAR = &H106`

Description   This is similar to the **WM_CHAR** message except that it detects Alt key combinations (characters entered when the Alt key is pressed) and characters entered when no window has the focus (in which case the message is sent to the active window).

■ WM_SYSCOLORCHANGE

VB Declaration   Global Const WM_SYSCOLORCHANGE = &H15

Description   This message is sent to applications to inform them that a system color has changed. System colors are those used for standard Windows objects.

Use with VB   None.

Use with Subclassing   Update any drawing that used colors based on the WIN.INI initialization file entries for window colors.

■ WM_SYSCOMMAND

VB Declaration   Global Const WM_SYSCOMMAND = &H112

Description   This message is sent to an application when a system menu command has been selected by the user.

Use with VB   It is possible to execute system menu commands under program control by posting these messages to a form.

Use with Subclassing   Can be used to intercept system menu commands.

Parameter	Description
wParam	The system command posted. Refer to the constants with the **SC_** prefix in the file APICONST.TXT. They are self-explanatory.
lParam	If the mouse was used to trigger this system menu command, the X mouse coordinate will be in the low 16 bits of **lParam** and the Y mouse coordinate will be in the high 16 bits of **lParam**. Otherwise this parameter is not used.

■ WM_SYSDEADCHAR

VB Declaration   Global Const WM_SYSDEADCHAR = &H107

Description   This is similar to the **WM_CHAR** message except that it indicates a character that is to be combined with another character; for example, the accent mark used on many non-English character sets. Refer to the **WM_CHAR** message for information on use with VB, subclassing, and parameters. This message only detects Alt key combinations or characters entered when no window has the focus.

■ WM_SYSKEYDOWN

VB Declaration   Global Const WM_SYSKEYDOWN = &H104

Description   Sent to a window when a key is pressed that is a system character. This message occurs when no window has the input focus or if the Alt key is pressed.

Use with VB   None. Refer to the discussion of keyboard control in Chapter 5 for further information.

Use with Subclassing   Allows detection of Alt key combinations.

Parameter	Description
wParam	The virtual key number of the character.
lParam	Same as that defined for the **WM_CHAR** message except that bit 31 is always zero. If bit 29 is zero, no window has the focus and this message is being received by the active window.

■ WM_SYSKEYUP

VB Declaration   Global Const WM_SYSKEYUP = &H105

Description   Sent to a window when a key is released that is a system character. This message occurs when no window has the input focus or if the Alt key is pressed.

Use with VB   None. Refer to the discussion of keyboard control in Chapter 5 for further information.

Use with Subclassing   Allows detection of Alt key combinations.

Parameter	Description
wParam	The virtual key number of the character.
lParam	Same as that defined for the **WM_CHAR** message except that bit 31 is always one. If bit 29 is zero, no window has the focus and this message is being received by the active window.

■ WM_TIMECHANGE

VB Declaration   Global Const WM_TIMECHANGE = &H1E

Description   This message is sent to all top level windows in the system when the system time has been changed.

Use with VB   If the system time is changed from Visual Basic, this message should be sent via the **SendMessage** function to all windows.

**Use with
Subclassing**   Useful for applications that display the time.

Parameter	Description
wParam	Not used—set to zero.
lParam	Not used—set to zero.

■ WM_UNDO

VB Declaration   `Global Const WM_UNDO = &H304`

Description   This message can be sent to a text box to undo the effect of the most recent editing operation.

Use with VB   No problem; however, this function does not undo changes made by assigning a string to the **Text** or **SelText** property of the text box. It will undo the effects of the **WM_CUT** or **WM_CLEAR** message, and will undo the most recent keyboard operation.

Parameter	Description
wParam	Not used—set to zero.
lParam	Not used—set to zero.

■ WM_VSCROLL

VB Declaration   `Global Const WM_VSCROLL = &H115`

Description   This message is sent to a window when the user clicks on the window's vertical scroll bar. It is also sent in response to user clicks on a vertical scroll control. Refer to the section on scroll bars in Chapter 15 for further information.

Use with VB   None.

**Use with
Subclassing**   Can be used to change the behavior of the window or scroll control. For example, if you intercept this message and do not send it to the control, you can manually control the thumb position instead of letting the normal positioning take effect. This could allow you to simulate scrolling through ranges greater than 64k in size.

Parameter	Description
wParam	One of the following constants: **SB_BOTTOM**: Scroll all the way to the bottom. **SB_ENDSCROLL**: End of dragging. **SB_LINEDOWN**: Scroll one unit down. **SB_LINEUP**: Scroll one unit up. **SB_PAGEDOWN**: Scroll one page down. **SB_PAGEUP**: Scroll one page up. **SB_THUMBPOSITION**: The thumb was dragged and released at the position specified in the low word of **lParam**. The possible values depend on the minimum and maximum settings as set by **SetScrollRange**.

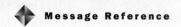

Parameter	Description
wParam (continued)	**SB_THUMBTRACK**: The thumb is in the process of being dragged. The current thumb position is specified in the low word of **lParam**. **SB_TOP**: Scroll all the way to the top.
lParam	Low word: As specified in the description of **wParam**. Unused otherwise. High word: If the scroll bar is a control, this is the handle of the control window. Zero otherwise.

■ WM_WINDOWPOSCHANGED

VB Declaration   `Global Const WM_WINDOWPOSCHANGED = &H47`

Description   This message is sent to a window whose size or position is changed after a call to the **SetWindow-Pos** function.

Use with VB   None.

Use with Subclassing   If this message is handled directly, it is up to the application to send **WM_SIZE** and **WM_MOVE** messages to the window.

Parameter	Description
lParam	The address of a **WINDOWPOS** function. Refer to the Comments section for a definition of this structure.

Comments   The **WINDOWPOS** function is defined as follows:

```
Type WINDOWPOS
    hwnd As Integer
    hwndInsertAfter As Integer
    x As Integer
    y As Integer
    cx As Integer
    cy As Integer
    flags As Integer
End Type
```

The meanings of these parameters are the same as the definitions of the parameters to the **SetWindowPos** function defined in Chapter 4.

■ WM_WINDOWPOSCHANGING

VB Declaration   `Global Const WM_WINDOWPOSCHANGING = &H46`

Description   This message is sent to a window whose size or position is changed after a call to the **SetWindow-Pos** function.

Use with VB   None.

Use with Subclassing

Changes made to the **WINDOWPOS** structure referred to by the **lParam** parameter at this time will be effective.

Parameter	Description
lParam	The address of a **WINDOWPOS** function. Refer to the Comments section of the **WM_WINDOWPOSCHANGED** message for a definition of this structure.

■ WM_WININICHANGE

VB Declaration   `Global Const WM_WININICHANGE = &H1A`

Description   This message is sent to all top level windows when a change is made to the WIN.INI initialization file.

Use with VB   This message should be sent to all windows via the **SendMessage** function when changes are made to the WIN.INI file. Refer to the description of the **WriteProfileString** function in Chapter 13 for further information.

Use with Subclassing

Useful for programs that base any part of their display or execution on the contents of the WIN.INI file.

Parameter	Description
lParam	A string containing the name of the section that has been changed.

18

Edit Control Messages

THIS CHAPTER DISCUSSES MESSAGES THAT CAN BE USED WITH VISUAL basic controls that are based on the Windows edit control, including the Visual Basic text control. These messages can significantly extend the capabilities of these controls. A sample program, TextMsgs, illustrates the use of many of these messages.

The Text Control

The text control is typically used for entering and editing text. It is subclassed from the standard Windows edit control, so it supports all of the edit control messages. The techniques presented here will also work on other controls provided by third-party vendors that are based on the Windows edit control class.

The combo box control is a combination of a text control and list box. It supports combo box messages that are very similar to the edit control messages described in this chapter. These messages are reviewed in Chapter 19.

The edit control messages are divided into a number of functional groups, which are described below.

Undo Capability

Edit controls maintain a single-level undo buffer for most editing operations. This means that in most cases the previous editing operation can be reversed. The messages listed in Table 18.1 relate to the use of the undo buffer in edit controls.

Table 18.1   **Edit Control Undo Messages**

Message	Description
EM_CANUNDO	Determines if the last editing operation can be reversed.
EM_EMPTYUNDOBUFFER	Clears the control's undo buffer, making it impossible to undo the previous editing operation.
EM_UNDO	Reverses the previous editing operation.

Text Formatting

The edit control messages provide a number of capabilities for internal formatting of data within the control.

Multiline edit controls maintain information internally regarding where soft line breaks occur. A soft line break is one that is inserted by the edit control in order to make the text fit within the control. Hard line breaks are those specified by the programmer by inserting a CR-LF (carriage return-line feed combination) into the text.

Edit controls keep track of soft line breaks by inserting a CR-CR-LF character sequence into the text string. Normally these soft line breaks are hidden from the programmer—they are not included in the text retrieved using the Visual Basic **Text** property.

You can force the edit control to include the soft line break characters in the text string by sending the **EM_FMTLINES** message to the control.

Each edit control has a formatting rectangle associated with it. On close examination of this type of control, you can see that the text does not extend all the way to the side of the control window. The formatting rectangle is the rectangle within the edit control that contains the text. Windows provides functions that allow you to determine the size of the formatting rectangle or to change it.

The edit control messages also provide the ability to set flexible tab stops for text within the control.

The messages listed in Table 18.2 are related to text formatting in edit controls.

Table 18.2   **Text Formatting Messages for Edit Controls**

Message	Description
EM_FMTLINES	Determines whether to include soft line breaks in retrieved text strings.
EM_GETRECT	Retrieves the formatting rectangle for an edit control.
EM_LIMITTEXT	Limits the length of text in an edit control.
EM_SETRECT	Sets the formatting rectangle for an edit control.
EM_SETRECTNP	Same as **EM_SETRECT** except that the control is not redrawn.
EM_SETTABSTOPS	Sets tab spacing within an edit control.

Selection and Display

The Visual Basic text control provides a flexible set of properties for controlling text selection and display. Version 2.0 added properties to support some of the more requested features such as password characters and setting of a maximum text length. As always, it is generally better and easier to use a VB property when one is available rather than a Windows message.

There are, however, several areas where messages still provide significantly improved capability when compared with the standard VB properties. This is especially true in the area of line vs. character orientation on multiline edit controls.

The contents of an edit control can be thought of as a single string. This is the string that is set and retrieved using the Visual Basic **Text** property. Positions within the edit control can be described as an offset to a character from the start of the string. With multiline edit controls, the control breaks the string into lines, but this process is hidden from the programmer who still sees the text as a single string.

Windows provides a set of edit control messages that make it possible to treat a multiline edit control as a series of lines instead of a single string. Messages are provided that let you determine the number of lines in the control, the length of each line, and the offset of the first character in a given line from the start of the string. It is possible to retrieve individual lines from the control.

These messages also provide the important capability of determining the number of the first line that is actually visible (though this is supported only for Windows 3.1 and later). This, combined with the line-scrolling message **EM_LINESCROLL**, makes it possible to control most aspects of an edit control's display from a Visual Basic program. One example of where this might be useful is in an edit control to scroll through very large files. The TextMsgs demonstration program discussed later in this chapter illustrates some of the techniques that are possible using these messages.

Table 18.3 lists the selection and display messages that are available for edit controls.

Table 18.3   Selection and Display Messages for Edit Controls

Message	Description
EM_GETFIRSTVISIBLELINE	Determines the first line that is displayed in an edit control.
EM_GETLINE	Retrieves a line from an edit control.
EM_GETLINECOUNT	Determines the number of lines in an edit control.
EM_GETMODIFY	Determines if the contents of an edit control have been changed.
EM_GETPASSWORDCHAR	Retrieves the password character for an edit control.
EM_GETSEL	Determines the start and end locations of a selection in an edit control.
EM_LINEFROMCHAR	Determines the line on which a specified character appears.

Table 18.3   Selection and Display Messages for Edit Controls (Continued)

Message	Description
EM_LINEINDEX	Determines the number of the first character on a specified line.
EM_LINELENGTH	Determines the length of a line.
EM_LINESCROLL	Scroll an edit control.
EM_REPLACESEL	Replaces the current selection in an edit control with the specified text.
EM_SETMODIFY	Used to set or clear the modification flag for an edit control.
EM_SETPASSWORDCHAR	Sets the password character for the specified control.
EM_SETREADONLY	Used to specify if an edit control is read only or not.
EM_SETSEL	Sets the start and end location of a selection in an edit control.

Example: TextMsgs—A Demonstration of Edit Control Messages

TextMsgs is a program that demonstrates the use of edit control messages to perform a number of operations that are not possible using the standard Visual Basic Text control properties. It emphasizes use of line-oriented access to multiline text controls.

Figure 18.1 shows the runtime screen for the TextMsgs program.

Figure 18.1
TEXTMSGS.FRM
runtime screen

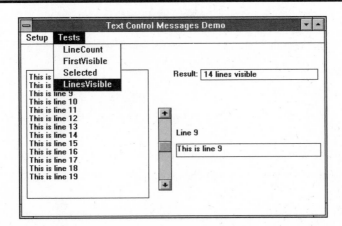

Using TextMsgs

The TextMsgs Setup menu has one entry, FillText, which is used to fill the text box with 20 lines of text for use in the demonstration. The Tests menu has entries for four different tests that can be performed.

The LineCount command determines the total number of lines in the text control and records the result in the **LabelResult** label control. The FirstVisible command displays the number of the first visible line. The Selected command displays the start and end locations of the current selection. The LinesVisible command (illustrated in Figure 18.1) calculates the number of lines that are visible in the text control based on the size of the control and the current font, and displays the result.

The **VScroll1** and **LabelShowline** scroll and label controls demonstrate how the programmer can take control of scrolling for a text control using a standard vertical scroll bar control. The scroll bar is used to select a line to display in the **LabelShowline** label control. If the selected line is not visible, it scrolls the text control to make sure the specified line is displayed.

Project Description

The TextMsgs project includes four files. TEXTMSGS.FRM is the only form used in the program. TEXTMSGS.BAS is the only module in the program and contains the constant type and global definitions. APIDECS.BAS is the type-safe API declaration file provided with this book. APIGUIDE.BAS contains the declarations for the APIGUIDE.DLL dynamic link library.

Listing 18.1 shows the project file for the TextMsgs program.

Listing 18.1 **Project Listing TEXTMSGS.MAK**

```
TEXTMSGS.FRM
TEXTMSGS.BAS
APIDECS.BAS
APIGUIDE.BAS
ProjWinSize=175,439,248,215
ProjWinShow=4
```

Form Description

Listing 18.2 contains the header from file TEXTMSGS.FRM that describes the control setup for the form.

Listing 18.2 Form Description TEXTMSGS.FRM

```
VERSION 2.00
Begin Form TextMsgs
   Caption          =   "Text Control Messages Demo"
   Height           =   4710
   Left             =   1035
   LinkMode         =   1  'Source
   LinkTopic        =   "Form1"
   ScaleHeight      =   4020
   ScaleWidth       =   7365
   Top              =   1140
   Width            =   7485
```

The **VScroll1** control is used to scroll through lines from the **Text1** control. The selected line is displayed in the **LabelShowLine** control.

```
Begin VScrollBar VScroll1
   Height           =   1935
   LargeChange      =   5
   Left             =   3360
   Max              =   1
   TabIndex         =   4
   Top              =   1500
   Width            =   315
End
Begin TextBox Text1
   Height           =   3015
   Left             =   120
   MultiLine        =   -1  'True
   TabIndex         =   0
   Text             =   "Text control example"
   Top              =   600
   Width            =   3015
End
Begin Label LabelShowLine
   BorderStyle      =   1  'Fixed Single
   Caption          =   ""
   Height           =   315
   Left             =   3780
   TabIndex         =   6
   Top              =   2340
   Width            =   3495
End
Begin Label LabelLinenum
   Caption          =   ""
   Height           =   315
   Left             =   3780
   TabIndex         =   5
```

```
    Top              =   1980
    Width            =   1455
End
```

The **LabelResult** label control is used to display the results of the various Tests menu commands.

```
Begin Label LabelResult
    BorderStyle      =   1  'Fixed Single
    Caption          =   ""
    Height           =   255
    Left             =   4380
    TabIndex         =   2
    Top              =   600
    Width            =   2835
End
Begin Label Label1
    Alignment        =   1  'Right Justify
    Caption          =   "Result:"
    Height           =   255
    Left             =   3420
    TabIndex         =   1
    Top              =   600
    Width            =   915
End
Begin Menu MenuSetup
    Caption          =   "Setup"
    Begin Menu MenuFillText
        Caption          =   "FillText"
    End
End
Begin Menu MenuTests
    Caption          =   "Tests"
    Begin Menu MenuLineCount
        Caption          =   "LineCount"
    End
    Begin Menu MenuFirstVisible
        Caption          =   "FirstVisible"
    End
    Begin Menu MenuSelected
        Caption          =   "Selected"
    End
    Begin Menu MenuLinesVisible
        Caption          =   "LinesVisible"
    End
End
End
```

TextMsgs Listings

Module TEXTMSGS.BAS contains the constant declarations and global variables used by the program.

Listing 18.3   Module TEXTMSGS.BAS

```
' TextMsgs program example


Global Const WM_NULL = &H0
Global Const WM_SETREDRAW = &HB
Global Const WM_SETTEXT = &HC
Global Const WM_GETTEXT = &HD
Global Const WM_GETTEXTLENGTH = &HE
Global Const WM_CLOSE = &H10
Global Const WM_SETFONT = &H30
Global Const WM_GETFONT = &H31
Global Const WM_COMMAND = &H111
Global Const WM_CUT = &H300
Global Const WM_COPY = &H301
Global Const WM_PASTE = &H302
Global Const WM_CLEAR = &H303
Global Const WM_UNDO = &H304


Global Const WM_USER = &H400
Global Const EM_GETSEL = WM_USER + 0
Global Const EM_SETSEL = WM_USER + 1
Global Const EM_GETRECT = WM_USER + 2
Global Const EM_SETRECT = WM_USER + 3
Global Const EM_SETRECTNP = WM_USER + 4
Global Const EM_SCROLL = WM_USER + 5
Global Const EM_LINESCROLL = WM_USER + 6
Global Const EM_GETMODIFY = WM_USER + 8
Global Const EM_SETMODIFY = WM_USER + 9
Global Const EM_GETLINECOUNT = WM_USER + 10
Global Const EM_LINEINDEX = WM_USER + 11
Global Const EM_GETTHUMB = WM_USER + 14
Global Const EM_LINELENGTH = WM_USER + 17
Global Const EM_REPLACESEL = WM_USER + 18
Global Const EM_SETFONT = WM_USER + 19
Global Const EM_GETLINE = WM_USER + 20
Global Const EM_LIMITTEXT = WM_USER + 21
Global Const EM_CANUNDO = WM_USER + 22
Global Const EM_UNDO = WM_USER + 23
Global Const EM_FMTLINES = WM_USER + 24
Global Const EM_LINEFROMCHAR = WM_USER + 25
Global Const EM_SETWORDBREAK = WM_USER + 26
```

Listing 18.3 **Module TEXTMSGS.BAS (Continued)**

```
Global Const EM_SETTABSTOPS = WM_USER + 27
Global Const EM_SETPASSWORDCHAR = WM_USER + 28
Global Const EM_EMPTYUNDOBUFFER = WM_USER + 29
Global Const EM_MSGMAX = WM_USER + 30
Global Const EM_GETFIRSTVISIBLELINE = (WM_USER + 30)
Global Const EM_SETREADONLY = (WM_USER + 31)
Global Const EM_SETWORDBREAKPROC = (WM_USER + 32)
Global Const EM_GETWORDBREAKPROC = (WM_USER + 33)
Global Const EM_GETPASSWORDCHAR = (WM_USER + 34)
```

Listing 18.4 **Form Listing TEXTMSGS.FRM**

```
Sub Form_Load ()
    ' Initialize the display line command
    UpdateDisplayLine
End Sub
```

(The form header and object descriptions for this file can be found in Listing 18.2.)

There is no direct way to determine how many lines are actually visible in an edit control; however, Windows provides all the tools necessary to calculate this value. The number of lines displayed obviously depends on two factors: the size of the control and the height of the font used by the control.

In order to determine the size of the control, this function uses the **EM_GETRECT** message to determine the size of the internal formatting rectangle for the text. This allows you to determine the height, in pixels, of the area in which text is displayed.

Determining the height of a font is a bit trickier. Here we take advantage of the **WM_GETFONT** message to retrieve a handle to the logical font that the control is using. The font returned by this message is affected by the Visual Basic font properties, so there is no problem with compatibility with Visual Basic. Next, a device context is obtained for the text control. The **SelectObject** API function is used to select the logical font into the device context. This makes it possible to retrieve the actual text metrics for the font including the font height. Chapter 10 describes this process in detail.

Once the height of the font has been obtained, it is very easy to calculate the number of lines that can actually be displayed by the control.

```
'
' Determines the number of lines actually visible in the
' text control.
```

```
'
Function GetVisibleLines% ()
    Dim rc As RECT
    Dim hdc%
    Dim lfont%, oldfont%
    Dim tm As TEXTMETRIC
    Dim di%

    ' Get the formatting rectangle - this describes the
    ' rectangle in the control in which text is placed.
    lc% = SendMessage(Text1.hWnd, EM_GETRECT, 0, rc)

    ' Get a handle to the logical font used by the control.
    ' The VB font properties are accurately reflected by
    ' this logical font.
    lfont% = SendMessageBynum(Text1.hWnd, WM_GETFONT, 0, 0&)

    ' Get a device context to the text control.
    hdc% = GetDC(Text1.hWnd)

    ' Select in the logical font to obtain the exact font
    ' metrics.
    If lfont% <> 0 Then oldfont% = SelectObject(hdc%, lfont%)

    di% = GetTextMetrics(hdc%, tm)
    ' Select out the logical font
    If lfont% <> 0 Then lfont% = SelectObject(hdc%, oldfont%)

    ' The lines depends on the formatting rectangle and font height
    GetVisibleLines% = (rc.bottom - rc.top) / tm.tmHeight

    ' Release the device context when done.
    di% = ReleaseDC(Text1.hWnd, hdc%)
End Function

' Fill the text control with 20 lines of text
'
Sub MenuFillText_Click ()
    Dim x%
    Dim t$
    For x% = 0 To 19
        t$ = t$ + "This is line" + Str$(x%) + Chr$(13) + Chr$(10)
    Next x%
    Text1.Text = t$

End Sub

'
' Determine the number of the first line visible in the text control
'
Sub MenuFirstVisible_Click ()
    Dim lc%
```

```
    lc% = SendMessageBynum(Text1.hWnd, EM_GETFIRSTVISIBLELINE, 0, 0&)
    LabelResult.Caption = "Line" + Str$(lc%) + " at top"

End Sub


' Determine the number of lines of text in the text control
'
Sub MenuLineCount_Click ()
    Dim lc%
    lc% = SendMessageBynum(Text1.hWnd, EM_GETLINECOUNT, 0, 0&)
    LabelResult.Caption = Str$(lc%) + " lines"
End Sub


' Determine the number of visible lines in the text control.
'
Sub MenuLinesVisible_Click ()
    LabelResult.Caption = Str$(GetVisibleLines()) + " lines visible"
End Sub


' Determine the start and end position of the current selection
'
Sub MenuSelected_Click ()
    Dim ls&
    ls& = SendMessageBynum&(Text1.hWnd, EM_GETSEL, 0, 0&)

    LabelResult.Caption = "Chars" + Str$(CInt(ls& And &HFFFF&)) + " to" + ⇔
    Str$(CInt(ls& / &H10000))


End Sub


' Update the display line information on change
'
Sub Text1_Change ()
    ' Make sure the vertical scroll range matches the number
    ' of lines in the text control
    lc% = SendMessageBynum(Text1.hWnd, EM_GETLINECOUNT, 0, 0&)
    VScroll1.Max = lc% - 1
    UpdateDisplayLine

End Sub
```

The **UpdateDisplayLine** function shows how individual lines can be extracted from an edit control. First the **EM_LINEINDEX** message is used to determine the offset in the edit control string to the first character in the line that you wish to retrieve. The **EM_LINELENGTH** message can then be used to determine the length of the line that contains that character.

The **EM_GETLINE** function requires that the first two bytes in the buffer represent the maximum length of the buffer. This function demonstrates how to load those bytes with the buffer length. Note how the first character contains the low-order byte of the integer and the second character contains the high-order byte. This is consistent with the byte ordering described in Chapter 16.

```
' This function updates the line displayed based on the
' current position of the scroll bar.
'
Sub UpdateDisplayLine ()
    Dim linetoshow%, linelength%
    Dim linebuf$
    Dim lc%
    Dim linechar%

    linetoshow% = VScroll1.Value
    ' Show the number of the line being displayed
    LabelLinenum.Caption = "Line" + Str$(linetoshow%)

    ' Find out the character offset to the first character
    ' in the specified line
    linechar% = SendMessageBynum(Text1.hWnd, EM_LINEINDEX, linetoshow%, 0&)

    ' The character offset is used to determine the length of the line
    ' containing that character.
    lc% = SendMessageBynum(Text1.hWnd, EM_LINELENGTH, linechar%, 0&) + 1

    ' Now allocate a string long enough to hold the result
    linebuf$ = String$(lc% + 2, 0)
    Mid$(linebuf$, 1, 1) = Chr$(lc% And &HFF)
    Mid$(linebuf$, 2, 1) = Chr$(lc% / &H100)

    ' Now get the line
    lc% = SendMessageByString(Text1.hWnd, EM_GETLINE, linetoshow%, linebuf$)
    LabelShowLine.Caption = Left$(linebuf$, /c%)

End Sub

' Whenever the scroll bar changes, display the requested
' line in the LabelShowLine label box
'
Sub VScroll1_Change ()
    Dim lc%
    Dim dl&
    Dim firstvisible%, lastvisible%

    ' Make sure value is in range
    lc% = SendMessageBynum(Text1.hWnd, EM_GETLINECOUNT, 0, 0&)
    If VScroll1.Value > lc% - 1 Then
        VScroll1.Value = lc% - 1
```

```
      Exit Sub
   End If
   UpdateDisplayLine ' Update the display


   ' Get the number of the first and last visible line
   firstvisible% = SendMessageBynum(Text1.hWnd, EM_GETFIRSTVISIBLELINE, 0, 0&)
   lastvisible% = GetVisibleLines%() + firstvisible% - 1

   ' Scroll it into view if necessary
   If (VScroll1.Value < firstvisible%) Then
       dl& = SendMessageBynum(Text1.hWnd, EM_LINESCROLL, 0, ⇔
       CLng(VScroll1.Value - firstvisible%))
   End If
   If (VScroll1.Value > lastvisible%) Then
       dl& = SendMessageBynum(Text1.hWnd, EM_LINESCROLL, 0, ⇔
       CLng(VScroll1.Value - lastvisible%))
   End If


End Sub
```

Notification Messages

Edit controls send **WM_COMMAND** messages to their parent window that notify it when certain events take place. Most of these messages are mapped into Visual Basic events for the VB text control. Those that are not cannot be accessed directly by the Visual Basic programmer, but may prove useful when using the advanced subclassing techniques described in Chapter 17.

All notification messages are sent using the **WM_COMMAND** message to the parent window of the control. The **wParam** parameter always refers to the numeric identifier of the control, a value that is not used in Visual Basic. The **lParam** parameter is divided into two parts. The low word contains the window handle of the control. This can be used to determine which control sent the notification message. The high word contains the notification type. In other words, the **EN_KILLFOCUS** notification would contain the constant **EN_KILLFOCUS** in the high-order word of the **lParam** parameter.

■ EN_CHANGE

VB Declaration   `Global Const EN_CHANGE = &H300`

Description   Sent any time the contents of the edit control change.

Use with VB   This message generates a **Change** event in the standard text control. The message is sent after the changes have already been displayed.

■ EN_ERRSPACE

VB Declaration   `Global Const EN_ERRSPACE = &H500`

Description   Sent any time an editing operation fails because there is insufficient memory to perform the operation.

Use with VB   Visual Basic will trigger this type of error during assignment to the **Text** property through its normal error notification system.

■ EN_HSCROLL

VB Declaration   `Global Const EN_HSCROLL = &H601`

Description   Sent whenever the user clicks anywhere on the horizontal scroll bar belonging to an edit control. This message is sent before the control display is updated.

Use with VB   None.

Use with Subclassing   Could be used to control the behavior of the horizontal scroll bar or to perform other operations when scrolling takes place.

■ EN_KILLFOCUS

VB Declaration   Global Const EN_KILLFOCUS = &H200

Description   Sent when the control loses the input focus.

Use with VB   This message generates the VB **LostFocus** event.

Use with
Subclassing   The Visual Basic **LostFocus** event is posted, so it occurs at some indeterminate time after this message is sent. This means that the VB event cannot be used to destroy a custom caret. Also, this event is not triggered when the focus is lost due to the activation of another application. The **EN_KILLFOCUS** message, however, can be used to provide full support of custom carets and to detect loss of focus in all circumstances.

■ EN_MAXTEXT

VB Declaration   Global Const EN_MAXTEXT = &H501

Description   Sent whenever the user attempts to enter text that exceeds the limit specified by the **EM_LIMIT-TEXT** message or VB **MaxLength** property. This message is also sent when automatic horizontal scrolling is not enabled and the insertion would exceed the width of the control, or automatic vertical scrolling is not enabled and the insertion would exceed the height of the control.

Use with VB   None.

Use with
Subclassing   Could be used to provide a prompt to the user whenever this type of error occurred.

■ EN_SETFOCUS

VB Declaration   Global Const EN_SETFOCUS = &H100

Description   Sent when the control receives the input focus.

Use with VB   This message generates the VB **GotFocus** event.

Use with
Subclassing   The Visual Basic **GotFocus** event is posted, so it occurs at some indeterminate time after this message is sent. This probably won't be a problem, so subclassing this message should not be necessary.

■ EN_UPDATE

VB Declaration   Global Const EN_UPDATE = &H400

Description   Sent before a control displays text that has been changed. This is similar to the **EN_CHANGE** notification except that it occurs before the text is displayed.

Use with VB   None.

Use with Subclassing   Could be used to customize text display for an edit control.

■ EN_VSCROLL

VB Declaration   `Global Const EN_VSCROLL = &H602`

Description   Sent whenever the user clicks anywhere on the vertical scroll bar belonging to an edit control. This message is sent before the control display is updated.

Use with VB   None.

Use with Subclassing   Could be used to control the behavior of the vertical scroll bar or to perform other operations when scrolling takes place.

Edit Control Messages

The following messages can be used to control the operation of any Visual Basic control based on the Windows edit class. This includes the standard Visual Basic text control.

As usual, the return value refers to the value returned by the **SendMessage** function used to send the message to the control.

These messages are numbered as offsets from the message **WM_USER**, which under Windows 3.0 and 3.1 is &H400.

■ EM_CANUNDO

VB Declaration   `Global Const EM_CANUNDO = WM_USER+22`

Description   Determines if the undo buffer for an edit control contains information that can be used to reverse the previous editing operation.

Use with VB   No problem.

Parameter	Description
wParam	Not used—set to zero.
lParam	Not used—set to zero.

Return Value   **Integer**—TRUE (nonzero) on success, zero otherwise.

■ EM_EMPTYUNDOBUFFER

VB Declaration   `Global Const EM_EMPTYUNDOBUFFER = WM_USER+29`

Description   Clears the undo buffer for an edit control. After this message is sent, the previous editing operation for the control will not be reversible.

Use with VB   No problem.

Parameter	Description
wParam	Not used—set to zero.
lParam	Not used—set to zero.

■ EM_FMTLINES

VB Declaration   `Global Const EM_FMTLINES = WM_USER+24`

Description   Determines whether soft line breaks are returned when the edit control string is read using the **WM_GETTEXT** message. This also applies to the Visual Basic **Text** property. A soft line break is indicated by the appearance of a CR-CR-LF sequence in the text string as follows:

`chr$(13)+chr(13)+chr$(10)`

Use with VB   No problem. Only applies to multiline edit controls.

Parameter	Description
wParam	TRUE (nonzero) to return soft line breaks. FALSE to return to normal operation.
lParam	Not used—set to zero.

■ EM_GETFIRSTVISIBLELINE

VB Declaration   `Global Const EM_GETFIRSTVISIBLELINE = WM_USER+30`

Description   Retrieves the number of the first line that is visible in the edit control. Lines are numbered starting with zero.

Use with VB   No problem. Only applies to multiline edit controls.

Parameter	Description
wParam	Not used—set to zero.
lParam	Not used—set to zero.

■ EM_GETLINE

VB Declaration   `Global Const EM_GETLINE = WM_USER+20`

Description	Retrieves a line from the edit control. Lines are numbered starting with zero.
Use with VB	No problem.

Parameter	Description
wParam	The number of the line to retrieve. Lines are numbered starting with zero. This value is not used on single-line edit controls.
lParam	The address of a string buffer to load with the line. The first two bytes of this buffer contain an integer representing the maximum number of characters that can be loaded into the buffer.

Return Value	The number of characters loaded into the string buffer. Zero is returned if an invalid line is specified.
Comments	If **linebuf$** is the string buffer to load and **lc%** is the length of the buffer – 1, the following lines can be used to load the string buffer with the value **lc%**:

```
Mid$(linebuf$, 1, 1) = Chr$(lc% And &HFF)
Mid$(linebuf$, 2, 1) = Chr$(lc% \ &H100)
```

■ EM_GETLINECOUNT

VB Declaration	Global Const EM_GETLINECOUNT = WM_USER+10
Description	Retrieves the number of lines in an edit control.
Use with VB	No problem. Only applies to multiline edit controls.

Parameter	Description
wParam	Not used—set to zero.
lParam	Not used—set to zero.

■ EM_GETMODIFY

VB Declaration	Global Const EM_GETMODIFY = WM_USER+8
Description	Each edit class control has an internal flag called the modify flag. This flag bit is set to 1 any time the contents of the control are modified. You can use the **EM_SETMODIFY** message to clear this flag, then later use this message to determine if the contents of the control have changed.

Use with VB   The Visual Basic **Change** event provides an effective way to determine if the contents of an edit control are modified.

Parameter	Description
wParam	Not used—set to zero.
lParam	Not used—set to zero.

Return Value   **Integer**—TRUE (nonzero) if the modify flag has been set, indicating that a change has occurred in the edit control since this flag was last cleared.

■ EM_GETPASSWORDCHAR

VB Declaration   Global Const EM_GETPASSWORDCHAR = (WM_USER+34)

Description   Retrieves the current password character for an edit control. This is the character displayed in the control when the user enters text.

Use with VB   Works only with controls that have the **ES_PASSWORD** style. This is not supported under Visual Basic 1.0. With Visual Basic 2.0 and later, you can use the **PasswordChar** property to retrieve the password character.

Parameter	Description
wParam	Not used—set to zero.
lParam	Not used—set to zero.

Return Value   The ASCII value of the password character. Zero if there is no password character set.

■ EM_GETRECT

VB Declaration   Global Const EM_GETRECT = WM_USER+2

Description   Retrieves the formatting rectangle for an edit control. Refer to "Text Formatting," earlier in this chapter, for a description of formatting rectangles.

Use with VB   No problem.

Parameter	Description
wParam	Not used—set to zero.
lParam	An address of a **RECT** structure to load with the formatting rectangle.

■ EM_GETSEL

VB Declaration Global Const EM_GETSEL = WM_USER+0

Description Retrieves the current selection state of the edit control.

Use with VB No problem, but the standard **SelStart** and **SelLength** properties are easier to use.

Parameter	Description
wParam	Not used—set to zero.
lParam	Not used—set to zero.

Return Value Long—The low word contains the character offset of the start of the selection, the high word contains the character offset of the character after the last selected character.

■ EM_LIMITTEXT

VB Declaration Global Const EM_LIMITTEXT = WM_USER+21

Description Used to specify the maximum number of characters that can be contained in an edit control.

Use with VB Useful under Visual Basic 1.0 to limit the contents of a text control and to extend it past 32k (up to nearly 64k). The Visual Basic 2.0 and later **MaxLength** property serves this purpose and is the preferred way to set the maximum text length.

Parameter	Description
wParam	The maximum length of the text that can be entered into an edit control. Zero to set the length to 65,535 characters.
lParam	Not used—set to zero.

■ EM_LINEFROMCHAR

VB Declaration Global Const EM_LINEFROMCHAR = WM_USER+25

Description Determines the line number of the line containing the character specified.

Use with VB No problem.

Parameter	Description
wParam	The offset of the character in the edit control text string to check.
lParam	Not used—set to zero.

Return Value The number of the line containing the specified character. Lines are numbered starting at zero.

■ EM_LINEINDEX

VB Declaration Global Const EM_LINEINDEX = WM_USER+11

Description Determines the character offset of the first character in the specified line.

Use with VB No problem.

Parameter	Description
wParam	The number of a line in an edit control. Lines are numbered starting at zero. –1 specifies the number of the line containing the caret.
lParam	Not used—set to zero.

Return Value The character offset of the first character in the line specified, –1 on error.

■ EM_LINELENGTH

VB Declaration Global Const EM_LINELENGTH = WM_USER+17

Description Determines the length of the line containing the character specified.

Use with VB No problem.

Parameter	Description
wParam	The offset of the character in the edit control text string to check.
lParam	Not used—set to zero.

Return Value The length of the line containing the specified character. Lines are numbered starting at zero.

■ EM_LINESCROLL

VB Declaration Global Const EM_LINESCROLL = WM_USER+6

Description Scrolls the contents of an edit control.

Use with VB   This is frequently used in conjunction with the **EM_GETFIRSTVISIBLELINE** message to display a particular line or lines in a multiline text control. This message is not supported for horizontal scrolling on single-line text controls.

Parameter	Description
wParam	Not used—set to zero.
lParam	The low word contains the number of lines to scroll vertically: positive to scroll the display up, negative to scroll it down. The high word contains the number of lines to scroll horizontally: positive to scroll the display left, negative to scroll it right.

■ EM_REPLACESEL

VB Declaration   `Global Const EM_REPLACESEL = WM_USER+18`

Description   Replaces the selected text in an edit control with the string specified.

Use with VB   No problem, but assignment to the **SelText** property is an easier way to perform this operation.

Parameter	Description
wParam	Not used—set to zero.
lParam	A pointer to a null terminated string.

Comments   If no text is selected, the specified string is inserted at the location of the caret.

■ EM_SETMODIFY

VB Declaration   `Global Const EM_SETMODIFY = WM_USER+9`

Description   Each edit class control has an internal flag called the modify flag. This flag bit is set to 1 any time the contents of the control are modified. You can use the this message to clear this flag, then later use the **EM_GETMODIFY** message to determine if the contents of the control have changed.

Use with VB   The Visual Basic **Change** event provides an effective way to determine if the contents of an edit control are modified.

Parameter	Description
wParam	TRUE (nonzero) to set the modify flag bit to 1, zero to clear it.
lParam	Not used—set to zero.

Return Value   Integer—TRUE (nonzero) or FALSE (zero) according to the new setting of the modify flag.

■ EM_SETPASSWORDCHAR

VB Declaration   Global Const EM_SETPASSWORDCHAR = WM_USER+28

Description   Sets the current password character for an edit control. This is the character displayed in the control when the user enters text.

Use with VB   Works only with controls that have the **ES_PASSWORD** style. This is not supported under Visual Basic 1.0. With Visual Basic 2.0 and later, you can use the **PasswordChar** property to retrieve the password character.

Parameter	Description
wParam	The ASCII value of the new password character.
lParam	Not used—set to zero.

Return Value   TRUE (nonzero) if the message has been successfully sent.

■ EM_SETREADONLY

VB Declaration   Global Const EM_SETREADONLY = (WM_USER+31)

Description   Allows you to see if an edit control is read only. When a control is read only, it is not possible to edit the contents of the control.

Use with VB   No problem.

Parameter	Description
wParam	TRUE (nonzero) to make the control read only. FALSE (zero) to clear the read only state.
lParam	Not used—set to zero.

■ EM_SETRECT

VB Declaration   Global Const EM_SETRECT = WM_USER+3

Description   Sets the formatting rectangle for an edit control. Refer to "Text Formatting," earlier in this chapter, for a description of formatting rectangles.

Use with VB   No problem.

Parameter	Description
wParam	Not used—set to zero.
lParam	An address of a **RECT** structure to set as the new formatting rectangle.

Comments   The formatting rectangle may exceed the size of the control, in which case text that is in the formatting rectangle but outside of the control's window will be clipped (not shown).

■ EM_SETRECTNP

VB Declaration   Global Const EM_SETRECTNP = WM_USER+4

Description   Sets the formatting rectangle for an edit control. Refer to "Text Formatting," earlier in this chapter, for a description of formatting rectangles. This is the same as the **EM_SETRECT** message except that the control is not redrawn.

Use with VB   No problem.

Parameter	Description
wParam	Not used—set to zero.
lParam	An address of a **RECT** structure to set as the new formatting rectangle.

Comments   See the comments for the **EM_SETRECT** message.

■ EM_SETSEL

VB Declaration   Global Const EM_SETSEL = WM_USER+1

Description   Retrieves the current selection state of the edit control.

Use with VB   No problem, but the standard **SelStart** and **SelLength** properties are easier to use. This message does, however, provide control over scrolling during the selection process.

Parameter	Description
wParam	Normally, the caret is scrolled onto the display when selection takes place based on the new position of the caret. Set this value to TRUE (nonzero) to prevent this from occurring.
lParam	The low word of this parameter specifies the character offset of the first character in the selection. The high word specifies the character offset of the first character after the selection. This is also the new caret location.

Return Value   **Integer**—TRUE (nonzero) if successfully sent to an edit control.

■ EM_SETTABSTOPS

VB Declaration   Global Const EM_SETTABSTOPS = WM_USER+27

Description	Used to specify tab stops in an edit control. Tabs can be placed in a text string using the tab character, **chr$(9)**. Tab stops are specified in dialog base units, which are described in "Miscellaneous Functions" in Chapter 16. Each dialog base unit represents one-fourth of the average character width.
Use with VB	No problem.

Parameter	Description
wParam	The number of tab stops to set. Zero to set the default of one tab stop every 32 dialog units. One to set tab stops every *N* dialog units where *N* is the first entry in an integer array specified by **lParam**. Otherwise, this specifies the number of tab stops to set based on the integer array specified by **lParam**.
lParam	The address of the first entry in an integer array containing tab stops to set. The tab stops should be given in order.

Comments	This function does not redraw the control. Use **InvalidateRect** or the Visual Basic **Refresh** method to redraw the text control in order for the new tab stops to take effect. The following code demonstrates how tab stops are set. In this example, the first tab stop is after the fourth character (16 dialog units divided by 4 is about 4 characters), followed by the sixth, eighth, and tenth character positions.

```
Sub Settabs
    ReDim tabvals%(8)
    tabvals%(0) = 16
    tabvals%(1) = 24
    tabvals%(2) = 32
    tabvals%(3) = 40

    di& = SendMessage(Text1.hWnd, EM_SETTABSTOPS, 4, tabvals%(0))
End Sub
```

■ EM_UNDO

VB Declaration	Global Const EM_UNDO = WM_USER+23
Description	Reverses the most recent editing operation. The **EM_CANUNDO** buffer can be used to determine if the previous operation can be reversed. This message has the same effect as the **WM_UNDO** operation described in Chapter 17.
Use with VB	No problem.

Parameter	Description
wParam	Not used—set to zero.
lParam	Not used—set to zero.

19

List Box, Combo Box, and Button Messages

THIS CHAPTER DISCUSSES MESSAGES USED WITH VISUAL BASIC CONTROLS that are based on the Windows list box, combo box, and button controls. These include the Visual Basic list control, file control, combo controls, and all button style controls including command buttons and check boxes. The messages described here can be used to provide features that are not supported by the standard Visual Basic events and properties for those controls. In many cases they will improve the performance of common operations.

The sample program APIcons is also discussed. This is perhaps the most useful utility program provided in this book. It can be used to load in the API-CONST.TXT file, which contains all of the Windows API constants used by the various functions and messages. Once loaded, individual constants can be easily found and transferred into the Windows clipboard for inclusion in any Visual Basic application.

The List Control

A list control is used to display and select lists of strings. The control can be configured in several different ways. The standard list control allows you to select only a single entry at a time. The Visual Basic **MultiSelect** property allows a standard list control to be configured as a multiple selection list box. These two configurations must be considered when using list control messages, as some messages are specific to one configuration or another.

Note that Visual Basic 1.0 did not provide multiple select functionality, so those messages relating to multiple select configurations would not work on the standard VB 1.0 list control. However, they do generally work on add-on products that include multiple select list boxes.

The list control messages divide into a number of functional groups, which are described below.

Selection and Data Functions

The Visual Basic selection and item entry properties can be used to set and select individual entries in a list control, and are adequate for most applications. Though many of the list control messages duplicate this functionality, in some cases they can provide improved performance. For example, the **LB_SELITEMRANGE** message can be used to select a group of entries in a multiple selection list box.

The **LB_FINDSTRING** and **LB_FINDSTRINGEXACT** functions can be used to perform search operations on a list control that are significantly faster than those possible in Visual Basic.

Table 19.1 lists the messages associated with adding and deleting list box entries, and controlling the list selections.

Table 19.1	Selection and Data Messages

Message	Description
LB_ADDSTRING	Adds a string to the list control.
LB_DELETESTRING	Removes a string from the list control.
LB_DIR	Adds a list of files to a list control.
LB_FINDSTRING	Finds an entry that matches a specified prefix.
LB_FINDSTRINGEXACT	Finds an entry that matches a specified string.
LB_GETCOUNT	Retrieves the number of entries in the list control.
LB_GETCURSEL	Retrieves the index of the currently selected entry in a single selection list control.
LB_GETSEL	Determines the selection state of an entry in a multiple selection list control.
LB_GETSELCOUNT	Determines the number of entries that are selected in a multiple select list control.
LB_GETSELITEMS	Loads an array with a list of selected items.
LB_GETTEXT	Retrieves a text entry from the control.
LB_GETTEXTLEN	Determines the length of a list control entry.
LB_INSERTSTRING	Inserts a string into a list control at a specified location.
LB_RESETCONTENT	Clears a list control.
LB_SELECTSTRING	Searches a list control for a string and selects it if found.
LB_SELITEMRANGE	Selects a range of entries in a list control.
LB_SETCURSEL	Selects or deselects an entry in a single selection list control.
LB_SETSEL	Selects or deselects an entry in a multiple selection list control.

Display Functions

The API messages provide a great deal of flexibility in controlling the display of the contents of a list control.

The WM_SETREDRAW Message

The **WM_SETREDRAW** message defined in Chapter 17 is occasionally useful when performing long operations on a list control. Normally, any time a string is added, deleted, or changed, the control becomes invalidated—

flagged for update during event processing. If you are allowing events to run, you can improve performance by preventing update of the list control display until after all modifications have been completed. Note that this applies only when you are adding or deleting data using Windows messages. The Visual Basic **AddItem** and **RemoveItem** methods invalidate the control window and thus override the setting of the **Redraw** flag.

Listing 19.1 illustrates how the **WM_SETREDRAW** message can be used to disable the update of a list control during event processing.

Listing 19.1   Using the WM_SETREDRAW Message

```
VERSION 2.00
Begin Form Form1
    Caption         =   "Form1"
    Height          =   4425
    Left            =   1035
    LinkTopic       =   "Form1"
    ScaleHeight     =   4020
    ScaleWidth      =   7365
    Top             =   1140
    Width           =   7485
    Begin CommandButton Command1
        Caption     =   "Command1"
        Height      =   735
        Left        =   3960
        TabIndex    =   1
        Top         =   840
        Width       =   1590
    End
    Begin ListBox List1
        Height      =   2175
        Left        =   660
        TabIndex    =   0
        Top         =   780
        Width       =   2595
    End
End
Option Explicit

Sub Command1_Click ()
    Dim x%, d%
    Dim WM_SETREDRAW%, LB_ADDSTRING%

    WM_SETREDRAW% = &HB
    LB_ADDSTRING% = &H401

    d% = SendMessageBynum(list1.hWnd, WM_SETREDRAW, 0, 0)
    For x% = 0 To 200
```

Listing 19.1   Using the WM_SETREDRAW Message (Continued)

```
        Print Str$(x%)
        d% = SendMessageBystring(list1.hWnd, LB_ADDSTRING, 0, Str$(x%))
        d% = DoEvents()
    Next x%
    d% = SendMessageBynum(list1.hWnd, WM_SETREDRAW, 1, 0)

End Sub
```

Horizontal and Vertical Scrolling

List controls automatically display a vertical scroll bar when the number of entries exceeds those that can be displayed. Normally, when the length of an entry exceeds the width of the control window, it is clipped—in other words, the entry seems to go off the right side of the list control and cannot be seen.

It is possible to add a horizontal scroll bar to a list control in cases like this so that long entries can be viewed. This is accomplished by specifying an extent greater than the width of the control using the **LB_SETHORIZONTALEXTENT** message. For example, if a list box is 200 pixels wide, setting the extent to 300 will cause a horizontal scroll bar to appear and allow entries up to 300 pixels wide to be displayed.

The **WS_HSCROLL** style must be set for a list control in order for horizontal scrolling to work. This style bit is set by default for the Visual Basic list control.

Display Positioning Messages

Windows messages can also be used to control the list box display. The **LB_GETCARETINDEX** message allows you to determine which entry in a list control has the focus selection. The **LB_SETCARETINDEX** message can then be used to set the focus position.

The **LB_GETITEMRECT** and **LB_GETITEMHEIGHT** messages can be used to determine the size of each entry in the list control. This in turn can be used to determine the number of entries that can be displayed. The **LB_SETITEMHEIGHT** message can be used to change the height of each entry, in effect allowing you to control the amount of space between lines in the list control.

The **LB_GETTOPINDEX** and **LB_SETTOPINDEX** messages can be used to control which entry is displayed at the top of the list control. This allows you to scroll the list box under program control.

Finally, the **LB_SETTABSTOPS** message can be used to set tab stops in a list control in a manner identical to that described in Chapter 18 for edit controls.

Display Message Summary

Table 19.2 lists those list control messages related to control of the display.

Table 19.2   **Display Control Messages**

Function	Description
LB_GETCARETINDEX	Determines which entry is displaying the focus rectangle.
LB_GETHORIZONTALEXTENT	Determines the logical extent of an edit control. If this value is larger than the width of the control window, a horizontal scroll bar appears that allows viewing of the entire logical display.
LB_GETITEMHEIGHT	Determines the height of each list control entry.
LB_GETITEMRECT	Retrieves a bounding rectangle for the specified entry.
LB_GETTOPINDEX	Determines the number of the first entry displayed in the list control.
LB_SETCARETINDEX	Sets the focus rectangle to the specified entry.
LB_SETCOLUMNWIDTH	Allows you to change the width of each column when multi-column mode is specified. Refer to the **Column** property in your Visual Basic manuals.
LB_SETHORIZONTALEXTENT	Sets the logical extent of an edit control. If this value is larger than the width of the control window, a horizontal scroll bar appears that allows viewing the entire logical display.
LB_SETITEMHEIGHT	Sets the height of each list control entry. This effectively controls spacing of the lines in the list box.
LB_SETTABSTOPS	Allows you to specify positions of tab stops in a list box.
LB_SETTOPINDEX	Sets the number of the first entry displayed in the list control.

The Combo Box Control

The combo box control is a combination of an edit control with an attached list control. The combo box messages thus combine many of the features of edit and list controls and in many cases are identical. Table 19.3 lists the combo box messages and the equivalent edit or list control message where appropriate. The list box messages affect the list box part of the combo box and the edit control messages affect the edit control portion of the combo box. Edit control message equivalents have an **EM_** prefix; they can be found in

Chapter 18. List control message equivalents have an **LB_** prefix; they are described in this chapter.

Table 19.3 **Combo Box Messages**

Message	Description
CB_ADDSTRING	Equivalent to **LB_ADDSTRING**. Adds a string to the list control.
CB_DELETESTRING	Equivalent to **LB_DELETESTRING**. Removes a string from the list control.
CB_DIR	Equivalent to **LB_DIR**. Adds a list of files to the list control.
CB_FINDSTRING	Equivalent to **LB_FINDSTRING**. Finds an entry in the list control that matches a specified prefix.
CB_FINDSTRINGEXACT	Equivalent to **LB_FINDSTRINGEXACT**. Finds an entry that matches a specified string.
CB_GETCOUNT	Equivalent to **LB_GETCOUNT**. Retrieves the number of entries in the list control.
CB_GETCURSEL	Equivalent to **LB_GETCURSEL**. Retrieves the index of the currently selected entry in the list control.
CB_GETDROPPEDCONTROLRECT	Determines the size and position of the dropped-down list box portion of a combo box.
CB_GETDROPPEDSTATE	Determines if the list box portion of a combo box is visible.
CB_GETEDITSEL	Equivalent to **EM_GETSEL**. Determines the start and end locations of a selection in the edit control.
CB_GETEXTENDEDUI	Determines the user interface mode of the combo box.
CB_GETITEMHEIGHT	Equivalent to **LB_GETITEMHEIGHT**. Determines the height of each list control entry.
CB_GETLBTEXT	Equivalent to **LB_GETTEXT**. Retrieves a text entry from the list control.
CB_GETLBTEXTLEN	Equivalent to **LB_GETTEXTLEN**. Determines the length of a list control entry.
CB_INSERTSTRING	Equivalent to **LB_INSERTSTRING**. Inserts a string into the list control at a specified location.
CB_LIMITTEXT	Equivalent to **EM_LIMITTEXT**. Limits the length of text in the edit control.
CB_RESETCONTENT	Equivalent to **LB_RESETCONTENT**. Clears the list control.

Table 19.3   Combo Box Messages (Continued)

Message	Description
CB_SELECTSTRING	Equivalent to **LB_SELECTSTRING**. Searches the list control for a string and selects it if found.
CB_SETCURSEL	Equivalent to **LB_SETCURSEL**. Selects or deselects an entry in a single selection list control.
CB_SETEDITSEL	Equivalent to **EM_SETSEL**. Sets the start and end location of a selection in an edit control.
CB_SETEXTENDEDUI	Sets the user interface mode of the combo box.
CB_SETITEMHEIGHT	Equivalent to **LB_SETITEMHEIGHT**. Sets the height of each list control entry. This effectively controls spacing of the lines in the list control.
CB_SHOWDROPDOWN	Used to show or hide the list box portion of the combo box.

The combo box control has several different styles available, as specified by the Visual Basic **Style** property. An extended user interface is available to combo boxes in which the list control drops down when the down arrow key is pressed. This extended mode is specified using the **CB_SETEXTENDEDUI** message.

The extended user interface affects the appearance of the drop-down box. Normally, the drop-down list box does not appear unless you either click on the drop-down arrow or press the F4 function key. If the drop-down list box is not visible, the up and down arrow keys scroll through the contents of the list box but do not cause the list box to appear.

When the extended user interface is enabled, the down arrow key causes the drop-down list box to appear. The F4 key is disabled. Clicking on the static control when the Combo Box **Style** property is set to 2 (Drop-down List) causes the drop-down list box to appear as well.

Button Controls

The Windows button style controls include command buttons, check boxes, and option buttons (referred to in the Windows documentation as radio buttons). These are among the simplest controls to use and the Windows messages provide little added functionality.

It is worthwhile to take a moment and review the difference between the *state* of a button and the *checked* status of a button. The checked status applies only to those buttons that can be checked or unchecked, such as the check box and option button. The general state of a button includes whether it is checked, but also other attributes such as whether the button is high-lighted (pressed), or has the focus.

Table 19.4 lists the Windows messages that are used with button style controls.

Table 19.4 **Button Control Messages**

Message	Description
BM_GETCHECK	Determines if a button style control is checked or unchecked.
BM_GETSTATE	Determines the current state of a button style control.
BM_SETCHECK	Checks or unchecks a button style control.
BM_SETSTATE	Sets the current state of a button style control.

One interesting application of these messages is to implement a "sticky" button—one that toggles between the pressed and unpressed appearance each time it is clicked.

In the following example, a static variable is used to keep track of the current state of the button. Each time the button is clicked, the variable is toggled. The **BM_SETSTATE** message is then sent to the command button to set it into either the normal (unpressed) or highlighted (pressed) state.

```
Sub Command1_Click ()
    Static downstate%
    Dim BM_SETSTATE%
    BM_SETSTATE% = &H403
    downstate% = Not downstate%
    di% = SendMessageBynum(command1.hWnd, BM_SETSTATE, downstate%, 0)
End Sub
```

Example: APICons—A Tool to Select API Constants

Three types of information are needed for using Windows API functions and messages. You need the actual function declarations, the type definitions of structures used under Windows, and the definitions of constants used by functions and used to define the values of the various messages. Microsoft provides this information in a single file in the professional edition of Visual Basic called WINAPI.TXT or WIN31API.TXT (depending on whether you are using Windows 3.0 or Windows 3.1 declarations).

Unfortunately, this file is much too large to include in a single Visual Basic module. Not only that, but defining all of the Windows constants exceeds the memory limitations of Visual Basic. The professional tool kit therefore recommends that you load the declaration file into the Windows Write application (Notepad cannot handle that large a file), edit out all those constants and declarations that are not needed, and then copy the remaining information into your Visual Basic module using the clipboard.

This book takes a slightly different approach by providing the information in the Windows declaration file in three parts. The APIDECS.TXT file contains all the function declarations. The APITYPES.TXT file contains all the type declarations. These are combined into a Visual Basic module, APIDECS.BAS, that can simply be added to your application. You will probably want to remove unused declarations and types to improve efficiency and reduce program load times, but it is not necessary. The declaration and type information can easily be handled by Visual Basic.

The Windows constants are defined in file APICONST.TXT. The APICons program described here can be used to simplify the task of copying these constants into your application. It also demonstrates the use of Windows messages to provide additional functionality to list controls.

Using APICons

Figure 19.1 shows the APICons program in action. The Load command (found under the File menu) is used to load a constant declaration file. It defaults to file APICONST.TXT, but can be used with any text file containing **Global Const** declarations. Any line in that file that begins with '' (a double comment) is loaded into the combo box and indexed for rapid lookup.

Figure 19.1
APICons runtime screen

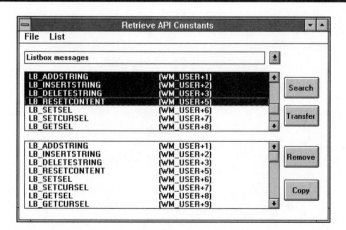

In Figure 19.1, the bulk of the screen is occupied by two list controls. The upper list box is loaded with every global constant declaration in the file. Once one or more declarations have been selected by the user, the Transfer button or menu command (in the List menu) can be used to copy those declarations into the lower list box. The transfer process makes sure that the declarations are not yet present in that list box in order to prevent duplications.

This process is repeated until a complete set of declarations has been loaded into the lower list box. A number of tools are provided to simplify editing. The Remove button can be used to delete any constants that are mistakenly copied. The Search button allows you to search for a declaration based on a name or prefix. The combo box is loaded with comments from the original source file and can be used to quickly position the upper list box to the first declaration that followed the comment in the source file, as shown in Figure 19.2.

Figure 19.2

Using the combo box in APICons

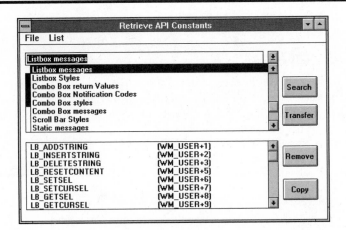

Once the lower list box has been loaded with a desired set of constants, the Copy button can be used to copy the constant declarations into the Windows clipboard, from which they can easily be transferred to a Visual Basic module.

You've probably noticed that the entire declaration is not loaded into the list box. The **Global Const** term is removed from the string before it is inserted into the list control, both for aesthetic reasons and to conserve memory. At the same time, the = character is replaced with a tab character in order to allow the constants to be aligned neatly.

Project Description

The APIcons project includes four files. APICONS.FRM is the only form used
in the program. APICONSM.BAS is the only module in the program and contains the constant type and global definitions and some program code.
APIDECS.BAS is the type-safe API declaration file provided with this book.
CMDIALOG.VBX is the common dialog box control provided with the professional edition of Visual Basic. If you do not have the professional edition, you
will need to replace the code in the **MenuLoadText_Click** function with your
own file selection routine. Listing 19.2 shows the project file for the APICons
program.

Listing 19.2   Project Listing APICONS.TXT

```
APICONS.FRM
CMDIALOG.VBX
APIDECS.BAS
APICONSM.BAS
ProjWinSize=152,402,248,215
ProjWinShow=9
Title="APICONS"
```

Form Description

Listing 19.3 contains the header from file APICONS.FRM that describes the
control setup for the form.

Listing 19.3   Form Description APICONS.FRM

```
VERSION 2.00
Begin Form ApiCons
    Caption         =    "Retrieve API Constants"
    Height          =    4815
    Icon            =    APICONS.FRX:0000
    Left            =    960
    LinkMode        =    1   'Source
    LinkTopic       =    "Form1"
    ScaleHeight     =    4125
    ScaleWidth      =    7425
    Top             =    1440
    Width           =    7545
    Begin ListBox List2
        Height      =       1590
        Left        =        120
```

Listing 19.3   Form Description APICONS.FRM (Continued)

```
            MultiSelect      =   2   'Extended
            TabIndex         =   6
            Top              =   2280
            Width            =   6135
         End
         Begin ListBox List1
            Height           =   1395
            Left             =   120
            MultiSelect      =   2   'Extended
            TabIndex         =   5
            Top              =   660
            Width            =   6135
         End
         Begin CommonDialog CMDialog1
            CancelError      =   -1  'True
            DialogTitle      =   "Select API Constant File"
            Filename         =   "Apiconst.Txt"
            Filter           =   "Constant Files (*.txt)|*.txt"
            Flags            =   4096
            Left             =   6540
            Top              =   60
         End
         Begin ComboBox Combo1
            Height           =   300
            Left             =   120
            TabIndex         =   3
            Top              =   180
            Width            =   6150
         End
         Begin CommandButton CmdSearch
            Caption          =   "Search"
            Height           =   495
            Left             =   6360
            TabIndex         =   4
            Top              =   780
            Width            =   855
         End
         Begin CommandButton CmdTransfer
            Caption          =   "Transfer"
            Height           =   495
            Left             =   6360
            TabIndex         =   0
            Top              =   1440
            Width            =   855
         End
         Begin CommandButton CmdRemove
            Caption          =   "Remove"
            Height           =   495
```

Listing 19.3   Form Description APICONS.FRM (Continued)

```
      Left           =   6360
      TabIndex       =   1
      Top            =   2400
      Width          =   855
   End
   Begin CommandButton CmdCopy
      Caption        =   "Copy"
      Height         =   495
      Left           =   6360
      TabIndex       =   2
      Top            =   3180
      Width          =   855
   End
```

The menu commands in the **MenuList** menu are duplicates of the commands invoked by the command buttons described above.

```
Begin Menu MenuFile
   Caption        =   "File"
   Begin Menu MenuLoadText
      Caption        =   "&Load Text"
   End
End
Begin Menu MenuList
   Caption        =   "List"
   Begin Menu MenuSearch
      Caption        =   "&Search"
      Shortcut       =   ^S
   End
   Begin Menu MenuTransfer
      Caption        =   "&Transfer"
      Shortcut       =   ^T
   End
   Begin Menu MenuRemove
      Caption        =   "&Remove"
      Shortcut       =   ^R
   End
   Begin Menu MenuCopy
      Caption        =   "&Copy"
      Shortcut       =   ^C
   End
End
End
```

APICons Listings

Module APICONSM.BAS (see Listing 19.4) contains the constant declarations and global variables used by the program. It also contains the **LoadConstants** function that is used to load a constant file and initialize the associated data structures.

Listing 19.4   Module APICONSM.BAS

```
' APICONSM.BAS
'
' Constant and Global definition file for APIcons

Global Const WM_USER = &H400
Global Const LB_CTLCODE = 0&
Global Const LB_OKAY = 0
Global Const LB_ERR = (-1)
Global Const LB_ERRSPACE = (-2)
Global Const LBN_ERRSPACE = (-2)
Global Const LBN_SELCHANGE = 1
Global Const LBN_DBLCLK = 2
Global Const LBN_SELCANCEL = 3
Global Const LBN_SETFOCUS = 4
Global Const LBN_KILLFOCUS = 5
Global Const LB_ADDSTRING = (WM_USER + 1)
Global Const LB_INSERTSTRING = (WM_USER + 2)
Global Const LB_DELETESTRING = (WM_USER + 3)
Global Const LB_RESETCONTENT = (WM_USER + 5)
Global Const LB_SETSEL = (WM_USER + 6)
Global Const LB_SETCURSEL = (WM_USER + 7)
Global Const LB_GETSEL = (WM_USER + 8)
Global Const LB_GETCURSEL = (WM_USER + 9)
Global Const LB_GETTEXT = (WM_USER + 10)
Global Const LB_GETTEXTLEN = (WM_USER + 11)
Global Const LB_GETCOUNT = (WM_USER + 12)
Global Const LB_SELECTSTRING = (WM_USER + 13)
Global Const LB_DIR = (WM_USER + 14)
Global Const LB_GETTOPINDEX = (WM_USER + 15)
Global Const LB_FINDSTRING = (WM_USER + 16)
Global Const LB_GETSELCOUNT = (WM_USER + 17)
Global Const LB_GETSELITEMS = (WM_USER + 18)
Global Const LB_SETTABSTOPS = (WM_USER + 19)
Global Const LB_GETHORIZONTALEXTENT = (WM_USER + 20)
Global Const LB_SETHORIZONTALEXTENT = (WM_USER + 21)
Global Const LB_SETCOLUMNWIDTH = (WM_USER + 22)
Global Const LB_SETTOPINDEX = (WM_USER + 24)
Global Const LB_GETITEMRECT = (WM_USER + 25)
Global Const LB_GETITEMDATA = (WM_USER + 26)
Global Const LB_SETITEMDATA = (WM_USER + 27)
```

Listing 19.4   Module APICONSM.BAS (Continued)

```
Global Const LB_SELITEMRANGE = (WM_USER + 28)
Global Const LB_MSGMAX = (WM_USER + 33)
Global Const LB_SETCARETINDEX = (WM_USER + 31)
Global Const LB_GETCARETINDEX = (WM_USER + 32)
Global Const LB_SETITEMHEIGHT = (WM_USER + 33)
Global Const LB_GETITEMHEIGHT = (WM_USER + 34)
Global Const LB_FINDSTRINGEXACT = (WM_USER + 35)
Global Const CB_GETEDITSEL = (WM_USER + 0)
Global Const CB_LIMITTEXT = (WM_USER + 1)
Global Const CB_SETEDITSEL = (WM_USER + 2)
Global Const CB_ADDSTRING = (WM_USER + 3)
Global Const CB_DELETESTRING = (WM_USER + 4)
Global Const CB_DIR = (WM_USER + 5)
Global Const CB_GETCOUNT = (WM_USER + 6)
Global Const CB_GETCURSEL = (WM_USER + 7)
Global Const CB_GETLBTEXT = (WM_USER + 8)
Global Const CB_GETLBTEXTLEN = (WM_USER + 9)
Global Const CB_INSERTSTRING = (WM_USER + 10)
Global Const CB_RESETCONTENT = (WM_USER + 11)
Global Const CB_FINDSTRING = (WM_USER + 12)
Global Const CB_SELECTSTRING = (WM_USER + 13)
Global Const CB_SETCURSEL = (WM_USER + 14)
Global Const CB_SHOWDROPDOWN = (WM_USER + 15)
Global Const CB_GETITEMDATA = (WM_USER + 16)
Global Const CB_SETITEMDATA = (WM_USER + 17)
Global Const CB_GETDROPPEDCONTROLRECT = (WM_USER + 18)
Global Const CB_MSGMAX = (WM_USER + 19)
Global Const CB_SETITEMHEIGHT = (WM_USER + 19)
Global Const CB_GETITEMHEIGHT = (WM_USER + 20)
Global Const CB_SETEXTENDEDUI = (WM_USER + 21)
Global Const CB_GETEXTENDEDUI = (WM_USER + 22)
Global Const CB_GETDROPPEDSTATE = (WM_USER + 23)
Global Const CB_FINDSTRINGEXACT = (WM_USER + 24)
Global Const CBN_ERRSPACE = (-1)
Global Const CBN_SELCHANGE = 1
Global Const CBN_DBLCLK = 2
Global Const CBN_SETFOCUS = 3
Global Const CBN_KILLFOCUS = 4
Global Const CBN_EDITCHANGE = 5
Global Const CBN_EDITUPDATE = 6
Global Const CBN_DROPDOWN = 7
Global Const CBN_CLOSEUP = 8
Global Const CBN_SELENDOK = 9
Global Const CBN_SELENDCANCEL = 10
```

Listing 19.4   Module APICONSM.BAS (Continued)

```
Global IndexList%(256)

' Define the position of the tabstop
Global Const TabPosition% = 25
```

Function **LoadConstants** scans a file containing constants. It removes the **Global Const** term and any trailing constant in order to conserve space in the list box. The = character in the line is changed into a tab in order to let the values and constant names line up in columns.

Any line that is preceded with two comment characters is loaded into the combo box. The value of the current position in the upper list box is recorded in the global **IndexList** array. Later, when the user selects an entry in the combo box, this value is used to scroll to the corresponding position in the list box.

```
'   Loads all lines in file fname $ that have the format:
'   Global Const ..........
'   Into list1, strips off the Global Const to save space
'   Removes comments and trailing spaces as well
'   Loads comments preceded by '' into Combo1, keeping
'   an index list to where it is in the list boxes.
'   The = signs are replaced with a tab to make things
'   easy to see.
'
Sub LoadConstants (fname$)
    Dim Filenum%, OldMousePointer%
    Dim CommentLoc%
    Dim EqualLoc%
    Dim fline$
    Dim comboentry%, di%

    Filenum% = FreeFile
    Open fname$ For Input Access Read As #Filenum%

    OldMousePointer = Screen.MousePointer
    Screen.MousePointer = 11
    Do Until EOF(Filenum%)
      Line Input #Filenum%, fline$
      If UCase$(Left$(fline$, 12)) = "GLOBAL CONST" Then
          ' This line is a constant, add it to the list
          CommentLoc% = InStr(fline$, "'")
          If CommentLoc% Then
          fline$ = Left$(fline$, CommentLoc% - 1)
          End If
          EqualLoc% = InStr(fline$, "=")
          ' Replace the = with a tab.
          If EqualLoc% > 0 Then Mid$(fline$, EqualLoc%, 1) = Chr$(9)
          ' And strip off the Global Const part as well
```

```
            apicons.List1.AddItem RTrim$(Mid$(fline$, 13))
        End If
        If Left$(fline$, 2) = "'" Then
            ' This line is a constant that should be added
            ' to the combo box and indexed
            fline$ = LTrim$(Mid$(fline$, 3))
            apicons.Combo1.AddItem fline$
            comboentry% = apicons.Combo1.ListCount - 1
            IndexList%(comboentry%) = apicons.List1.ListCount
        End If
    Loop
    Screen.MousePointer = OldMousePointer
    Close #Filenum%
End Sub
```

The form header and object descriptions for Listing 19.5 can be found in Listing 19.3.

The **CmdCopy_Click** function reconstructs the global declarations in the lower list box and compiles them into a string, which is then placed in the clipboard.

Listing 19.5   Form Listing APICONS.FRM

```
'   Copy the contents of list2 into the clipboard
'
Sub CmdCopy_Click ()
    Dim totcount%, indexnum%
    Dim OldMousePointer%
    Dim strpos&
    Dim usestring$
    Dim liststring$
    Dim tabposition%

    totcount% = List2.ListCount
    OldMousePointer% = Screen.MousePointer
    Screen.MousePointer = 11
    Do While indexnum% < totcount%
        liststring$ = List2.List(indexnum%)
        tabposition% = InStr(liststring$, Chr$(9))
        Mid$(liststring$, tabposition%, 1) = "="
        usestring$ = usestring$ + "Global Const" + ⇔
        liststring$ + Chr$(13) + Chr$(10)
        indexnum% = indexnum% + 1
    Loop
    Clipboard.SetText usestring$
    Screen.MousePointer = OldMousePointer%


End Sub
```

Listing 19.5   Form Listing APICONS.FRM (Continued)

```
'    Remove all selected entries in List2
'
Sub CmdRemove_Click ()
    Dim totcount%, indexnum%
    Dim OldMousePointer%
    Dim strpos&
    Dim usestring$

    totcount% = List2.ListCount
    OldMousePointer% = Screen.MousePointer
    Screen.MousePointer = 11
    Do While indexnum% < totcount%
        If List2.Selected(indexnum%) Then
            List2.RemoveItem indexnum%
            indexnum% = indexnum% - 1
            totcount% = totcount% - 1
        End If
        indexnum% = indexnum% + 1
    Loop
    Screen.MousePointer = OldMousePointer%

End Sub
```

The **CmdSearch_Click** function illustrates the use of the **LB_FIND-STRING** message to find the first string in a list box that has a specified prefix. The **LB_SETTOPINDEX** message is then used to scroll the string into view.

```
Sub CmdSearch_Click ()
    Dim srchstring$
    Dim prompt$
    prompt$ = "Enter the prefix of the string to search for"
    srchstring$ = InputBox$(prompt$, "Search for string")
    If (srchstring$ <> "") Then
        srchstring$ = " " + srchstring$
        strpos& = SendMessageByString&(List1.hWnd, LB_FINDSTRING, 0, ⟺
        srchstring$)
        If strpos& >= 0 Then
            di% = SendMessageByNum(List1.hWnd, LB_SETTOPINDEX, CInt(strpos&), 0)
        End If
    End If

End Sub
```

The **CmdTransfer_Click** function copies selected entries from the upper to the lower list box. The **LB_FINDSTRING** message is used here to prevent duplicate entries from being copied.

```
'   Transfer all selected entries in List1 to List2
'   Do not transfer duplicates
'
Sub CmdTransfer_Click ()
    Dim totcount%, indexnum%
    Dim OldMousePointer%
    Dim strpos&
    Dim usestring$

    totcount% = List1.ListCount
    OldMousePointer% = Screen.MousePointer
    Screen.MousePointer = 11
    For indexnum% = 0 To totcount% - 1
        If List1.Selected(indexnum%) Then
            ' Get the selected strings
            usestring$ = List1.List(indexnum%)
            ' Try to find the string in List2
            strpos& = SendMessageByString&(List2.hWnd, ⇔
            LB_FINDSTRING, 0, usestring$)
            ' If it's not there, add it
            If strpos& < 0 Then List2.AddItem usestring$
        End If
    Next indexnum%
    List1.Selected(-1) = 0
    Screen.MousePointer = OldMousePointer%
End Sub
```

```
'   Scroll to the appropriate place
'
Sub Combo1_Click ()
    Dim curentry%
    If Combo1.ListIndex < 0 Then Exit Sub
    curentry% = IndexList%(Combo1.ListIndex)
    List1.TopIndex = curentry%
End Sub
```

Tab stops are set for list boxes in much the same way as they are for edit controls. The **tabposition** constant defines the approximate desired tab position based on the average character width in the current font. This number is multiplied by four to obtain the tab stop location in dialog units.

```
'   Set the tabstop location for both list boxes
'
Sub Form_Load ()
    ReDim t%(2)
```

```
                    ' Note that dialog units are 4* the average char width
                    t%(0) = tabposition% * 4
                    ' We place a second tab stop just in case of very
                    ' long variables
                    t%(0) = (tabposition% + 5) * 4

                    di% = SendMessage(List1.hWnd, LB_SETTABSTOPS, 2, t%(0))
                    di% = SendMessage(List2.hWnd, LB_SETTABSTOPS, 2, t%(0))

End Sub

Sub MenuCopy_Click ()
        CmdCopy.Value = -1
End Sub

Sub MenuLoadText_Click ()
        On Error Resume Next
        CMDialog1.Action = 1
        If Err = 0 Then
            List1.Clear
            LoadConstants (CMDialog1.Filename)
        End If
End Sub
```

The menu entries shown below simply trigger the associated command button.

```
Sub MenuRemove_Click ()
        CmdRemove.Value = -1
End Sub

Sub MenuSearch_Click ()
        CmdSearch.Value = -1
End Sub

Sub MenuTransfer_Click ()
        CmdTransfer.Value = -1

End Sub
```

Notification Messages

Edit controls send **WM_COMMAND** messages to their parent window that notify it when certain events take place. Most of these messages are mapped into Visual Basic events for the VB list or combo control. Those that are not, cannot be accessed directly by the Visual Basic programmer, but may prove useful when using the advanced subclassing techniques described in Chapter 17.

All notification messages are sent to the parent window of the control using the **WM_COMMAND** message. The **wParam** parameter always refers to the numeric identifier of the control, a value that is not used in Visual Basic. The **lParam** parameter is divided into two parts. The low word contains the window handle of the control. This can be used to determine which control sent the notification message. The high word contains the notification type. In other words, the **LBN_KILLFOCUS** notification would contain the constant **LBN_KILLFOCUS** in the high order word of the **lParam** parameter.

■ CBN_CLOSEUP

VB Declaration   Global Const CBN_CLOSEUP = 8

Description   Sent when the list box portion of a combo box is closed. The **CBN_SELCHANGE** message may be sent before or after this message if a change occurs when the list box is closed.

Use with VB   None.

Use with Subclassing   Could be used to detect a user action that closes the list box without causing a change to the contents.

■ CBN_DBLCLK

VB Declaration   Global Const CBN_DBLCLK = 2

Description   Sent when the user double clicks on an entry in the list box part of a combo box. This notification is only sent with simple combo controls as a click on a drop-down combo control causes the list box to be hidden.

Use with VB   This notification triggers the Visual Basic **DblClick** event.

■ CBN_DROPDOWN

VB Declaration   Global Const CBN_DROPDOWN = 7

Description   Sent when the list box portion of a drop-down combo box is about to be made visible.

Use with VB   This notification triggers the Visual Basic **DropDown** event.

■ CBN_EDITCHANGE

VB Declaration   Global Const CBN_EDITCHANGE = 5

Description   Sent any time the contents of the edit control part of a combo control changes.

Use with VB   This message generates a Visual Basic **Change** event in the standard combo control. The message is sent after the changes have already been displayed.

■ CBN_EDITUPDATE

VB Declaration   Global Const CBN_EDITUPDATE = 6

Description   Sent before the edit control part of a combo control displays text that has been changed. This is similar to the **CBN_EDITCHANGE** notification except that it occurs before the text is displayed.

Use with VB   None.

Use with Subclassing   Could be used to customize text display for the edit control part of a combo box.

■ CBN_ERRSPACE

VB Declaration   Global Const CBN_ERRSPACE = (-1)

Description   Sent any time an operation fails because there is insufficient memory to perform the operation.

Use with VB   Visual Basic will trigger an error through its normal error notification system when this type of error occurs.

■ CBN_KILLFOCUS

VB Declaration   Global Const CBN_KILLFOCUS = 4

Description   Sent when the control loses the input focus.

Use with VB   This message generates the VB **LostFocus** event.

Use with Subclassing   The Visual Basic **LostFocus** event is posted, which means that it occurs at some indeterminate time after this message is sent. Also, this event is not sent when the focus is lost due to the activation of another application. This message, however, can be used to detect loss of focus in all circumstances.

■ CBN_SELCHANGE

VB Declaration   Global Const CBN_SELCHANGE = 1

Description   This message is sent any time the selection in the list control part of a combo control changes.

Use with VB   This message generates the Visual Basic **Click** event for combo box controls.

■ CBN_SELENDCANCEL

VB Declaration   Global Const CBN_SELENDCANCEL = 10

Description   Sent before the **CBN_CLOSEUP** notification when the list box portion of a combo control is about to be hidden due to the user selecting or clicking outside of the combo control. This is used to indicate that the user's selection should be ignored. On simple combo boxes, this message is sent even though the list box is not hidden.

Use with VB   None.

Use with Subclassing   Can be used to detect the end of a list box selection operation.

■ CBN_SELENDOK

VB Declaration   Global Const CBN_SELENDOK = 9

Description   Sent before the **CBN_CLOSEUP** notification when the list box portion of a combo control is about to be hidden due to the user pressing the Enter key or clicking inside a combo control. This is used to indicate that the user's selection is valid. On simple combo boxes, this message is sent even though the list box is not hidden.

Use with VB   None.

Use with Subclassing   Can be used to detect the end of a list box selection operation.

■ CBN_SETFOCUS

VB Declaration   Global Const CBN_SETFOCUS = 3

Description   Sent when the control receives the input focus.

Use with VB   This message generates the VB **GotFocus** event.

Use with Subclassing   The Visual Basic **GotFocus** event is posted, which means that it occurs at some indeterminate time after this message is sent. This is unlikely to be a problem, so subclassing this message should not be necessary.

■ LBN_DBLCLK

VB Declaration   Global Const LBN_DBLCLK = 2

Description   Sent when the user double clicks on an entry in a list box.

Use with VB   This notification triggers the Visual Basic **DblClick** event.

■ LBN_ERRSPACE

VB Declaration   Global Const LBN_ERRSPACE = (-2)

Description   Sent any time an operation fails because there is insufficient memory to perform the operation.

Use with VB   Visual Basic will trigger an error through its normal error notification system when this type of error occurs.

■ LBN_KILLFOCUS

VB Declaration   Global Const LBN_KILLFOCUS = 5

Description   Sent when the control loses the input focus.

Use with VB   This message generates the VB **LostFocus** event.

Use with Subclassing   The Visual Basic **LostFocus** event is posted, which means that it occurs at some indeterminate time after this message is sent. Also, this event is not sent when the focus is lost due to the activation of another application. This message, however, can be used to detect loss of focus in all circumstances.

■ LBN_SELCANCEL

VB Declaration   Global Const LBN_SELCANCEL = 3

Description   Sent when a list box selection is canceled. This is typically due to the user selecting or clicking outside of the control.

Use with VB   None.

Use with Subclassing   Can be used to detect the end of a list box selection operation.

■ LBN_SELCHANGE

VB Declaration   Global Const LBN_SELCHANGE = 1

Description   This message is sent any time the selection in the list control changes.

Use with VB   This message generates the Visual Basic **Click** event for list box controls.

■ LBN_SETFOCUS

VB Declaration   Global Const LBN_SETFOCUS = 4

Description   Sent when the control receives the input focus.

Use with VB   This message generates the VB **GotFocus** event.

Use with Subclassing   The Visual Basic **GotFocus** event is posted, which means that it occurs at some indeterminate time after this message is sent. This is unlikely to be a problem, so subclassing this message should not be necessary.

Combo Box Control Messages

The following messages can be used to control the operation of any Visual Basic control based on the Windows Combo Box class. This includes the standard Visual Basic combo control.

Most of the messages defined here are exact duplicates of edit control messages defined in Chapter 18 or list control messages defined in the next section. In those cases, the entry simply refers you to the corresponding edit or list control message. The message applies to the corresponding part of the combo box (which consists of an edit control and a list box).

These messages are numbered as offsets from the message **WM_USER**, which is &H400 under Windows 3.0 and 3.1.

■ CB_ADDSTRING

VB Declaration   Global Const CB_ADDSTRING = (WM_USER+3)

Description   See the description of the **LB_ADDSTRING** message in this chapter.

■ CB_DELETESTRING

VB Declaration   Global Const CB_DELETESTRING = (WM_USER+4)

Description   See the description of the **LB_DELETESTRING** message in this chapter.

■ CB_DIR

VB Declaration   Global Const CB_DIR = (WM_USER+5)

Description   See the description of the **LB_DIR** message in this chapter.

■ CB_FINDSTRING

VB Declaration   Global Const CB_FINDSTRING = (WM_USER+12)

Description   See the description of the **LB_FINDSTRING** message in this chapter.

■ CB_FINDSTRINGEXACT

VB Declaration   Global Const CB_FINDSTRINGEXACT = (WM_USER+24)

Description   See the description of the **LB_FINDSTRINGEXACT** message in this chapter.

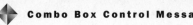

■ CB_GETCOUNT

VB Declaration   Global Const CB_GETCOUNT = (WM_USER+6)

Description   See the description of the **LB_GETCOUNT** message in this chapter.

■ CB_GETCURSEL

VB Declaration   Global Const CB_GETCURSEL = (WM_USER+7)

Description   See the description of the **LB_GETCURSEL** message in this chapter.

■ CB_GETDROPPEDCONTROLRECT

VB Declaration   Global Const CB_GETDROPPEDCONTROLRECT = (WM_USER+18)

Description   Determines the dimensions of the drop-down list box for a combo control. The dimensions are specified in pixel screen coordinates.

Use with VB   No problem.

Parameter	Description
wParam	Not used—set to zero.
lParam	The address of a **RECT** structure to load with the list box dimensions.

■ CB_GETDROPPEDSTATE

VB Declaration   Global Const CB_GETDROPPEDSTATE = (WM_USER+23)

Description   Determines if the list box portion of a combo box is visible.

Use with VB   No problem.

Parameter	Description
wParam	Not used—set to zero.
lParam	Not used—set to zero.

Return Value   Integer—TRUE (nonzero) if the list box is visible, zero otherwise.

■ CB_GETEDITSEL

VB Declaration   Global Const CB_GETEDITSEL = (WM_USER+0)

Description   Equivalent to the **EM_GETSEL** message. Retrieves the current selection state of the edit control portion of the combo box.

Use with VB   No problem, but the standard **SelStart** and **SelLength** properties are easier to use.

Parameter	Description
wParam	Not used—set to zero.
lParam	Not used—set to zero.

Return Value   **Long**—The low word contains the character offset of the start of the selection, the high word contains the character offset of the character after the last selected character.

■ CB_GETEXTENDEDUI

VB Declaration   Global Const CB_GETEXTENDEDUI = (WM_USER+22)

Description   Determines if the combo control has the extended user interface enabled. The extended user interface is described in "The Combo Box Control," earlier in this chapter.

Use with VB   No problem.

Parameter	Description
wParam	Not used—set to zero.
lParam	Not used—set to zero.

Return Value   **Integer**—1 if the extended user interface is enabled.

■ CB_GETITEMHEIGHT

VB Declaration   Global Const CB_GETITEMHEIGHT = (WM_USER+20)

Description   See the description of the **LB_GETITEMHEIGHT** message in this chapter.

■ CB_GETLBTEXT

VB Declaration   Global Const CB_GETLBTEXT = (WM_USER+8)

Description   See the description of the **LB_GETLBTEXT** message in this chapter.

■ CB_GETLBTEXTLEN

VB Declaration   Global Const CB_GETLBTEXTLEN = (WM_USER+9)

Description   See the description of the **LB_GETLBTEXTLEN** message in this chapter.

CB_INSERTSTRING

VB Declaration Global Const CB_INSERTSTRING = (WM_USER+10)

Description See the description of the **LB_INSERTSTRING** message in this chapter.

CB_LIMITTEXT

VB Declaration Global Const CB_LIMITTEXT = (WM_USER+1)

Description Used to specify the maximum number of characters that can be contained in the edit control portion of a combo box.

Use with VB The standard Visual Basic combo box does not support the **MaxLength** property, so this message can used to set the maximum length of text that can be entered into the edit control part of a combo control.

Parameter	Description
wParam	The maximum length of the text that can be entered into an edit control. Zero to set the length to 65535 characters.
lParam	Not used—set to zero.

CB_RESETCONTENT

VB Declaration Global Const CB_RESETCONTENT = (WM_USER+11)

Description See the description of the **LB_RESETCONTENT** message in this chapter.

CB_SELECTSTRING

VB Declaration Global Const CB_SELECTSTRING = (WM_USER+13)

Description See the description of the **LB_SELECTSTRING** message in this chapter.

CB_SETCURSEL

VB Declaration Global Const CB_SETCURSEL = (WM_USER+14)

Description See the description of the **LB_SETCURSEL** message in this chapter.

CB_SETEDITSEL

VB Declaration Global Const CB_SETEDITSEL = (WM_USER+2)

Description Retrieves the current selection state of the edit control part of a combo box.

Use with VB   No problem, but the standard **SelStart** and **SelLength** properties are easier to use. This message does, however, provide control over scrolling during the selection process.

Parameter	Description
wParam	Normally, the caret is scrolled onto the display when selection takes place based on the new position of the caret. Set this value to TRUE (nonzero) to prevent this from occurring.
lParam	The low word of this parameter specifies the character offset of the first character in the selection. The high word specifies the character offset of the first character after the selection. This is also the new caret location.

Return Value   Integer—TRUE (nonzero) if successfully sent to the edit control.

■ CB_SETEXTENDEDUI

VB Declaration   `Global Const CB_SETEXTENDEDUI = (WM_USER+21)`

Description   Enables or disables the extended user interface for a combo control. The extended user interface is described in "The Combo Box Control," earlier in this chapter.

Use with VB   No problem.

Parameter	Description
wParam	One to enable the extended user interface for a combo control, zero to disable the extended user interface.
lParam	Not used—set to zero.

■ CB_SETITEMHEIGHT

VB Declaration   `Global Const CB_SETITEMHEIGHT = (WM_USER+19)`

Description   See the description of the **LB_SETITEMHEIGHT** message in this chapter.

■ CB_SHOWDROPDOWN

VB Declaration   `Global Const CB_SHOWDROPDOWN = (WM_USER+15)`

Description   Used to show or hide the drop down list box part of a combo control.

Use with VB   No problem.

Parameter	Description
wParam	TRUE (nonzero) to show the list box. Zero to hide it.
lParam	Not used—set to zero.

List Box Control Messages

The following messages can be used to control the operation of any Visual Basic control based on the Windows List class. This includes the standard Visual Basic list control and file control.

As usual, the return value refers to the value returned by the **SendMessage** function used to send the message to the control.

These messages are numbered as offsets from the message **WM_USER** which is &H400 under Windows 3.0 and 3.1.

▧ LB_ADDSTRING

VB Declaration   Global Const LB_ADDSTRING = (WM_USER+1)

Description   This message is used to add a string to a list box. If the list box is sorted, the new string will be inserted in the correct location. Otherwise, the string will be added to the end of the list box.

Use with VB   No problem. The Visual Basic **AddItem** method performs the same task.

Parameter	Description
wParam	Not used—set to zero.
lParam	Address of a null terminated string to add to the list box.

Return Value   The entry number of the new string, where entry zero is the first string in the list box. –1 on error.

▧ LB_DELETESTRING

VB Declaration   Global Const LB_DELETESTRING = (WM_USER+3)

Description   Deletes a string from a list box.

Use with VB   No problem. The Visual Basic **RemoveItem** method performs the same task.

Parameter	Description
wParam	The entry number of the string to delete. Entry zero is the first entry in the list box.
lParam	Not used—set to zero.

Return Value   The number of strings remaining in the list control. –1 on error.

▧ LB_DIR

VB Declaration   Global Const LB_DIR = (WM_USER+14)

Description   Fills a list control with a list of file names.

Use with VB   No problem. The Visual Basic file control is much easier to use for file management.

Parameter	Description
wParam	One or more of the following mask values can be combined to choose the files to load: &H1—Read only files. &H2—Hidden files. &H4—System files. &H10—**lParam** specifies a directory name. &H20—Files with the archive bit set. &H4000—All files matching the **lParam** specification are loaded. &H8000—Only files that match all of the attributes are loaded.
lParam	The address of a null terminated string specifying a DOS file specification. This can include the ? and * wild card characters.

Return Value   The entry number of the last file added to the list box. –1 on error.

■ LB_FINDSTRING

VB Declaration   `Global Const LB_FINDSTRING = (WM_USER+16)`

Description   Finds an entry in a list box that matches the specified prefix. This search is not case sensitive.

Use with VB   No problem.

Parameter	Description
wParam	The number of the list box entry from which to start the search. –1 to search the entire control starting from the beginning. The search will wrap around to the start if the last entry is reached without a match.
lParam	The address of a null terminated string containing a prefix to search for.

Return Value   The entry number of the new string, where entry zero is the first string in the list box. –1 on error. For example, to search for a string in a list box that begins with the letters "LB_", starting the search from the sixth entry, you could use the command:

```
entrynum% = SendMessageByString(List1.hWnd, LB_FINDSTRING, 5, "LB_")
```

■ LB_FINDSTRINGEXACT

VB Declaration   `Global Const LB_FINDSTRINGEXACT = (WM_USER+35)`

Description   Finds an entry in a list box that matches the specified string. This search is not case-sensitive. This differs from **LB_FINDSTRING** in that the entire string must match.

Use with VB	No problem.

Parameter	Description
wParam	The number of the list box entry from which to start the search. –1 to search the entire control starting from the beginning. The search will wrap around to the start if the last entry is reached without a match.
lParam	The address of a null terminated string to search for.

Return Value The entry number of the new string, where entry zero is the first string in the list box. –1 on error.

■ LB_GETCARETINDEX

VB Declaration `Global Const LB_GETCARETINDEX = (WM_USER+32)`

Description When a multiple selection list box has the focus, a focus rectangle appears on one of entries. This message can be used to determine which entry has the focus rectangle.

Use with VB No problem.

Parameter	Description
wParam	Not used—set to zero.
lParam	Not used—set to zero.

Return Value The entry number of the string that has the focus, where entry zero is the first string in the list box. On single selection list boxes, the entry number of the selected string if one exists.

■ LB_GETCOUNT

VB Declaration `Global Const LB_GETCOUNT = (WM_USER+12)`

Description Used to determine the number of entries in a list box.

Use with VB No problem. The Visual Basic **ListCount** property performs the same task and is easier to use.

Parameter	Description
wParam	Not used—set to zero.
lParam	Not used—set to zero.

Comments The number of entries in the list box.

■ LB_GETCURSEL

VB Declaration `Global Const LB_GETCURSEL = (WM_USER+9)`

Description Used to determine the entry number of the selected string if one exists in a single selection list box. Do not use this message on multiple selection list boxes.

Use with VB   No problem. The Visual Basic **ListIndex** property performs the same task and is easier to use.

Parameter	Description
wParam	Not used—set to zero.
lParam	Not used—set to zero.

Return Value   The entry number of the current selection if one exists. –1 if no selection exists. The first entry in the list control is entry number zero.

■ LB_GETHORIZONTALEXTENT

VB Declaration   `Global Const LB_GETHORIZONTALEXTENT = (WM_USER+20)`

Description   Determines the current horizontal extent of the list control. If this value is greater than the width of the list box, a horizontal list scroll bar appears that allows scrolling the contents of the control.

Use with VB   No problem.

Parameter	Description
wParam	Not used—set to zero.
lParam	Not used—set to zero.

Return Value   The horizontal extent of the list box in pixels.

■ LB_GETITEMHEIGHT

VB Declaration   `Global Const LB_GETITEMHEIGHT = (WM_USER+34)`

Description   Determines the height of each entry in the list control in pixels.

Use with VB   No problem.

Parameter	Description
wParam	Not used—set to zero.
lParam	Not used—set to zero.

Return Value   The height of each entry in the list box in pixels.

■ LB_GETITEMRECT

VB Declaration   `Global Const LB_GETITEMRECT = (WM_USER+25)`

Description   Determines the dimensions of an entry in the list control. The dimensions are specified in list control client pixel coordinates.

Use with VB	No problem.	
	Parameter	**Description**
	wParam	The number of the entry for which to retrieve dimensions. The first entry is entry number zero.
	lParam	The address of a **RECT** structure to load with the entry dimensions.

Return Value   –1 on error.

■ LB_GETSEL

VB Declaration   Global Const LB_GETSEL = (WM_USER+8)

Description   Determines the selection state of an entry in a multiple select list box.

Use with VB	No problem. The Visual Basic **Selected** property performs the same task and is easier to use.	
	Parameter	**Description**
	wParam	The number of the entry to check. The first entry is entry number zero.
	lParam	Not used—set to zero.

Return Value   A result greater than zero if the entry is selected, zero if it is not selected, and –1 on error.

■ LB_GETSELCOUNT

VB Declaration   Global Const LB_GETSELCOUNT = (WM_USER+17)

Description   Determines the total number of selected entries in a multiple select list box.

Use with VB	No problem.	
	Parameter	**Description**
	wParam	Not used—set to zero.
	lParam	Not used—set to zero.

Return Value   The number of selected entries selected in the list box. –1 on error or if it is a single selection list box.

■ LB_GETSELITEMS

VB Declaration   Global Const LB_GETSELITEMS = (WM_USER+18)

Description   Fills an integer array with the numbers of all selected entries in a multiple selection list box.

Use with VB   No problem.

Parameter	Description
wParam	The maximum number of entries to load into the array specified by **lParam**. **lParam** must be large enough to contain this many integers.
lParam	The address of the first entry in an integer array that has at least **wParam** entries. After this message returns, this array will be loaded with the numbers of all selected entries up to the number of entries specified by **wParam**.

Return Value   −1 on error or if this message is sent to a single selection list box.

■ LB_GETTEXT

VB Declaration   `Global Const LB_GETTEXT = (WM_USER+10)`

Description   Retrieves the string for the specified list box entry.

Use with VB   No problem. The Visual Basic **List** property performs the same task and is easier to use.

Parameter	Description
wParam	The number of the entry to retrieve. The first entry is entry number zero.
lParam	The address of a string buffer to load with the list box text. This string must be preallocated to a length adequate to hold the string and null terminator. Use the **LB_GETTEXTLEN** message to determine the necessary buffer size.

Return Value   The length of the string loaded.

■ LB_GETTEXTLEN

VB Declaration   `Global Const LB_GETTEXTLEN = (WM_USER+11)`

Description   Retrieves the length of the string for the specified list box entry.

Use with VB   No problem.

Parameter	Description
wParam	The number of the entry to check. The first entry is entry number zero.
lParam	Not used—set to zero.

Return Value   The length of the string for the specified entry.

■ LB_GETTOPINDEX

VB Declaration   Global Const LB_GETTOPINDEX = (WM_USER+15)

Description   Determines which entry appears at the top of the list control display.

Use with VB   No problem.

Parameter	Description
wParam	Not used—set to zero.
lParam	Not used—set to zero.

Comments   The number of the first entry visible in the list box. The first string in the list box is entry zero.

■ LB_INSERTSTRING

VB Declaration   Global Const LB_INSERTSTRING = (WM_USER+2)

Description   This message is used to insert a string into a list box at a specified location. If the list box is sorted, the new string will be inserted into the specified location without regard for the sort order.

Use with VB   No problem. The Visual Basic **AddItem** method performs the same task.

Parameter	Description
wParam	The entry location at which to insert this string. –1 to append the string to the end of the list box. The first entry is entry number zero.
lParam	Address of a null terminated string to insert into the list box.

Return Value   The entry number of the new string, where entry zero is the first string in the list box. The constant **LB_ERR** on error, **LB_ERRSPACE** if there is insufficient memory to insert the string.

■ LB_RESETCONTENT

VB Declaration   Global Const LB_RESETCONTENT = (WM_USER+5)

Description   Clears the contents of the list box.

Use with VB   No problem. The Visual Basic **Clear** method performs the same task for Visual Basic 2.0.

Parameter	Description
wParam	Not used—set to zero.
lParam	Not used—set to zero.

■ LB_SELECTSTRING

VB Declaration   Global Const LB_SELECTSTRING = (WM_USER+13)

Description   Finds an entry in a list box that matches the specified prefix and selects it. This search is not case-sensitive.

Use with VB   No problem.

Parameter	Description
wParam	The number of the list box entry from which to start the search. –1 to search the entire control starting from the beginning. The search will wrap around to the start if the last entry is reached without a match.
lParam	The address of a null terminated string containing a prefix to search for.

Return Value   The entry number of the selected string if one is found, where entry zero is the first string in the list box. –1 if no match is found.

■ LB_SELITEMRANGE

VB Declaration   Global Const LB_SELITEMRANGE = (WM_USER+28)

Description   Used to select or deselect a range of entries in a multiple select list box. This message can be used only on multiple selection list boxes.

Use with VB   No problem.

Parameter	Description
wParam	TRUE (nonzero) to select the specified entries, FALSE (zero) to clear the selection.
lParam	The low 16 bits specify the first entry to select or deselect. The high 16 bits specify the last entry to select or deselect.

Return Value   –1 on error.

■ LB_SETCARETINDEX

VB Declaration   Global Const LB_SETCARETINDEX = (WM_USER+31)

Description   When a multiple selection list box has the focus, a focus rectangle appears on one of entries. This message can be used to set the focus rectangle to a particular entry. The string that is given the focus will be scrolled onto the display if necessary.

Use with VB	No problem.	
	Parameter	**Description**
	wParam	The entry number that is to receive the focus rectangle.
	lParam	The low 16 bits are set to TRUE (nonzero) to specify that the entire entry should be visible after this operation. Otherwise it is possible that it will be only partially visible after scrolling. The high 16 bits are not used and should be set to zero.

Return Value   −1 on error.

■ LB_SETCOLUMNWIDTH

VB Declaration   Global Const LB_SETCOLUMNWIDTH = (WM_USER+22)

Description   Sets the width of each column on a multiple column list control.

Use with VB	No problem. The **Columns** property of the standard list control must be greater than zero.	
	Parameter	**Description**
	wParam	The width of each column in pixels.
	lParam	Not used—set to zero.

■ LB_SETCURSEL

VB Declaration   Global Const LB_SETCURSEL = (WM_USER+7)

Description   Used to select an entry in a single selection list box. Do not use this message on multiple selection list boxes.

Use with VB	No problem. The Visual Basic **ListIndex** property performs the same task and is easier to use.	
	Parameter	**Description**
	wParam	The entry number to select. The first entry in the list box is entry zero. −1 to clear any selection.
	lParam	Not used—set to zero.

■ LB_SETHORIZONTALEXTENT

VB Declaration   Global Const LB_SETHORIZONTALEXTENT = (WM_USER+21)

Description   Sets the current horizontal extent of the list control. If this value is greater than the width of the list box, a horizontal list scroll bar appears that allows scrolling the contents of the control.

Use with VB	No problem.	
	Parameter	**Description**
	wParam	The new horizontal extent of the list control in pixels.
	lParam	Not used—set to zero.

◼ LB_SETITEMHEIGHT

VB Declaration	`Global Const LB_SETITEMHEIGHT = (WM_USER+33)`

Description Sets the height of each entry in the list control in pixels. This can be effectively used to set line spacing in a list control.

Use with VB	No problem.	
	Parameter	**Description**
	wParam	Not used—set to zero.
	lParam	The low 16 bits are set to the height of each list box entry in pixels. The high 16 bits are not used and must be set to zero.

Return Value −1 if the height specified is invalid.

◼ LB_SETSEL

VB Declaration	`Global Const LB_SETSEL = (WM_USER+6)`

Description Sets the selection state of an entry in a multiple select list box.

Use with VB	No problem. The Visual Basic **Selected** property performs the same task and is easier to use.	
	Parameter	**Description**
	wParam	TRUE (nonzero) to select the entry, FALSE to clear the entry.
	lParam	The low 16 bits contain the number of the entry to check. The first entry is entry number zero. −1 to apply the selection operation to all entries. The high 16 bits are not used and should be set to zero.

Return Value A result greater than zero if the entry is selected, zero if it is not selected, and −1 on error.

◼ LB_SETTABSTOPS

VB Declaration	`Global Const LB_SETTABSTOPS = (WM_USER+19)`

Description Used to specify tab stops in a list control. Tabs can be placed in a text string using the tab character, **chr$(9)**. Tab stops are specified in dialog base units which are described in "Miscellaneous Functions" in Chapter 16. Each dialog base unit represents one-fourth of the average character width in the current font.

Use with VB   No problems.

Parameter	Description
wParam	The number of tab stops to set. Zero to set the default of one tab stop every two dialog units. One to set tab stops every N dialog units where N is the first entry in an integer array specified by **lParam**. Otherwise, this specifies the number of tab stops to set based on the integer array specified by **lParam**.
lParam	The address of the first entry in an integer array containing tab stops to set. The tab stops should be given in order.

Comments   This function does not redraw the control. Use **InvalidateRect** or the Visual Basic **Refresh** method to redraw the text control in order for the new tab stops to take effect.

The following code demonstrates how tab stops are set. In this example, the first tab stop is after the fourth character (16 dialog units divided by 4 is about four characters), followed by the sixth, eighth, and tenth character positions.

```
Sub Settabs
    ReDim tabvals%(8)
    tabvals%(Ø) = 16
    tabvals%(1) = 24
    tabvals%(2) = 32
    tabvals%(3) = 40

    di& = SendMessage(List1.hWnd, LB_SETTABSTOPS, 4, tabvals%(Ø))
End Sub
```

■ LB_SETTOPINDEX

VB Declaration   `Global Const LB_SETTOPINDEX = (WM_USER+24)`

Description   Scrolls the list box so that the specified entry appears at the top of the list control display, or as close as possible to the top if the maximum scroll range has been reached.

Use with VB   No problem.

Parameter	Description
wParam	The number of the entry to scroll to the top of the display. The first entry is entry number zero.
lParam	Not used—set to zero.

Comments   –1 on error.

Button Control Messages

The following messages can be used to control the operation of any Visual Basic control based on the Windows Button class. This includes the standard Visual Basic command button, check box, and option buttons.

These messages are numbered as offsets from the message **WM_USER**, which is &H400 under Windows 3.0 and 3.1.

■ BM_GETCHECK

VB Declaration   Global Const BM_GETCHECK = WM_USER+0

Description   Used to determine if a button style control is checked or unchecked.

Use with VB   No problem. The Visual Basic **Value** property performs this task and is easier to use.

Parameter	Description
wParam	Not used—set to zero.
lParam	Not used—set to zero.

Return Value   0 if the button is unchecked, 1 if checked, 2 if it is in a third state (typically grayed).

Comments   This message has no effect on command buttons.

■ BM_GETSTATE

VB Declaration   Global Const BM_GETSTATE = WM_USER+2

Description   Used to determine the state of a button style control.

Use with VB   No problem.

Parameter	Description
wParam	Not used—set to zero.
lParam	Not used—set to zero.

Return Value   A bit field that is defined as follows:
Bits 0–1: The checked state of the button. 0 if the button is unchecked, 1 if checked, 2 if it is in a third state (typically grayed).
Bit 2: One if the button is highlighted (pressed).
Bit 3: One if the button has the focus.

■ BM_SETCHECK

VB Declaration   Global Const BM_SETCHECK = WM_USER+1

Description   Used to check or uncheck a button style control.

Use with VB   No problem. The Visual Basic **Value** property performs this task and is easier to use.

Parameter	Description
wParam	0 to uncheck the button. 1 to check the button. 2 to place it in its third state if applicable (gray, for example).
lParam	Not used—set to zero.

Comments   This message has no effect on command buttons.

■ BM_SETSTATE

VB Declaration   Global Const BM_SETSTATE = WM_USER+3

Description   Used to set the highlight state for a button style control. A button is highlighted when it is pressed; that is, the user clicks the left mouse button over the control. The button remains highlighted until the mouse button is released.

Use with VB   No problem.

Parameter	Description
wParam	0 to clear the highlighting. Nonzero to highlight the button.
lParam	Not used—set to zero.

Using APIGUIDE.DLL and CBK.VBX

Visual Basic can access the vast majority of the Windows API functions. There are, however, a significant number of API functions that are not directly compatible with Visual Basic, but can be used with the help of a few DLL functions that are not part of the Windows API or of Visual Basic.

The disk that comes with this book contains a dynamic link library APIGUIDE.DLL and a custom control CBK.VBX, which will both prove useful in accessing the Windows API functions.

The functions in APIGUIDE.DLL serve several tasks:

- Provide access to Visual Basic system information.

- Manipulate memory and obtain addresses of VB objects.

- Port I/O.

- Coordinate data conversions.

- Provide access to printer driver functions.

CBK.VBX is a custom control that enables use of Windows API functions that require callback function addresses. Both APIGUIDE.DLL and CBK.VBX programs can be used freely and distributed with your Visual Basic applications. This appendix describes the use of these two programs.

CBK.VBX—Generic Callback Custom Control

CBK.VBX is a custom control that enables use of Windows API callback functions. This control is a subset of the Generic Callback custom control provided with Desaware's SpyWorks-VB program.

How Do Callback Functions Work?

In a number of situations, you may wish to enumerate objects. Consider the problem of listing all of the top level windows in the system. One way to do this is to use the **EnumWindows** API function. This function works by calling a user-defined function for each window. Similar enumeration functions follow the same principle for enumerating fonts, properties, GDI objects, and so on.

How do enumeration functions know which user-defined function to call? Like data objects, the code for functions is present in memory and has a memory address associated with it. The enumeration functions require as one of their parameters the address of a user-defined function to call. Figure A.1 illustrates the program flow used during such enumeration. The Windows application passes the address of a callback function to Windows. Windows then calls the function for each object being enumerated.

Figure A.1

Use of callback functions by traditional Windows applications

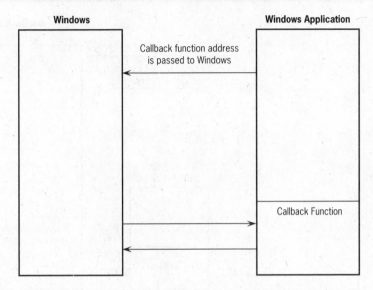

Visual Basic does not provide any mechanism for obtaining the address of a VB function. In order to make it possible to use enumeration functions, the CBK.VBX custom control contains a built-in pool of five function addresses that can be provided to an enumeration function. These addresses are obtained using the **ProcAddress** property. Figure A.2 illustrates the program flow in this case. The Visual Basic application obtains the address of a callback function in CBK.VBX using the **ProcAddress** property and passes it to Windows. Windows then calls the callback function, which in turn triggers a Visual Basic event for each object being enumerated.

Enumeration functions not only expect a function address, but they expect it to be a function of a certain type—it accepts certain parameters and returns certain values. The CBK.VBX custom control has a **Type** property that specifies the type of enumeration function in use. When the enumeration function calls the callback function address provided by the CBK.VBX custom control, the custom control triggers a Visual Basic event corresponding to the type of enumeration.

Most enumeration functions provide a mechanism for stopping the enumeration process. CBK.VBX supports this capability by including a return value parameter to the Visual Basic event. This return value can be set by your program to specify the value that will be returned by the callback function. This return value usually determines whether the enumeration should continue. Refer to the description of each event in "Callback Types and Events," later in this chapter, for information on required return values.

Figure A.2

Use of callback functions in Visual Basic using the CBK.VBX custom control

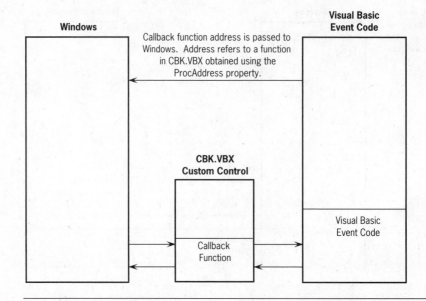

Most enumeration functions provide a user-defined parameter that is passed to the enumeration function and in turn is passed to the callback function each time it is called. The value is then passed to the appropriate Visual Basic event. This parameter can be used in any way you choose. One common technique is to pass the address of a structure or block of memory. This block of memory can then be used to save information during the enumeration process so that when the original enumeration function returns it has all of the accumulated data available. This provides an alternative to using global variables to pass information back to the calling function.

Using CBK.VBX

The CBK.VBX custom control is added into your Visual Basic controls' toolbox using the File-Add command in the same way as any other Visual Basic custom control. Like the timer control, the CBK custom control is not displayed at runtime.

You can have as many controls loaded as you wish. The control does not actually obtain a function address from the pool until it is enabled using the **Type** property. The control maintains a pool of five function addresses that are shared by all controls and all applications. If other programs are using all of the function addresses, an error will occur when the **Type** property is set.

When you wish to use an enumeration function, you simply set the **Type** property to the type of callback you wish to use. Table A.1 lists the properties for the CBK.VBX custom control. You can then use the **ProcAddress** property to obtain a long function address that can be passed as a parameter to the enumeration function.

Table A.1   **CBK.VBX Properties**

Property	Description
(About)	When the "..." button in the property window is clicked, it will display information about the version and capabilities of the CBK.VBX custom control.
Type	Refer to "Callback Types and Events," later in this chapter, for a description of the callback function types supported by this version of CBK.VBX.
ProcAddress	When the **Type** property is not zero (disabled), this property returns the address of a callback function that can be passed to an enumeration function.
Hwnd	Can be read to obtain the window handle of the CBK.VBX custom control.

When you are finished with the enumeration, you can set the **Type** property back to 0 (Disabled) to return the function address to the pool of callback functions.

During enumeration, the CBK.VBX event corresponding to the callback type will be triggered for each object being enumerated.

Callback Types and Events

This section describes the types of callbacks supported by the version of the CBK.VBX custom control provided with this book. Each section describes the associated **Type** property value and corresponding Visual Basic event. You should not modify the values of parameters passed by this VB event unless otherwise noted in the description for that parameter.

■ AbortProc

Type property = 1—AbortProc

Description

The **ProcAddress** property provides the address for a function suitable for use with the **SetAbortProc** API function. Refer to the Chapter 11 function reference for more information on this function. The callback function is called periodically during printing to provide the user with the opportunity to cancel printing.

Visual Basic Event Triggered

AbortProc (hPr%, code%, retval%)

Event Parameter	Description
hPr	**Integer**—A handle to a device context for the printer.
code	**Integer**—Nonzero indicates that a printer error occurred. The constant **SB_OUTOFDISK** indicates that there is insufficient disk space for the output spool file on disk. When this occurs there is a chance that disk space will be freed up by other applications, so you need not abort printing.
retval	**Integer**—Set this value to zero to cancel printing.

■ CommEvent

Type property = Use 0—Disabled

Description

The **CommEvent** function is triggered upon receipt of a **WM_COMMNOTIFY** message by the control. The **EnableCommNotification** API function described in Chapter 14 is used to enable receipt of these messages by a window. This event differs from the others in that the **EnableCommNotification** function uses a window handle instead of a function address. The window handle for the CBK.VBX control can be obtained using the **hWnd** property.

Visual Basic Event Triggered

CommEvent(DeviceID%, NotifyStatus%)

Event Parameter	Description
DeviceID	**Integer**—The identifier of the serial port triggering the notification.

Event Parameter	Description
NotifyStatus	**Integer**—A combination of one or more of the following constant flags ORed together: **CN_EVENT**: An event notification. Serial I/O events are enabled using the **SetCommEventMask** API function. **CN_RECEIVE**: Enough characters have been received to cause the input buffer to exceed a user-defined limit. **CN_TRANSMIT**: The output buffer has dropped below a user-defined limit.

■ Disabled

Type property = 0—Disabled

Description This control is not active. No function is allocated from the internal function pool and the **ProcAddress** property value is not valid.

Visual Basic Event Triggered None.

■ EnumFonts

Type property = 2—EnumFonts

Description The **ProcAddress** property provides the address for a function suitable for use with the **EnumFonts** and **EnumFontFamilies** API functions. Refer to the Chapter 10 function reference for more information on these functions. This callback function is called for each font that is enumerated.

Visual Basic Event Triggered EnumFonts(lpLogFont&, lpTextMetrics&, nFontType%, lpData&, retval%)

Event Parameter	Description
lpLogFont	**Long**—A 32-bit address to a **LOGFONT** data structure containing information about the enumerated font. A description of this structure can be found in Chapter 10.
lpTextMetrics	**Long**—A 32-bit address to a **NEWTEXTMETRIC** structure for TrueType fonts, or a **TEXTMETRIC** structure for non-TrueType fonts. A description of this structure can be found in Chapter 10.
nFontType	**Integer**—A combination of zero or more of the following constants ORed together: **DEVICE_FONTTYPE** if this is a device font. **RASTER_FONTTYPE** if this is a bitmap raster font. **TRUETYPE_FONTTYPE** if this is a TrueType font.
lpData	**Long**—This is the same value passed by your program as the **lP-Data** parameter to the **EnumFonts** function. This is typically used to pass information to the callback function.

Event Parameter	Description
retval	Integer—Set this value to zero to stop the enumeration.

EnumMetaFile

```
Type property = 3—EnumMetaFile
```

Description The **ProcAddress** property provides the address for a function suitable for use with the **Enum-MetaFile** API function. Refer to the Chapter 7 function reference for more information on this function. This callback function is called for each record in a metafile.

**Visual Basic
Event Triggered** EnumMetaFile (hDC%, lpHTable&, lpMFR&, nObj%, lpClientData&, retval%)

Event Parameter	Description
hDC	Integer—A handle to the device context associated with the metafile.
lpHTable	Long—A 32-bit address to an integer table of GDI objects that are used by the metafile. This can include pens, brushes, and so on.
lpMFR	Long—A 32-bit address to a **METARECORD** structure defining a metafile record. A description of this structure can be found in Appendix B.
nObj	Integer—The number of object handles contained in the object table referred to by **lpHTable**.
lpClientData	Long—This is the same value passed by your program as the **lP-ClientData** parameter to the **EnumMetaFile** function. This is typically used to pass information to the callback function.
retval	Integer—Set this value to zero to stop the enumeration.

EnumObjects

```
Type property = 4—EnumObjects
```

Description The **ProcAddress** property provides the address for a function suitable for use with the **EnumOb-jects** API function. Refer to the Chapter 7 function reference for more information on this function. This callback function is called for each GDI object that is enumerated.

**Visual Basic
Event Triggered** EnumObjects (lpLogObject&, lpData&, retval%)

Event Parameter	Description
lpLogObject	**Long**—A 32-bit address to a **LOGPEN** or **LOGBRUSH** data structure depending on the type of object being enumerated. A description of this structure can be found in Appendix B.
lpData	**Long**—This is the same value passed by your program as the **lP-Data** parameter to the **EnumObjects** function. This is typically used to pass information to the callback function.
retval	**Integer**—Set this value to zero to stop the enumeration.

■ EnumProps

Type property = 5—EnumProps

Description The **ProcAddress** property provides the address for a function suitable for use with the **Enum-Props** API function. Refer to the Chapter 16 function reference for more information on this function. This callback function is called for each property that is enumerated. Note that property in this case does not refer to Visual Basic properties but rather to Windows properties, as defined in Chapter 16.

**Visual Basic
Event Triggered** EnumProps (hWnd%, lpString$, hData%, retval%)

Event Parameter	Description
hWnd	**Integer**—A handle to the windows whose properties are being enumerated.
lpString	**String**—The string associated with the property being enumerated.
hData	**Integer**—The data associated with the property being enumerated.
retval	**Integer**—Set this value to zero to stop the enumeration.

Warning

■ Do not perform any operation that could yield control to other applications (such as the VB **DoEvents** function) during this event.

■ Do not add new properties during this event.

■ Do not remove properties during this event (except for the property being enumerated).

■ EnumWindows

Type property = 6—EnumWindows

Description The **ProcAddress** property provides the address for a function suitable for use with the **Enum-Windows** or **EnumTaskWindows** API functions. Refer to the Chapter 4 function reference for more information on these functions. This callback function is called for each window that is enumerated.

**Visual Basic
Event Triggered**   `EnumWindows(hWnd%, lParam&, retval%)`

Event Parameter	Description
hWnd	**Integer**—A handle to the window being enumerated.
lpParam	**Long**—This is the same value passed by your program as the **lParam** parameter to the **EnumWindows** or **EnumTaskWindows** function. This is typically used to pass information to the callback function.
retval	**Integer**—Set this value to zero to stop the enumeration.

■ GrayString

`Type property = 7-GrayString`

Description   The **ProcAddress** property provides the address for a function suitable for use with the **Gray-String** API function. Refer to the Chapter 10 function reference for more information on this function. This callback is typically used when you want to draw a grayed string (like those used when a control is disabled), but wish to customize the text output.

**Visual Basic
Event Triggered**   `GrayString(hDC%, lpData&, nCount%, retval%)`

Event Parameter	Description
hDC	**Integer**—A device context on which to draw the string. The string specified by **lpData** and **nCount** should be drawn at coordinates 0,0 of this device context.
lpData	**Long**—A 32-bit address of the string to draw.
nCount	**Integer**—The number of characters to draw.
retval	**Integer**—Set this value to TRUE (nonzero) to indicate that the drawing was successful. Zero on error. This result will be reflected in the result of the **GrayString** API function.

■ LineDDA

`Type property = 8-LineDDA`

Description   The **ProcAddress** property provides the address for a function suitable for use with the **LineDDA** API function. Refer to the Chapter 7 function reference for more information on this function. This callback function is used to determine the x,y coordinates of each point in a line.

Visual Basic
Event Triggered   LineDDA (x%, y%, lpData&, retval%)

Event Parameter	Description
x%, y%	**Integer**—The x and y coordinate of a point in a line specified by the **LineDDA** API function.
lpData	**Long**—This is the same value passed by your program as the **lpData** parameter to the **LineDDA** function. This is typically used to pass information to the callback function.
retval	**Integer**—Not used.

■ WndProc

Type property = 9—WndProc

Description   The **ProcAddress** property provides the address for a function suitable for use with a function that uses the standard Windows message protocol. It is included for the sake of completeness, but does not have any application at this time. Do not attempt to use this callback to implement subclassing of a window other than on an experimental basis.

Visual Basic
Event Triggered   WndProc(hwnd%, msg%, wp%, lp%, res&)

Event Parameter	Description
hWnd	**Integer**—A handle to a window.
msg	**Integer**—A message number.
wp	**Integer**—The 16-bit parameter to the message.
lp	**Long**—The 32-bit parameter to the message.
res	**Long**—The value to return from the callback function.

APIGUIDE.DLL

The functions described in this section are part of the APIGUIDE.DLL dynamic link library.

■ agCopyData, agCopyDataBynum

VB Declaration Declare Sub agCopyData Lib "Apiguide.dll" (source as any, dest as any, ByVal ⇔ nCount%)

Declare Sub agCopyDataBynum Lib "Apiguide.dll" Alias "agCopyData" (ByVal ⇔ source&, ByVal dest&, ByVal nCount%)

Description This function is provided to copy data from one object to another. Two forms of this function are provided; the first accepts any type of object. If the two objects were of the same type, you could simply use the Visual Basic **LSet** function; however, this function can be used for copying only the specified part of the object.

   The second form accepts **Long** parameters. It is typically used to copy data between Visual Basic structures and string buffers or memory blocks. Chapter 12 demonstrates the use of this function for transferring data to and from global memory blocks.

Use with VB No problem.

Parameter	Type/Description
source	**Long**—The address of the start of a block of memory to copy.
dest	**Long**—The address of the beginning of a destination block of memory.
nCount	**Integer**—The number of bytes to copy.

Comments Be very careful that the parameters to this function are valid and that the entire range specified by **nCount** is also valid.

   This function does not handle blocks greater than 64k in size. Use the Windows **hmemcpy** and **hmemcpyBynum** functions for huge memory blocks.

   The source and destination memory ranges may overlap.

■ agDeviceCapabilities

VB Declaration Declare Function agDeviceCapabilities& Lib "Apiguide.dll" (ByVal hlib%, ByVal ⇔ lpszDevice$, ByVal lpszPort$, ByVal fwCapability%, ByVal lpszOutput&, ByVal ⇔ lpdm&)

Description This function is described in the function reference for APIGUIDE.DLL functions in Chapter 10.

■ agDeviceMode

VB Declaration   Declare Function agDeviceMode% Lib "Apiguide.dll" (ByVal hWnd%, ByVal ⇔ hModule%, ByVal lpszDevice$, ByVal lpszOutput$)

Description   This function is described in the function reference for APIGUIDE.DLL functions in Chapter 10.

■ agDWORDto2Integers

VB Declaration   Declare Sub agDWORDto2Integers Lib "Apiguide.dll" (ByVal l&, lw%, lh%)

Description   Many Windows API functions return a long variable that contains two integers. This function provides an efficient way to separate the two integers.

Use with VB   No problem.

Parameter	Type/Description
l	**Long**—The source **Long** variable.
lw	**Integer**—This variable is set to the low 16 bits of parameter l.
lh	**Integer**—This variable is set to the high 16 bits of parameter l.

■ agExtDeviceMode

VB Declaration   Declare Function agExtDeviceMode% Lib "Apiguide.dll" (ByVal hWnd%, ByVal ⇔ hDriver%, ByVal lpdmOutput&, ByVal lpszDevice$, ByVal lpszPort$, ByVal ⇔ lpdmInput&, ByVal lpszProfile&, ByVal fwMode%)

Description   This function is described in the function reference for APIGUIDE.DLL functions in Chapter 10.

■ agGetAddressForObject, agGetAddressForInteger, agGetAddressForLong, agGetAddressForLPSTR

VB Declaration   Declare Function agGetAddressForObject& Lib "Apiguide.dll" (object As Any)

Declare Function agGetAddressForInteger& Lib "Apiguide.dll" Alias ⇔ "agGetAddressForObject" (intnum%)

Declare Function agGetAddressForLong& Lib "Apiguide.dll" Alias ⇔ "agGetAddressForObject" (intnum&)

Declare Function agGetAddressForLPSTR& Lib "Apiguide.dll" Alias ⇔ "agGetAddressForObject" (ByVal lpstring$)

Description   Many of the API declarations found in this book require 32-bit (long) addresses as parameters. These functions can be used to determine the address of a Visual Basic variable. Three type-safe declarations are provided for integers, longs, and strings.

        The function **agGetAddressForObject** is defined to retrieve the addresses of variables and user-defined structures. This should not be confused with the new Visual Basic 2.0 object type that is used to hold forms and controls.

Use with VB   Addresses obtained using this function should be used immediately because Visual Basic variable objects can move in memory. Generally, you should call these functions to obtain an address each time you need it.

Parameter	Type/Description
object	**Any**—The object for which to obtain an address.

Return Value   **Long**—The address of the object.

■ agGetAddressForVBString

VB Declaration   `Declare Function agGetAddressForVBString& Lib "Apiguide.dll" (vbstring$)`

Description   Retrieves the address of a Visual Basic string. This function bypasses the conversion to a null terminated string that is used with function **agGetAddressForLPSTR**.

Use with VB   Addresses obtained using this function should be used immediately because Visual Basic strings can move in memory. Generally, you should call these functions to obtain an address each time you need it.

Parameter	Type/Description
vbstring	**String**—String for which to obtain an address.

Return Value   **Long**—The address of the object.

■ agGetControlHwnd

VB Declaration   `Declare Function agGetControlHwnd% Lib "Apiguide.dll" (hctl As Control)`

Description   Retrieves the window handle for a control.

Use with VB   Most Visual Basic 2.0 and later controls have a **hWnd** property that can be used to retrieve the window handle of a control. This function can be used with Visual Basic 1.0 controls and other controls that do not have a **hWnd** property.

Parameter	Type/Description
hctl	**Control** or **Form**—The control or form for which to obtain a window handle.

Return Value   Integer—The window handle for a control. Zero if the control is a VB 2.0 graphical control.

■ agGetControlName

VB Declaration   Declare Function agGetControlName$ Lib "Apiguide.dll" (ByVal hWnd%)

Description   Retrieves the name of a Visual Basic control.

Use with VB   No problem.

Parameter	Type/Description
hWnd	Integer—A handle to a window.

Return Value   String—The control name of a Visual Basic control that has window **hWnd**. An empty string if the window is not a Visual Basic control.

■ agGetInstance

VB Declaration   Declare Function agGetInstance% Lib "Apiguide.dll" ()

Description   Retrieves the instance handle of the current application. The instance handle is used by a number of Windows API functions.

Use with VB   No problem.

Return Value   Integer—A handle to the current instance.

■ agGetStringFromLPSTR

VB Declaration   Declare Function agGetStringFromLPSTR$ Lib "Apiguide.dll" (ByVal lpstring&)

Description   A number of Windows API functions return pointers to NULL terminated strings. This function provides an easy way to convert these strings into Visual Basic strings.

Use with VB   No problem.

Parameter	Type/Description
lpstring	Long—The address of a block of memory containing a null terminated string.

Return Value   String—A Visual Basic string containing the string referred to by the **lpstring** block.

■ agHugeOffset

VB Declaration   Declare Function agHugeOffset& Lib "Apiguide.dll" (ByVal addr&, ByVal offset&)

Description   Address calculations that could cross a 64k segment boundary cannot be performed with simple arithmetic. The problems of calculating address offsets on huge (>64k) memory blocks are discussed at length in Chapter 10.

This function can be used to add or subtract an offset to a 32-bit address.

Use with VB   No problem.

Parameter	Type/Description
addr	**Long**—A valid 32-bit memory address.
offset	**Long**—An offset to add to the address (this address may be negative to perform subtraction).

Return Value   **Long**—The resulting 32-bit address.

■ agInp, agInpw

VB Declaration   Declare Function agInp% Lib "Apiguide.dll" (ByVal portid%)

Declare Function agInpw% Lib "Apiguide.dll" (ByVal portid%)

Description   These functions are used to input data from an I/O port.

Use with VB   No problem.

Parameter	Type/Description
portid	**Integer**—I/O port address.

Return Value   **Integer**—The byte (**agInp**) or integer (**agInpw**) read from the port.

Comments   Direct port access under Windows may not work depending on the device. This function is typically used for accessing specialized interfaces for which a Windows driver does not exist.

■ agOutp, agOutpw

VB Declaration   Declare Sub agOutp Lib "Apiguide.dll" (ByVal portid%, ByVal outval%)

Declare Sub agOutpw Lib "Apiguide.dll" (ByVal portid%, ByVal outval%)

Description   These functions are used to send data to an I/O port.

Use with VB	No problem.

Parameter	Type/Description
portid	**Integer**—I/O port address.
outval	**Integer**—The Byte or Integer to write out to the I/O port.

Comments   Direct port access under Windows may not work depending on the device. This function is typically used for accessing specialized interfaces for which a Windows driver does not exist.

■ agPOINTAPItoLong

VB Declaration   Declare Function agPOINTAPItoLong& Lib "Apiguide.dll" (pt As POINTAPI)

Description   Converts a **POINTAPI** structure into a **Long**, placing the X field in the low 16 bits of the result and the Y field in the high 16 bits of the result. This function is convenient for Windows API functions that expect **POINTAPI** structures to be passed as **Long** parameters.

Use with VB   No problem.

Parameter	Type/Description
pt	**POINTAPI**—A **POINTAPI** structure.

Return Value   **Long**—A **Long** representation of the **POINTAPI** structure.

■ agVBClientToScreen

VB Declaration   Declare Sub agVBClientToScreen Lib "Apiguide.dll" (ctl As Control, pap As ⇔ POINTAPI)

Description   Used to convert client coordinates to screen coordinates of a control.

Use with VB   This function can be used to perform coordinate conversions for Visual Basic graphical controls. This function requires Visual Basic version 2.0.

Parameter	Type/Description
ctl	**Control**—Control defining the client coordinate system to use.
pap	**POINTAPI**—Structure containing the point on the screen in client coordinates of the specified control. This function loads the structure with the corresponding screen coordinates.

■ agVBGetVersion

VB Declaration `Declare Function agVBGetVersion% Lib "Apiguide.dll" ()`

Description Determines the version of Visual Basic that this program is running under.

Use with VB No problem.

Return Value **Integer**—&H100 if this is Visual Basic 1.0, &H200 if this is Visual Basic 2.0.

■ agVBScreenToClient

VB Declaration `Declare Sub agVBScreenToClient Lib "Apiguide.dll" (ctl As Control, pap As ⇔`
`POINTAPI)`

Description Used to convert screen coordinates to client coordinates of a control.

Use with VB This function can be used to perform coordinate conversions for Visual Basic graphical controls. This function requires Visual Basic version 2.0.

Parameter	Type/Description
ctl	**Control**—Control defining the client coordinate system to use.
pap	**POINTAPI**—Structure containing the point on the screen in screen coordinates. This function loads the structure with the corresponding client coordinates based on the specified control.

■ agVBSendControlMsg

VB Declaration `Declare Function agVBSendControlMsg& Lib "Apiguide.dll" (ctl As Control, ⇔`
`ByVal msg%, ByVal wp%, ByVal lp&)`

Description This function is identical to the **SendMessage** function except that it accepts a control handle as a parameter instead of a window handle.

Use with VB This function can be used to send messages to graphical controls. Note that graphical controls do not respond to all Windows messages.

Parameter	Type/Description
ctl	**Control**—A Visual Basic control.
wMsg	**Integer**—Message ID.
wParam	**Integer**—16-bit parameter depending on message.
lParam	Varies—32-bit **Long** or **String** parameter depending on the message.

Return Value   **Long**—Depends on the message.

Comments   If **lParam** is a handle or pointer to a global memory block, that block must be allocated with the **GMEM_SHARE** flag. See Chapter 16 for details.

■ agXPixelsToTwips, agYPixelsToTwips

VB Declaration   Declare Function agXPixelsToTwips& Lib "Apiguide.dll" (ByVal pixels%)

Declare Function agYPixelsToTwips& Lib "Apiguide.dll" (ByVal pixels%)

Description   Converts screen pixels into twips. Note the separate functions for horizontal and vertical conversions. Be careful to use the correct one.

Use with VB   The VB 2.0 Screen object **TwipsPerPixelX** and **TwipsPerPixelY** properties can be used to perform these calculations.

Parameter	Type/Description
pixels	**Integer**—A number of pixels to convert into twips.

Return Value   **Long**—The number of twips.

■ agVBSetControlFlags

VB Declaration   Declare Function agVBSetControlFlags& Lib "Apiguide.dll" (ctl As Control, ByVal mask&, ByVal value&)

Description   This function is used to control the palette status of a control and returns the current status of the control.

Use with VB   Can be used to specify or determine when a control is palette, and whether or not it is currently owns a palette. In practice, this is only effective for determining status. You can use this function to set the palette awareness of a control only if you take over all aspects of selecting and resizing palettes. This requires a subclassing tool capable of detecting both the windows palette messages and the Internal Visual Basic palette messages.

Parameter	Type/Description
ctl	A control or form
mask	Set a bit in the mask to 1 to indicate that it should be changed according to the value parameter.
value	Indicates the new value for the bits specified by the mask parameter. Bit 0 is set to 1 to indicate that the control owns a palette. Bit 1 is set to 1 to indicate that the control is palette aware.

Return Value   **Long**—A value describing the current state of the control.

■ agXTwipsToPixels, agYTwipsToPixels

VB Declaration   `Declare Function agXTwipsToPixels% Lib "Apiguide.dll" (ByVal twips&)`

`Declare Function agYTwipsToPixels% Lib "Apiguide.dll" (ByVal twips&)`

Description   Converts twips to screen pixels. Note the separate functions for horizontal and vertical conversions. Be careful to use the correct one.

Use with VB   The VB 2.0 Screen object **TwipsPerPixelX** and **TwipsPerPixelY** properties can be used to perform these calculations.

Parameter	Type/Description
twips	**Long**—A number of twips to convert into pixels.

Return Value   **Integer**—The number of pixels.

Windows Data Structures

This appendix lists the data structures used by Microsoft Windows that are useful under Visual Basic. These type definitions can be found in file API-TYPES.TXT provided with this book and are also included in the module APIDECS.BAS.

■ ABC

VB Declaration

```
Type ABC      '6 Bytes
     abcA As Integer
     abcB As Integer
     abcC As Integer
End Type
```

Description

Describes spacing of TrueType fonts.

Field	Type/Description
abcA	**Integer**—TrueType character 'A' spacing.
abcB	**Integer**—TrueType character 'B' spacing.
abcC	**Integer**—TrueType character 'C' spacing.

Comments

Refer to the description of TrueType fonts in Chapter 10.

■ BITMAP

VB Declaration

```
Type BITMAP '14 bytes
     bmType As Integer
     bmWidth As Integer
     bmHeight As Integer
     bmWidthBytes As Integer
     bmPlanes As String * 1
     bmBitsPixel As String * 1
     bmBits As Long
End Type
```

Description

This structure defines a logical device-dependent bitmap.

Field	Type/Description
bmType	**Integer**—Must be 0.
bmWidth	**Integer**—Width of the bitmap in pixels.
bmHeight	**Integer**—Height of the bitmap in pixels.

Field	Type/Description
bmWidthBytes	**Integer**—The number of bytes of data in a raster line. Must be an even number.
bmPlanes	**Character**—The number of color planes in the bitmap.
bmBitPixel	**Character**—The number of bits per pixel on each plane.
bmBits	**Long**—Address of the actual bitmap data.

■ BITMAPCOREHEADER

VB Declaration
```
Type BITMAPCOREHEADER '12 bytes
    bcSize as Long
    bcWidth As Integer
    bcHeight As Integer
    bcPlanes As Integer
    bcBitCount As Integer
End Type
```

Description This is the device-independent bitmap (DIB) structure used by OS/2-compatible DIBs. It is not generally used by Windows applications.

Field	Type/Description
bcSize	**Long**—The size of this structure—currently 12.
bcWidth	**Integer**—The width of the bitmap.
bcHeight	**Integer**—The height of the bitmap.
bcPlanes	**Integer**—The number of planes. Always 1.
bcBitCount	**Integer**—1 for monochrome, 4 for 16 colors, 8 for 256 colors, and 24 for 24-bit RGB color.

■ BITMAPCOREINFO

VB Declaration
```
Type BITMAPCOREINFO  'Varies
    bmciHeader As BITMAPCOREHEADER
    bmciColors As String * 48 ' Array length depends on the bitmap.
End Type
```

Description A structure that includes a **BITMAPCOREINFO** structure followed by a color table. The size of the color table needed depends on the **biBitCount** field of the **bmciHeader BITMAPCORE-HEADER** structure as follows:

bcBitCount	Number of Colors	Size of Color Table in Bytes
1	2	6

bcBitCount	Number of Colors	Size of Color Table in Bytes
4	16	48
8	256	768
24	2^{24}	0 (not used for 24-bit color)

■ BITMAPFILEHEADER

VB Declaration
```
Type BITMAPFILEHEADER    '14 Bytes
        bfType As Integer
        bfSize As Long
        bfReserved1 As Integer
        bfReserved2 As Integer
        bfOffBits As Long
End Type
```

Description   This structure appears at the beginning of a Windows device-independent bitmap file (.BMP file).

Field	Type/Description
bfType	**Integer**—The two bytes in this integer contain the characters BM (the value &H4D42).
bfSize	**Long**—The size of the file.
bfReserved1	**Integer**—Not used.
bfReserved2	**Integer**—Not used.
bfOffBits	**Long**—The offset from the end of this structure to the beginning of the actual bitmap data in the file.

■ BITMAPINFO

VB Declaration
```
Type BITMAPINFO   'Varies
       bmiHeader as BITMAPINFOHEADER
       bmiColors As String * 64 ' Array length depends on the bitmap
End Type
```

Description   A structure that includes a **BITMAPINFOHEADER** structure followed by a color table. The size of the color table needed depends on the **biBitCount** field of the **bmiHeader BITMAPINFO-HEADER** structure as follows:

biBitCount	Number of Colors	Size of Color Table in Bytes
1	2	8
4	16	64

biBitCount	Number of Colors	Size of Color Table in Bytes
8	256	1024
24	2^{24}	0 (not used for 24-bit color)

■ BITMAPINFOHEADER

VB Declaration
```
Type BITMAPINFOHEADER '40 bytes
    biSize As Long
    biWidth As Long
    biHeight As Long
    biPlanes As Integer
    biBitCount As Integer
    biCompression As Long
    biSizeImage As Long
    biXPelsPerMeter As Long
    biYPelsPerMeter As Long
    biClrUsed As Long
    biClrImportant As Long
End Type
```

Description
A device-independent bitmap consists of two parts. The first of these is a **BITMAPINFO** structure, which in turn begins with a **BITMAPINFOHEADER** structure. This structure defines the characteristics of the device-independent bitmap including the size, color information, and type of compression used.

Use with VB
Detailed information on using device-independent bitmaps can be found in "Device-Independent Bitmaps" in Chapter 8.

Field	Type/Description
biSize	**Long**— 40 (the size of this structure).
biWidth	**Long**—The width of the bitmap in pixels.
biHeight	**Long**—The height of the bitmap in pixels.
biPlanes	**Integer**—1 (DIBs always have one plane).
biBitCount	**Integer**—1 for monochrome, 4 for 16 colors, 8 for 256 color, and 24 for 24-bit RGB color.
biCompression	**Long**—See Table B.1.
biSizeImage	**Long**—The size of the image in bytes. May be zero if **biCompression** is **BI_RGB**.
biXPelsPerMeter	**Long**—Number of horizontal pixels per meter for which this DIB was designed.
biYPelsPerMeter	**Long**—Number of vertical pixels per meter for which this DIB was designed.

Field	Type/Description
biClrUsed	**Long**—Number of entries in the DIB color table that are actually used. Zero if all are used. Must be zero or the actual color table size for packed DIBs (see Chapter 8 for details).
biClrImportant	**Long**—Number of entries in the DIB color table that are important. Zero to specify all colors.

Table B.1 **Bitmap Compression Types**

biCompression	Description
BI_RGB	No compression is used.
BI_RLE8	RLE compression for an 8-bit bitmap. Bytes are paired. The first byte indicates the number of pixels to draw, the second indicates the index into the color table of the color to use. If the first byte is zero, the second byte has one of the following values: 0—Mark end of line. 1—Mark end of bitmap. 2—The next two bytes indicate an X,Y offset to the next pixel from the current pixel. 3-256—The next three to 256 bytes are set according to the data that follows. The data run must be aligned on a 16-bit boundary (pad with nulls if necessary).
BI_RLE4	Similar to **BI_RLE8** except that the color data byte contains two four-bit color indexes. The color used alternates using the high four bits, then the low four bits, then the high four bits again, and so on.

■ COMSTAT

VB Declaration
```
Type COMSTAT   '5 Bytes
    Bits As String * 1
    cbInQue As Integer
    cbOutQue As Integer
End Type
```

Description   Refer to "Obtaining Serial Port Status" in Chapter 14 for a description of this structure.

■ DCB

VB Declaration
```
Type DCB    '25 Bytes
    Id As String * 1
```

```
        BaudRate As Integer
        ByteSize As String * 1
        Parity As String * 1
        StopBits As String * 1
        RlsTimeout As Integer
        CtsTimeout As Integer
        DsrTimeout As Integer
        Bits1 As String * 1
        Bits2 As String * 1
        XonChar As String * 1
        XoffChar As String * 1
        XonLim As Integer
        XoffLim As Integer
        PeChar As String * 1
        EofChar As String * 1
        EvtChar As String * 1
        TxDelay As Integer
End Type
```

Description   Refer to "Configuring Serial Ports and the Device Control Block" in Chapter 14 for a description of this structure.

■ DEVMODE

VB Declaration
```
Type DEVMODE      ' 68 Bytes
{
        dmDeviceName As String *32
        dmSpecVersion As Integer
        dmDriverVersion As Integer
        dmSize As Integer
        dmDriverExtra As Integer
        dmFields As Long
        dmOrientation As Integer
        dmPaperSize As Integer
        dmPaperLength As Integer
        dmPaperWidth As Integer
        dmScale As Integer
        dmCopies As Integer
        dmDefaultSource As Integer
        dmPrintQuality As Integer
        dmColor As Integer
        dmDuplex As Integer
        dmYResolution As Integer
        dmTTOption As Integer
End Type
```

Description   This structure is used to describe the configuration of an output device such as a printer. It is described in detail in "Printer Settings and the DEVMODE Structure" in Chapter 11.

■ DOCINFO

VB Declaration
```
Type DOCINFO    ' 10 Bytes
     cbSize As Integer
     lpszDocName As Long
     lpszOutput As Long
End Type
```

Description   Refer to the **StartDoc** API function description in Chapter 11.

■ EVENTMSG

VB Declaration
```
Type EVENTMSG '10 Bytes
     message As Integer
     paramL As Integer
     paramH As Integer
     time As Long
End Type
```

Description   This structure is used to describe event messages as used by event macro recorders.

Use with VB   Visual Basic provides no access to the low-level system hooks that use this structure, so it is unlikely to be of use to the VB programmer.

Field	Type/Description
message	**Integer**—The message number.
ParamL, ParamH	**Integers**—16-bit parameters to the message. The meaning of these fields depends on the message.
time	**Long**—The time at which the message was added to the message queue. Measured in number of milliseconds from the time the system was started.

■ FIXED

VB Declaration
```
Type FIXED   '4 Bytes
     fract As Integer
     value As Integer
End Type
```

Description   A fixed-point number consisting of an integer and fractional part used by TrueType fonts.

Parameter	Type/Description
fract	**Integer**—Fractional part of the number.
value	**Integer**—Integer portion of the number.

■ FIXEDFILEINFO

VB Declaration

```
Type FIXEDFILEINFO ' 52 Bytes
        dwSignature As Long
        dwStrucVersion As Long
        dwFileVersionMS As Long
        dwFileVersionLS As Long
        dwProductVersionMS As Long
        dwProductVersionLS As Long
        dwFileFlagsMask As Long
        dwFileFlags As Long
        dwFileOS As Long
        dwFileType As Long
        dwFileSubtype As Long
        dwFileDateMS As Long
        dwFileDateLS As Long
End Type
```

Description   This structure is used to obtain version information for a file that contains version stamping information. It is described in detail in "The Version Data Structures" in Chapter 13.

■ GLYPHMETRICS

VB Declaration

```
Type GLYPHMETRICS ' 12 Bytes
        gmBlackBoxX As Integer
        gmBlackBoxY As Integer
        gmptGlyphOrigin As POINTAPI
        gmCellIncX As Integer
        gmCellIncY As Integer
End Type
```

Description   Determines the size and position of the character within a character cell. The character area is referred to as the glyph. The **BlackBox** is the smallest rectangle that completely encloses the glyph.

Field	Type/Description
gmBlackBoxX, gmBlackBoxY	**Integers**—The width and height of the **BlackBox** for the character.
gmptGlyphOrigin	**POINTAPI**—The X,Y coordinates of the **BlackBox** within the character cell.
gmCellIncX, gmCellIncY	**Integers**—The horizontal and vertical distance to the next character cell.

■ HANDLETABLE

VB Declaration

```
Type HANDLETABLE
        objectHandle As String * 512
End Type
```

Description   This structure is part of a metafile and is used to hold handles to GDI objects such as pens, brushes, and fonts.

Field	Type/Description
objectHandle	**String**—This is a buffer of arbitrary length that holds an array of GDI object handles.

■ HELPWININFO

VB Declaration
```
Type HELPWININFO  ' 12 Bytes + length of rgchMember
    wStructSize As Integer
    x As Integer
    y As Integer
    dx As Integer
    dy As Integer
    wMax As Integer
    rgchMember As String *2 'Length varies depending on the window name
End Type
```

Description   This structure is used by the **WinHelp** API function to specify the position and size of the help application window. The Windows help system uses a coordinate system of 1024x1024 with the upper left corner of the display being point 0,0.

Use with VB   No problem.

Field	Type/Description
wStructSize	**Integer**—The size of this structure. Fourteen bytes as defined above.
x,y	**Integer**—The x,y coordinates of the upper left corner of the help application window in help system coordinates.
dx,dy	**Integer**—The width and height of the help window in help system coordinates.
wMax	**Integer**—0 to base the window size on the x, y, dx, and dy parameters. 1 to maximize the help window.
rgchMember	**String**—The window name.

■ LOGBRUSH

VB Declaration
```
Type LOGBRUSH      '8 Bytes
    lbStyle As Integer
    lbColor As Long
    lbHatch As Integer
End Type
```

Description	Data structure used to define a logical brush. The actual physical brush will depend on the capabilities of the device.
Use with VB	No problem.

Field	Type/Description
lbStyle	**Integer**—One of the following constants: **BS_DIBPATTERN**: A pattern brush based on a device-independent bitmap. **BS_HATCHED**: A hatched brush according to field **lbHatch**. **BS_HOLLOW**: A hollow brush. **BS_PATTERN**: A pattern brush based on a bitmap. **BS_SOLID**: A solid brush.
lbColor	**Long**—Depends on the value of **lbStyle**: For **BS_SOLID** refer to the description of the **crColor** parameter of the **CreateSolidBrush** API function (see Chapter 7). For **BS_HATCHED** refer to the description of the **crColor** parameter of the **CreateHatchBrush** API function (see Chapter 7). For **BS_DIBPATTERN** refer to the description of the **wUsage** parameter of the **CreateDIBPatternBrush** API function (see Chapter 7).
lbHatch	**Integer**—If **lbStyle** is **BS_DIBPATTERN**, this field contains the handle to a packed DIB (refer to description of the **hPackedDIB** parameter to the **CreateDIBPatternBrush** API function in Chapter 7 for details). If **lbStyle** is **BS_HATCHED**, this field is the same as the **nIndex** parameter to the **CreateHatchBrush** API function (see Chapter 7).

■ LOGFONT

VB Declaration

```
Type LOGFONT    ' 50 Bytes
        lfHeight As Integer
        lfWidth As Integer
        lfEscapement As Integer
        lfOrientation As Integer
        lfWeight As Integer
        lfItalic As String * 1
        lfUnderline As String * 1
        lfStrikeOut As String * 1
        lfCharSet As String * 1
        lfOutPrecision As String * 1
        lfClipPrecision As String * 1
        lfQuality As String * 1
        lfPitchAndFamily As String * 1
        lfFaceName As String * 32
End Type
```

Description   Description of a logical font. It is used either to request a font from Windows or to report on the characteristics of a font using the **GetObject** API function. Refer to Chapter 10 for a full description of the fields used in this structure.

■ LOGPALETTE

VB Declaration
```
Type LOGPALETTE
        palVersion As Integer
        palNumEntries As Integer
        palPalEntry As String * varies
End Type
```

Description
This structure defines a logical palette and is used when you are creating a palette with the **CreatePalette** API function. The **palPalEntry** field is a buffer that holds **PALETTEENTRY** structures. The **agCopyData** and **agCopyDataBynum** functions can be used to copy **PALETTEENTRY** structures into this string array.

Use with VB
As described in "Color Palettes" in Chapter 16.

Field	Type/Description
palVersion	**Integer**—The version of this **LOGPALETTE** structure. Should be &H300.
palNumEntries	**Integer**—Specifies the number of palette entries. The **palPalEntry** buffer must be large enough to hold this many **PALETTEENTRY** structures. Thus if a palette has 64 entries, this buffer must be 64*4 = 256 characters long.
palPalEntry	**String**—A string buffer that contains **palNumEntries PALETTE-ENTRY** structures. Under Visual Basic you will need to copy the structures into the string directly as described in the description of this function.

■ LOGPEN

VB Declaration
```
'  Logical Pen
    Type LOGPEN      '10 Bytes
    lopnStyle As Integer
    lopnWidth As POINTAPI
    lopnColor As Long
End Type
```

Description
Data structure used to define a logical pen. The actual physical pen will depend on the capabilities of the device.

Use with VB
No problem.

Field	Type/Description
lopnStyle	**Integer**—Refer to the **nPenStyle** parameter of the **CreatePen** function (see Chapter 7).
lopnWidth	**POINTAPI**—X field contains the width of the pen in logical units. The Y field is not used.

Field	Type/Description
lopnColor	**Long**—RGB color of the pen.

▣ MAT2

VB Declaration
```
Type MAT2    '16 Bytes
    eM11 As FIXED
    eM12 As FIXED
    eM21 As FIXED
    eM22 As FIXED
End Type
```

Description Refer to the TrueType Font specification available from Microsoft for further information on this structure.

▣ MENUITEMTEMPLATE

VB Declaration
```
Type MENUITEMTEMPLATE    'Length Varies
    mtOption As Integer
    mtID As Integer
    mtString As String * 1
End Type
```

Description Defines an entry in a menu resource.

Use with VB Not particularly useful.

Field	Type/Description
mtOption	**Integer**—One or more menu flag constants as defined for the **ModifyMenu** function in Chapter 9. Only the following constants may be used: **MF_CHECKED**, **MF_GRAYED**, **MF_HELP**, **MF_MENUBARBREAK**, **MF_MENUBREAK**, **MF_OWNERDRAW**, **MF_POPUP**.
mtID	**Integer**—The menu ID for this entry. This entry does not exist for entries that have popup windows attached.
mtString	**String**—A null terminated string containing the name of the menu entry.

▣ MENUITEMTEMPLATEHEADER

VB Declaration
```
Type MENUITEMTEMPLATEHEADER    '4 Bytes
    versionNumber As Integer
    offset As Integer
End Type
```

Description A header for a menu resource. It is followed by one or more **MENUITEMTEMPLATE** data structures.

Use with VB   Not particularly useful.

Field	Type/Description
versionNumber	**Integer**—Set to zero.
offset	**Integer**—Offset to the first **MENUITEMTEMPLATE** structure. Set to 4.

■ METAFILEHEADER

VB Declaration

```
Type METAFILEHEADER    ' 22 bytes
    Key As Long
    hmf As Integer
    bbox As RECT
    inch As Integer
    reserved As Long
    checksum As Integer
End Type
```

Description   This structure usually appears at the beginning of a disk metafile (.WMF extension) before the **METAHEADER** structure for the metafile. It is used to define what is known as a "placeable" metafile—a metafile that includes information on scaling that can be used to accurately specify the appearance of the metafile.

Use with VB   No problem.

Field	Type/Description
key	**Long**—The value &H9AC6CDD7&.
hmf	**Integer**—Unused, set to zero.
bbox	**RECT**—A rectangle specifying the bounding rectangle for the metafile (that is, the metafile will be contained within this rectangle). The units of this rectangle are specified by the inch field.
inch	**Integer**—The number of metafile units per inch. This value should be less than 1,440. Typical values are 576 or 1,000.
reserved	**Long**—Not used, set to zero.
checksum	**Integer**—The value of the first ten 16-bit integers of this structure combined using the Xor operation.

Comments   The Windows **GetMetaFile** function cannot read a placeable metafile (one that has this structure). In order to read a placeable metafile, you must strip off this 22-byte structure, load the rest of the metafile into a global memory block, and then use the **SetMetaFileBits** function to create the metafile.

This structure does not appear in file APITYPES.TXT or APIDECS.BAS.

■ METAFILEPICT

VB Declaration

```
Type METAFILEPICT      '8 Bytes
        mm As Integer
        xExt As Integer
        yExt As Integer
        hMF As Integer
End Type
```

Description   This is the structure contained in a global memory block that is used when a metafile is held in the clipboard.

Use with VB   No problem.

Field	Type/Description
mm	**Integer**—The mapping mode used when the metafile was created. The mapping mode is defined by a constant with the **MM_** prefix. Mapping modes are described in Chapter 6.
xExt, yExt	**Integers**—The extents that were used when the metafile was created. If these numbers are negative, then these values specify only the desired aspect ratio, and not the actual magnitude of the extents.
hMF	**Integer**—A handle to a memory metafile. Refer to "Metafiles" in Chapter 7 for further information.

■ METAHEADER

VB Declaration

```
Type METAHEADER        '18 Bytes
        mtType As Integer
        mtHeaderSize As Integer
        mtVersion As Integer
        mtSize As Long
        mtNoObjects As Integer
        mtMaxRecord As Long
        mtNoParameters As Integer
End Type
```

Description   This structure is the header for a metafile. It precedes the metafile records in the memory block that hold a metafile and appears before the start of a disk metafile (files with the .WMF extension), but it may follow a **METAFILEHEADER** structure.

Use with VB   No problem.

Field	Type/Description
mtType	**Integer**—The type of metafile. 1 for memory metafiles, 2 for disk metafiles.

Field	Type/Description
mtHeaderSize	**Integer**—The size of this header in 16-bit integers. Should be 9.
mtVersion	**Integer**—&H300 for metafiles that support device-independent bit-maps. &H100 for older metafiles.
mtSize	**Long**—The size of the file in 16-bit integers.
mtNoObjects	**Integer**—The number of GDI objects that the metafile can require at one time.
mtMaxRecord	**Long**—The size of the largest metafile record in 16-bit integers.
mtNoParameters	**Integer**—Reserved, currently unused.

Comments   Refer to "Metafiles" in Chapter 7 for further information on metafiles.
Note that the sizes specified in this structure are in 16-bit integers (words) instead of bytes.

■ METARECORD

VB Declaration
```
Type METARECORD
    rdSize As Long
    rdFunction As Integer
    rdParm As String * 512 ' Array length is arbitrary
End Type
```

Description   A metafile is a recording of GDI operations. Each of those operations is described in a **METARECORD** structure in a metafile. Refer to the function reference for each function to determine the use of the function and required parameters.

Field	Type/Description
rdSize	**Long**—The size of this record.
rdFunction	**Integer**—A number identifying the GDI operation to be performed. Refer to Table B.2 for a listing of numbers for each GDI function.
rdParm	**String**—A buffer containing the parameters for the GDI function. Generally speaking, this contains the parameters to the function in reverse order (the final parameter appears first in the buffer) except that the device context parameter is not included. Some functions are more complex, as shown in Table B.3.

Table B.2 lists the metafile record numbers for the various GDI functions. Several functions are listed twice. The version listed as obsolete was used before version 3.0 of Windows and is device-dependent.

  The metafile records for most GDI functions are easy to determine based on the parameter list for the function. Typically, the parameters appear in the **rdParm** buffer of the **METARECORD** structure in reverse order. Some functions, however, require special parameters for metafiles. Functions that normally expect pointers to structures as parameters are handled by placing the

entire structure in the **rdParm** field. Examples of these include the **CreateBrushIndirect, Create-FontIndirect, CreatePalette,** and **CreatePenIndirect** functions.

Table B.2   Metafile Record Functions

GDI Function	Metafile Identifier (Hex)
AnimatePalette	&H0436
Arc	&H0817
BitBlt	&H0940
BitBlt (obsolete)	&H0922
Chord	&H0830
CreateBrushIndirect	&H02FC
CreateFontIndirect	&H02FB
CreatePalette	&H00F7
CreatePatternBrush	&H0142
CreatePatternBrush (obsolete)	&H01F9
CreatePenIndirect	&H02FA
CreateRegion	&H06FF
DeleteObject	&H01F0
Ellipse	&H0418
Escape	&H0626
ExcludeClipRect	&H0415
FloodFill	&H0419
IntersectClipRect	&H0416
LineTo	&H0213
MoveTo	&H0214
OffsetClipRgn	&H0220
OffsetViewportOrg	&H0211
OffsetWindowOrg	&H020F

Table B.2 **Metafile Record Functions (Continued)**

GDI Function	Metafile Identifier (Hex)
PatBlt	&H061D
Pie	&H081A
Polygon	&H0324
Polyline	&H0325
PolyPolygon	&H0538
RealizePalette	&H0035
Rectangle	&H041B
ResizePalette	&H0139
RestoreDC	&H0127
RoundRect	&H061C
SaveDC	&H001E
ScaleViewportExt	&H0412
ScaleWindowExt	&H0400
SelectClipRgn	&H012C
SelectObject	&H012D
SelectPalette	&H0234
SetBkColor	&H0201
SetBkMode	&H0102
SetDIBitsToDevice	&H0D33
SetMapMode	&H0103
SetMapperFlags	&H0231
SetPaletteEntries	&H0037
SetPixel	&H041F
SetPolyFillMode	&H0106
SetROP2	&H0104
SetStretchBltMode	&H0107

Table B.2   **Metafile Record Functions (Continued)**

GDI Function	Metafile Identifier (Hex)
SetTextAlign	&H012E
SetTextCharExtra	&H0108
SetTextColor	&H0209
SetTextJustification	&H020A
SetViewportExt	&H020E
SetViewportOrg	&H020D
SetWindowExt	&H020C
SetWindowOrg	&H020B
StretchBlt	&H0B41
StretchBlt (obsolete)	&H0B23
StretchDIBits	&H0F43
TextOut	&H0521

Table B.3 describes the contents of the **rdParm** buffer for additional special cases.

Table B.3   **Metafile Record Parameters**

Function	rdparm Parameter List
AnimatePalette	**start**—Integer: the number of the first palette entry to animate.
	numentries—Integer: the number of entries to animate.
	A series of **PALETTEENTRY** structures containing the new palette entries.
BitBlt (Obsolete—device-dependent version)	**raster-op**—Long: The raster operation.
	SY, **SX**—Integers: The X,Y source origin.
	DYE, **DXE**—Integers: The destination height and width.
	DY, **DX**—Integers: The X,Y destination origin.
	bmWidth—Integer: The width of the bitmap.

Table B.3   Metafile Record Parameters (Continued)

Function	rdparm Parameter List
BitBlt (Obsolete—device-dependent version, continued)	**bmHeight**—Integer: The height of the bitmap.
	bmWidthBytes—Integer: Bytes/raster line.
	bmPlanes—Integer: Number of color planes.
	bmBitsPixel—Integer: Bits/Pixel.
	The bitmap data.
BitBlt	**raster-op**—Long: The raster operation.
	SY, **SX**—Integers: The X,Y source origin.
	DYE, **DXE**—Integers: The destination height and width.
	DY, **DX**—Integers: The X,Y destination origin.
	BitMapInfo—A **BITMAPINFO** structure defining a DIB.
	The bitmap data.
CreatePatternBrush (Obsolete—device-dependent version)	**bmWidth**—Integer: The width of the bitmap.
	bmHeight—Integer: The height of the bitmap.
	bmWidthBytes—Integer: Bytes/raster line.
	bmPlanes—Integer: Number of color planes.
	bmBitsPixel—Integer: Bits/Pixel.
	The bitmap data.
CreatePatternBrush	**Integer**: Value **BS_PATTERN** to use the **CreatePatternBrush** function; **BS_DIBPATTERN** to use the **CreateDIBPatternBrush** function.
	Value **DIB_RGB_COLORS** to use RGB colors, **DIB_PAL_COLORS** if the DIB that follows contains palette relative indexes.
	A **BITMAPINFO** structure defining a DIB.
	The bitmap data.
DeleteObject	An integer index into the metafile handle table defining the GDI object to delete.

Table B.3   Metafile Record Parameters (Continued)

Function	rdparm Parameter List
Escape	The integer number of the **Escape**.
	The number of bytes that follow.
	The parameters to the **Escape** function.
ExtTextOut	**y,x**—Integer: Location to start drawing the string.
	Integer: The length of the string.
	Integer: The **wOptions** parameter to the **ExtTextOut** function.
	A **RECT** structure defining the **lpRect** parameter to the **ExtTextOut** function.
	A string buffer to print.
	An optional integer array defining the **lpDx** parameter to the **ExtTextOut** function.
Polygon	**Integer**: The number of points.
	POINTAPI structures: The array of points.
PolyPolygon	**Integer**: The number of polygons.
	An integer array of polygon sizes (the number of points in each).
	POINTAPI structures: Arrays of points for each polygon.
PolyLine	Same as **Polygon**.
SelectClipRgn SelectObject SelectPalette	An integer index into the metafile handle table defining the GDI object to use in the operation.
SetDIBitsToDevice	The following parameters from the **SetDIBitsToDevice** function (in order):
	wUsage, **NumScans**, **Scan**, **SrcY**, **SrcX**, **dY**, **dX**, **Y**, **X**.
	Followed by:
	A **BITMAPINFO** structure defining the DIB.
	The bitmap data.
SetPaletteEntries	Same as **AnimatePalette**.

Table B.3 **Metafile Record Parameters (Continued)**

Function	rdparm Parameter List
StretchBlt (Obsolete—device-dependent version)	The following parameters from the **StretchBlt** function (in order): **dwROP** (low word followed by high word), **nSrcHeight**, **nSrcWidth**, **YSrc**, **XSrc**, **nHeight**, **nWidth**, **Y**, **X**, Followed by: **bmWidth**—The width of the bitmap. **bmHeight**—The height of the bitmap. **bmWidthBytes**—Bytes/raster line. **bmPlanes**—Number of color planes. **bmBitsPixel**—Bits/pixel. The bitmap data.
StretchBlt	The following parameters from the **StretchBlt** function (in order): **dwROP** (low word followed by high word), **nSrcHeight**, **nSrcWidth**, **YSrc**, **XSrc**, **nHeight**, **nWidth**, **Y**, **X**. Followed by: A **BITMAPINFO** structure defining the DIB. The bitmap data.
StretchDIBits	The following parameters from the **StretchDIBits** function (in order): **dwROP** (low word followed by high word), **wUsage**, **wSrcHeight**, **wSrcWidth**, **SrcY**, **SrcX**, **dY**, **dX**, **Y**, **X**. Followed by: A **BITMAPINFO** structure defining the DIB. The bitmap data.
TextOut	**Integer**: The length of the string. The string data. **Integers**: The Y, X coordinates of the start point for the string.

■ MSG

VB Declaration

```
Type MSG      '18 Bytes
        hwnd As Integer
        message As Integer
        wParam As Integer
        lParam As Long
        time As Long
        pt As POINTAPI
End Type
```

Description   This structure is used to describe a message to a window. It is used by the **PeekMessage** function to retrieve message information.

Use with VB   As described in "Message Processing" in Chapter 16.

Field	Type/Description
hwnd	**Integer**—A handle to the window that is to receive the message.
message	**Integer**—The message number.
wParam	**Integer**—A 16-bit parameter to the message. The meaning of this field depends on the message. Refer to Part 3 of this book for further information.
lParam	**Long**—A 32-bit parameter to the message. The meaning of this field depends on the message. Refer to Part 3 of this book for further information.
time	**Long**—The time at which the message was added to the message queue. Measured in number of milliseconds from the time the system was started.
pt	**POINTAPI**—The location of the cursor in pixel screen coordinates at the time the message was added to the message queue.

■ MULTIKEYHELP

VB Declaration

```
Type MULTIKEYHELP
        mkSize As Integer
        mkKeylist As String * 1
        szKeyphrase As String * 253
End Type
```

Description   This structure is used by the **WinHelp** API function to specify a topic keyword out of a help file keyword table. Refer to your help compiler documentation for further information.

Use with VB   No problem.

Field	Type/Description
mkSize	**Integer**—The number of bytes in this structure. 256 as defined here.

Field	Type/Description
mkKeyList	**String**—A single character that specifies which help file keyword table to search.
szKeyphrase	**String**—The keyword to search for. This string may be of any size.

■ NEWLOGFONT

VB Declaration

```
Type NEWLOGFONT    ' 146 Bytes
        lfHeight As Integer
        lfWidth As Integer
        lfEscapement As Integer
        lfOrientation As Integer
        lfWeight As Integer
        lfItalic As String * 1
        lfUnderline As String * 1
        lfStrikeOut As String * 1
        lfCharSet As String * 1
        lfOutPrecision As String * 1
        lfClipPrecision As String * 1
        lfQuality As String * 1
        lfPitchAndFamily As String * 1
        lfFaceName As String * 32
        lfFullName As String * 64
        lfStyle As String *32
End Type
```

Description Description of a logical TrueType font. It is used when enumerating fonts using the **EnumFont-Families** API function. Refer to Chapter 10 for a full description of the fields used in this structure.

■ NEWTEXTMETRIC

VB Declaration

```
Type NEWTEXTMETRIC    '41 Bytes
        tmHeight As Integer
        tmAscent As Integer
        tmDescent As Integer
        tmInternalLeading As Integer
        tmExternalLeading As Integer
        tmAveCharWidth As Integer
        tmMaxCharWidth As Integer
        tmWeight As Integer
        tmItalic As String * 1
        tmUnderlined As String * 1
        tmStruckOut As String * 1
        tmFirstChar As String * 1
        tmLastChar As String * 1
        tmDefaultChar As String * 1
        tmBreakChar As String * 1
        tmPitchAndFamily As String * 1
```

```
              tmCharSet As String * 1
              tmOverhang As Integer
              tmDigitizedAspectX As Integer
              tmDigitizedAspectY As Integer
              ntmFlags As Long
              ntmSizeEM As Integer
              ntmCellHeight As Integer
              ntmAvgWidth As Integer
        End Type
```

Description   This structure holds information about a physical TrueType font as retrieved by the **GetTextMet-rics** and **EnumFontFamilies** functions. Refer to Chapter 10 for a detailed description of the fields for this function.

■ OFSTRUCT

VB Declaration
```
       '  OpenFile() Structure
       Type OFSTRUCT  '136 Bytes
            cBytes As String * 1
            fFixedDisk As String * 1
            nErrCode As Integer
            reserved As String * 4
            szPathName As String * 128
       End Type
```

Description   This structure is described in detail in "Files and Directories" in Chapter 13.

■ OUTLINETEXTMETRIC

VB Declaration
```
       Type OUTLINETEXTMETRIC  '112 Bytes
            otmSize As Integer
            otmTextMetrics As TEXTMETRIC
            otmFIller As String * 1
            otmPanoseNumber As PANOSE
            otmfsSelection As Integer
            otmfsType As Integer
            otmsCharSlopeRise As Integer
            otmsCharSlopeRun As Integer
            otmEMSquare As Integer
            otmAscent As Integer
            otmDescent As Integer
            otmLineGap As Integer
            otmCapEmHeight As Integer
            otmXHeight As Integer
            otmrcFontBox As RECT
            otmMacAscent As Integer
            otmMacDescent As Integer
            otmMacLineGap As Integer
            otmusMinimumPPEM As Integer
            otmptSubscriptSize As POINTAPI
```

```
            otmptSubscriptOffset As POINTAPI
            otmptSuperscriptSize As POINTAPI
            otmptSuperscriptOffset As POINTAPI
            otmsStrikeoutSize As Integer
            otmsStrikeoutPosition As Integer
            otmsUnderscoreSize As Integer
            otmsUnderscorePosition As Integer
            otmpFamilyName As Integer
            otmpFaceName As Integer
            otmpStyleName As Integer
            otmpFullName As Integer
End Type
```

Use with VB   This structure requires use of 16-bit near pointers, which are difficult to implement in Visual Basic. Refer to the TrueType font specification provided by Microsoft for information on this structure.

■ PAINTSTRUCT

VB Declaration
```
Type PAINTSTRUCT      '32 Bytes
            hdc As Integer
            fErase As Integer
            rcPaint As RECT
            fRestore As Integer
            fIncUpdate As Integer
            rgbReserved As String * 16
End Type
```

Description   This structure is used when painting an application.

Use with VB   Not useful unless you are subclassing the **WM_PAINT** message.

Field	Type/Description
hdc	**Integer**—Device context to use when drawing.
fErase	**Integer**—TRUE (nonzero) if the background needs to be drawn.
rcPaint	**RECT**—A rectangle specifying the area that needs to be painted.
fRestore	**Integer**—Used internally by Windows.
fIncUpdate	**Integer**—Used internally by Windows.
rgbReserved	**String * 16**—Used internally by Windows.

■ PALETTEENTRY

VB Declaration
```
Type PALETTEENTRY     '4 Bytes
            peRed As String * 1
            peGreen As String * 1
            peBlue As String * 1
```

```
        peFlags As String * 1
End Type
```

Description   Describes an entry in a logical palette.

Use with VB   As described in "Color Palettes" in Chapter 16.

Field	Type/Description
peRed	**Integer**—An eight-bit value describing the red component of an RGB color.
peGreen	**Integer**—An eight-bit value describing the green component of an RGB color.
peBlue	**Integer**—An eight-bit value describing the blue component of an RGB color.
peFlags	**Integer**—An eight-bit value containing one of the following values: **0**: Map this entry normally. **PC_EXPLICIT**: The low order word (combination of the **peRed** and **pe-Green** fields) contains an index into the system palette. This allows you to display the system palette colors. **PC_NOCOLLAPSE**: This color is mapped into an unused system palette entry and will not be mapped to an existing color. Subsequent palettes may map colors to this entry. **PC_RESERVED**: This color is mapped to an unused system palette entry and no other logical palettes will be mapped to that entry. By restricting the system palette entry to this logical entry, color cycling involving direct changes to the system palette becomes possible. Refer to the description of the **AnimatePalette** function in Chapter 16.

▧ PANOSE

VB Declaration
```
Type PANOSE ' 10 Bytes
    bFamilyType As String * 1
    bSerifStyle As String * 1
    bWeight As String * 1
    bProportion As String * 1
    bContrast As String * 1
    bStrokeVariation As String * 1
    bArmStyle As String * 1
    bLetterform As String * 1
    bMidline As String * 1
    bXHeight As String * 1
End Type
```

Description   Refer to the TrueType Font specification provided by Microsoft for further information on this structure.

■ PARAMETERBLOCK

VB Declaration

```
Type PARAMETERBLOCK  '14 Bytes
       wEnvSeg As Integer
       lpCmdLine As Long
       lpCmdShow As Long
       dwReserved As Long
End Type
```

Description This structure is passed as a parameter to the **LoadModule** API function to specify the parameters to a Windows application that is being loaded.

Use with VB No problem.

Field	Type/Description
wEnvSeg	**Integer**—If zero, the new application receives a duplicate of the parent application's environment block. Otherwise, this should be set to a segment address of a global memory block containing the environment to use.
lpCmdLine	**Long**—A pointer to a string containing the command line for the program to launch (not including the program name). Must not be zero.
lpCmdShow	**Long**—A pointer to a string specifying how to show the launched program. This matches the **nCmdShow** parameter to the **ShowWindow** API function described in Chapter 4.
dwReserved	**Long**—Set to zero.

■ POINTAPI

VB Declaration

```
Type POINTAPI  '4 Bytes - Synonymous with LONG
       x As Integer
       y As Integer
End Type
```

Description Point. Refer to Chapter 4 for a detailed description of this structure.

■ POINTFX

VB Declaration

```
Type POINTFX   ' 8 Bytes
       x As FIXED
       y As Fixed
End Type
```

Description Used to describe a point in a TrueType font. Refer to the TrueType Font specification available from Microsoft for further information on this structure.

The **FIXED** structure is defined earlier in this appendix.

■ RASTERIZERSTATUS

VB Declaration

```
Type RASTERIZERSTATUS    '6 Bytes
    nSize As Integer
    wFlags As Integer
    nLanguageID As Integer
End Type
```

Description

Used by the **GetRasterizerCaps** function to retrieve information on the configuration of Windows with regard to scalable fonts.

Field	Type/Description
nSize	**Integer**—The size of this structure. Currently 6.
wFlags	**Integer**—Flags indicating the rasterizer capabilities based on the following constants: **TT_AVAILABLE**: At least one TrueType font is available on the system. **TT_ENABLED**: TrueType fonts are enabled on the system.
nLanguageID	**Integer**—The language ID as specified in the Windows SETUP.INF setup information file.

■ RECT

VB Declaration

```
Type RECT    '8 Bytes
    left As Integer
    top As Integer
    right As Integer
    bottom As Integer
End Type
```

Description

Rectangle. Refer to Chapter 4 for a detailed description of this structure.

■ RGBQUAD

VB Declaration

```
Type RGBQUAD        '4 Bytes
    rgbBlue as String * 1
    rgbGreen As String * 1
    rgbRed As String * 1
    rgbReserved As String * 1
End Type
```

Description

A four-byte structure holding an RGB value. This structure is used with device-independent bitmaps (see the **BITMAPINFO** structure) and is a subset of the **PalleteEntry** structure (which is identical except for the use of the **rgbReserved** field).

Field	Type/Description
rgbBlue	**Character**—The 256 level blue component of an RGB color.
rgbGreen	**Character**—The 256 level green component of an RGB color.
rgbRed	**Character**—The 256 level red component of an RGB color.
rgbReserved	**Character**—Reserved. Set to zero.

■ RGBTRIPLE

VB Declaration
```
Type RGBTRIPLE     '3 Bytes
    rgbtBlue As String * 1
    rgbtGreen As String * 1
    rgbtRed As String * 1
End Type
```

Description   A three-byte structure holding an RGB value. This is provided for compatibility with OS/2 bit-maps and is not generally used under Windows.

Field	Type/Description
rgbtBlue	**Character**—The 256 level blue component of an RGB color.
rgbtGreen	**Character**—The 256 level green component of an RGB color.
rgbtRed	**Character**—The 256 level red component of an RGB color.

■ SIZEAPI

VB Declaration
```
Type SIZEAPI '4 Bytes - Synonymous with LONG
    x As Integer
    y As Integer
End Type
```

Description   Size: X and Y refer to the width and height of an object.

■ TEXTMETRIC

VB Declaration
```
Type TEXTMETRIC    '31 Bytes
    tmHeight As Integer
    tmAscent As Integer
    tmDescent As Integer
    tmInternalLeading As Integer
    tmExternalLeading As Integer
    tmAveCharWidth As Integer
    tmMaxCharWidth As Integer
    tmWeight As Integer
    tmItalic As String * 1
```

```
        tmUnderlined As String * 1
        tmStruckOut As String * 1
        tmFirstChar As String * 1
        tmLastChar As String * 1
        tmDefaultChar As String * 1
        tmBreakChar As String * 1
        tmPitchAndFamily As String * 1
        tmCharSet As String * 1
        tmOverhang As Integer
        tmDigitizedAspectX As Integer
        tmDigitizedAspectY As Integer
    End Type
```

Description   This structure holds information about a physical font as retrieved by the **GetTextMetrics** and **EnumFont** functions. Refer to Chapter 10 for a detailed description of the fields for this function.

■ TTPOLYCURVE

VB Declaration
```
Type TTPOLYCURVE        ' 12 Bytes
    wType As Integer
    cpfx As Integer
    apfx As POINTFX
end Type
```

Description   Used to describe a segment in a TrueType font. Refer to the TrueType Font specification available from Microsoft for further information on this structure.

■ TTPOLYGONHEADER

VB Declaration
```
Type TTPOLYGONHEADER        ' 16 Bytes
    cb As Long
    dw As Long
    pfxStart As POINTFX
end Type
```

Description   The header for a segment in a TrueType font. Refer to the TrueType Font specification provided by Microsoft for further information on this structure.

■ WINDOWPLACEMENT

VB Declaration
```
Type WINDOWPLACEMENT        '22 Bytes
    length As Integer
    flags As Integer
    showCmd As Integer
    ptMinPosition AS POINTAPI
    ptMaxPosition AS POINTAPI
    rcNormalPosition As RECT
End Type
```

Description   This structure is used by the **GetWindowPlacement** and **SetWindowPlacement** functions to retrieve and set the position and visibility of a window.

Use with VB   No problem.

Field	Type/Description
length	**Integer**—The size of this structure. Must be 22.
flags	**Integer**—One or both of the following constants: **WPF_SETMINPOSITION**: The **ptMinPosition** specifies the x,y location of the window when minimized. **WPF_RESTORETOMAXIMIZED**: The **SW_SHOWMINIMIZED** constant must be specified in the **showCmd** parameter. Indicates that the window should be maximized the next time it is restored.
ShowCmd	**Integer**—Visibility flags. Refer to the **nCmdShow** parameter to the **ShowWindow** function in Chapter 4.
ptMinPosition	**POINTAPI**—The x,y location of the window when minimized.
ptMaxPosition	**POINTAPI**—The x,y location of the window location when maximized.
rcNormalPosition	**RECT**—The position and size of the window when it is restored (normal condition).

■ WNDCLASS

VB Declaration
```
Type WNDCLASS '26 Bytes
    style As Integer
    lpfnWndProc As Long
    cbClsExtra As Integer
    cbWndExtra As Integer
    hInstance As Integer
    hIcon As Integer
    hCursor As Integer
    hbrBackground As Integer
    lpszMenuName As Long
    lpszClassName As Long
End Type
```

Description   This structure is used when registering a new class of window to define the attributes of that class.

Use with VB   This structure is of little use to the VB programmer since new classes are not registered from within Visual Basic. The class attributes for a window that correspond to the fields in this structure can be obtained using the **GetClassWord** and **GetClassLong** functions.

Field	Type/Description
style	**Integer**—One or more style constants as shown in Table B.4.
lpfnWndProc	**Long**—The address of the default class window function to use for windows of this class.
cbClsExtra	**Integer**—The number of extra bytes to allocate in the class structure. These extra bytes may be accessed using the **GetClassWord**, **GetClassLong**, **SetClassWord**, and **SetClassLong** functions, and are shared by all windows of this class.
cbWndExtra	**Integer**—The number of extra bytes to allocate in the window structure for each window of this class. These extra bytes may be accessed using the **GetWindowWord**, **GetWindowLong**, **SetWindowWord**, and **SetWindowLong** functions.
hInstance	**Integer**—The handle of the module or instance that owns this class. The class is destroyed when this module is freed.
hIcon	**Integer**—A handle of the default icon to use when minimizing windows of this class. This may be NULL, in which case the application must draw an appropriate icon whenever it is minimized.
hCursor	**Integer**—A handle of the default cursor to use when the mouse is over a window of this class. If NULL, the application is responsible for setting the cursor.
hbrBackground	**Integer**—A handle to a brush to use to fill the background of windows of this class. It may also be a color value as defined by constants with the **COLOR_** prefix in APICONST.TXT by specifying the constant plus one. In other words, to use the default menu color you would specify **COLOR_MENU+1**.
lpszMenuName	**Long**—The resource identifier to the menu to use for windows of this class. May be a string address or a resource ID (in which case the low word contains the ID and the high word contains zero). This field may be NULL.
lpszClassName	**Long**—The address of a string containing the name of the class.

Table B.4   **Class Style Constant Definitions**

Style Constant	Description
CS_BYTEALIGNCLIENT	The client area of the window will always be aligned on an eight-bit boundary. This tends to improve performance.

Table B.4   **Class Style Constant Definitions (Continued)**

Style Constant	Description
CS_BYTEALIGNWINDOW	The entire window will always be aligned on an eight-bit boundary. This tends to improve performance.
CS_CLASSDC	All windows of this class share a single device context.
CS_DBLCLKS	Windows of this class receive double-click messages.
CS_GLOBALCLASS	Other applications may use this class. This is typically used when a class is defined by a dynamic link library. All applications that use the DLL may create windows that belong to this class.
CS_HREDRAW	Redraw the window if the width of the window changes.
CS_NOCLOSE	The close entry in the system menu is disabled.
CS_OWNDC	Each window of this class has its own device context. This option requires approximately 800 extra bytes per window.
CS_PARENTDC	Each window of this class uses the device context of its parent window.
CS_SAVEBITS	When this window appears, Windows attempts to save the screen image of the underlying windows so that they may be quickly restored. This is useful for windows that appear and disappear quickly, such as menus and dialog boxes.
CS_VREDRAW	Redraws the window if the height of the window changes.

Windows File Formats

This appendix describes the file formats for some of the common file types used under Windows. In most cases the file contains a series of data structures, some of which are described here and some of which are described in Appendix B.

Bitmap File Format

Bitmap files—those with a .BMP extension—consist of three parts. The file begins with a **BIT-MAPFILEHEADER** structure that describes the file. It is followed by a **BITMAPINFO** structure (described in Appendix B and in Chapter 8). It contains the header and color table for a device-independent bitmap. The **BITMAPINFO** structure is followed by the bitmap data.

The **BITMAPFILEHEADER** structure is defined as follows:

■ BITMAPFILEHEADER

VB Declaration

```
Type BITMAPFILEHEADER    ' 14 Bytes
    bfType As Integer
    bfSize As Long
    bfReserved1 As Integer
    bfReserved2 As Integer
    bfOffBits As Long
```

Description   This structure appears at the beginning of a bitmap file.

Field	Type/Description
bfType	**Integer**—The string "BM" (hex value &H424D).
bfSize	**Long**—The size of the file, measured in bytes.
bfReserved1	**Integer**—Not used, set to zero.
bfReserved2	**Integer**—Not used, set to zero.
bfOffBits	**Long**—The start offset of the bitmap data in the file.

Icon File Format

An icon file, with an .ICO extension, can in fact contain any number of icons. Generally, each icon will be a rendition of an icon image designed for a particular display device. Thus a single icon file may contain icons for CGA, monochrome, VGA, and super VGA devices.

An icon file begins with an **ICONDIR** structure as described below:

ICONDIR

VB Declaration

```
Type ICONDIR     ' 6 Bytes
    idReserved As Integer
    idType As Integer
    idCount As Integer
End Type
```

Description   This structure appears at the beginning of an icon file.

Field	Type/Description
idReserved	**Integer**—Not used, set to zero.
idType	**Integer**—1.
idCount	**Integer**—The number of icons in the file. This specifies the number of **ICONDIRENTRY** structures that follow this structure in the file.

A series of **ICONDIRENTRY** structures immediately follows the **ICONDIR** structure at the start of the file. Each of these structures defines the characteristics of one of the icons in the file. This structure is defined as follows:

ICONDIRENTRY

VB Declaration

```
Type ICONDIRENTRY
    bWidth As String * 1
    bHeight As String * 1
    bColorCount As String * 1
    bReserved As String * 1
    wPlanes As Integer
    wBitCount As Integer
    dwBytesInRes As Long
    dwImageOffset As Long
End Type
```

Description   Each icon in an icon file has an **ICONDIRENTRY** structure associated with it that describes the characteristics of the icon.

Field	Type/Description
bWidth	**String * 1**—The width of the icon. This may be 16, 32, or 64. Most Windows icons are 32x32.
bHeight	**String * 1**—The height of the icon. This may be 16, 32, or 64. Most Windows icons are 32x32.
bColorCount	**String * 1**—The number of colors used by the icons. This may be 2, 8, or 16.
bReserved	**String * 1**—Not used, set to zero.

Field	Type/Description
wPlanes	**Integer**—The number of color planes in the icon.
wBitCount	**Integer**—The number of bits per pixel in the icon.
dwBytesInRes	**Long**—The size of the icon specified in bytes.
dwImageOffset	**Long**—The offset of the specified icon from the beginning of the file.

This structure provides enough information for Windows or an application to match the icon to the display device. You would usually choose the icon in the file that most closely matches the actual display.

The icon data appears after all of the **ICONDIRENTRY** structures. Each icon consists of two bitmaps: an XOR bitmap defining the exclusive-or part of the icon, and an AND bitmap defining the AND mask. These are defined in "Icons and Cursors" in Chapter 8. The XOR bitmap appears first and consists of a device-independent bitmap. This bitmap may be monochrome or color. (Device-independent bitmaps are described in Chapter 8. The data structures used by DIBs are listed in Appendix B.) Only the **biSize** through **biBitCount** fields of the DIB's **BIT-MAPINFOHEADER** structure are used with icons. The **biHeight** field of the **BITMAPINFO-HEADER** structure is equal to the sum of the height of the DIB and mask bitmaps. Thus for a 32×32 pixel icon, the **biHeight** field will have a value of 64, not 32 as one might expect.

After the XOR bitmap DIB, the AND bitmap appears. This is a monochrome bitmap with the same dimensions as the XOR bitmap.

Cursor File Format

An icon file with a .CUR extension can also contain any number of cursors. Generally, each cursor will be a rendition of a cursor image designed for a particular display device.

A cursor file begins with a **CURSORDIR** structure as described here:

■ CURSORDIR

VB Declaration

```
Type CURSORDIR    ' 6 Bytes
      cdReserved As Integer
      cdType As Integer
      cdCount As Integer
End Type
```

Description   This structure appears at the beginning of a cursor file.

Field	Type/Description
idReserved	**Integer**—Not used, set to zero.
idType	**Integer**—2.

Field	Type/Description
idCount	**Integer**—The number of cursors in the file. This specifies the number of **CURSORDIRENTRY** structures that follow this structure in the file.

A series of **CURSORDIRENTRY** structures immediately follows the **CURSORDIR** structure at the start of the file. Each of these structures defines the characteristics of one of the cursors in the file. This structure is defined as follows:

■ CURSORDIRENTRY

VB Declaration
```
Type CURSORDIRENTRY
      bWidth As String * 1
      bHeight As String * 1
      bColorCount As String * 1
      bReserved As String * 1
      wXHotspot As Integer
      wYHotspot As Integer
      dwBytesInRes As Long
      dwImageOffset As Long
End Type
```

Description   Each cursor in a cursor file has a **CURSORDIRENTRY** structure associated with it that describes the characteristics of the cursor.

Field	Type/Description
bWidth	**String * 1**—The width of the cursor. This may be up to 32 for Windows 3.x.
bHeight	**String * 1**—The height of the cursor. This may be up to 32 for Windows 3.x.
bColorCount	**String * 1**—The number of colors used by the cursor. This is 2 for Windows 3.x.
bReserved	**String * 1**—Not used, set to zero.
wXHotspot, wYHotspot	**Integers**—The offset of the hot spot for the cursor. This specifies the pixel within the cursor that the cursor is actually pointing to.
dwBytesInRes	**Long**—The size of the cursor specified in bytes.
dwImageOffset	**Long**—The offset of the specified cursor from the beginning of the file.

The rest of the cursor file is identical to that of an icon file with the exception that the XOR bitmap of a cursor must be monochrome.

Metafile Format (.WMF extension)

There are two types of metafiles, with the .WMF extension, available under Windows. The standard metafile begins with a **METAHEADER** structure, which was defined in Appendix B. This structure is followed by one or more **METARECORD** structures, each of which describes a GDI graphic command that is executed when the record is played.

The second type of metafile is known as a placeable metafile. This metafile contains additional information describing the desired appearance of the metafile drawing. The standard metafile is preceded with a **METAFILEHEADER** structure.

Visual Basic-to-DLL Calling Conventions: A Technical Review

Chapter 3 of this book discusses in detail how a Visual Basic programmer can use the VB **Declare** statement to access virtually any dynamic link library function. This appendix reviews this same process from the other point of view—that of the C or C++ language programmer who wishes to write dynamic link library functions for use by Visual Basic applications. Even if you never expect to write your own DLL, this information can be useful in providing a better understanding of how the Visual Basic-to-DLL interface works.

Calling Conventions

Visual Basic supports the standard Microsoft Pascal calling conventions. This calling convention is of course supported by Microsoft's compilers, and should be supported by any other compiler that allows you to create Windows dynamic link libraries. Refer to the mixed-language guide for your compiler or contact your compiler vendor to verify compatibility.

If you wish to use Visual Basic specific data types such as VB strings (**HLSTR**) and variants, you will also need the Control Development Kit (CDK) for Visual Basic, which is currently available as part of the professional edition of Visual Basic. This kit contains the library VBAPI.LIB that contains a set of functions for handling Visual Basic strings directly, eliminating the need for VB to convert them into null terminated format for DLL processing.

Two calling conventions are supported in Visual Basic for data types other than strings. The default is known as *call by reference*. In this scheme your VB function actually transfers a pointer to the variable. The DLL function can then use the pointer to access the data. Any changes made to that data will be reflected in the Visual Basic variable once the function returns.

The second scheme is known as *call by value*. In this case, VB passes a copy of the data to the DLL function. Call by value is specified by placing the **ByVal** keyword before the variable name in the function declaration.

Calling Conventions by Data Type

All of Visual Basic's data types can be passed as parameters to DLL functions. Some of the data types, such as the Visual Basic string type and currency type, are not supported directly by the C language. However, in most cases it is possible to write additional code to handle those data types.

Numeric Data Types

The numeric data types **Integer**, **Long**, **Single**, and **Double** are easily handled from Visual Basic. Variables can be passed by value or by reference and DLL functions may return numeric values directly.

Currency Data Types

The currency data type has no direct equivalent in C. This type uses eight bytes in a fixed precision format. A DLL designed to handle currency could use a structure to define the variable as shown below:

```
typedef struct currencystruct {
    char cbuf[8];
} currency;

currency FAR PASCAL ReceivesCurrency(currency curr)
{
    // You can access the curr parameter within the
    // function and return it as well.
    return(curr);
}
```

This takes advantage of the fact that C supports passing of structures by value and returning structures as results of functions.

The eight bytes of the currency structure form a single 64-bit integer that is a fixed-point representation of a floating-point currency number with four digits after the decimal point. In other words, the value $12.53 would be represented by the number 125,300 in a 64-bit number.

String Data Types

Strings in Visual Basic are handled differently from numeric data. They are always called by reference. The **ByVal** keyword is still used, however, to differentiate between two types of strings. When **ByVal** is specified, Visual Basic makes a copy of the string that is null terminated. This produces a string in the standard format expected by Windows API functions. When the DLL function returns, Visual Basic copies the string data back into the string variable (hence the DLL can modify the string even though **ByVal** is specified). Note that Visual Basic strings may have embedded nulls. Passing such a string to a DLL using this method will lead to truncation of the string.

When modifying a string parameter in a DLL that was passed using this method, it is critical that you do not modify any data past the null terminator unless you are certain that enough space has been allocated in the string. Doing so will almost certainly cause a system error sooner or later. You must initialize the string to the largest length that you expect to need before passing it as a parameter. This is commonly accomplished by using fixed length strings or setting the string length with the **String$()** function before the DLL call.

When **ByVal** is absent, the string is passed as an **HLSTR** data type—or a handle to a Visual Basic string. You must have the Control Development Kit for Visual Basic to make use of this data type. It includes the file VBAPI.LIB that contains the functions listed in Table D.1.

Table D.1 **Visual Basic CDK String Functions**

Function	Description
VBCreateHlstr()	Allocates a VB string
VBCreateTempHlstr	Allocates a temporary VB string.
VBDerefHlstr()	Retrieves a pointer to the data in a VB string.
VBDerefZeroTermHlstr	Retrieves a pointer to the data in a VB string that is null terminated.
VBDestroyHlstr()	Deletes a VB string.
VBGetHlstr	Copies a VB string into a buffer.
VBGetHlstrLen	Returns the length of a VB string.
VBResizeHlstr	Changes the size of a VB string.
VBSetHlstr()	Changes the contents of a VB string.

There are a number of advantages in using Visual Basic strings directly. By eliminating the need to make a null terminated copy, this method should have slightly better performance. It allows you to use Visual Basic's string management facilities, eliminating the need to preallocate buffers of a particular length. Also, it is possible for a DLL function to be defined as a string type and thus have it return a string directly in the form

```
a$ = dllfunc$()
```

Be aware that Visual Basic strings may contain nulls. Your DLL code must take this into account. Also, destroying VB strings in a DLL that are passed as parameters from Visual Basic will probably lead to trouble. Use **VBSetHlstr()** to change the contents of these strings.

Forms and Controls

Forms and controls are available as parameter types in the **Declare** statement. Every control and form in Visual Basic has a control handle (**HCTL**) that can be passed as a parameter to a DLL. It is important to note that this handle is absolutely useless unless you have the Control Development Kit and its VBAPI.LIB library. Do not use **ByVal** with this type of parameter.

User-Defined Types

User-defined types can be called by reference only and cannot be returned. The C function receives a pointer to the user-defined structure. The user-defined structures may contain strings; however, these strings will not be converted into null terminated strings. Fixed-length strings in user-defined structures can be treated as arrays of characters of the specified length since Visual Basic allocates enough space for each fixed-length string inside the structure. Arrays in user-defined types can be accessed directly, as Visual Basic allocates enough space in the structure for the entire array. You will need to copy the fixed-length string to a temporary buffer and add a null terminating character before using the string. Variable-length strings within structures are represented by the 32-bit Visual Basic string handle (**HLSTR**). The Visual Basic documentation implies that a variable-length string entry in a user-defined type may have a null value if it is not yet initialized (though this has not been demonstrated by the author). If a string entry in a user-defined structure has a null value, you should be able to use **VBCreateHlstr()** to insert the string into the structure.

Arrays

There are two ways to work with arrays in Visual Basic. The first involves using the call-by-reference protocol and passing the first element in the array as a parameter to the DLL function. Be very careful when using this technique—it is easy to accidentally access memory outside the array boundaries (by not using the first element of the array in the VB call, or through an indexing error in the DLL). As usual, this type of error will likely cause a system error. Control arrays cannot be passed as parameters to a DLL using this technique. A sample declaration of this type is:

```
Declare Sub dllfunc Lib "dlllib.dll" (xentry As Integer)
```

Note that **xentry** is not defined as an array. This works because all of the elements in a numeric array are arranged in sequence in memory. Using this technique on string arrays passes the first element in an array of **HLSTR** Visual Basic string handles.

If the DLL is designed for use with Visual Basic, it may be designed to accept Visual Basic arrays as parameters. In this case Visual Basic passes a special array handle known as an **HAD** as a parameter. As with VB strings, the CDK provides functions for working with Visual Basic arrays. This is a typical declaration for using VB arrays with DLL functions:

```
Declare Sub dllfunc Lib "dlllib.dll" (xentry() As Integer)
```

Note that the **xentry** parameter is an array rather than a single value. When passing string arrays to a DLL, you should always use the latter (Visual Basic array) technique. Since it is necessary to have the VB control development kit to use Visual Basic strings in the first place, any DLL that can handle string arrays can, by definition, also use the proper Visual Basic array functions.

Variants

Visual Basic Variant types can be passed to DLL functions both by value and by reference and can be returned from DLL functions. The CDK is required to write DLL functions that can use variants.

The method for returning variants from a C DLL function is not obvious and does not follow the standard C calling convention. The Visual Basic declaration for the function must specify the return of a variant as follows:

```
Declare Function myfunc Lib "libname" (param1, param2) As Variant
```

where **myfunc** and **libname** are the names of the function and DLL respectively, and **param1**, **param2** represents zero or more parameters to the function.

The C function must be declared to return void (no return value) and have an extra parameter specifying the address in which to store the variant as follows:

```
void _far _pascal myfunc(param1type param1, param2type param2, VARIANT FAR ⇔
*lpres)
```

In order to return the variant, you must set a variant into the location pointed by **lpres** using the **VBSetVariantValue** function as follows:

```
VBSetVariantValue(lpres, vartype, lpval)
```

where **vartype** is a constant specifying the type of variant and **lpval** is a pointer to the value. Refer to the description of variants and variant functions in the Visual Basic CDK for further information.

You must set the result using **VBSetVariantValue**. Do not attempt to copy an existing variant into the area pointed to by **lpval**. This is because the size of variants may change and only this function is guaranteed to be compatible with the space allocated on the stack for the result.

Summary of Parameter Passing Conventions

Table D.2 summarizes the legal calling conventions for the Visual Basic-to-DLL interface.

Table D.2   **Visual Basic to DLL Calling Conventions**

Data Type	Convention	Parameter	Comments
Integer	By value	16-bit integer	—
Long	By value	32-bit long value	—
Single	By value	32-bit single (float) value	—
Double	By value	64-bit double	Points to temporary copy of double.
Currency	By value	64-bit currency value	Points to temporary copy of a 64-bit currency variable.
String	By value	32-bit address	Points to a null terminated copy of the string. Copy will be set into the VB variable on return (thus this is actually call by reference).
Integer	By reference	32-bit address	Points to 16-bit VB integer variable.
Long	By reference	32-bit address	Points to 32-bit VB long variable.
Single	By reference	32-bit address	Points to 32-bit VB single variable.
Double	By reference	32-bit address	Points to 64-bit VB double variable.
Currency	By reference	32-bit address	Points to 64-bit VB currency variable.
String	By reference	32-bit VB string handle (HLSTR)	VB string handle as described in the VB CDK.
Form or control	Special	32-bit control handle (HCTL)	You can use **VBGetControlHwnd()** to obtain a window handle from this parameter. Requires the VB CDK.
User-defined type	By reference	32-bit address	Points to the structure.
Array (first method)	By reference	32-bit address	Points to the first element of the array by reference.
Array (second method)	By reference	32-bit VB array handle (HAD)	VB array handle as described in the VB CDK.

Table D.2   Visual Basic to DLL Calling Conventions (Continued)

Data Type	Convention	Parameter	Comments
Variant	By value	14-byte variant structure	The actual **VARIANT** structure as defined in the VB CDK.
Variant	By reference	32-bit address	Points to a **VARIANT** structure as defined in the VB CDK.

Table D.3 summarizes the legal return conventions for the Visual Basic-to-DLL interface. Values are returned in the AX and DX registers as specified in the table. Address offset and selector combine to form a 32-bit FAR pointer.

Table D.3   Visual Basic-to-DLL Function Return Conventions

Data Type	AX	DX	Comments
Integer	16-bit integer	—	—
Long	Low word (16-bit) of long	High word (16-bit) of long	—
Single	Address offset	Address selector	Points to temporary 32-bit single value.
Double	Address offset	Address selector	Points to temporary 64-bit double variable.
Currency	Address offset	Address selector	Points to temporary 64-bit VB currency variable.
String	Low word (16-bit) of VB string handle	High word (16-bit) of VB string handle	Refer to CDK for Visual Basic for information on VB string functions.
Variant	—	—	Refer to the chapter text for details on returning variants.

Avoiding General Protection Faults

Visual Basic guarantees that any DLL function calls in your program will match the expected parameters and return values in the declaration for that function. This means that if you have declared a function as accepting an integer parameter and call it from VB with a double parameter, VB will convert that parameter into an integer before calling the DLL function just as it would for any other VB function. Once a DLL function has been correctly declared, you are unlikely to run into any difficulties with general protection faults due to programming errors in Visual Basic unless you intentionally turned off error checking for a parameter by using the **As Any** type definition.

Visual Basic and Windows perform absolutely no error checking or detection when it comes to making sure that the VB declaration for a DLL function is in any way compatible with the DLL function itself. Given these facts, the following techniques should help when it comes to creating DLLs for use with Visual Basic.

- Save your work frequently!

- Declare VOID DLL functions as VB subroutines (**SUB**), and DLL functions returning values as VB functions (**FUNCTION**).

- Be sure that the DLL return value type matches the VB declaration. This is especially critical for the double, currency, and variant data types.

- Be sure that all DLL function parameters are defined correctly in the VB declaration. Pay special attention to call by value and call by reference considerations, and to the two string types available.

- When passing regular string parameters, be sure that your DLL does not modify any part of the string after the NULL terminator.

- When passing parameters by reference, be sure that your DLL does not exceed the boundaries of the data (especially for user-defined data types and arrays).

- Test your DLL thoroughly. If you have the Microsoft Windows SDK, use the debugging version of Windows in your testing—it detects error conditions that the retail version may miss.

Index of API Functions and Declarations

This appendix contains a list of the Windows API functions included in file APIDECS.TXT. The *Chapter* column indicates in which chapter's function reference section a detailed description of the function can be found. *NA* in this column indicates that the function cannot be used from within Visual Basic. These functions are listed here for completeness, but are not documented further in this book.

   If the *Version* column contains a 3.1, the particular function has been added for version 3.1 of Windows. If you wish your application to be compatible with both Windows 3.0 and Windows 3.1 it should not use API functions that contain a 3.1 in this column. Keep in mind that the declaration must be placed on a single line in Visual Basic.

Function Name	Chapter	Version	Declaration
AbortDoc	11	3.1	Declare Function AbortDoc% Lib "GDI" (ByVal hDC%)
AccessResource	12		Declare Function AccessResource% Lib "Kernel" (ByVal hInstance%, ByVal hResInfo%)
AddAtom	16		Declare Function AddAtom% Lib "Kernel" (ByVal lpString$)
AddFontResource	10		Declare Function AddFontResource% Lib "GDI" (ByVal lpFilename As Any)
AddFontResourceByname	10		Declare Function AddFontResourceByname% Lib "GDI" Alias "AddFontResource" (ByVal lpFilename$)
AddFontResourceByHandle	10		Declare Function AddFontResourceByHandle% Lib "GDI" Alias "AddFontResource" (ByVal lpFilename&)
AdjustWindowRect	4		Declare Sub AdjustWindowRect Lib "User" (lpRect As RECT, ByVal dwStyle&, ByVal bMenu%)
AdjustWindowRectEx	4		Declare Sub AdjustWindowRectEx Lib "User" (lpRect As RECT, ByVal dsStyle&, ByVal bMenu%, ByVal dwEsStyle&)
AllocDStoCSAlias	NA		Declare Function AllocDStoCSAlias% Lib "Kernel" (ByVal wSelector%)
AllocResource	12		Declare Function AllocResource% Lib "Kernel" (ByVal hInstance%, ByVal hResInfo%, ByVal dwSize&)
AllocSelector	NA		Declare Function AllocSelector% Lib "Kernel" (ByVal wSelector%)
AnimatePalette	16		Declare Sub AnimatePalette Lib "GDI" (ByVal hPalette%, ByVal wStartIndex%, ByVal wNumEntries%, lpPaletteColors As PALETTEENTRY)
AnsiLower	10		Declare Function AnsiLower& Lib "User" (ByVal lpString$)
AnsiLowerBuff	10		Declare Function AnsiLowerBuff% Lib "User" (ByVal lpString$, ByVal aWORD%)
AnsiNext	16		Declare Function AnsiNext& Lib "User" (ByVal lpString$)

Function Name	Chapter Version	Declaration
AnsiNextBynum	16	Declare Function AnsiNextBynum& Lib "User" Alias "AnsiNext" (ByVal lpString&)
AnsiPrev	16	Declare Function AnsiPrev& Lib "User" (ByVal lpString$, ByVal lpCurrent&)
AnsiPrevBynum	16	Declare Function AnsiPrevBynum& Lib "User" Alias "AnsiPrev" (ByVal lpString&, ByVal lpCurrent&)
AnsiToOem	5	Declare Function AnsiToOem% Lib "Keyboard" (ByVal lpAnsiStr$, ByVal lpOemStr$)
AnsiToOemBuff	5	Declare Sub AnsiToOemBuff Lib "Keyboard" (ByVal lpAnsiStr$, ByVal lpOemStr$, ByVal nLength%)
AnsiUpper	10	Declare Function AnsiUpper& Lib "User" (ByVal lpString$)
AnsiUpperBuff	10	Declare Function AnsiUpperBuff% Lib "User" (ByVal lpString$, ByVal aWORD%)
AnyPopup	4	Declare Function AnyPopup% Lib "User" ()
AppendMenu	9	Declare Function AppendMenu% Lib "User" (ByVal hMenu%, ByVal wFlags%, ByVal wIDNewItem%, ByVal lpNewItem As Any)
AppendMenuByNum	9	Declare Function AppendMenuByNum% Lib "User" Alias "AppendMenu" (ByVal hMenu%, ByVal wFlags%, ByVal wIDNewItem%, ByVal lpNewItem&)
AppendMenuByString	9	Declare Function AppendMenuByString% Lib "User" Alias "AppendMenu" (ByVal hMenu%, ByVal wFlags%, ByVal wIDNewItem%, ByVal lpNewItem$)
Arc	7	Declare Function Arc% Lib "GDI" (ByVal hDC%, ByVal X1%, ByVal Y1%, ByVal X2%, ByVal Y2%, ByVal X3%, ByVal Y3%, ByVal X4%, ByVal Y4%)
ArrangeIconicWindows	4	Declare Function ArrangeIconicWindows% Lib "User" (ByVal hWnd%)
BeginDeferWindowPos	4	Declare Function BeginDeferWindowPos Lib "User" (ByVal nNumWindows%)
BeginPaint	NA	Declare Function BeginPaint% Lib "User" (ByVal hWnd%, lpPaint As PAINTSTRUCT)
BitBlt	8	Declare Function BitBlt% Lib "GDI" (ByVal hDestDC%, ByVal X%, ByVal Y%, ByVal nWidth%, ByVal nHeight%, ByVal hSrcDC%, ByVal XSrc%, ByVal YSrc%, ByVal dwRop&)
BringWindowToTop	4	Declare Sub BringWindowToTop Lib "User" (ByVal hWnd%)
BuildCommDCB	14	Declare Function BuildCommDCB% Lib "User" (ByVal lpDef$, lpDCB As DCB)

Function Name	Chapter	Version	Declaration
CloseSound	15		Declare Sub CloseSound Lib "Sound" ()
CloseWindow	4		Declare Sub CloseWindow Lib "User" (ByVal hWnd%)
CombineRgn	6		Declare Function CombineRgn% Lib "GDI" (ByVal hDestRgn%, ByVal hSrcRgn1%, ByVal hSrcRgn2%, ByVal nCombineMode%)
CopyLZFile	13		Declare Function CopyLZFile& Lib "lzexpand" (ByVal hfSource%, ByVal hfDest%)
CopyMetaFile	7		Declare Function CopyMetaFile% Lib "GDI" (ByVal hMF%, ByVal lpFilename$)
CopyMetaFileBynum	7		Declare Function CopyMetaFileBynum% Lib "GDI" (ByVal hMF%, ByVal hDest&)
CopyCursor	5	3.1	Declare Function CopyCursor% Lib "User" (ByVal hinst%, ByVal hcur%)
CopyIcon	8	3.1	Declare Function CopyIcon% Lib "User" (ByVal hinst%, ByVal hicon%)
CopyRect	4		Declare Function CopyRect% Lib "User" (lpDestRect As RECT, lpSourceRect As RECT)
CountClipboardFormats	15		Declare Function CountClipboardFormats% Lib "User" ()
CountVoiceNotes	15		Declare Function CountVoiceNotes% Lib "Sound" (ByVal nVoice%)
CreateBitmap	8		Declare Function CreateBitmap% Lib "GDI" (ByVal nWidth%, ByVal nHeight%, ByVal nPlanes%, ByVal nBitCount%, ByVal lpBits As Any)
CreateBitmapBynum	8		Declare Function CreateBitmapBynum% Lib "GDI" Alias "CreateBitmap" (ByVal nWidth%, ByVal nHeight%, ByVal nPlanes%, ByVal nBitCount%, ByVal lpBits&)
CreateBitmapBystring	8		Declare Function CreateBitmapBystring% Lib "GDI" Alias "CreateBitmap" (ByVal nWidth%, ByVal nHeight%, ByVal nPlanes%, ByVal nBitCount%, ByVal lpBits$)
CreateBitmapIndirect	8		Declare Function CreateBitmapIndirect% Lib "GDI" (lpBitmap As BITMAP)
CreateBrushIndirect	7		Declare Function CreateBrushIndirect% Lib "GDI" (lpLogBrush As LOGBRUSH)
CreateCaret	5		Declare Sub CreateCaret Lib "User" (ByVal hWnd%, ByVal hBitmap%, ByVal nWidth%, ByVal nHeight%)
CreateCompatibleBitmap	8		Declare Function CreateCompatibleBitmap% Lib "GDI" (ByVal hDC%, ByVal nWidth%, ByVal nHeight%)
CreateCompatibleDC	6		Declare Function CreateCompatibleDC% Lib "GDI" (ByVal hDC%)

Function Name	Chapter	Version	Declaration
CreateCursor	8		Declare Function CreateCursor% Lib "User" (ByVal hInstance%, ByVal nXhotspot%, ByVal nYhotspot%, ByVal nWidth%, ByVal nHeight%, ByVal lpANDbitPlane As Any, ByVal lpXORbitPlane As Any)
CreateCursorBynum	8		Declare Function CreateCursorBynum% Lib "User" Alias "CreateCursor" (ByVal hInstance%, ByVal nXhotspot%, ByVal nYhotspot%, ByVal nWidth%, ByVal nHeight%, ByVal lpANDbitPlane&, ByVal lpXORbitPlane&)
CreateCursorBystring	8		Declare Function CreateCursorBystring% Lib "User" Alias "CreateCursor" (ByVal hInstance%, ByVal nXhotspot%, ByVal nYhotspot%, ByVal nWidth%, ByVal nHeight%, ByVal lpANDbitPlane$, ByVal lpXORbitPlane$)
CreateDC	6		Declare Function CreateDC% Lib "GDI" (ByVal lpDriverName$, ByVal lpDeviceName$, ByVal lpOutput$, ByVal lpInitData&)
CreateDIBitmap	8		Declare Function CreateDIBitmap% Lib "GDI" (ByVal hDC%, lpInfoHeader As BITMAPINFOHEADER, ByVal dwUsage&, ByVal lpInitBits$, lpInitInfo As BITMAPINFO, ByVal wUsage%)
CreateDIBitmapBynum	8		Declare Function CreateDIBitmapBynum% Lib "GDI" Alias "CreateDIBitmap" (ByVal hDC%, lpInfoHeader As BITMAPINFOHEADER, ByVal dwUsage&, ByVal lpInitBits&, lpInitInfo As BITMAPINFO, ByVal wUsage%)
CreateDIBPatternBrush	7		Declare Function CreateDIBPatternBrush% Lib "GDI" (ByVal hPackedDIB%, ByVal wUsage%)
CreateDiscardableBitmap	8		Declare Function CreateDiscardableBitmap% Lib "GDI" (ByVal hDC%, ByVal nWidth%, ByVal nHeight%)
CreateEllipticRgn	6		Declare Function CreateEllipticRgn% Lib "GDI" (ByVal X1%, ByVal Y1%, ByVal X2%, ByVal Y2%)
CreateEllipticRgnIndirect	6		Declare Function CreateEllipticRgnIndirect% Lib "GDI" (lpRect As RECT)
CreateFont	10		Declare Function CreateFont% Lib "GDI" (ByVal H%, ByVal W%, ByVal E%, ByVal O%, ByVal W%, ByVal I%, ByVal U%, ByVal S%, ByVal C%, ByVal OP%, ByVal CP%, ByVal Q%, ByVal PAF%, ByVal F$)
CreateFontIndirect	10		Declare Function CreateFontIndirect% Lib "GDI" (lpLogFont As LOGFONT)
CreateHatchBrush	7		Declare Function CreateHatchBrush% Lib "GDI" (ByVal nIndex%, ByVal crColor&)
CreateIC	6		Declare Function CreateIC% Lib "GDI" (ByVal lpDriverName$, ByVal lpDeviceName$, ByVal lpOutput$, ByVal lpInitData$)

Function Name	Chapter Version	Declaration
CreateIcon	8	Declare Function CreateIcon% Lib "User" (ByVal hInstance%, ByVal nWidth%, ByVal nHeight%, ByVal nPlanes%, ByVal nBitsPixel%, ByVal lpANDbits As Any, ByVal lpXORbits As Any)
CreateIconBynum	8	Declare Function CreateIconBynum% Lib "User" Alias "CreateIcon" (ByVal hInstance%, ByVal nWidth%, ByVal nHeight%, ByVal nPlanes%, ByVal nBitsPixel%, ByVal lpANDbits&, ByVal lpXORbits&)
CreateIconBystring	8	Declare Function CreateIconBystring% Lib "User" Alias "CreateIcon" (ByVal hInstance%, ByVal nWidth%, ByVal nHeight%, ByVal nPlanes%, ByVal nBitsPixel%, ByVal lpANDbits$, ByVal lpXORbits$)
CreateMenu	9	Declare Function CreateMenu% Lib "User" ()
CreateMetaFile	7	Declare Function CreateMetaFile% Lib "GDI" (ByVal lpString As Any)
CreateMetaFileBynum	7	Declare Function CreateMetaFileBynum% Lib "GDI" Alias "CreateMetaFile" (ByVal lpString&)
CreateMetaFileBystring	7	Declare Function CreateMetaFileBystring% Lib "GDI" Alias "CreateMetaFile" (ByVal lpString$)
CreatePalette	16	Declare Function CreatePalette% Lib "GDI" (lpLogPalette As LOGPALETTE)
CreatePatternBrush	7	Declare Function CreatePatternBrush% Lib "GDI" (ByVal hBitmap%)
CreatePen	7	Declare Function CreatePen% Lib "GDI" (ByVal nPenStyle%, ByVal nWidth%, ByVal crColor&)
CreatePenIndirect	7	Declare Function CreatePenIndirect% Lib "GDI" (lpLogPen As LOGPEN)
CreatePolygonRgn	6	Declare Function CreatePolygonRgn% Lib "GDI" (lpPoints As POINTAPI, ByVal nCount%, ByVal nPolyFillMode%)
CreatePolyPolygonRgn	6	Declare Function CreatePolyPolygonRgn% Lib "GDI" (lpPoints As POINTAPI, lpPolyCounts%, ByVal nCount%, ByVal nPolyFillMode%)
CreatePopupMenu	9	Declare Function CreatePopupMenu% Lib "User" ()
CreateRectRgn	6	Declare Function CreateRectRgn% Lib "GDI" (ByVal X1%, ByVal Y1%, ByVal X2%, ByVal Y2%)
CreateRectRgnIndirect	6	Declare Function CreateRectRgnIndirect% Lib "GDI" (lpRect As RECT)
CreateRoundRectRgn	6	Declare Function CreateRoundRectRgn% Lib "GDI" (ByVal X1%, ByVal Y1%, ByVal X2%, ByVal Y2%, ByVal X3%, ByVal Y3%)

Function Name	Chapter	Version	Declaration
CreateScalableFontResource	10	3.1	Declare Function CreateScalableFontResource% Lib "GDI" (ByVal fHidden%, ByVal lpszResourceFile$, ByVal lpszFontFile$, ByVal lpszCurrentPath$)
CreateSolidBrush	7		Declare Function CreateSolidBrush% Lib "GDI" (ByVal crColor&)
CreateWindow	NA		Declare Function CreateWindow% Lib "User" (ByVal lpClassName$, ByVal lpWindowName$, ByVal dwStyle&, ByVal X%, ByVal Y%, ByVal nWidth%, ByVal nHeight%, ByVal hWndParent%, ByVal hMenu%, ByVal hInstance%, ByVal lpParam$)
CreateWindowEx	NA		Declare Function CreateWindowEx% Lib "User" (ByVal dwExStyle&, ByVal lpClassName$, ByVal lpWindowName$, ByVal dwStyle&, ByVal X%, ByVal Y%, ByVal nWidth%, ByVal nHeight%, ByVal hWndParent%, ByVal hMenu%, ByVal hInstance%, ByVal lpParam$)
DebugBreak	NA		Declare Sub DebugBreak Lib "Kernel" ()
DefDlgProc	NA		Declare Function DefDlgProc& Lib "User" (ByVal hDlg%, ByVal wMsg%, ByVal wParam%, ByVal lParam As Any)
DeferWindowPos	4		Declare Function DeferWindowPos% Lib "User" (ByVal hWinPosInfo%, ByVal hWnd%, ByVal hWndInsertAfter%, ByVal x%, ByVal y%, ByVal cx%, ByVal cy%, ByVal wFlags%)
DefFrameProc	NA		Declare Function DefFrameProc& Lib "User" (ByVal hWnd%, ByVal hWndMDIClient%, ByVal wMsg%, ByVal wParam%, ByVal lParam&)
DefHookProc	NA		Declare Function DefHookProc& Lib "User" (ByVal code%, ByVal wParam%, ByVal lParam%, ByVal lplpfnNextHook&)
DefMDIChildProc	NA		Declare Function DefMDIChildProc& Lib "User" (ByVal hWnd%, ByVal wMsg%, ByVal wParam%, ByVal lParam&)
DefWindowProc	NA		Declare Function DefWindowProc& Lib "User" (ByVal hWnd%, ByVal wMsg%, ByVal wParam%, Byval lParam As Any)
DeleteAtom	16		Declare Function DeleteAtom% Lib "Kernel" (ByVal nAtom%)
DeleteDC	6		Declare Function DeleteDC% Lib "GDI" (ByVal hDC%)
DeleteMenu	9		Declare Function DeleteMenu% Lib "User" (ByVal hMenu%, ByVal nPosition%, ByVal wFlags%)
DeleteMetaFile	7		Declare Function DeleteMetaFile% Lib "GDI" (ByVal hMF%)
DeleteObject	7		Declare Function DeleteObject% Lib "GDI" (ByVal hObject%)
DestroyCaret	5		Declare Sub DestroyCaret Lib "User" ()

Function Name	Chapter Version	Declaration
DestroyCursor	5	Declare Function DestroyCursor% Lib "User" (ByVal hCursor%)
DestroyIcon	8	Declare Function DestroyIcon% Lib "User" (ByVal hIcon%)
DestroyMenu	9	Declare Function DestroyMenu% Lib "User" (ByVal hMenu%)
DestroyWindow	4	Declare Function DestroyWindow% Lib "User" (ByVal hWnd%)
DirectedYield	NA	Declare Sub DirectedYield Lib "Kernel" (ByVal htask%)
DispatchMessage	NA	Declare Function DispatchMessage& Lib "User" (lpMsg As MSG)
DlgDirList	NA	Declare Function DlgDirList% Lib "User" (ByVal hDlg%, ByVal lpPathSpec$, ByVal nIDListBox%, ByVal nIDStaticPath%, ByVal wFiletype%)
DlgDirListComboBox	NA	Declare Function DlgDirListComboBox% Lib "User" (ByVal hDlg%, ByVal lpPathSpec$, ByVal nIDComboBox%, ByVal nIDStaticPath%, ByVal wFileType%)
DlgDirSelect	NA	Declare Function DlgDirSelect% Lib "User" (ByVal hDlg%, ByVal lpString$, ByVal nIDListBox%)
DlgDirSelectComboBox	NA	Declare Function DlgDirSelectComboBox% Lib "User" (ByVal hDlg%, ByVal lpString$, ByVal nIDComboBox%)
DPtoLP	6	Declare Function DPtoLP% Lib "GDI" (ByVal hDC%, lpPoints As POINTAPI, ByVal nCount%)
DragAcceptFiles	16	Declare Sub DragAcceptFiles Lib "shell.dll" (ByVal hwnd%, ByVal fAccept%)
DragFinish	16	Declare Sub DragFinish Lib "shell.dll" (ByVal hDrop%)
DragQueryFile	16	Declare Function DragQueryFile% Lib "shell.dll" (ByVal hDrop%, ByVal iFile%, ByVal lpszFile$, ByVal cb%)
DragQueryPoint	16	Declare Function DragQueryPoint% Lib "shell.dll" (ByVal hDrop%, lppt As POINTAPI)
DrawFocusRect	7	Declare Sub DrawFocusRect Lib "User" (ByVal hDC%, lpRect As RECT)
DrawIcon	8	Declare Function DrawIcon% Lib "User" (ByVal hDC%, ByVal X%, ByVal Y%, ByVal hIcon%)
DrawMenuBar	9	Declare Sub DrawMenuBar Lib "User" (ByVal hWnd%)
DrawText	10	Declare Function DrawText% Lib "User" (ByVal hDC%, ByVal lpStr$, ByVal nCount%, lpRect As RECT, ByVal wFormat%)
Ellipse	7	Declare Function Ellipse% Lib "GDI" (ByVal hDC%, ByVal X1%, ByVal Y1%, ByVal X2%, ByVal Y2%)

Function Name	Chapter	Version	Declaration
EmptyClipboard	15		Declare Function EmptyClipboard% Lib "User" ()
EnableCommNotification	14	3.1	Declare Function EnableCommNotification% Lib "User" (ByVal idComDev%, ByVal hWnd%, ByVal cbWriteNotify%, ByVal cbOutQueue%)
EnableHardwareInput	5		Declare Function EnableHardwareInput% Lib "User" (ByVal bEnableInput%)
EnableMenuItem	9		Declare Function EnableMenuItem% Lib "User" (ByVal hMenu%, ByVal wIDEnableItem%, ByVal wEnable%)
EnableScrollBar	15		Declare Function EnableScrollBar% Lib "User" (ByVal hWnd%, ByVal fnSBFlags%, ByVal fuArrowFlags%)
EnableWindow	4		Declare Function EnableWindow% Lib "User" (ByVal hWnd%, ByVal aBOOL%)
EndDeferWindowPos	4		Declare Sub EndDeferWindowPos Lib "User" (ByVal hWinPosInfo%)
EndDialog	NA		Declare Sub EndDialog Lib "User" (ByVal hDlg%, ByVal nResult%)
EndDocAPI	11		Declare Function EndDocAPI% Lib "GDI" (ByVal hDC%)
EndPage	11	3.1	Declare Function EndPage% Lib "GDI" (ByVal hDC%)
EndPaint	NA		Declare Sub EndPaint Lib "User" (ByVal hWnd%, lpPaint As PAINTSTRUCT)
EnumChildWindows	4		Declare Function EnumChildWindows% Lib "User" (ByVal hWndParent%, ByVal lpEnumFunc&, ByVal lParam&)
EnumClipboardFormats	15		Declare Function EnumClipboardFormats% Lib "User" (ByVal wFormat%)
EnumFontFamilies	10	3.1	Declare Function EnumFontFamilies% Lib "GDI" (ByVal hDC%, ByVal lpszFamily$, ByVal lpFontFunc&, ByVal lpData&)
EnumFontFamiliesBynum	10	3.1	Declare Function EnumFontFamiliesBynum% Lib "GDI" Alias "EnumFontFamilies" (ByVal hDC%, ByVal lpszFamily&, ByVal lpFontFunc&, ByVal lpData&)
EnumFonts	10		Declare Function EnumFonts% Lib "GDI" (ByVal hDC%, ByVal lpFacename$, ByVal lpFontFunc&, ByVal lpData&)
EnumFontsBynum	10		Declare Function EnumFontsBynum% Lib "GDI" Alias "EnumFonts" (ByVal hDC%, ByVal lpFacename&, ByVal lpFontFunc&, ByVal lpData&)
EnumMetaFile	7		Declare Function EnumMetaFile% Lib "GDI" (ByVal hDC%, ByVal hMF%, ByVal lpCallbackFunc&, ByVal lpClientData&)
EnumObjects	7		Declare Function EnumObjects% Lib "GDI" (ByVal hDC%, ByVal nObjectType%, ByVal lpObjectFunc&, ByVal lpData&)

Function Name	Chapter	Version	Declaration
EnumProps	16		Declare Function EnumProps% Lib "User" (ByVal hWnd%, ByVal lpEnumFunc&)
EnumTaskWindows	4		Declare Function EnumTaskWindows% Lib "User" (ByVal hTask%, ByVal lpEnumFunc&, ByVal lParam&)
EnumWindows	4		Declare Function EnumWindows% Lib "User" (ByVal lpEnumFunc&, ByVal lParam&)
EqualRect	4		Declare Function EqualRect% Lib "User" (lpRect1 As RECT, lpRect2 As RECT)
EqualRgn	6		Declare Function EqualRgn% Lib "GDI" (ByVal hSrcRgn1%, ByVal hSrcRgn2%)
Escape	11		Declare Function Escape% Lib "GDI" (ByVal hDC%, ByVal nEscape%, ByVal nCount%, lpInData As Any, lpOutData As Any)
EscapeBynum	11		Declare Function EscapeBynum% Lib "GDI" Alias "Escape" (ByVal hDC%, ByVal nEscape%, ByVal nCount%, ByVal lpInData&, ByVal lpOutData&)
EscapeBystring	11		Declare Function EscapeBystring% Lib "GDI" Alias "Escape" (ByVal hDC%, ByVal nEscape%, ByVal nCount%, ByVal lpInData$, ByVal lpOutData$)
EscapeCommFunction	14		Declare Function EscapeCommFunction% Lib "User" (ByVal nCid%, ByVal nFunc%)
ExcludeClipRect	6		Declare Function ExcludeClipRect% Lib "GDI" (ByVal hDC%, ByVal X1%, ByVal Y1%, ByVal X2%, ByVal Y2%)
ExcludeUpdateRgn	6		Declare Function ExcludeUpdateRgn% Lib "User" (ByVal hDC%, ByVal hWnd%)
ExitWindows	5		Declare Function ExitWindows% Lib "User" (ByVal dwReserved&, wReturnCode)
ExitWindowsExec	5	3.1	Declare Function ExitWindowsExec% Lib "User" (ByVal lpszExe$, ByVal lpszParams$)
ExtFloodFill	7		Declare Function ExtFloodFill% Lib "GDI" (ByVal hDC%, ByVal X%, ByVal Y%, ByVal crColor&, ByVal wFillType%)
ExtTextOut	10		Declare Function ExtTextOut% Lib "GDI" (ByVal hDC%, ByVal X%, ByVal Y%, ByVal wOptions%, lpRect As Any, ByVal lpString$, ByVal nCount%, lpDx As Any)
ExtTextOutBynum	10		Declare Function ExtTextOutBynum% Lib "GDI" Alias "ExtTextOut" (ByVal hDC%, ByVal X%, ByVal Y%, ByVal wOptions%, ByVal lpRect&, ByVal lpString$, ByVal nCount%, ByVal lpDx&)

Function Name	Chapter Version	Declaration
ExtTextOutByrect	10	Declare Function ExtTextOutByrect% Lib "GDI" Alias "ExtTextOut" (ByVal hDC%, ByVal X%, ByVal Y%, ByVal wOptions%, lpRect as RECT, ByVal lpString$, ByVal nCount%, Byval lpDx&)
ExtractIcon	8	Declare Function ExtractIcon% Lib "shellapi.dll" (ByVal hisnt%, ByVal lpszExeName$, ByVal iIcon%)
FatalAppExit	NA	Declare Sub FatalAppExit Lib "Kernel" (ByVal wAction%, ByVal lpMessageText$)
FatalExit	NA	Declare Sub FatalExit Lib "Kernel" (ByVal Code%)
FillRect	7	Declare Function FillRect% Lib "User" (ByVal hDC%, lpRect As RECT, ByVal hBrush%)
FillRgn	7	Declare Function FillRgn% Lib "GDI" (ByVal hDC%, ByVal hRgn%, ByVal hBrush%)
FindAtom	16	Declare Function FindAtom% Lib "Kernel" (ByVal lpString$)
FindExecutable	12	Declare Function FindExecutable% Lib "shellapi.dll" (ByVal lpszFile$, ByVal lpszDir$, ByVal lpszResult$)
FindResource	12	Declare Function FindResource% Lib "Kernel" (ByVal hInstance%, ByVal lpName$, ByVal lpType As Any)
FindResourceByname	12	Declare Function FindResourceByname% Lib "Kernel" Alias "FindResource" (ByVal hInstance%, ByVal lpName$, ByVal lpType$)
FindResourceBynum	12	Declare Function FindResourceBynum% Lib "Kernel" Alias "FindResource" (ByVal hInstance%, ByVal lpName$, ByVal lpType&)
FindWindow	4	Declare Function FindWindow% Lib "User" (ByVal lpClassName As Any, ByVal lpWindowName As Any)
FindWindowBynum	4	Declare Function FindWindowBynum% Lib "User" Alias "FindWindow" (ByVal lpClassName&, ByVal lpWindowName&)
FindWindowBystring	4	Declare Function FindWindowBystring% Lib "User" Alias "FindWindow" (ByVal lpClassName$, ByVal lpWindowName$)
FlashWindow	4	Declare Function FlashWindow% Lib "User" (ByVal hWnd%, ByVal bInvert%)
FloodFill	7	Declare Function FloodFill% Lib "GDI" (ByVal hDC%, ByVal X%, ByVal Y%, ByVal crColor&)
FlushComm	14	Declare Function FlushComm% Lib "User" (ByVal nCid%, ByVal nQueue%)
FrameRect	7	Declare Function FrameRect% Lib "User" (ByVal hDC%, lpRect As RECT, ByVal hBrush%)

Function Name	Chapter	Version	Declaration
FrameRgn	7		Declare Function FrameRgn% Lib "GDI" (ByVal hDC%, ByVal hRgn%, ByVal hBrush%, ByVal nWidth%, ByVal nHeight%)
FreeLibrary	12		Declare Sub FreeLibrary Lib "Kernel" (ByVal hLibModule%)
FreeModule	12		Declare Sub FreeModule Lib "Kernel" (ByVal hModule%)
FreeResource	12		Declare Function FreeResource% Lib "Kernel" (ByVal hResData%)
FreeSelector	NA		Declare Function FreeSelector% Lib "Kernel" (ByVal wSelector%)
GetActiveWindow	4		Declare Function GetActiveWindow% Lib "User" ()
GetAspectRatioFilter	10		Declare Function GetAspectRatioFilter& Lib "GDI" (ByVal hDC%)
GetAspectRationFilterEx	10	3.1	Declare Function GetAspectRationFilterEx% Lib "GDI" (ByVal hDC%, lpAspectRation As SIZEAPI)
GetAsyncKeyState	5		Declare Function GetAsyncKeyState% Lib "User" (ByVal vKey%)
GetAtomName	16		Declare Function GetAtomName% Lib "Kernel" (ByVal nAtom%, ByVal lpBuffer$, ByVal nSize%)
GetBitmapBits	8		Declare Function GetBitmapBits& Lib "GDI" (ByVal hBitmap%, ByVal dwCount&, ByVal lpBits As Any)
GetBitmapBitsBynum	8		Declare Function GetBitmapBitsBynum& Lib "GDI" Alias "GetBitmapBits" (ByVal hBitmap%, ByVal dwCount&, ByVal lpBits&)
GetBitmapBitsBystring	8		Declare Function GetBitmapBitsBystring& Lib "GDI" Alias "GetBitmapBits" (ByVal hBitmap%, ByVal dwCount&, ByVal lpBits$)
GetBitmapDimension	8		Declare Function GetBitmapDimension& Lib "GDI" (ByVal hBitmap%)
GetBitmapDimensionEx	8	3.1	Declare Function GetBitmapDimensionEx% Lib "GDI" (ByVal hBitmap%, lpDimension As SIZEAPI)
GetBkColor	7		Declare Function GetBkColor& Lib "GDI" (ByVal hDC%)
GetBkMode	7		Declare Function GetBkMode% Lib "GDI" (ByVal hDC%)
GetBoundsRect	6	3.1	Declare Function GetBoundsRect% Lib "GDI" (ByVal hDC%, lprcBounds As RECT, ByVal flags%)
GetBrushOrg	7		Declare Function GetBrushOrg& Lib "GDI" (ByVal hDC%)
GetBrushOrgEx	7	3.1	Declare Function GetBrushOrgEx% Lib "GDI" (ByVal hDC%, lpPoint As POINTAPI)

Function Name	Chapter	Version	Declaration
GetCapture	5		Declare Function GetCapture% Lib "User" ()
GetCaretBlinkTime	5		Declare Function GetCaretBlinkTime% Lib "User" ()
GetCaretPos	5		Declare Sub GetCaretPos Lib "User" (lpPoint As POINTAPI)
GetCharABCWidths	10	3.1	Declare Function GetCharABCWidths Lib "GDI" (ByVal hDC%, ByVal uFirstChar%, ByVal uLastChar%, lpabc As ABC)
GetCharWidth	10		Declare Function GetCharWidth% Lib "GDI" (ByVal hDC%, ByVal wFirstChar%, ByVal wLastChar%, lpBuffer%)
GetClassInfo	4		Declare Function GetClassInfo% Lib "User" (ByVal hInstance%, ByVal lpClassName$, lpWndClass as WNDCLASS)
GetClassLong	4		Declare Function GetClassLong& Lib "User" (ByVal hWnd%, ByVal nIndex%)
GetClassName	4		Declare Function GetClassName% Lib "User" (ByVal hWnd%, ByVal lpClassName$, ByVal nMaxCount%)
GetClassWord	4		Declare Function GetClassWord% Lib "User" (ByVal hWnd%, ByVal nIndex%)
GetClientRect	4		Declare Sub GetClientRect Lib "User" (ByVal hWnd%, lpRect As RECT)
GetClipboardData	15		Declare Function GetClipboardData% Lib "User" (ByVal wFormat%)
GetClipboardFormatName	15		Declare Function GetClipboardFormatName% Lib "User" (ByVal wFormat%, ByVal lpString$, ByVal nMaxCount%)
GetClipboardOwner	15		Declare Function GetClipboardOwner% Lib "User" ()
GetClipboardViewer	NA		Declare Function GetClipboardViewer% Lib "User" ()
GetClipBox	6		Declare Function GetClipBox% Lib "GDI" (ByVal hDC%, lpRect As RECT)
GetClipCursor	5	3.1	Declare Sub GetClipCursor Lib "User" (lprc As Rect)
GetCommError	14		Declare Function GetCommError% Lib "User" (ByVal nCid%, lpStat As COMSTAT)
GetCommEventMask	14		Declare Function GetCommEventMask% Lib "User" (ByVal nCid%, ByVal nEvtMask%)
GetCommState	14		Declare Function GetCommState% Lib "User" (ByVal nCid%, lpDCB as DCB)
GetCurrentPDB	NA		Declare Function GetCurrentPDB% Lib "Kernel" ()
GetCurrentPosition	7		Declare Function GetCurrentPosition& Lib "GDI" (ByVal hDC%)

Function Name	Chapter	Version	Declaration
GetCurrentPositionEx	7	3.1	Declare Function GetCurrentPositionEx% Lib "GDI" (ByVal hDC%, lpPoint As POINTAPI)
GetCurrentTask	12		Declare Function GetCurrentTask% Lib "Kernel" ()
GetCurrentTime	5		Declare Function GetCurrentTime& Lib "User" ()
GetCursor	5	3.1	Declare Function GetCursor% Lib "User" ()
GetCursorPos	5		Declare Sub GetCursorPos Lib "User" (lpPoint As POINTAPI)
GetDC	6		Declare Function GetDC% Lib "User" (ByVal hWnd%)
GetDCEx	6	3.1	Declare Function GetDCEx% Lib "User" (ByVal hWnd%, ByVal hrgnClip%, ByVal fdwOptions&)
GetDCOrg	6		Declare Function GetDCOrg& Lib "GDI" (ByVal hDC%)
GetDesktopHwnd	4		Declare Function GetDesktopHwnd% Lib "User" ()
GetDesktopWindow	4		Declare Function GetDesktopWindow% Lib "User" ()
GetDeviceCaps	6		Declare Function GetDeviceCaps% Lib "GDI" (ByVal hDC%, ByVal nIndex%)
GetDialogBaseUnits	16		Declare Function GetDialogBaseUnits& Lib "User" ()
GetDIBits	8		Declare Function GetDIBits% Lib "GDI" (ByVal aHDC%, ByVal hBitmap%, ByVal nStartScan%, ByVal nNumScans%, ByVal lpBits$, lpBI As BITMAPINFO, ByVal wUsage%)
GetDIBitsBynum	8		Declare Function GetDIBitsBynum% Lib "GDI" Alias "GetDIBits" (ByVal aHDC%, ByVal hBitmap%, ByVal nStartScan%, ByVal nNumScans%, ByVal lpBits&, lpBI As BITMAPINFO, ByVal wUsage%)
GetDlgCtrlID	NA		Declare Function GetDlgCtrlID% Lib "User" (ByVal hWnd%)
GetDlgItem	NA		Declare Function GetDlgItem% Lib "User" (ByVal hDlg%, ByVal nIDDlgItem%)
GetDlgItemInt	NA		Declare Function GetDlgItemInt% Lib "User" (ByVal hDlg%, ByVal nIDDlgItem%, lpTranslated%, ByVal bSigned%)
GetDlgItemText	NA		Declare Function GetDlgItemText% Lib "User" (ByVal hDlg%, ByVal nIDDlgItem%, ByVal lpString$, ByVal nMaxCount%)
GetDOSEnvironment	13		Declare Function GetDOSEnvironment& Lib "Kernel" ()
GetDoubleClickTime	5		Declare Function GetDoubleClickTime% Lib "User" ()
GetDriveType	13		Declare Function GetDriveType% Lib "Kernel" (ByVal nDrive%)

Function Name	Chapter	Version	Declaration
GetEnvironment	NA		Declare Function GetEnvironment% Lib "GDI" (ByVal lpPortName$, lpEnviron As Any, ByVal nMaxCount%)
GetEnvironmentBystring	NA		Declare Function GetEnvironmentBystring% Lib "GDI" Alias "GetEnvironment" (ByVal lpPortName$, Byval lpEnviron$, ByVal nMaxCount%)
GetEnvironmentBynum	NA		Declare Function GetEnvironmentBynum% Lib "GDI" Alias "GetEnvironment" (ByVal lpPortName$, Byval lpEnviron&, ByVal nMaxCount%)
GetExpandedName	13		Declare Function GetExpandedName% Lib "lzexpand" (ByVal lpszSource$, ByVal lpszBuffer$)
GetFileResource	13		Declare Function GetFileResource% Lib "ver.dll" (ByVal lpszFileName$, ByVal lpszResType&, ByVal lpszResID&, ByVal dwFileOffset&, ByVal dwResLen&, ByVal lpvData&)
GetFileResourceSize	13		Declare Function GetFileResourceSize& Lib "ver.dll" (ByVal lpszFileName$, ByVal lpszResType&, ByVal lpszResID&, dwFileOffset&)
GetFileVersionInfo	13		Declare Function GetFileVersionInfo% Lib "ver.dll" (ByVal lpszFileName$, ByVal handle&, ByVal cbBuf&, ByVal lpvData&)
GetFileVersionInfoSize	13		Declare Function GetFileVersionInfoSize% Lib "ver.dll" (ByVal lpszFileName$, lpdwHandle&)
GetFocus	4		Declare Function GetFocus% Lib "User" ()
GetFontData	10	3.1	Declare Function GetFontData& Lib "GDI" (ByVal hDC%, ByVal dwTable&, ByVal dwOffset&, ByVal lpvBuffer$, ByVal cbData&)
GetFreeSpace	5		Declare Function GetFreeSpace& Lib "Kernel" (ByVal wFlags%)
GetFreeSystemResources	5		Declare Function GetFreeSystemResources% Lib "User" (ByVal fuSysResource%)
GetGlyphOutline	10	3.1	Declare Function GetGlyphOutline& Lib "GDI" (ByVal hDC%, ByVal uChar%, ByVal fuFormat%, lpgm As GLYPHMETRICS, ByVal cbBuffer&, lppt As POINTAPI, lpmat2 As MAT2)
GetInputState	5		Declare Function GetInputState% Lib "User" ()
GetInstanceData	NA		Declare Function GetInstanceData% Lib "Kernel" (ByVal hInstance%, ByVal pData%, ByVal nCount%)
GetKBCodePage	5		Declare Function GetKBCodePage% Lib "Keyboard" ()
GetKeyboardState	5		Declare Sub GetKeyboardState Lib "User" (LpKeyState As Any)
GetKeyboardStateBystring	5		Declare Sub GetKeyboardStateBystring Lib "User" Alias "GetKeyboardState" (ByVal LpKeyState$)

Function Name	Chapter	Version	Declaration
GetKeyboardType	5		Declare Function GetKeyboardType% Lib "Keyboard" (ByVal nTypeFlag%)
GetKeyNameText	5		Declare Function GetKeyNameText% Lib "Keyboard" (ByVal lParam&, ByVal lpBuffer$, ByVal nSize%)
GetKeyState	5		Declare Function GetKeyState% Lib "User" (ByVal nVirtKey%)
GetLastActivePopup	4		Declare Function GetLastActivePopup% Lib "User" (ByVal hwndOwnder%)
GetMapMode	6		Declare Function GetMapMode% Lib "GDI" (ByVal hDC%)
GetMenu	9		Declare Function GetMenu% Lib "User" (ByVal hWnd%)
GetMenuCheckMarkDimensions	9		Declare Function GetMenuCheckMarkDimensions& Lib "User" ()
GetMenuItemCount	9		Declare Function GetMenuItemCount% Lib "User" (ByVal hMenu%)
GetMenuItemID	9		Declare Function GetMenuItemID% Lib "User" (ByVal hMenu%, ByVal nPos%)
GetMenuState	9		Declare Function GetMenuState% Lib "User" (ByVal hMenu%, ByVal wId%, ByVal wFlags%)
GetMenuString	9		Declare Function GetMenuString% Lib "User" (ByVal hMenu%, ByVal wIDItem%, ByVal lpString$, ByVal nMaxCount%, ByVal wFlag%)
GetMessage	NA		Declare Function GetMessage% Lib "User" (lpMsg As MSG, ByVal hWnd%, ByVal wMsgFilterMin%, ByVal wMsgFilterMax%)
GetMessageExtraInfo	16	3.1	Declare Function GetMessageExtraInfo& Lib "User" ()
GetMessagePos	16		Declare Function GetMessagePos& Lib "User" ()
GetMessageTime	5		Declare Function GetMessageTime& Lib "User" ()
GetMetaFile	7		Declare Function GetMetaFile% Lib "GDI" (ByVal lpFilename$)
GetMetaFileBits	7		Declare Function GetMetaFileBits% Lib "GDI" (ByVal hMF%)
GetModuleFileName	12		Declare Function GetModuleFileName% Lib "Kernel" (ByVal hModule%, ByVal lpFilename$, ByVal nSize%)
GetModuleHandle	12		Declare Function GetModuleHandle% Lib "Kernel" (ByVal lpModuleName$)
GetModuleUsage	12		Declare Function GetModuleUsage% Lib "Kernel" (ByVal hModule%)
GetNearestColor	7		Declare Function GetNearestColor& Lib "GDI" (ByVal hDC%, ByVal crColor&)

Function Name	Chapter	Version	Declaration
GetNearestPaletteIndex	16		Declare Function GetNearestPaletteIndex% Lib "GDI" (ByVal hPalette%, ByVal crColor&)
GetNextDlgGroupItem	NA		Declare Function GetNextDlgGroupItem% Lib "User" (ByVal hDlg%, ByVal hCtl%, ByVal bPrevious%)
GetNextDlgTabItem	NA		Declare Function GetNextDlgTabItem% Lib "User" (ByVal hDlg%, ByVal hCtl%, ByVal bPrevious%)
GetNextWindow	4		Declare Function GetNextWindow% Lib "User" (ByVal hWnd%, ByVal wFlag%)
GetNumTasks	12		Declare Function GetNumTasks% Lib "Kernel" ()
GetObjectAPI	7		Declare Function GetObjectAPI% Lib "GDI" Alias "GetObject"(ByVal hObject%, ByVal nCount%, ByVal lpObject&)
GetOpenClipboardWindow	15	3.1	Declare Function GetOpenClipboardWindow% Lib "User" ()
GetOutlineTextMetrics	10		Declare Function GetOutlineTextMetrics& Lib "GDI" (ByVal hDC%, ByVal cbData%, lpOTM As OUTLINETEXTMETRIC)
GetPaletteEntries	16		Declare Function GetPaletteEntries% Lib "GDI" (ByVal hPalette%, ByVal wStartIndex%, ByVal wNumEntries%, lpPaletteEntries As PALETTEENTRY)
GetParent	4		Declare Function GetParent% Lib "User" (ByVal hWnd%)
GetPixel	7		Declare Function GetPixel& Lib "GDI" (ByVal hDC%, ByVal X%, ByVal Y%)
GetPolyFillMode	7		Declare Function GetPolyFillMode% Lib "GDI" (ByVal hDC%)
GetPriorityClipboardFormat	15		Declare Function GetPriorityClipboardFormat% Lib "User" (lpPriorityList%, ByVal nCount%)
GetPrivateProfileInt	13		Declare Function GetPrivateProfileInt% Lib "Kernel" (ByVal lpApplicationName$, ByVal lpKeyName$, ByVal nDefault%, ByVal lpFileName$)
GetPrivateProfileString	13		Declare Function GetPrivateProfileString% Lib "Kernel" (ByVal lpApplicationName$, ByVal lpKeyName As Any, ByVal lpDefault$, ByVal lpReturnedString$, ByVal nSize%, ByVal lpFileName$)
GetProcAddress	12		Declare Function GetProcAddress& Lib "Kernel" (ByVal hModule%, ByVal lpProcName$)
GetProfileInt	13		Declare Function GetProfileInt% Lib "Kernel" (ByVal lpAppName$, ByVal lpKeyName$, ByVal nDefault%)
GetProfileString	13		Declare Function GetProfileString% Lib "Kernel" (ByVal lpAppName$, ByVal lpKeyName As Any, ByVal lpDefault$, ByVal lpReturnedString$, ByVal nSize%)

Function Name	Chapter	Version	Declaration
GetProp	16		Declare Function GetProp% Lib "User" (ByVal hWnd%, ByVal lpString As Any)
GetPropBystring	16		Declare Function GetPropBystring% Lib "User" Alias "GetProp" (ByVal hWnd%, ByVal lpString$)
GetPropBynum	16		Declare Function GetPropBynum% Lib "User" Alias "GetProp" (ByVal hWnd%, ByVal lpString&)
GetQueueStatus	5	3.1	Declare Function GetQueueStatus& Lib "User" (ByVal fuFlags%)
GetRasterizerCaps	10	3.1	Declare Function GetRasterizerCaps% Lib "GDI" (lpraststat As RASTERIZERSTATUS, ByVal cb%)
GetRgnBox	6		Declare Function GetRgnBox% Lib "GDI" (ByVal hRgn%, lpRect As RECT)
GetROP2	7		Declare Function GetROP2% Lib "GDI" (ByVal hDC%)
GetScrollPos	15		Declare Function GetScrollPos% Lib "User" (ByVal hWnd%, ByVal nBar%)
GetScrollRange	15		Declare Sub GetScrollRange Lib "User" (ByVal hWnd%, ByVal nBar%, lpMinPos%, lpMaxPos%)
GetSelectorBase	NA		Declare Function GetSelectorBase& Lib "Kernel" (ByVal uSelector%)
GetSelectorLimit	NA		Declare Function GetSelectorLimit& Lib "Kernel" (ByVal uSelector%)
GetStockObject	7		Declare Function GetStockObject% Lib "GDI" (ByVal nIndex%)
GetStretchBltMode	8		Declare Function GetStretchBltMode% Lib "GDI" (ByVal hDC%)
GetSubMenu	9		Declare Function GetSubMenu% Lib "User" (ByVal hMenu%, ByVal nPos%)
GetSysColor	5		Declare Function GetSysColor& Lib "User" (ByVal nIndex%)
GetSysModalWindow	4		Declare Function GetSysModalWindow% Lib "User" ()
GetSystemDebugState	NA	3.1	Declare Function GetSystemDebugState& Lib "User" ()
GetSystemDirectory	13		Declare Function GetSystemDirectory% Lib "Kernel" (ByVal lpBuffer$, ByVal nSize%)
GetSystemMenu	9		Declare Function GetSystemMenu% Lib "User" (ByVal hWnd%, ByVal bRevert%)
GetSystemMetrics	5		Declare Function GetSystemMetrics% Lib "User" (ByVal nIndex%)

Function Name	Chapter	Version	Declaration
GetSystemPaletteEntries	16		Declare Function GetSystemPaletteEntries% Lib "GDI" (ByVal hDC%, ByVal wStartIndex%, ByVal wNumEntries%, lpPaletteEntries As PALETTEENTRY)
GetSystemPaletteUse	16		Declare Function GetSystemPaletteUse% Lib "GDI" (ByVal hDC%)
GetTabbedTextExtent	10		Declare Function GetTabbedTextExtent& Lib "GDI" (ByVal hDC%, ByVal lpString$, ByVal nCount%, ByVal nTabPositions%, lpnTabStopPositions%)
GetTempDrive	13		Declare Function GetTempDrive% Lib "Kernel" (ByVal cDriveLetter%)
GetTempFileName	13		Declare Function GetTempFileName% Lib "Kernel" (ByVal cDriveLetter%, ByVal lpPrefixString$, ByVal wUnique%, ByVal lpTempFileName$)
GetTextAlign	10		Declare Function GetTextAlign% Lib "GDI" (ByVal hDC%)
GetTextCharacterExtra	10		Declare Function GetTextCharacterExtra% Lib "GDI" (ByVal hDC%)
GetTextColor	10		Declare Function GetTextColor& Lib "GDI" (ByVal hDC%)
GetTextExtent	10		Declare Function GetTextExtent& Lib "GDI" (ByVal hDC%, ByVal lpString$, ByVal nCount%)
GetTextExtentPoint	10	3.1	Declare Function GetTextExtentPoint% Lib "GDI" (Byval hDC%, ByVal lpszString$, ByVal cbString%, lpSize As SIZEAPI)
GetTextFace	10		Declare Function GetTextFace% Lib "GDI" (ByVal hDC%, ByVal nCount%, ByVal lpFacename$)
GetTextMetrics	10		Declare Function GetTextMetrics% Lib "GDI" (ByVal hDC%, lpMetrics As TEXTMETRIC)
GetThresholdEvent	15		Declare Function GetThresholdEvent% Lib "Sound" ()
GetThresholdStatus	15		Declare Function GetThresholdStatus% Lib "Sound" ()
GetTickCount	5		Declare Function GetTickCount& Lib "User" ()
GetTimerResolution	5		Declare Function GetTimerResolution& Lib "User" ()
GetTopWindow	4		Declare Function GetTopWindow% Lib "User" (ByVal hWnd%)
GetUpdateRect	4		Declare Function GetUpdateRect% Lib "User" (ByVal hWnd%, lpRect As RECT, ByVal bErase%)
GetUpdateRgn	6		Declare Function GetUpdateRgn% Lib "User" (ByVal hWnd%, ByVal hRgn%, ByVal fErase%)

Function Name	Chapter	Version	Declaration
GetVersion	5		Declare Function GetVersion& Lib "Kernel" ()
GetViewportExt	6		Declare Function GetViewportExt& Lib "GDI" (ByVal hDC%)
GetViewportExtEx	6	3.1	Declare Function GetViewportExtEx% Lib "GDI" (ByVal hDC%, lpSize As SIZEAPI)
GetViewportOrg	6		Declare Function GetViewportOrg& Lib "GDI" (ByVal hDC%)
GetViewportOrgEx	6	3.1	Declare Function GetViewportOrgEx% Lib "GDI" (ByVal hDC%, lpSize As SIZEAPI)
GetWinDebugInfo	NA		Declare Function GetWinDebugInfo% Lib "Kernel" (lpwdi As WINDEBUGINFO, ByVal flags%)
GetWindow	4		Declare Function GetWindow% Lib "User" (ByVal hWnd%, ByVal wCmd%)
GetWindowDC	6		Declare Function GetWindowDC% Lib "User" (ByVal hWnd%)
GetWindowExt	6		Declare Function GetWindowExt& Lib "GDI" (ByVal hDC%)
GetWindowExtEx	6	3.1	Declare Function GetWindowExtEx% Lib "GDI" (ByVal hDC%, lpSize As SIZEAPI)
GetWindowLong	4		Declare Function GetWindowLong& Lib "User" (ByVal hWnd%, ByVal nIndex%)
GetWindowOrg	6		Declare Function GetWindowOrg& Lib "GDI" (ByVal hDC%)
GetWindowOrgEx	6	3.1	Declare Function GetWindowOrgEx% Lib "GDI" (ByVal hDC%, lpSize As SIZEAPI)
GetWindowPlacement	4	3.1	Declare Function GetWindowPlacement% Lib "User" (ByVal hWnd%, lpwndpl As WINDOWPLACEMENT)
GetWindowRect	4		Declare Sub GetWindowRect Lib "User" (ByVal hWnd%, lpRect As RECT)
GetWindowsDirectory	13		Declare Function GetWindowsDirectory% Lib "Kernel" (ByVal lpBuffer$, ByVal nSize%)
GetWindowTask	12		Declare Function GetWindowTask% Lib "User" (ByVal hWnd%)
GetWindowText	4		Declare Function GetWindowText% Lib "User" (ByVal hWnd%, ByVal lpString$, ByVal aint%)
GetWindowTextLength	4		Declare Function GetWindowTextLength% Lib "User" (ByVal hWnd%)
GetWindowWord	4		Declare Function GetWindowWord% Lib "User" (ByVal hWnd%, ByVal nIndex%)

Function Name	Chapter	Version	Declaration
GetWinFlags	5		Declare Function GetWinFlags& Lib "Kernel" ()
GlobalAddAtom	16		Declare Function GlobalAddAtom% Lib "User" (ByVal lpString$)
GlobalAlloc	12		Declare Function GlobalAlloc% Lib "Kernel" (ByVal wFlags%, ByVal dwBytes&)
GlobalCompact	12		Declare Function GlobalCompact& Lib "Kernel" (ByVal dwMinFree&)
GlobalDeleteAtom	16		Declare Function GlobalDeleteAtom% Lib "User" (ByVal nAtom%)
GlobalFindAtom	16		Declare Function GlobalFindAtom% Lib "User" (ByVal lpString$)
GlobalFix	12		Declare Sub GlobalFix Lib "Kernel" (ByVal hMem%)
GlobalFlags	12		Declare Function GlobalFlags% Lib "Kernel" (ByVal hMem%)
GlobalFree	12		Declare Function GlobalFree% Lib "Kernel" (ByVal hMem%)
GlobalGetAtomName	16		Declare Function GlobalGetAtomName% Lib "User" (ByVal nAtom%, ByVal lpbuffer$, ByVal nSize%)
GlobalHandle	12		Declare Function GlobalHandle& Lib "Kernel" (ByVal wMem%)
GlobalLock	12		Declare Function GlobalLock& Lib "Kernel" (ByVal hMem%)
GlobalLRUNewest	12		Declare Function GlobalLRUNewest% Lib "Kernel" (ByVal hMem%)
GlobalLRUOldest	12		Declare Function GlobalLRUOldest% Lib "Kernel" (ByVal hMem%)
GlobalReAlloc	12		Declare Function GlobalReAlloc% Lib "Kernel" (ByVal hMem%, ByVal dwBytes&, ByVal wFlags%)
GlobalSize	12		Declare Function GlobalSize& Lib "Kernel" (ByVal hMem%)
GlobalUnfix	12		Declare Function GlobalUnfix% Lib "Kernel" (ByVal hMem%)
GlobalUnlock	12		Declare Function GlobalUnlock% Lib "Kernel" (ByVal hMem%)
GrayString	10		Declare Function GrayString% Lib "User" (ByVal hDC%, ByVal lpOuputFunc&, ByVal lpData&, ByVal nCount%, ByVal X%, ByVal Y%, ByVal nWidth%, ByVal nHeight%)
GrayStringBystring	10		Declare Function GrayStringBystring% Lib "User" Alias "GrayString" (ByVal hDC%, ByVal lpOuputFunc&, ByVal lpData$, ByVal nCount%, ByVal X%, ByVal Y%, ByVal nWidth%, ByVal nHeight%)

Function Name	Chapter	Version	Declaration
HideCaret	5		Declare Sub HideCaret Lib "User" (ByVal hWnd%)
HiliteMenuItem	9		Declare Function HiliteMenuItem% Lib "User" (ByVal hWnd%, ByVal hMenu%, ByVal wIDHiliteItem%, ByVal wHilite%)
hmemcpy	12	3.1	Declare Sub hmemcpy Lib "Kernel" (hpvDest As Any, hpvSource As Any, ByVal cbCopy&)
hmemcpyBynum	12		Declare Sub hmemcpyBynum Lib "Kernel" Alias "hmemcpy" (ByVal hpvDest&, ByVal hpvSource&, ByVal cbCopy&)
hread	13	3.1	Declare Function hread& Lib "Kernel" Alias "_hread" (ByVal hf%, ByVal hpvBuffer&, ByVal cbBuffer&)
hwrite	13	3.1	Declare Function hwrite& Lib "Kernel" Alias "_hwrite" (ByVal hf%, ByVal hpvBuffer&, ByVal cbBuffer&)
InflateRect	4		Declare Sub InflateRect Lib "User" (lpRect As RECT, ByVal X%, ByVal Y%)
InitAtomTable	16		Declare Function InitAtomTable% Lib "Kernel" (ByVal nSize%)
InSendMessage	NA		Declare Function InSendMessage% Lib "User" ()
InsertMenu	9		Declare Function InsertMenu% Lib "User" (ByVal hMenu%, ByVal nPosition%, ByVal wFlags%, ByVal wIDNewItem%, ByVal lpNewItem As Any)
InsertMenuBynum	9		Declare Function InsertMenuBynum% Lib "User" Alias "InsertMenu" (ByVal hMenu%, ByVal nPosition%, ByVal wFlags%, ByVal wIDNewItem%, ByVal lpNewItem&)
InsertMenuBystring	9		Declare Function InsertMenuBystring% Lib "User" Alias "InsertMenu" (ByVal hMenu%, ByVal nPosition%, ByVal wFlags%, ByVal wIDNewItem%, ByVal lpNewItem$)
IntersectClipRect	6		Declare Function IntersectClipRect% Lib "GDI" (ByVal hDC%, ByVal X1%, ByVal Y1%, ByVal X2%, ByVal Y2%)
IntersectRect	4		Declare Function IntersectRect% Lib "User" (lpDestRect As RECT, lpSrc1Rect As RECT, lpSrc2Rect As RECT)
InvalidateRect	4		Declare Sub InvalidateRect Lib "User" (ByVal hWnd%, lpRect As RECT, ByVal bErase%)
InvalidateRectBynum	4		Declare Sub InvalidateRectBynum Lib "User" Alias "InvalidateRect (ByVal hWnd%, ByVal lpRect&, ByVal bErase%)
InvalidateRgn	6		Declare Sub InvalidateRgn Lib "User" (ByVal hWnd%, ByVal hRgn%, ByVal bErase%)
InvertRect	7		Declare Sub InvertRect Lib "User" (ByVal hDC%, lpRect As RECT)

Function Name	Chapter	Version	Declaration
InvertRgn	7		Declare Function InvertRgn% Lib "GDI" (ByVal hDC%, ByVal hRgn%)
IsBadCodePtr	NA	3.1	Declare Function IsBadCodePtr% Lib "Kernel" (ByVal lpfn&)
IsBadHugeReadPtr	12	3.1	Declare Function IsBadHugeReadPtr% Lib "Kernel" (ByVal lp&, ByVal cb&)
IsBadHugeWritePtr	12	3.1	Declare Function IsBadHugeWritePtr% Lib "Kernel" (ByVal lp&, ByVal cb&)
IsBadReadPtr	12	3.1	Declare Function IsBadReadPtr% Lib "Kernel" (ByVal lp&, ByVal cb%)
IsBadStringPtr	12	3.1	Declare Function IsBadStringPtr% Lib "Kernel" (ByVal lpsz&, ByVal cb%)
IsBadWritePtr	12	3.1	Declare Function IsBadWritePtr% Lib "Kernel" (ByVal lp&, ByVal cb%)
IsCharAlpha	10		Declare Function IsCharAlpha% Lib "User" (ByVal cChar%)
IsCharAlphaNumeric	10		Declare Function IsCharAlphaNumeric% Lib "User" (ByVal cChar%)
IsCharLower	10		Declare Function IsCharLower% Lib "User" (ByVal cChar%)
IsCharUpper	10		Declare Function IsCharUpper% Lib "User" (ByVal cChar%)
IsChild	4		Declare Function IsChild% Lib "User" (ByVal hWndParent%, ByVal hWnd%)
IsClipboardFormatAvailable	15		Declare Function IsClipboardFormatAvailable% Lib "User" (ByVal wFormat%)
IsDBCSLeadByte	5	3.1	Declare Function IsDBCSLeadByte% Lib "Kernel" (ByVal bTestChar%)
IsDialogMessage	NA		Declare Function IsDialogMessage% Lib "User" (ByVal hDlg%, lpMsg As MSG)
IsDlgButtonChecked	NA		Declare Function IsDlgButtonChecked% Lib "User" (ByVal hDlg%, ByVal nIDButton%)
IsGDIObject	7		Declare Function IsGDIObject% Lib "GDI" (ByVal hobj%)
IsIconic	4		Declare Function IsIconic% Lib "User" (ByVal hWnd%)
IsMenu	9	3.1	Declare Function IsMenu% Lib "User" (ByVal hMenu%)
IsRectEmpty	4		Declare Function IsRectEmpty% Lib "User" (lpRect As RECT)
IsTask	12	3.1	Declare Function IsTask% Lib "Kernel" (ByVal htask%)

Function Name	Chapter	Version	Declaration
IsWindow	4		Declare Function IsWindow% Lib "User" (ByVal hWnd%)
IsWindowEnabled	4		Declare Function IsWindowEnabled% Lib "User" (ByVal hWnd%)
IsWindowVisible	4		Declare Function IsWindowVisible% Lib "User" (ByVal hWnd%)
IsZoomed	4		Declare Function IsZoomed% Lib "User" (ByVal hWnd%)
KillTimer	NA		Declare Function KillTimer% Lib "User" (ByVal hWnd%, ByVal nIDEvent%)
lclose	13		Declare Function lclose% Lib "Kernel" Alias "_lclose" (ByVal hFile%)
lcreat	13		Declare Function lcreat% Lib "Kernel" Alias "_lcreat" (ByVal lpPathName$, ByVal iAttribute%)
LimitEmsPages	NA		Declare Sub LimitEmsPages Lib "Kernel" (ByVal dwKbytes&)
LineDDA	7		Declare Sub LineDDA Lib "GDI" (ByVal X1%, ByVal Y1%, ByVal X2%, ByVal Y2%, ByVal lpLineFunc&, ByVal lpData&)
LineTo	7		Declare Function LineTo% Lib "GDI" (ByVal hDC%, ByVal X%, ByVal Y%)
llseek	13		Declare Function llseek& Lib "Kernel" Alias "_llseek" (ByVal hFile%, ByVal lOffset&, ByVal iOrigin%)
LoadAccelerators	NA		Declare Function LoadAccelerators% Lib "User" (ByVal hInstance%, ByVal lpTableName$)
LoadBitmap	8		Declare Function LoadBitmap% Lib "User" (ByVal hInstance%, ByVal lpBitmapName As Any)
LoadBitmapBynum	8		Declare Function LoadBitmapBynum% Lib "User" Alias "LoadBitmap" (ByVal hInstance%, ByVal lpBitmapName&)
LoadBitmapBystring	8		Declare Function LoadBitmapBystring% Lib "User" Alias "LoadBitmap" (ByVal hInstance%, ByVal lpBitmapName$)
LoadCursor	5		Declare Function LoadCursor% Lib "User" (ByVal hInstance%, ByVal lpCursorName As Any)
LoadCursorBystring	5		Declare Function LoadCursorBystring% Lib "User" Alias "LoadCursor" (ByVal hInstance%, ByVal lpCursorName$)
LoadCursorBynum	5		Declare Function LoadCursorBynum% Lib "User" Alias "LoadCursor" (ByVal hInstance%, ByVal lpCursorName&)
LoadIcon	8		Declare Function LoadIcon% Lib "User" (ByVal hInstance%, ByVal lpIconName As Any)
LoadIconBynum	8		Declare Function LoadIconBynum% Lib "User" Alias "LoadIcon" (ByVal hInstance%, ByVal lpIconName&)

Function Name	Chapter	Version	Declaration
LoadIconBystring	8		Declare Function LoadIconBystring% Lib "User" Alias "LoadIcon" (ByVal hInstance%, ByVal lpIconName$)
LoadLibrary	12		Declare Function LoadLibrary% Lib "Kernel" (ByVal lpLibFileName$)
LoadMenu	9		Declare Function LoadMenu% Lib "User" (ByVal hInstance%, ByVal lpString$)
LoadMenuIndirect	9		Declare Function LoadMenuIndirect% Lib "User" (lpMenuTemplate As MENUITEMTEMPLATE)
LoadModule	12		Declare Function LoadModule% Lib "Kernel" (ByVal lpModuleName$, lpParameterBlock As PARAMETERBLOCK)
LoadResource	12		Declare Function LoadResource% Lib "Kernel" (ByVal hInstance%, ByVal hResInfo%)
LoadString	12		Declare Function LoadString% Lib "User" (ByVal hInstance%, ByVal wID%, ByVal lpBuffer$, ByVal nBufferMax%)
LocalAlloc	NA		Declare Function LocalAlloc% Lib "Kernel" (ByVal wFlags%, ByVal wBytes%)
LocalCompact	NA		Declare Function LocalCompact% Lib "Kernel" (ByVal wMinFree%)
LocalDiscard	NA		Declare Function LocalDiscard% Lib "Kernel" (ByVal hMem%)
LocalFlags	NA		Declare Function LocalFlags% Lib "Kernel" (ByVal hMem%)
LocalFree	NA		Declare Function LocalFree% Lib "Kernel" (ByVal hMem%)
LocalHandle	NA		Declare Function LocalHandle% Lib "Kernel" (ByVal wMem%)
LocalInit	NA		Declare Function LocalInit% Lib "Kernel" (ByVal wSegment%, ByVal pStart%, ByVal pEnd%)
LocalLock	NA		Declare Function LocalLock% Lib "Kernel" (ByVal hMem%)
LocalReAlloc	NA		Declare Function LocalReAlloc% Lib "Kernel" (ByVal hMem%, ByVal wBytes%, ByVal wFlags%)
LocalShrink	NA		Declare Function LocalShrink% Lib "Kernel" (ByVal hSeg%, ByVal wSize%)
LocalSize	NA		Declare Function LocalSize% Lib "Kernel" (ByVal hMem%)
LocalUnlock	NA		Declare Function LocalUnlock% Lib "Kernel" (ByVal hMem%)
LockInput	5	3.1	Declare Function LockInput% Lib "User" (ByVal hReserved%, ByVal hwndInput%, ByVal fLock%)
LockResource	12		Declare Function LockResource& Lib "Kernel" (ByVal hResData%)

Function Name	Chapter	Version	Declaration
LockSegment	NA		Declare Function LockSegment% Lib "Kernel" (ByVal wSegment%)
LockWindowUpdate	4	3.1	Declare Function LockWindowUpdate% Lib "User" (ByVal hWnd%)
LogError	NA	3.1	Declare Sub LogError Lib "Kernel" (ByVal uErr%, lpvInfo As Any)
LogParamError	NA	3.1	Declare Sub LogParamError Lib "Kernel" (ByVal uErr%, ByVal lpfn&, lpvInfo As Any)
lopen	13		Declare Function lopen% Lib "Kernel" Alias "_lopen" (ByVal lpPathName$, ByVal iReadWrite%)
LPtoDP	6		Declare Function LPtoDP% Lib "GDI" (ByVal hDC%, lpPoints As POINTAPI, ByVal nCount%)
lread	13		Declare Function lread% Lib "Kernel" Alias "_lread" (ByVal hFile%, ByVal lpBuffer$, ByVal wBytes%)
lstrcat	16		Declare Function lstrcat& Lib "Kernel" (ByVal lpString1 As Any, ByVal lpString2 As Any)
lstrcmp	16		Declare Function lstrcmp% Lib "User" (ByVal lpString1 As Any, ByVal lpString2 As Any)
lstrcmpi	16		Declare Function lstrcmpi% Lib "User" (ByVal lpString1 As Any, ByVal lpString2 As Any)
lstrcpy	16		Declare Function lstrcpy& Lib "Kernel" (ByVal lpString1 As Any, ByVal lpString2 As Any)
lstrlen	16		Declare Function lstrlen% Lib "Kernel" (ByVal lpString As Any)
lwrite	13		Declare Function lwrite% Lib "Kernel" Alias "_lwrite" (ByVal hFile%, ByVal lpBuffer$, ByVal wBytes%)
LZClose	13		Declare Sub LZClose Lib "lzexpand" (ByVal hf%)
LZCopy	13		Declare Function LZCopy& Lib "lzexpand" (ByVal hfSource%, ByVal hfDest%)
LZDone	13		Declare Sub LZDone Lib "lzexpand" ()
LZInit	13		Declare Function LZInit% Lib "lzexpand" (ByVal hfSrc%)
LZOpenFile	13		Declare Function LZOpenFile% Lib "lzexpand" (ByVal lpszFile$, lpof As OFSTRUCT, ByVal style%)
LZRead	13		Declare Function LZRead% Lib "lzexpand" (ByVal hf%, ByVal lpvBuf&, ByVal cb%)
LZSeek	13		Declare Function LZSeek& Lib "lzexpand" (ByVal hf%, ByVal lOffset&, ByVal nOrigin%)

Function Name	Chapter	Version	Declaration
LZStart	13		Declare Function LZStart% Lib "lzexpand" ()
MapDialogRect	16		Declare Sub MapDialogRect Lib "User" (ByVal hDlg%, lpRect As RECT)
MapVirtualKey	5		Declare Function MapVirtualKey% Lib "Keyboard" (ByVal wCode%, ByVal wMapType%)
MapWindowPoints	4	3.1	Declare Sub MapWindowPoints Lib "User" (ByVal hwndFrom%, ByVal hwndTo%, lppt As POINTAPI, ByVal cPoints%)
MessageBeep	15		Declare Sub MessageBeep Lib "User" (ByVal wType%)
MessageBox	16		Declare Function MessageBox% Lib "User" (ByVal hWnd%, ByVal lpText$, ByVal lpCaption$, ByVal wType%)
ModifyMenu	9		Declare Function ModifyMenu% Lib "User" (ByVal hMenu%, ByVal nPosition%, ByVal wFlags%, ByVal wIDNewItem%, ByVal lpString As Any)
ModifyMenuBynum	9		Declare Function ModifyMenuBynum% Lib "User" Alias "ModifyMenu" (ByVal hMenu%, ByVal nPosition%, ByVal wFlags%, ByVal wIDNewItem%, ByVal lpString&)
ModifyMenuBystring	9		Declare Function ModifyMenuBystring% Lib "User" Alias "ModifyMenu" (ByVal hMenu%, ByVal nPosition%, ByVal wFlags%, ByVal wIDNewItem%, ByVal lpString$)
MoveTo	7		Declare Function MoveTo& Lib "GDI" (ByVal hDC%, ByVal X%, ByVal Y%)
MoveToEx	7	3.1	Declare Function MoveToEx% Lib "GDI" (ByVal hDC%, ByVal nX%, ByVal nY%, lpPoint As POINTAPI)
MoveWindow	4		Declare Sub MoveWindow Lib "User" (ByVal hWnd%, ByVal X%, ByVal Y%, ByVal nWidth%, ByVal nHeight%, ByVal bRepaint%)
MulDiv	16		Declare Function MulDiv% Lib "GDI" (ByVal nNumber%, ByVal nNumerator%, ByVal nDenominator%)
OemKeyScan	5		Declare Function OemKeyScan& Lib "Keyboard" (ByVal wOemChar%)
OemToAnsi	5		Declare Function OemToAnsi% Lib "Keyboard" (ByVal lpOemStr$, ByVal lpAnsiStr$)
OemToAnsiBuff	5		Declare Sub OemToAnsiBuff Lib "Keyboard" (ByVal lpOemStr$, ByVal lpAnsiStr$, ByVal nLength%)
OffsetClipRgn	6		Declare Function OffsetClipRgn% Lib "GDI" (ByVal hDC%, ByVal X%, ByVal Y%)
OffsetRect	4		Declare Sub OffsetRect Lib "User" (lpRect As RECT, ByVal X%, ByVal Y%)

Function Name	Chapter	Version	Declaration
OffsetRgn	6		Declare Function OffsetRgn% Lib "GDI" (ByVal hRgn%, ByVal X%, ByVal Y%)
OffsetViewportOrg	6		Declare Function OffsetViewportOrg& Lib "GDI" (ByVal hDC%, ByVal X%, ByVal Y%)
OffsetViewportOrgEx	6	3.1	Declare Function OffsetViewportOrgEx% Lib "GDI" (ByVal hDC%, ByVal X%, ByVal Y%, lpPoint As POINTAPI)
OffsetWindowOrg	6		Declare Function OffsetWindowOrg& Lib "GDI" (ByVal hDC%, ByVal X%, ByVal Y%)
OffsetWindowOrgEx	6	3.1	Declare Function OffsetWindowOrgEx% Lib "GDI" (ByVal hDC%, ByVal X%, ByVal Y%, lpPoint As POINTAPI)
OpenClipboard	15		Declare Function OpenClipboard% Lib "User" (ByVal hWnd%)
OpenComm	14		Declare Function OpenComm% Lib "User" (ByVal lpComName$, ByVal wInQueue%, ByVal wOutQueue%)
OpenFile	13		Declare Function OpenFile% Lib "Kernel" (ByVal lpFileName$, lpReOpenBuff As OFSTRUCT, ByVal wStyle%)
OpenIcon	8		Declare Function OpenIcon% Lib "User" (ByVal hWnd%)
OpenSound	15		Declare Function OpenSound% Lib "Sound" ()
OutputDebugString	NA		Declare Sub OutputDebugString Lib "Kernel" (ByVal lpOutputString$)
PaintRgn	7		Declare Function PaintRgn% Lib "GDI" (ByVal hDC%, ByVal hRgn%)
PatBlt	8		Declare Function PatBlt% Lib "GDI" (ByVal hDC%, ByVal X%, ByVal Y%, ByVal nWidth%, ByVal nHeight%, ByVal dwRop&)
PeekMessage	16		Declare Function PeekMessage% Lib "User" (lpMsg As MSG, ByVal hWnd%, ByVal wMsgFilterMin%, ByVal wMsgFilterMax%, ByVal wRemoveMsg%)
Pie	7		Declare Function Pie% Lib "GDI" (ByVal hDC%, ByVal X1%, ByVal Y1%, ByVal X2%, ByVal Y2%, ByVal X3%, ByVal Y3%, ByVal X4%, ByVal Y4%)
PlayMetaFile	7		Declare Function PlayMetaFile% Lib "GDI" (ByVal hDC%, ByVal hMF%)
PlayMetaFileRecord	7		Declare Sub PlayMetaFileRecord Lib "GDI" (ByVal hDC%, lpHandletable%, lpMetaRecord As METARECORD, ByVal nHandles%)
Polygon	7		Declare Function Polygon% Lib "GDI" (ByVal hDC%, lpPoints As POINTAPI, ByVal nCount%)
Polyline	7		Declare Function Polyline% Lib "GDI" (ByVal hDC%, lpPoints As POINTAPI, ByVal nCount%)

Function Name	Chapter	Version	Declaration
PolyPolygon	7		Declare Function PolyPolygon% Lib "GDI" (ByVal hDC%, lpPoints As POINTAPI, lpPolyCounts%, ByVal nCount%)
PostAppMessage	4		Declare Function PostAppMessage% Lib "User" (ByVal hTask%, ByVal wMsg%, ByVal wParam%, lParam As Any)
PostAppMessageBynum	4		Declare Function PostAppMessageBynum% Lib "User" Alias "PostAppMessage" (ByVal hTask%, ByVal wMsg%, ByVal wParam%, Byval lParam&)
PostAppMessageBystring	4		Declare Function PostAppMessageBystring% Lib "User" Alias "PostAppMessage" (ByVal hTask%, ByVal wMsg%, ByVal wParam%, Byval lParam$)
PostMessage	4		Declare Function PostMessage% Lib "User" (ByVal hWnd%, ByVal wMsg%, ByVal wParam%, lParam As Any)
PostMessageBynum	4		Declare Function PostMessageBynum% Lib "User" Alias "PostMessage" (ByVal hWnd%, ByVal wMsg%, ByVal wParam%, Byval lParam&)
PostMessageBystring	4		Declare Function PostMessageBystring% Lib "User" Alias "PostMessage" (ByVal hWnd%, ByVal wMsg%, ByVal wParam%, Byval lParam$)
PostQuitMessage	NA		Declare Sub PostQuitMessage Lib "User" (ByVal nExitCode%)
PtInRect	4		Declare Function PtInRect% Lib "User" (lpRect As RECT, ByVal Pnt As Any)
PtInRectBynum	4		Declare Function PtInRectBynum% Lib "User" Alias "PtInRect" (lpRect As RECT, ByVal Pnt&)
PtInRegion	6		Declare Function PtInRegion% Lib "GDI" (ByVal hRgn%, ByVal X%, ByVal Y%)
PtVisible	6		Declare Function PtVisible% Lib "GDI" (ByVal hDC%, ByVal X%, ByVal Y%)
QuerySendMessage	NA	3.1	Declare Function QuerySendMessage% Lib "User" (ByVal hreserved1%, hreserved2%, hreserved3%, lpMessage As MSG)
ReadComm	14		Declare Function ReadComm% Lib "User" (ByVal nCid%, ByVal lpBuf$, ByVal nSize%)
RealizePalette	16		Declare Function RealizePalette% Lib "User" (ByVal hDC%)
Rectangle	7		Declare Function Rectangle% Lib "GDI" (ByVal hDC%, ByVal X1%, ByVal Y1%, ByVal X2%, ByVal Y2%)
RectInRegion	6		Declare Function RectInRegion% Lib "GDI" (ByVal hRgn%, lpRect As RECT)
RectVisible	6		Declare Function RectVisible% Lib "GDI" (ByVal hDC%, lpRect As RECT)

Function Name	Chapter	Version	Declaration
RedrawWindow	4	3.1	Declare Function RedrawWindow% Lib "User" (ByVal hWnd%, lprcUpdate As RECT, ByVal hrgnUpdate%, ByVal fuRedraw%)
RegisterClass	NA		Declare Function RegisterClass% Lib "User" (lpWndClass As WNDCLASS)
RegisterClipboardFormat	15		Declare Function RegisterClipboardFormat% Lib "User" (ByVal lpString$)
RegisterWindowMessage	M		Declare Function RegisterWindowMessage% Lib "User" (ByVal lpString$)
ReleaseCapture	5_		Declare Sub ReleaseCapture Lib "User" ()
ReleaseDC	6		Declare Function ReleaseDC% Lib "User" (ByVal hWnd%, ByVal hDC%)
RemoveFontResource	10		Declare Function RemoveFontResource% Lib "GDI" (ByVal lpFilename As Any)
RemoveFontResourceBynum	10		Declare Function RemoveFontResourceBynum% Lib "GDI" Alias "RemoveFontResource" (ByVal lpFilename&)
RemoveFontResourceBystring	10		Declare Function RemoveFontResourceBystring% Lib "GDI" Alias "RemoveFontResource" (ByVal lpFilename$)
RemoveMenu	9		Declare Function RemoveMenu% Lib "User" (ByVal hMenu%, ByVal nPosition%, ByVal wFlags%)
RemoveProp	16		Declare Function RemoveProp% Lib "User" (ByVal hWnd%, ByVal lpString$)
RemovePropBynum	16		Declare Function RemovePropBynum% Lib "User" Alias "RemoveProp" (ByVal hWnd%, ByVal lpString&)
ReplyMessage	NA		Declare Sub ReplyMessage Lib "User" (ByVal lReply&)
ResetDC	11		Declare Function ResetDC% Lib "GDI" (ByVal hDC%, lpdm As DEVMODE)
ResizePalette	16		Declare Function ResizePalette% Lib "GDI" (ByVal hPalette%, ByVal nNumEntries%)
RestoreDC	6		Declare Function RestoreDC% Lib "GDI" (ByVal hDC%, ByVal nSavedDC%)
RoundRect	7		Declare Function RoundRect% Lib "GDI" (ByVal hDC%, ByVal X1%, ByVal Y1%, ByVal X2%, ByVal Y2%, ByVal X3%, ByVal Y3%)
SaveDC	6		Declare Function SaveDC% Lib "GDI" (ByVal hDC%)
ScaleViewportExt	6		Declare Function ScaleViewportExt& Lib "GDI" (ByVal hDC%, ByVal Xnum%, ByVal Xdenom%, ByVal Ynum%, ByVal Ydenom%)

Function Name	Chapter	Version	Declaration
ScaleViewportExtEx	6	3.1	Declare Function ScaleViewportExtEx& Lib "GDI" (ByVal hDC%, ByVal nXnum%, ByVal nXdenom%, ByVal nYnum%, ByVal nYdenom%, lpSize As SIZEAPI)
ScaleWindowExt	6		Declare Function ScaleWindowExt& Lib "GDI" (ByVal hDC%, ByVal Xnum%, ByVal Xdenom%, ByVal Ynum%, ByVal Ydenom%)
ScaleWindowExtEx	6	3.1	Declare Function ScaleWindowExtEx& Lib "GDI" (ByVal hDC%, ByVal nXnum%, ByVal nXdenom%, ByVal nYnum%, ByVal nYdenom%, lpSize As SIZEAPI)
ScreenToClient	4		Declare Sub ScreenToClient Lib "User" (ByVal hWnd%, lpPoint As POINTAPI)
ScrollDC	6		Declare Function ScrollDC% Lib "User" (ByVal hDC%, ByVal dx%, ByVal dy%, lprcScroll As RECT, lprcClip As RECT, ByVal hRgnUpdate%, lprcUpdate As RECT)
ScrollWindow	4		Declare Sub ScrollWindow Lib "User" (ByVal hWnd%, ByVal XAmount%, ByVal YAmount%, lpRect As RECT, lpClipRect As RECT)
ScrollWindowEx	4	3.1	Declare Sub ScrollWindowEx Lib "User" (ByVal hWnd%, ByVal dx%, ByVal dy%, lprcScroll As RECT, lprcClip As RECT, ByVal hrgnUpdate%, lprcUpdate As Rect, ByVal fuScroll%)
SelectClipRgn	6		Declare Function SelectClipRgn% Lib "GDI" (ByVal hDC%, ByVal hRgn%)
SelectObject	7		Declare Function SelectObject% Lib "GDI" (ByVal hDC%, ByVal hObject%)
SelectPalette	16		Declare Function SelectPalette% Lib "User" (ByVal hDC%, ByVal hPalette%, ByVal bForceBackground%)
SendDlgItemMessage	NA		Declare Function SendDlgItemMessage& Lib "User" (ByVal hDlg%, ByVal nIDDlgItem%, ByVal wMsg%, ByVal wParam%, lParam As Any)
SendMessage	4		Declare Function SendMessage& Lib "User" (ByVal hWnd%, ByVal wMsg%, ByVal wParam%, lParam As Any)
SendMessageBynum	4		Declare Function SendMessageBynum& Lib "User" Alias "SendMessage" (ByVal hWnd%, ByVal wMsg%, ByVal wParam%, Byval lParam&)
SendMessageBystring	4		Declare Function SendMessageBystring& Lib "User" Alias "SendMessage" (ByVal hWnd%, ByVal wMsg%, ByVal wParam%, Byval lParam$)
SetAbortProc	11	3.1	Declare Function SetAbortProc% Lib "GDI" (ByVal hDC%, ByVal abrtprc&)
SetActiveWindow	4		Declare Function SetActiveWindow% Lib "User" (ByVal hWnd%)

Function Name	Chapter	Version	Declaration
SetBitmapBits	8		Declare Function SetBitmapBits& Lib "GDI" (ByVal hBitmap%, ByVal dwCount&, ByVal lpBits As Any)
SetBitmapBitsBynum	8		Declare Function SetBitmapBitsBynum& Lib "GDI" Alias "SetBitmapBits" (ByVal hBitmap%, ByVal dwCount&, ByVal lpBits&)
SetBitmapBitsBystring	8		Declare Function SetBitmapBitsBystring& Lib "GDI" Alias "SetBitmapBits" (ByVal hBitmap%, ByVal dwCount&, ByVal lpBits$)
SetBitmapDimension	8		Declare Function SetBitmapDimension& Lib "GDI" (ByVal hBitmap%, ByVal X%, ByVal Y%)
SetBitmapDimensionEx	8	3.1	Declare Function SetBitmapDimensionEx% Lib "GDI" (ByVal hBitmap%, ByVal nX%, ByVal nY%, lpSize As SIZEAPI)
SetBkColor	7		Declare Function SetBkColor& Lib "GDI" (ByVal hDC%, ByVal crColor&)
SetBkMode	7		Declare Function SetBkMode% Lib "GDI" (ByVal hDC%, ByVal nBkMode%)
SetBoundsRect	6	3.1	Declare Function SetBoundsRect% Lib "GDI" (ByVal hDC%, lprcBounds As RECT, ByVal flags%)
SetBrushOrg	7		Declare Function SetBrushOrg& Lib "GDI" (ByVal hDC%, ByVal X%, ByVal Y%)
SetCapture	5_		Declare Function SetCapture% Lib "User" (ByVal hWnd%)
SetCaretBlinkTime	5		Declare Sub SetCaretBlinkTime Lib "User" (ByVal wMSeconds%)
SetCaretPos	5		Declare Sub SetCaretPos Lib "User" (ByVal X%, ByVal Y%)
SetClassLong	4		Declare Function SetClassLong& Lib "User" (ByVal hWnd%, ByVal nIndex%, ByVal dwNewLong&)
SetClassWord	4		Declare Function SetClassWord% Lib "User" (ByVal hWnd%, ByVal nIndex%, ByVal wNewWord%)
SetClipboardData	15		Declare Function SetClipboardData% Lib "User" (ByVal wFormat%, ByVal hMem%)
SetClipboardViewer	NA		Declare Function SetClipboardViewer% Lib "User" (ByVal hWnd%)
SetCommBreak	14		Declare Function SetCommBreak% Lib "User" (ByVal nCid%)
SetCommEventMask	14		Declare Function SetCommEventMask& Lib "User" (ByVal nCid%, nEvtMask%)
SetCommState	14		Declare Function SetCommState Lib "User" (lpdcb As DCB)

Function Name	Chapter Version	Declaration
SetCursor	5	Declare Function SetCursor% Lib "User" (ByVal hCursor%)
SetCursorPos	5	Declare Sub SetCursorPos Lib "User" (ByVal X%, ByVal Y%)
SetDIBits	8	Declare Function SetDIBits% Lib "GDI" (ByVal aHDC%, ByVal hBitmap%, ByVal nStartScan%, ByVal nNumScans%, ByVal lpBits$, lpBI As BITMAPINFO, ByVal wUsage%)
SetDIBitsBynum	8	Declare Function SetDIBitsBynum% Lib "GDI" Alias "SetDIBits" (ByVal aHDC%, ByVal hBitmap%, ByVal nStartScan%, ByVal nNumScans%, ByVal lpBits&, lpBI As BITMAPINFO, ByVal wUsage%)
SetDIBitsToDevice	8	Declare Function SetDIBitsToDevice% Lib "GDI" (ByVal hDC%, ByVal X%, ByVal Y%, ByVal dX%, ByVal dY%, ByVal SrcX%, ByVal SrcY%, ByVal Scan%, ByVal NumScans%, ByVal Bits$, BitsInfo As BITMAPINFO, ByVal wUsage%)
SetDIBitsToDeviceBynum	8	Declare Function SetDIBitsToDeviceBynum% Lib "GDI" Alias "SetDIBitsToDevice" (ByVal hDC%, ByVal X%, ByVal Y%, ByVal dX%, ByVal dY%, ByVal SrcX%, ByVal SrcY%, ByVal Scan%, ByVal NumScans%, ByVal Bits&, BitsInfo As BITMAPINFO, ByVal wUsage%)
SetDlgItemInt	NA	Declare Sub SetDlgItemInt Lib "User" (ByVal hDlg%, ByVal nIDDlgItem%, ByVal wValue%, ByVal bSigned%)
SetDlgItemText	NA	Declare Sub SetDlgItemText Lib "User" (ByVal hDlg%, ByVal nIDDlgItem%, ByVal lpString$)
SetDoubleClickTime	5	Declare Sub SetDoubleClickTime Lib "User" (ByVal wCount%)
SetEnvironment	NA	Declare Function SetEnvironment% Lib "GDI" (ByVal lpPortName$, ByVal lpEnviron$, ByVal nCount%)
SetErrorMode	NA	Declare Function SetErrorMode% Lib "Kernel" (ByVal wMode%)
SetFocusAPI	4	Declare Function SetFocusAPI% Lib "User" Alias "SetFocus" (ByVal hWnd%)
SetHandleCount	13	Declare Function SetHandleCount% Lib "Kernel" (ByVal wNumber%)
SetKeyboardState	5	Declare Sub SetKeyboardState Lib "User" (lpKeyState As Any)
SetKeyboardStateByname	5	Declare Sub SetKeyboardStateByname Lib "User" Alias "SetKeyboardState" (Byval lpKeyState$)
SetMapMode	6	Declare Function SetMapMode% Lib "GDI" (ByVal hDC%, ByVal nMapMode%)
SetMapperFlags	10	Declare Function SetMapperFlags& Lib "GDI" (ByVal hDC%, ByVal dwFlag&)

Function Name	Chapter	Version	Declaration
SetMenu	9		Declare Function SetMenu% Lib "User" (ByVal hWnd%, ByVal hMenu%)
SetMenuItemBitmaps	9		Declare Function SetMenuItemBitmaps% Lib "User" (ByVal hMenu%, ByVal nPosition%, ByVal wFlags%, ByVal hBitmapUnchecked%, ByVal hBitmapChecked%)
SetMessageQueue	NA		Declare Function SetMessageQueue% Lib "User" (ByVal cMsg%)
SetMetaFileBits	7		Declare Function SetMetaFileBits% Lib "GDI" (ByVal hMem%)
SetMetaFileBitsBetter	7	3.1	Declare Function SetMetaFileBitsBetter% Lib "GDI" (ByVal hmf%)
SetPaletteEntries	16		Declare Function SetPaletteEntries% Lib "GDI" (ByVal hPalette%, ByVal wStartIndex%, ByVal wNumEntries%, lpPaletteEntries As PALETTEENTRY)
SetParent	4		Declare Function SetParent% Lib "User" (ByVal hWndChild%, ByVal hWndNewParent%)
SetPixel	7		Declare Function SetPixel& Lib "GDI" (ByVal hDC%, ByVal X%, ByVal Y%, ByVal crColor&)
SetPolyFillMode	7		Declare Function SetPolyFillMode% Lib "GDI" (ByVal hDC%, ByVal nPolyFillMode%)
SetProp	16		Declare Function SetProp% Lib "User" (ByVal hWnd%, ByVal lpString$, ByVal hData%)
SetPropBynum	16		Declare Function SetPropBynum% Lib "User" Alias "SetProp" (ByVal hWnd%, ByVal lpString&, ByVal hData%)
SetRect	4		Declare Sub SetRect Lib "User" (lpRect As RECT, ByVal X1%, ByVal Y1%, ByVal X2%, ByVal Y2%)
SetRectEmpty	4		Declare Sub SetRectEmpty Lib "User" (lpRect As RECT)
SetRectRgn	6		Declare Sub SetRectRgn Lib "GDI" (ByVal hRgn%, ByVal X1%, ByVal Y1%, ByVal X2%, ByVal Y2%)
SetROP2	7		Declare Function SetROP2% Lib "GDI" (ByVal hDC%, ByVal nDrawMode%)
SetScrollPos	15		Declare Function SetScrollPos% Lib "User" (ByVal hWnd%, ByVal nBar%, ByVal nPos%, ByVal bRedraw%)
SetScrollRange	15		Declare Sub SetScrollRange Lib "User" (ByVal hWnd%, ByVal nBar%, ByVal nMinPos%, ByVal nMaxPos%, ByVal bRedraw%)
SetSelectorBase	NA		Declare Function SetSelectorBase% Lib "Kernel" (ByVal selector%, ByVal dwBase&)
SetSelectorLimit	NA		Declare Function SetSelectorLimit% Lib "Kernel" (ByVal selector%, ByVal dwBase&)

Function Name	Chapter	Version	Declaration
SetSoundNoise	15		Declare Function SetSoundNoise% Lib "Sound" (ByVal nSource%, ByVal nDuration%)
SetStretchBltMode	8		Declare Function SetStretchBltMode% Lib "GDI" (ByVal hDC%, ByVal nStretchMode%)
SetSwapAreaSize	5		Declare Function SetSwapAreaSize& Lib "Kernel" (ByVal rsSize%)
SetSysColors	5		Declare Sub SetSysColors Lib "User" (ByVal nChanges%, lpSysColor%, lpColorValues&)
SetSysModalWindow	4		Declare Function SetSysModalWindow% Lib "User" (ByVal hWnd%)
SetSystemPaletteUse	16		Declare Function SetSystemPaletteUse% Lib "GDI" (ByVal hDC%, ByVal wUsage%)
SetTextAlign	10		Declare Function SetTextAlign% Lib "GDI" (ByVal hDC%, ByVal wFlags%)
SetTextCharacterExtra	10		Declare Function SetTextCharacterExtra% Lib "GDI" (ByVal hDC%, ByVal nCharExtra%)
SetTextColor	10		Declare Function SetTextColor& Lib "GDI" (ByVal hDC%, ByVal crColor&)
SetTextJustification	10		Declare Function SetTextJustification% Lib "GDI" (ByVal hDC%, ByVal nBreakExtra%, ByVal nBreakCount%)
SetViewportExt	6		Declare Function SetViewportExt& Lib "GDI" (ByVal hDC%, ByVal X%, ByVal Y%)
SetViewportExtEx	6	3.1	Declare Function SetViewportExtEx% Lib "GDI" (ByVal hDC%, ByVal nX%, ByVal nY%, lpSize As SIZEAPI)
SetViewportOrg	6		Declare Function SetViewportOrg& Lib "GDI" (ByVal hDC%, ByVal X%, ByVal Y%)
SetViewportOrgEx	6	3.1	Declare Function SetViewportOrgEx% Lib "GDI" (ByVal hDC%, ByVal X%, ByVal Y%, lpSize As SIZEAPI)
SetVoiceAccent	15		Declare Function SetVoiceAccent% Lib "Sound" (ByVal nVoice%, ByVal nTempo%, ByVal nVolume%, ByVal nMode%, ByVal nPitch%)
SetVoiceEnvelope	15		Declare Function SetVoiceEnvelope% Lib "Sound" (ByVal nVoice%, ByVal nShape%, ByVal nRepeat%)
SetVoiceNote	15		Declare Function SetVoiceNote% Lib "Sound" (ByVal nVoice%, ByVal nValue%, ByVal nLength%, ByVal nCdots%)
SetVoiceQueueSize	15		Declare Function SetVoiceQueueSize% Lib "Sound" (ByVal nVoice%, ByVal nBytes%)
SetVoiceSound	15		Declare Function SetVoiceSound% Lib "Sound" (ByVal nVoice%, ByVal lFrequency&, ByVal nDuration%)

Function Name	Chapter	Version	Declaration
SetVoiceThreshold	15		Declare Function SetVoiceThreshold% Lib "Sound" (ByVal nVoice%, ByVal nNotes%)
SetWinDebugInfo	NA		Declare Function SetWinDebugInfo% Lib "Kernel" (lpwdi As WINDEBUGINFO)
SetWindowExt	6		Declare Function SetWindowExt& Lib "GDI" (ByVal hDC%, ByVal X%, ByVal Y%)
SetWindowExtEx	6	3.1	Declare Function SetWindowExtEx% Lib "GDI" (ByVal hDC%, ByVal X%, ByVal Y%, lpSize As SIZEAPI)
SetWindowLong	4		Declare Function SetWindowLong& Lib "User" (ByVal hWnd%, ByVal nIndex%, ByVal dwNewLong&)
SetWindowOrg	6		Declare Function SetWindowOrg& Lib "GDI" (ByVal hDC%, ByVal X%, ByVal Y%)
SetWindowOrgEx	6	3.1	Declare Function SetWindowOrgEx% Lib "GDI" (ByVal hDC%, ByVal X%, ByVal Y%, lpSize As SIZEAPI)
SetWindowPlacement	4	3.1	Declare Function SetWindowPlacement% Lib "User" (ByVal hWnd%, lpwndpl As WINDOWPLACEMENT)
SetWindowPos	4		Declare Sub SetWindowPos Lib "User" (ByVal hWnd%, ByVal hWndInsertAfter%, ByVal X%, ByVal Y%, ByVal cx%, ByVal cy%, ByVal wFlags%)
SetWindowText	4		Declare Sub SetWindowText Lib "User" (ByVal hWnd%, ByVal lpString$)
SetWindowWord	4		Declare Function SetWindowWord% Lib "User" (ByVal hWnd%, ByVal nIndex%, ByVal wNewWord%)
ShellExecute	12		Declare Function ShellExecute% Lib "shell.dll" (ByVal hwnd%, ByVal lpszOp$, ByVal lpszFile$, ByVal spszParams$, ByVal lpszDir$, ByVal fsShowCmd%)
ShellExecuteBynum	12		Declare Function ShellExecuteBynum% Lib "shell.dll" Alias "ShellExecute" (ByVal hwnd%, ByVal lpszOp&, ByVal lpszFile$, ByVal spszParams&, ByVal lpszDir$, ByVal fsShowCmd%)
ShowCaret	5		Declare Sub ShowCaret Lib "User" (ByVal hWnd%)
ShowCursor	5		Declare Function ShowCursor% Lib "User" (ByVal bShow%)
ShowOwnedPopups	4		Declare Sub ShowOwnedPopups Lib "User" (ByVal hWnd%, ByVal fShow%)
ShowScrollBar	4		Declare Sub ShowScrollBar Lib "User" (ByVal hWnd%, ByVal wBar%, ByVal bShow%)
ShowWindow	4		Declare Function ShowWindow% Lib "User" (ByVal hWnd%, ByVal nCmdShow%)

Function Name	Chapter	Version	Declaration
SizeofResource	12		Declare Function SizeofResource% Lib "Kernel" (ByVal hInstance%, ByVal hResInfo%)
StartDoc	11	3.1	Declare Function StartDoc% Lib "GDI" (ByVal hDC%, lpdi As DOCINFO)
StartPage	11	3.1	Declare Function StartPage% Lib "GDI" (ByVal hDC%)
StartSound	15		Declare Function StartSound% Lib "Sound" ()
StopSound	15		Declare Function StopSound% Lib "Sound" ()
StretchBlt	8		Declare Function StretchBlt% Lib "GDI" (ByVal hDC%, ByVal X%, ByVal Y%, ByVal nWidth%, ByVal nHeight%, ByVal hSrcDC%, ByVal XSrc%, ByVal YSrc%, ByVal nSrcWidth%, ByVal nSrcHeight%, ByVal dwRop&)
StretchDIBits	8		Declare Function StretchDIBits% Lib "GDI" (ByVal hDC%, ByVal X%, ByVal Y%, ByVal dX%, ByVal dY%, ByVal SrcX%, ByVal SrcY%, ByVal wSrcWidth%, ByVal wSrcHeight%, ByVal lpBits$, lpBitsInfo As BITMAPINFO, ByVal wUsage%, ByVal dwRop&)
StretchDIBitsBynum	8		Declare Function StretchDIBitsBynum% Lib "GDI" Alias "StretchDIBits" (ByVal hDC%, ByVal X%, ByVal Y%, ByVal dX%, ByVal dY%, ByVal SrcX%, ByVal SrcY%, ByVal wSrcWidth%, ByVal wSrcHeight%, ByVal lpBits&, lpBitsInfo As BITMAPINFO, ByVal wUsage%, ByVal dwRop&)
SubtractRect	4		Declare Function SubtractRect% Lib "User" (lprcDest As RECT, lprcSource1 As RECT, lprcSource2 As RECT)
SwapMouseButton	5		Declare Function SwapMouseButton% Lib "User" (ByVal bSwap%)
SwitchStackBack	NA		Declare Sub SwitchStackBack Lib "Kernel" ()
SwitchStackTo	NA		Declare Sub SwitchStackTo Lib "Kernel" (ByVal wStackSegment%, ByVal wStackPointer%, ByVal wStackTop%)
SyncAllVoices	15		Declare Function SyncAllVoices% Lib "Sound" ()
SystemParametersInfo	5	3.1	Declare Function SystemParametersInfo% Lib "User" (ByVal uAction%, ByVal uParam%, lpvParam As Any, ByVal fuWinIni%)
SystemParametersInfoByval	5		Declare Function SystemParametersInfoByval% Lib "User" (ByVal uAction%, ByVal uParam%, ByVal lpvParam As Any, ByVal fuWinIni%)
TabbedTextOut	10		Declare Function TabbedTextOut& Lib "User" (ByVal hDC%, ByVal X%, ByVal Y%, ByVal lpString$, ByVal nCount%, ByVal nTabPositions%, lpnTabStopPositions%, ByVal nTabOrigin%)
TextOut	10		Declare Function TextOut% Lib "GDI" (ByVal hDC%, ByVal X%, ByVal Y%, ByVal lpString$, ByVal nCount%)

Function Name	Chapter Version	Declaration
Throw	NA	Declare Sub Throw Lib "Kernel" (lpCatchBuf As Any, ByVal nThrowBack%)
ToAscii	5	Declare Function ToAscii% Lib "Keyboard" (ByVal wVirtKey%, ByVal wScanCode%, lpKeyState As Any, lpChar As Any, ByVal wFlags%)
ToAsciiBystring	5	Declare Function ToAsciiBystring% Lib "Keyboard" Alias "ToAscii" (ByVal wVirtKey%, ByVal wScanCode%, ByVal lpKeyState$, lpChar&, ByVal wFlags%)
TrackPopupMenu	9	Declare Function TrackPopupMenu% Lib "User" (ByVal hMenu%, ByVal wFlags%, ByVal x%, ByVal y%, ByVal nReserved%, ByVal hWnd%, lpRect As Any)
TrackPopupMenuBynum	9	Declare Function TrackPopupMenuBynum% Lib "User" Alias "TrackPopupMenu" (ByVal hMenu%, ByVal wFlags%, ByVal x%, ByVal y%, ByVal nReserved%, ByVal hWnd%, ByVal lpRect&)
TranslateAccelerator	NA	Declare Function TranslateAccelerator% Lib "User" (ByVal hWnd%, ByVal hAccTable%, lpMsg As MSG)
TranslateMDISysAccel	NA	Declare Function TranslateMDISysAccel% Lib "User" (ByVal hWndClient%, lpMsg As MSG)
TranslateMessage	NA	Declare Function TranslateMessage% Lib "User" (lpMsg As MSG)
TransmitCommChar	14	Declare Function TransmitCommChar% Lib "User" (ByVal nCid%, ByVal cChar%)
UngetCommChar	14	Declare Function UngetCommChar% Lib "User" (ByVal nCid%, ByVal cChar%)
UnionRect	4	Declare Function UnionRect% Lib "User" (lpDestRect As RECT, lpSrc1Rect As RECT, lpSrc2Rect As RECT)
UnlockSegment	NA	Declare Function UnlockSegment% Lib "Kernel" (ByVal wSegment%)
UnrealizeObject	7	Declare Function UnrealizeObject% Lib "GDI" (ByVal hObject%)
UnregisterClass	NA	Declare Function UnregisterClass% Lib "User" (ByVal lpClassName$, ByVal hInstance%)
UpdateColors	16	Declare Function UpdateColors% Lib "GDI" (ByVal hDC%)
UpdateWindow	4	Declare Sub UpdateWindow Lib "User" (ByVal hWnd%)
ValidateCodeSegments	NA	Declare Sub ValidateCodeSegments Lib "Kernel" ()
ValidateFreeSpaces	NA	Declare Function ValidateFreeSpaces& Lib "Kernel"()

Function Name	Chapter Version	Declaration
ValidateRect	4	Declare Sub ValidateRect Lib "User" (ByVal hWnd%, lpRect As RECT)
ValidateRgn	6	Declare Sub ValidateRgn Lib "User" (ByVal hWnd%, ByVal hRgn%)
VerFindFile	13	Declare Function VerFindFile% Lib "ver.dll" (ByVal fl%, ByVal FileName$, ByVal WinDir&, ByVal AppDir$, ByVal CurrDir$, CurDirLen%, ByVal DestDir$, DestDirLen%)
VerInstallFile	13	Declare Function VerInstallFile& Lib "ver.dll" (ByVal fl%, ByVal SrcFile$, ByVal DstFile$, ByVal SrcDir$, ByVal DstDir$, ByVal CurrDir$, ByVal TmpFile$, TmpFileLen%)
VerLanguageName	13	Declare Function VerLanguageName% Lib "ver.dll" (ByVal Lang%, ByVal lpszLang$, ByVal cbLang%)
VerQueryValue	13	Declare Function VerQueryValue% Lib "ver.dll" (ByVal lpvBlock&, ByVal SubBlock$, lpBuffer&, lpcb%)
VkKeyScan	5	Declare Function VkKeyScan% Lib "Keyboard" (ByVal cChar%)
WaitMessage	NA	Declare Sub WaitMessage Lib "User" ()
WaitSoundState	15	Declare Function WaitSoundState% Lib "Sound" (ByVal nState%)
WindowFromPoint	4	Declare Function WindowFromPoint% Lib "User" (ByVal Pnt As Any)
WindowFromPointBynum	4	Declare Function WindowFromPointBynum% Lib "User" Alias "WindowFromPoint" (ByVal Pnt&)
WinExec	12	Declare Function WinExec% Lib "Kernel" (ByVal lpCmdLine$, ByVal nCmdShow%)
WinHelp	15	Declare Function WinHelp% Lib "User" (ByVal hWnd%, ByVal lpHelpFile$, ByVal wCommand%, dwData As Any)
WinHelpBynum	15	Declare Function WinHelpBynum% Lib "User" Alias "WinHelp" (ByVal hWnd%, ByVal lpHelpFile$, ByVal wCommand%, ByVal dwData&)
WNetAddConnection	13	Declare Function WNetAddConnection% Lib "User" (ByVal lpszNetPath$, ByVal lpszPassword$, ByVal lpszLocalName$)
WNetCancelConnection	13	Declare Function WNetCancelConnection% Lib "User" (ByVal lpszName$, ByVal fForce%)
WNetGetConnection	13	Declare Function WNetGetConnection% Lib "User" (ByVal lpszLocalName$, ByVal lpszRemoteName$, cbRemoteName%)
WriteComm	14	Declare Function WriteComm% Lib "User" (ByVal nCid%, ByVal lpBuf$, ByVal nSize%)

Function Name	Chapter	Version	Declaration
WritePrivateProfileString	13		Declare Function WritePrivateProfileString% Lib "Kernel" (ByVal lpApplicationName$, ByVal lpKeyName$, ByVal lpString$, ByVal lplFileName$)
WritePrivateProfileString Bynum	13		Declare Function WritePrivateProfileStringBynum% Lib "Kernel" Alias "WritePrivateProfileString" (ByVal lpApplicationName$, ByVal lpKeyName&, ByVal lpString&, ByVal lplFileName$)
WriteProfileString	13		Declare Function WriteProfileString% Lib "Kernel" (ByVal lpApplicationName$, ByVal lpKeyName$, ByVal lpString$)
WriteProfileStringBynum	13		Declare Function WriteProfileStringBynum% Lib "Kernel" Alias "WriteProfileString" (ByVal lpApplicationName$, ByVal lpKeyName&, ByVal lpString&)
wvsprintf	16		Declare Function wvsprintf% Lib "User" (ByVal lpszOutput$, ByVal lpszFormat$, lpvArglist%)
Yield	NA		Declare Sub Yield Lib "Kernel" ()

Index of Windows Messages and Values

This appendix contains a list of the Windows messages included in file API-CONST.TXT. A 3.1 in the version column indicates that the message has been added for version 3.1 of Windows. If you wish your application to be compatible with both Windows 3.0 and Windows 3.1 it should not use Windows messages in this column.

The **Global Const** term has been removed from the beginning of each declaration to make it easier to look up particular messages. Some of the message are based on the **WM_USER** constant. This constant has value &H400 in Windows 3.0 and 3.1. To determine the value to use, simply add this value. Therefore, the **BM_GETSTATE** message, which is defined as **WM_USER+2**, will have the value &H402.

The detailed descriptions of these messages can be found in the chapter in Part 3 of this book that corresponds to the type of message. All messages with the **WM_** prefix are in Chapter 17. Messages with the **EM_** prefix are in Chapter 18. All others can be found in Chapter 19. Messages that are not listed in the message reference section of the corresponding chapter are not compatible with Visual Basic.

Version	Constant Declaration
	BM_GETCHECK = WM_USER+0
	BM_GETSTATE = WM_USER+2
	BM_SETCHECK = WM_USER+1
	BM_SETSTATE = WM_USER+3
	BM_SETSTYLE = WM_USER+4
	BN_CLICKED = 0
	BN_DISABLE = 4
	BN_DOUBLECLICKED = 5
	BN_HILITE = 2
	BN_PAINT = 1
	BN_UNHILITE = 3
	CB_ADDSTRING = (WM_USER+3)
	CB_DELETESTRING = (WM_USER+4)

Version	Constant Declaration
	CB_DIR = (WM_USER+5)
	CB_FINDSTRING = (WM_USER+12)
3.1	CB_FINDSTRINGEXACT = (WM_USER+24)
	CB_GETCOUNT = (WM_USER+6)
	CB_GETCURSEL = (WM_USER+7)
3.1	CB_GETDROPPEDCONTROLRECT = (WM_USER+18)
3.1	CB_GETDROPPEDSTATE = (WM_USER+23)
	CB_GETEDITSEL = (WM_USER+0)
3.1	CB_GETEXTENDEDUI = (WM_USER+22)
	CB_GETITEMDATA = (WM_USER+16)
3.1	CB_GETITEMHEIGHT = (WM_USER+20)
	CB_GETLBTEXT = (WM_USER+8)
	CB_GETLBTEXTLEN = (WM_USER+9)
	CB_INSERTSTRING = (WM_USER+10)
	CB_LIMITTEXT = (WM_USER+1)
	CB_MSGMAX = (WM_USER+19)
	CB_RESETCONTENT = (WM_USER+11)
	CB_SELECTSTRING = (WM_USER+13)
	CB_SETCURSEL = (WM_USER+14)
	CB_SETEDITSEL = (WM_USER+2)
3.1	CB_SETEXTENDEDUI = (WM_USER+21)
	CB_SETITEMDATA = (WM_USER+17)
3.1	CB_SETITEMHEIGHT = (WM_USER+19)

Version	Constant Declaration
	CB_SHOWDROPDOWN = (WM_USER+15)
3.1	CBN_CLOSEUP = 8
	CBN_DBLCLK = 2
	CBN_DROPDOWN = 7
	CBN_EDITCHANGE = 5
	CBN_EDITUPDATE = 6
	CBN_ERRSPACE = (-1)
	CBN_KILLFOCUS = 4
	CBN_SELCHANGE = 1
3.1	CBN_SELENDCANCEL = 10
3.1	CBN_SELENDOK = 9
	CBN_SETFOCUS = 3
	EM_CANUNDO = WM_USER+22
	EM_EMPTYUNDOBUFFER = WM_USER+29
	EM_FMTLINES = WM_USER+24
3.1	EM_GETFIRSTVISIBLELINE = (WM_USER+30)
	EM_GETLINE = WM_USER+20
	EM_GETLINECOUNT = WM_USER+10
	EM_GETMODIFY = WM_USER+8
3.1	EM_GETPASSWORDCHAR = (WM_USER+34)
	EM_GETRECT = WM_USER+2
	EM_GETSEL = WM_USER+0
	EM_GETTHUMB = WM_USER+14
3.1	EM_GETWORDBREAKPROC = (WM_USER+33)

Version	Constant Declaration
	EM_LIMITTEXT = WM_USER+21
	EM_LINEFROMCHAR = WM_USER+25
	EM_LINEINDEX = WM_USER+11
	EM_LINELENGTH = WM_USER+17
	EM_LINESCROLL = WM_USER+6
	EM_MSGMAX = WM_USER+30
	EM_REPLACESEL = WM_USER+18
	EM_SCROLL = WM_USER+5
	EM_SETFONT = WM_USER+19
	EM_SETMODIFY = WM_USER+9
	EM_SETPASSWORDCHAR = WM_USER+28
3.1	EM_SETREADONLY = (WM_USER+31)
	EM_SETRECT = WM_USER+3
	EM_SETRECTNP = WM_USER+4
	EM_SETSEL = WM_USER+1
	EM_SETTABSTOPS = WM_USER+27
	EM_SETWORDBREAK = WM_USER+26
3.1	EM_SETWORDBREAKPROC = (WM_USER+32)
	EM_UNDO = WM_USER+23
	EN_CHANGE = &H300
	EN_ERRSPACE = &H500
	EN_HSCROLL = &H601
	EN_KILLFOCUS = &H200
	EN_MAXTEXT = &H501

Version	Constant Declaration
	EN_SETFOCUS = &H100
	EN_UPDATE = &H400
	EN_VSCROLL = &H602
	LB_ADDSTRING = (WM_USER+1)
	LB_DELETESTRING = (WM_USER+3)
	LB_DIR = (WM_USER+14)
	LB_FINDSTRING = (WM_USER+16)
3.1	LB_FINDSTRINGEXACT = (WM_USER+35)
	LB_GETCARETINDEX = (WM_USER+32)
	LB_GETCOUNT = (WM_USER+12)
	LB_GETCURSEL = (WM_USER+9)
	LB_GETHORIZONTALEXTENT = (WM_USER+20)
	LB_GETITEMDATA = (WM_USER+26)
3.1	LB_GETITEMHEIGHT = (WM_USER+34)
	LB_GETITEMRECT = (WM_USER+25)
	LB_GETSEL = (WM_USER+8)
	LB_GETSELCOUNT = (WM_USER+17)
	LB_GETSELITEMS = (WM_USER+18)
	LB_GETTEXT = (WM_USER+10)
	LB_GETTEXTLEN = (WM_USER+11)
	LB_GETTOPINDEX = (WM_USER+15)
	LB_INSERTSTRING = (WM_USER+2)
	LB_MSGMAX = (WM_USER+33)
	LB_RESETCONTENT = (WM_USER+5)

Version	Constant Declaration
	LB_SELECTSTRING = (WM_USER+13)
	LB_SELITEMRANGE = (WM_USER+28)
	LB_SETCARETINDEX = (WM_USER+31)
	LB_SETCOLUMNWIDTH = (WM_USER+22)
	LB_SETCURSEL = (WM_USER+7)
	LB_SETHORIZONTALEXTENT = (WM_USER+21)
	LB_SETITEMDATA = (WM_USER+27)
3.1	LB_SETITEMHEIGHT = (WM_USER+33)
	LB_SETSEL = (WM_USER+6)
	LB_SETTABSTOPS = (WM_USER+19)
	LB_SETTOPINDEX = (WM_USER+24)
	LBN_DBLCLK = 2
	LBN_ERRSPACE = –2
	LBN_KILLFOCUS = 5
	LBN_SELCANCEL = 3
	LBN_SELCHANGE = 1
	LBN_SETFOCUS = 4
	STM_GETICON = (WM_USER+1)
	STM_SETICON = (WM_USER+0)
	WM_ACTIVATE = &H6
	WM_ACTIVATEAPP = &H1C
	WM_ASKCBFORMATNAME = &H30C
	WM_CANCELMODE = &H1F

Version	Constant Declaration
	WM_CHANGECBCHAIN = &H30D
	WM_CHAR = &H102
	WM_CHARTOITEM = &H2F
	WM_CHILDACTIVATE = &H22
	WM_CLEAR = &H303
	WM_CLOSE = &H10
	WM_COMMAND = &H111
3.1	WM_COMMNOTIFY = &H44
	WM_COMPACTING = &H41
	WM_COMPAREITEM = &H39
	WM_COPY = &H301
	WM_CREATE = &H1
	WM_CTLCOLOR = &H19
	WM_CUT = &H300
	WM_DEADCHAR = &H103
	WM_DELETEITEM = &H2D
	WM_DESTROY = &H2
	WM_DESTROYCLIPBOARD = &H307
	WM_DEVMODECHANGE = &H1B
	WM_DRAWCLIPBOARD = &H308
	WM_DRAWITEM = &H2B
	WM_DROPFILES = &H233
	WM_ENABLE = &HA

Version	Constant Declaration
	WM_ENDSESSION = &H16
	WM_ENTERIDLE = &H121
	WM_ERASEBKGND = &H14
	WM_FONTCHANGE = &H1D
	WM_GETDLGCODE = &H87
	WM_GETFONT = &H31
	WM_GETMINMAXINFO = &H24
3.1	WM_GETTEXT = &HD
3.1	WM_GETTEXTLENGTH = &HE
	WM_HSCROLL = &H114
	WM_HSCROLLCLIPBOARD = &H30E
	WM_ICONERASEBKGND = &H27
	WM_INITDIALOG = &H110
	WM_INITMENU = &H116
	WM_INITMENUPOPUP = &H117
	WM_KEYDOWN = &H100
	WM_KEYFIRST = &H100
	WM_KEYLAST = &H108
	WM_KEYUP = &H101
	WM_KILLFOCUS = &H8
	WM_LBUTTONDBLCLK = &H203
	WM_LBUTTONDOWN = &H201
	WM_LBUTTONUP = &H202
	WM_MBUTTONDBLCLK = &H209

Version	Constant Declaration
	WM_MBUTTONDOWN = &H207
	WM_MBUTTONUP = &H208
	WM_MDIACTIVATE = &H222
	WM_MDICASCADE = &H227
	WM_MDICREATE = &H220
	WM_MDIDESTROY = &H221
	WM_MDIGETACTIVE = &H229
	WM_MDIICONARRANGE = &H228
	WM_MDIMAXIMIZE = &H225
	WM_MDINEXT = &H224
	WM_MDIRESTORE = &H223
	WM_MDISETMENU = &H230
	WM_MDITILE = &H226
	WM_MEASUREITEM = &H2C
	WM_MENUCHAR = &H120
	WM_MENUSELECT = &H11F
	WM_MOUSEACTIVATE = &H21
	WM_MOUSEFIRST = &H200
	WM_MOUSELAST = &H209
	WM_MOUSEMOVE = &H200
	WM_MOVE = &H3
	WM_NCACTIVATE = &H86
	WM_NCCALCSIZE = &H83

Version	Constant Declaration
	WM_NCCREATE = &H81
	WM_NCDESTROY = &H82
	WM_NCHITTEST = &H84
	WM_NCLBUTTONDBLCLK = &HA3
	WM_NCLBUTTONDOWN = &HA1
	WM_NCLBUTTONUP = &HA2
	WM_NCMBUTTONDBLCLK = &HA9
	WM_NCMBUTTONDOWN = &HA7
	WM_NCMBUTTONUP = &HA8
	WM_NCMOUSEMOVE = &HA0
	WM_NCPAINT = &H85
	WM_NCRBUTTONDBLCLK = &HA6
	WM_NCRBUTTONDOWN = &HA4
	WM_NCRBUTTONUP = &HA5
	WM_NEXTDLGCTL = &H28
	WM_NULL = &H0
	WM_PAINT = &HF
	WM_PAINTCLIPBOARD = &H309
	WM_PAINTICON = &H26
	WM_PALETTECHANGED = &H311
	WM_PALETTEISCHANGING = &H310
	WM_PARENTNOTIFY = &H210
	WM_PASTE = &H302

Version	Constant Declaration
3.1	WM_POWER = &H48
	WM_QUERYDRAGICON = &H37
	WM_QUERYENDSESSION = &H11
	WM_QUERYNEWPALETTE = &H30F
	WM_QUERYOPEN = &H13
	WM_QUEUESYNC = &H23
	WM_QUIT = &H12
	WM_RBUTTONDBLCLK = &H206
	WM_RBUTTONDOWN = &H204
	WM_RBUTTONUP = &H205
	WM_RENDERALLFORMATS = &H306
	WM_RENDERFORMAT = &H305
	WM_SETCURSOR = &H20
	WM_SETFOCUS = &H7
	WM_SETFONT = &H30
	WM_SETREDRAW = &HB
3.1	WM_SETTEXT = &HC
	WM_SHOWWINDOW = &H18
	WM_SIZE = &H5
	WM_SIZECLIPBOARD = &H30B
	WM_SPOOLERSTATUS = &H2A
	WM_SYSCHAR = &H106
	WM_SYSCOLORCHANGE = &H15
	WM_SYSCOMMAND = &H112

Version	Constant Declaration
	WM_SYSDEADCHAR = &H107
	WM_SYSKEYDOWN = &H104
	WM_SYSKEYUP = &H105
	WM_SYSTEMERROR = &H17
	WM_TIMECHANGE = &H1E
	WM_TIMER = &H113
	WM_UNDO = &H304
	WM_USER = &H400
	WM_VKEYTOITEM = &H2E
	WM_VSCROLL = &H115
	WM_VSCROLLCLIPBOARD = &H30A
3.1	WM_WINDOWPOSCHANGED = &H47
3.1	WM_WINDOWPOSCHANGING = &H46
	WM_WININICHANGE = &H1A

Raster Operation Table

Table G.1 lists the raster operations available under Windows. Each has a 32-bit value that can be used as a parameter to functions that use raster-ops. The third column shows the constant name for those raster operations that are defined in the APICONST.TXT file. These are the operations most commonly used in Windows.

Table G.1 **Raster Operations**

RPN Raster-Op Equation	32-Bit Raster-Op Parameter Value in Hex	Constant Name
0	00000042	BLACKNESS
1	00FF0062	WHITENESS
D	00AA0029	
Dn	00550009	DSTINVERT
DPa	00A000C9	
DPan	005F00E9	
DPna	000A0329	
DPno	00AF0229	
DPo	00FA0089	
DPon	000500A9	
DPSaa	008003E9	
DPSaan	007F03C9	
DPSana	002A0CC9	
DPSanan	00D50CE9	
DPSano	00BF08C9	
DPSao	00EA02E9	
DPSaon	001502C9	

Table G.1 **Raster Operations (Continued)**

RPN Raster-Op Equation	32-Bit Raster-Op Parameter Value in Hex	Constant Name
DPSax	006A01E9	
DPSaxn	009501C9	
DPSDanax	00DA1CE9	
DPSDaox	005206C9	
DPSDaoxn	00AD06E9	
DPSDnaox	005E1B29	
DPSDnoax	007A1E29	
DPSDoax	004A0789	
DPSDoaxn	00B507A9	
DPSDonox	005B18A9	
DPSDPaoxx	00B616E9	
DPSDPoaxx	009217A9	
DPSDxax	00CA0749	
DPSDxox	005C0649	
DPSDxoxn	00A30669	
DPSnaa	00200F09	
DPSnao	00BA0B09	
DPSnaon	00450B29	
DPSnax	009A0709	
DPSnoa	00A20E09	

Table G.1 **Raster Operations (Continued)**

RPN Raster-Op Equation	32-Bit Raster-Op Parameter Value in Hex	Constant Name
DPSnoan	005D0E29	
DPSnoo	00FB0A09	PATPAINT
DPSnox	00590609	
DPSoa	00A803A9	
DPSoan	00570389	
DPSona	00020C89	
DPSono	00AB0889	
DPSonon	005408A9	
DPSoo	00FE02A9	
DPSoon	00010289	
DPSox	005601A9	
DPSoxn	00A90189	
DPSxa	00280369	
DPSxan	00D70349	
DPSxna	00820C49	
DPSxnan	007D0C69	
DPSxno	00EB0849	
DPSxnon	00140869	
DPSxo	00BE0269	
DPSxon	00410249	
DPSxx	00960169	

Table G.1   **Raster Operations (Continued)**

RPN Raster-Op Equation	32-Bit Raster-Op Parameter Value in Hex	Constant Name
DPx	005A0049	PATINVERT
DSa	008800C6	SRCAND
DSan	007700E6	
DSna	00220326	
DSno	00BB0226	MERGEPAINT
DSo	00EE0086	SRCPAINT
DSon	001100A6	NOTSRCERASE
DSPDaox	004606C6	
DSPDaoxn	00B906E6	
DSPDoax	00620786	
DSPDoaxn	009D07A6	
DSPDSanaxxn	00E95CE6	
DSPDSaoxx	009E16E6	
DSPDSaoxxn	006116C6	
DSPDSoaxx	008617A6	
DSPDSoaxxn	00791786	
DSPDSonoxxn	006858A6	
DSPDxax	00E20746	
DSPDxaxn	001D0766	
DSPDxox	00740646	
DSPDxoxn	008B0666	

Table G.1   **Raster Operations (Continued)**

RPN Raster-Op Equation	32-Bit Raster-Op Parameter Value in Hex	Constant Name
DSPnao	00AE0B06	
DSPnaon	00510B26	
DSPnax	00A60706	
DSPnoa	008A0E06	
DSPnoan	00750E26	
DSx	00660046	SRCINVERT
DSxn	00990066	
P	00F00021	PATCOPY
PDna	00500325	
PDno	00F50225	
PDSana	00700CC5	
PDSanan	008F0Ce5	
PDSano	00F708C5	
PDSao	00F802E5	
PDSaon	000702C5	
PDSax	007801E5	
PDSaxn	008701C5	
PDSnao	00F20B05	
PDSnaon	000D0B25	
PDSnax	00D20705	
PDSnoa	00B00E05	

Table G.1   **Raster Operations (Continued)**

RPN Raster-Op Equation	32-Bit Raster-Op Parameter Value in Hex	Constant Name
PDSnoan	004F0E25	
PDSnox	004B0605	
PDSoa	00E003A5	
PDSoan	001F0385	
PDSona	00100C85	
PDSono	00F10885	
PDSonon	000E08A5	
PDSox	001E01A5	
PDSoxn	00E10185	
PDSPanaxn	00251CC5	
PDSPaox	001A06C5	
PDSPaoxn	00E506E5	
PDSPDaoxxn	004916C5	
PDSPDoaxxn	006D1785	
PDSPnaoxn	00A11B05	
PDSPnoaxn	00851E05	
PDSPoax	00580785	
PDSPoaxn	00A707A5	
PDSPonoxn	00A41885	
PDSPxax	00D80745	

Table G.1 **Raster Operations (Continued)**

RPN Raster-Op Equation	32-Bit Raster-Op Parameter Value in Hex	Constant Name
PDSPxox	004E0645	
PDSPxoxn	00B10665	
PDSxa	00600365	
PDSxan	009F0345	
PDSxna	00900C45	
PDSxnan	006F0C65	
PDSxno	00F90845	
PDSxnon	00060865	
PDSxo	00F60265	
PDSxon	00090245	
PDSxxn	00690145	
PDxn	00A50065	
Pn	000F0001	
PSa	00C000CA	MERGECOPY
PSan	003F00EA	
PSDnaa	00400F0A	
PSDnao	00F40B0A	
PSDnaon	000B0B2A	
PSDnax	00B4070A	
PSDnoa	00D00E0a	
PSDnoan	002F0E2A	

Table G.1   Raster Operations (Continued)

RPN Raster-Op Equation	32-Bit Raster-Op Parameter Value in Hex	Constant Name
PSDnoo	00FD0A0A	
PSDnox	002D060A	
PSDPaox	001C06CCCA	
PSDPaoxn	00E306EA	
PSDPoax	0038078A	
PSDPoaxn	00C707AA	
PSDPSanaxx	00165CCA	
PSDPSaoxx	00D616EA	
PSDPSaoxxn	002916CA	
PSDPSoaxx	009417AA	
PSDPSoaxxn	006B178A	
PSDPSonoxx	0097588A	
PSDPxax	00B8074A	
PSDPxaxn	0047076A	
PSDPxox	002E064A	
PSDPxoxn	00D1066A	
PSna	0030032A	
PSno	00F3022A	
PSo	00FC008A	
PSon	000300AA	

Table G.1 **Raster Operations (Continued)**

RPN Raster-Op Equation	32-Bit Raster-Op Parameter Value in Hex	Constant Name
PSx	003C004A	
PSxn	00C3006A	
S	00CC0020	SRCCOPY
SDna	00440328	SRCERASE
SDno	00DD0228	
SDPana	004C0CC8	
SDPanan	00B30CE8	
SDPano	00DF08C8	
SDPao	00EC02E8	
SDPaon	001302C8	
SDPax	006C01E8	
SDPnaa	00080F08	
SDPnao	00CE0B08	
SDPnaon	00310B28	
SDPnax	00C60708	
SDPnoa	008C0E08	
SDPnoan	00730E28	
SDPnoo	00EF0A08	
SDPnox	00650606	
SDPoa	00C803A8	
SDPoan	00370388	

Table G.1   **Raster Operations (Continued)**

RPN Raster-Op Equation	32-Bit Raster-Op Parameter Value in Hex	Constant Name
SDPona	00040C88	
SDPono	00CD0888	
SDPox	003601A8	
SDPSanax	00E61CE8	
SDPSanaxn	00191CC8	
SDPSaox	002606C8	
SDPSaoxn	00D906E8	
SDPSnaox	00761B28	
SDPSnaoxn	00891B08	
SDPSnoax	006E1E28	
SDPSnoaxn	00911E08	
SDPSoaxn	009B07A8	
SDPSonox	006718A8	
SDPSonoxn	00981888	
SDPSoox	00320688	
SDPSxax	00E40748	
SDPSxaxn	001B0768	
SDPSxnox	00271868	
SDPSxox	00720648	
SDPSxoxn	008D0668	

Table G.1   Raster Operations (Continued)

RPN Raster-Op Equation	32-Bit Raster-Op Parameter Value in Hex	Constant Name
SDPxa	00480368	
SDPxan	00B70348	
SDPxna	00840C48	
SDPxnan	007B0C68	
SDPxno	00ED0848	
SDPxnon	00120868	
SDPxo	00DE0268	
SDPxon	00210248	
SDxPDxa	00420D5D	
SDxPDxan	00BD0D7D	
Sn	00330008	NOTSRCCOPY
SPDaxn	009301C4	
SPDnao	00DC0B04	
SPDnax	009C0704	
SPDnoa	00C40E04	
SPDnoan	003B0E24	
SPDnox	00390604	
SPDoxn	00C90184	
SPDSanax	00BC1CE4	
SPDSanaxn	00431CC4	
SPDSaox	003406C4	

Table G.1	Raster Operations (Continued)		
RPN Raster-Op Equation	**32-Bit Raster-Op Parameter Value in Hex**	**Constant Name**	
SPDSaoxn	00CB06E4		
SPDSnaox	003E1B24		
SPDSnaoxn	00C11B04		
SPDSnoax	007C1E24		
SPDSnoaxn	00831E04		
SPDSoax	002C0784		
SPDSoaxn	00D307A4		
SPDSonox	003D18A4		
SPDSonoxn	00C21884		
SPDSxax	00AC0744		
SPDSxaxn	00530764		
SPDSxnox	00351864		
SPDSxox	003A0644		
SPDSxoxn	00C50664		
SPna	000C0324		
SPno	00CF0224		
SPxDSxa	00240D55		
SPxDSxan	00DB0D75		
SPxDSxo	007E0955		
SPxDSxon	00810975		

Table G.1   **Raster Operations (Continued)**

RPN Raster-Op Equation	32-Bit Raster-Op Parameter Value in Hex	Constant Name
SPxPDxa	00180D59	
SPxPDxan	00E70D79	
SSDxPDxax	008E1D7C	
SSDxPDxaxn	00711D5C	
SSPxDSxax	00E81D74	
SSPxDSxaxn	00171D54	
SSPxDSxox	00B21974	
SSPxDSxoxn	004D1954	
SSPxPDxax	00D41D78	
SSPxPDxaxn	002B1D58	

About the Accompanying Disk

This appendix briefly describes the contents of the disk included with this book and the necessary installation procedures. If you would like to exchange the disk for a 3 ½-inch disk, refer to the disk exchange offer at the back of the book.

Installation

The easiest way to install the software on the enclosed disk is to use the setup program included. Insert the disk into the appropriate floppy-disk drive, then use the program manager to run the program SETUP.EXE on the disk. Follow the instructions that appear.

Many of the files on the disk are compressed. The Expand utility that comes with Microsoft Windows can be used to expand individual files. The setup program used was written with the setup toolkit provided with the professional edition of Visual Basic 2.0.

Disk Contents

Refer to the file README.TXT for information on any last-minute changes or corrections that were added after the book went to press.

Following is a summary of the files included on the disk. Table H.1 lists the example projects and their file names. Table H.2 lists other files included on the disk.

Table H.1   **Example Project Files**

Project Names and File Functions	File Name
APICONS	APICONS.MAK
Demonstrates list box API functions. Used for extracting API constants from text files.	APICONS.FRX
	APICONS.FRM
	APICONSM.BAS
CH12CODE	CH12CODE.MAK
Chapter 12 sample code. Includes memory API functions.	CH12CODE.FRM

Table H.1 **Example Project Files (Continued)**

Project Names and File Functions	File Name
CH15CODE	CH15CODE.MAK
Chapter 15 sample code. Includes sound and multimedia examples.	CH15CODE.FRM
	CH15CODE.FRX
	MMTEST.FRM
	MMTEST.BAS
CH16CODE	CH16CODE.MAK
Demonstrates property enumeration and file drag/drop API functions.	CH16CODE.FRM
ClipView	CLIPVIEW.MAK
Demonstrates region and clipping functions.	CLIPVIEW.FRM
	CLIPVIEW.BAS
CommDemo	COMMDEMO.MAK
Demonstrates serial port I/O API functions.	COMMDEMO.FRM
	COMMCFG.FRM
	COMMUTIL.BAS
DevView	DEVVIEW.MAK
Demonstrates device context API functions.	DEVVIEW.FRM
	DEVVIEW.BAS
ExecDemo	EXECDEMO.MAK
Demonstrates API functions for shelling applications.	EXECDEMO.FRM
FileDemo	FILEDEMO.MAK
Demonstrates version API functions.	FILEDEMO.FRM
	FILEDEMO.BAS

Table H.1   **Example Project Files (Continued)**

Project Names and File Functions	File Name
FontView	FONTVIEW.MAK
Demonstrates font API functions.	FONTVIEW.FRM
	FONTVIEW.BAS
MenuLook	MENULOOK.MAK
Demonstrates menu API functions.	MENULOOK.FRM
	MENULOOK.BAS
	MENULOOK.FRX
PalTest	PALTEST.MAK
Demonstrates color palette API functions.	PALTEST.FRM
	PALTEST.BAS
PicPrint	PICPRINT.MAK
Demonstrates API functions used for printing.	PICPRINT.FRM
	PICPRINT.FRX
	ABORTFOR.FRM
Puzzle	PUZZLE.MAK
Demonstrates bitmap API functions.	PUZZLE2.FRM
	PUZZLE.BAS
	PUZZLE.FRX
QuikDraw	QUIKDRAW.MAK
Demonstrates drawing and metafile API functions.	QUIKDRAW.FRM
	QUIKDRAW.BAS

Table H.1 **Example Project Files (Continued)**

Project Names and File Functions	File Name
RectPlay	RECTPLAY.FRM
Demonstrates rectangle API functions.	RECTPLAY.MAK
	RECTPLAY.BAS
StockBMs	STOCKBMS.MAK
Stock bitmap and icon viewer.	STOCKBMS.FRM
	STOCKBMS.BAS
SysInfo	SYSINFO.MAK
Demonstrates system information API functions.	SYSINFO.FRM
	SYSINFO.BAS
TextDemo	TEXTDEMO.MAK
Demonstrates text and font API functions.	TEXTDEMO.FRM
	TEXTDEMO.BAS
TextMsgs	TEXTMSGS.MAK
Demonstrates sending messages to text controls.	TEXTMSGS.FRM
	TEXTMSGS.BAS
WinView	WINVIEW.MAK
Demonstrates API functions for obtaining information on windows.	WINVIEW.FRM
	WINVIEW.BAS

Table H.2 **Additional Disk Files**

File Name	Description
APICONST.TXT	Windows 3.1 API constants for VB.

Table H.2   Additional Disk Files (Continued)

File Name	Description
APIDECS.BAS	Windows 3.1 API declarations and types.
APIDECS.TXT	Windows 3.1 type-safe API declarations for VB.
APIGUIDE.BAS	VB declarations for dynamic link library APIGUIDE.DLL.
APIGUIDE.DLL	Dynamic link library containing many useful functions. Required for several of the example programs.
APITYPES.TXT	Windows 3.1 API structure definitions for VB.
CBK.VBX	Generic callback custom control. Required for several of the example programs.
MMCONST.TXT	Windows multimedia extensions API constant declarations for VB.
MMDECS.BAS	Windows multimedia extensions API declarations and types.
MMDECS.TXT	Windows multimedia extensions API declarations for VB.
README.TXT	File containing an updated file list and important additional last-minute information.

Distributing Files

All of the example files include complete source code. You may use, modify, and distribute them as you wish. These example files are provided as-is, and no guarantees are made regarding their fitness for any application.

Every effort has been made to ensure the accuracy of the Visual Basic declaration files. They may also be modified and distributed as you wish. The multimedia extensions declaration files are based on the original files from the Windows Software Development Kit, but have not undergone extensive testing under Visual Basic. They are intended to serve as a starting point.

The dynamic link library APIGUIDE.DLL may be distributed with your applications as well.

The custom control CBK.VBX is a subset of Desaware's SpyWorks package. It may also be distributed with your application on a royalty-free basis. If you do so, be careful during the installation of your application not to overwrite a later version of the CBK.VBX control that may already be present on the target system. This control contains internal version control information identifying it as version 1.*x*. The CBK.VBX provided with SpyWorks has version 2.0 or greater.

INDEX

Numbers in **boldface** type indicate tables or figures